COMMUNITY POLICING

1455728500

Anderson Publishing

6th

2011

COMMUNITY POLICING
A Contemporary Perspective

6th **Edition**

Victor E. **KAPPELER**

Eastern Kentucky University

Larry K. **GAINES**

California State University–San Bernardino

ELSEVIER

AMSTERDAM • BOSTON • HEIDELBERG • LONDON
NEW YORK • OXFORD • PARIS • SAN DIEGO
SAN FRANCISCO • SINGAPORE • SYDNEY • TOKYO

Anderson Publishing is an imprint of Elsevier

Acquiring Editor: Shirley Decker-Lucke
Development Editor: Gregory Chalson
Project Manager: André Cuello
Designer: Dennis Schaefer

Anderson Publishing is an imprint of Elsevier
225 Wyman Street, Waltham, MA 02451, USA

Notices
Knowledge and best practice in this field are constantly changing. As new research and experience broaden our understanding, changes in research methods or professional practices, may become necessary.

Practitioners and researchers must always rely on their own experience and knowledge in evaluating and using any information or methods described herein. In using such information or methods they should be mindful of their own safety and the safety of others, including parties for whom they have a professional responsibility.

To the fullest extent of the law, neither the Publisher nor the authors, contributors, or editors, assume any liability for any injury and/or damage to persons or property as a matter of products liability, negligence or otherwise, or from any use or operation of any methods, products, instructions, or ideas contained in the material herein.

Library of Congress Cataloging-in-Publication Data
Application submitted

British Library Cataloguing-in-Publication Data
A catalogue record for this book is available from the British Library.

ISBN: 978-1-4557-2850-3

Printed in the United States of America
11 12 13 14   10 9 8 7 6 5 4 3 2 1

Working together to grow
libraries in developing countries

www.elsevier.com | www.bookaid.org | www.sabre.org

ELSEVIER   BOOK AID International   Sabre Foundation

For information on all Anderson publications visit our website at www.andersonpublishing.com

CONTENTS

ABOUT THE AUTHORS

Victor E. Kappeler is Chair and Foundation Professor of Criminal Justice at Eastern Kentucky University in Richmond, Kentucky. He received his Ph.D. from Sam Houston State University. He has published a number of books and articles in the areas of police liability, police deviance and ethics, the media and crime, community policing, and police and society. His current interests include the social construction of crime, ideology and crime, and crime and popular culture.

Larry K. Gaines is Chair and Professor of Criminal Justice at California State University–San Bernardino. He received his Ph.D. from Sam Houston State University. He has published a number of books and articles in the areas of police operations, police administration, criminal justice, drugs, and gangs. His current interests include police traffic stop studies, law enforcement response to gangs and drugs, and implementation of community policing.

The legitimate object of government is to do for a community of people whatever they need to have done, but cannot do at all, or cannot so well do for themselves, in their separate and individual capacities.

—Abraham Lincoln

CHAPTER 1   The Idea of Community Policing

LEARNING OBJECTIVES

After reading the chapter, you should be able to:

1. Discuss the ways in which the community impacts the police mandate when a department has implemented community policing.
2. Describe why community policing encourages decentralized police service and changes in patrol.
3. Discuss the sources of confusion surrounding the implementation of community policing.
4. List and describe the four major facets of community policing.
5. Understand why community policing is an overarching philosophy, not a technique.
6. Discuss how community policing entails the use of discretion and working with other agencies to find other means of dealing with problematic situations.
7. List and discuss what community policing does NOT constitute.
8. Discuss how community policing is sometimes used as a cover for aggressive police tactics.
9. Describe how community policing affects officer activity.

The Community Policing Revolution

Community policing is the first substantive reform in the American police institution since it embraced the professional model nearly a century ago. It is a dramatic change in the philosophy that determines the way police agencies engage the public. It incorporates a philosophy that broadens the police mission from a narrow focus on crime and law enforcement to a mandate encouraging the exploration of creative solutions for a host of community concerns—including crime, fear of crime, perceptions of disorder, quality of life, and neighborhood

3

conditions. Community policing, in its ideal form, not only addresses community concerns, but it is a philosophy that turns traditional policing on its head by empowering the community rather than dictating to the community. In this sense, policing derives it role and agenda from the community rather than dictating to the community. Community policing rests on the belief that only by working together with people will the police be able to improve quality of life. This implies that the police must assume new roles and go about their business in a very different way. In addition to being law enforcers, they must also serve as advisors, facilitators, supporters, and leaders of new community-based initiatives. The police must begin to see themselves as part of the community rather than separate from the community. In its ideal form, community policing is a grassroots form of participation, rather than a representative top-down approach to addressing contemporary community life. In this sense, police become active participants in a process that changes power configurations in communities. It empowers the police to bring real-life problems of communities to those governmental authorities with the capacity to develop meaningful public policy and provide needed services to their communities (see Reisig & Parks, 2004).

Community policing consists of two primary components: community partnerships and problem solving. It is a partnership or enhanced relationship between the police and the community they serve. It is a partnership in that the police must assist people with a multitude of problems and social conditions including crime, and it is a partnership because the police must solicit support and active participation in dealing with these problems (Wood & Bradley, 2009). It is an enhanced relationship, since the police must deal with substantive issues. They must go beyond merely responding to crime and calls for service. They must recognize and treat the causes of these problems so that they are resolved. When problems are resolved, there is a higher level of civility and tranquility in a community. Thus, the two primary components of community policing are community partnerships and problem solving. **Community partnerships** are the engagement by the police with the community to cooperatively resolve community problems. On the other hand, **problem solving** is where community policing officers (CPOs) attempt to deal with the conditions that cause crime and negatively affect the quality of life in a community. Problem solving is an important part of community policing.

Community policing also embodies an **organizational strategy** that allows police departments to decentralize service and reorient patrol (Skogan & Hartnett, 1997). The focus is on the police officer who works closely with people and their problems. This CPO has responsibility for a specific beat or geographical area, and works as a generalist who considers making arrests as only one of many viable tools, if only temporarily, to address community problems. As the community's conduit for positive change, the CPO enlists people in the process of policing and improving the quality of life in a community. The CPO serves as the community's ombudsman to other public and private agencies that can offer help. If police officers are given stable assignments to geographical areas, they are able not only to focus on current problems, but also to become directly involved in strategies that may forestall long-range problems. Also, by giving people the power to set local police agendas, community policing challenges both police officers and community members to cooperate in finding new and creative ways to accurately identify and solve problems in their communities.

What started as an experiment using foot patrols (Trojanowicz, 1982) and problem solving in a few departments (Goldstein, 1990) exploded into a national mandate. As a result of the Violent Crime Control and Law Enforcement Act of 1994 and its provision to fund 100,000 more CPOs, most police departments in the United States now say they ascribe to community policing. In the 1990s, community policing became an institutionalized and publicly understood form of policing (Morabito, 2010; NIJ, 1997; Gallup, 1996). In 2010, Reaves (2010) reported that 53 percent of police departments have community policing as part of their mission statements. As shown in Table 1.1,

Table 1.1
Local Police Deaprtments Using Full-Time Community Policing Officers, by Size of Population Served, 1997–2007

Population served

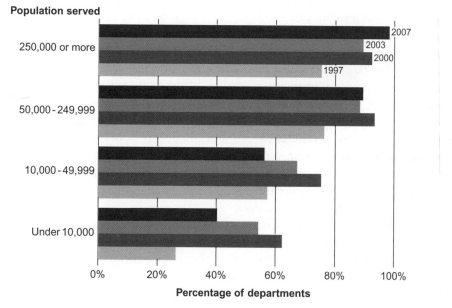

Percentage of departments

community policing has become an important part of policing in all but the smallest police departments.

Even the media presented a limited but very positive depiction of community policing (Mastrofski & Ritti, 1999; Chermak & Weiss, 2006). "Community policing, or variations of it, has become the national mantra of American policing. Throughout the United States, the language, symbolism, and programs of community policing have sprung up in urban, suburban, and even rural police departments" (Greene, 2000:301). Additionally, community policing became a standard in many other countries. Police departments all over the world embraced the language of community policing. It has become ingrained throughout departments as managers attempt to develop strategies and tactics to deal with day-to-day issues and community problems.

Despite this impressive progress, many people, both inside and outside police departments, do not know precisely what "community policing" is and what it can do (Chappell, 2009). Although most everyone has heard of community policing, and most police departments say that they have adopted the philosophy, few actually understand how it works and the possibilities it has for police agencies and communities. Indeed, it is viewed from a number of different perspectives. Is community policing simply a new name for police-community relations? Is it foot patrol? Is it crime prevention? Is it problem solving? Is it a political gimmick, a fad, or a promising trend, or is it a successful new way of policing? Perhaps David Bayley (1988:225) best summarized the confusion about community policing:

> Despite the benefits claimed for community policing, programmatic implementation of it has been very uneven. Although widely, almost universally, said to be important, it means different things to different people—public relations campaigns, shop fronts, and mini-stations, re-scaled patrol beats, liaisons with ethnic groups, permission for rank-and-file to speak to the press, Neighborhood Watch, foot patrols, patrol-detective teams, and door-to-door visits by police officers. Community policing on the ground often seems less a program than a set of aspirations wrapped in a slogan.

There is substantial confusion surrounding community policing (Colvin & Goh, 2006). It stems from a variety of factors that, if not attended to, can undermine a department's efforts to successfully implement community policing. The sources of confusion are:

- Community policing's introduction into American policing has been a long, complicated process. It is rooted in team policing, police-community relations, and crime prevention (Rosenbaum & Lurigio, 1994);

- Some police departments are using community policing as a cover for aggressive law enforcement tactics rather than serving the needs of their communities. When this happens, confusion arises about a police department's real commitment to the community;

- The movement continues to suffer because some police departments claim to have implemented community policing, but they violate the spirit or the letter of what true community policing involves and demands;

- Most police agencies have adopted the language of community policing, but have yet to change their organizational structures and value systems to bring them into line with the community policing philosophy (Kappeler & Kraska, 1998a);

- Community policing threatens the status quo, which always generates resistance and spawns controversy within police organizations (Gaines & Worrall, 2012). This is because community policing challenges basic beliefs, which have become the foundation for traditional policing. It requires substantive changes in the way police officers and commanders think, the organizational structure of police departments, and the very definition of police work;

- Community policing may generate public expectations that go unfulfilled, thus creating a backlash against community policing and the department (Klockars, 1988; Manning, 1988);

- Community policing is often confused with problem-oriented policing and community-oriented policing. Community policing is not merely problem-oriented policing or becoming "oriented" toward the community. While community policing does use problem-solving approaches, unlike problem-oriented policing community policing always engages the community in the identification of and solution to problems rather than seeing the police as the sole authority in this process.

Selected Comparisons between Problem-Oriented Policing and Community Policing Principles

Principle	Problem-oriented policing	Community policing
Primary emphasis	Substantive social problems within police mandate	Engaging the community in the policing process
When police and community collaborate	Determined on a problem-by-problem basis	Always or nearly always
Emphasis on problem analysis	Highest priority given to thorough analysis	Encouraged, but less important than community collaboration
Preference for responses	Strong preference for alternatives to criminal law enforcement be explored	Preference for collaborative responses with community
Role for police in organizing and mobilizing community	Advocated only if warranted within the context of the specific problem being addressed	Emphasizes strong role for police
Importance of geographic decentralization of police and continuity of officer assignment to community	Preferred, but not essential	Essential
Degree to which police share decision-making authority with community	Strongly encourages input from community while preserving ultimate decision-making authority to police	Emphasizes sharing decision-making authority with community
Emphasis on officers' skills	Emphasizes intellectual and analytical skills	Emphasizes interpersonal skills
View of the role or mandate of police	Encourages broad but not unlimited role for police, stresses limited capacities of police, and guards against creating unrealistic expectations of police	Encourages expansive role for police to achieve ambitious social objectives

Source: Scott, M. (2000). *Problem-Oriented Policing: Reflections on the First 20 Years.* Washington, DC: Office of Community-Oriented Policing Services, U.S. Department of Justice, p. 99.

The Philosophical and Structural Facets of Community Policing

Although community policing has taken a number of directions, there is a common overarching logic and structure to it. Four major facets occur when community policing is implemented: (1) the **philosophical facet**, (2) the **organizational and personnel facet**, (3) the **strategic facet**, and (4) the **programmatic facet** (see Colvin & Goh, 2006). All four facets must exist if a department is indeed implementing community policing. The following section explains the philosophy and structure of community policing.

The Philosophical Facet

Historically, even though there have been sporadic variations in the underpinnings or theme for American law enforcement, it has remained substantively a legal-bureaucratic organization focusing on professional law enforcement (Gaines & Worrall, 2012; Gaines & Swanson, 1997). Outputs such as numbers of arrests, reductions and increases in crime rates, volume of recovered property, numbers of citations issued, and a rapid response to calls have been more important than the end result of police work. This philosophy translated into a reactive police institution that does little to deal tangibly with social problems. A substantial body of research that began in the 1970s questions a number of the basic assumptions associated with the legal-bureaucratic model (Bittner, 1970; Wilson, 1968; Reiss & Bordua, 1967). Consequently, people began to search for a new philosophy and way to conduct police work.

Philosophically, community policing consists of a number of community-based elements that differentiate it from the traditional professional model. Some of community policing's core ideas are: (1) **broad police function** and **community focus**, (2) **community input** (3) **concern for people**, (4) **developing trust,** (5) **sharing power**, (6) **creativity**, and (7) **neighborhood variation**.

Broad Police Function and Community Focus

Community policing is a philosophy of policing, based on the concept that police officers and people working together in creative ways can help solve contemporary community problems related to crime, fear of crime, quality of life, and neighborhood conditions. The philosophy is predicated on the belief that achieving these goals requires that police departments develop a new relationship with people by expanding their role in the community, allowing ordinary

Figure 1.1
The Philosophical Facet of Community Policing

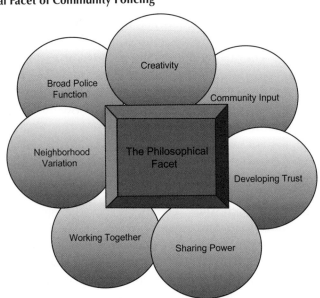

people the power to set local police priorities, and involving them in efforts to improve the overall quality of life in their neighborhoods. It shifts the focus of police work from responding to random crime calls to proactively addressing community concerns.

Community policing dictates that police departments move from law enforcement or crime fighting as the primary function. The police should have a **broader function** that incorporates fear reduction, order maintenance, and community health. Indeed, fear reduction, order maintenance, and a community's overall health become the primary goals for the department, supplanting crime reduction as the central organizing theme of police work. Research demonstrates that community policing can reduce people's fear of crime (Weisburd & Eck, 2004; Roh & Oliver, 2005).

This change in police philosophy emanates from three general observations. First, research examining police operations and crime statistics show that police are not effective, nor will they become effective, in controlling crime by law enforcement alone. Crime is a product of socioeconomic conditions and poor public policy; therefore, it cannot be controlled through police action alone. Crime can be affected only through the control and manipulation of social conditions and public policy. The police can, at best, only manage and document most crime. Order maintenance and addressing the health of a community are legitimate police goals in themselves. For the police to have an impact on crime they must first impact social conditions and public policy.

Second, fear has a far greater debilitating effect on a community or individuals than does actual crime or crime rates. The fear of crime results in persons becoming virtual prisoners in their own homes; it inhibits commerce; and it imposes a subtle psychological cost to everyone (Hale, 1996). Fear destroys community because it isolates people and causes apprehension and suspicion. Research shows that oftentimes an individual's level of fear of crime bears no relationship to the actual amount of crime or victimization (Jackson & Gray, 2010). The traditional approach to fear reduction, however, has been to attack crime, hoping that reducing crime will ultimately lessen fear. Because traditional policing relies primarily on motor patrol, which is basically reactive, there are obvious structural limitations that make it difficult to provide an effective means of confronting fear of crime separately and directly. The simple fact of the matter is that most crime in American society is not committed or solved on the streets, nor is it committed by strangers (Kappeler & Potter, 2005). Though crime prevention and police-community relations programs have helped broaden the traditional police role in ways that impinge on fear of crime, these peripheral attempts tended to chip away at problems that demand a bulldozer. Police-sponsored fear-reduction programs have the potential to yield positive results in a number of areas: community participation in crime prevention programs, increased crime reporting, and positive relations with people (see Zhao, Scheider & Thurman, 2002).

Community policing recognizes that fear of crime can be as much of a problem as crime itself. It is fear of crime that can trap the elderly in their homes or can make people afraid to venture out alone. Traditional policing efforts have had little, if any, ability to reduce fear. Fear was not even a consideration or objective in traditional policing. Periodically the police would make arrests that might have had a short-lived impact on fear, but for the most part, people sustained a fairly significant level of fear for which the police did little. This fear adversely affected people's daily lives. An important ingredient in community policing is active police involvement with people through a wide range of programs designed to reduce fear. Police must get people out of their homes and get actively involved in their communities. This means police must become directly involved in community activities and become organizers of community. Police must also be careful not to promote unnecessary fear of crime to gain short-lived political and community support. Even more important, the police must address the sources that cause fear of crime—most often the politicization of crime and the media's construction of crime (Kappeler & Potter, 2005).

Historically, political leaders and the media used fear of crime to promote their own interests and agendas. Today, they use terrorism for the same purposes.

Third, we have long debated the primary role of the police in society (Wilson, 1968; Manning, 1997), and over the past 30 years we have come to the point whereby everyone accepts that the police role has expanded well beyond law enforcement and "crook catching." In fact, reviews of police activities show that the majority of calls and the vast amount of time police spend on the job are of a non-crime nature (see Gaines & Kappeler, 2012). The advent of community policing has resulted in a broader police mission evolving. Today, police should see crime, fear of crime, and the general quality of life all as being important parts of the police mission. Indeed, all of these societal factors are intertwined and interact with one another.

Community Input

The police have traditionally developed and implemented programs that involved community members. For the most part, however, these programs bordered on public relations schemes with little consideration given to community or human needs. Team policing programs of the 1970s and some of the police-community relations programs of earlier years never seriously involved and considered people; for the most part, the police were concerned with educating the public about their own needs rather than listening to the public about community needs. One of the most difficult aspects of community policing is determining the needs, concerns, and desires of the community. Real community policing requires the police to set aside their own agendas to fairly and accurately measure the needs of the communities they serve. This requires not only listening to people but also acting on their concerns.

Community policing employs methods that cause the police to work more closely with people. To develop a better relationship, police departments have attempted to collect information about people's attitudes toward crime problems and the effectiveness of the police. For example, the police in Baltimore County, Reno, Atlanta, Newport News, St. Louis, and other cities have requested that community members complete surveys. Other departments have attempted to collect information by holding town or neighborhood meetings or by regularly meeting with minority and business groups. Gathering information from people allows the police to accomplish several tasks. Survey information can be used to evaluate the effectiveness of police programs in terms of fear reduction or attitudes toward the police. They also gauge behavior such as victimization or crime prevention efforts. Finally, they can also be used to collect data to assist the police in establishing community goals and priorities (Peak & Glensor, 2007).

Community policing gets people involved in developing communities through two-way communication. Only by engaging the people and by collecting information from the public can the police begin to understand the needs and concerns of the community and begin to develop a community-based agenda rather than merely fostering traditional police agendas.

Concern for People

The professional model of policing was institutionalized in the early 1900s. It dictated that police officers remain aloof and detached from the people they served. Police administrators believed that if officers were "professional" in their interactions with people, as defined by this aloofness and detachment, then there would be less possibility of police corruption and political intervention into police affairs, which were two significant problems at the time (Bracey, 1992). The professional model resulted in police departments and police officers having little concern or knowledge about community and neighborhood problems. Officers acted more like robots who responded to one call after another. This detachment resulted in people having little confidence in the police, and it negatively affected police departments' ability to serve communities.

Police officers, to be effective, must be concerned with the welfare of people and the community. The primary role of the police is not to arrest people, write citations, or answer calls. These activities are merely tools by which to accomplish the police's primary objective, ensuring the safety and domestic tranquility of a community. This equates to the police being concerned with people and their problems. It means the police must understand community problems and effectively respond to them.

Developing Trust

Community policing suggests that to get "the facts," the police must do more than attempt to impose their authority and sense of order on a community, that they must find new ways to promote cooperation between community members and the police. Information is the lifeblood of both traditional and community policing. Without information, police officers cannot solve crimes or social problems. The challenge the police face in getting information is that there must be some level of trust for people to cooperate with the police. Historically, the affluent and middle-class segments of a community had a great deal of trust for their police, but relationships with most poor and minorities left a great deal to be desired (Kappeler, Sluder & Alpert, 1998; Carter, 1985; Scaglion & Condon, 1980). In many instances, the police were seen as armed, uniformed strangers who could hurt you, but would not help you. The police were intimidating. For far too many in the community and for far too many years, contact with the police could lead to nothing good. Today, officers must continue fostering better relations with all segments of society. They must attempt to gain all community members' trust so that they can also gain their cooperation.

A prime example of the trust problem occurred in New Orleans in the mid-1990s. During that period, the police department was rife with corruption and the police were known for their brutality. The police essentially were out of control. The problem came to a culmination with the shooting of a police officer by another officer who was committing an armed robbery. During the period, people had good reason not to trust the police. Some people stated that when cases went to court, they would have more faith in the defendants' testimony than that of police officers. Not only was there a lack of trust of the police, but people were afraid of them. After national attention and substantial public outcry, the city began a reform of the police department. History shows that it is a long and arduous process for a police department to reform itself and regain public support and trust (Kappeler, Sluder & Alpert, 1998).

In contrast, a central part of community policing is building trust. An important strategy is for community officers to directly communicate with as many individuals and groups of people as possible. CPOs not only portray themselves as friends and partners in the community—they must become friends and partners with the community. This philosophy ultimately fosters greater trust and cooperation.

Sharing Power

The third dramatic departure from the past is that a community policing agenda is influenced by the community's needs and desires, not just the dictates of the department. Historically, politicians and police administrators have set the agenda for policing, often without any regard or input from the people who were being policed. The police, from chief to line police officer, must recognize that people have a legitimate right to make demands on the police and control their agenda. Police departments, in addition to being law enforcement organizations, are service organizations, and as such, they should provide the best level of service possible. This means asking all community members, not just those supportive of the police or those with political power, about the kinds and levels of services they need and want. There is a wide divide in American society between those who have power and those who experience the victimization of crime—power sharing can close this divide.

Empowering a community requires an important adjustment in the line officer's thinking. Traditional officers who believe their authority should be sufficient to demand compliance may find it difficult to make the shift to sharing power as demanded by community policing. A traditional officer might find it difficult or unwieldy to chat with people about seemingly petty concerns, but this is an important part of community policing. It builds a bond between the police and community members, and it allows officers to gather information about what they should be doing (Reisig & Parks, 2004). The best CPOs understand that people are not obstacles the officer must overcome to do the job, but a tremendous resource that can be tapped to make the community a safer, more harmonious environment. It also takes the sustained presence of a CPO to persuade people that the department now sees them in this new light, and that there is a real commitment to **sharing power**.

The community policing challenge includes involving people directly in efforts to identify and solve problems in the community. Community policing is not just a tactic to make people the eyes and ears of the department, but it solicits their direct participation in identifying and solving problems. In this regard, community policing goes well beyond other programs such as foot patrol, neighborhood watch, crime prevention, or police-community relations. It might mean encouraging volunteers to help staff the local office. It could mean urging groups of parents to volunteer their time to coach summer athletic activities for kids. It often means asking businesses to donate goods, services, or expertise for neighborhood projects. Perhaps more importantly, it means organizing people to bring pressure on policy makers who have ignored community problems. The goal is for the CPO to recruit as many volunteers as possible and to organize them, so that the community has dozens of people working together to make a difference. Generating community involvement is one of the most difficult aspects of community policing (Skogan & Hartnett, 1997).

Creativity

The "Profiles in Community Policing," featured at the end of this book, demonstrate that community policing can work in any kind of police department, from large municipalities to small towns. Community policing can be successful because it is not a static program. It represents a philosophy whereby problems are identified and the community, not just the police, determines strategies and tactics. As Weisburd and Eck (2004) advise, police officers must possess a variety of tools with which to deal with community problems. Community policing, in its ideal sense, is a form of accountable creativity whereby officers are allowed to experiment with a variety of tactics that directly involve people (Spelman, 2004). Community input and participation can be a rich source of innovation and creativity—it opens up possibilities that the police and political leaders may never consider. Since community members come from all walks of life and have a rich diversity of knowledge and occupational experience, they can be a vital source of innovation. If police view people as know-nothings who have little knowledge or nothing to contribute, then innovation and creativity is not really possible. Accountability is interjected into the process because officers are forced not only to successfully address specific problems and community concerns but also to seek community involvement in possible solutions. This is a departure from traditional policing whereby a police department had a limited repertoire of enforcement-based programs, and all problems were essentially addressed using the same strategies and tactics. Also, officers in traditional policing were evaluated on response times, the numbers of arrests they made, and the numbers of citations they issued. These measures have little to do with community policing or the quality of police work (Stephens, 1996). Community policing demands that the people become the judges of the quality of police service, rather than just relying on the cold crime accounting practices of the past.

Neighborhood Variation

Traditional, professional policing mandated that officers disavow the existence of discretion, and police every situation and neighborhood as if they were the same. That is, the police cultivated the image of full or uniform enforcement of the law. This, however, has never been a reality. There has always existed variation in law enforcement and service across communities and different neighborhoods and among people (Williamson, Ashby & Webber, 2006). Community policing, on the other hand, recognizes that a political jurisdiction is composed of a number of communities or neighborhoods, each with its own set of problems and expectations. Suttles (1972) notes that people develop "cognitive maps" where they designate certain places as theirs, or their neighborhood. Stable neighborhoods have relative homogeneity of activity, people, and values. Because neighborhoods are defined by ethnic, religious, and socioeconomic factors and geographical boundaries, differential expectations evolve within neighborhoods. Particular neighborhoods develop expectations not only about what the police should do, but also about what types of behavior by residents and nonresidents is acceptable or unacceptable—police cannot afford to ignore these variations.

Community policing dictates that the police follow the "will of the community" when dealing with situations and enforcing the law. This means that police must first learn to accurately read the will of the community rather than projecting their will on the community. This requires the police to get out of their cars, engage the community, collect information, and begin a dialog with the people living in the neighborhoods they police. It also requires the police to become more open minded and think outside their occupation filters and their own socialization. For the most part, there is little variation in how the police react to serious crimes or felonies. However, the police must be cognizant of community standards when policing minor infractions of the law and dealing with activities that may be acceptable in one neighborhood, but not another. For example, a person working on his car while parked on the street would not be acceptable in many upper- and middle-class neighborhoods, but it is a way of life for many people residing in poor neighborhoods. Police must begin to realize these variations and that the law is a tool that can be used to either build community or to cause conflict. Police officers must rely on community or neighborhood standards when encountering such situations. The police must maintain a balance between neighborhood values and overall legal goals and objectives. A poor person cited by the police for repairing his car on the street is not very likely to be either supportive of the police or to provide much needed information to solve a serious crime. In this situation police have not gained a partner but rather alienated a member of the community. The overall mission of the police should not be subordinated to the issuance of a traffic ticket or the enforcement of a city ordinance. Police must recognize variation in communities and use the law as a responsive tool rather than a tool of repression.

The Organizational and Personnel Facet

Community policing requires both a philosophical shift in the way that police think about their mission, as well as a commitment to the structural changes this form of policing demands. Police organizations must decentralize their organizations to be more responsive to the community. Community policing provides a new way for the police to provide decentralized and personalized service that offers every community member an opportunity to become active in the police process. In this way, people who have been isolated or disenfranchised, either because of economics or the lack of political power, can have both a voice in police activities and an interest in the development and health of their community. Community policing can help mitigate some of the harsh realities of modern life. Community policing is more than involving people in crime control; it is active involvement in enhancing the health of the community.

Figure 1.2
The Organizational and Personnel Facet of Community Policing

This helps explain why it is crucial to understand that community policing is a philosophy that offers a coherent strategy that departments can use to guide them in making the structural changes that allow the concept to become real. Community policing is not just a tactic that can be applied to solve a particular problem—one that can be abandoned once the goal is achieved. It implies a profound difference in the way the police view their role and their relationship with the community. Just adopting one or more tactics associated with community policing is not enough. Police must change their organizational structures, modify their personnel's orientation, and adjust their value systems to allow for community policing.

A police department's philosophy sets the stage for the development and implementation of strategies and specific tactics. A philosophical change, as required with the implementation of community policing, generally is enumerated in a department's mission statement. Mission statements should endorse the most essential aspect of the community policing philosophy: giving people the power to set the police agenda and developing people-based accountability of the police. Also a mission statement must find its expression in coherent strategies. That is, strategies must be employed that will further the overarching philosophy or mission of the department. In fact, Reaves (2010) found that 53 percent of departments have a community policing policy. This means that about half of American police departments have not formally endorsed community policing as an organizational imperative. A philosophy serves as the department's rudder, which helps guide the department as it serves the public.

Community officers answer calls and make arrests, just like any other police officer, but these activities actually are only a small part of the job. The community police officer acts as an innovator, looking beyond individual crime incidents for new ways to solve problems. They are the police department's direct link to the community, providing policing with a human touch as an officer who people know on a first-name basis and as a friend who can help. They act as catalysts, involving people in efforts to police themselves. They are mini-chiefs in beat areas, with the autonomy to do what it takes to solve problems. They are referral specialists, the community's ombudsman who can link people to the public and private services that can help and who can jog reluctant bureaucracies to do the jobs they are supposed to do.

The hallmark of community policing is that policing is tailored to neighborhood needs. In some programs, the officers operate out of offices in schools, public housing, or even in shopping malls. Police service and access are decentralized so that the police are more approachable to community members. When the police are accessible, people are more likely to cooperate with them, to have a reduced fear of crime, and to provide crime-related information.

SPOTLIGHT ON COMMUNITY POLICING PRACTICE

Community Policing: Home Sweet Home

It's been nearly 20 years since the Racine (WI) Police Department embraced the community policing philosophy and changed how the organization delivers police services. Their approach? Where crime was its worst was where the police department wanted to be. Rather than saturating officers to a crime hot spot, they moved in. Literally. "We explored the storefront idea," said Deputy Chief Smetana, "but, we could never get what we wanted." So instead, the police department decided to invest in the community by building its own house and setting an example for the neighborhood. Making this possible was state funding directed

(Continued)

towards local initiatives and a partnership with the Racine Community Outpost, a local non-profit organization currently run by three retired Racine officers: Dave Voss, Marty DeFatte, and former Chief Richard Polzin.

The purpose of these Community Oriented Policing (COP) Houses is long-term stabilization by way of building relationships with the community, improving the quality of life, reducing crime, consolidating resources, and providing programming. The COP Houses have become an anchor of their community. Initially, the communities were not enthusiastic. The first House was built in a drug-infested neighborhood and was fire-bombed. But now they have become a hub of positive activity. "If we asked the community," said Lt. Mark Esch, "we would have ten. Everyone wants one in their neighborhood." Today there are six.

The COP Houses have served as catalysts of change, leading to improved property maintenance and lower crime. In some COP House neighborhoods crime has been reduced up to 70 percent. And, it is crime that is one of the primary driving forces behind where a COP House is located. The criteria for establishing a community policing house is based on factors such as Part I crime, calls for service, and nuisance calls for service. "After being through some years of having 18–19 homicides and shots fired," said Deputy Chief Smetana, "calls for service are now complaints about loud car stereos."

Being assigned to a COP House has become a premier assignment in the department, with only 12 positions available among the 202 sworn personnel. Officers go through a competitive application and interview process. They need to demonstrate their communication and problem-solving skills. "Our agency has emphasized problem-solving throughout the department. It comes from the top down and we promote qualified candidates with an emphasis on the importance of problem-solving," said Deputy Chief Smetana. "What we look for is self-motivated officers and we give them the latitude and freedom to make decisions." Officers realize it's labor intensive work, but rewarding. Their focus is helping people and this is a chance for them to do that in a specific neighborhood and see the fruits of their efforts every day.

The COP Houses also serve as "Positive Alternative Centers," providing a positive and structured environment focused on learning. The police department provides the classroom and a computer lab, while the program provides everything from help with homework to arts and crafts. Every semester students from local Carthage College volunteer their time to the program and the kids. Carthage even offers independent study credits to students who become leaders of the program—that's how much emphasis and value they place on the partnership.

Through the establishment of the COP Houses, "the police department is closer to the community, closer to their neighbors, and cooperation is tremendous," said Deputy Chief Smetana. "The community feels comfortable because they trust us."

Amy Schapiro
Senior Social Science Analyst
The COPS Office

Source: The e-newsletter of the COPS Office, Volume 4, Issue 4, April 2011.

Some officers walk the beat, while others may ride a horse or a bike. The mode of transportation is not as important as the commitment to ensuring that the officer has the time and opportunity to talk with people formally and informally. The police mode of transportation is merely the vehicle by which officers get into contact with the members of the community.

The Strategic Facet

The police must develop strategies by which to implement the philosophy of community policing. Strategies provide guidelines for the development of specific programs. Community policing has at least three strategic facets. These facets include: (1) **geographic focus and ownership**, (2) direct, daily, **face-to-face contact**, and (3) **prevention focus**. These three parameters should guide operational planning when implementing community policing.

Figure 1.3
The Strategic Facet of Community Policing

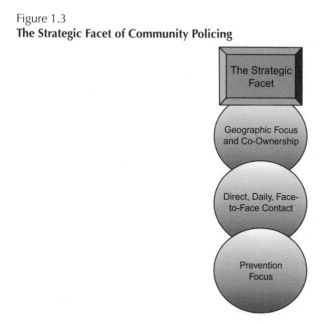

Geographic Focus and Co-Ownership

Traditional law enforcement focuses on time, function, and place as opposed to geographies within a community. In terms of time, police departments revolve around shift work. Patrol officers, detectives, and other officers are assigned to shifts. Police effectiveness is measured by activities across time, that is, what occurred on a particular shift. In terms of function, police departments are highly specialized with a number of different units, patrol, criminal investigation, traffic, community relations, etc., responsible for their own unique tasks. Officers assigned to one functional area seldom have the time or inclination to work on or worry about activities that fall into another functional area. In fact, typically only the chief in small and medium departments and precinct commanders in large departments have full responsibility for a given geographical area. Specialization by time and task inhibits the evaluation, or even articulation, of policing at the neighborhood level.

For community policing to be successful, there must be some level of geographical permanence. Officers must work a geographical area on a permanent basis so that they become familiar with residents, activities, and social problems. Geography is not a sole matter of place, territory, or location; it is the product of complex human interactions. Furthermore, if police officers are permanently assigned to an area, they hopefully will come to identify with the area and take greater care in safeguarding it and working to solve its problems. While the **territorial imperative** does not end, police must begin to understand the human geography of the areas in which they work. Command staff must also come to identify with and take responsibility for "geographical" areas. Once there is a level of geographical accountability within police departments, officers and units will respond more effectively to human and neighborhood needs and demands.

The importance of stationing a CPO permanently in a specific beat rests on allowing the officer to co-own that particular piece of turf and to begin to understand how that space is created and given meaning by human subjects. The optimal size of each beat can differ dramatically from place to place, but it will always involve people and human interactions. The goal is to keep the geographic area small enough so that the officer can get around the entire beat often enough to maintain direct contact with the people who create it. In high-density areas, an officer might only be able to handle a few blocks at most, while in a relatively tranquil residential area of single-family homes, the officer's ability to cover the physical distance might be the primary limiting factor.

Another important consideration in setting up beats is for the department to identify areas of community cohesion. Whenever possible, it pays to not divide a distinct neighborhood so that it falls into two or more beats. Along these same lines, it is not a good idea to have more than one distinct neighborhood group in the same beat. The goal is to decentralize police service by dividing the area into natural and manageable units that are derived from human interactions not maps, so that people can receive quality police service regardless of whether they live in little-town, Texas, or mid-town Manhattan. Beats should be as homogeneous and natural as possible.

A major misunderstanding about community policing stems from the misconception that the reward reaped for freeing officers from patrol cars transforms them into visible deterrents to crime. While that may be seen as a useful by-product of freeing officers from the patrol car or even a specific tactic in a high-crime area, the more important purpose is to involve the officer in the life of the community. This allows officers to integrate into the community. Obviously, the size of the beat significantly affects the quality of this integration process.

Direct, Daily, Face-to-Face Contact

Community policing also rests on maintaining the same officers in the same beat every day. The goal is to involve officers so deeply in the life of the community that the officers feel responsible for what happens in their beats, and the people who live there learn to trust them and work with them, and hold them accountable for their successes and failures. Community officers should not be used to back-fill vacancies elsewhere in the department, nor should they be rotated in and out of different beats. The only way that community policing can work is when both the officers and the residents can count on a continued, daily presence. This breeds familiarity on the part of the officers and community members, which is an important ingredient in community policing.

There is considerable debate around the question of whether community officers should be allowed to use cars for at least part of their shifts, simply to get around their beat areas more quickly. The optimal situation allows officers to walk or ride a horse, motor-scooter, or bicycle around the beat area, at least some of the time. These modes of transportation make it easy to stop and chat and to reassure people that the officer is concerned with them and their problems. Freeing officers from patrol cars altogether may be an essential step in reversing the pitfalls of traditional policing. The foot patrol studies in Flint, Michigan, affirmed this important concept (Trojanowicz, 1982).

The danger in the traditional system's reliance on the patrol car is that the patrol car becomes a barrier to communication with people in the community. Officers trapped inside cars are segregated from the public. They become slaves to the police radio, which serves less as a link to people in the community and more as a means for the department to control the officers' behavior and activities. This is especially true in large cities where officers run from one dispatched call to another. In some cities, officers never have the opportunity to talk with pedestrians or business owners in their beat areas.

Prevention Focus

As previously alluded to, community policing dictates that the police be proactive rather than reactive to problems and situations. A crucial part of proactive policing is prevention. Prevention is a much more attractive alternative when dealing with crime as compared to enforcement because it reduces the level of victimization in a community. Prevention subsumes a number of operational possibilities. Prevention refers to ferreting out the problems and conditions that cause crime. In essence, the police must examine the conditions surrounding crime in an effort to develop effective measures of eliminating it. This requires thinking about crime in a very different way. For literally hundreds of years, police have seen crime as a product of the individual actions of "bad" people who make the decision to engage in crime, rather than viewing crime as an act of "agency" (the ability to freely choose) that is carried out under real social conditions "structure" (the social, political, and economic conditions that guide a decision) before structure. Patrol, criminal investigation, and other operational units must become actively involved in prevention and seeing the structural and social conditions that contribute to individual crimes. Crime prevention units in police departments must become more involved and broaden their range of activities. Historically, crime prevention in a given police agency has centered on a few activities such as home and business surveys, neighborhood watches, and presentations to the community. Crime prevention units must become more active, and in addition to regular target-hardening activities, CPOs should assist operational units by serving as a resource when dealing with specific crime problems or **hot spots**, and they should work closely with crime analysis and operational units to identify crime, problems, and solutions.

A part of a police department's crime prevention responsibility includes attacking the conditions that contribute to, or result in, crime. Police departments must take the lead in implementing programs that attack causes of crime. Here, the police can assume a number of social welfare roles. Police departments now have programs to assist and refer people in need to appropriate social welfare agencies; they have initiated educational and recreational programs aimed at providing wholesome life skills experiences for underprivileged youth; and in some cases, police departments have begun to provide direct services to the needy. Crime prevention also means helping people at risk attain a minimum standard of living.

The Programmatic Facet

The above philosophy and strategies must be operationalized into specific tactics or programs. For the most part, community policing comes to life through: (1) **reoriented police operations**, (2) **problem solving** and **situational crime prevention**, and (3) **community engagement**.

Figure 1.4
The Programmatic and Personnel Facet of Community Policing

Reoriented Police Operations

The traditional police response to crime primarily consisted of random, routine patrols. It was believed that random patrols would deter crime through a consistent, unpredictable police presence. If patrols were unable to prevent crime, then officers, as a result of their distribution across beats, would be in a good position to observe the criminal activity and apprehend criminals. Finally, if this failed, detectives would be dispatched to investigate the crime and make arrests.

Community policing requires going beyond this reactive strategy. It means not waiting to be called, but instead identifying and targeting problems and implementing solutions. Police operational units must use foot patrols, directed patrols, surveys, and alternatives to random patrol to target community problems. In other words, the police must devise and implement police strategies based on the problems at hand. Community policing requires the police to tailor services to community needs. The police must ensure that they have an intensified police presence through larger numbers of positive community contacts.

Problem Solving and Situational Crime Prevention

Two primary tactics in community policing include problem solving (Eck & Spelman, 1987) and situational crime prevention (Clarke, 1992). Problem-oriented policing evolved as a result of the writings of Herman Goldstein and work by the Police Executive Research Forum (PERF). Goldstein (1979; 1990) observed that American police had devolved into call-takers. That is, police officers typically responded rapidly to calls for service, attempted to deal with problems or issues as quickly as possible, and then returned to their cars so as to be available to respond to another call. Goldstein noted that the police did little substantively when responding to calls for service, and if the police were to be effective, officers must devote more time and attention to calls. They must attempt to understand the issue at hand and provide some meaningful, not just short-term, solution. In other words, the police should engage in problem solving, rather than focusing solely on responding. Goldstein's idea evolved into problem solving, which now falls under the umbrella of community policing.

Problem solving consists of the following four-step process: (1) specific identification of the problem, (2) careful analysis of the problem and its attributes, (3) identification of possible solutions, and (4) implementation of a solution and a subsequent evaluation to measure the effectiveness of the solution. Simple questions such as What is the problem? What is causing the problem? and What can I do to resolve it? should be asked by officers when attempting to solve problems. Effective solutions require comprehensive responses. When effective problem solving occurs, solutions that go beyond traditional police responses become the norm. Such solutions include encouraging the city to demolish an abandoned building being used as a crack house; strictly enforcing alcohol laws in and around bars and taverns that experience high levels of crime; or encouraging people to construct fences around residential areas to prevent transients from entering the neighborhood and committing property crimes. Problem solving ventures beyond responding to and documenting calls. It represents a sincere attempt by the police to eliminate the conditions and problems that result in community problems and calls to the police.

Situational crime prevention, a form of problem solving, comprises "opportunity-reducing measures that: (1) are directed at highly specific forms of crime, (2) involve the management, design, or manipulation of the immediate environment in as systematic and permanent a way as possible, and

(3) reduce the rewards as perceived by a wide range of offenders" (Clarke, 1992:4). Adherents to situational crime prevention believe that crime is a product of "rational choice" where criminals weigh the likelihood of being discovered with the potential benefits of the act (Cornish & Clarke, 1987). They believe increases in difficulty in committing crime or likelihood of apprehension result in reduced levels of crime. This approach, however, does not really get at the social conditions that generate crime. Often it only diverts or displaces crime from one location to another and does not involve community development as a crime prevention effort. While situational crime prevention and problem solving play a role in community policing, they are not by themselves community policing.

In essence, community policing requires that police officers be creative when devising solutions and attacking community problems. Police must think "outside the box" and consider nontraditional solutions to community problems. Too often, police officers restrict their thinking to the same old responses to problems. Problem solving requires a substantial amount of innovativeness, and police managers must give officers the freedom to innovate.

Community Engagement

Community engagement implies that the police must depart from the professional model, and work with individuals and groups. Community policing dictates that the community become involved in protecting itself. People must realize that crime is not the exclusive domain of the police and government. People can become involved in a variety of ways. They can form neighborhood watches or patrols, report criminal or suspicious activities, become involved in sports or educational activities for disadvantaged youth, assist nongovernmental agencies in providing social services to the disadvantaged, or volunteer services. The police must encourage, motivate, or otherwise induce people to become involved in their communities. This is best with police supporting opportunities for involvement. In other words, create a need, and the police and the community will fulfill it with the appropriate amount of effort.

The police must also become involved in community building and empowerment. In some cases, a neighborhood or community will be so disorganized that it does not have the resources to become involved in helping itself. In these instances, the police must engage the community, identify leaders, and begin building the community. The police must work with religious and civic leaders to increase the level of neighborhood governance, and they must work to improve governance even when a neighborhood has a strong infrastructure.

There should be a reduction in crime concomitant with increases in local governance. In essence, the police must assist in building a neighborhood's ability to ward off crime.

Community engagement is often best accomplished through the establishment of partnerships. Not only must the police partner with community and neighborhood leaders, but the police must also work with other governmental and private agencies. Many governmental agencies have not embraced the concept of community policing. Rather, they still view their roles in the community as bureaucracies whose purpose is to follow bureaucratic rules when serving clients. The police must be leaders in identifying partner agencies and encouraging their involvement in addressing community problems.

The above sections provide a theoretical foundation for community policing. Community policing, as a model, is very complex because it entails implementation throughout a police department, not just selected units or officers. It is complex because it requires that the police department, at a number of levels, be in synchronization with the community it serves. Finally, it is complex because it requires not only that police agencies do different things (i.e., meet with the community, allow the community to decide police operations, or emphasize order maintenance over law enforcement), but it also means that police departments perform many of their old tasks differently.

There is an obvious danger in suggesting that police administrators can consider the elements that make up community policing as a shopping list from which they can pick and choose the things that sound easy to adopt and ignore those that are difficult to implement. We will discuss the consequences and practice of picking and choosing among the various programs and tactics that have become associated with community policing in the concluding chapter of the book. Yet, community policing can and must take different forms in different areas, depending on the internal dynamics of the department and the external situations in the community (Gaines & Kappeler, 2012). Ultimately, the sincerity of the commitment to the philosophy probably matters more than the particular strategies or tactics, and some departments may have good reason to phase in aspects of community policing over time.

What Community Policing Does Not Constitute

The above sections provide a fairly in-depth discussion of the idea of community policing. Community policing is a comprehensive philosophy that affects every person and part of a police department. It is also an overarching philosophy that dictates a department's operational strategies and tactics. To reinforce understanding of what community policing is, it is important to understand what community policing does not constitute. By understanding what does not constitute community policing, we get a better idea of what needs to occur if it is to be implemented correctly.

Traditional versus Community Policing Models

Question	Traditional policing (TPM)	Community policing (CPM)
1. Who are the police?	A *government agency* principally responsible for law enforcement.	*Police are the public* and the public are the police; police officers are those who are paid to give full-time attention to the duties of every citizen.
2. What is the relationship of the police to other public service departments?	*Priorities often conflict.*	The police are *one department among many responsible* for improving the quality of life.
3. What is the role of the police?	Focusing on *solving crimes.*	A broader *problem-solving* approach.
4. How is the police efficiency measured?	By detection and *arrest rates.*	By the *absence of crime and disorder.*
5. What are the highest priorities?	*Crimes* that are high value (e.g., bank robberies) and those involving violence.	Whatever *problems* disturb the community most.
6. What specifically do police deal with?	*Incidents.*	Citizens' *problems* and concerns.
7. What determines the effectiveness of police?	*Response* times.	*Public cooperation.*
8. What view do police take of service calls?	Deal with them only if there is no *real police work* to do.	Vital function and great *opportunity.*
9. What is police professionalism?	Swift/effective response to *serious crime.*	Keeping close to the *community.*

(Continued)

Question	Traditional policing (TPM)	Community policing (CPM)
10. What kind of intelligence is most important?	*Crime intelligence* (study of particular crimes or series of activities crimes).	Criminal intelligence *(information about* individuals or *groups).*
11. What is the essential nature of police accountability?	*Highly centralized;* governed by rules, regulations, and policy directives; accountable to the *law.*	Emphasis on *local accountability* to community needs.
12. What is the role of headquarters?	To provide the necessary *rules and policy* directives.	To preach organizational *values.*
13. What is the role of the press liaison department?	To *keep the "heat"* off operational officers so they can get on with the job.	To *coordinate* an essential channel of communication with the community.
14. How do the police regard prosecutions?	As an *important goal.*	As *one tool* among many.

Source: Adapted from M. Sparrow (1988). *Implementing Community Policing. Perspectives on Policing,* pp. 8–9. Washington, DC: National Institute of Justice and Harvard University.

Community policing is not a technique. Many police departments have moved away from the old quasi-military model, but many others are rapidly embracing military tactics under the language of community policing (Kappeler & Kraska, 1998; Kraska & Kappeler, 1997). Additional movement and redirection by many departments is required if they are to embrace the spirit of community policing successfully. Regardless, community policing is not a technique that departments can apply to a specific problem, but an entirely new way of thinking about the role of the police in the community. It says that the police must focus on addressing community concerns rather than their own agendas.

Community policing is not public relations. Improved public relations is a welcome by-product of community policing, though not its sole or even primary goal. Public relations units, however, tended not to attempt to help the community or focus on community needs, but rather they were designed to "sell" the police department. The underlying philosophy was that a substantial amount of dissatisfaction with the police was the result of people not understanding the police and the difficulties facing them as they enforce the law

(Wintersmith, 1976). Police-community relations programs were seen as vehicles to educate the public and lessen the strains between the police and community. Community policing, on the other hand, enhances the department's image because it is a sincere change in the way the department interacts with people in the community. Police-community relations, by and large, was appearance, while community policing is substantive. It treats people as partners and establishes a new relationship based on mutual trust and shared power. The traditional system often makes people feel that the police do not care about their needs (see, Reisig & Parks, 2000; Sampson & Jeglum-Bartusch, 1998). In traditional departments, officers often see people in the community as "them," those nameless and faceless strangers whose reluctance to cooperate and share what they know makes them indistinguishable from the criminals (see Van Maanen, 2006). Community policing instead treats people in the community as an extension of "us."

Community policing is not soft on crime. Critics suggest that community policing's broad mandate, its focus on the community as opposed to crime, and its use of tactics other than arrest to solve problems detract from a proper focus on serious crime. CPOs often face ridicule from fellow officers who call them "lollicops" or the "grin-and-wave" squad. The reality is that CPOs make arrests just like other officers do, but CPOs deal with a broader variety of community problems in addition to crime, not as a substitute for addressing serious crime. In fact, as Scott and Goldstein (2005:2) observe, "There is growing evidence that by addressing the conditions that underlie crime and disorder problems, rather than merely looking to arrest offenders, police can more effectively prevent and control such problems." The major difference is that CPOs ask themselves whether an arrest will solve the problem or make matters worse, and what solutions can prevent this problem from happening again in the future.

Crime analysis routinely shows that the majority of calls for service come from a relatively small number of locations (Braga & Weisburd, 2010; Sherman, 1987). An important ingredient of community policing is to focus on these "hot spots." But merely focusing on the hot spots fails to recognize that police behavior and programs influence who will and who will not call the police for assistance. Furthermore, applying location-oriented policing based on traditional notions of what calls are worthy of a police response violates the spirit of community policing. If people call the police, the problem is important to them and CPOs should see this as an opportunity no matter how trivial the call seems. CPOs must dissect these areas, determine what is occurring in terms of problems, and develop strategies for reducing problems. CPOs must also be mindful that their behaviors, programs, and data collection techniques, at least in part, determine what a "hot spot" is. By way of example, one rarely hears police speak of a concentrated group of drug users as a hot spot for the transmission of HIV, a hotbed of unemployment, or an area in the city with juvenile crime problems as devoid of social activities for youth. Community policing dictates that officers consider strategies and tactics, which include, but are not limited to, arrest and suppression. This does not mean that community policing is soft on crime; it means that community policing is smart about crime and open to suggestions on solving broader social problems that generate crime.

Community policing is not flamboyant. When a SWAT team successfully disarms or kills a sniper or a barricaded person, their work makes the headlines. When police officers engage in high-speed pursuits, it often makes the nightly news. When a CPO helps organize a summer softball league for idle neighborhood youngsters, the long-term impact may be equally as dramatic, but the effort will not rate a feature on the nightly TV news. It is unlikely to be picked up by the media. An officer may not experience the cultural satisfaction associated with the crime-fighter image. The media reinforces the image of the macho police officer whose job is glamorous, tough, and often dangerous (Kappeler & Potter, 2005; Kasinsky, 1994). The hero myth and "warrior fantasy" (Kraska, 1996; Crank, 2004), which accounts for a substantial degree of resistance to community policing, also appeals to police officers themselves. Community policing recognizes that the job gets done through steady, hard work, not warrior images and tactical exercises. CPOs must learn to defer traditional-cultural sources of gratification and notoriety and focus on the job and the long-term benefits of community building.

Community policing is not paternalistic. Police departments are organized as a paramilitary hierarchy where those at the top, to some extent, expect to set the department's agenda, based on their experience and expertise. This organizational structure and mentality often extend beyond the police department itself and are manifested in the way officers typically interact with the community (Kappeler, Sluder & Alpert, 1998). In its most extreme form, the message to the average person is that the police think people do not know enough about police work to do much more than pay taxes and respond to officers when questions are asked. The traditional, paternalistic police attitude suggests that crime is so complex and difficult that it must be left in the hands of skilled professionals specifically trained for the job. How many police officers, however, are trained at creating jobs and social activities for youth? How many police officers know the signs of mental and physical health problems? How many police officers know the relationship between crime, mental health, and the provision of meaningful activities for youth? Community policing threatens those who enjoy the traditional system, because it requires that police superiors empower officers and people with the decision-making authority to properly serve communities.

Community policing is not an independent entity within the department. Ultimately, the community policing philosophy must inundate the entire department. There are a number of ways of implementing community policing, including doing so gradually. Piecemeal arrangements include the formation of a special unit or concentration on specific geographical areas. In fact, it is virtually impossible to suddenly and comprehensively implement community policing in all but the smallest departments. When community policing is implemented piecemeal, it can generate tremendous pressure on the CPOs, who are the most visible expression of the new commitment. The challenge is finding ways to demonstrate to noncommitted members of the department how the community policing philosophy works.

Patrol officers in particular must be shown that CPOs not only help them by providing information, but also that they help ease tensions between the police and the community, which can be a particular problem in minority neighborhoods. In the Flint, Michigan, experiment, a foot patrol officer arrived on the scene shortly after patrol officers had responded to a call about a man brandishing a gun. The foot officer was able to tell his motor patrol peers that the man inside was known as a heavy drinker, and that his wife routinely visited her sister when he got drunk. A phone call there confirmed that the wife was safe and had her children with her, and that the man was probably asleep in the back bedroom. When the officers entered, they found the man passed out in bed as predicted. By working together, the motor officers and the CPO solved the problem with the least risk to themselves and others and avoided using a SWAT team. This is quite a different approach to the problem when compared to the use of paramilitary teams using force to extract people from their homes. CPOs are able to assist other officers because of the intimate knowledge they amass as a result of close ties with the community—thus, hopefully reducing the need for force-based actions.

Community policing is not cosmetic. Unlike crime prevention and police-community relations programs, community policing goes beyond providing information and expressing goodwill. Community policing requires that departments make substantive changes in how the department interacts with the public. Community policing broadens the police mandate to focus on proactive efforts to solve problems. CPOs are simply the patrol officers who serve as community outreach specialists, offering direct, decentralized, and personalized police service as part of a full-spectrum community policing approach that involves the entire department in new community-based efforts to solve problems.

Unlike limited proactive or community-relations efforts of the past, community policing not only broadens the agenda to include the entire spectrum of community concerns, but it offers greater continuity, follow-up, and accountability. It is important to understand that community policing goes beyond handing out brochures, making speeches, talking with community leaders, telling people how to guard against crime, and urging fellow officers to treat people with respect. As line officers directly involved in the community, CPOs have the opportunity to make real, substantive changes.

In Florida, a CPO concerned about the poverty and high unemployment in his beat area actively solicited leads on jobs, which he posted in the neighborhood community policing office. Officers in the Jefferson County, Kentucky, Police Department participated in neighborhood programs in public housing where youths were tutored in reading and mathematics. Community policing's proactive focus goes beyond target hardening, street sweeps of so-called hot spots, and other relatively superficial solutions, to initiating creative efforts that attack the very social fiber of crime problems. Such solutions hold the promise of long-term changes whose full impact may not become fully evident for years.

Community policing is not just another name for social work. The broad constellations of problems that plague society, especially in the inner city, defy simple solutions. Yet critics of community policing think that involving officers in efforts that have not traditionally been viewed as part of the police mandate is not only wasteful, but also silly. Traditionalists insist that the police have their hands full trying to battle serious crime, so efforts that detract from that effort not only waste valuable time and money, but they can erode the credibility and authority of the police. Their attitude is that the police should leave social work to the social workers, so that the police can focus all their energies on their real and important job of fighting crime.

Yet, this position ignores the fact that serious crime constitutes only a very small portion of what the police are called upon to do (Greene & Klockars, 1991). Further, Famega (2005) examined police workload studies and found that about 75 percent of officers' time is not devoted to answering crime-related calls for service. Indeed, if the police actually attempted to limit their mandate solely to crime, it would be almost impossible for most departments to justify the bulk of their budgets, especially since crime is declining dramatically (Kappeler & Potter, 2005). The fact is police officers are already involved in many non-law-enforcement activities that have little, if anything, to do with serious crime. These activities include: crowd control at public events, protecting politicians, issuing traffic tickets, providing people with directions, investigating accidents, and helping stranded motorists. The issue is not whether the police should become involved in efforts that do not directly focus on serious crime, but what other kinds of services the police should provide. Is it more effective to have another police officer issuing traffic citations or to have an officer in public schools speaking to youths about the hazards of drinking and driving or the unsafe operation of motor vehicles?

The police officer must be many things, law enforcer and peace officer, armed symbol of authority and part-time social worker. It is this blend of force and compassion that makes the job so potent and unique. No other job in civilian society permits a person to choose from an array of responses that range from flashing a friendly smile to using deadly force.

Community policing is not elitist. One of the biggest difficulties that CPOs often face is that they are heroes in the community, but objects of sarcasm and scorn among their peers. Some of the resentment stems from CPOs receiving seemingly preferential treatment or special consideration by the department. Left unchecked, this friction can erupt into outright hostility. Departments that launch new community policing efforts must pay particular attention to educating everyone in the department about the community policing philosophy, the role of the CPO, and how this new way of policing can benefit everyone in the department directly. It takes constant reinforcement from the top to explain that CPOs are not being treated like an elite corps, but as the department's direct link to the community. It is also important to establish CPO standards and allow everyone the opportunity to become involved. If everyone is given an opportunity to participate, it generally reduces some of the hostility.

Community policing is not designed to favor the rich and powerful. The dramatic surge in drug-related murders in Washington, DC, prompted more than one commentator to suggest that if these murders were occurring in an affluent enclave nearby such as Georgetown, the police would be forced to take more action.

That damning indictment that the police pay more attention to the problems of the rich and powerful deserves a closer look because it offers more than a kernel of truth. The fact is, of course, that the odds are that an upscale community like Georgetown will never suffer a similar spate of drug-related murders. The mistake is to think that this is because most of the residents of Georgetown obey the law, while the majority of those who live in poor neighborhoods in the District of Columbia do not. But what it does mean is that the high price tag required to afford to live in Georgetown means the community does not suffer from poverty, unemployment, illiteracy, over crowdedness, substandard education, declining health care, or despair, the myriad of social ills that plague many inner-city neighborhoods. Crime clusters in neighborhoods that already suffer from social and economic problems, and these problems can overwhelm the people forced to live there.

Yet there may well be more than a little truth to the persistent allegations that the police often accede to pressures to pay more attention to the wants and needs of the rich and powerful. Though this can include paying attention to even the most serious crime of murder, any gap in the level of service between rich and poor is likely to grow even wider in the level of response for less important calls for service. In fact, one of the most common complaints from inner-city residents is under-enforcement of the law. Inner-city residents complain that the police do not give their problems the same consideration that they give to problems in more affluent communities.

It is easy to see why the police might hustle faster to investigate an abandoned car, up on blocks with no wheels, if the call comes from a senator in Georgetown rather than someone from a bad section in the District. The first reason is that the police in Georgetown may well be far less busy, because there are fewer emergency calls demanding an immediate response. Second, that abandoned car would be a relative rarity in Georgetown, which makes it seem more suspicious. And the unfortunate and unavoidable third reason is that a senator who is unhappy with the police response can do far more to make problems for the department. The senator may well know the chief personally and would have few qualms about calling at home to complain. Senators also have access to the media, a bully pulpit from which they can denounce the department's inefficiency. Poor people, on the other hand, seldom have any access whatsoever when they feel grieved as a result of government inaction or insufficient action.

Community policing is egalitarian in the sense that it says that regardless of whether you have money and power, and despite whether you do or do not vote or pay taxes, all people deserve direct assistance and support from the police. For example, today some people are outraged over undocumented immigrants residing in their communities and advocate that they should not receive any form of government service. Yet in order to maintain community tranquility and ensure justice, the police should treat these people no differently than citizens. Community policing requires that every area within a city be evaluated and serviced. Community policing mandates that the police not disregard the needs of the poor, disadvantaged, or least powerful in society (see Bursik, 2000; Taylor, 2001; Velez, 2001). Research shows that officers who value equality are more willing to work with minorities (Zhao, He & Lovrich, 1999). In fact, the police can play an important role in leveling many of the disadvantages created by the political and economic system in which we live.

Community policing is not "safe." Allowing officers the freedom to attempt creative solutions to problems carries with it the risk of mistakes that can range from the embarrassing to the disastrous. The traditional system instead focuses on routinizing tasks and codifying procedures as a way to eliminate the potential for mistakes that can threaten the department's reputation.

At issue, of course, is whether police officers are educated professionals who can be trusted to do their jobs. Community policing dictates that police departments must learn to suffer the occasional mistakes, so that officers can bring the full impact of their education, training, experience, professional instincts, and imagination to bear on solving community problems. History shows that the traditional approach is far from being error-free, and that treating personnel as if they cannot be trusted cannot eliminate problems.

The preceding sections have laid out the idea of community policing. Our discussion shows that community policing represents a significant departure from the way policing has been thought about in the past.

Community policing is not a series or bundle of programs. Although many departments have implemented a number of new programs under the rubric of community policing, they have not yet achieved an operational level whereby they should declare themselves a community policing department. Too often, programs are implemented in a vacuum, whereby they have little contact with other units and programs. Administrators fail to recognize that, for most problems, there is no quick fix, and that problems are complex, often requiring substantial effort to solve. Previous sections of this chapter considered the comprehensiveness of community policing in terms of philosophy, organization, strategy, and programming. Each of these dimensions must be addressed for a department to truly implement community policing effectively. A series or bundle of programs, although having the appearance of community policing, will not be as effective as a comprehensive approach.

Community policing is not merely problem-oriented policing. Problem-oriented policing emphasizes social problems and holds the police solely accountable and responsible for addressing these concerns. Community policing recognizes that the police alone cannot solve social problems and that the community must be engaged in a meaningful way if change is to occur. Under the problem-oriented policing approach, the community

> You can learn more about the various forms of community policing by going to http://www.cops.usdoj.gov/.

may or may not be engaged in the identification and control of a community problem. Under community policing, there is always a collaborative level of cooperation between the police and the community. In fact under community policing the police mobilize the community for problem solving. Michael Scott (2000:98) summarized the difference in the following passage:

> Community policing strongly emphasizes organizing and mobilizing the community, almost to the point that doing so becomes a central function of the police; problem-oriented policing advocates such efforts only if they are warranted in the specific context of addressing a particular problem. Under community policing, certain features of police organizational structure and policy, like geographic decentralization and

continuity in officer assignments to neighborhoods, are deemed essential; under problem-oriented policing, many of these features are seen as helpful, but not essential—problem-oriented policing can be done under a variety of organizational arrangements. Community policing emphasizes that the police share more decision-making authority with the community; problem-oriented policing seeks to preserve more ultimate decision making authority for the police.

Problem-oriented policing without community control retains the traditional authoritarian top-down approach to community problems and does not involve the power sharing necessary to make real changes in the community. If the police are not willing to share power and decision making with the community, there is little chance that the community will embrace the police, the problems the police deem necessary to address, or the solutions they come up with in isolation. Problem-oriented policing without community policing can quickly erode into aggressive law enforcement practices that foster conflict and divide the police from the community. In such a situation police are merely moving crime around like deck chairs on the Titanic, all the while ignoring that they are heading for an iceberg. Problem-oriented policing without community policing is merely the repackaging of traditional policing which has been shown to have devastating social consequences (we trace these consequences in the next chapter).

Reconciling Law Enforcement with Community Policing

Community policing represents a departure from traditional reactive law enforcement. It de-emphasizes the law enforcement function and emphasizes service to the community, order maintenance, and community building. Indeed, only a small percentage of police activities and calls for service relate to the law enforcement function. There has been some criticism of community policing and its new direction. For example, Johnson (1997) notes that the community development goals of community policing are noble, but it is questionable whether the police can actually change value systems and cultural norms. He argues that family, peer, and community pressures and influences play a larger role in shaping identities than do surrogate associations with police officers. While there is truth to this assertion, values and culture are expressions of the real concrete living conditions within a community—not some ether that magically appears from abstract values. Changing the concrete conditions in which people live changes values, and police have an important role in changing community conditions. Regardless, the police must realize that they are confronting a monumental task when attempting to change a community's culture. Some would even argue that this falls outside the scope of law enforcement—but at some point, the scope of policing must be revolutionized.

The advent of community policing has witnessed resurgence in focused law enforcement activities. Police departments across the country are using saturation patrols, undercover operations, field interrogations, and other highly visible enforcement tactics (Gaines, 1996). Such tactics are being justified as a part of community policing. Police managers maintain that these tactics are efforts to "take back the streets" or regain control over areas that have been lost to crime. The emergence of these aggressive tactics is grounded in a failed philosophy rooted in Wilson and Kelling's (2006) "Broken Windows" theory and the U.S. Justice Department's funding of "Weed and Seed" programs. **Broken Windows** postulates that, if unchecked, a neighborhood in decline will continue to decline and the number of disorder and crime problems will increase. Therefore, the police and government must intervene and attempt to reverse neighborhood deterioration. **Weed and Seed** is an extension of Broken Windows. Under Weed and Seed, police departments across the country were funded to clean up drug-prone neighborhoods, and, once the cleanup was complete, to engage the community and assist in revitalizing it.

Decades of using aggressive law enforcement practices where the police wage a war against certain segments of the community have shown this to be a failed practice that only furthers community problems, reinforces the "crime-fighter" orientation of the police, and oftentimes leads to riots and civil unrest. Far too often, after police have aggressively "weeded" communities with law enforcement tactics, political leaders have failed to provide the promised "seed" to revitalize these communities, leaving the police with still another community

> *You can learn more about the Weed and Seed program by going to*
> *http://www.ojp.usdoj.gov/ccdo/ws/welcome.html.*

relations nightmare. Worse yet, these tactics have been used in the interests of big business to displace residents for the purposes of development and gentrification (see Zimmer, 1997). Unfortunately, a number of police departments see aggressive law enforcement as a potent tool in the policing arsenal. These are, however, tools that are not in keeping with the spirit of community policing and were the hallmarks of the failed traditional model of policing.

The Weed and Seed Strategy

In 1991, the U.S. Department of Justice established Operation Weed and Seed—a community-based multi-agency approach to law enforcement, crime prevention, and neighborhood restoration. The Community Capacity Development Office (CCDO), Office of Justice Programs, administers Operation Weed and Seed. The goals of Weed and Seed are to control violent crime, drug trafficking, and drug-related crime in designated high-crime neighborhoods and provide a safe environment free of crime and drug use for residents. The Weed and Seed strategy brings together federal, state, and local crime-fighting agencies, social service providers, representatives of the public and private sectors, prosecutors, business owners, and neighborhood residents under the shared goal of weeding out violent crime and gang activity while seeding in social services and economic revitalization. Weed and Seed began with three pilot sites in 1991 and has spread quickly to more than 300 high-crime neighborhoods across the nation.

The Weed and Seed strategy is a two-pronged approach to crime control and prevention:

- Law enforcement agencies and prosecutors cooperate in "weeding out" criminals from the designated area.
- "Seeding" brings prevention, intervention, treatment, and neighborhood revitalization services to the area.

The Weed and Seed approach is unique when compared with traditional crime prevention approaches of the past. The strategy is based on collaboration, coordination, community participation, and leveraging resources. Weed and Seed sites maximize existing programs and resources by coordinating and integrating existing federal, state, local, and private sector initiatives, criminal justice efforts, and social services. The strategy also puts heavy emphasis on community participation. Residents of Weed and Seed neighborhoods are actively involved in problem solving in their community. Neighborhood watches, citizen marches and rallies, cleanup events, drug-free zones, and graffiti removal are some of the common programs that encourage community participation and help prevent crime.

Source: Office of Justice Programs (2004). *The Weed and Seed Strategy,* pp. 1–2. Washington, DC: U.S. Department of Justice, Office of Justice Programs.

Perhaps the best known of these aggressive programs is New York City's **zero-tolerance** policing (McArdle & Ezren, 2001). Here, the police lowered their tolerance and enforced many minor infractions that historically were ignored by the police. The failed idea was that minor law violations ultimately lead to more serious crime, and by attacking minor crime the police can have an impact on serious crime (broken windows). At the same time, the department also began to target high-crime areas with highly aggressive law enforcement. The result was large numbers of arrests and a misguided belief that these practices resulted in a decline in serious violent crime. One must remember that almost every American city, even those that have not employed aggressive zero-tolerance practices, has experienced significant reductions in crime over the last few decades. Aggressive policing also resulted in an increase in complaints against the police. Greene (1999) questions the effectiveness of New York's aggressive policing. She notes that other cities, particularly San Diego, experienced similar drops in crime without aggressive policing. San Diego was able to lower crime rates while adhering to a brand of community policing that emphasized community partnerships. The research is mixed regarding aggressive patrol's impact on crime. Novak and his colleagues (1999) found that it had no impact, while Sherman and Weisburd (1995) and Weiss and Freels (1996) found a very weak relationship. The research can be only marginally characterized as mixed, but the historical result of aggressive policing is more than clear. These police practices result in alienation of the community (Reisig & Parks, 2000; Sampson & Jeglum-Bartusch, 1998), riots and civil disorder, and a distrust of the police.

SPOTLIGHT ON COMMUNITY POLICING PRACTICE

Broken Windows and Community Policing

The notion of broken windows has provided important insights and innovation to the field of policing. At times, however, these ideas have been misunderstood, misapplied, and often viewed outside the context of community policing. Broken windows is based on the notion that signs of incivility, like broken windows, signify that nobody cares, which leads to greater fear of crime and a reduction of community efficacy, which in turn can lead to more serious crimes and greater signs of incivility, repeating the cycle and causing a potential spiral of decay. For police, the insight of broken windows is that they are called on to address minor quality-of-life offenses and incidents of social disorder to prevent more serious crime, and that they must take specific steps to increase the capacity of communities to exert informal social control. Just as many have inaccurately reduced community policing to community relations, others have incorrectly reduced broken windows to merely zero-tolerance or order enforcement policies, with little regard for community concerns or outcomes. In fact, broken windows advocates for the careful implementation of these specific police tactics so that individual rights and community interests are respected. In addition, broken windows stresses the importance of including communities in the change process, with the primary goal being the development of informal social control mechanisms within the communities in question and not merely increased enforcement of minor offenses.

(Continued)

Later articulations of broken windows place it squarely within the context of community policing and attempt to address some of the legal and moral implications of its adoption. As Sousa and Kelling (2006:90) state, "we believe that order maintenance should represent a policy option in support of police and community efforts to be implemented as problem-analysis and problem-solving dictates." An application of a one-size-fits-all order maintenance program is unlikely to have universally positive effects on all of the various crimes and serious problems confronted by police departments and is not advocated for by broken windows theory. Rather, from the perspective of community policing, broken windows represents an important potential response to crime and disorder problems that may or may not be dictated through problem-solving processes, and broken-windows-style interventions should be conducted in partnership with community stakeholders.

Broken windows is more narrow in scope than the overarching community policing philosophy and fits well within the community policing context. For example, unlike the community policing philosophy, broken windows does not attempt to identify specific organizational changes in law enforcement agencies that are necessary to institutionalize these types of police interventions. Situating broken windows within the broader community policing philosophy can help to advance the organizational changes necessary to make broken windows interventions (when they are called for through careful analysis) successful and sustainable. For example, broken windows can benefit from community policing's focus on hiring different kinds of officers (who pay attention to disorder and have skills in community capacity building), building stronger analytical functions to support proper analysis, and making specific efforts to engage communities and increase trust to facilitate order-maintenance interventions.

When broken windows is correctly understood within a broader community policing philosophy, improper implementation of its central tenets through such things as ignoring community concerns, applying a zero-tolerance one-size-fits-all approach to minor offenses, and conducting cursory or no analysis of problems is less likely to occur. Appreciating the true scope of broken windows policing concepts within the context of community policing will enable these innovations to flourish and be most effective.

Matthew C. Scheider, Ph.D.
Assistant Director
The COPS Office

Source: The e-newsletter of the COPS Office, Volume 2, Issue 1, January 2009 [citation omitted].

Law enforcement remains a central part of the police mission. Aggressive policing has become a frequently used tactic by departments that say they adhere to community policing. We would argue that aggressive law enforcement is anti-community policing. Others would argue that the police must take control of "lost" neighborhoods before more positive relationships and actions can develop. Police executives must begin to take a cold, hard, and sober look at the politics underlying policing and crime control. They must ask some hard questions like: What public policies and political decisions led to the creation of communities that needed "weeding"? Did the very people who failed to provide the necessary "seed" to grow healthful communities make these decisions? Whose interests are really being served when long time residents are pushed out of communities for development? Were the police abandoned to deal with the consequences of poor public policy and politically motivated decisions? Is aggressive policing a fix for communities or for political leaders?

Community Policing and Homeland Security

The 9/11 attacks on New York City and Washington, DC, had a devastating impact on the United States both psychologically and in terms of public policy. It also affected the role and function of law enforcement. Police departments, as a result of the attacks, became more concerned with terrorists and homeland security. Homeland security is a multi-faceted endeavour. The Office of Homeland Security (2002) identified four primary goals for homeland security: (1) prevent and disrupt terrorist attacks, (2) protect the American people, critical infrastructure, and key resources, (3) respond to and recover from incidents that do occur, and (4) continue to strengthen the foundation to ensure long-term success. These four goals not only have implications for the federal government, but also apply to the state and local level. Local departments were instructed by political leaders, the media, and federal officials to identify possible terrorists to better safeguard communities and were encouraged to develop plans for responding to potential terrorist attacks and other catastrophes. In the midst of the fear generated by 9/11, the role of the police in addressing the "other catastrophes" aspect of homeland security has become obscured in favor of a monolithic focus on waging a war on terrorism. The police have an important role to play in helping communities following natural disasters like the 2011 flooding in the Midwest and the hurricanes and tornados that have devastated many communities. This important community service role has been all but lost in the obsession with terrorism. There is, however, an important role that community policing can play in the prevention of terrorism.

On the surface it might appear that preventing terrorism at the local level is the antithesis of community policing. This is certainly the case when the police are instructed to "wage war" against segments of the community. The "war against crime" and the "drug war" are two prime examples of the police being turned against their communities with little positive result. A "war on terrorism" would likewise require the police to use intrusive, aggressive, and militaristic tactics to ferret out "hidden" terrorists and terrorist plots. It implies that the police should revert to traditional and very aggressive tactics. Such tactics are intrusive and alienate people who are subjected to them—they are the antithesis of community policing (Brown, 2007).

We find, however, that preventing terrorism can be complementary to community policing (Murray, 2005; Pelfrey, 2007). The police, to a large extent, must depend on the public to supply them information to effectively prevent terrorism. A police department at war with the community it serves is unlikely to find very many people willing to partner with it to achieve any objective. If the police only swoop down into the community when it's time to catch the bad guys and can't be found in the wake of a natural disaster, they are not likely to find many people willing to share information. The police depend on the public to observe and report suspicious activities. In most instances, people become aware of suspicious persons and activities long before the police. Community policing fosters reporting and cooperation with the public, which are necessary if the police are to prevent terrorist activity. Thus, community policing can contribute significantly to the first line of defense against terrorism—information collection. It should not be de-emphasized in favor of aggressive police tactics.

> You can learn more about crime prevention by going to http://www.ncpc.org/programs/crime-prevention-coalition-of-america.

If the police have not developed good or positive relationships with members of the community, people are less likely to report suspicious activity. Too often people, and sometimes police officers, view minorities as terrorists even when they are law-abiding. This leads to problems with the relations between the police and minority groups. This is counterproductive to any crime prevention effort. If the police have good relations with all the people they serve and assist people in their times of need, they more likely will receive critical information about possible attacks.

Summary

Community policing represents a new, bold approach to law enforcement. Not since the beginning of the 1900s has law enforcement moved back to its social service roots. Community policing represents a comprehensive attack on community problems. It signals a time whereby the police are concerned with people and their problems as opposed to focusing solely on responding to calls for service and making arrests. Community policing truly is a paradigm shift.

It is important for the police administrator to not mistake some strategy or tactic for community policing. While community policing employs a number of strategies and tactics, the essence of community policing (empowerment of the community, community engagement, problem solving, and community partnerships) represents the glue that holds these strategies and tactics together. Community policing requires that police work as closely as possible with people to identify and solve their problems. Under community policing, crime reduction and "crook-catching" are not primary objectives, but represent strategies that are a part of a rich, over arching philosophy of community service.

KEY TERMS IN CHAPTER 1

- aggressive tactics
- broad police function
- broken windows
- community engagement
- community focus
- community input
- community partnerships
- community policing
- community policing officer (CPO)
- concern for people
- creativity
- decentralize
- developing trust
- face-to-face contact
- fear of crime
- geographic focus
- hot spots
- law enforcement function
- neighborhood variation
- order maintenance
- organizational and personnel facet
- organizational strategy
- philosophical facet
- prevention focus
- proactive
- problem solving
- problem-oriented policing
- professional model
- programmatic facet
- reoriented operations
- sharing power
- situational crime prevention
- strategic facet
- Weed and Seed
- zero tolerance

DISCUSSION QUESTIONS

1. Discuss the idea that community policing is little more than a continuation of police agencies telling communities what types of police services they need and will therefore receive.
2. Discuss and describe the sources of confusion surrounding the implementation of community policing.
3. Have a discussion on what exactly community policing is.
4. Discuss and describe major facets of community policing.
5. Briefly discuss how neighborhood variation can impact community policing efforts.
6. What is situational crime prevention, and how is it related to community policing?

7. Discuss the role of the CPO in community engagement. Include a discussion of the obstacles that may be present and how the officer can work to overcome them.
8. The text lists several concepts that are NOT a part of community policing. Discuss four.
9. Discuss "broken windows" theory. How does it relate to "Weed and Seed" programs? Is this an effective approach to helping communities?
10. Discuss the role community policing can play in homeland security. What are some of the pitfalls of a narrow police focus on terrorism?

References

Bayley, D. H. (1988). Community Policing: A Report from the Devil's Advocate. In J. Greene & S. Mastrofski (Eds.), *Community Policing: Rhetoric or Reality?* (pp. 225–238). New York, NY: Praeger.

Bittner, E. (1970). *The Functions of the Police in Modern Society.* Rockville, MD: National Institute of Mental Health, Center for Studies of Crime and Delinquency.

Bracey, D. (1992). Police Corruption and Community Relations: Community Policing. *Police Studies, 15*(4), 179–183.

Braga, A., & Weisburd, D. (2010). *Policing Problem Places: Crime Hot Spots and Effective Prevention.* New York: Oxford.

Brown, B. (2007). Community Policing in Post-September 11 America: A Comment on the Concept of Community-Oriented Counterterrorism. *Police Practice and Research, 8,* 239–251.

Bursik, R. J. (2000). The Systemic Theory of Neighborhood Crime Rates. In S. S. Simpson (Ed.), *Of Crime & Criminality: The Use of Theory in Everyday Life.* Boston, MA: Pine Forge Press.

Carter, D. (1985). Hispanic Perception of Police Performance: An Empirical Assessment. *Journal of Criminal Justice, 13,* 487–500.

Chappell, A. (2009). The Philosophical Versus Actual Adoption of Community Policing: A Case Study. *Criminal Justice Review, 34,* 5–24.

Chermak, S., & Weiss, A. (2006). Community Policing in the News Media. *Police Quarterly, 9*(2), 135–160.

Clarke, R.V. (1992). *Situational Crime Prevention: Successful Case Studies.* New York, NY: Harrow and Heston.

Colvin, C. A., & Goh, A. (2006). Elements Underlying Community Policing: Validation of the Construct. *Police Practice and Research, 7*(1), 19–33.

Cornish, D. B., & Clarke, R.V. (1987). Understanding Crime Displacement: An Application of Rational Choice Theory. *Criminology, 25,* 933–947.

Crank, J. P. (2004). *Understanding Police Culture* (2nd ed.). Newark, NJ: LexisNexis Matthew Bender/Anderson Publishing.

Eck, J., & Spelman, W. (1987). Newport News Tests Problem-Oriented Policing. *NIJ Reports,* (Jan.–Feb.), 2–8.

Famega, C. (2005). Variation in Officer Downtime: A Review of the Research. *Policing: An International Journal of Police Strategies & Management, 28*, 388-414.

Gaines, L. K. (1996). Specialized Patrol. In G. Cordner, L. Gaines, & V. Kappeler (Eds.), *Police Operations* (pp. 115-130). Cincinnati, OH: Anderson Publishing Co.

Gaines, L. K., & Kappeler, V. E. (2012). *Policing in America* (7th ed.). Waltham, MA: Anderson.

Gaines, L. K., & Swanson, C. R. (1997). Empowering Police Officers: A Tarnished Silver Bullet? *Police Forum, 7*(4), 1-7.

Gaines, L. K., & Worrall, J. (2012). *Police Administration*. Clifton Park, NY: Delmar.

Gallup (1996). Community Policing Survey. October.

Goldstein, H. (1979). Improving Policing: A Problem-Oriented Approach. *Crime & Delinquency, 25*, 236-258.

Goldstein, H. (1990). *Problem-Oriented Policing*. New York, NY: McGraw-Hill.

Greene, J. A. (1999). Zero Tolerance: A Case Study of Police Policies and Practices in New York City. *Crime & Delinquency, 45*(2), 171-188.

Greene, J. (2000). Community Policing in America: Changing the Nature, Structure, and Function of the Police. In *Criminal Justice 2000, Volume 3, Policies, Processes, and Decisions of the Criminal Justice System* (pp. 299-370). Washington, DC: National Institute of Justice.

Greene, J., & Klockars, C. (1991). What Police Do. In C. Klockars & S. Mastrofski (Eds.), *Thinking About Police: Contemporary Readings* (2nd ed.). New York, NY: McGraw-Hill.

Hale, C. (1996). Fear of Crime: A Review of the Literature. *International Review of Victimology*, (4), 79-150.

Jackson, J., & Gray, E. (2010). Functional fear and public insecurities about crime. *British Journal of Criminology, 50*, 1-22.

Johnson, R. A. (1997). Integrated Patrol: Combining Aggressive Law Enforcement and Community Policing. *FBI Law Enforcement Bulletin, 66*(11), 6-11.

Kappeler, V. E., & Kraska, P. B. (1998). Police Adapting to High Modernity: A Textual Critique of Community Policing. *Policing: An International Journal of Police Strategies and Management, 21*(2), 293-313.

Kappeler, V. E., & Kraska, P. B. (1998). Police Modernity: Scientific and Community Based Violence on Symbolic Playing Fields. In S. Henry, & D. Milovanovic (Eds.), *Constitutive Criminology at Work*. Albany, NY: SUNY Press.

Kappeler, V. E., & Potter, G. W. (2005). *The Mythology of Crime and Criminal Justice* (4th ed.). Prospect Heights, IL: Waveland Press.

Kappeler, V. E., Sluder, R. D., & Alpert, G. P. (1998). *Forces of Deviance: Understanding the Dark Side of the Force* (2nd ed.). Prospect Heights, IL: Waveland Press.

Kasinsky, R. (1994). Patrolling the Facts: Media, Cops, and Crime. In G. Barak (Ed.), *Media, Process, and the Social Construction of Crime* (pp. 203-234). New York, NY: Garland Publishing, Inc.

Klockars, C. B. (1988). The Rhetoric of Community Policing. In J. Greene & S. Mastrofski (Eds.), *Community Policing: Rhetoric or Reality* (pp. 239-258). New York, NY: Praeger.

Kraska, P. B. (1996). Enjoying Militarism: Political/Personal Dilemmas in Studying U.S. Paramilitary Units. *Justice Quarterly, 13*(3), 405-429.

Kraska, P. B., & Kappeler, V. E. (1997). Militarizing American Police: The Rise and Normalization of Paramilitary Units. *Social Problems, 44*(1), 1-18.

Manning, P. K. (1988). Community Policing as a Drama of Control. In J. Greene & S. Mastrofski (Eds.), *Community Policing: Rhetoric or Reality* (pp. 27-46). New York, NY: Praeger.

Manning, P. K. (1997). *Police Work* (2nd ed.). Prospect Heights, IL: Waveland Press.

Mastrofski, S., & Ritti, R. R. (1999). *Patterns of Community Policing: A View from Newspapers in the United States. COPS Working Paper.* Washington, DC: USDOJ.

McArdle, A., & Ezren, T. (2001). *Zero Tolerance: Quality of Life and the New Police Brutality in New York City.* New York: NYU Press.

Morabito, M. (2010). Understanding Community Policing as an Innovation: Patterns of Adaptation. *Crime & Delinquency, 56*, 564-587.

Murray, J. (2005). Policing Terrorism: A Threat to Community Policing or Just a Shift in Priorities? *Police Practice and Research, 6*, 347-361.

National Institute of Justice. (1997). *Criminal Justice Research under the Crime Act—1995 to 1996.* Washington, DC: U.S. Department of Justice.

Novak, K. J., Hartman, J. L., Holsinger, A. M., & Turner, M. G. (1999). The Effects of Aggressive Policing of Disorder on Serious Crime. *Policing: An International Journal of Police Strategies and Management, 22*(2), 171-190.

Office of Homeland Security. (2002). *The National Strategy for Homeland Security.* Washington, DC: Author.

Peak, K. J., & Glensor, R. W. (2007). *Community Policing & Problem Solving: Strategies and Practices* (5th ed.). Upper Saddle River, NJ: Prentice-Hall.

Pelfrey, W. (2007). Local Law Enforcement Terrorism Prevention Efforts: A State Level Case Study. *Journal of Criminal Justice, 35*, 313-321.

Reaves, B. (2010). *Local Police Departments, 2007.* Washington, DC: Bureau of Justice Statistics.

Reiss, A., & Bordua, D. (1967). Environment and Organization: A Perspective on the Police. In D. Bordua (Ed.), *The Police: Six Sociological Essays.* New York: John Wiley.

Reisig, M. D., & Parks, R. B. (2000). Experience, Quality of Life, and Neighborhood Context: A Hierarchical Analysis of Satisfaction with Police. *Justice Quarterly, 17*, 607-630.

Reisig, M. D., & Parks, R. B. (2004). Can Community Policing Help the Truly Disadvantaged? *Crime & Delinquency, 50*(2), 139-167.

Roh, S., & Oliver, W. (2005). Effects of Community Policing upon Fear of Crime: Understanding the Causal Linkage. *Policing, 28*, 670-683.

Rosenbaum, D., & Lurigio, A. (1994). An Inside Look at Community Policing Reform: Definitions, Organizational Changes, and Evaluation Findings. *Crime & Delinquency, 40*, 299-314.

Sampson, R. J., & Jeglum-Bartusch, D. (1998). Legal Cynicism and (Subcultural?) Tolerance of Deviance: The Neighborhood Context of Racial Differences. *Law & Society Review, 32*, 777-804.

Scaglion, R., & Condon, R. G. (1980). Determinants of Attitudes toward City Police. *Criminology, 17*(4), 485-494.

Scott, M. (2000). *Problem-Oriented Policing: Reflections on the First 20 Years* (p. 99). Washington, DC: Office of Community-Oriented Policing Services, U.S. Department of Justice.

Scott, M. S., & Goldstein, H. (2005). *Shifting and Sharing Responsibility for Public Safety Problems. Problem-Oriented Guides for Police, Response Guide Series* (*Vol. 3*, pp. 1-53).

Sherman, L. (1987). Repeat Calls for Service: Policing the "Hot Spots." In *Crime Control Reports*. Washington, DC: Crime Control Institute.

Sherman, L., & Weisburd, D. (1995). General Deterrent Effects of Police Patrol in Crime "Hot Spots": A Randomized, Controlled Trial. *Justice Quarterly, 12*, 625-648.

Skogan, W. G., & Hartnett, S. M. (1997). *Community Policing: Chicago Style*. New York, NY: Oxford University Press.

Sousa, W. H., & Kelling, G. L. (2006). Of "broken windows", criminology, and criminal justice. In D. Weisburd, & A. A. Braga (Eds.), *Police Innovation: Contrasting Perspectives* (pp. 77-97). Cambridge: Cambridge University Press.

Sparrow, M. (1988). *Implementing Community Policing. Perspectives on Policing* (No. 9). Washington, DC: National Institute of Justice and Harvard University.

Spelman, W. (2004). Optimal Targeting of Incivility-Reduction Strategies. *Journal of Quantitative Criminology, 20*(1), 63-89.

Spelman, W., & Eck, J. (1987). Newport News Tests Problem-Oriented Policing. *National Institute of Justice Reports*, (Jan.-Feb.), 2-8.

Stephens, D. (1996). Community Problem-Oriented Policing: Measuring Impacts. In L. Hoover (Ed.), *Quantifying Quality in Policing*. Washington, DC: PERF.

Suttles, G. D. (1972). *The Social Construction of Communities*. Chicago, IL: University of Chicago Press.

Taylor, R. B. (2001). *Breaking Away from Broken Windows*. Boulder, CO: Westview.

Trojanowicz, R. (1982). *An Evaluation of the Neighborhood Foot Patrol Program in Flint, Michigan*. East Lansing, MI: Michigan State University.

Van Maanen, J. (2006). The Asshole. In V. Kappeler (Ed.), *The Police & Society: Touch Stone Readings* (3rd ed.). Prospect Heights, IL: Waveland Press.

Velez, M. B. (2001). The Role of Public Social Control in Urban Neighborhoods: A Multi-Level Analysis of Victimization Risk. *Criminology, 39*, 837-864.

Weisburd, D., & Eck, J. (2004). What Can Police Do to Reduce Crime, Disorder, and Fear? *Annals of the American Academy of Political and Social Science*, *593*, 42–65.

Weiss, A., & Freels, S. (1996). The Effects of Aggressive Policing: The Dayton Traffic Enforcement Experiment. *American Journal of Police*, *15*, 45–64.

Williamson, T., Ashby, B., & Webber, R. (2006). Classifying Neighborhoods for Reassurance Policing. *Policing & Society*, *16*, 189–208.

Wilson, J. Q. (1968). Dilemmas of Police Administration. *Public Administration Review*, (Sept./Oct.), 407–416.

Wilson, J. Q., & Kelling, G. (2006). Broken Windows. In V. Kappeler (Ed.), *The Police & Society: Touch Stone Readings* (3rd ed., pp. 154–167). Prospect Heights, IL: Waveland Press.

Wintersmith, R. F. (1976). The Police and the Black Community: Strategies for Improvement. In A. Cohn, & E. Viano (Eds.), *Police Community Relations* (pp. 422–433). Philadelphia, PA: J.B. Lippincott.

Wood, J., & Bradley, D. (2009). Embedding Partnership Policing: What We've Learned from the Nexus Policing Project. *Police Practice & Research*, *10*, 133–144.

Zhao, J., He, N., & Lovrich, N. P. (1999). Value Change among Police Officers at a Time of Organizational Reform: A Follow-up Study Using Rokeach Values. *Policing: An International Journal of Police Strategies and Management*, *22*(2), 152–170.

Zhao, S., Scheider, M., & Thurman, Q. (2002). The Effect of Police Presence on Public Fear Reduction and Satisfaction: A Review of the Literature. *The Justice Professional*, *15*, 273–299.

Zimmer, L. (1997). Proactive Policing against Street-level Drug Trafficking. In L. Gaines, & P. Kraska (Eds.), *Drug, Crime, and Justice* (pp. 249–296). Prospect Heights, IL: Waveland.

Perhaps it is not true that history repeats itself; it is only that man remains the same.

—*Walter Sorrell*

CHAPTER 2 A History of Communities and Policing

LEARNING OBJECTIVES

After reading the chapter, you should be able to:

1. List the five interrelated pressures that influenced the historical shift from informal to formal policing in America.
2. Describe the development of policing in England.
3. Describe the development of policing in America.
4. Describe the spoils system and the problems with policing during this era.
5. List and describe the three rationalizations of vigilantism.
6. Discuss the impact of the Volstead Act on police corruption.
7. List August Vollmer's 10 principles of police reform.
8. Discuss the problematic relationship police have historically had with minorities.
9. Describe the role of the 1960s in the birth of community policing.
10. List the factors that set the stage for community policing.

The Lessons of History

The saying that "people receive the kind of policing they deserve" ignores the role power plays in the kind, quality, and distribution of police service. The police are social control agents, an institution of government that imposes the force of law on the public. Power, therefore, resides with those who make the laws and those who have the ability to influence the course of law. By extension, then, power is vested in those who determine police structures, set the police agenda, and choose the tactics police employ. This power arrangement can be as formal as political leaders passing new laws that direct police

53

attention or as informal as influential people and interest groups bringing pressure on political leaders to change police programs and tactics.

This power arrangement is an obvious invitation to abuse because the system permits the few to impose their will on the many, with the police controlled by an elite group. Ideally, the people make the laws through their elected representatives, but the organization and operation of the police can vary greatly from agency to agency, and from place to place, depending on the ability of social groups to influence police practice.

A main challenge in the United States has been to fashion a structure for the police that insulates departments from the corrupting influence of politics, without risking a department so autonomous that it is isolated from accountability to the people. Finding the proper balance between the need for police independence and the need for public accountability has been difficult. Examining the history of American policing can help us see what we have learned—and forgotten—as modern policing evolved.

Policing shifted from an informal to a formal system; this change also meant a shift away from direct community input and control. As we will see, most transformations in policing were the result of five interrelated pressures: (1) continued population growth; (2) the shift from an agrarian to an industrial economy; (3) increased complexity and inequity in the distribution of material resources; (4) the crowding of people into cities; and (5) advances in technology.

At the beginning of English policing, hundreds of years ago, people simply policed themselves. Volunteers or those conscripted into service carried out police functions. Policing became formalized with the adoption of regular night watches manned by volunteers that ultimately culminated in paid forces that provided service around the clock. These forces underwent reform that **professionalized** (bureaucratized) and attempted to depoliticize the police. In this process, police narrowed their mandate to "crime-fighting," and motorized patrol replaced foot patrol with the police rapidly adopting more modern technology. The bulk of modern police history shows that each succeeding advance inadvertently distanced the police further and further from the people they ostensibly served. Each effort to improve police efficiency and effectiveness was a response to an obvious social problem, but few recognized the downside to each change was increasing **isolation** from the community. The riots and civil unrest of the late 1960s were a vivid reminder that a society will not accept a police force that is alienated from and systematically uses violence against a large segment of society—regardless of the use of technology or the effectiveness or efficiency of the tactics.

The purpose of looking retrospectively at policing is to identify the best of the past we must keep, as it warns us of mistakes we dare not repeat.

The history of modern policing therefore serves to show why the emergence of community policing was a hopeful response to a system that was not in touch with its ideal function, which was to involve all people in improving society.

When people feel that the police do not understand or respond to their wants and needs, when police use violence to stifle progress or maintain an order that a significant number of people have no vested interest in, the result is either apathy, vigilantism, or revolution. History proves that safety and order are not commodities the police can effectively impose on communities; instead, they are the hallmarks of communities that participate in social equity and self-governance to improve the quality of life for all people.

The British Roots of Policing

The United States is undeniably a diverse society, with various ethnic groups who continue to arrive in search of the "American dream." While this unlikely mix has blended together to produce a uniquely American culture, with its distinct way of doing things, most of this country's institutions still show the profound early influence of the British with a strange mix of Puritan values. Therefore, understanding this country's law enforcement tradition requires a brief excursion into British police history. According to William H. Hewitt (1965), the history of law enforcement in England can be divided into three distinct, successive periods:

- The era when citizens were responsible for law and order among themselves;

- A system where the justice of the peace both meted out justice and maintained the peace; and

- A paid police force (Hewitt, 1965:4).

From our modern gaze, it is hard to imagine a time when there were no paid police officers and community residents policed themselves. Under Alfred the Great (870-901), citizens had to help apprehend wrongdoers or risk being fined. During that era, communities were organized into **tithings**, hundreds, and shires. Every 10 citizens constituted a tithing and every 10 tithings made up a **hundred**. A **constable**, appointed by a local nobleman, was in charge of each hundred; his job was to make sure citizens reported problems and tracked down offenders. A group of hundreds was organized into a **shire**, the rough equivalent of a county. A shire-reeve, or sheriff, whose role narrowed over time to apprehending lawbreakers, supervised shires. During the reign of Edward I (1272-1307), the constable was formally given a force to help protect property in large towns; the force was funded by pledges and manned by unpaid citizen volunteers.

In 1326, Edward II established a new office, justice of the peace, filled by noblemen appointed by the king. The justice of the peace, with the constable serving as his assistant, eventually refined his role to that of judge—the first official split of the judicial and law enforcement functions.

It is important to understand that the king and his noblemen had a vested interest in maintaining social order, because both crime and rebellion ultimately threatened the taxes upon which the feudal system depended. The people supported the upper classes, in exchange for which they received some protections. As economic pressures began to erode the feudal system, the pledge system that supported these local law enforcement efforts broke down and participation decreased.

The dramatic rise of the **Industrial Revolution** in the eighteenth century significantly accelerated the pace of social change. As people were pushed from the countryside and flocked to the cities, the older forms of community control broke down as newly vested interests arose with economic change. One of the most significant changes during this period was the enclosure movement. During the eighteenth and nineteenth centuries, lands that were used by entire communities, called the "**commons**," were consolidated and privatized with a series of acts of Parliament, called the "**Enclosure Acts**." These laws effectively took away lands that had been open to the public for use, divided and fenced them, and created private property. The enclosure movement took away the traditional right of the people to make a living upon these common areas, forcing many into the cities in search of work and destroying many villages. Ironically, because of industrialization, once these displaced and disposed people arrived in the cities they often found little or no work. One historian describes these changes as "a plain enough case of class robbery" (Thompson, 1991:239).

Between 1795 and 1800 a series of laws were passed to control workers. The "**Combination Laws**" prohibited workers from meeting, organizing, and striking against their "masters" to improve working conditions. Harsh penalties for these new "crimes" were enacted. At one point, stealing a loaf of bread was a hanging offense—one of 160 capital crimes. In that era, people vied for rewards that were paid for turning in offenders, and the guilty were given long sentences or deported to America or Australia, yet crime caused by dispossession continued to plague urban areas.

The King's Proclamations Respecting Seditious Meetings, November 1795

By the King—A Proclamation

Whereas it has been represented to us, that immediately before the opening of the present session of parliament, a great number of persons were collected in fields in the neighbourhood of the metropolis, by advertisements and handbills, and that divers inflammatory discourses were delivered to the persons so collected; and divers proceedings were had, tending to create groundless jealousy and discontent, and to endanger the public peace, and the quiet and safety of our faithful subjects: and whereas it hath also been represented to us, that divers seditions and treasonable papers have been lately distributed, tending to excite evil disposed persons to acts, endangering our royal person. And whereas such proceedings have been following on the day on which the present session of parliament commenced by acts of tumult and violence, and by daring and highly criminal outrages, in direct violation of the public peace, to the immediate danger of our royal person, and to the interruption of our royal person, and to the interruption of our passage to and from our parliament. And whereas great uneasiness and anxiety hath been produced in the minds of our faithful subjects, by rumours and apprehensions, that seditious and lawful assemblies are intended to be held by evil disposed persons; and that such other criminal practices, as aforesaid, are intended to be repeated: We therefore have thought fit, by and with the advice of our privy council, to enjoin and require, all justices of the peace, sheriffs, mayors, bailiffs, constables, and all other our loving subjects throughout our kingdom, to use the utmost diligence to discourage, prevent, and suppress all seditious and unlawful assemblies: and we do specially enjoin and command all our loving subjects, who shall have cause to suspect that any such assemblies are intended to be held in any part of our kingdom, to give the earliest information thereof to the magistrates of the several districts, within which it shall be suspected that the same are intended to be held; and if such assemblies shall nevertheless in any case be actually held, to be aiding and assisting, on being required thereto by the civil magistrate, in causing persons delivering inflammatory discourses in such assemblies, and other principal actors therein, to be forthwith apprehended, in order that they may be dealt with according to law. And we have also thought fit, by and with the advice aforesaid, to enjoin and require all justices of the peace, sheriffs, mayors, bailiffs, constables, and all other our loving subjects, throughout our kingdom, to be in like manner aiding and assisting in bringing to justice all persons distributing such seditious and treasonable papers as aforesaid.

Given at our court at St. James's the 4th day of November, in the 36th year of our reign.
God Save the King
George R.

Source: *The Parliamentary History of England,* Vol. XXXII. London: Hansard, 1818.

The need for new solutions became even more urgent when the people began to rebel against military intervention. In 1818, troops were called in to quell a disturbance at a lecture in Manchester, and 11 people were killed, with many more injured. For the first time, the people balked at using soldiers to deal with civil unrest, and the resulting public outcry set the stage for dramatic reform.

During the eighteenth century, Britain's population grew from about 6 million persons to 12 million persons (Critchley, 1985). Ironically, people moving to cities looking for work found "increasing mechanization which meant that manufacturers needed fewer and fewer workers. Accordingly, many job seekers found themselves unemployed and impoverished. Because so many workers were displaced, resentment developed that often pitted the industrialists against labor—a condition that drastically changed the nature of policing" (Kappeler, Sluder & Alpert, 1998:33). Social conditions in the eighteenth century worsened for most people. While the rich isolated themselves in enclaves with private security forces, others faced more difficult times. Evidence of disorder could be found everywhere. Riots occurred throughout Europe over food shortages, high prices, the introduction of machinery, and religious prejudice (Richardson, 1974). Public drunkenness became a common sight, and intoxicated mobs often engaged in unpredictable and violent activities (Rubinstein, 1973), many of which were directed at the industrialists and their factories because of the exploitation of workers. Urbanization was accompanied by homelessness, sewage, and air pollution. By mid-century, vast, crime-riddled slums had sprung up in the industrial cities, and frightened officials and industrialist supporters created a host of erratic and overlapping groups that launched a draconian war on the poor.

The Combination Act of 1800

An Act to repeal an Act, passed in the last Session of Parliament, intitulated, "An Act to prevent Unlawful Combinations of Workmen"; and to substitute other provisions in lieu thereof.

I. Whereas it is expedient to explain and amend an Act [39 Geo. III, c. 81] ... to prevent unlawful combinations of workmen ... be it enacted ... that from ... the passing of this Act, the said Act shall be repealed; and that all contracts, covenants and agreements whatsoever ... at any time ... heretofore made ... between any journeymen manufacturers or other persons ... for obtaining an advance of wages of them or any of them, or any other journeymen manufacturers or workmen, or other persons in any manufacture, trade or business, or for lessening or altering their or any of their usual hours or nine of working, or for decreasing the quantity of work (save and except any contract made or to be made between any master and his journeyman or manufacturer, for or on account of the work or service of such journeyman or manufacturer with whom such contract may be made), or for preventing or hindering any person or persons from employing whomsoever he, she, or they shall think proper to employ ... or for controlling or anyway affecting any person or persons carrying on any manufacture, trade or business, in the conduct or management thereof, shall be ... illegal, null and void. ...

II. ... No journeyman, workman or other person shall at any time after the passing of this Act make or enter into, or be concerned in the making of or entering into any such contract, covenant or agreement, in writing or not in writing ... and every ... workman ... who, after the passing of this Act, shall be guilty of any of the said offences, being thereof lawfully convicted, upon his own confession, or the oath or oaths of one or more credible witness or witnesses, before any two justices of the Peace ... within three calendar months next after the offence shall have been committed, shall, by order of such justices, be committed to and confined in the common gaol, within his or their jurisdiction, for any time not exceeding 3 calendar months, or at the discretion of such justices shall be committed to some House of Correction within the same jurisdiction, there to remain and to be kept to hard labour for any time not exceeding 2 calendar months.

III. ... Every ... workman ... who shall at any time after the passing of this Act enter into any combination to obtain an advance of wages, or to lessen or alter the hours or duration of the time of working, or to decrease the quantity of work, or for any other purpose contrary to this Act, or who shall, by giving money, or by persuasion, solicitation or intimidation, or any other means, wilfully and maliciously endeavour to prevent any unhired or unemployed journeyman or workman, or other person, in any manufacture, trade or business, or any other person wanting employment in such manufacture, trade or business, from hiring himself to any manufacturer or tradesman, or person conducting any manufacture, trade or business, or who shall, for the purpose of obtaining an advance of wages, or for any other purpose contrary to the provisions of this Act, wilfully and maliciously decoy, persuade, solicit, intimidate, influence or prevail, or attempt or endeavour to prevail, on any journeyman or workman, or other person hired or employed, or to be hired or employed in any such manufacture, trade or business, to quit or leave his work, service or employment, or who shall wilfully and maliciously hinder or prevent any manufacturer or tradesman, or other person, from employing in his or her manufacture, trade or business, such journeymen, workmen and other persons as he or she shall think proper, or who, being hired or employed, shall, without any just or reasonable cause, refuse to work with any other journeyman or workman employed or hired to work therein, and who shall be lawfully convicted of any of the said offences, upon his own confession, or the oath or oaths of one or more credible witness or witnesses, before any two justices of the Peace for the county ... or place where such offence shall be committed, within 3 calendar months ... shall, by order of such justices, be committed to ... gaol for any time not exceeding 3 calendar months; or otherwise be committed to some House of Correction ... for any time not exceeding 2 calendar months.

IV. And for the more effectual suppression of all combinations amongst journeymen, workmen and other persons employed in any manufacture, trade or business, be it further enacted, that all and every persons and person whomsoever (whether employed in any such manufacture, trade or business, or not) who shall attend any meeting had or held for the purpose of making or entering into any contract, covenant or agreement, by this Act declared to be illegal, or of entering into, supporting, maintaining, continuing, or carrying on any combination for any purpose by this Act declared to be illegal, or who shall summons, give notice to, call upon, persuade, entice, solicit, or by intimidation, or any other means, endeavour to induce any journeyman, workman, or other person,

(Continued)

employed in any manufacture, trade or business, to attend any such meeting, or who shall collect, demand, ask, or receive any sum of money from any such journeyman, workman, or other person, for any of the purposes aforesaid, or who shall persuade, entice, solicit, or by intimidation, or any other means, endeavour to induce any such journeyman, workman or other person to enter into or be concerned in any such combination, or who shall pay any sum of money, or make or enter into any subscription or contribution, for or towards the support or encouragement of any such illegal meeting or combination, and who shall be lawfully convicted of any of the said offences, upon his own confession, or the oath or oaths of one or more credible witness or witnesses, before any two justices of the Peace ... within 3 calendar months ... shall ... be committed to and confined in the common gaol ... for any time not exceeding 3 calendar months, or otherwise be committed to some House of Correction ... for any time not exceeding 2 calendar months.

Source: Statutes at Large, (39 and 40 Geo. III, c. 106), LIII, pp. 847-862.

Against this backdrop of chaos, **Sir Robert Peel** became Home Secretary in 1822, inheriting a fragmented system where there was one police force for business, one for shipping, and one for parishes, as well as a host of vigilante groups. The visionary Peel, acknowledged as the father of modern policing, introduced the **Metropolitan Police Act of 1829**. How the bill passed without dissent remains a mystery, since it radically restructured the status quo. Randal Williams' (2003:324) remarks shed light on the passage of the Act: "We know that the criminalization of the laboring poor was a decisive factor in garnering widespread elite and middle-class support for an idea which had long been stymied on grounds that it was an institution antithetical to liberty and democracy." The Act abolished existing efforts and, in their place, established a Police Office, administered by justices (commissioners) in charge of planning. It also created the Metropolitan Police District, staffed by paid constables.

> You can learn more about the Metropolitan Police Act of 1829 by going to http://www.historyhome.co.uk/peel/laworder/metact.htm.

The virtually unknown Charles Rowan and Richard Mayne were the commissioners Peel appointed to organize and run the new department. The duo set up operation in the back of London's Whitehall Place, which opened onto a courtyard used by the kings of Scotland—Scotland Yard. There they fashioned a plan to deploy six divisions of 1,000 men each, with each division divided into eight patrol sections, with those sections divided into eight beats.

To be an officer, candidates had to provide three character references and prove they could read and write. Despite the dismal pay—and the fact that becoming an officer cost the men their right to vote in parliamentary and municipal elections—more than 12,000 applied for the 6,000 jobs as a Bobby (a nickname honoring Sir Robert). Most of the officers selected came from cities other than London, which further distanced the police from the community (Richardson, 1974). The turnover was high, with more than 11,000 officers leaving the force during the first three years (Richardson, 1974), in part because of low pay (Stead, 1985), but also because of misconduct (Kappeler, Sluder & Alpert, 1998) and the public's initial resistance to the new police force. After the first year, people called for the force to be disbanded.

Yet the twin problems of low status and low pay persisted even after the force won acceptance. For years, British police officers were considered unskilled laborers, and it was not until 1890 that they were granted pensions. A police strike in 1918 led to legislation the following year that established a police federation that set pay scales and adopted a professional code. Of the nine principles typically attributed to Peel (which were, in fact, drafted by Rowan and Mayne), the seventh principle addresses how the police should treat the public:

> To maintain at all times a relationship with the public that gives reality to the historic tradition that the police are the public and that the public are the police; the police being only members of the public who are paid to give full-time attention to duties which are incumbent on every citizen in the interests of community welfare and existence (Reith, 1952:154).

Colonial Law Enforcement in Cities and Towns

Against this brief backdrop of British history, we can now trace the American law enforcement tradition to its beginnings in Colonial times. While the history of American policing can be traced to its English origins, the American system of policing evolved from an amalgamation of systems from England, France, and Spain. "Many policing problems plagued the new cities of America. They included controlling certain classes, including slaves and Indians; maintaining order; regulating specialized functions such as selling in the market, delivering goods, making bread, packing goods for export; maintaining health and sanitation; ensuring the orderly use of the streets by vehicles; controlling liquor; controlling gambling and vice; controlling weapons; managing pests and other animals" (Nalla & Newman, 1994:304). These early police services had little to do with crime control and were performed by volunteer citizens who served on slave patrols or night watches. Many modern American police organizations were birthed from these early slave patrols.

> You can learn more about colonial policing by going to http://law.jrank.org/pages/1640/Police-History-Early-policing-in-colonial-America.html.

Slave patrols and **night watches**, which later became police departments, had different primary objectives depending on the part of the country in which they were located. For example, New England settlers appointed Indian constables to police Native Americans (National Constable Association, 1995) and many southern police departments began as slave patrols. In 1704 the colony of Carolina developed the nation's first slave patrol. Slave patrols helped to maintain the economic order and to assist the wealthy landowners recover and punish slaves who essentially were considered their property. Virginia, for example, enacted more than 130 slave statutes between 1689 and 1865. Slavery was, however, not merely a southern affair; Connecticut, New York, and other colonies enacted laws to criminalize and control slaves. **Fugitive Slave Laws**, laws allowing the detention and return of escaped slaves, were also passed by Congress in 1793 and 1850. As Turner, Giacopassi, and Vandiver (2006:186) remark, "the literature clearly establishes that a legally sanctioned law enforcement system existed in America before the Civil War for the express purpose of controlling the slave population and protecting the interests of slave owners. The similarities between the slave patrols and modern American policing are too salient to dismiss or ignore. Hence, the slave patrol should be considered a forerunner of modern American law enforcement."

Select Virginia Statutes Concerning Slaves

September 1663-ACT XVIII. An act prohibiting servants to go abroad without a lycence.

FOR better suppressing the unlawful meetings of servants, it is thought fitt and enacted by this present grand assembly and the authority thereof that all masters of ffamilies be enjoyned and take especiall care that their servants doe not depart from their houses on Sundayes or any other dayes without perticuler lycence from them, and that the severall respective counties (as they find cause) to take espetiall care to make such by laws within themselves, as by the act dated the thrid of December 1662, they are impowred as may cause a further restraint of all unlawfull meetings of servants and punish the offenders.

September 1672-ACT VIII. An act for the apprehension and suppression of runawayes, negroes and slaves.

FORASMUCH as it hath beene manifested to this grand assembly that many negroes have lately beene, and now are out in rebellion in sundry parts of this country, and that noe meanes have yet beene found for the apprehension and suppression of them from whome many mischeifes of very dangerous consequence may arise to the country if either other negroes, Indians or servants should happen to fly forth and joyne with them; for the prevention of which, be it enacted by the governour, councell and burgesses of this grand assembly, and by the authority thereof, that if any negroe, molatto, Indian slave, or servant for life, runaway and shalbe persued by the warrant or hue and crye, it shall and may be lawfull for any person who shall endeavour to take them, upon the resistance of such negroe, molatto, Indian slave, or servant for life, to kill or wound him or them soe resisting; Provided alwayes, and it is the true intent and meaning hereof, that such negroe, molatto, Indian slave, or servant for life, be named and described in the hue and crye which is alsoe to be signed by the master or owner of the said runaway. And if it happen that such negroe, molatto, Indian slave, or servant for life doe dye of any wound in such their resistance received the master or owner of such shall receive satisfaction from the publique for his negroe, molatto, Indian slave, or servant for life, soe killed or dyeing of such wounds; and the person who shall kill or wound by virtue of any such hugh and crye any such soe resisting in manner as aforesaid shall not be questioned for the same, he forthwith giveing notice thereof and returning the hue and crye or warrant to the master or owner of him or them soe killed or wounded or to the next justice of peace. And it is further enacted by the authority aforesaid that all such negroes and slaves shalbe valued at ffowre thousand five hundred pounds of tobacco and caske a peece, and Indians at three thousand pounds of tobacco and caske a peice, And further if it shall happen that any negroe, molatto, Indians slave or servant for life, in such their resistance to receive any wound whereof they may not happen to dye, but shall lye any considerable tyme sick and disabled, then alsoe the master or owner of the same soe sick or disabled shall receive from the publique a reasonable satisfaction for such damages as they shall make appeare they have susteyned thereby at the county court, who shall thereupon grant the master or owner a certificate to the next assembly of what damages they shall make appeare; And it is further enacted that the neighbouring Indians doe and hereby are required and enjoyned to seize and apprehend all runawayes whatsoever that shall happen to come amongst them, and to bring them before some justice of the peace whoe upon the receipt of such servants, slave, or slaves, from the Indians, shall pay unto the said Indians for a recompence twenty armes length of Roanoake or the value thereof in goods as the Indians shall like of, for which the said justice of peace shall receive from the publique two hundred and fifty pounds of tobacco, and the said justice to proceed in conveying the runaway to his master according to the law in such cases already provided; This act to continue in force till the next assembly and noe longer unlesse it be thought fitt to continue.

August 1701-ACT II. An act for the more effectuall apprehending an outlying negro who hath commited divers robberyes and offences.

WHEREAS one negro man named Billy, slave to John Tillit, but lately the slave of Thomas Middleton, and formerly of James Bray, gentleman, of James City county, has severall years unlawfully absented himselfe from his masters services, lying out and lurking in obscure places suposed within the countys of James City, York, and New-Kent, devouring and destroying the socks and crops, robing the houses of and committing and threatening other injuryes to severall of his majestyes good and leige people within this his colony and dominion of Virginia in contempt of the good laws thereof.

Be it therefore enacted by the governour, councell and burgesses of this present generall assembly, and the authority therefor, and it is hereby enacted, That the said negro slave Billy stand and be adjudged by the authority of this present act convicted of unlawfully lying out, lurking and

(Continued)

destroying the stocks and crops and comiting robberyes as aforesaid, and that he suffer the paines of death. And for further encouragement in a more speedy and effectual apprehending or destroying the said negro and discovering and punishing his accomplices,

Be it enacted by the authority aforesaid, and it is hereby enacted, That whosoever shall kill or destroy the said negro slave Billy and apprehend and deliver him to justice in this colony and dominion, he, she or they shall be paid and allowed for the same by the publick one thousand pounds of tobacco: and that all persons whatsoever within this his majestyes colony and dominion that from and after the publication of this act shall witingly and wilingly enteraine, assist, harbour, conceale, truck or trade with the said negroe Billy, and every of them, shall be and by authority of this present act be adjudged guilty of felony and incur the paines, penaltyes and forfeitures lyable by law to be inflicted for felony, any thing in this act or any other act contained to the contrary in any wise notwithstanding. Provided alwayes, that if the said negro Billy shall be kiled in pursuance of this act, his master or owner shall be paid by the publick four thousand pounds of tobacco, as is provided by a former act in the like cases.

In the American colonies, constables were among the first law enforcement officers. Their numbers varied depending upon the size of the city they policed. Constables were charged with surveying land, checking weights and measures, serving warrants, and meting out punishment. The first constable on record in the colonies was Joshua Pratt. Pratt served as Constable for the Plymouth Colony in 1634 (National Constable Association, 1995). Constables were often assigned to oversee night watches, many of which later developed into police departments.

Perhaps the earliest organized law enforcement effort was the night watch first established in a Boston town meeting in 1636. Unless they could provide a "good excuse," all males over the age of 18 were expected to serve. No doubt the most famous night watchman was Paul Revere, the Revolutionary War hero who roused the people with the cry, "The British are coming, the British are coming."

In New York, a scout and rattle watch was established in 1651. The rattle was an actual "rattle," used to sound the alarm by a watcher, who made 48 cents for his 24-hour duty. The system was not without problems, particularly because offenders were often sentenced to this same duty as punishment. Once pay rates rose, however, so did the number of applicants eager for jobs.

Over time, watch systems in various towns became more sophisticated and more organized. By 1705, in Philadelphia, the Common Council divided the city into 10 patrol areas, each with a constable who recruited citizen volunteers to keep the watch with him. Incredible as it seems today, all these early law enforcement efforts only provided formal protection at night. In fact, captains assigned to various areas of New York (Colony) chose to interpret sunrise as occurring anywhere from 3 a.m. to 5 a.m., so they could shorten their duty. "In the larger industrial cities in the East and Northeast, a watch system was adopted. Because the South was more rural and agriculturally based, a county system of government emerged with the office of the Sheriff providing law enforcement services. As the Midwest and West began to develop, citizens preferred law enforcement services provided by constables and sheriffs—both of whom were elected officials" (Kappeler, Sluder & Alpert, 1994:39). Though the system had serious flaws, night watches functioned fairly well as long as America remained primarily an agrarian society—keep in mind that it was not until 1790 that six cities finally reached a population of 8,000. However, at the turn of the nineteenth century, the drawbacks were becoming difficult to ignore. One major problem was that local watchmen were notoriously lax, to the degree that they had become the butt of jokes about their ineptitude.

As commerce and population in the eastern states grew, labor and crime problems there began to mirror those in England that were fueled by the Industrial Revolution. Meanwhile, continued western expansion into the seemingly unlimited frontier created a different set of law enforcement problems. Understanding how these different traditions were ultimately wedded into one distinctly American approach requires looking at each historical trend separately.

The Rise of Municipal Police

As noted above, early law enforcement efforts in the few American cities large enough to require organized efforts consisted primarily of night watches, manned by citizens who were supervised by constables assigned to various districts. Major problems with this system were that they operated only at night, enforcement was erratic and inefficient, and the competence and character of the individuals selected or forced to serve were often suspect.

Between the Revolutionary War and the Civil War, rapid population growth and increasing industrialization pressured police departments to become more effective and more efficient. However, the downside to organizing the police into one structured department was that concentrating power into the hands of paid police without providing the proper safeguards ushered in an era marked by widespread corruption. Political elites, rather than the community, became the controllers of the police.

In Philadelphia, the first of a series of so-called Negro riots occurred, causing widespread death and destruction, including the burning of Pennsylvania Hall. The rioting broke out again in 1842 and 1844. Around 1835, a series of riots swept through the country. About 15,000 Irish citizens and firemen clashed in

Boston in 1837; riots in Philadelphia left scores of people dead; and in 1844, Native American riots lasted for three months, leaving many persons dead or wounded and much property damage. Similar episodes of mass violence took place in most other major cities. In New York, for example, 1834 was christened the "year of the riots" following repeated outbreaks of civil disorder (Miller, 1977). "Since there were no full-time police forces, cities had to resort to calling out the militia to restore order. Given problems of civil disorder, coupled with an increase in citizens' fear of crime, many cities had few options other than to create full-time, organized police forces" (Kappeler, Sluder & Alpert, 1994). As a result, police forces were formed in New York City in 1845, New Orleans and Cincinnati in 1852, Boston and Philadelphia in 1854, Chicago in 1855, Baltimore in 1857, and St. Louis in 1861 (Kappeler, 1989). By the mid-1860s, police forces had been created in virtually every major city and several smaller ones in the United States (Johnson, 1981).

As early as 1833, Philadelphia made a dramatic effort to organize an independent, competent, 24-hour-a-day police force, supported by patron Steven Girard, who left a large inheritance to fund police reform. Philadelphia passed a model ordinance that provided two dozen police, who would serve both day and night, with officers appointed by the mayor's office, and control of the force vested in one officer. In addition, the new law required that promotions would be based on skill and integrity.

While this sounds like a giant leap forward—and it was—within two decades, partisan politics undid Girard's "good intentions," with the police force consolidated under a marshal (later, a police chief), elected for a two-year term. While that change may sound benign, it meant that the police department was not insulated from partisan politics. Without safeguards, such as **civil service**, the spoils system prevailed. That term comes from the motto, "To the victors go the spoils," used in this sense to mean that the political party that wins and election can use patronage (political favors) as a means of consolidating and perpetuating its power. The **Spoils Era** in American history refers to the period prior to passage of the **Civil Service Act of 1883** when many federal officials considered a government post a private fiefdom. Once elected, politicians solidified their power by taking care of the cronies who had helped them win election. Every decision, from who would receive lucrative government contracts to who would be hired or promoted, was dictated by politics rather than merit.

State and local governments were far from immune to political corruption. Within local police departments, the spoils system meant that political favoritism dictated who was hired and who was promoted. In their dealings with the public, corrupt departments did the politicians' bidding, which meant looking the other way when politicians and their friends broke the law, while using the law to punish political enemies. This kind of corruption also promoted the harassment of Black people and immigrant ethnic minorities, many of whom could not vote, and the police were also used to wage outright war against strikers who threatened powerful business interests. In short, police were used to control and regulate the two major economic engines of the times—slaves and industrial workers.

Adding to opportunity for corruption as well was the fact that the police in those days also handled a number of other administrative tasks totally unrelated to what we think of today as part of the police role. In many cities, the police issued licenses for everything from taverns to ice-cream parlors, boarding houses to dog breeders. Even honest cops who were not tempted by monetary bribes could do little to defy a system where such licenses were dispensed as political favors.

In the Spoils Era, a police chief whose sole qualification was that he would do the bidding of the politician or politicians who gave him his job routinely headed police departments. Lack of qualified and independent leadership at the top was a major problem in American policing for many years.

In cities such as Baltimore and Cincinnati, the police force was used primarily to rig elections. Until 1844, New York City had actually had two police forces, one for daytime duty, and one for nighttime duty, with each dispensing patronage. The New York police reform act passed that same year became a model for the American police system, though it lagged years behind Peelian reform in England. The major problem with the law was that it allowed aldermen and assistant aldermen to appoint the police captain, assistant captains, and patrolmen for their wards to one-year terms. The police chief, appointed by the mayor, was little more than a figurehead. While the new system attempted, in theory, to consolidate and upgrade the police into one unit controlled by a police chief, in practice, it institutionalized political corruption.

In some municipalities, police officials were elected; in others, the mayor, the city council, or some other administrative body appointed them. Even uniforms were not standardized. As late as 1853, New York policemen wore civilian clothes and could only be identified by the 33-inch clubs they carried. Initial efforts at standardization often did little to lessen confusion, since each ward adopted its own style. For instance, the summer uniforms in some wards consisted of suits made of white duck cloth, while others opted to wear colors, and some even chose to wear straw hats.

By 1860, Philadelphia decided to adopt a standard police uniform, which consisted of single-breasted blue frock coats with brass buttons, white pants with black stripes down the sides, and an old-style broad-top cap with a leather visor. It was not until the next year that a new badge was adopted, and a few years later the trousers were changed to matching blue, inaugurating the blue look associated with police uniforms today.

As these anecdotes demonstrate, the history of policing in this era was marked by occasional enlightened efforts to upgrade the force, but few efforts addressed the underlying corruption in any systematic way. For example, in 1871, leading police officials of the time met in Philadelphia, where they devised and implemented the first uniform crime-reporting system, a valuable attempt to find new ways to identify crime trends. Yet, this development was a first major step toward institutionalizing the police and making them a crime-fighting bureaucracy of limited responsiveness to people's concerns. It, in effect, created a measure of police performance based on reported crime rather than community input and concern. By that time, pay scales for police officers had also improved, and, by the mid-1880s, police officers in many metropolitan areas could retire at half pay after 20 years of service.

Graft was endemic. The **Lexow investigation** of the New York City Police Department in 1894 confirmed that officers had to pay to be hired, with higher payoffs for promotions. From their first contact with the department, rookies learned that bribery and political pull were part of the system.

> You can read more about the Lexow investigation by going to http://teacher.sduhsd.k12.ca.us/tpsocialsciences/us_history/guildedage/lexow.htm.

Civil service reform helped clean up some abuses, particularly in hiring and promotion, and periodic, highly touted investigations of corruption in big-city departments also spurred change, though in many cases, those gains faded when the headlines stopped (Kappeler, Sluder & Alpert, 1998). However, as long as police leadership remained deeply politicized, the taint of corruption hovered around many municipal police departments well into the twentieth century.

While nineteenth-century law enforcement in the eastern United States was primarily a study in learning how to develop structures suited to increasingly populous cities, the law enforcement challenge in the Wild West during this period focused on how to make the frontier a safer place, which involved different kinds of problems, because people were scattered far apart and communication between settlements was almost non existent. As we will see later, no sector of the United States was free of vigilantism, but, on the frontier, even authorized efforts dispensed street justice.

Frontier Justice

The westward expansion that characterized the nineteenth century meant that White people ventured into the wilderness first, and then formal institutions followed. Movies about this era tend to glorify the violence associated with the lawlessness of the frontier, but there were many bloody clashes between various interest groups—sheepherders versus cattlemen, farmers versus ranchers, settlers versus Native Americans, various ethnic groups against each other, and in many cases the police against themselves. Perhaps the story of the Texas Rangers best describes the bloody conflict of frontier justice and policing. The **Texas Rangers** are said to be the first state police organization. While the history of the Texas Rangers can be traced to 1823, the name did not appear in legislation until 1874. In 1823, Stephen F. Austin—often called the "Father of Texas"—wrote about the need for a small group of men to protect his fledgling colony. In August of that same year, Austin sent a proclamation to Land Commissioner Baron de Bastrop and on the back of that document wrote that he would "employ ten men ... to act as rangers for the common defense ... the wages I will give said ten men is fifteen dollars a month payable in property."

These initial Rangers only convened when needed and worked on a voluntary basis. By 1835, a local council created a "Corps of Rangers" to provide frontier settlements protection from Native Americans.

The Texas Rangers became the stuff of legend in 1841, with the slaughter of Comanche peoples under the direction of Captain Jack Hayes. The movement of the capital of Texas from Houston to Austin began a cycle of conflict between the Rangers and the Comanches, when the Rangers began surveying the Comanches' holy mountains. The Rangers became even more infamous when the war with Mexico was declared in 1846 and Zachary Taylor commissioned Texas Ranger Samuel Walker to the United States military. Samuel Walker and his Texas Rangers developed a reputation for engaging in activities that even the military could not condone. Among Mexicans, the Rangers became know as "Los Diablos Tejanos"—the Texas Devils. As one Texas Ranger put it, their objective was to "demand blood for blood." Eventually, Taylor sent the Texas Rangers packing. For a decade after the Mexican War, the Rangers reverted to their volunteer status. Settlers were also not only easy prey for con men and swindlers offering phony land deals, but isolated families alone on the prairie had little protection from thieves and rustlers (Gaines & Kappeler, 2011).

The laws in place were also a curious blend of criminal codes and so-called **blue laws**, a peculiar American phenomenon where religious groups successfully lobbied to make custom criminal laws. Many of these laws related to the sale and consumption of alcohol, either restricting its sale to certain times or places or banning it outright in specific areas. In other cases, blue laws regulated everything from store hours to public dancing. There was a certain irony in the fact that many

> *You can learn more about the blue laws by going to* http://law.jrank.org/pages/1640/Police-History-Early-policing-in-colonial-America.html.

frontier communities had rigid laws governing social behavior, when, at the same time, it was doubtful they had mechanisms in place to enforce laws against major crimes. A similar desire to control morals was exhibited in the eastern part of the United States. The Massachusetts State Police force was created in 1865, making it one of the oldest statewide law enforcement agencies in the nation. The creation of the Massachusetts State Police evolved out of the desire to control vice-related crime in rural Massachusetts (Gaines & Kappeler, 2011).

In many cases as well, it was difficult to tell much difference between formal law enforcement and vigilantism. The prevailing system in most frontier towns was a sheriff serving as the chief law enforcement official. The sheriff could deputize citizen volunteers to track down offenders, and visiting circuit judges made periodic rounds of outlying territories to conduct trials. When the town or territory could afford to do so, the sheriff was a paid official, but the candidates for the job often had few skills beyond a willingness to take what was often a thankless job.

Vigilantism

Because of an inadequate justice system and the violent nature of American frontier life, many people had few qualms with taking the law into their own hands. Drawing the line between "responsible" efforts of organized civilian volunteers and vigilantism can thus be difficult. After all, looking back on the British experience, groups of unpaid citizens constituted the bulk of early law enforcement efforts. However, as the concept of justice evolved, it recognized that victims and their families and friends must be removed from the formal process, since they could not be expected to be "objective"—if you damage my property, that should be a capital crime, whereas if I damage yours, that is merely a forgivable accident.

What makes **vigilantism** different from "responsible citizen action" is that it often operates in opposition to formal legal norms and is often driven by xenophobia, racism, and prejudice. As more than one sheriff learned, standing in the way of vigilantes intent on enforcing their own brand of justice could be more dangerous than dealing with other criminals. Among the first recorded examples of vigilantism were the South Carolina regulators who operated between 1767 and 1769. This extralegal citizens' group served as a model for later vigilante efforts. Astute filmgoers will note that Marlon Brando played a regulator hired to kill rustlers in *The Missouri Breaks,* certifying "regulator" as the preferred term for a vigilante until the mid-nineteenth century.

According to Richard M. Brown in *Violence in America*, vigilantism is based on three rationalizations:

- **Self-preservation**—Just as self-defense is a valid defense for what would otherwise be murder, this idea justifies vigilantism by arguing that citizens must be willing to kill or be killed when the official system fails to provide adequate protection. Newspapers of the era often endorsed this sentiment. An editorial in the *San Francisco Herald* in 1851 said: "Whenever the law becomes an empty name, has not the citizen the right to supply its deficiencies?" (Gard, 1949:158).

- **Right of revolution**—Unlike the Canadians, for instance, people of the United States come from a tradition of violent revolution, and early framers of the Constitution argued that periodic revolt might be necessary to prevent government tyranny. Part of the American psyche embraces the idea that when something fails to work properly, revolution is as valid a response as reform.

- **Economic rationale**—The development and maintenance of an effective criminal justice system is an expensive proposition, and this position argued that frontier towns should not bear the expense, when vigilantism did the job efficiently for free (Brown, 1969:140).

Echoes of all three justifications can be heard in this particular warning, posted outside Las Vegas, New Mexico, in 1880, a citizen manifesto similar to many of that era:

The citizens of Las Vegas are tired of robbery, murder, and other crimes that have made this town a byword in every civilized community. They are resolved to put a stop to crime, even if, in obtaining that end, they have to forget the law and resort to a speedier justice than it will afford. All such characters are notified that they must either leave this town or conform themselves to the requirement of the law or they will be severely dealt with. The flow of blood must and shall be stopped in this community and good citizens of both the old and new towns have been determined to stop it if they have to hang by the strong arm of force every violator of law in this country—Vigilantes (Otem, 1935:205-206).

The impulse to vigilantism may be understandable, but a system with no controls is an invitation to abuse. All too often, the innocent were hung along with or instead of the guilty. In addition, whenever groups operate with no oversight, there is nothing to prevent people's worst instincts from taking over. On the frontier in the South, and also in the major cities of the East, prejudice ran high against various groups—Native peoples, people of African descent, Mexicans, and immigrants. Many formal law enforcement efforts were often tainted by a two-track system of justice, where offenses committed by members of unpopular groups rated punishment far beyond what White Americans suffered, especially if the victims were White.

Because vigilantes, by definition, have no external restraints, lynch mobs had a justified reputation for hanging minorities first and asking questions later. Because of its tradition of slavery, which rested on the racist rationalization that Blacks were sub-human, the South had a long and shameful history of mistreating people of color, long after the end of the Civil War. Perhaps the most infamous American vigilante group, the Ku Klux Klan, was notorious for assaulting and killing Black men for transgressions that would not be considered crimes at all, had a White man committed them.

Minutemen Gather to Patrol U.S.-Mexico Border

An organization of volunteers known as the Minuteman Project is planning to begin patrolling a 23-mile stretch of the Arizona-Mexico border in the search for illegal immigrants. The project is described as the "nation's largest neighborhood watch group" by Minuteman field operations director Chris Simcox.

The goal of the project is to make Americans aware of porous and undefended American borders. They are motivated by concern about illegal drug trafficking, the availability of entry points for potential terrorists, and a lack of effective enforcement of immigration laws by U.S. federal and state officials, and the name Minuteman was used in order for the group to portray itself as a "grassroots effort to bring Americans to the defense of their homeland, similar to the way the original Minutemen from Massachusetts (and other U.S. colonies) did in the late 1700s," according to the group's website.

The activities of the Minutemen are protected by legal rights found in the U.S. Constitution, according to various commentators. Says Arizona Gov. Janet Napolitano, "People are entitled to exercise their First Amendment rights and entitled to assemble....That's why you can't stop the Minutemen from coming even though, from a law enforcement perspective, it's worrisome to have untrained people, potentially armed, performing what should be a law enforcement function." Some of the Minutemen plan to be armed in order to defend themselves in case of aggressive action by potential armed illegal immigrants and those who transport them. The carrying of handguns is allowed under Arizona law and is protected by the Second Amendment.

The Minutemen are not allowed by law to arrest or detain potential illegal immigrants, and any such action is forbidden by the group's organizers. The project's goal is to survey the area using planes and binoculars and to alert the appropriate authorities and follow suspected illegal immigrants until they are detained. Observers from various groups, most prominently the American Civil Liberties Union (ACLU), plan to be on hand to monitor the activities of the Minutemen with a view to mounting possible legal challenges against them.

Critics, such as some Arizona Hispanic lawmakers, are planning to show up at the public gatherings and press conferences of the Minutemen, in order to raise criticism and present contrary points of view to the public about what they believe to be the current state of illegal immigration. Some opponents have also complained that many participants may be motivated by racism or vigilantism; however, the organizers of the Project make a point of emphasizing their lack of participation with separatist or supremacist groups and the racial diversity and inclusiveness of their volunteers.

Illegal immigrants and their public benefits have come under increasing scrutiny in recent months in Arizona, with the passing of Proposition 200 on November 2, 2004 by a margin of 56% of voters in favor. This proposition attempts to prevent illegal immigrants from voting or receiving some government services. The effort to define what benefits they can legally be excluded from is ongoing, for example, with the recent failure of HB2264 to pass an Arizona senate committee; the bill would have required some illegal immigrants to pay higher out-of-state rates for college tuition.

Similar efforts to the current Minuteman Project have been organized in the past few years, but with few participants and without notable success. Some local residents were concerned that possible violence could erupt from the presence of additional armed individuals, either among the Minutemen or the illegal immigrants. Others welcomed the presence of the Minutemen, considering them tourists helping the local economy and appreciating their drawing attention to the perceived lax enforcement of border control by federal authorities. Their activities are planned to last for about a month.

Source: *Wikinews* (2005). Minutemen Gather to Patrol U.S.-Mexico Border in April. April 1, 2005.

Hundreds of Southern Blacks were hanged by lynch mobs for crimes like whistling at a White woman or failing to show proper respect to a White person. This story of "Southern" racism, however, masks the systemic nature of racism across the country as well as the police role in this period of American history. Racism and violence toward Blacks was not just occurring in the South among civilians, in fact history shows the majority of lynchings occurred in northern states and the police were active participates in this form of injustice. Adding to the climate of terror such outrages perpetuated was the fact that many law enforcement officers actually participated in or gave tacit approval to Klan activities; some vigilante groups enjoyed a quasi-legal status or were at least tolerated by the establishment. The **Civil Rights Act of 1871**, which has become the modern-day foundation for police legal liability for civil rights violations (Kappeler, 2005), passed in large part because of involvement of law enforcement in the activities of the Ku Klux Klan.

Twentieth-Century Policing

While the foregoing might seem like a uniformly grim and pessimistic view of the history of law enforcement, there were undeniable problems in law enforcement at the turn of the century, including the taint of corruption, shortcomings and confusion in leadership, vigilantism, and inequities in application of laws. Though civil service reform helped introduce increased fairness in hiring and promotion, without effective leadership at the top, many police departments continued to wallow in corruption.

Part of the problem was structural, since police boards that rarely provided a single, strong leader who could speak with authority for the department and to the department controlled many big-city departments. Awareness of this flaw led to efforts to invest leadership in one person, so that by 1921, only 14 out of the 52 cities in the United States with a population of 100,000 or more were still run by police boards. This reform, however, served to highlight another major defect—men who had no practical or educational background in law enforcement headed too many departments.

Once New York City adopted the single-administrator form, during roughly the next two decades, a parade of army officers, newspapermen, lawyers, and professional politicians were tapped to fill the post. In Philadelphia, during the first 20 years of the twentieth century, a candy manufacturer, an insurance broker, a banker, an electric company official, and five lawyers filled the position of director of public safety.

This also indicates the tremendous problem many departments had with turnover, since civil service reforms did little to insulate the top spot from politics. Not only were most top police administrators incompetent for the job, but also they served at the whim of politicians. Police Commissioner Woods of New York City testified in 1912:"The police department is peculiarly the victim of this principle of transient management. Most of the commissioners are birds of passage. The force gets a glimpse of them flying over, but hardly has time to determine the species" (Fosdick, 1921:68).

At that time, New York had seen 12 commissioners in 19 years, with an average term on the job of less than two years, and the shortest term only lasting 33 days. In comparison, by 1912, London had seen only seven police commissioners during the preceding 91 years. The problem was not limited to New York; in the early twentieth century, the director, chief, or commissioner's office in major cities seemed to have a revolving door. For example, Philadelphia had 13 directors in 33 years; Cincinnati had 4 in 7 years; Cleveland had 5 in 12 years; Chicago had 25 in 49 years; and Detroit had 9 in 19 years.

Adding to the host of problems that plagued police departments in that era, legislative control tied chiefs' hands making them an instrument of the law, such that they could not innovate or experiment. In addition, low pay for police added to problems with morale and increased the likelihood of bribery. In 1900, a blue-ribbon commission known as **The Fifteen** found New York City officers had been blackmailing prostitutes, requiring a sliding scale of payoffs, to "look the other way."

In September 1919, the Boston police went on strike for higher wages. When word spread that there were no police on duty, people looted stores and smashed windows, forcing the mayor to call out the troops. A hastily organized group of citizen volunteers was deployed to maintain order, but when they killed two people, that touched off intermittent rioting and violence that lasted for days. Massachusetts Governor Calvin Coolidge (later president) announced: "There is no right to strike against the public safety by anybody, anywhere, anytime" (Allen, 1959:44). In response, Boston recruited an entirely new police force, but the incident left a negative mark against the police that extended far beyond the city, because the story made headlines nationwide.

Corruption also increased with passage of the **Volstead Act of 1919**, which made Prohibition the law of the land. This ushered in the Roaring Twenties, also called the "Jazz Age" or the "Flapper Era." It was a time when bootleggers and owners of speakeasies openly paid off police, and many people "winked" at the no-alcohol law. Mirroring in some ways today's problems with illegal drugs, huge profits from rum-running often meant huge payoffs to police. While many decried this open rebellion, a large segment of society viewed Prohibition as a laughable nuisance, and even gangsters like Al Capone and Lucky Luciano became folk heroes. Vast wealth was amassed not only by organized crime figures but by, the soon to be prominent, families involved in organized crime like the Kennedys, whose wealth can be traced to Prohibition.

The blatant disregard of Prohibition also fostered widespread disrespect for the law in general and, by extension, disrespect for police. The 1920s were a heady time, a live-for-today response to the grimness of World War I. It was also the era of the easy buck, when people could buy stock on margin for as little as 10 percent down, which meant even busboys and cab drivers were playing the stock market. More than a few became millionaires overnight, as a result of a stock tip from a well-connected patron with insider information.

It should also be noted that one of the quickest ways for an ambitious politician to further his career was to launch an investigation of corruption in police departments. In New York, both Theodore Roosevelt and, much later, Thomas Dewey, catapulted onto the national political scene by using the springboard of police reform. The press was also eager to jump on this issue, because expressions of moral outrage about police corruption, coupled with sordid examples of abuses, helped sell newspapers.

This is not to suggest that there were not serious problems within police departments, but honest and dedicated individuals who were trying to make a difference faced tremendous odds, in no small part because the general public held the police in such low regard. A widely read article of the period said:

> Every large American police department is under suspicion. The suspicion amounts to this: that for-money crimes are not only tolerated but encouraged. The higher the rank of the police officer, the stronger the suspicion. Now it is only one step from the encouragement of vice, for the purposes of loot, to an alliance with criminals. Indeed, in some of our large cities, the robbery of drunken men is permitted already by police on the profit-sharing plan (Matthews, 1901:1314).

The Stock Market Crash of 1929 and the resulting Great Depression ended the giddy atmosphere of the 1920s with a bang, touching off a politically volatile period of re-examination. The crisis of confidence in the police set the stage for the dramatic police reform movement launched in the 1930s that shaped the face of American policing for the next half-century.

Police Reform in the 1930s

Just as the principles attributed to Sir Robert Peel provided the foundation for British policing, Oakland, California, Police Chief **August Vollmer** is credited with launching the American police reform movement. As head of the National Commission on Law Observance and Enforcement established by President Herbert Hoover in 1929, Vollmer supervised the preparation of 10 principles he considered vital in reforming the police:

- The corrupting influence of politics should be removed from the police organization;

- The head of the department should be selected at large for competence, a leader, preferably a man of considerable police experience, and removable from office only after preferment of charges and a public hearing;

- Patrolmen should be able to rate a "B" on the Alpha test, be able-bodied and of good character, weigh 150 pounds, measure 5-feet 9-inches tall, and be between 21 and 31 years of age. These requirements may be disregarded by the chief for good and sufficient reason;

- Salaries should permit decent living standards, housing should be adequate, eight hours of work, one day off weekly, annual vacation, fair sick leave with pay, just accident and death benefits when in performance of duty, reasonable pension provisions on an actuarial basis;

- Adequate training for recruits, officers, and those already on the roll is imperative;

- The communication system should provide for call boxes, telephones, recall system, and (in appropriate circumstances) teletype and radio;

- Records should be complete, adequate, but as simple as possible. They should be used to secure administrative control of investigations and of department units in the interest of efficiency;

- A crime-prevention unit should be established if circumstances warrant this action and qualified women police should be engaged to handle juvenile delinquents' and women's cases;

- State police forces should be established in states where rural protection of this character is required; and

- State bureaus of criminal investigation and information should be established in every state (Wickersham Commission, 1931:140).

Though some of Vollmer's specifics may seem dated, this progressive doctrine established important concepts that served as the underpinning for modern policing:

- The necessity of eliminating political corruption;

- The need for an independent chief;

- The importance of an educated and trained police force that would be compensated as professionals;

- The judicious use of the latest technology;

- An awareness of the benefits of preventing crime;

- The beginning of an expanded role for women;

- An understanding of the need for different police approaches for urban and rural areas; and

- The importance of the service role in policing.

In their analysis of this reform movement, George L. Kelling and Mark H. Moore propose that Vollmer's moral vision, coupled with O.W. Wilson's work in police administration, revolutionized policing in seven areas:

- Authorization—In the past, police authority rested on politics and the law; the Reform Era replaced that underpinning with professionalism and the law.

- Function—The reform movement also narrowed the police function from a broad array of social services to crime control.

- Organizational design—Reformers also shifted departments from their previous decentralized model into a classical, centralized form.

- Demand for services—In the past, police responded to a community's needs, but the reform movement instead sold the public on the police role as crime-fighters.

- Relationship to environment—To insure against corruption and improve professionalism, the police were encouraged to abandon their intimate community ties and instead adopt a sort of professional aloofness.

- Tactics/technology—The foot patrols of the past gave way to preventive motor patrol, with an additional emphasis on rapid response to calls for service.

- Outcomes—The police of the past sought to satisfy both politicians and mainstream citizens, whereas the reform movement measured success by how well the police controlled crime (Kelling & Moore, 1987:38).

As Kelling and Moore point out, big-city police departments took a lesson from J. Edgar Hoover, who made the Federal Bureau of Investigation (FBI) a widely popular and respected agency by narrowing its mandate to specific crimes that were both highly visible and relatively easy to solve, then selling the public on the force's successes. The FBI has not been without criticism.

Public policy analysts and agents alike have leveled scathing criticism against the FBI, especially when Hoover was Director. Historically, the FBI has experienced two different periods of decline and criticism: the Teapot Dome-Attorney General Stone era of 1924-1936 and the Watergate era of 1972-1977. The **Teapot Dome** scandal involved large-scale corruption in the Office of the President and Congress and resulted in numerous criminal indictments and convictions. During the 1960s and 1970s, the FBI sustained substantial criticism because of its spying on noncriminal groups. For example, it was learned that from 1962 through 1968, the FBI planted numerous wiretaps and hidden microphones to monitor the movements of civil rights leader Dr. Martin Luther King, Jr., and the FBI routinely maintained surveillance on political and civic groups that were deemed to be "enemies." President Richard Nixon revealed in 1973 that the FBI had been involved in a number of burglaries for the purpose of "gathering intelligence (Gaines & Kappeler, 2011). Despite the FBI's ability to cultivate a professional crime-fighting image, local police did not have the luxury of picking and choosing which crimes they would pursue; the reformers could see great wisdom in narrowing the police function to crime control, not only because relative success would be easier to measure, but because involving the police in a whole host of other duties, such as political spying and issuing liquor licenses, seemed to invite corruption.

It is also important to understand the panorama of societal change that provided the backdrop against which these reforms took place. Not only had Hoover professionalized the FBI, but also this was a time when it seemed every problem, including social ills, could be solved by properly applying scientific principles and the new science of management theory. As proof, believers could point to the giant strides made by industry, where moguls such as Henry Ford introduced revolutionary concepts such as the assembly line that dramatically increased productivity by stressing efficiency. It was an era when change was synonymous with progress, and there appeared to be no limits on what could be achieved.

That seems naïve today, now that we have learned there is always a price, though sometimes initially hidden, that must be paid when any new technology is introduced, and that people do not always behave rationally. However, back then, as the country struggled to overcome the effects of the Great Depression, the idea that American ingenuity could create a perfect world was an article of faith, seemingly substantiated over time by this country's victory in World War II.

Vollmer's precepts signaled an organized approach to resolving the problems of the past, while offering a new course for the future. Change does not come overnight, but these principles gained momentum as the wave of the future for policing, which meant many metropolitan police departments adopted new ways to extract politics from the process. As Kelling and Moore point out, such efforts helped make many police chiefs more autonomous than any other local government official. For example, Los Angeles and Cincinnati adopted civil service examinations for chiefs, while Milwaukee provided police chiefs lifetime tenure, with removal only for cause. This insulation from politics, however, gave chiefs in these cities great power and autonomy. More recent history shows that these police departments have been plagued with police violence and the abuse of minorities as well as a focus on crime fighting to the exclusion of community service and responsiveness (see Kappeler, Sluder & Alpert, 1998). LAPD's beating of motorist Rodney King and the subsequent acquittal of the officers involved by an all-White jury sparked the worst riots in American history; Milwaukee's mishandling of the Jeffrey Dahmer case which allowed a child to die at the hands of a serial killer brought renewed charges of racism in the police department, and recent acts of brutality by police officers in Cincinnati, Ohio, and Oakland, California, have rekindled concerns over police violence.

As the reform movement took hold in urban police departments, the frontier and Southern sheriff tradition continued to evolve into the model for rural areas nationwide, and state police departments were initiated to fill gaps between local and federal efforts to control society's economic engine as well as selected groups in society. Pressures to professionalize the police increased throughout the system, but history suggests that concentrating people in dire circumstances and confining spaces in cities appears to increase crime problems, which means urban police face challenges in scope and scale beyond what other departments do. Because crime clusters in poor neighborhoods, because police have historically focused on minority populations for control, this helps explain why minorities can serve as convenient scapegoats for all types of social problems.

The Police and Minorities

The history of policing is, in reality, a record of how one group of people attempts to control the behavior of others, as individuals and as groups. A closer examination of early law enforcement efforts in England shows that even within a seemingly cohesive culture, where everyone seemed to share the same ethnic roots, the same language, and the same customs, differences in class determined application of the law. Under the feudal system, the nobility claimed rights that the serfs did not enjoy. A group of noblemen on a foxhunt could destroy serfs' crops with impunity. Ironically, it was not until 2005 that the British parliament outlawed this class-based leisure activity that had become such a part of English culture. It was, however, not only in the pursuit of the hunt that nobles enjoyed legally sanctioned exploitation of the powerless. The infamous *droit du seigneur* gave landlords the right to deflower the virginal daughters of their tenants—legalized rape.

While it is often claimed that the United States was founded on the ideal of establishing a classless society, nothing could be further from the truth. In practice, various groups have been discriminated against because of their skin color, ethnic heritage, immigrant status, religious beliefs, gender, or income level. Since law enforcement is part of the overall social and economic fabric, these groups also suffered at the hands of police.

During the Spoils Era it was not uncommon to find entire departments harassing minorities, as a way of solidifying mainstream support. In a capitalist society, supply and demand operate unfettered, at least in theory. This means the job goes to the lowest bidder, which means that impoverished immigrants and disenfranchised people of African descent were forced to work for lower wages than Whites. This situation was perceived by businessmen as a boon—and as a serious threat by workers who feared being displaced. American history is littered with the politicalization of race and labor, where American political leaders and the media have used fear of minorities to consolidate their power with language that borders on fascism. Until or unless these groups could establish political and economic clout, it was popular to use the police to "keep them in line."

In a capitalist society, money and votes mean power. Immigrants often arrive with little more than the clothes they are wearing, and the process of becoming a naturalized citizen takes time. In the South, poll taxes and literacy tests were effective ways of excluding Blacks from the electoral process, and statistics verify that Blacks have never enjoyed income levels comparable to Whites in this country. Even today, the poor, the underclass, and many minority groups are the least likely to vote. The powerless make inviting targets for exploitation—and for society's frustrations.

Sadly, the history of modern policing includes countless incidents where police unfairly harassed minorities, and under certain circumstances, white skin was no protection against abuse. Jews faced widespread anti-Semitism, including harsh treatment by police, especially in cities like New York where immigrant Jewish families often settled. The Irish, Poles, Italians, Germans, and other central and eastern European immigrants also suffered injustice, a sadly predictable political rite of passage in the transition to assimilation.

As this litany confirms, the have-nots, those without substantial clout, often had good reason to fear the police. Waves of immigrants hit this country's shores because of problems at home—the Irish faced famine, eastern Europeans fled revolution, the Jews tried to escape persecution. Lured by the myth that this country's streets were paved with gold, hordes of displaced persons flooded into the land of opportunity only to face the stark reality of low-paying and often dangerous jobs as unskilled workers. Attempts of workers to organize for improved job conditions were often smashed by the police at the direction of politicians in league with industrialists.

One bloody episode occurred in 1897 when 21 Polish and Hungarian strikers who had organized a march outside Hazleton, Pennsylvania, were killed when the local police fired upon them after the owners of the local coal company convinced the police the protest was illegal. As this example demonstrates, police violence against minorities often exhibited the interwoven themes of rich against poor, as well as us against them.

As Jack L. Kuykendall explains, these incidents are evidence of power clashes that reinforce the negative stereotyping of one group by another (Kuykendall, 1970:47,52). Ethnic minorities cling together because of culture, heritage, language, and rejection and oppression by the mainstream, yet this in turn is perceived by the mainstream as evidence of secretive and clannish behavior that justifies further abuse. Completing the vicious cycle, minorities who suffer indignities and brutality at the hands of police learn, in turn, to see the police as paid thugs and oppressors. Once people are divided by an "us against them" mind-set, it becomes much easier for each side to justify aggression against the other.

> You can learn more about police brutality by going to http://www.drury.edu/ess/irconf/DMangan.html.

Though having white skin did not prevent discrimination, being White undoubtedly made it easier for ethnic minorities to assimilate into the mainstream. The additional burden of racism has made that transition much more difficult for those whose skin is black, brown, red, or yellow. In no small part because of the tradition of slavery, Blacks have long been a target of abuse. The use of patrols to capture runaway slaves was one of the precursors of formal police forces, especially in the South. This unfortunate legacy persisted as an element of the police role. In some cases, police harassment simply meant people of African descent were more likely to be stopped and questioned, while at the other extreme, they have suffered beatings, and even murder, at the hands of White police. Questions still arise periodically today about the disproportionately high numbers of people of African descent killed, beaten, and arrested by police in major cities.

Most worrisome is that some law enforcement officials made it clear that they not only tolerated but also encouraged their officers to keep people of color "in their place." Though we still wince at news footage of notorious southern lawman "Bull" Connor loosing police dogs on Civil Rights marchers in Birmingham, Alabama, the police in the North have not always treated people of African descent much better. More than one northern, big-city police chief used racism to secure his power, by currying favor with Whites by thinly veiled assurances that police power would be used against people of color.

Latinos have fared little better, and border states in particular have a checkered record in their dealings with Mexican immigrants, dating back even before the notorious incident in the 1940s, when zoot suiters and police clashed in riots in Los Angeles in 1943. Cubans in Miami and Puerto Ricans in New York have also reported notable problems with police brutality. The same held true for Native Americans.

Asians have also been the targets of hostility. "Coolies" who worked laying railroad track were seen by many as taking jobs away from "real" Americans, which led to riots in 1871. American citizens of Japanese origin were interned in concentration camps during World War II. The "boat people" from Vietnam and Cambodia faced problems in many communities, where they were perceived as straining the local economy, as evidenced in the bloody clashes between White and Asian fishermen in Texas, and California continues to be a hot spot for conflicts between people over immigration. Today, undocumented Latino immigrants are suffering the same fate, especially in border states such as Texas, California, and especially Arizona. The important issues such as homeland security are being used in a political struggle, with large, multi-national corporations being desirous of cheap immigrant labor and political leaders and the media speaking of "broken borders" and "terrorism" and scapegoating Latinos over job losses and economic problems associated with a post-industrial economy. Time after time, history shows that political leaders are more than willing to place social problems on the backs of minorities, concealing their role in developing failed public policy and all the while allowing their supporters to amass great sums of wealth.

Initial Attempts to Reach the Community

The police reform movement launched by Vollmer in the 1920s, which took hold in the 1930s, seemed to offer the promise that society was on the brink of solving the riddle of crime. Police departments were now increasingly insulated from the political pressures that had spawned a variety of abuses, and they were organized according to the principles of scientific management theory, which promised increased efficiency and effectiveness. Over time, educated and highly trained officers roamed the streets in new squad cars that gave them the mobility to swoop down quickly on problems. As home telephones became increasingly affordable, it seemed there would be no way crooks could escape the ever-tightening net of police technology. The use of new tactics and technology ushered in the "professionalization" of the police.

The professionalization movement, however, had its problems. As Jack Greene (2000:305) notes, the police were "isolated from the publics they serve, relied on personal as opposed to constitutional authority, and lacked the communal attachments necessary for effective citizen-police interaction. Contributing to the **communal isolation** of the American police has been a shift in organizational strategy emphasized throughout most of the twentieth century. This shift to professionalize the police generally separated these professionals from their clients, often in profound ways." By the 1950s, blemishes had begun to appear in that model of perfection. Many police departments found themselves the target of mounting complaints. Many accusations seemed relatively trivial—perhaps the officer appeared indifferent to the caller's seemingly petty concerns such as broken streetlights or barking dogs. Often the charges were serious and well founded, such as minorities' accusations of police harassment and brutality.

While concern about the isolation of the police from their constituency had not reached crisis proportions, the increasing pressure to find a way to build bridges to the community fostered interest in **police-community relations** (PCR) efforts. The best PCR programs represented sincere efforts to reach out and address a host of community concerns. The worst PCR programs were half-hearted, understaffed, and underfunded attempts to blunt public criticism without making any substantive change. The worst PCR programs were often little more than attempts to legitimize past police practices, protect political leaders, and secure business interests.

In 1955, the National Institute on Community and Police Relations, co-sponsored by the School of Police Administration and Public Safety of Michigan State University and the National Conference of Christians and Jews, convened to help police become aware of their problems. Later, the National Association of Police Community Relations Officers outlined seven objectives of a good PCR program, paraphrased below:

- Improve communication, reduce hostility, and identify tensions between the police and the community;

- Assist both the police and the community in acquiring skills to promote improved crime detection and prevention;

- Define the police role, emphasizing equal protection;

- Adopt a teamwork approach, including the police department, the public, and other public service agencies;

- Instill in each officer a proper attitude and appreciation of good police-community relations;

- Enhance mutual understanding between the police and the community; and

- Stress that the administration of justice is a total community responsibility that necessitates total community involvement (NAPCRO, 1971).

As these laudable goals suggest, PCR efforts aimed high, but they fell short on structure and tactics. In practice, PCR units operated as separate entities within the department, never fully integrating into the police milieu. In the organizational scheme, the PCR unit was usually in the service track, not part of the operations bureau, which meant the jobs were filled with staff and not line officers. While this made sense, given the unit's mandate, it meant PCR officers were not viewed as real cops. The officer's mission was not to handle crime on a daily basis, but to "make nice." In some cases, the PCR director was a civilian, further distancing the effort from service-based policing.

With the benefit of 20/20 hindsight, another structural flaw was to have PCR officers communicate with the community through community leaders. Tactics included organizing an advisory council made up of civic and church leaders. Though this seemed wise at the time, experience shows that community leaders are not always fully in touch with the real concerns in the community, so PCR units rarely received the broadest possible input about the community's real concerns. This was also, in part, because police brought their own law enforcement agenda to these meetings and most often it did not include a desire for real change.

In part because of these structural weaknesses, PCR tactics often translated into well-meaning activities of limited scope. PCR officers staffed a speaker's bureau that gave talks on crime prevention or recruiting to various civic groups. Officers also made presentations in schools. Another typical PCR function was press relations. PCR officers also served as the liaison to other public and private agencies. Many PCR officers spent much of their day hosting tours of police facilities. Though PCR officers were encouraged to solicit suggestions, many were under orders not to handle actual complaints, but to refer those to the administration. In short, while perhaps well meaning, PCRs managed the appearance of the police, but did little to foster police accountability.

While most PCR officers winced at being labeled public relations flak-catchers, the structure of the unit and nature of their daily activities made it difficult for them to do more. The friendly PCR officer who discussed concerns with minority leaders often bore little resemblance to the tough motor patrol officer who arrived later to handle a call. Their role in press relations was often perceived as putting a good face on a department's mistakes.

PCR programs overall suffered two major interrelated problems because of the inherent lack of follow-up and accountability. Though people might have felt flattered by the attention when a PCR officer asked for suggestions, the officer lacked clout within the department to address specific complaints. In addition, the PCR officer who gave the talk on crime prevention to the Senior Citizens Club was never the officer who had to handle the call later, if those preventive efforts failed.

The stated objective of using PCR officers to reverse minority abuse within the department was obviously doomed, since the most aggressive officers were usually the first to call PCR officers "wimps." Also, especially in departments where PCR units were established as a reluctant gesture to defuse community criticism, police administrators used the unit as a dumping ground for problem officers, further undermining internal and external credibility.

The 1950s also saw the introduction of new **Crime Prevention Units**, a proactive approach aimed at the community. Depending on the size of the department and the funding available, some departments provided a separate Crime Prevention Unit or officer, while others rolled both Crime Prevention and PCR into one.

Like PCR, civilian staff rather than line officers staffed crime prevention units. The unit's goal was to educate the businesses and community residents about specific measures they could take, such as target-hardening, to reduce their likelihood of victimization and thereby help decrease the crime rate overall. Obviously, the units' strengths and weaknesses mirrored those of PCR units, and although many such efforts helped inform the public about things they could do to help prevent crime, it was nevertheless an overly optimistic, over-reliance on "scientific" surface solutions to human, political, and economic problems facing communities.

The Challenge of the Late 1960s

Though PCR efforts were decidedly a step in the right direction, the programs' inherent weaknesses became dramatically apparent during the domestic upheaval that began in the late 1960s. As Baby Boomers will attest, the early 1960s was a time of great optimism, fueled by the idealism of the millions of young people who dominated the culture by their sheer numbers. President John F. Kennedy tapped into this youthful enthusiasm when he challenged the entire generation to "ask not what your country can do for you, but what you can do for your country." His new Peace Corps attracted thousands of energetic young people who believed in their collective ability to change the world overnight.

Despite Kennedy's assassination in 1963, his successor, Lyndon B. Johnson, announced his commitment to carry on Kennedy's civil rights agenda, embodied in the Great Society programs that were supposedly designed to promote equality between Blacks and Whites and narrow the gap between rich and poor. This was the era when Martin Luther King's dream of a colorblind society seemed within reach. Within policing, it seemed the continued adoption and expansion of PCR and Crime Prevention Units would provide the last link in fulfilling the promise of a full-service, professionalized police force, capable of handling any challenge.

Shockingly, within just a few short years, the country was instead plunged into domestic chaos, and policing encountered perhaps its most formidable challenge—a direct and frontal assault on the legitimacy of the police and indeed the legal and economic systems. The civil rights and Vietnam anti-war movements, as well as the emerging youth culture of the 1960s, effectively merged two groups that had previously been socially and politically separated—minorities, particularly Blacks, and urban and suburban middle-class White youth. The convergence of these social and political movements confronted American policing in direct and visible ways (Greene, 2000:307).

Talk of revolution filled the air, as cities burned, and crime rates soared. The Civil Rights Movement and decades of oppression spawned the militant Black Power Movement, which included groups such as the Black Panthers, whose bloody clashes with police heightened tensions on both sides. Race riots erupted summer after summer—in Watts, Newark, and Detroit, and then in cities nationwide in the spring of 1968 when Martin Luther King Jr. was assassinated.

Meanwhile, protests on college campuses became increasingly violent, as the focus narrowed to the pressing issues of the Vietnam War and the draft. The nightly news was filled with images of students, armed with lists of nonnegotiable demands, taking over university administration buildings as riot police lobbed tear gas into the crowds. History repeated itself; or, as we have observed at the onset of this chapter, the same tactics and mistakes were repeated. For example, the military units were called out to control a student protest at Kent State University, which resulted in the killing of four students by national guardsmen.

The upheaval pitted hawks against doves, Blacks against Whites, students against the establishment, and the powerful against the powerless, in an atmosphere of increasing fury on all sides. As representatives of the establishment whose job included maintaining domestic peace, the police often found themselves on one side of the barricades facing any one of a number of widely diverse groups collectively known as the **New Left**.

The New Left was a loose coalition of groups demanding a variety of social, economic, and political changes, under the overall umbrella phrase "social justice." Their unifying slogan was "Power to the People." The agenda ranged from legalizing marijuana and other drugs to ending the draft, from sexual freedom to equality for people of color and women. Protests covered the spectrum, from nonviolent actions to bombings conducted by small, ultra-radical groups like the Weathermen, who had split from Students for a Democratic Society (SDS) over the issue of violence. The underground Weathermen served as a model for other groups, such as the Symbionese Liberation Army (SLA) that made headlines when they kidnapped heiress Patty Hearst.

> You can learn more about the Kerner
> Commission by going to
> http://historymatters.gmu.edu/d/6545/.

Gross characterizations took place. To the police, the New Left was made up of mindless hippies and longhairs, an unlikely mix of spoiled college kids and draft-dodgers, who had turned their backs on the culture that subsidized them, and "murderous Black criminals," who cloaked their "reverse racism" in rhetoric about equality. Perhaps the most dramatic confrontation occurred in Chicago during the 1968 Democratic convention, when TV cameras rolled as the late Mayor Richard J. Daley's police waded into crowds of young protesters. Wielding nightsticks, their badge numbers hidden, the police cracked heads in what the **Kerner Commission** would later call a police riot—confirmation of the New Left's concerns. Again, social change was to be forestalled by the brute force of the police rather than progressive political policy.

Those on the political right issued a call for "law and order"—which those on the left interpreted as a euphemism for heavy-handed police crackdowns on minorities and students. Those on the political left protested against police brutality, suggesting the police had become the Gestapo. Despite the infusion of new technology funded by the **Law Enforcement Assistance Act** (LEAA), escalating criminal and political violence continued into the early 1970s, underscoring the need for the police to find new ways to heal old wounds.

In this climate, the growing rift within society could not be healed by ineffectual PCR and Crime Prevention efforts. Quite obviously, the bitterness brewing between the police and various splintered and polarized elements within communities required a bolder approach. Though many police departments had not previously adopted a PCR or Crime Prevention program, they now did so as a way of addressing the need to find ways to break down barriers between the police and the community—a cheap ointment for gaping social wounds.

As the limitations of both PCR and Crime Prevention efforts became increasingly obvious, numerous experiments were conducted to see if some new way could be found to build bridges to the community. One promising new approach that became popular beginning in the early 1970s was **team policing**, which involved maintaining a permanent team of officers that responded to crime problems within a particular geographic area.

Team policing recognized that one of PCR's main defects was its reliance on staff and not line officers. However, though team policing involved line officers,

> You can learn more about team policing by going to
> http://www.policefoundation.org/docs/
> foundation.html.

it was often applied as if it were no more than a limited tactic, rather than as a strategic approach, so it typically lacked the commitment required to make any substantive and lasting impact on improving overall, long-term police relations within the community. In essence, team policing also suffered because it was still basically a reactive approach, with officers rushing from one crisis to the next. Team policing also failed because it ignored the power of mid-level police supervisors and vested decision-making authority with street-level officers. This created a situation where police supervisors' authority and power were challenged. This is a major reason why community policing calls for an alteration in police organizational structure.

The Birth of Community Policing

Nothing in the history of the American police institution made community policing "the" inevitable transformation to occur in policing. Rather, history dictated that some major transformation had to occur because of changes in the political, economic, and social structures. It was evident that police were no longer going to accept the racism that plagued America or the use of police violence to repress change. Community policing emerged because a set of historical forces created by an environment where some major transformation in policing had to happen. As history demonstrates, many factors set the stage for the birth of community policing:

- Police and political reformers advancing their agenda;

- The influx of government funding for community policing;

- The alienation of the police from the community;

- The narrowing of the police mission to crime fighting;

- An over-reliance on scientific management that stressed efficiency and effectiveness;

- Increased reliance on high-tech gadgetry instead of human interaction;

- Insulation of police administration from community control and accountability;

- A long-standing concern about police violation of human rights; and

- Failed PCR, Crime Prevention, and team policing units.

Most of these elements share two common themes—the isolation of the police from the public and a growing use of overt and symbolic violence to control groups in society. The resulting alienation fostered an "us against them" mind-set on the part of both the police and the community. Community policing therefore rose like a phoenix from the ashes of burned cities, embattled campuses, and crime-riddled neighborhoods, a new response to the chaos of that turbulent era. Beginning in the early 1970s, the basic issues and ideas that would ultimately coalesce into the community policing concept were discussed in various books and articles, though the cohesive philosophy and the specific organizational changes that would have to be made to achieve these new goals had not yet solidified (Trojanowicz, 1973; Trojanowicz & Dixon, 1974; Trojanowicz, Trojanowicz & Moss, 1975; Goldstein, 1977, 1979). Later, in some cases, it was called foot patrol, then Neighborhood Policing, Neighborhood-Oriented Policing, Community-Oriented Policing, Community-Based Policing, or Community Policing. But regardless of the name used, this growing new movement attempted to learn from the past and strived to save the best from each successive advance.

A Summary of the Lessons Learned and Mistakes Not to Be Repeated

The Reform Movement of the 1930s brought about many changes in policing, some of which are contained in the philosophy of community policing. Community policing retains, for example, commitment to upgrading the education and training of police officers. It also recognizes the limits of technology and science in dealing with human problems and encourages the judicious use of new technology. The philosophy embraces and encourages the recruitment and employment of talented women officers. Most importantly, the movement seeks the insulation of the police from politics, so that today's community policing officer cannot fall into the trap of the foot patrol officers of the past, whose agenda was dictated by politicians and special-interest groups, while recognizing that lack of accountability to the community can lead to abuse of authority.

The PCR and Crime Prevention movement also changed the face of policing and the lessons police must learn. Community policing retains from these lessons of history a sincere commitment to improving police relations with minorities and a concerted effort to end police brutality. Community policing embraces an outreach into schools, in the hope of preventing problems in the future, and provides a liaison with other organizations and agencies. History, however, also instructs that police are too prone to use technology and gimmicks to enlist support and the police themselves often undermine even well-meaning efforts. Police cannot rely merely on the pretense of service and commitment to community; they must embrace the spirit of service, accountability, and responsiveness.

No doubt changing times and changing needs will spawn yet another reform movement in the future, but today's community policing revolution is the most dynamic and innovative response to finding ways to involve the community in policing itself that has come along in 60 years. From its birth as pilot programs in places like Newark and Flint, to its widespread practical application nationwide today, community policing has made the crucial transition from being a promising philosophy to a professed norm.

The lesson of history teaches that the biggest challenge the police face is finding a way to enlist the cooperation and support of average people in efforts to make their lives safer and more enjoyable, a way to earn dignity and respect. Community policing reminds us of the importance of balancing efforts aimed at the top with those that focus on the street where most people live. It also reminds us that people are the police department's most valuable resource and should be treated as valued partners in the police process.

What history also shows is that change takes time and that, at any given moment, the past and the future coexist. Even today, some departments have not fully embraced all the reforms Vollmer outlined in the 1930s, meanwhile other departments are leading the way into the future that others will follow. Still, signs of the past can often repeat themselves and reformers must be concerned that history finds well-meaning solutions to the problems of crime, policing, and accountability stifled and abused by institutional and social forces.

KEY TERMS IN CHAPTER 2

- August Vollmer
- blue laws
- Civil Rights Act of 1871
- civil service
- Civil Service Act of 1883
- Combination Laws
- commons
- communal isolation
- constable
- crime prevention units
- economic rationale
- Enclosure Acts
- Fugitive Slave Laws
- hundreds
- Industrial Revolution
- justice of the peace
- Kerner Commission
- Law Enforcement Assistance Act (LEAA)
- Lexow investigation
- Metropolitan Police Act of 1829
- New Left
- night watch
- police-community relations (PCR)
- professionalized
- right of revolution
- self-preservation
- shire
- Sir Robert Peel
- slave patrols
- Spoils Era
- team policing
- Texas Rangers
- The Fifteen
- tithings
- vigilantism
- Volstead Act of 1919

DISCUSSION QUESTIONS

1. The first sentence of Chapter 2 reads, "The saying that 'people receive the kind of policing they deserve' ignores the role power plays in the kind, quality, and distribution of police service." Discuss what this sentence means in the context of contemporary policing in the United States.
2. Discuss the social developments that preceded the passage of the Metropolitan Police Act.
3. Discuss and describe the five interrelated pressures that shifted policing from an informal to a formal system.
4. Consider what social, economic, and political factors led to the creation of full-time, organized police forces in most major cities in the United States in the mid-1800s.
5. When was the Spoils Era in the United States? Briefly discuss how the government worked under this system. What factors led to the demise of the Spoils Era?
6. What factors were tied to extensive vigilantism in the frontier areas of the country through the 1800s?
7. Discuss when and why the Volstead Act passed. What ramifications, if any, did the Volstead Act have on police operations?
8. Beginning in 1929, August Vollmer, as head of the National Commission on Law Observance and Enforcement, established 10 principles vital in reforming the police. Discuss the importance of the principles in providing the underpinnings for modern policing.
9. Describe the seven areas revolutionized by Vollmer and Wilson's work in police administration.
10. Discuss the effectiveness of police-community relations programs implemented by police beginning in the 1950s and 1960s.

References

Allen, F. L. (1959). *Only Yesterday*. New York, NY: Harper & Row, Publishers.

Bell, D. (1960). *The End of Ideology: On the Exhaustion of Political Ideas in the Fifties*. New York, NY: The Free Press.

Bittner, E. (1970). *The Functions of the Police in Modern Society*. Chevy Chase, MD: National Institute of Mental Health, Center for Studies of Crime and Delinquency.

Brown, R. (1969). *The American Vigilante Tradition, Violence in America, A Staff Report to the National Commission on the Causes and Prevention of Violence*. Washington, DC: U.S. Government Printing Office.

Crank, J. P., & Langworthy, R. (1992). An Institutional Perspective of Policing. *The Journal of Criminal Law & Criminology*, *83*(2), 338–363.

Critchley, T. A. (1985). Constables and Justices of the Peace. In W. C. Terry (Ed.), *Policing Society: An Occupational View*. New York, NY: John Wiley and Sons.

Davies, R. W. (1977). Augustus Caesar: A Police System in the Ancient World. In P. J. Stead (Ed.), *Pioneers in Policing* (pp. 12–32). Montclair, NJ: Patterson-Smith.

Douthit, N. (1975). Enforcement and Nonenforcement Roles in Policing: A Historical Inquiry. *Journal of Police Science and Administration*, *3*(3), 336–345.

Drago, H. (1975). *The Legend Makers: Tales of the Old-Time Peace Officers and Desperadoes of the Frontier*. New York, NY: Dodd, Mead & Co.

Fogelson, R. (1977). *Big-City Police*. Cambridge, MA: Harvard University Press.

Fosdick, R. (1921). *American Police Systems*. New York, NY: The Century Co.

Gaines, L. K., & Kappeler, V. E. (2011). *Policing in America* (7th ed.). Waltham, MA: Anderson.

Gard, W. (1949). *Frontier Justice*. Norman, OK: University of Oklahoma Press.

Goldstein, H. (1977). *Policing in a Free Society*. Cambridge, MA: Ballinger.

Goldstein, H. (1979). Improving Policing: A Prom Approach. *Crime & Delinquency, 25*, 236-258.

Greene, J. (2000). Community Policing in America: Changing the Nature, Structure, and Function of the Police. In *Criminal Justice 2000, Volume 3, Policies, Processes, and Decisions of the Criminal Justice System* (pp. 299-370). Washington, DC: National Institute of Justice.

Haller, M. H. (1992). Historical Roots of Police Behavior: Chicago, 1890-1925. In E. H. Monkkonen (Ed.), *Policing and Crime Control*. New York, NY: K.G. Saur.

Harring, S. L. (1981). Policing a Class Society: The Expansion of the Urban Police in the Late Nineteenth and Early Twentieth Centuries. In D. F. Greenburg (Ed.), *Crime and Capitalism*. Palo Alto, CA: Mayfield Publishing.

Harring, S. L. (1992). Class Conflict and the Suppression of Tramps in Buffalo, 1892-1894. In E. H. Monkkonen (Ed.), *Policing and Crime Control*. New York, NY: K.G. Saur.

Harring, S. L., & McMullin, L. M. (1992). The Buffalo Police 1872-1900: Labor Unrest, Political Power and the Creation of the Police Institution. In E. H. Monkkonen (Ed.), *Policing and Crime Control*. New York, NY: K.G. Saur.

Hewitt, W. H. (1965). *British Police Administration*. Springfield, IL: Charles C Thomas.

Johnson, D. R. (1981). *American Law Enforcement: A History*. St. Louis, MO: Forum Press.

Kappeler, V. E. (1989). St. Louis Police Department. In W. G. Bailey (Ed.), *The Encyclopedia of Police Science*. New York, NY: Garland Publishing, Inc.

Kappeler, V. E. (2005). *Critical Issues in Police Civil Liability* (4th ed.). Prospect Heights, IL: Waveland Press.

Kappeler, V. E., Sluder, R., & Alpert, G. P. (1994). *Forces of Deviance: Understanding the Dark Side of Policing*. Prospect Heights, IL: Waveland Press.

Kelling, G. L., & Moore, M. H. (1987). From Political to Reform to Community: The Evolving Strategy of Police. A paper produced at Harvard University's Kennedy School of Government: Cambridge, MA.

Kelling, G. L., & Moore, M. H. (1988). *The Evolving Strategy of Policing*. (NCJ114213). Washington, DC: National Institute of Justice.

Kelly, M. A. (1973). The First Urban Policeman. *Journal of Police Science and Administration, 1*(1), 56-60.

Kleinig, J., & Zhang, Y. (1993). *Professional Law Enforcement Codes: A Documentary Collection*. Westport, CT: Greenwood Press.

Knapp Commission Report on Police Corruption. (1973). New York, NY: George Braziller.

Kuykendall, J. L. (1970). Police and Minority Groups: Toward a Theory of Negative Contacts. *Police*, *15*(1), 47, 52.

Louis, P. (1989). New York Police Department. In W. G. Bailey (Ed.), *The Encyclopedia of Police Science*. New York, NY: Garland Publishing, Inc.

Matthews, F. (1901). *The Character of the American Police, The World's Work 2*. New York, NY: Doubleday, Page & Co.

Miller, W. R. (1977). *Cops and Bobbies: Police Authority in New York and London, 1830-1870*. Chicago, IL: University of Chicago Press.

Moore, M. H., & Kelling, G. L. (1976). To Serve and Protect: Learning from Police History. In A. S. Blumberg & E. Neiderhoffer (Eds.), *The Ambivalent Force*. New York, NY: Holt, Rinehart and Winston.

Murray, C. (1985). Images of Fear. *Harper's Magazine*, (May), 41.

Nalla, M. K., & Newman, G. R. (1994). Is White-Collar Policing, Policing? *Policing and Society*, *3*, 303–318.

NAPCRO. (1971). *Get the Ball Rolling: A Guide to Police Community Relations Programs*. New Orleans, LA: National Association of Police Community Relations Officers.

National Advisory Commission on Civil Disorders. (1968). *Report of the National Advisory Commission on Civil Disorders*. New York, NY: Bantam Books.

National Constables Association. (1995). Constable. In W. G. Bailey (Ed.), *The Encyclopedia of Police Science* (2nd ed., pp. 114–119). New York, NY: Garland Press.

Otem, M. (1935). *My Life on the Frontier, 1864-1882*. New York, NY: The Press of the Pioneers.

President's Commission on Law Enforcement and Administration of Justice. (1967). *The Challenge of Crime in a Free Society*. Washington, DC: U.S. Government Printing Office.

Pringle, P. (n.d.). *Hue and Cry: The Story of Henry and John Fielding and Their Bow Street Runners*. Bangay, Suffolk, Great Britain: Richard Clay and Company.

Reichel, P. L. (1992). The Misplaced Emphasis on Urbanization in Police Development. *Policing and Society*, *3*, 1–12.

Reith, C. (1952). *The Blind Eye of History*. London, England: Faber & Faber Ltd.

Richardson, J. F. (1974). *Urban Police in the United States*. Port Washington, NY: National University Publications, Kennikat Press.

Robinson, C. D., Scaglion, R., & Olivero, J. M. (1994). *Police in Contradiction*. Westport, CT: Greenwood Press.

Rubinstein, J. (1973). *City Police*. New York, NY: Farrar, Straus and Giroux.

Samaha, J. (1974). *Law and Order in Historical Perspective*. New York, NY: Academic Press.

Stead, P. J. (1985). *The Police of Britain*. New York, NY: Macmillan.

Strecher, V. (2006). Revising the Histories and Futures of Policing. In V. E. Kappeler (Ed.) *The Police & Society: Touch Stone Readings* (3rd ed.). Prospect Heights, IL: Waveland Press.

Thompson, E. P. (1991). *The Making of the English Working Class*. New Edition. New York, NY: Penguin.

Thorwald, J. (1966). *Crime and Science*. New York, NY: Harcourt, Brace & World, Inc.

Tobias, J. J. (1979). *Crime and Police in England, 1700-1900*. Dublin, England: Macmillan.

Trojanowicz, R. C. (1973). *Juvenile Delinquency: Concepts and Control*. Englewood Cliffs, NJ: Prentice Hall.

Trojanowicz, R. C., & Dixon, S. L. (1974). *Criminal Justice and the Community*. Englewood Cliffs, NJ: Prentice Hall.

Trojanowicz, R. C., Trojanowicz, J. M., & Moss, F. M. (1975). *Community Based Crime Prevention*. Pacific Palisades, CA: Goodyear Publishing Co.

Turner, K. B., Giacopassi, D., & Vandiver, M. (2006). Ignoring the Past: Coverage of Slavery and Slave Patrols in Criminal Justice Texts. *Journal of Criminal Justice Education, 17*(1), 181-195.

Uchida, C. D. (1993). The Development of the American Police: An Historical Overview. In R. C. Dunham & G. P. Alpert (Eds.), *Critical Issues in Policing: Contemporary Readings* (2nd ed.). Prospect Heights, IL: Waveland Press.

Walker, S. (1977). *A Critical History of Police Reform*. Lexington, MA: Lexington Books.

Walker, S. (1992). The Origins of the American Police-Community Relations Movement: The 1940s. In E. H. Monkkonen (Ed.), *Policing and Crime Control, Part III*. New York, NY: K.G. Saur.

Walker, S. (2006). "Broken Windows" and Fractured History: The Use and Misuse of History in Recent Police Patrol Analysis. In V. E. Kappeler (Ed.), *The Police & Society: Touch Stone Readings* (2nd ed., pp. 51-65). Prospect Heights, IL: Waveland Press.

Walker, D. B., & Richards, M. (1995). British Policing. In W. G. Bailey (Ed.), *The Encyclopedia of Police Science* (2nd ed., pp. 41-48). New York, NY: Garland Press.

Whitehouse, J. (1973). Historical Perspectives on the Police Community Service Function. *Journal of Police Science and Administration, 1*(1), 87-92.

Wickersham Commission. (1931). *Report on Police*. National Commission on Law Observance and Enforcement. Washington, DC: U.S. Government Printing Office.

Williams, R. (2003). A State of Permanent Exception: The Birth of Modern Policing in Colonial Capitalism. *Interventions, 5*(3), 322-344.

•

The difference between the right word and the almost right word is the difference between lightning and the lightning bug.

— Mark Twain

CHAPTER 3   The Changing Meaning of Community

LEARNING OBJECTIVES

After reading the chapter, you should be able to:

1. Understand the importance of defining community.
2. Understand how communities have changed over the course of time.
3. Describe differing definitions of community and list their common elements.
4. Understand the difference between community and neighborhood.
5. Describe the historical development of suburbs.
6. List the factors that have contributed to a growing underclass in American society.
7. Describe the role of technology in the evolution of community.
8. List and describe the three-tiered "hierarchy of community" based on class.
9. Discuss the role of the police in building a sense of community.

The Importance of Definitions

Like any profession or highly skilled craft, policing abounds in jargon—terms understood by insiders, which function as shorthand so that members of the profession can communicate ideas to each other easily and quickly. In a practical sense, of course, there is the danger that jargon can cause confusion, both inside and outside a profession, when people do not understand a term's real meaning or its history. In a more abstract sense, words and phrases have embedded meanings, values, and connotations. Words and phrases do not simply carry with them a variety of meanings that cause the potential for misunderstanding;

they are representations of reality that provide bridges to other words, meanings, and history. Words change with the social context in which they are created and deployed. Words also inform and guide practice.

Confusion and misunderstanding can also arise when two people think they are talking about the same thing, when they both use the same term, without realizing each has a different idea concerning what the word actually means. The likelihood of this kind of misunderstanding is magnified with a phrase like "community policing," since those two simple words are used to convey a subtle but sophisticated philosophy, as well as an organizational strategy that police departments can use to put the philosophy into practice. The phrase "community policing" has its connotations and linkages to the past.

Because accurate and complete definitions are so important, the first chapter defined the philosophy of community policing. The purpose of this chapter is to clear up any confusion concerning what the word "community" means in the context of community policing. As we shall see, the very meaning of community has changed as communities themselves have been transformed throughout modern history.

A History of the Meaning of Community

To understand the full implications of community policing requires a clear understanding of what community means and how communities have changed over time. The definition of community has evolved to take into account the changing nature of communities themselves. In the past, defining community seemed simpler, because a sense of community was based on people's shared interests and interdependence, which typically overlapped a geographic location, but as we shall see, that is not always the case. Technological, political, economic, and communicative changes have all had a dramatic impact on community life and have altered the very nature of modern communities.

The term "community" is perhaps one of the most difficult concepts to define and one of the most abused terms in modern sociology and criminology. The term can be used in both the concrete and the abstract. In the concrete sense, one sociologist defined community as "any area in which people with a common culture share common interests" (Fessler, 1976:7). More often than not, the geographic area referred to in the definition of community is a neighborhood. The problem with that broad a definition is that it could span "a rural village of half a hundred families" to "one of our major cities" (Fessler, 1976:7). Additionally, this definition fails to note the use of the term "community" in the abstract as well as the social ascriptions often thrust upon the term.

Community does not always refer to an area, location, or neighborhood; often it refers only to a group of people drawn together by common interests—like a "community of scholars" or a "religious community." At least initially, these notions of community were coupled to places like university or church. Today, communities of interest can be tied together through social media and communications technology. Community can also convey a sentiment like "a sense of community" that makes us feel a certain way rather than think of a particular location or group of people. This sentiment too can be simulated through social media and communications technology. As we shall see, however, these are hardly replacements for communities tied to a geographic location where people share going social interactions in real time and space.

The German sociologist **Ferdinand Tönnies** (1887) was perhaps the first sociologist to make an important distinction about communities. In his book *Gemeinschaft und Gesellschaft,* Tönnies distinguished between the local community (**gemeinschaft**) versus the larger society (**gesellschaft**). He also made a clear distinction between **community relationships** that were defined by intimacy and durability where kin relations determined status, power, and behavior and where community relationships were rational, calculated, contractual, and based on merit and achievement. This later use of the term "community" is not what people meant when they talked about community, because of the depersonalization that dominates relations in large cities and militates against a cohesive sense of community. Thus, the tangible aspects of community like location, social interaction, and social relations interact to create a feeling of community.

In the early 1800s, when this country was primarily an agrarian society with less than one-half the population living in cities, the term "community" hardly seemed to require definition. Community expressed the idea of a distinct area where people shared a common geography and a seemingly common culture, as well as elements of mutual dependence. Increasing industrialization drove people from farms and small villages into the cities and, in the first decade of the last century, more than nine million people immigrated into cities, but the term "community" still seemed to serve fairly well in describing how even the largest cities broke down into smaller, often ethnic-based, communities.

In the 1920s, the **Chicago School**, comprised of sociologists such as Robert E. Park, continued attempts to refine the rural model so that it could be applied to communities within major metropolitan areas. The Chicago School's technique relied on identifying central locators, such as businesses, churches, and schools, and then drawing the community's boundary lines by finding those living the farthest away who still used those services. As Thomas Meenaghan

(1972:94) wrote in his treatise *What Means Community,* "Park saw the community as a group of people living in a specific geographic area and conditioned by the subcultural or life processes of competition, cooperation, assimilation, and conflict. The unplanned life processes created so-called natural areas that not only had a defined territorial frame, but also shared special or unique cultural and social characteristics."

In less formal terms, this meant people took on identifiable marks of membership in the community just by living there and creating community-based social institutions that allowed residents to interact. Even when individuals or groups within a community were in conflict, their constant interaction and interdependence, perhaps their shared interests, helped shape their identities and values. Living in the community was a potent force in influencing what people thought, how they felt, and what they believed. People do not make a conscious decision to take on the colorations and nuances of their communities, but instead this occurs as a seemingly natural outgrowth of living together under a variety of conditions and bumping up against the behavior and attitudes of other community members in the course of daily life. In this sense, community has a moral dimension because collective sentiments and beliefs are often shared by members of a community and are passed on to generations and people moving into a community.

In the 1930s, social scientists began focusing their definitions on **legal constructs** of community. One author wrote that a community is defined as a "geographical area with definite legal boundaries, occupied by residents engaged in interrelated economic activities and constituting a politically self-governing unit" (*Encyclopaedia of Social Sciences*, 1949:102ff). While not all communities are defined in legal terms or represent a political subdivision, communities can have political properties. Perhaps the most important aspect of this definition is the ability of a community to be organized and to take political action based on its members' shared beliefs and interests. This activity may flow through not only formal political structures like city government but can also be linked to community institutions like workplaces, churches, schools, or neighborhood associations.

By the 1950s, there were so many definitions of community that George A. Hillery, Jr., of the University of Atlanta, attempted to classify 94 different definitions, by content, to see whether he could identify areas of common agreement. His conclusion was that, "Most ... are in basic agreement that community consists of persons in social interaction within a geographic area and having one or more additional ties" (Hillery, 1955:111). In this sense, community is not a fixed set of attributes but rather an ongoing process resulting from social interactions over time. This means that, by altering social interactions, the community as a whole changes. For the police, the implications of this observation are profound. Police must inject themselves in this complex of social interactions because they shape communities.

This makes it easy to see how the term "community" began to become synonymous with "neighborhood." A neighborhood, however, is a physical area where "there is a collective life that emerges from the social networks that have arisen among the residents and the sets of institutional arrangements that overlap these networks. That is, the neighborhood is inhabited by people who perceive themselves to have a common interest in that area and to whom a common life is available. Finally, the neighborhood has some tradition of identity and continuity over time" (Bursik & Grasmick, 1993:6). In Hillery's time, a decade after World War II, when most cities were still dominated by clear-cut, virtually self-contained, ethnic neighborhoods, drawing such distinctions seemed like needless hairsplitting. But we must understand that existing social arraignments and networks often determined the conditions of social life and how dominant groups treated people.

In her paper "The Neighborhood," Suzanne Keller (1982) defined neighborhood in terms that echo past definitions of community, demonstrating that confusion about these terms persisted. She saw neighborhoods as being marked by "boundaries—either physical or symbolic and usually both—where streets, railway lines, or parks separate off an area and its inhabitants or where historical and social traditions make people view an area as a distinctive unit. Usually these two boundaries reinforce each other: the physical unit encourages symbolic unity, and symbolic boundaries come to be attached to physical ones" (1982:9). Common phrases like a person "comes from the wrong side of the tracks" captures the physical, racial, economic, and cultural separation between neighborhoods in the 1950s. Depending, of course, on which side of tracks one came from likely determined whether communities were a positive or negative force in one's life and often determined how people were viewed and treated. This point illustrates the double-edged aspect of community. Communities are defined as much by who and what they exclude as they are by who and what they include.

Though community study had, to a great degree, fallen out of fashion in the 1960s, efforts to update and refine the definition of community in the 1970s focused on identifying new, unifying principles. The University of Chicago's Albert Hunter (cited in Watman, 1980), in his book *Symbolic Communities,* noted the close association among the words "common," "communication," and "community." He argued that both language and shared symbols help identify what he called the **natural community**. Meenaghan (1972:95) focused on social-area analysis, which used census tract information to break out urban groups of 3,000 to 6,000 people, so that data on the homogeneity of economic, family, and ethnic characteristics could then be used to identify the boundaries of communities. While this form of analysis assists in constructing ideas about some characteristics that can be used to mark the boundaries of community, there is nothing inherently "natural" about them. Likewise, census data tell us very little about the social interactions that take place within a community. The characteristics of communities emerge from social forces that compel people to live together in a geographic location under a set of concrete conditions. Communities are created and defined by social forces that act upon and structure social interactions.

Worsley (1987) has argued that despite the complex and different definitional issues associated with the term "community," there seem to be three base components to communities. First, there is the **geographical aspect** of the term that refers to human settlements within a fixed location. Second, the term refers to the network of **social relations and interactions** among a group of people who constitute a community. Third, community has been referred to as a quality of particular types of social interrelations where the phrases "**sense of community**" and "community spirit" capture the essence of this usage (Figure 3.1).

> You can learn more about the elements of community by going to http://www.newsalem.com/communitysummit/kbase/elements.htm.

We can summarize our review of the definitions of community by noting that communities are, to a lesser or greater extent, composed of the following elements:

- A particular geographic area or location where a group of people live and/or work;

- A location or node where an interrelated series of economic, political, and social interactions occur regularly;

Figure 3.1
Elements of Community

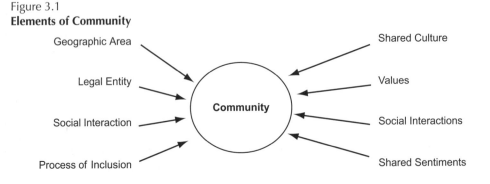

- A recognized legal entity or unit of governance. At the very least a community provides for social and political action;

- A network of social interactions that include a division of labor and sense of interdependence;

- A group of individuals who have a shared culture, interest, outlook, or perspective;

- A moral dimension where values are transmitted;

- A process by which social interactions collectively shape character;

- A processes of inclusion and exclusion; and

- A shared sentiment; a sense of belonging and feeling of interdependence.

It is important for community policing officers and police executives to be able to identify where a community exists within their legal jurisdiction. This knowledge is essential for the assignment of officers, the collection of information about people's needs, and the provision of community services. The following features may also mark a community:

- The presence or absence of businesses;

- The location of churches, schools, community associations, or neighborhood centers;

- Residential groupings and points of transition from single-family to multi-family units or apartments;

- Homogeneity of economic, occupational, or ethnic characteristics;

- Physical characteristics like railroads, streets, parks, and gated residences; or

- An extensive and continued network of human interaction; or

- A collection of people with shared interests.

Virtual Community

In the age of information and communication technology, more and more people are connecting in virtual rather than physical space. People are often drawn together through their shared interests in particular types of information or a desire to communicate about particular topics or issues facing their community. People living in a community can now communicate or learn about their communities through Internet technology. A **virtual community** is a communicative network of people who interact through technologies for social purposes and to exchange information and ideas about mutual interests. This type of community can arise through various mediums including email, message boards, chat rooms, or social networking sites designed to allow people to communicate. Some of the most popular forms of virtual communities are hosted on commercial websites like Facebook, Twitter, and Myspace.

As we shall see, while these forms of social communication are far from the face-to-face social relations that are developed and needed to sustain real communities they do offer community policing officers the possibility of reaching out to the community in new ways and perhaps even establishing some sense of belonging or attachment to a community. While these technologies were initially used by police departments to allow them to connect to other agencies, they can be used to provide community members with information and forums for participating with their police department. In essence, virtual communities are just one more way for the police to engage the community.

Matthew J. Simeone, Jr. (2008: 6-8), has identified and commented on law enforcement's use of four Internet-based technologies that create, and possibly sustain, a virtual community that enhances the communication between the police and the public. Use of these technologies can affect the practice of both law enforcement and community members. It is hoped that more information sharing will lead to the active involvement of people in the business of policing and crime control.

- **Email**—The presence of computers and Internet access in virtually all large businesses and in most homes today provides the tools needed to implement an email-based system. Email allows near instant access to potentially thousands of end users, and, equally important, it allows for a direct means of communication back to the agency.

- **Web portals**—These can provide virtually unlimited access to large numbers of users. Reports and notifications can be archived, and links to other agencies and resources can make volumes of information easily accessible. In addition, more sophisticated sites are offering content in the form of podcasts or enabling users to sign up for RSS feeds. Such uses of technology typically engage a younger, more technologically savvy demographic.

- **Web forums**—These have the potential to become virtual communities where people gather online to participate in a community of interest. In some cases, a community of interest may even develop into a community of practice, where people deepen their knowledge and expertise in an area and further the practice by interacting on an ongoing basis. Web forums can be open to the public or limited to a certain group of members. For neighborhood watch leaders, agencies should consider making a forum accessible to the general public, as it will allow it to grow by giving those with an interest in crime prevention an opportunity to either join in the discussions or just stand on the sidelines and observe.

- **Groove**—Microsoft Office Groove offers a potentially powerful tool for providing a secure environment for sharing information. Designed to facilitate collaboration, Groove provides a law enforcement agency with the ability to invite specific users into a secure virtual workspace. Once invited into a workspace, individuals would be able to share information, conduct discussion threads, and collaborate on documents, all with encryption end-to-end in a secure environment within Groove.

Another powerful tool for reaching out to the community and creating communities of interest is social media. As Lauir Stevens (2011:7) explains, "Social media tools offer police departments a way to listen to their citizens and hear what is being said about the department, crime, the quality of life, and events. They also offer the department the ability to shape the conversation." She describes how the Ocean City, Maryland, Police Department uses social media like email, Twitter, Facebook, YouTube, and a blog to engage the community. The agency provides "crime prevention information and community-related news in a matter of seconds. Press releases detail current police-involved incidents. The department blog has posts on Internet scams, and citizens are encouraged to add their comments and experiences. Since Ocean City is a beach community with a high number of summer visitors, other postings have addressed such beach-specific topics as heavy rain storms and hurricane season as well as many other topics including bicycle, moped, and scooter safety; sexual assault awareness; pedestrian safety; traffic safety tips; and public transportation. Social media not only allows the police to reach the public, but also allows the public to communicate with the police."

Assaults on Community

A serious danger in any discussion about changes in what is meant by the word "community," and changes that have occurred within communities, is that such discussion is unconsciously colored by a wistful longing for what may only seem like a better past. As Victor Azarya (1985:135) of the Hebrew University in Jerusalem wrote about many of the definitions of community analyzed by Hillery: "These approaches are clearly mixed with some nostalgia for a glorious past in which people were thought to be more secure, less alienated, and less atomized." Certainly there is a healthy measure of nostalgia and romanticism in the notion that communities of the past were all safe harbors and free of conflict. This certainly was not the case then, nor is it the case today. Victor G. Strecher (2006b) makes the following observations on today's notion and uses of the term "community":

> An "American community" is a warm, comforting phrase. In this concept there is the overtone of the small society—the community of neighbors who know each other (to the third generation), and whose offspring develop their self-awareness in an atmosphere of warmth, trust and a wish to become like those who have gone before.... The small, simple, pre-industrial, consensual, almost primitive aspect of community does not require much secular law...—not much beyond the Ten Commandments. There is no big government, no regulatory laws and agencies..., no tension between the sermons heard in church and the high school curriculum. "Community" is a realization of the romanticized melting pot. Where do we find this small, uncomplicated, unspecialized, unstratified colony of believers who are clustered around an agreeable moral code? Chicago? Miami? San Francisco? Minneapolis? Maybe those are too large. Bangor? Rocky Mount? Wausau? Dothan? Waco? Nogales? Butte? Poplar Bluff? Bakersfield? Boulder? Eugene?

American society, however, is different today than it was decades ago. In the early 1900s, wave after wave of immigrants arrived in the United States, primarily from Europe, settling most often into expanding ethnic neighborhoods in major cities, where they could also continue to maintain their various cultural traditions. The popular movie *Gangs of New York* portrayed the negative side of immigration and the ethic divides that plagued many American urban centers. In addition, Blacks from the rural South continued to migrate to northern cities in search of higher-paying jobs in industry and to escape the treatment they received in the South. They settled in specific city neighborhoods, dictated not only by choice but also by discriminatory housing practices. Victor G. Strecher (2006b) describes this exodus:

Between 1910 and 1963 it is estimated that more than 5,000,000 African Americans migrated from the South, mostly to the large cities of the North and the West, in two distinctive patterns. Between 1910 and 1940, about 1,750,000 migrants moved northward to the large cities directly in their paths '... from South Carolina to New York, from Georgia to Philadelphia, from Alabama to Detroit, and from Mississippi to Chicago.' Between 1940 and 1963 migration largely followed the second pattern. During that period most of the 3,300,000 African Americans who left the South migrated to the western as well as to the northern cities. Frequently, the reason for moving was a desire to leave the South rather than a specific attraction of the destination (citations omitted).

One major difference is U.S. cities have become poorer. The **White flight** of the 1950s from the cities to the suburbs was succeeded by the **Black flight** of African Americans that began roughly a decade later. Serious social problems persuaded those who could to move to the suburbs. This shift was also fueled by the continuing rise in the overall standard of living created by an expanding economy, which allowed some people the opportunity to be upwardly mobile. Being upwardly mobile also meant being horizontal—moving out.

White flight from cities was also the result of a notoriously unethical real estate practice, called **blockbusting**. Blockbusting stampeded White homeowners into selling their houses because of the fear that African American families moving in would inevitably cause property values to plunge. Some unscrupulous real estate agents would intentionally line up an African American home buyer for a house in an all-White neighborhood, and the agents would either keep the buyer's race secret or offer the seller an inflated price to ensure the sale would go through. Then they would prey on the racial fears of the other White homeowners, warning them that unless they sold quickly, they would be trapped in homes worth a fraction of their current value. This practice exploited a self-fulfilling prophecy, since panic selling did depress price, which meant those previously stable neighborhoods quickly degenerated into chaos—leaving only the real estate agents and bankers to profit.

> You can learn more about blockbusting by going to http://www.encyclopedia.chicagohistory.org/pages/147.html.

Not only did the influx of newcomers lack a shared history together, late arrivals were able to purchase homes for a fraction of what the early arrivals had paid, which often meant the new community suffered inevitable internal tensions in trying to blend people of vastly different socio economic classes in one confined geographic area. Only the real estate agents benefited, because they were able to turn tidy profits on the huge volume of sales that blockbusting promoted.

> You can learn more about McDonalization by going to http://www.umsl .edu/~keelr/010/mcdonsoc.html.

The full implications of these dislocations were somewhat masked, as long as the rising standard of living held the false promise of offering ever-increasing opportunities for advancement to anyone willing to work hard—the "American dream." Then the dramatic rise of oil prices in the early 1970s, followed by stagflation, then the recession of 1982, and globalization culminated in the loss of high-paid, unskilled jobs in industry and manufacturing, with more of the new jobs created in the lower-paying service fields, and with many of those jobs in the suburbs. An increasing trend toward corporatizing, the **Walmarting** and **McDonaldization** of American businesses, dislodged many "mom-and-pop" operations and drastically lowered workers' wages and stripped communities of their local economic base—forever changing the face and "place" of community.

Manufacturing was moved to rural areas or foreign countries in search of inexpensive, often child-based, labor. This trend continued well into the 1990s with corporate downsizing and the decline of workers' real wages. Even when adjusted for inflation, median family income declined over the last three decades. The shifting economic picture of America was coupled with a growing negative view of welfare and governmental assistance. People who were dislodged from jobs also found it more difficult to look to the government for a helping hand as they attempted to make the transition from industry to the service sector. As a society, we have not yet grasped the full implications of what it will mean if most people cannot expect to improve their condition, and the young have good reason to worry they may not be able to achieve the same standard of living enjoyed by their parents or even grandparents.

Although the most educated generations in American history, the **X, Y, and Z generations**, people now in their early twenties and thirties, earn less than their parents did when they were the same age. The only factor keeping household income at pace with inflation is that more and more women are entering the workforce and contributing to family income (Ellis, 2007). Expression of this condition can be found among the **X generation's** willingness to reject the traditional work ethic of the past and adopt an alternative culture and worldview that gives up economic drive in favor of a freer lifestyle. The cultural sentiments of this generation were expressed in serious movies like *Reality Bites* and *Fight Club* to comedies like *Ferris Bueller's Day Off* and *Slacker.* The most current adult generation, often referred to as **Generation Z** (today's teenagers and 20-somethings), is experiencing a new array of social problems. Although they are said to be the most technologically savvy of the generations, their problems run from an inability to secure affordable housing (resulting in young adults never leaving home, moving back in with parents following college, or living in non-traditional housing arrangements), to the potential for lower educational attainment (because of governmental cutbacks and increased costs of education), to the inability to secure meaningful

> You can learn more about Generation Z by going to http://sparxoo.com/2010/02/23/examining-generation-z-stats-demographics-segments-predictions/.

employment. The plight of these generations is no accident—it is the consequence of the way work, business, and the political economy have been reorganized over the last half century.

Using Detroit as an example, between 1955 and 1990, the city lost more than 850,000 people—enough to qualify as this nation's eleventh largest city. According to the *Detroit Free Press,* during that same time, other important community assets were also lost: "Detroit ... lost about 100 movie theaters, J.L. Hudson's flagship department store, the headquarters of the AAA-Michigan, Stroh's brewery, the Pistons professional basketball team, the Lions pro football team, countless factories" (McGraw & Blossom, 1988:2B). In addition, Cardinal Szoka announced in the fall of 1988 that he planned to close one-third (43) of Detroit's remaining Catholic churches, leaving the city with only one-half the number it boasted in 1968 (Ager, 1988:15A). Since 2005, 14 parishes have closed in Detroit, and archdiocese officials are concerned that many of the remaining 55 will also have to be closed. More than 30,000 buildings now stand vacant in that city, and many are in need of demolition.

In 1956, Michigan employed 412,000 in the auto industry, down to 288,000 in the second quarter of 1988 (Jackson, 1988:1C) and down to 260,000 by 2008 (University of Michigan, 2008). By 2011, even the most optimistic forecasts predicted that the Michigan auto industry could recover to about 160,000 workers. In the midst of the great recession labor was forced to make great concessions that eroded the quality of workers' lives. In 2008, Ford Motor Company planned to buy out or retire early at least 54,000 U.S. hourly workers, about 93 percent of its hourly workforce, and to replace those leaving workers with lower-paid ones.

Chrysler and GM's negotiated bankruptcies allowed new workers to be hired at significantly lower wages. In all, since 2000 Michigan has lost more than 800,000 jobs.

While this suggests future workers will need more education to secure good jobs, the high school graduation rate for Detroit was estimated to have dropped to about 48 percent (*Detroit News, 2008*). More young people are leaving school rather than are graduating. Detroit is still suffering the consequences of a shifting economy and an aggressive attack on workers and their benefits. Most recently, this political attack has extended to states such as Ohio, Indiana, and Minnesota where political leaders are attempting to pit private workers against their public counterparts. The state of Michigan has recently begun a campaign to attract people to the state and into a service-based economy, but major urban centers across the country are still strapped for an economic base and the countless number of abandoned houses and businesses serve as markers of communities in distress.

SPOTLIGHT ON COMMUNITY POLICING PRACTICE

A Partnership That Builds Communities: Chesapeake Habitat for Humanity and the Baltimore Police Department

The work of Chesapeake Habitat for Humanity (CHH) has an impact well beyond the bricks and mortar of the homes that it builds. CHH has made a commitment to develop strategic partnerships that, together with the time and resources invested in building homes in the community, seek to create a family, neighborhood, and community transformation.

With this goal in mind, CHH has recently partnered with the Baltimore (Maryland) Police Department (BPD) to improve public safety. The collaboration aims to achieve five outcomes:

1. Increased community stabilization.
2. Expanded education for CHH homeowners.
3. Improved officer/community relations.
4. Increased public safety awareness.
5. Enhanced teamwork among district commanders and their officers.

Laying the Foundation for Community Stabilization

In April 2007, CHH partnered with the Southern District police force through a community safe zone in the Washington Village/Pigtown area of Baltimore, along with other area nonprofit entities, to provide access to services within the designated safe zone area.

In early March of this year, the department presented a course at police headquarters, during which CHH homebuyers were given constructive examples of how they could become actively engaged in the public safety of their neighborhoods, such as through Community

---

Relations Councils and Citizens on Patrol groups. Families also learned about the Crime Watch program, which allows 911 calls to be made anonymously, visited the Communications Center where all 911 and 311 calls are answered, and toured the Intelligence Watch Center. In a presentation on Baltimore's city-wide Camera Project, they learned how police responded to events captured on camera and how the video evidence had been used in court.

In just a few short hours, homebuyer perceptions about police and safety in Baltimore were significantly changed for the better. The BPD will benefit from the engagement of new community members, while those community members, in turn, will gain the knowledge they need to protect their families and become leaders in their communities.

Expanding Our Collective Impact

To increase interaction among the police commanders, volunteers, and future CHH homebuyers, enhance department teamwork, and contribute to neighborhood stabilization objectives, CHH invited police commanders from each of Baltimore's nine districts to spend a day alongside CHH volunteers on a build site. During the joint build, a CHH staff member will provide an overview, from the nonprofit perspective, of public safety issues surrounding vacant buildings.

Furthermore, CHH will be incorporated into the BPD's officer training program this spring. The program will rotate a full shift off duty for 30 days, during which officers will alternate between 2 weeks of firearms training and 2 weeks of communication training. During the latter 2 weeks, an entire shift of 35 officers will volunteer on a CHH construction site.

Long-Term Vision

Chesapeake Habitat for Humanity has a history of bringing about many positive outcomes, both socially and economically, by building and renovating homes in Baltimore communities. Its presence injects new stakeholders and resources into the city by increasing the homeownership rate, adding to the tax base, and adding new social capital within the community. Chesapeake Habitat for Humanity has a history of bringing about many positive outcomes, both socially and economically, by building and renovating homes in Baltimore communities. Its presence injects new stakeholders and resources into the city by increasing the homeownership rate, adding to the tax base, and adding new social capital within the community.

Through partnerships such as this one with the BPD, CHH has been able to fulfill its mission to work as a positive catalyst for change, not only in the lives of homeowner families, but in the communities where they live. This, ultimately, is part of the greater goal to build a better and safer city for all Baltimore residents. Together, the CHH and the BPD aim to demonstrate how decent housing, community revitalization, and public safety are deeply interconnected and require strong community-police partnerships to create a safer city.

Mike Mitchell
Chief Executive Officer
Chesapeake Habitat for Humanity

Source: The e-newsletter of the COPS Office, Volume 2, Issue 5, May 2009.

Figure 3.2
Long-Term Unemployment Rose to Historic Highs

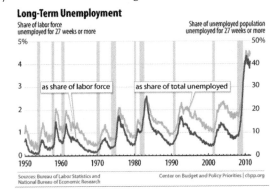

Source: CBPP (2010). *Chart Book: The Legacy of the Great Recession*. Center on Budget and Policy Priorities, Washington, DC, p. 19.

These economic shifts have contributed to a growing **underclass** in American society: more than 43 million Americans now live in poverty. The number of people in poverty in 2009 was the largest number in 51 years of data collection by the U.S. Census Bureau. Nearly 21 percent of America's children, some 15.1 million, live in poverty (U.S. Census, 2011). Among children from all kinds of families, more than one in four is born poor, and at least one in three will be on welfare at some point in their lives, with millions living in a single-parent household headed by a female (U.S. Census, 2011). Today, more than 8 million Americans are unemployed, and about the same number are forced to work part-time when they need full-time employment to support their families (Figure 3.2).

Economic changes, particularly the growing outsourcing of labor, the inequity in the distribution of material resources, as well as the dislocations wrought by globalization and greed have ruptured the tie between geography and community.

The Technological and Corporate Divide

The economic changes and the explosion of technology since the end of World War II disrupted the status quo, so established definitions of community and neighborhood began to take on new meaning. What many researchers failed to take into account was that a community of interest did not have to be tied to a particular geographic area. Likewise, work and economic relations were becoming detached from community geography. In particular, the impact of mass transit, communications technologies, mass media and globalization, as well as economic pressures disrupted previously stable, but very often far less than equal, communities, leaving in their wake areas where people still live together in geographic areas, but do not interact in the same ways as before.

Affordable technology, such as the automobile, the telephone, and the Internet, now allow those with sufficient resources to make bonds based on "community of interest" without regard for geography or mutual dependency. If trouble strikes, a person today picks up the telephone, shoots off an email, or Facebooks a friend across town or across the country. If the problem is serious enough, that friend can climb into a car or board a plane to go help. If someone is lonely, they can access a chat-line on the Internet and simulate social interaction. In the same faceless sense, people now look to corporations to provide the necessities of life rather than looking to each other or to someone in the community. Similarly, business decisions are made based on efficiency and cost rather than by a sense of community responsibility. Often, community-based businesses suffer because people now have the ability and willingness to procure goods from hundreds of miles away with the click of a mouse and little thought to how these changing forms of commerce affect their neighbor's business or their community.

The emergence of large, even multinational, corporations has played a big role in the destruction of both the economics of community as well as a sense of community. Fast-food chains, mall-like department stores, and multinational oil corporations have driven businesses that were locally owned and operated out of existence. They have shifted jobs to places on the globe where the cheapest labor sources can be found and when unable to move factories or outsource work they have used immigration to import labor to drive down workers' wages—all this with the assistance of the government and lawmakers. In the aftermath of these economic changes, a sense of loyalty to a community, its economic interests, and the sense of responsibility that comes with being a business owner who lives in the community in which he or she works is lost. Money is stripped from the communities in which these corporations locate, wages are lowered, choices are limited, and the sense of interdependence among members of the community is lost—people are alienated from their work, a geographic place to work, and members of their community.

In the past, before the advent of the telephone and the automobile, people were forced to trust and depend upon their neighbors, whether they shared much in common or not. Today, it takes less effort to call or Facebook a friend hundreds of miles away for advice, comfort, or assistance, than to walk 50 feet to the person who lives next door. This makes it far easier to associate with people of the same class, same educational level, same religion, same politics, and same interests, regardless of whether they live nearby—a community of self-interest driven by technology.

These changes, of course, have altered the nature of police and community interaction. People have become more dependent on corporate and government ordering. In the same sense that a person might pick up the telephone to call a friend hundreds of miles away rather than turning to a neighbor, people will call the police to complain about and ask for assistance with the loud music coming from next door rather than merely walking those same 50 feet to ask the neighbor to turn down the stereo. Our tolerance for diversity and ability to solve human problems has been limited by reliance on formal social institutions and a growing alienation from community.

Though the effects of mass transportation and mass communication on the community have been well documented, the role of mass media also deserves mention. Journalists and advertisers alike understand demographics, which means that their audience breaks down in part by geography, but more strongly by lifestyle, made up of age, income, race, religion, marital status, education, career, politics, social status, and leisure-time interests. The advertising medium now attempts to capture cultural sentiments and accentuate differences for the purposes of increasing sales. Many in our society now define themselves by labels, reinforced by the mass media—Baby Boomer, born-again Christian, feminist, yuppie, New-Ager, or member of the X, Y, or Z generations. Some people identify most strongly with career, while others identify more closely with family or leisure activities. Freed from the link to place, many people can shift gears into and out of various communities of interest during the day without having any real connection to community.

Using politics as an example, it becomes clear how this context of community has changed. Before television and social media, politicians and their supporters relied on campaigning door-to-door within neighborhoods for support. Today, the politician stages a photo opportunity in a particular neighborhood where background symbols that appeal to particular demographic groups are manipulated to transmit a message to those who share that community of interest—regardless of where they live, community is used as a media backdrop. A political leader stands before us on television with

> You can learn more about social media and its political use by going to http://www.npr.org/templates/story/story.php?storyId=130873983.

a backdrop of shipping boxes stamped "Made in America" to create an illusion of caring while he quietly endorses the outsourcing of jobs or he takes a photo opportunity aboard a naval ship to show he cares about the troops, but refuses to visit the widows and orphans left behind in the community. A presidential hopeful takes a hunting trip for the cameras to show he is "just a good old boy" and then hosts a lavish dinner complete with servants. Another political hopeful has a "shot and a beer" at a local pub to illustrate her affection for the working class. Another political figure tells us, "Yes, we can," as he quietly agrees to extend tax breaks for the most affluent while agreeing to cut support for the most needy. Today, politicians engage their supporters with "email blasts" asking for contributions, all the while targeting populations with messages suited for their demographic. If you're wealthy, they will help you stay that way; if you're poor, they will give you a hand up. Like-minded political followers are allowed to track their favorite politicians on Twitter to receive the textual equivalent of a "sound bite" response to an emerging social issue or community problem.

While communities and political leaders of the past were far from being glorious, that does not mean today's communities and leaders do not fall even further short of that imperfect model. Likewise, it is somewhat simplistic to solely blame urbanization on the decline of "traditional" communities. The very nature of social interaction has changed and continues to change today—well after the Industrial Revolution.

These changes alone do not tell the full story about the impact on our sense of community or the lives of people. The answer in such cases lies in looking not at what science or politicians tell us, but at literature. As author **Kurt Vonnegut** notes, this need to be part of a community, tied to a place where people interact together in their daily lives, has universal appeal:

> This is a lonesome society that's been fragmented by the factory system. People have to move from here to there as jobs move, as prosperity leaves one area and appears somewhere else. People don't live in communities permanently anymore. But they should: Communities are very comforting to human beings. I was talking to a United Mine Workers lawyer in a bar down in the Village the other day, and he was telling me how some miners in Pennsylvania damn well will not leave, even though the jobs are vanishing, because of the church centered communities there, and particularly because of the music. They have choirs that are 100 years old, some of them extraordinary choirs, and they are not going to go to San Diego, and build ships or airplanes. They're going to stay in Pennsylvania because that's home.... Until recent times, you know, human beings usually had a permanent community of relatives. They had dozens of homes to go to. So when a married couple had a

fight, one or the other could go to a house three doors down and stay with a close relative until he was feeling tender again. Or if a kid got so fed up with his parents that he couldn't stand it, he could march over to his uncle's for a while. And this is no longer possible. Each family is locked into its little box. The neighbors aren't relatives. There aren't other houses where people can go and be cared for....We're lonesome. We don't have enough friends or relatives anymore. And we would if we lived in real communities (Vonnegut, 1965-74:241-242).

Vonnegut says the craving for community runs so deep that people who have no drinking problem join Alcoholics Anonymous because of the extended family and sense of community it provides them. The movie *Fight Club* depicted the desperate lives that many people live showing the actors in the film arguing about who would attend various self-help groups just to belong to something. Vonnegut cites the longing for community as a factor in drug use. "The fact that they use drugs gives them a community. If you become a user of any drug, you can pick up a set of friends you see day after day, because of the urgency of getting drugs all the time. And you'll get a community where you might not ordinarily have one" (Vonnegut, 1965-74:250). Vonnegut's observation only becomes more powerful when one looks at the consequences of social media, gated communities, retirement villages, and the power of the media to shape sentiments about **social interactions**. Take for example the AT&T commercial where a husband is jetting off on business to some far away location. The traveler faxes a message to his wife to meet him on the porch of their house for a "date." He then calls her up on a cellular phone while still in flight. Both are mutually satisfied by the technological encounter and business goes on. This commercial is aimed at changing the cultural sentiment about social relations and implies that technology is a viable replacement for real human interaction. If the introduction of technology and the careful crafting of social sentiment by the media can modify views and personal relationships, communities can be altered to an even greater extent. The emotional need to belong in a society where few opportunities exist has produced "a proud but meaningless association of human beings" (Vonnegut, 1965-74:xv). The theme in many of Vonnegut's writings is that a true sense of community has been lost, replaced by the illusion of community that fails to satisfy the basic human need of belonging.

But even technological interactions are not evenly distributed across all segments of society. What is clear as well is that many who live in poverty—the underclass—lack the resources to enjoy even this weakened sense of belonging based solely on interests or the simulation of meaningful social interaction. While some may be able to tune in to the mass culture offered on TV, fewer have the money for a telephone, a car, or an Internet connection, so they have no easy access to people outside their own neighborhoods. Different as well is the increased likelihood that the person behind the counter in the neighborhood store is not a member of the community. Chances are likely that the person behind the counter is not the owner, but a hired clerk, someone who has no authority to extend credit to customers or to make allowances for customers' family problems. The clerk more often than not works for some corporation located hundreds of miles away from the community. The underlying racial tensions, cultural differences, and pervasive mistrust make it far more likely that if the young boy shoplifts, the clerk will not confront the family privately but instead will call the police—or even take the law into his own hands. And somehow, though the face of the law makes no distinction, shoplifting from an impersonal corporation rather than the mom-and-pop stores of old is a different kind of crime.

These changes have accentuated the **three-tiered hierarchy** of community based on class:

- **Underclass** inner-city neighborhoods house those who are too poor to escape, permanently, through upward mobility, or symbolically and temporarily, by automobile, telephone, or Internet. These blighted areas have lost many important anchors, including town meeting halls, industry, businesses, shops, schools, and churches—interactions that not only helped hold the community together, but also provided meaningful ways for people to fill their lives. Despite a shared geography and the common-thread fear of crime, many people in such communities are too fearful to interact in ways that can rebuild a sense of community. This desperation was perhaps best captured in singer Tracey Chapman's song "Fast Car."

- For the **working class**, community spans a wider range of options. On one end are lower class neighborhoods that may or may not show active signs of community life, filled with people who hope to rise higher, but fear slipping lower. On the other end of that spectrum are upper-working class communities— gentrified areas in major cities and upscale suburban and ex-urban enclaves. In those areas, people usually have the resources that allow them to interact with others who share their interests, regardless of geography. These interactions, however, are becoming more meaningless, less direct, and certainly less social. As disposable income increases for some, people can also afford to partake of social and cultural activities both within the geographic community and elsewhere—movies, plays, clubs, sporting events, health clubs. The more money an individual or family has, the better they can afford to develop and enjoy a community of interests that need not be tied to the geographic area in which they live. Participation in any community life available within the geographic area where they live becomes voluntary, a matter of choice no longer based on mutual dependence or determined by social responsibility but rather by the desire and ability to pay.

- By virtue of their income, the **upper class** can afford all the security they want and need, yet, even with bodyguards, the affluent cannot guarantee perfect safety, especially because their wealth makes them inviting targets for crime. There is also, no doubt, a sense of community associated with wealthy areas such as Palm Springs, California, and Grosse Pointe, Michigan, but community involvement usually means heading charitable organizations or becoming a patron of the arts, which implies service to others rather than mutual dependence; it often amounts to little more than pulling out a checkbook for their pet cause and a getting a tax deduction. The affluent also have the wherewithal to travel wherever a community of interest draws them. Additionally, they have the resources to influence social policy and practices that are in their best interests rather than those of the community; and when a community fails, they simply move to another one.

Not only has American society become more stratified in this classed hierarchy, but communities have also changed because of the fairly recent emergence of planned communities. Planned communities upset the so-called natural balance, whether it is a low-income public housing project or an upscale suburban enclave. What all planned communities share in common is that their rapid appearance thrusts large numbers of people together who have no history. They also displace people who have had a sense of history. Likewise, they are simulations of community and serve to isolate people from larger social groups and problems. Can one really argue that celebrities like Paris Hilton or the Kardashians understand or care about the problems in poor urban communities?

Figure 3.3
Income Gains at the Top Dwarf Those of Low- and Middle-Income Households

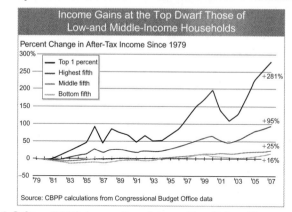

Source: Sherman, A., & C. Stone (2010). *Income Gaps Between Very Rich and Everyone Else More Than Tripled in Last Three Decades, New Data Show*. Center on Budget and Policy Priorities, Washington, DC, p. 2.

Lexington, Kentucky, is a classic example of how communities are destroyed and new policing problems are created by the greed associated with "development." During the latter part of the 2000s, entire inner-city neighborhoods in Lexington were demolished to create "safe and affordable housing" by developers. The residents of these neighborhoods, most minorities, were forced out to make way for new housing. Upon completion of the projects, prior residents found that the new housing was hardly affordable. Many of residents were forced out of public housing to the suburbs of Lexington into subdivisions that had been historically White.

Figure 3.4
Significant Changes in Public Housing

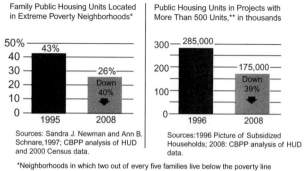

Source: CBPP (2010). *Center on Budget and Policy Priorities Annual Repot, 2009*. Center on Budget and Policy Priorities, Washington, DC, p. 19.

Within a short period of time police began to get calls from long time residents in the suburbs complaining about rising levels of crime. When officers responded to these calls, they found that residents could not explain their newfound fear of crime with concrete incidents and that statistics did not indicate any rise in crime in the suburbs. The Police Commander in charge of the area told us that merely seeing unfamiliar people, particularly people of color, in the neighborhood invoked a racist fear of crime. This is not to suggest that communities need to be homogeneous, but rather to illustrate that communities are not always created naturally and that people are often forced together by economic conditions. It also illustrates that communities take time to develop and that misguided ideas about race and crime still persist.

Sparking an immediate sense of community is difficult because there is no established base upon which to build. In the case of many suburban developments, a sense of community may develop over time, because the people who move there share enough in common, though it may never run deep. This is far different than when an organic community assimilates an infusion of newcomers into an already functioning system. The emotional loss may be masked in affluent suburbs, because people in such circumstances often have the money to travel and indulge their hobbies and amusements. Among those who are financially strapped, however, the move from a stable city neighborhood to a new suburb offers undeniable improvements, yet it may also exact a penalty in the loss of an important source of social support, meaningful activities, and real social interaction.

In the case of public housing projects, the same kinds of barriers to generating a natural community exist, but experience also shows they are prone to even more serious problems. The kinds of low-income housing projects popular during the 1940s through the 1960s put huge numbers of people into a confined space virtually overnight. Unlike the suburbs, such projects usually housed renters, not owners. As residences were converted to places of profits, as developers dislodged entire populations to build affluent housing projects, people were pushed into high-rise slums and community relations were destroyed. This meant residents had less of a stake in maintaining property, and they typically also had fewer resources to do so.

The lack of an existing cohesive community allowed people to exploit this lack of community, which, in turn, could prevent or at least slow the growth of a natural community. Unlike in the suburbs, where homeowners typically enjoyed a rising standard of living, many of the people trapped in housing projects found their standard of living declining instead, especially as welfare payments failed to keep pace with inflation or were cut altogether. Home ownership also allowed those who bought homes in new suburbs to enjoy the benefits of increasing equity, inflating home prices, and write-offs of mortgage interest on their income tax returns. Their counterparts in low-income public housing were not building any equity, and, for them, inflation simply meant an increased risk of rising rents and expenses beyond what their income could cover. While the police were directed to "weed" these communities during the Clinton administration, political leaders began cutting the safety net of social programs out from under these communities—pitting the poor against the working class with discussions about welfare mothers and cheaters. The administration of George W. Bush was perhaps no better, using fear to pit younger workers against the retired elderly to destroy one of the last vestiges of the "great society"—social security. The greed of investment banks in the 1990s, which led to predatory lending practices in housing, is gutting communities in this decade, dislodging and literally leaving hundreds of thousands of people without homes. In 2011, 1 out of every 605 homes was in foreclosure and one-third of all homeowners were underwater on their loans. Today, attacks against social programs continue and labor organizations are under siege by political leaders. President Barack Obama seems more than willing to compromise with his political opponents, as long it is merely the working class or social programs for the poor that suffer.

Figure 3.5
Foreclosure Rates, 2000-2008

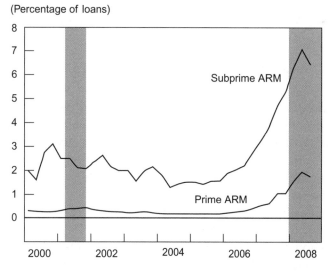

Sources: Congressional Budget Office; Mortgage Bankers Association.

Notes: ARM = adjustable-rate mortgage.

Data are quarterly and are plotted through the third quarter of 2008.

Source: CBO (2009). *The Budget and Economic Outlook: Fiscal Years 2009 to 2019*. The Congress of the United States Congressional Budget Office: Washington, DC, p. 7.

For those whose basic standard of living is comfortable, the loss of community may simply mean greater self-reliance, perhaps explaining the boom in self-help books offering advice to people on how they can become their own best friends and handle personal problems on their own, as well as the types of service calls police officers receive every day. As Suzanne Keller (1984:288) wrote, "It is now possible for individuals to travel throughout the globe without ever leaving home, while others are at home wherever they set foot. Expanding spiritual and physical horizons have severed the original link between place and community." For those left behind without access to social media and a raise each year, the gap between the life of the haves and the have-nots can be an unbridgeable gulf.

Without overly romanticizing the past, the alienation fostered by the loss of a sense of community takes an increasing toll on people. Membership in a strong community of the past implied belonging to a group who held fast together against the world. If community no longer provides that emotionally satisfying feeling of security and shared struggle, people are forced to rely more on themselves or on family. For those without the resources to enjoy the culture beyond what a TV screen or an Internet connection provides, the loss of geographically viable communities threatens to differentially erode the quality of life.

How Community Policing Can Build a Sense of Community

The purpose in this analysis is not to belabor the growing gap between rich and poor, the problems posed by racism, the blight of the inner city, and the pernicious problems of the underclass. Instead the goal is to examine today's reality and the dynamics that have eroded the strong communities of the past, to better understand the unique role community policing can play in meeting the obvious challenges.

Part of the challenge for community policing is to help revive the idea that those who live in the same area can improve the quality of community life by understanding how they share a community of mutual interests. Perhaps ironically, the **threat of crime** or even terrorism can be a catalyst to make people see that they do share a community of interest based on mutual geography. Of great consequence as well is that unless fear is channeled into positive change, it can degenerate into apathy, social isolation, or even vigilantism and rioting. Community policing holds the promise of using fear of crime as an impetus to improve the overall quality of community life. It is a pivot point from which change can take place.

The issues of crime and fear of crime within any geographic community offer police their best and most logical opportunity for unifying people in ways that help rebuild that traditional sense of community. Yet as the discussion of the three-tiered class hierarchy of community also shows, money can mask some of the downside of a loss of a sense of community, and community policing can play an important role wherever people cluster together. The department in Clearwater, Florida, for instance, first introduced community policing in the Greenwood Avenue area, a low-income, high-crime community. The approach's success there persuaded the administration to implement community policing on the beach, where many problems involved helping local businesses and residents cope with the influx of tourists. In the effort, community policing officers (CPOs) wearing shorts patrol the beach, easing tensions when young visitors who are far away from home often feel the urge to behave in ways they would not behave in their home communities— which also shows how a sense of community can shape people's behavior.

Regardless of the neighborhood, any new community policing effort starts first with face-to-face meetings with average people, not just so-called community leaders. This part of the start-up process involves average people in setting the priorities the police should pursue first and that alone can help people regain a sense of personal control over their collective destiny. One must be mindful, however, that **initiatives** must come from the community itself and not just from police or elites who desire to impose their vision of community onto a neighborhood. Bursik and Grasmick (1993:3) recount the consequences of this failed attempt at revitalization in the following observation:

> Several cities also have experienced a sometimes violent resistance to the movement of upper-middle-class residents into traditionally lower- and working-class areas, that is, the process that has been referred to as gentrification. For example, the Knight-Ridder News Service released a story about the tensions that have evolved between the Polish, Italian, and German blue-collar residents of the Manayunk section of Philadelphia and the recent wave of artists, white-collar workers, and merchants who have tried to transform its working-class shopping district into a "hip row of pastel-colored shops that some compare to Coconut Grove without the palms or Sausalito without the San Francisco." The resistance to this change rapidly escalated from the exchange of verbal insults to broken windows, scratched cars, and assaults (citations omitted).

As Bruce Benson, who was a lieutenant in the Flint foot patrol experiment, noted, a survey comparing why people chose one bank over another, despite the fact all the banks in the area offered virtually the same services and benefits, related strongly to whether the patrons felt they received personalized service. If tellers smiled and made comments about anything other than the business at hand, people responded positively to this personalized attention. A police department infused with the community policing philosophy understands that the benefits of making people feel they are being treated as human beings not only makes the police more popular within the community, but it enhances the feeling of community cohesion. We must be mindful, however, that false responsiveness, technological gimmicks, and institutionalized niceties like cheerful bank tellers calling you by your first name because it appears on your bank deposit slip or the smiling Walmart or restaurant greeter undermines the spirit of community policing and will be quickly detected as an attempt by police to manage their appearances and impose their will on the community.

Perhaps, more importantly, community policing has the ability to change our communities. If only one lesson is to be learned from our examination of community it is that social interactions and processes make communities. In this sense the police have the ability to change social interactions and invoke processes that directly affect the quality of community life. The police should be, by definition of their role, members of the communities that they serve. Police can choose to be isolated, faceless store clerks that are accountable to select political leaders and they can subscribe to values that are far removed from the health of the community or they can choose to actively engage the community. An engagement of the community with a sense of its needs, a knowledge of the values and social arrangements that mark community, and an insight into the way social, economic, and political changes affect community are the hallmarks of real community policing as well as a the starting point for improving the quality of American communities.

SPOTLIGHT ON COMMUNITY POLICING PRACTICE

Indio Police Department Tackles the Foreclosure Crisis

Between 2002 and 2007, the city of Indio, California experienced a housing boom, but by late 2007 found itself on the leading edge of what is now a national foreclosure crisis. Faced with increasing numbers of citizen complaints of poorly maintained properties as well as concerns that neighborhood blight was leading to more serious crime and disorder, the Indio Police Department launched a multipronged project to contain the impact of vacant properties on the surrounding neighborhoods.

Indio and Its Foreclosure Problem

Indio, California is a city of 84,000 people located 120 miles southeast of Los Angeles in Riverside County. Although not a new city—it incorporated in the 1930s—approximately 40 percent of the current housing stock was built in the most recent housing boom. Typical of the time, much of it was bought and financed through loans that were eventually packaged together into mortgage-backed securities. The rapid escalation of home prices brought an increase in investment purchasers and non-owner-occupied homes. By January 2008, 1,400 homes were in foreclosure or preforeclosure, representing 4 percent of the city's housing stock, at a time when the national rate was still less than 1 percent. The number of foreclosures continued to grow throughout the year, so that by January 2009 the rate had increased to 8 percent of Indio's homes.

As the number of foreclosed properties increased, so too did the number of vacant properties. Approximately one-third of the foreclosure properties were vacant and both the neighbors and the police were taking notice. According to Lieutenant Rich Bitonti of the Shadow Hills District, "In some of our neighborhoods you could drive down the street and see many as 10 foreclosed properties on the same street. The overgrown yards, damaged gates, and broken windows made it very inviting for local thieves." Citizen complaints of code violations were climbing steadily, and increases in property crimes associated with these properties, in particular metal theft, were tying up police time. Even within gated communities, the Indio Police Department was seeing entire homes stripped down to the drywall of anything of value. This was making these properties harder to resell and staying on the market without capable guardianship for longer amounts of time.

The Police Department Responds

The Indio Police Department is the largest, most visible branch of the city government, with 85 sworn officers, 60 civilians, and a tradition of incorporating partnerships and problem-solving activities into its work. Somewhat unusually, the police department is also responsible for enforcing all municipal and public nuisance laws, and maintains a 12-member code enforcement team for that purpose. It was logical that the department would take the lead in developing a response to the city's foreclosure problem. It also was no surprise to others in the city that this response would result in the shifting and sharing of responsibilities with the city council, social services, and even the banking industry.

To start, the Indio Police Department wanted to better understand the nature of the problem. Department personnel analyzed code enforcement data and citizen complaints of nuisance violations, and conducted windshield surveys to determine the locations and conditions of foreclosure properties. They found no patterns to the foreclosures, which crossed the city and affected every neighborhood and every economic class. They established that properties that were vacant were a bigger source of disorder problems than those that were still occupied. They also knew from experiences in the economic downturn of the mid-1990s that

(Continued)

getting banks to take responsibility for the conditions of vacant properties would be a serious challenge. They researched the state foreclosure laws and discovered a gap that resulted in lenders not being required to secure or maintain properties during the foreclosure, a process that typically takes more than 300 days to complete. They also found that there was no one source of accurate and timely information about property owners. "This lack of information meant that staff were spending a tremendous amount of time and resources trying to track down the responsible parties," said Jason Anderson, an Indio code enforcement officer.

From this work, Indio Police Department personnel developed a three-pronged solution: 1. They created a comprehensive foreclosure registration and maintenance ordinance; 2. They ensured that the Code Enforcement Team had the necessary tools to enforce the new ordinance; and 3. They created a Housing Resource Center focused on keeping people in their homes so that the properties would not become vacant. A media blitz, continuing education programs, and ongoing informal meetings helped inform lenders, homeowners associations, and the general public of the program.

The foreclosure registration and maintenance ordinance was passed by the city council in February 2008. It requires lenders to inspect property prior to filing a Notice of Default or Deed of Trust and determine if it is vacant. The lender must then register all vacant properties with the police department so that code enforcement has accurate records of who is responsible for the property's maintenance. The information is stored in the department's CAD system so that officers responding for calls for service to those properties know whom to contact. The ordinance further holds the lenders responsible for securing and monitoring the property against criminal activity and blight. Lenders pay a registration fee for each property to offset the cost of enforcement. Violations of the ordinance are misdemeanors and can result in arrest and/or administrative fines up to $25,000 per violation.

The Code Enforcement Team took the lead in educating lenders, realtors, and community members about the new ordinance. They built partnerships with local realtors, property managers, and homeowner associations, recognizing that they were the local individuals who would have the most vested interests in the maintenance of the properties. They also increased their enforcement efforts, establishing that noncompliance would not be tolerated.

Code enforcement officers also took an active role in promoting the third prong of the approach, referring homeowners at risk of foreclosure to the new Housing Resource Center. The Center, the first city-sponsored housing resource center in the region, opened in August 2008. Trained housing counselors from the Inland Fair Housing and Mediation Board (a HUD-certified, nonprofit housing agency) provide free, confidential default- and foreclosure-prevention counseling services. The Indio Redevelopment Agency provides office space for the Center, as well as funding for facility maintenance and advertising.

The Signs of Success

In the short time since the project was fully implemented, the Indio Police Department has already seen results. Two hundred-fifty properties have been registered in accordance with the new ordinance, resulting in the collection of $41,250 in registration fees. During the last quarter of 2008, the Code Enforcement Team inspected more than 5,000 properties in the city. More than 500 notices were issued on vacant properties, and more than 200 administrative citations (totaling more than $30,000 in fines) were issued to lenders, realtors, and property managers. Even the largest national lenders have begun to actively maintain their foreclosure properties to avoid the administrative citation and fine.

The department has discovered that realtors are a key partner in their success. Realtor-listed homes registered and maintained in accordance with the ordinance are selling faster and at higher prices than bank-sold foreclosures, so there is a strong financial incentive for realtors to work with these otherwise undesirable properties.

The Housing Resource Center has conducted 140 formal counseling sessions and has helped keep 139 families in their homes. It has also received more than 450 phone calls and more than 200 walk-ins from homeowners interested in receiving counseling or foreclosure process information. As a result of this immediate success, the city intends to continue funding the operation of the Center.

Lessons Learned

The Indio Police Department believes that without these efforts the city would have seen an increase in the number of families displaced from their community, the number of unmaintained vacant homes, and the number of crimes associated with those properties. Based on these experiences, the department suggests that the development of a national foreclosure policy and registry is warranted. Allowing for local governments to obtain accurate information in a timely manner would be a huge first step in helping local law enforcement agencies understand their foreclosure problem. In addition, as Officer Anderson noted, "having accurate information is vital when an officer responds to a call and needs to know who is responsible for the property then and there, not after hours of research."

Deborah Spence
Senior Social Science Analyst
The COPS Office

Source: The e-newsletter of the COPS Office, Volume 2, Issue 3, March 2009.

For police officers and police departments to begin to meaningfully engage the community and improve the quality of life for members of the community, a transformation in the way police measure their own activities must take place. These measurements must become community-based. Policing can no longer afford to use arrest rates, service calls, crime rates, and the issuance of traffic tickets as the measures of their success; they must begin to measure attributes of the community and community interactions. Jack Greene (2000:314), for example, remarks that

Measuring success in a community policing framework requires that the police capture much more information about communities, social control, and local dynamics and link their efforts to community stabilization and capacity building. Quite often, this shifts the measurement of policing activities from reported crime to calls for police service, a measure thought to better reflect the range of problems communities confront (citation omitted). In addition, measures of community health might also include willingness to use public places, community volunteerism, business starts, home ownership increases or decreases, home improvements in neighborhoods (an indirect measure of homeowner confidence in the neighborhood), and local perceptions about safety and the police.

Community policing is not a panacea—it alone cannot be expected to revive that sense of community or reverse the economic devastation thrust upon communities. What community policing can provide, however, is an important first step in many ways:

- Community officers can *bring neighborhood people together* in efforts to enhance the community, so that they can begin to re-establish a pattern of interacting face-to-face, which fosters the mutual trust and support that is necessary to build a sense of community;

- Community officers can assist in educating the public on *what builds and what destroys communities*;

- By *making communities safer and more attractive* places to live, people can begin to enjoy the emotional support that participating in community life can provide;

- By giving people *the power to set the police agenda* for their area, community policing can help people develop confidence in their ability to control their collective destiny;

- In contrast to the adversarial relationship implicit in the traditional system, the community policing philosophy encourages the department to *humanize all interactions with people,* focusing on ways to solve community concerns. By decentralizing police service and by personalizing all the department's interactions with average people, it fosters an atmosphere of mutual trust and respect, which is essential in promoting a positive community atmosphere;

- Many community policing efforts specifically target the most vulnerable—the elderly, women, children, and minorities. Singling them out for protection and help offers the promise of *encouraging everyone to participate* more fully in a community life enriched by their involvement. Community policing can focus on the positive inclusive aspect of community rather than the negative exclusive way of community building;

- Fear of crime traps many people in their homes, where television reinforces the perception that the streets are even more dangerous than, in fact, they are. By encouraging people to band together for support and by providing personal protection, community policing *reduces the fear of crime* that stifles community involvement;

- At least initially, many cities used community policing in inner-city neighborhoods. Besides the logic of addressing the most serious problems first, a renewed sense of community may provide part of the answer in addressing current social and community conditions. This offers the promise of involving police in *new efforts to reach the underclass,* encouraging and supporting their efforts to make positive changes;

- A welcome by-product of community policing is *improved race relations,* and racial tensions remain a major barrier in developing a true sense of community. Exclusion produces conflict while inclusion builds communities; and

- Community policing officers can become a supportive source of community organizing and education—they can be agents for social and political change.

Summary

In summary, we see that the sense of community that existed in many neighborhoods has disappeared, as a result of dramatic economic and technological changes in a relatively short period of time. Those above the poverty line at least have some opportunity to use their resources to find the emotional sustenance once provided by neighborhood life, but many problems are magnified where people cannot escape impoverished communities, either physically or symbolically.

In many ways, these changes occurred so suddenly that people stunned by the changes have not yet fully identified how to set things right. The advent of a society rich enough so that the majority can afford their own homes, automobiles, telephones, televisions, and Internet connections seemed to offer unlimited progress. Given enough time, it seemed those left behind would catch up. What we see today instead, however, is a culture still reeling from change, with many falling behind and perhaps even more falling altogether. The once seemingly secure upper middle class is also beginning to feel the effects of these social and economic changes.

As our understanding grows, we see that a community based solely on a community of interest, with no geographic or economic tie, can provide some level of emotional sustenance to some segments of society as long as it is reinforced with meaningful, face-to-face involvement. The problem of crime, however, requires that people who live in the same area find ways to revitalize that sense of community in their neighborhoods, especially in those places where people cannot afford to buy as much protection as they want and need.

As this discussion demonstrates, community policing attempts to renew the link to a place that was historically an important part of society. It says that people who live in the same place must again become sensitive to the need to care for their neighbors, and that the police must become good neighbors to the people they serve—not an alien force.

KEY TERMS IN CHAPTER 3

- adversarial
- Black flight
- blockbusting
- Chicago School
- community relationships
- exclusion
- Ferdinand Tönnies
- *gemeinschaft*
- *gesellschaft*
- hierarchy
- inclusion
- initiatives
- Kurt Vonnegut
- legal constructs
- McDonaldization
- natural community
- neighborhood
- social interactions
- threat of crime
- three-tiered hierarchy
- underclass
- upper class
- viural community
- Walmarting
- White flight
- working class
- X, Y, Z generations

DISCUSSION QUESTIONS

1. Discuss the difference between a community and a neighborhood.
2. Discuss the importance of the distinctions about communities made by Tönnies.
3. What were the contributions of the Chicago School in studies of the community?
4. Identify an example from contemporary times to illustrate the authors' point that a community of interest does not have to be tied to a particular geographic area.
5. Discuss the major elements that make up a community as they are listed in the text.
6. Consider why is it important to assess the concept of community when studying the idea of community policing.
7. Describe and discuss migration and immigration patterns as they impact communities.
8. Describe the eight ways community policing can enhance the sense of community.
9. Discuss how technology has affected communities of interest in the United States.
10. Discuss the influence that the Internet and social networking has had on communities in the United States.
11. Discuss and identify the three-tiered hierarchy of community based on class.

References

Ager, S. (1988). Catholics Took Road to Closings. *Detroit Free Press*, (October 2), 15A.

Azarya, V. (1985). In A. Kuper & J. Kuper (Eds.), *Community in the Social Science Encyclopedia*. London, England: Routledge & Kegan Paul.

Bursik, R. J., & Grasmick, H. J. (1993). *Neighborhoods and Crime*. New York, NY: Lexington Books.

Detroit News. (2008). Cost of Quitting School: Dropouts Strain Strapped State. *Special Report*, Sunday, May 29, 2005.

Ellis, D. (2007). Making less than dad did: report reveals that american men in their 30s earn less than their fathers did, as family income growth decelerates. *CNN Money*, May 25, 2007.

Encyclopaedia of Social Sciences. (1949). New York: Macmillan. pp. 102ff.

Fessler, D. R. (1976). *Facilitating Community Change: A Basic Guide*. San Diego, CA: University Associate.

Greene, J. (2000). Community Policing in America: Changing the Nature, Structure, and Function of the Police. In *Criminal Justice 2000, Volume 3, Policies, Processes, and Decisions of the Criminal Justice System*. pp. 299–370. Washington, DC: National Institute of Justice.

Hillery, G. A. (1955). Definitions of Community: Areas of Agreement. *Rural Sociology*, 20(4), 111.

Jackson, L. (1988). State's Auto Jobs Continue Decline. *Detroit Free Press*, (August 15), 1C.

Keller, S. (1982). The Neighborhood. In R. H. Baylor (Ed.), *Neighborhoods in Urban America*. Baylor Port Washington, NY: Kennikat Press.

Keller, S. (1984). Community and Community Feeling. In A. Whittick (Ed.), *The Encyclopedia of Urban Planning*. New York, NY: McGraw-Hill.

McGraw, B., & Blossom, T. (1988). Losings Deal Another Blow to a City Losing People, Businesses, Institutions. *Detroit Free Press*, (September 30), 2B.

Meenaghan, T. M. (1972). What Means Community. *Social Work, 19*(6), 94.

Simeone, M. (2008). Integrating Virtual Public-Private Partnerships into Local Law Enforcement for Enhanced Intelligence-Led Policing. *Homeland Security Affairs*, (Suppl. 2), 1–22.

Stevens, L. (2011). Technology Talk Social Media in Policing: Nine Steps for Success. *Police Chief*, (June), 12–14.

Strecher, V. G. (2006a). People Who Don't Even Know You. In V. Kappeler (Ed.), *The Police & Society: Touch Stone Readings*. (3rd ed.). Prospect Heights, IL: Waveland Press.

Strecher, V. G. (2006b). Revising the Histories and Futures of Policing. In V. Kappeler (Ed.), *The Police & Society: Touch Stone Readings* (3rd ed.). Prospect Heights, IL: Waveland Press.

Tönnies, F. (1887, Eng. Trans. 1955). *Community and Society*. London, England: Routledge.

U.S. Census (2011). *Income, Poverty and Health Insurance Coverage in the United States: 2009*. Washington, DC: US Gov. Printing Office.

University of Michigan. (2008). Automotive Industry Creates Four Jobs for Every Worker It Employs. *News Service*, March 15, 2001.

Vonnegut, K. (1965-1974). *Wampeters, Foma & Granfalloons (Opinions)*. New York, NY: Delacorte/Seymour Lawrence.

Watman, W. S. (1980). *A Guide to the Language of Neighborhoods*. Washington, DC: National Center for Urban Ethnic Affairs.

Worsley, P. (1987). *New Introductory Sociology* (3rd ed.). London, England: Penguin.

Young, M., & Wilmott, P. (1960). *Family and Kinship in East London*. Harmondsworth: Penguin.

The adjustment of reality to the masses and of the masses to reality is a process of unlimited scope, as much for thinking as for perception.

—Walter Benjamin

CHAPTER 4   The Police and Community Perception

In the previous chapter, we discussed the meaning of community. It was noted that although we often envision the existence of a community or numerous communities, the envisioned areas are often disorganized to the point that they cannot be distinguished or considered real communities. Such areas are comprised of people with no inter-connectiveness. The areas have no leadership and few informal mechanisms for social control. They often are awash with poverty and crime. We attempted to demonstrate that the police often face significant problems in such areas, especially when attempting to organize the community to participate in crime prevention and social control activities. In many cases, the police must engage in community building and development. They must endeavor to build an area's ability to develop a sense of community

135

and to work with people to solve social problems. Viable communities must have a social fiber, a human network, an economic foundation, and political organization.

In this chapter, we provide an examination of people's views of police. CPOs must not only understand the community, but they must also understand how different groups view the police. Different groups of people have various perspectives about the police in terms of service, support, and ability to control crime. Too often, police officers use stereotypical views when interacting with people. Such stereotypes cut across gender, race, social class, ethnicity and politics. In some cases, these stereotypes are global. Skolnick (1966) noted that police officers often viewed people as **symbolic assailants**, while Van Maanen (2006) wrote that police officers divide people into three distinct groups: (1) **suspicious persons** who the police believe have committed a serious offense, (2) **assholes**, people who refuse to accept police authority, and (3) **know nothings**, people who are not in the first two categories, but nonetheless are of little importance. Skolnick and Van Maanen demonstrate that the police often have negative, preconceived notions about the character of the people they serve. These views are a direct result of the way the police role has been historically developed and defined.

Police officers often develop negative stereotypes as a result of their jobs. Much of what police officers do consists of negative confrontations with people. Officers write tickets; they place people under arrest; they tell people what to do or what not to do; and they often cannot solve a person's problem because of the limitations of the law, or because the problem is seen as outside officers' duties and responsibilities. The nature of police work often engenders negative attitudes on the part of the police, and these attitudes deter developing positive relations with people, which is an important part of community policing. Moreover, when officers use negative stereotypical ideas about people, they fail to recognize that not all people are the same. Many, and perhaps the majority of, people have a desire to cooperate and work with the police to build better communities and enhance their quality of life.

People's Attitudes Toward Police

Before discussing specific attitudes toward the police, it may be helpful to discuss attitudes within a general cultural context. Our society consists of numerous ethnic and racial groups. The United States has historically maintained a liberal immigration policy resulting in the United States being one of the most multi-cultural countries in the world. As people are raised within their respective cultures, they develop their own culturally defined worldview of how society is and should be ordered. This worldview can remain fairly stable throughout life. Within this context, liberal, conservative, or radical ideology affects how people perceive the police (Miller, 1973; Packer, 1968; Reed & Gaines, 1982). Also, attributes such as socioeconomic class and values affect the nature of people's attitudes toward police and to some extent, the type of interactions they have with police. Finally, the interactions people have with the police affect attitudes. Both negative and positive experiences with police affect people's attitudes.

Table 4.1
Reported Confidence in the Police by Demographic Characteristics, United States, 2010

Question: "I am going to read you a list of institutions in American society. Please tell me how much confidence you, yourself, have in each one–a great deal, quite a lot, some, or very little: the police?"				
	Great deal/ quite a lot	Some	Very little	None[a]
National	59%	27%	12%	1%
Politics				
Republican	69	23	7	1
Democrat	54	29	14	2
Independent	58	28	13	[b]
Ideology				
Conservative	63	25	10	1
Moderate	63	24	12	1
Liberal	49	34	14	1

Note: Sample sizes vary from year to year; the data for 2010 are based on telephone interviews with a randomly selected national sample of 1,020 adults, 18 years of age and older, conducted July 8-11, 2010. The "don't know/refused" category has been omitted.
[a] Response volunteered.
[b] Less than 0.5%.

Source: *Sourcebook of Criminal Justice Statistics* (2011). Table 2.12. Washington, DC: Bureau of Justice Statistics.

Ideology also affects what people see as being right and wrong. Different groups of individuals often disagree with laws as a result of their beliefs. For example, we have seen right-wing religious fanatics kill abortion doctors and blow up abortion clinics, while others who disagree with the government have blown up public buildings or assassinated judges and other public officials, and still others are caught on camera spitting on African American political leaders. When such acts are committed, perpetrators often feel that they are morally justified. Thus, ideologies can result in the commission of criminal acts in extreme forms. In less extreme forms, it may result in distrust of police, the belief that certain minor violations of law are acceptable, or an avoidance of police, such as in the case of many immigrants. It must be remembered, however, that ideology as well as values and beliefs are not created in a vacuum—they are birthed from the conditions in which people live.

For the most part, however, the general public tends to view the police positively (Benedict et al., 2000; Kaminski & Jefferis, 1998; Reisig & Giacomazzi, 1998). People see the police as an important part of society. However, there are problems. There are those who have negative views of the police, or they view police less positively as compared to the public as a whole.

There is a need for people to view the police positively. This is important because public perceptions of what the police do and how effective they are determines public participation in crime reduction programs, political support for the police, police programs, and crime-related legislation. Also, public support is a key consideration when making budgetary and other administrative and operational decisions that affect police departments. There are a number of benefits to the police and community when good relations exist:

- Greater cooperation and harmony between police and all the people in the community;

- A decrease in rates of crime and delinquency;

- Establishment of communication lines into the community so that community problems can be worked on and resolved;

- Improved working relationships with individuals and groups;

- Greater numbers of people interested in police careers, thus enhancing the recruitment and selection of police officers;

- Increased governmental support in terms of higher salaries and resources for new programs;

- Creation of a better working environment for officers, which promotes good mental and physical health; and

- Good relations with the community just makes police work easier.

Essentially, the police have a vested interest in maintaining positive relations with all individuals and groups in the community.

When examining attitudes toward the police, it is important to realize that there are numerous groups and subgroups of people within every community, and these various groups may have differing perceptions of the police and their effectiveness in dealing with community problems (Brown & Benedict, 2002). In most cities there is no such thing as one community; each jurisdiction is composed of many communities. These communities of interest are created by geographical boundaries such as rivers or major highways, by ethnic or racial groups settling together, such as a "Little Italy" or "Chinatown," which occurs in a number of larger American cities, or by service landmarks or centers such as when shopping centers and malls tend to serve as hubs in a city and draw upon a specific clientele. All cities are broken down into various neighborhoods. For this reason, public perceptions of the police are examined in general and in terms of the various groups that exist in most communities.

Most researchers have found that, in general, people view the police positively. For example, the Bureau of Justice Statistics and Office of Community-Oriented Policing Services surveyed more than 13,000 people in 13 cities and found that nearly 80 percent of the respondents were satisfied with the police (Smith et al., 1999). Gallup poll research, however, shows that nationally only a slight majority of people, about 59 percent, have confidence in the police (Sourcebook, 2011). Confidence in the police differs drastically by demographics. Even though people support the police, this support is not uniform across all groups of people. Perhaps the best way to study and understand support for the police is to study the levels of support across demographic and community variables. Decker (1981) and Worrall (1999) note that individual and community variables serve to mold and describe the types and levels of support that exist in a community. Demographic variables include factors such as gender, race, and personal experience with the police. On the other hand, community variables include factors such as socioeconomic status, likelihood of victimization, general community attitudes toward the police, and crime rates. These factors are explored in the following sections.

Figure 4.1
Factors Affecting Citizen Attitudes Toward the Police

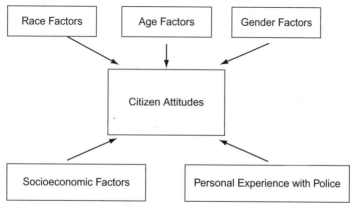

Age and Perception of Police

The consensus among researchers is that older persons tend to view the police more positively than do younger people (Cao et al., 1996; Chermak et al., 2001; Reisig & Giacomazzi, 1998). Some research indicates that even very young children have a poor view of the police. Powell, Skouteris, and Murfett (2008) conducted interviews with 112 children between the ages of 5 and 8 and found that even when controlling for experience, age, and television exposure to police shows, children emphasized the punitive role of police and few could identify positive roles police might play. Older people, especially seniors, possess higher levels of fear of crime, so they tend to see police as their allies and are supportive of the police (Zevitz & Rettammel, 1990). Survey research consistently indicates that younger people have a more negative view of the police than do older people (Sourcebook, 2011). Whether the question is on confidence in the police or their honesty and ethics, youths tend to view police more negatively than their older counterparts (Sourcebook, 2011). Another consistent finding on attitudes toward the police is that officer demeanor affects perception. A few officers with poor attitudes can undo the work of any police-community relations program.

Table 4.2
Reported Confidence in the Police by Demographic Characteristics, United States, 2010

Question: "I am going to read you a list of institutions in American society. Please tell me how much confidence you, yourself, have in each one–a great deal, quite a lot, some, or very little: the police?"

	Great deal/ quite a lot	Some	Very little	None[a]
National	59%	27%	12%	1%
Age				
18 to 29 years	52	28	19	1
30 to 49 years	58	28	13	1
50 to 64 years	65	26	8	2
50 years and older	64	25	8	1
65 years and older	64	24	9	[b]

Note: Sample sizes vary from year to year; the data for 2010 are based on telephone interviews with a randomly selected national sample of 1,020 adults, 18 years of age and older, conducted July 8-11, 2010. The "don't know/refused" category has been omitted.
[a] Response volunteered.
[b] Less than 0.5%.

Source: *Sourcebook of Criminal Justice Statistics* (2011). Table 2.12. Washington, DC: Bureau of Justice Statistics.

While the reasons for young people's negative views of the police are complex, they are likely a product of both police and youth behavior. First, police are more likely to stop younger people for non-criminal matters—often attempting exert a peace keeping or even parental role. Youth may view these interventions as being "hassled" by the police for "no good reason." Second, police are more likely to contact young people in negative situations and they are more likely to treat youth with less respect than their adult counterparts. Because youth have less economic and political power and because they are often seen as unlikely to file complaints against police, police may be more aggressive and treat youth more disrespectfully than adults. Third, younger people tend to be more involved in dangerous behavior such as traffic violations, substance abuse, and frequenting nightclubs and bars, which results in more negative contacts with police. Younger people, as a result of participating in more dangerous behavior, are more likely to be victimized, which sometimes results in negative views of the police. Fourth, younger people often are distrustful of authority figures, which make them more prone to having negative contacts with the police. Finally, it may be that police differentially interact with youth—often only having contact with young people when they are trouble. There needs to be more incentive for police to have greater and more positive interaction with young people. Regardless of reasoning, older people tend to foster more positive attitudes toward the police than do younger people. Police departments should attempt to alleviate this situation through better training and programs that produce more positive contact with younger people. Also, officers should be trained on non-confrontational communications skills to reduce friction with young people.

Race and Perception of Police

Over the years there has been a substantial amount of research examining how minorities view the police. Minorities tend to view the police positively, but less positively as compared to Whites. It appears that minorities generally have a more strained relationship with the police as compared to Whites. Race is perhaps the best predictor of attitudes toward police. There is consensus in the research that White people tend to view the police more positively than do minorities. Weitzer and Tuch (2004) note that Whites most often have higher opinions of police, are more supportive of aggressive crime control measures, and are suspicious of criticisms of police. White people tend to support the police more or less across the board. Moreover, they are in favor of oppressive crime control measures such as racial profiling, because they see these measures being enacted against "criminals." Whites tend to see themselves as victims rather than perpetrators of crime. Of course, crime statistics show that Whites commit the vast majority of crimes and that crime is generally an intra- rather than inter-racial event (see Kappeler & Potter, 2005). Racism still clouds the public's perception of crime.

African Americans, on the other hand, consistently rate the police lower (Huang & Vaughn, 1996; Murphy & Worrall, 1999; Reisig & Parks, 2000; Tuch & Weitzer, 1997; Worrall, 1999; Dowler & Sparks, 2008). Researchers tend to attri- bute these lower perceptions to mistreatment. Weitzer and Tuch (1999) found that African Americans were much more likely to report being mistreated by the police. Erez (1984) found that they were no more likely to be chased, questioned, or warned by the police, but tended to have more negative attitudes toward the police as compared to Whites. This finding, however, fails to note that police stop, search the vehicles of, and arrest minority people more frequently in these contacts, with less evidence, and for less serious offenses than their White counterparts.

Table 4.3
Reported Confidence in the Police by Demographic Characteristics, United States, 2010

Question: "I am going to read you a list of institutions in American society. Please tell me how much confidence you, yourself, have in each one–a great deal, quite a lot, some, or very little: the police?"

	Great deal/ quite a lot	Some	Very little	None[a]
National	59%	27%	12%	1%
Race				
White	62	27	10	1
Nonwhite	52	26	17	2
Black	35	33	25	4

Note: Sample sizes vary from year to year; the data for 2010 are based on telephone interviews with a randomly selected national sample of 1,020 adults, 18 years of age and older, conducted July 8-11, 2010. The "don't know/refused" category has been omitted.
[a] Response volunteered.

Source: *Sourcebook of Criminal Justice Statistics* (2011). Table 2.12. Washington, DC: Bureau of Justice Statistics.

Carter (1983, 1985) assessed the attitudes of Latinos toward the police. His findings coincided with the research on African America attitudes toward the police. Overall, he found that Latinos: (1) feel less safe concerning crime in com- parison to the general population, (2) do not feel that the police are capable of reducing the incidence of crime, (3) feel that they receive less than adequate protection from the police, and (4) generally evaluate the police lower relative to the general population. More specifically, Carter found that Latinos believed the police did a poor job. They believed that the police had a bad attitude, needed to do a better job of investigating crimes, needed to decrease response times, and in general should reduce the level of discrimination against Latinos.

However, Cheurprakobkit (2000) found that Latinos did have a more positive view of the police in comparison to African Americans, and Spanish-speaking Latinos were more cooperative and viewed the police more positively than did English-speaking Latinos. Many Latinos, though, are fearful of the police and fail to report crimes or seek assistance because of immigration status and fear of deportation (Walker, 1997). Police departments must recognize these problems, especially those involving Latino victimization, and develop programs to ensure better relations with the Latino community. A key here is that departments serving significant Latino populations or serving emerging Latino populations should hire bilingual officers and train officers to speak Spanish and understand how they are viewed.

Racial and ethnic diversity in a community or neighborhood affect attitudes. Apple and O'Brian (1988) found that as the proportion of African Americans in a neighborhood increases, there also is an increase in negative attitudes toward the police. Such concentrations may attract the police to the area, especially lower socioeconomic areas where crime rates and calls for police services are higher. It also provides an opportunity for like-minded, critical individuals to associate with others, often generating more negative sentiment toward the police. More recently, there have been a number of studies showing that there are few differences between races in multi-cultured communities. Chandek (1999) and Chermak et al. (2001) found little differences in attitudes among different racial groups in neighborhoods that were racially diverse.

There appear to be a multitude of explanations for the difference in attitudes across racial groups. First, minorities have a higher number of negative contacts with the police relative to non-minorities (Walker, 1997). Minorities tend to have a higher representation in arrest statistics, and based on racial profiling or traffic stop studies they tend to be stopped in greater numbers. Second, minorities tend to be victimized at higher rates relative to non-minorities. Victimization tends to adversely affect one's view of the police, especially when the police fail to apprehend the perpetrator or provide what is perceived as poor or inferior service. As the research suggests, it may be that police officers do in fact treat minority people differently than they treat White people. Police officers, especially White officers, typically do not comprehend or understand other cultures, which may cause them to treat minorities differently, and unfortunately, some officers are biased against minorities, which often affects how they treat minority suspects or victims.

Gender and Perception of Police

It has been commonly thought that females view police more positively than their male counterparts. It was perceived that they were less involved in crime, and they were more likely to call the police and fear victimization. However, the research does not support this hypothesis. There have been several studies that found females view the police more positively than males (Cao et al., 1996; Reisig & Giacomazzi, 1998), while other studies have found the opposite (Correia et al., 1996; Reisig & Correia, 1997; Sampson & Bartusch, 1998). Other studies have found no differences (Chermak et al., 2001; Huang & Vaughn, 1996). Thus, it appears based on the aggregate that females and males typically view the police about the same.

Table 4.4
Reported Confidence in the Police by Demographic Characteristics, United States, 2010

Question: "I am going to read you a list of institutions in American society. Please tell me how much confidence you, yourself, have in each one–a great deal, quite a lot, some, or very little: the police?"

	Great deal/ quite a lot	Some	Very little	None[a]
National	59%	27%	12%	1%
Sex				
Male	59	26	14	1
Female	61	27	10	1

Note: Sample sizes vary from year to year; the data for 2010 are based on telephone interviews with a randomly selected national sample of 1,020 adults, 18 years of age and older, conducted July 8-11, 2010. The "don't know/refused" category has been omitted.
[a] Response volunteered.

Source: *Sourcebook of Criminal Justice Statistics* (2011). Table 2.12. Washington, DC: Bureau of Justice Statistics.

Socioeconomic Status and Perception of Police

Socioeconomic status refers to an individual's social and economic class. It has implications for quality of life, and it affects one's connectiveness with the social and political system. It also appears that people often use global judgments when evaluating the police. If a person is disgruntled with government in general, he or she often automatically distrusts the police. Thus, problems with other parts of government may well affect attitudes toward the police.

People from lower socioeconomic backgrounds are less likely to view the police positively (Cao et al., 1996; Huang & Vaughn, 1996). Essentially, minorities in poor urban neighborhoods have some of the lowest approval ratings of the police. The reasons for these perceptions include injustice, lack of concern and attention on the part of the police, and ineffectiveness, especially in comparison to the level of services often provided to more wealthy neighborhoods in the same jurisdiction. Unfortunately, people's class often determines the type of service they will receive from both the police and government.

Kusow, Wilson, and Martin (1997) found that African Americans and Whites living in the suburbs viewed the police more positively than did residents of urban areas, and suburban African Americans viewed the police more positively than did urban Whites. However, Weitzer and Tuch (1999) found that socioeconomic status did not have an effect on attitudes toward the police. Other researchers have found that persons who are well educated and wealthy view the police less favorably than those with less education and income.

Table 4.5
Reported Confidence in the Police by Demographic Characteristics, United States, 2010

Question: "I am going to read you a list of institutions in American society. Please tell me how much confidence you, yourself, have in each one–a great deal, quite a lot, some, or very little: the police?"

	Great deal/ quite a lot	Some	Very little	None[a]
National	59%	27%	12%	1%
Education				
College post graduate	66	22	10	0
College graduate	74	21	6	0
Some college	60	30	9	1
High school graduate or less	52	28	18	2
Income				
$75,000 and over	66	23	10	0
$50,000 to $74,999	67	25	8	1
$30,000 to $49,999	55	30	14	0
$20,000 to $29,999	57	26	13	3
Under $20,000	49	29	17	3

Note: Sample sizes vary from year to year; the data for 2010 are based on telephone interviews with a randomly selected national sample of 1,020 adults, 18 years of age and older, conducted July 8-11, 2010. The "don't know/refused" category has been omitted.
[a] Response volunteered.

Source: *Sourcebook of Criminal Justice Statistics* (2011). Table 2.12. Washington, DC: Bureau of Justice Statistics.

Thus, the results from research examining socioeconomic status are inconclusive. An explanation for the mixed results may be that the socioeconomic extremes may have a more negative view of the police, while those in the middle class have more of a positive view. The middle class seems to be more dependent on police services as compared to the upper class, and the lower class often receives the brunt of police interventions. These differences are most likely a complex interaction between how policing is experienced by different groups and knowledge about the police, politics, and economics. In essence, what people know and what they have affect their perception of the police.

Personal Experience and Perception of Police

The police come into contact with many people each year as a result of traffic violations, being arrested, or being the victim of a crime. Jesilow et al. (1995) found that people often voice more dissatisfaction with the police after such encounters. In other cases, police officers provide people with an array of services, which produce positive outcomes. Contact with the police influences perceptions of the police; negative contacts tend to produce negative perceptions, while positive contacts tend to have a positive impact (Worrall, 1999). Little is know about which type of contact has the greatest impact although Cheurprakobkit (2000) and Huang and Vaughn (1996) found that positive contacts have a stronger influence relative to negative contacts.

People's perceptions are often mediated by the context of the contact. Reisig and Chandek (2001) found that people's satisfaction is based on their expectations. If police actions meet their expectations, they are satisfied, but if the police provide an inadequate level of service or exhibit what is perceived as negative demeanor, people become dissatisfied with the police. For example, crime victims often voice dissatisfaction with the police when they believe that officers do a poor job of investigating their victimization. Police service, not victimization, determines attitude. Police officers must use good judgment when interacting with people. Even though officers may be making an arrest or issuing a citation, they can do so with some measure of civility. This would lead to fewer confrontations and improved relations with the public.

Periodically, there are major police incidents that receive national media attention, which affect public perceptions of the police. Some of these incidents include the Rodney King incident in Los Angeles, the Rampart Division scandal in Los Angeles, the Abner Louima case in New York, and the racist attitudes of Mark Fuhrman in the O.J. Simpson case. Studies indicate that such incidents undermine public trust of the police and cause the public to question police integrity (Jesilow & Meyer, 1995; Kaminski & Jefferis, 1998). Moreover, such incidents have a global effect resulting in a decline in public support across the country. When such incidents occur, people begin questioning whether it could occur in their community. Police administrators must understand that these incidents, even though in faraway places, can have a rippling effect in their communities, and they must immediately respond to them by shoring up local support.

SPOTLIGHT ON COMMUNITY POLICING PRACTICE

Making Every Encounter Count: Building Trust and Confidence in the Police

Several years ago in the Flatbush neighborhood of Brooklyn, New York, police officers responded to a report of youths stealing from a street vendor. When the uniformed officers arrived on the scene, the youths reacted confrontationally: "Why are you harassing me? I'm just on my way home from school. How dare you! You're just doing this 'cause I'm black."

A large group of onlookers formed. One of the officers said that he sensed the youths were hoping to "get the crowd working against us … [so we would] … just back off." While the officer was explaining to the crowd why they were there, a woman in the crowd spoke up. "I remember this guy," she told the others. "I got my purse robbed 2 months ago and he was really good; he treated me well. I think he's a good cop and I trust him."

The woman's unsolicited comments quelled the crowd, which quickly dispersed without incident. The officer later reflected on the encounter. "I never forgot that lesson," he noted. "You never know when treating people well will pay off—not just in satisfying what you owe to citizens—but in this larger communal sense of gaining allies."

What Factors Affect Public Satisfaction with the Police?

Satisfaction with the police, while generally high, is unevenly distributed. Understanding why some people harbor negative views about police officers is the first and most important step in building a positive relationship with the community.

NIJ recently funded five studies exploring factors that influence satisfaction with the police. The research suggests that satisfaction is shaped by demographic variables, neighborhood crime conditions, and experiences with the police—whether firsthand or indirect. Race was not found to directly determine level of satisfaction. Instead, researchers concluded that race, due to its correlation with other demographic variables, neighborhood crime rates, and experiences with police, was an indirect influence on the level of satisfaction with the police.

Although community members' views about the police may be stubbornly resistant to change, police officers and policymakers should appreciate that treating individuals respectfully and professionally during each encounter can establish, build, and maintain crucial support for the police within the community.

(Continued)

The Importance of Quality Treatment

When people form opinions of the police based on their interactions, they tend to focus on the process more than the outcome. Impressions of police encounters are influenced by the demeanor as well as the actions of the officer. People pay close attention to the "neutrality of decision making, respectful and polite interpersonal treatment, and ... opportunities for input into decisions," noted Tom Tyler of New York University. Researchers often refer to this as a person's sense of "procedural justice."

People base their impressions of the police on their own personal experiences and on secondhand reports of police encounters. However, because most Americans do not directly interact with the police in any given year, they are forming their opinions on the basis of word-of-mouth accounts from others.

Early studies of satisfaction with police showed that a person's unpleasant experiences had a greater impact than pleasant experiences. Newer studies, however, have found that pleasant experiences have a greater influence than researchers originally thought. As illustrated by the Flatbush officer's experience described at the beginning of this article, positive experiences with the police can have a ripple effect throughout the community.

The implication: Every encounter—both pleasant and unpleasant—with the public can greatly affect the community's level of satisfaction with the police.

It also appears that people bring different expectations to their encounters with the police, depending upon whether those encounters are police- or citizen-initiated. In the past, it was widely assumed that police-initiated encounters had the greatest impact on citizen attitudes. But NIJ-funded research at the University of Illinois at Chicago contradicts that belief. Instead, researchers found that negative encounters have a greater tendency to erode satisfaction with the police when they are citizen-initiated. This finding raises the possibility that individuals' unmet expectations of how the police could or should have assisted them during an encounter may be as influential in forming opinions as the experience itself, regardless of whether citizens or police initiate the contact.

Race and the Context of Neighborhoods

Trust and confidence in the police, however, are built on more than police encounters. Recent NIJ studies also explored the role of race in the formation of opinions about the police.

Although the data show that Caucasians hold the police in higher regard than African Americans or Hispanics, race was not found to directly influence how people form opinions about police. In fact, when researchers controlled for factors such as the level of neighborhood crime, the reported quality of police-citizen encounters, and other demographic variables, such as age, income, and education, the effects of race disappeared entirely or were substantially reduced. Researchers concluded that race affects satisfaction with the police indirectly and in conjunction with other factors, including the level of crime within one's neighborhood.

People in low-crime neighborhoods tend to credit police officers with securing and maintaining low crime rates. As a result, perceptions of the police in those neighborhoods are mostly positive. In neighborhoods with higher crime rates—where racial and ethnic minorities are disproportionately represented—the level of community satisfaction with police is substantially lower. These findings illustrate that, in addition to unpleasant police encounters, individuals' dissatisfaction with crime rates in their community can negatively affect their view of police.

The Impact of Attitudes on Perceptions of Police

Some would argue that satisfaction with law enforcement is a dynamic concept, evolving with each citizen's interaction with the police. But recent research challenges that contention. Attitudes toward the police appear to be relatively stable, and people's preexisting views shape their perceptions of future encounters. Researchers at the University of Illinois at Chicago found that residents' initial attitudes toward the police played a critical role in determining their judgments of subsequent experiences and in the formation of future attitudes toward police.

The challenge for law enforcement officers is to treat each encounter—whether with a suspect, witness, or complainant—as if it is that person's first contact with police. If he or she believes that the officer was fair and professional, then that person is more likely to have positive impressions of future encounters with police. Making this effort with each and every interaction is an important investment in building goodwill within the community.

Steps to Enhancing a Positive Public Image

Public consent and support of law enforcement are two of the most critical tools on a police officer's "belt." People who believe that the police are performing their duties with professionalism and integrity are more likely to obey laws and support the system by acting as witnesses, for example.

NIJ's continuing research into the determinants of satisfaction, trust, and confidence in the police reveals that attitudes toward the police are shaped by a combination of demographic variables, neighborhood conditions, direct and vicarious police citizen encounters, and prior attitudes. The police cannot control some of these factors; others, however, are a direct consequence of an individual officer's actions and demeanor. Therefore, officers should focus their efforts where they can have the most direct impact: in each day-to-day interaction with the public.

The first step in building good relations with the community is to understand and respond to the expectations of people across a range of possible police encounters. Departments might also consider tracking the level of satisfaction through community surveys. This feedback could be used to design police training and intervention programs. In the end, NIJ's research illustrates that it behooves our Nation's police officers to pay close attention to developing what might be called their "bedside manner."

Jake Horowitz
Senior Associate
The Pew Charitable Trust

Source: Horowitz, J. (2007). "Making Every Encounter Count: Building Trust and Confidence in the Police." *NIJ Journal*, 256: 8-11 [citations omitted].

The research regarding individual and community differences and their effects on people's attitudes toward the police is striking. There are numerous differences as a result of these variables. These differences should be considered in police policymaking. Brown and Benedict (2002) have identified four areas that police administrators should consider as a result of the differences in public opinion about the police:

- Law enforcement tactics and strategies should be tailored to address different needs and individual communities or neighborhoods.

- The police should strive to improve relations with minorities and young people.

- The police should strive to maintain a professional demeanor, especially when dealing with the public.

- It is important for the police to develop good relations with the press to help mediate some of the problems the police have in the community.

We have demonstrated that an array of perceptions exists in every community. We have noted that it is important to address the needs of each group if police-community relations are to be maximized. However, this is no easy task. For example, Zatz and Portillos (2004) examined the gang problem in a barrio in Phoenix. They found that when the police attempted to intervene in the gang problem, they received a mixed reaction from the public. On one hand, many of the residents objected to the police using suppressive law enforcement tactics. They saw the tactics as harassment. They did not buy into the ways police were dealing with the gang problem. On the other hand, other residents believed the police were not doing enough about the gang problem. Those complaining about an inadequate response included small business owners and social activists who resided or worked in the area. The police essentially could not satisfy all residents. However, if the police had attempted to develop a better relationship with the community or had consulted with community members prior to the aggressive enforcement, they possibly could have mediated some of the complaints. Additionally, had the police developed partnerships with members of the community, rather than using aggressive law enforcement tactics, an alternative outcome may have prevailed. This example demonstrates the difficulty in addressing every group in a community, and it shows that unilateral enforcement without working with the community can result in community relation problems. It also shows that the police must consider the community as it plans and deploys crime control tactics.

It is important to reiterate that a police department can only be as effective as relations with people allow. Poor police-community relations lead to poor public perception. Better relations often equate to more effective law enforcement. The following section examines some of the barriers confronting the police when attempting to build a working partnership with the community.

Barriers to a Police-Community Partnership

The police, to be effective, must forge a partnership with the community. As previously noted, this partnership results in numerous benefits to both the police and the public. Because the police are charged with serving and protecting the public, working closely with people is important. Carter and Radelet (1999) identified five departmental behaviors that contribute to police problems in the community: **excessive force**, **corruption**, **rudeness**, **authoritarianism**, and **politics**. Police administrators must recognize these issues are real and not to be dismissed. They must make every effort to ensure that they are absent from the department and the communities they serve.

Excessive Force

Charges of **excessive force** for most departments are not commonplace, but nonetheless, in the aggregate, there are substantial numbers of cases of police use and abuse of force. Each case has the potential of significantly stigmatizing officers and departments. Police-community relations can be severely damaged with only one brutality incident. Minor cases of excessive force by police officers can become major public relations problems, especially if they occur with some frequency in the same community.

There are a number of mechanisms that police departments can use to substantially reduce excessive force problems. First and foremost, the department can ensure that officers are properly trained. Basic academies have use-of-force training, but too often, they focus on officer safety and neglect to encourage officers to avoid the use of force when possible. Officers must understand that less force often produces better outcomes.

> You can learn more about excessive force and community relations by going to
> http://www.justice.gov/crs/pubs/pdexcess.htm.

Second, a department should have a policy outlining when an officer can use force and the degree of force that can be used. Most departments use a use-of-force

Table 4.6

Respondents' Perceptions of Police Brutality in Their Area by Demographic Characteristics, United States, 2005

Question: "In some places in the nation there have been charges of police brutality. Do you think there is any police brutality in your area, or not?"			
	Yes	No	Don't know/refused
National	31%	65%	4%
Sex			
Male	30	65	5
Female	32	64	4
Race			
White	25	71	4
Nonwhite	54	40	6
Black	67	29	4
Age			
18 to 29 years	41	57	2
30 to 49 years	34	62	4
50 to 64 years	30	65	5
50 years and older	24	70	6
65 years and older	15	77	8
Education			
College post graduate	30	68	2
College graduate	28	65	7
Some college	34	62	4
High school graduate or less	31	64	5
Income			
$75,000 and over	24	74	2
$50,000 to $74,999	38	56	6
$30,000 to $49,999	34	61	5
$20,000 to $29,999	34	63	3
Under $20,000	32	64	4
Community			
Urban area	40	56	4
Suburban area	28	67	5
Rural area	26	71	3
Region			
East	27	66	7
Midwest	27	71	2
South	35	63	2
West	34	59	7
Politics			
Republican	20	76	4
Democrat	39	57	4
Independent	34	61	5

Source: *Sourcebook of Criminal Justice Statistics* (2011). Table 2.0002. Washington, DC: Bureau of Justice Statistics.

continuum that outlines when and to what degree force is appropriate (Gaines & Kappeler, 2011). Third, a department's supervisors should enforce the use of force policy. This means that each instance of use of force is reviewed. Many departments now require officers to complete a use of force report each time they use force, which allows for a review of individual cases and use of force in the aggregate. It also means that each complaint about the use of force must be investigated. This ultimately reduces use of force, and it provides people with some measure of assurance that the department is attempting to ensure that people are treated properly. Finally, wrongful use of force must be addressed by adequate disciplinary action and police officials must make that action known to their communities.

Research indicates that officers tend to use the greatest levels of force when encountering suspects involved in property crimes (McDonald, Manz & Alpert, 2003). Officers tend to be more coercive and make quick decisions in these situations. Also, younger officers are more likely to use force relative to older, veteran officers (McElvain & Kposowa, 2004). Officers are also more likely to use more force in neighborhoods that are disadvantaged and have high rates of crime (Terrill & Reisig, 2003), and when officers initially use force in a situation, the situation is more likely to escalate where more force is used (Terrill, 2003). These studies indicate that use of force often is situational, and the level of force sometimes is based on factors other than the level of suspect resistance. It also implies that if departments have proper training, policies, and supervision, the amount of force used by officers could be reduced.

Police Corruption

The Mollen Commission, upon investigating corruption in the New York City Police Department, noted that most officers begin their careers by viewing the job honestly and idealistically, but become corrupt over time through progressive stages (Mollen Commission, 1994). It seems that some officers' moral compass changes over time. There are numerous forms of police corruption. They range from accepting small gifts or payments from businesspeople to the protection of and involvement in criminal activities. America's drug problem has contributed notably to the corruption problem. The illegal drug industry is so widespread and embodies such vast amounts of money that police

> *You can learn more about the Mollen Commission investigation by going to http://www.nyc.gov/html/ccpc/html/about/about.shtml.*

are afforded numerous opportunities to engage in corrupt activities. Drugs have been related to a precipitous increase in police corruption (Kappeler, Sluder & Alpert, 1998).

Table 4.7

Respondents' Ratings of the Honesty and Ethical Standards of Police by Demographic Characteristics, United States, 2010

Question: "Please tell me how you would rate the honesty and ethical standards of people in these different fields–very high, high, average, low, or very low: Policemen?"

	Very high	High	Average	Low	Very low
National	12%	45%	33%	7%	3%
Sex					
Male	14	44	32	8	2
Female	11	45	34	7	3
Race					
White	12	49	31	6	2
Nonwhite	13	34	37	11	5
Black	13	25	37	21	4
Age					
18 to 29 years	7	39	38	11	5
30 to 49 years	15	48	27	6	4
50 to 64 years	14	45	33	8	1
50 years and older	13	46	33	7	1
65 years and older	12	46	34	7	1
Education					
College post graduate	10	48	35	6	2
College graduate	7	55	32	5	1
Some college	14	46	29	7	3
High school graduate or less	15	39	33	9	3
Income					
$75,000 and over	11	53	30	5	1
$50,000 to $74,999	16	42	30	9	1
$30,000 to $49,999	10	46	35	6	3
$20,000 to $29,999	18	45	25	11	1
Under $20,000	16	33	35	11	3
Region					
East	13	52	27	7	1
Midwest	10	47	35	6	1
South	14	40	34	9	4
West	12	41	34	8	4
Politics					
Republican	15	50	29	4	1
Democrat	12	40	35	11	2
Independent	11	44	32	8	4
Ideology					
Conservative	14	50	27	6	3
Moderate	13	43	35	7	2
Liberal	10	39	39	11	1

Note: These data are based on telephone interviews with a randomly selected national sample of 1,037 adults, 18 years of age and older, conducted November 19-21, 2010. The "don't know/refused" category has been omitted; therefore percents may not sum to 100.

Source: *Sourcebook of Criminal Justice Statistics* (2011). Table 2.21. Washington, DC: Bureau of Justice Statistics.

Two important dimensions associated with corruption must be mentioned. First, corruption that is uncovered in one city will affect people's attitudes in other cities. People tend to generalize about the police and evaluate them based on information that is usually provided by the mainstream media. Second, the severity of the corruption case has little bearing on the magnitude of the public relations backlash. Corruption, regardless of magnitude, is a violation of trust that cuts to the heart of public morale and feelings of safety and security.

Police scandals undermine the public's confidence in the police. For example, in 2000, the **Rampart Division scandal** in Los Angeles caused people and the courts to question the work of all Los Angeles police officers, and other communities pondered whether their officers were also engaged in planting evidence and lying in court. If the police are dishonest, who will protect the people?

Rudeness

Perhaps rudeness is the most frequently lodged complaint against the police. It is also the most frequent topic of conversation when people complain about the police. Rudeness seems to surface when officers are writing citations or making arrests, interviewing suspects and witnesses, and even during on-the-street encounters when people request assistance or directions. Rude behavior can occur in any police-citizen interaction.

This is not to say that all police officers are rude, or that police officers who tend to be rude are always rude. It is important to understand that rudeness is a matter of perception. Each officer must actively guard against the perception of rudeness. Rudeness has several sources. First, police officers traditionally have been taught to assume a businesslike demeanor when interacting with people. Some officers take an extreme approach and as a result are rude or appear to be rude. Although a professional, businesslike demeanor should never result in rudeness, it does have the potential to be misinterpreted as rudeness. Second, rudeness can result when the vast majority of contacts officers have with people are negative. Repeated negative contacts with people ultimately will take their toll even on well-intentioned officers. Community policing, with its emphasis on positive community contacts, may help ameliorate this problem. Third, rudeness can be a symptom of stress (either job-related or within the officer's personal life). Police officers are placed in a variety of stressful situations. Ultimately stress will affect the attitude and demeanor of officers if there is no attempt to provide alternative methods to cope with stress. Finally, some police officers just abuse their authority, and police organizations have a poor history of taking this problem seriously. Police management is responsible for ensuring that police treat all people with respect.

It is important to realize that police rudeness or disrespectful behavior can result in a situation escalating. For example, Reisig and his colleagues (2004) found that when officers were disrespectful to people or suspects, they responded in kind. On the other hand, they found that when officers used less coercive tactics or communications skills, the situation tended to deescalate. Let us be clear about this: any police officer with some experience on the streets knows that they can escalate or deescalate most situations by their demeanor and actions. Officer demeanor has a significant impact on the outcomes of interactions with people.

Perhaps the most prominent cases of rudeness are charges of racial profiling. When officers perform pretextual or investigative traffic stops, they often do so under the guise of a traffic violation. In many cases, these violations are minor, such as improper lane change or no license plate lamp. Officers often are unable to articulate a reasonable justification for the stop to the person. It appears that the stop is arbitrary, which results in hostility on the part of the person, and this is a reasonable reaction on the person's part. Police officers and departments should understand that the countless stops of people who are innocent erode public trust, and they should question if the problems associated with the stops are worth the few, minor arrests that are made. Police departments must do a better job at not just counting interactions but measuring the qualify of interactions in the community.

Authoritarianism

Essentially, **police authority**, when reduced to an act, is used when police officers take command and control of situations or people by issuing orders or directives. **Authoritarianism** is an attitude or approach used when exercising authority and is typically seen as negative or coercive. According to Kappeler, Sluder, and Alpert (1998), authoritarianism consists of cynicism, aggression, and rigid behavior. Barker and Carter (1991) found that authoritarianism is a dominant trait among police officers.

> *You can learn more about the authoritarian personality by going to http://en.wikipedia.org/wiki/Authoritarian_personality.*

Because police officers tend to become more authoritarian over time, management must attempt to reduce it and its behavioral consequences. Community policing, through more positive police-community contacts, may help reduce the degree of authoritarianism that develops in officers. Authoritarianism and community policing are incompatible. Police authority must be applied assertively within the context of the community's values and goals, and it must be applied within the appropriate context of the situation.

A large measure of the police officer's job is to get people to act in certain ways. For example, officers attempt to control others' behavior when they make an arrest or issue a traffic citation. Even when the contact is positive, the police officer is generally attempting to change the person's behavior, as in the case of a crime prevention program or DARE program. Police work is about getting others to do what police officers want them to do. Use of authority is a core component of the police job; however, the attitude with which authority is used must coincide with the rule of law and the service role of policing.

With this respect, officers are taught to take command of situations with the belief that such behavior will result in compliance and a reduction in the likelihood that force will be used. However, it appears that this is not the case. Terrill (2003) notes that this authoritarian approach often escalates rather than controls the situation. It results in officers having to use more force or be more coercive. Police essentially must learn a broader array of tactics to get people to do what they need to have done in problem situations.

Politics

Politics have long been a part of law enforcement (Gaines et al., 2011). From the earliest times, politicians have used the police to serve their ends. Internally, political influence has been exerted to control who was hired, promoted, or placed in specialized units such as criminal investigation or narcotics. Externally, politics were used to influence who was arrested or cited and which vice activities were allowed to continue without police interference. Politics almost always leads to some miscreants receiving preferential treatment.

Americans, for the most part, cling to the ideas of equality and justice. When people observe others receiving differential treatment, especially from their police, they immediately have disdain for the police. When the police allow some people to get away with violations while citing others, or when the police provide services to some while refusing others, most people's sense of justice is violated. Furthermore, the injustice as a result of the act is diffused across the spectrum of police activity. People tend to distrust the police in every respect.

An important issue regarding politics is that some segments of a community may perceive that they receive police services inferior to those received by others. Residents of lower socioeconomic neighborhoods often complain that residents in their neighborhood receive inferior services and are treated differently as compared to residents in more affluent neighborhoods. This problem is compounded by the fact that the police already have poor relations in these neighborhoods.

It is important for the police administrator to take measures to control each of these five problem areas. The police cannot successfully serve their constituents without trust and cooperation. When the police use excessive force, routinely or occasionally, engage in corruption, are rude, are authoritarian, or allow politics to influence enforcement decisions, people will very quickly lose faith in their police. The police always remain in the public eye, and they must measure up to people's expectations.

Summary

This chapter examines people's perceptions of the police and some of the factors that shape these perceptions. Historically, police officers reasoned that all persons should be treated the same, although this has not been the case. People have been treated differently because of race, gender, age, and economic position in a community. Regardless, officers should understand that police-community relations are important, and that their interactions with people over time will have an impact on those relations.

Research shows that minorities, persons living in disadvantaged areas, and younger people often have a more negative view of the police. Gender seems not to affect people's attitudes. The implications of these findings are that the police must be aware of differences in community perceptions, and officers must learn to adjust their behavior and reactions to people based on these differences. When officers recognize ethnic and cultural differences, they are more likely to have a productive encounter with people.

Finally, this chapter examined some of the broad problems that have impeded better relations with the community. They include excessive force, corruption, rudeness, authoritarianism, and politics. Each of these areas, when not properly managed, can adversely affect individuals' perspectives and the community's perspectives about the police and their effectiveness. When a department takes a proactive approach to managing these potential problem areas, it essentially reduces the probability of police-community relations problems.

KEY TERMS IN CHAPTER 4

- age and perception
- authoritarianism
- excessive force
- gender and perception
- Mollen Commission
- police authority
- police corruption
- race and perception

- Rampart scandal
- rudeness
- suspicious persons
- know nothings
- socioeconomic status
- symbolic assailants
- wealth and perception

DISCUSSION QUESTIONS

1. Discuss the three groups that police officers tend to use in categorizing people.
2. Briefly discuss the seven benefits to the police and community when good relations exist.
3. Discuss the effects of age, race, gender, and socioeconomic status on people's perceptions of the police.
4. Discuss and describe the role age plays in public perceptions of the police.
5. What is the relationship between race and public views of police?
6. Discuss whether race or socioeconomic status has a greater impact on people's views of police. Use information from the text to make your argument.
7. Describe the relationship between personal experience and public perceptions of the police.
8. Identify and discuss the five departmental behaviors that contribute to police problems in the community.
9. Discuss the ways that police corruption impacts public perception of police.
10. Discuss the importance of officer demeanor in contacts with the public.

References

Apple, N., & O'Brien, D. J. (1988). Neighborhood Racial Composition and Residents' Evaluation of Police Performance. *Journal of Police Science and Administration, 11,* 76-84.

Barker, T., & Carter, D. (1991). *Police Deviance* (2nd ed.). Cincinnati, OH: Anderson Publishing.

Benedict, W. R., Brown, B., & Bower, D. J. (2000). Perceptions of the Police and Fear of Crime in a Rural Setting: Utility of a Geographical Focused Survey for Police Services, Planning, and Assessment. *Criminal Justice Policy Review, 11*(4), 275-298.

Brown, B., & Benedict, W. R. (2002). Perceptions of the Police. *Policing: An International Journal of Police Strategies and Management, 25*(3), 543-580.

Cao, L., Frank, J., & Cullen, F. (1996). Race, Community Context, and Confidence in Police. *American Journal of Police, 15,* 3-22.

Carter, D. (1983). Hispanic Interaction with the Criminal Justice System in Texas: Experiences, Attitudes, and Perceptions. *Journal of Criminal Justice, 11,* 213-227.

Carter, D. (1985). Hispanic Perception of Police Performance: An Empirical Assessment. *Journal of Criminal Justice, 13,* 487-500.

Carter, D., & Radelet, L. (1999). *The Police and the Community.* Upper Saddle River, NJ: Prentice Hall.

Chandek, M. (1999). Race, Expectations and Evaluations of Police Performance: An Empirical Assessment. *Policing: An International Journal of Police Strategies & Management, 22,* 675-695.

Chermak, S., McGarrell, E. F., & Weiss, A. (2001). Citizens' Perceptions of Aggressive Traffic Enforcement Strategies. *Justice Quarterly, 18,* 365-391.

Cheurprakobkit, S. (2000). Police-Citizen Contact and Police Performance: Attitudinal Differences between Hispanics and Non-Hispanics. *Journal of Criminal Justice, 28,* 325-336.

Correia, M. E., Reisig, M. D., & Lovrich, N. P. (1996). Public Perceptions of State Police: An Analysis of Individual-Level and Contextual Variables. *Journal of Criminal Justice, 24,* 17-28.

Decker, S. H. (1981). Citizen Attitudes toward the Police: A Review of Past Findings and Suggestions for Future Policy. *Journal of Police Science and Administration, 9*(1), 80-87.

Dowler, K., & Sparks, R. (2008). Victimization, Contact with Police, and Neighborhood Conditions: Reconsidering African American and Hispanic Attitudes Toward the Police. *Police Practice and Research, 9*(5), 395-415.

Erez, E. (1984). Self-Defined "Desert" and Citizens' Assessment of the Police. *Journal of Criminal Law and Criminology, 75,* 1276-1299.

Gaines, L., & Kappeler, V. (2011). *Policing in America* (7th ed.). Waltham, MA: Anderson.

Gaines, L., Worrall, J., Southerland, M., & Angell, J. (2011). *Police Administration* (3rd ed.). New York, NY: McGraw-Hill.

Huang, W., & Vaughn, M. (1996). Support and Confidence: Public Attitudes toward the Police. In T. Flanagan & D. Longmire (Eds.), *Americans View Crime and Justice: A National Public Opinion Survey* (pp. 31-45). Thousand Oaks, CA: Sage Publications.

Jesilow, P., & Meyer, J. (1995). The Effect of Police Misconduct on Public Attitudes: A Quasi-Experiment. *Journal of Crime and Justice, 24,* 109-121.

Jesilow, P., Meyer, J., & Namazzi, J. (1995). Public Attitudes toward the Police. *American Journal of Police, 14,* 67-88.

Kaminski, R. J., & Jefferis, E. S. (1998). The Effect of a Violent Televised Arrest on Public Perceptions of the Police: A Partial Test of Easton's Theoretical Framework. *Policing: An International Journal of Police Strategies and Management, 21,* 683-706.

Kappeler, V. E., & Potter, G. W. (2005). *The Mythology of Crime and Criminal Justice* (4th ed.). Prospect Heights, IL: Waveland.

Kappeler, V., Sluder, R., & Alpert, G. (1998). *Forces of Deviance: Understanding the Dark Side of Policing* (2nd ed.). Prospect Heights, IL: Waveland Press.

Kusow, A., Wilson, L., & Martin, D. (1997). Determinants of Citizen Satisfaction with the Police: The Effects of Residential Location. *Policing: An International Journal of Police Strategies and Management, 20,* 655-664.

McDonald, J. M., Manz, P. W., & Alpert, G. P. (2003). Police Use of Force: Examining the Relationship between Calls for Service and the Balance of Police Force and Suspect Resistance. *Journal of Criminal Justice, 31*(2), 119-127.

McElvain, J., & Kposowa, A. (2004). Police Officer Characteristics and Internal Affairs Investigations for Use of Force Allegations. *Journal of Criminal Justice, 32*(3), 265-279.

Miller, W. (1973). Ideology and Criminal Justice Policy: Some Current Issues. *Journal of Criminal Law and Criminology, 64*, 141-162.

Mollen Commission to Investigate Allegations of Police Corruption. (1994). *Commission Report.* New York, NY: Author.

Murphy, D. W., & Worrall, J. L. (1999). Residency Requirements and Public Perceptions of the Police in Large Municipalities. *Policing: An International Journal of Police Strategies and Management, 22*, 327-342.

Packer, H. (1968). *The Limits of the Criminal Sanction.* Stanford, CA: Stanford University Press.

Powell, M. B., Skouteris, H., & Murfett, R. (2008). Children's Perceptions of the Role of Police: A Qualitative Study. *International Journal of Police Science & Management, 10*(4), 464-473.

Reed, T., & Gaines, L. K. (1982). Criminal Justice Models as a Function of Ideological Images: A Social Learning Alternative to Packer. *International Journal of Comparative and Applied Criminal Justice, 6*, 212-222.

Reisig, M. D., & Chandek, M. S. (2001). The Effects of Expectancy Disconfirmation on Outcome Satisfaction in Police-Citizen Encounters. *Policing: An International Journal of Police Strategies and Management, 24*, 87-99.

Reisig, M. D., & Correia, M. E. (1997). Public Evaluations of Police Performance: An Analysis Across Three Levels of Policing. *Policing, 20*, 311-325.

Reisig, M. D., & Giacomazzi, A. L. (1998). Citizen Perceptions of Community Policing: Are Attitudes Toward Police Important? *Policing: An International Journal of Police Strategies and Management, 21*, 547-561.

Reisig, M. D., & Parks, R. B. (2000). Experience, Quality of Life, and Neighborhood Context: A Hierarchical Analysis of Satisfaction with Police. *Justice Quarterly, 17*, 607-630.

Reisig, M. D., McCluskey, J. D., & Mastrofski, S. D. (2004). Suspect Disrespect toward the Police. *Justice Quarterly, 21*(2), 241-268.

Sampson, R. J., & Bartusch, D. J. (1998). Legal Cynicism and (Subcultural?) Tolerance of Deviance: The Neighborhood Context of Racial Differences. *Law & Society Review, 32*, 777-804.

Skolnick, J. (1966). *Justice without Trial.* New York, NY: Wiley.

Smith, S. K., Steadman, G. W., Minton, T. D., & Townsend, M. (1999). *Criminal Victimization and Perceptions of Community Safety in 12 Cities, 1998.* Washington, DC: U.S. Department of Justice.

Sourcebook. (2011). *Sourcebook of Criminal Justice Statistics.* Washington, DC: Bureau of Justice Statistics.

Terrill, W. (2003). Police Use of Force and Suspect Resistance: The Micro Process of the Police-Suspect Encounter. *Police Quarterly, 6*(1), 51-83.

Terrill, W., & Reisig, M. D. (2003). Neighborhood Context and Police Use of Force. *Journal of Research in Crime and Delinquency, 40*(3), 291-321.

Tuch, S.A., & Weitzer, R. (1997). The Polls: Racial Differences in Attitudes toward the Police. *Public Opinion Quarterly, 61,* 642-664.

Van Maanen, J. (2006). The Asshole. In V. Kappeler (Ed.), *The Police & Society: Touchstone Readings* (3rd ed.). Prospect Heights, IL: Waveland Press.

Walker, S. (1997). Complaints against the Police: A Focus Group Study of Citizen Perceptions, Goals, and Expectations. *Criminal Justice Review, 22,* 207-226.

Weitzer, R., & Tuch, S. (1999). Race, Class, and Perceptions of Discrimination by the Police. *Crime & Delinquency, 45,* 494-507.

Weitzer, R., & Tuch, S. (2004). Reforming the Police: Racial Differences in Public Support for Change. *Criminology, 42,* 391-416.

Worrall, J. L. (1999). Public Perceptions of Police Efficacy and Image: The "Fuzziness" of Support for the Police. *American Journal of Criminal Justice, 24,* 47-66.

Zatz, M., & Portillos, E. (2004). Voices from the Barrio: Chicano/A Gangs, Families, and Communities. In F. Esbensen, S. Tibbetts, & L. Gaines (Eds.), *American Youth Gangs at the Millennium* (pp. 113-141). Long Grove, IL: Waveland Press.

Zevitz, R. G., & Rettammel, R. J. (1990). Elderly Attitudes about Police Service. *American Journal of Police, 9*(2), 25-39.

Do we shrink from change? Why, what can come into being saved by change?

—*Marcus Aurelius*

CHAPTER 5   Managing and Implementing Community Policing

LEARNING OBJECTIVES

After reading the chapter, you should be able to:

1. Understand the historical role of the military model in policing.
2. List the principles of classical organizational theory.
3. Understand and define organic organization.
4. Describe the best way to organize a department for community policing.
5. Describe how organizational culture can hinder the implementation of community policing.
6. List and describe the factors of comprehensive change.
7. Identify and describe the eight steps of implementing community policing.
8. How COMSTAT can work with community policing.
9. Discuss why leadership is important to community policing.

Organizing the Police

Community policing, in its ideal form, represents a significant departure from the way American police departments have operated throughout the better part of the twentieth century. It is a philosophy that substantially broadens the role of police in society. Community policing is people-based as opposed to being bureaucratic or militaristic. It is about improving people's quality of life. Community policing officers (CPOs) must recognize that their primary function is to serve the public, not to provide law enforcement. Although law enforcement is important, it is recognized that it is only one part of the overall responsibility of the police. Today, too many police departments concentrate on "bean counting," or making large numbers of arrests or issuing numerous traffic citations, without considering whether such activities improve the community. Numbers of citations and arrests do not necessarily contribute to the quality of life in a community or enhance the image of police in the eyes of the community.

Police organization is about how to structure the department so that goals and objectives are achieved. From the community policing philosophy, organizing the police is about structuring the department so that community goals and objectives are achieved. A department must be organized so that it enhances the quality of life of the people it serves, while at the same time, services are provided efficiently, effectively, and equitably. This means that community policing should provide primary guidance when organizing or altering a department's organization. In Chapter 1, the facets constituting community policing were elaborated. When organizing the department, administrators must address each of these facets. This means that changes must be made in a department's leadership, mid-level management, and supervision. It also means that every element within the police department should be considered when implementing community policing. This sometimes is problematic. For example, Vito, Walsh, and Kunselman (2005) found that almost half of the police middle managers they surveyed stated that the organizational structure in their departments was an impediment to community policing. Police administrators must examine their departments' structure and ensure that it is conducive to community policing.

Principles of Organization and Police Administration

Police organization, for the most part, is based on **classical organizational theory** or the military or bureaucratic model. The military or bureaucratic model of police administration has its roots in the London Metropolitan Police Force in London. Sir Robert Peel created a police force organized along military lines when he established the force in 1829. At the time, the military was one of the best examples of how to administer large organizations. This military orientation was later adopted in the United States, and elements of this bureaucratic model remain a central part of police administration for many police departments today (Gaines & Kappeler, 2011).

The tenets of the military organization are found in classical organization theory. Although numerous newer organizational variations such as community policing, decentralization, participative management, and total quality management have been discussed and attempted in policing, classical organization or bureaucracy remains the foundation from which these innovations are attempted. Classical organization forms the foundation for American policing; its principles are enumerated below.

Classical Organization Principles

The German sociologist **Max Weber**, the founder of modern sociology, was the first to outline the principles of organization. Weber studied the church and army to understand why complex organizations were effective (Gaines & Worrall, 2012). It should be remembered that these early organizations were successful because they had a measure of order or organization to them. As a result of his study, Weber delineated six principles that have become the foundation of classical organizational theory and are used in many police departments today:

- The organization follows the **principle of hierarchy**—each lower officer is under the control and supervision of a higher one. This is called the chain of command in policing. It consists of ranks, including officer, sergeant, lieutenant, captain, major, assistant chief, and chief. Each rank is responsible for subordinate officers and a set of tasks. A negative side effect is that communication is inhibited whereas orders and commands flow down to the bottom of the department, but little information is passed upward. This creates a void when decisions are made.

- Specialization or **division of labor** exists whereby individuals are assigned a limited number of job tasks and responsibilities. This principle is exemplified in policing by organizational units such as patrol, traffic, criminal investigation, juvenile, planning, training, and records. Each unit has a distinct set of responsibilities, which clarifies their jobs and assists in managing workload. A negative side effect of specialization is that units often fail to coordinate their activities or work together when tackling complex problems. They also come to focus on their individual unit responsibilities and neglect the department's overall mission and goals.

- Official policies and procedures guide the activities of the organization. Police departments have large volumes of **policies and procedures**. They specify what can be done and what cannot be done. They are used by administrators to control subordinate behavior and to provide consistency in operation. Negative side effects from rulification include a failure to use innovative solutions to problems and to concentrate on procedures as opposed to solving problems.

- Administrative acts, decisions, and rules are **recorded** in writing. Bureaucracies tend to make formal records of all decisions and activities. This not only provides a permanent record, but the written records can also be used to hold subordinates accountable for deviations from decisions and policies. A negative side effect of recorded decisions is that too much emphasis is placed on ensuring that documents are properly completed and recorded while actual police work may be neglected. It also slows down decision making and the communication of decisions.

- **Authority** within the organization is associated with one's position. One's authority is based on rank. This ensures that the chain of command remains intact, and personnel understand who is responsible for specific tasks and responsibilities. A negative side effect of positional authority is that it often does not recognize the ability or expertise of lower-level subordinates who may be able to contribute to the solution of problems. A police department that has a highly centralized authority structure or chain of command, however, may be in a better position to mandate a change toward community policing (Morabito, 2010).

- Candidates are appointed on the basis of their **qualifications**, and training is a necessary part of the selection process. It is critical for the department to have employees who are competent and able to do the job. For this reason, police departments have extensive screening processes and mandated training. A problem with police training is that it often focuses on policies and procedures and fails to enhance officers' decision-making and problem-solving skills, especially as they relate to dealing with people.

These principles provide organizations a high degree of structure. They are similar to those used by the military, to an extent, and sometimes result in employees behaving as bureaucrats (see Gaines & Worrall, 2012). They are at the heart of organizing large numbers of employees and work. When these principles are followed, officers tend to focus on policies and procedures as opposed to providing effective services. They also can result in a high level of control that is useful in reducing corruption and other problems, such as improper use of force. Police managers see conformity as the primary means of reducing potential problems. It should be remembered that all organizations possess some measure of the above principles.

Burns and Stalker (1961) have referred to organizations that strictly adhere to these principles as mechanistic because of their centralized authority and rigidity. In other words, police organizations are designed to create a great deal of conformity by employees, and officers are discouraged from deviating from departmental norms and expectations. Control is given more credence than individualized services to people. Here, fear of potential problems trumps or overcomes the need to provide the best quality services. This obviously can hinder CPOs when attempting to tailor their services to meet the needs of the community.

Community policing, on the other hand, requires what Stalker refers to as an organic organization. **Organic organizations** are more open, and delegate higher levels of responsibility to subordinates at the operational levels of the organization. Community policing dictates that police officers develop a cooperative or personal, rather than a bureaucratic, relationship with people. This means that the police must develop relationships with people in every neighborhood and consider their concerns and problems when delivering police services. This recognizes that a middle-class community in suburbia will have different problems and expectations as compared to residents in a poor neighborhood. The police must be equally effective in both neighborhoods.

Organic organizations delegate decision making to the lowest level in the organization. Unit commanders, rather than top administrators, should be making decisions about priorities and which problems have a higher priority. These mid-level managers often have a better understanding of the problems and issues confronting the department at the street level. They should do this in consultation with officers working in the community. When officers work a beat or an assigned area for long periods of time, they gain familiarity and ideas about what needs to be done in their area. This is best accomplished through vertical staff meetings where officers of all ranks meet to discuss problems. Moreover, there should be meetings across units. For example, patrol, criminal investigation, traffic, and other tactical units should discuss how each could compliment or facilitate the work of other units to achieve objectives more effectively. Such meetings also engender more cooperation and an understanding of the issues facing other units within the department. Research demonstrates that this participatory style of management produces better results, and it leads to greater job satisfaction on the part of officers (Steinheider & Wuestawald, 2008).

Community policing entails allowing officers a great deal of discretion in handling calls for service and problems—discretion is more important than conformity. Therefore, the military or traditional model is totally inappropriate for community policing. Community policing requires that officers be given latitude in choosing options to solve problems rather than relying on standard departmental procedures that may not meet the needs of the problem. In other words, police officers must be released from the shackles of close supervision so that they can adequately perform their jobs. Officers must also be taught that problems are often unique to neighborhoods, and they often require unique responses. Officers must have an ever-expanding set of tools or tactics with which to deal with problems.

How can a police department's organization be altered to meet these needs? Zhao (1996) found that police departments' structure has, to some extent, changed as a result of community policing, but this change has been the result of community pressure as opposed to efforts to better incorporate community policing. Indeed, Maguire (1997) examined police departments and found that police departments that reported adopting community policing did not significantly change their organizational structure. Community policing may flourish within a department's current structure, but extreme changes have to be made in how it is managed. Administrators, managers, and supervisors must be committed and lead subordinates.

First, police leadership must be changed. Police administrators must be committed to community policing. Too often police administrators see community policing as a bundle of programs that have been cobbled together. Other police administrators see it as lip service to gain political support. In these instances, community policing is piecemeal and sporadic. It results in officers not having an understanding of community policing or a strong commitment to it. It results in role confusion and conflicts within the department as traditional law enforcement vies with the tenets of community policing (Greene et al., 1994; Lord, 1996).

Second, community policing consists of two very important elements: community partnerships and problem solving. These two elements must permeate the department from top to bottom. Officers must be committed to building community partnerships. The same is true for problem solving. Officers must have a commitment to solving problems, often by using nontraditional tools and tactics. Police administrators are responsible for instilling this commitment, and it requires an organizational structure that facilitates, rather than inhibits, community policing.

SPOTLIGHT ON COMMUNITY POLICING PRACTICE

The Purpose of Partnerships

Community policing encourages law enforcement agencies to forge partnerships with government agencies, community members and groups, nonprofits, service providers, private business, and the media. It is important to understand that partnerships within the context of community policing should serve the two interrelated goals of increasing trust and enhancing collaborative problem-solving efforts.

Partnerships to Increase Trust

One fundamental purpose of partnerships is to increase trust between law enforcement agencies and the customers they serve. Trust is the basis for any effective relationship, whether it is between two friends, between customers and a company, or between a public service agency and citizens. Citizens who do not trust the police are less likely to report crime and to participate in developing solutions to problems. They are also more likely to place blame for increases in crime on the shoulders of police. It takes only one volatile incident to create tension between the public and the police, even for the most respected police agencies. Community policing encourages agencies to build up accounts of trust and goodwill to call on when the inevitable crisis arises. Simply put, trust provides the necessary basis for fair and effective policing.

Partnerships for Collaborative Problem Solving

The second primary purpose of partnerships is to conduct collaborative problem-solving efforts. The first step of any problem-solving effort should be to prioritize crime and disorder problems. The roots of community policing are based on the belief that the public should have a say in how they are policed and in how the problems of their community are prioritized. It is not uncommon for law enforcement agencies to find that their priorities differ significantly from those of citizens. Part I violent and property crime will likely always be of interest to the public, but other public safety problems and fear of crime may be of greater importance than initially realized.

Once identified, the police can rarely solve crime and disorder problems alone. Long-term solutions to problems often require comprehensive responses, and enforcement typically represents only one aspect of an effective response. Other public service providers, nonprofits, or local government agencies can bring unique resources to bear on offenders, victims, and crime locations. Law enforcement agencies should seek to engage in SARA problem-solving processes with partners who have a stake in addressing specific problems and can play a significant role in developing innovative solutions.

(Continued)

Effective Partnerships

Forging collaborative partnerships is difficult and the vast majority of law enforcement agencies are familiar with public apathy when it comes to crime and disorder problems. Thus, law enforcement agencies need to be strategic about their partnerships and have very specific goals in mind at the outset. Is this partnership primarily for public relations or is it to develop a solution to a specific problem or set of problems? How will success be defined?

Collaborative problem-solving efforts work best with partners who have a stake in developing a solution to the problem and have specific identified resources that they can bring to bear on proposed solutions. Representatives of various agencies or constituencies should also have an appropriate degree of decision-making power to increase efficiency. Partnerships also work best when there are clear agendas and expectations among partners. Finally, although the police may have a natural leadership role in convening collaborative problem-solving groups, they should consider whether they are ultimately best positioned to serve in a membership or advisory role instead. When possible, police should seek to shift responsibility to, and share responsibility for public safety problems with, other entities.

Matthew Scheider
Assistant Director
Office of Community Oriented Policing Services

Source: The e-newsletter of the COPS Office, Volume 1, Issue 2, February 2008.

Third, the department must change its culture. It must move from a traditional police culture to one that is open and committed to community policing. This means that a department must examine its policies and procedures to ensure they facilitate and encourage community policing. Community policing must be incorporated in training; officers must be educated to the point they have a firm understanding of what must occur. Other personnel practices such as performance evaluations must be changed to include community policing (see Connors & Webster, 2001). As noted throughout this text, community policing must be comprehensive and permanent.

Organizing for Community Policing

What is the best way to implement community policing or to ensure that it has been implemented properly? The following sections examine some of the administrative issues that must be considered when attempting to successfully implement community policing. As noted in Chapter 1, there are several facets that must be considered, and the community policing philosophy, strategies, and operational programming must be implemented and coordinated throughout a department.

Strategic Planning

As noted in Chapter 1, the philosophical facet of community policing focuses on defining police work broadly using community needs to create partnerships in identifying and solving problems. This process begins with strategic planning. **Strategic planning** simply is the identification of goals and objectives, and a determination of how they will be achieved. What is the department attempting to accomplish and how is it going to do it? Strategic planning in the traditional police department generally has two components. First, the department tends to respond to crime and calls for police services as it has traditionally. Little emphasis is placed on problem identification or problem solving. It is more status quo policing. Second, the department reacts when a significant problem arises. Usually reaction occurs when a significant crime event occurs or when there is a general increase in crime or some category of crime such as murder, robbery, gang activity, or sexual assaults. Media coverage often precedes the department's recognition of the problem. The department responds reactively as opposed to being proactive. It is much more difficult to play catch-up after a problem has gotten out of hand as opposed to attempting to deal with it at the beginning stages.

Community policing dictates that police administrators establish goals and objectives after consultation with all the stakeholders in the community. Stakeholders should be given the opportunity to provide input; the subsequent information and data then must be collated, synthesized, and analyzed; and finally, goals and objectives are established based on community needs and problems. This is an arduous process requiring input from a variety of sources as depicted in Figure 5.1.

Figure 5.1 shows that there is a sharing of information between the police department and people in the community. The police department should be an open system whereby information about the quality of police services and crime problems are routinely solicited. In addition to obtaining information from the elected officials, police administrators should solicit information from all sorts of people within the community including civic organizations, business leaders, community leaders, neighborhood groups, and individuals. These groups will have different ideas and perspectives about problems, but the department must consider all of them (Skogan & Hartnett, 1997). The department must strive to provide an equitable level of service, and this means that the department must attend to all constituents' needs.

This process is facilitated by building relationships, sharing power, and trusting all constituents involved in the process. Working groups must be established that meet frequently to discuss issues and provide input. In the past, police

Figure 5.1
Strategic Planning Process

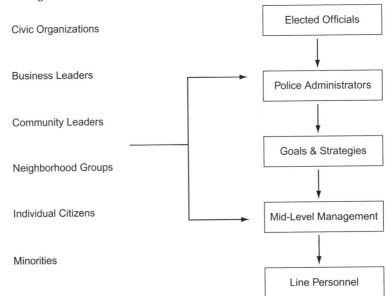

departments have established advisory groups, but too often, they were formed to rubber stamp police programming and activities. Police administrators would dictate and preach to the groups—not solicit input or cooperation. Roth (2000), in an examination of police-community partnerships, found that most were in name only—they lacked substance or a real desire to develop cooperative relationships. Such a process is not community policing. When police departments do not solicit and use information from constituents, it results in a closed system where community needs are not considered or met.

It is not an easy task to get people effectively involved in providing input to the police department. Many of the constituents will come to the table with preconceived notions and hidden agendas. They will attempt to influence the process so that the results will benefit them directly or the particular group they represent. They must be convinced that all parties win when the police equitably address everyone's issues or problems. Open dialog will, over time, reduce or remove many of the barriers to a cooperative, working relationship, especially if the participants sense a genuine interest on the part of the police to be guided by their needs. A genuine interest is best demonstrated by using people's input and such actions engender trust and further participation.

Gaining the cooperation of police subordinate personnel can be just as difficult as working with people. Police personnel are often cynical and resistant to community policing and changes in departmental direction and procedures. Moreover, police officers see their primary role as being law enforcement and often mistakenly believe that order maintenance and the provision of services are secondary or not important (Gaines & Kappeler, 2011). Police officers often take a "we versus them" attitude toward the public (Kappeler & Potter, 2005; Skolnick, 1966). Police officers must understand that they should be concerned with the overall health of the community, and that order maintenance and the provisions of service facilitate successful law enforcement.

It is critical for administrators to have open, honest dialog with line officers and supervisors. This means developing lines of communication outside or in conjunction with the chain of command. When communications are opened, administrators have an opportunity to sell their programs and achieve a higher level of commitment from line officers. It also enables line officers to communicate problems to administrators. When information is shared everyone benefits.

There are several mechanisms available to the police administrator that can be used to facilitate communications with the community. They include the following:

- **Neighborhood counsels**—Cities contain distinctive neighborhoods that are recognized as such by people and government. Police departments should encourage and facilitate the creation and strengthening of neighborhood counsels. These counsels often are comprised of leaders such as religious leaders, businesspeople, community activists, and ordinary people who have community concerns. Neighborhood counsels go beyond block watches. Whereas block watches are instruments of the police to assist in crime reduction, neighborhood counsels provide feedback on what are the most pertinent problems in a neighborhood and neighborhood expectations of the police. Such meetings would ideally include the chief or a member of his or her executive staff, patrol area commander, members of specialized units such as juvenile, criminal investigation, etc., and people. City or county elected officials should also be encouraged to attend counsel meetings. Inclusion of city or county elected leaders often contributes to the funding of new police initiatives in the neighborhoods. These meetings can lead to powerful partnerships.

- **Chief's advisory committee**— A number of departments have created advisory committees, but they often do not reach their potential. Committee members should represent large diverse constituencies. Such a committee can provide broad-based opinions and ideas about community problems and police initiatives. The committee can sometimes serve as a spokesperson for the police department to the media and government bodies. If the chief keeps an open mind to the concerns expressed by advisory committees, he or she will obtain valuable information about the department and the community. Care, however, must be taken not to include only those well-placed figures who support the police or political leaders.

- **Special committees**—Special community committees can be appointed to study individual problems that are occurring in the community or in a neighborhood. These committees are generally devoted to a particular problem or area. For example, if a neighborhood has a gang problem, people from the neighborhood along with police and other governmental officials can be appointed to a committee to study and work with the police on the problem. This accomplishes several objectives. First, it promotes an understanding on the part of people relative to police abilities and limitations. Second, it fosters a relationship whereby people may provide intelligence information to the police. Third, it possibly will foster neighborhood programs to help alleviate the problem.

Police administrators should attempt to improve communications within the department. As such, there are several vehicles that can be used, including:

- **Command or administrative staff meetings**—Police executives should meet periodically with departmental staff and unit commanders to discuss problems, programs, and goal achievement. Most chiefs hold staff meetings, but they often occur too infrequently, and they focus on personnel or administrative problems, not the achievement of police goals and objectives. At a minimum, they should occur weekly. They allow communications across police units and foster better coordination and cooperation when dealing with police problems. They should include program updates and progress reports as a part of the agenda. This increases the probability that new or unresolved problems will be identified.

- **Quality circles**—A number of departments have experimented with quality circles. Quality circles are formed to deal with significant problems in the department such as use of force, increase in auto thefts, or changes in policies. Various ranks, especially lower ranks, should be represented in the meetings, and depending on the problem, officers from several different units should be involved in the meetings. They are virtually vertical staff meetings. The quality circle meets periodically, keeps minutes of its meetings, and, ultimately, provides its recommendations to the police executive. Quality circles often can provide valuable input to decision makers about problems. Quality circles generally focus on a particular problem or issue.

- **Unit meetings**—Units should be afforded the time periodically where all officers assigned to the unit or at least a representative sample of officers can meet and discuss problems and unit objectives. Most units hold some form of roll call, but roll calls for the most part are the dissemination of information from the top down. Seldom are officers asked their opinions about unit priorities and the best way to achieve these priorities. Unit meetings can increase commitment to programs on the part of officers, and they can provide new and innovative strategies for dealing with problems.

In addition to increasing the flow of communications within the department and between the department and the larger community, the police executive must take measures to increase communications and foster cooperation between the department and other governmental agencies. That is, the chief must ensure that the department has a working relationship with other governmental agencies. The chief often attends city or county council meetings. Such meetings generally allow the chief to provide information to counsel members and answer questions, but they do not necessarily allow the chief to forge better working relationships with other departments.

There are several departments that can be helpful to the police including code enforcement, public housing, alcoholic beverage control, fire, recreation, parks and recreation, and sanitation. There are several noteworthy examples. Alcoholic beverage control can assist the police by closing a bar that serves alcohol to intoxicated patrons who later become disorderly. Code enforcement can be used to close and board up a crack house or other nuisance location. Many rowdy nightclubs and bars often exceed the permissible number of patrons as allowed by the fire code, so the police working with fire department inspectors can exert pressure on these establishments to maintain order. Police officials can work with parks and recreation personnel to provide recreation opportunities in neighborhoods that have juvenile and gang problems. The police can work with the sanitation department to clean up a neighborhood. These examples show that other governmental departments can be instrumental to the police department in dealing with a host of problems, and they represent critical partnerships to a community policing department.

The above processes contribute to the police department collecting information and forming relationships to achieve the philosophical facet of community policing. They contribute to creating a broad police function with a community focus, development of innovative strategies, community input, cooperation within the department and community, shared power, and developing trust at all levels of the department and community.

Once this information is received, it must be collated, analyzed, and reduced to strategic plans. In other words, the information must be reduced to action plans. Specifically, what issues will the department respond to and what will be the responses? The most effective way of collating the information is by geography. Police departments organize their service delivery system according to beats or other geographical subdivisions such as precincts or districts. The problems identified for each area should be sorted or collated. Information on the same or similar problems in an area should be linked. Once this process has occurred, police decision makers and community members can identify those problems that have the highest priority, and they can be assigned to operational units. One must be mindful, however, not to confuse causes, symptoms, and problems. Each of these is a symptom, not a cause. This process provides information relative to the "who," "what," "when," "where," and "how" of problems. The operational units then implement tactics or programs targeting the problems.

Such strategic planning identifies specific problems to be addressed, and it allows for better, more precise solutions. The process is more helpful than traditional goal statements that globally discuss eliminating or reducing crime. The process also allows for evaluation whereby the department can judge if it has been successful in addressing problems.

COMPSTAT

A growing number of police departments are using some form of COMSTAT. **COMPSTAT** was pioneered in New York City by William Bratton and Jack Maples and is an acronym for computer statistics in some locations, while others refer to it as compare statistics. It has been adopted by a large number of police departments (Weisburd et al., 2003). Today, police departments are collecting data for a variety of purposes. Table 5.1 shows how departments are now using data.

It is a managerial process that uses crime analysis information. COMPSTAT consists of periodic meetings, usually weekly or monthly, where unit commanders and management staff are assembled to discuss crime problems. The foundation of the meetings is crime maps showing the crimes and crime trends in the various patrol areas. The management staff asks the patrol, traffic, and detective commanders to provide a description of their priorities and what actions are being taken

Table 5.1

General Functions of Computers in Local Police Departments by Size of Population Served, 2007

Population served	Percent of departments using computers for—							
	Records management	Crime investigation	Personnel records	Information sharing	Dispatch	Automated booking	Fleet management	Resource allocation
All sizes	79%	60%	53%	50%	49%	32%	27%	20%
1,000,000 or more	85%	100%	85%	85%	100%	77%	100%	85%
500,000-999,999	97	90	94	100	94	65	100	77
250,000-499,999	100	93	96	89	93	54	78	80
100,000-249,999	95	89	85	80	97	58	65	62
50,000-99,999	96	86	78	76	95	59	67	56
25,000-49,999	97	84	74	72	90	61	50	42
10,000-24,999	94	77	67	63	79	49	44	29
2,500-9,999	84	64	55	52	51	31	29	19
Under 2,500	65	43	39	36	23	18	9	9

Source: Reaves, B. (2010). *Local Police Departments, 2007*. Washington, DC: Bureau of Justice Statistics.

to alleviate the problems. It enables decision makers to have immediate access to information about problems and to make tactical decisions based on real time crime information. It is a process where administrators in conjunction with patrol, traffic, and investigative commanders and personnel examine activities and cooperatively develop plans to address problems in specific geographical areas. It also adds accountability to the mix since it provides a constant level of feedback relative to the success of operations. In other words, if a problem persists, it means that departmental actions have not sufficiently addressed the problem. Administrators can then discuss the lack of progress or successes with commanders. COMPSTAT also ensures that problems are constantly monitored and receive adequate attention. They are not forgotten once an initial strategy or tactic has been deployed.

The process also consists of a comprehensive reporting system whereby all participants share crime information. Henry (2002) examined COMSTAT in New York and found that it consisted of three distinct, weekly reports.

- The **COMPSTAT Report** provides a ranking of the precincts by crime and arrests. This report allows management to make a determination about each precinct's problems and the efforts exerted to solve the problems. This report can also provide information on officer productivity to determine those officers who are making more and fewer arrests and issuing citations. This information would be helpful in identifying officers in need of additional supervision and training.

- The **Commander Profile Report** serves as a report card on how managers are dealing with their crime problems and their units. The report contains information on population and demographics for each command area, number of assigned personnel, complaints filed against officers in the command, vehicle crashes involving departmental vehicles, response time to calls for service, number of on-duty injuries to officers, and amount of overtime expenditures. This report allows administrators to examine individual commanders over time and compare each with the other commanders. Such a comparison can identify problem commands.

- The **Crime Mapping Report** provides commanders with visual accounts of crime and calls for service in their commands. Various maps can be generated examining individual or all major crimes for a short or extended period. This flexibility allows commanders to discover trends over time or in specific locations. The maps assist the commanders in developing better tactics for dealing with the problems in their areas.

In New York, there are weekly COMPSTAT meetings where administrators discuss these reports and the status of crime and police activity in each of the commands. Administrators query the commanders about their tactics and whether they are effective in dealing with identified problems. Silverman (1999) notes that discussions with commanders of high-profile cases and crime patterns reduce the bureaucratic entanglements and facilitate communication. This allows for better identification of goals and objectives and a rapid change in tactics to meet evolving problems. Commanders are held accountable for crime problems since they must make progress reports during the COMPSTAT meetings. When they fail to make progress on problems, they must account for the lack of progress.

A deficiency in many of the current COMPSTAT programs is that the analysis and discussions center exclusively on crime statistics and often do not include input or information from members of the community. Currently, COMPSTAT, although seen as a police innovation, is actually more attuned with traditional policing as opposed to community policing since there is an absence of community input. The current system presents three problems. First, it deems people and community input as being irrelevant. COMPSTAT does not collect or consider community member input data. Second, problems identified through community member input may be more important or critical, at least to the people who are affected by the problems, but such problems are ignored. Finally, merging community member input with crime analysis and

COMPSTAT data may result in a more comprehensive understanding of crime problems and the identification of more effective solutions. Police agencies using COMPSTAT should develop mechanisms to resolve this issue. For example, COMPSTAT information could be supplemented with community surveys. Magers (2004) advises that police departments must synthesize COMPSTAT with community policing; they essentially compliment each other. This means focusing on management and supervision as a system rather than contemplating elements of management and supervision individually.

An important rationale for using COMPSTAT is that crime is not equally distributed geographically. Research shows that crime and disorder are clustered in locations or hot spots (Braga & Weisburd, 2010). In the first study to examine hot spots, Sherman, Gartin, and Buerger (1989) found that three percent of the addresses in Minneapolis accounted for 50 percent of the crime. These results have been confirmed in other research (Eck, Gersh & Taylor, 2000; Weisburd, Maher & Sherman, 1992). Also, Weisburd and his colleagues (2004) found that the concentration of crime in hot spots is fairly stable over time. Also, there are different types of hot spots: street drug markets (Weisburd & Green, 1995); gun violence (Sherman & Rogan, 1995); violent crime (Braga et al., 1999) and crime and disorder (Braga & Bond, 2008). This research demonstrates that COMPSTAT can be useful in identifying and diagnosing hot spots.

> *You can learn more about COMPSTAT by going to http://www.policefoundation.org/pdf/ compstatinpractice.pdf.*

Personnel Development

In addition to articulating the department's mission and vision by developing goals and objectives, police administrators must ensure that the workforce or officers are capable and prepared to engage in community policing activities. Thus, it is pertinent to examine police training issues. As noted throughout this text, community policing represents a substantial departure from traditional, mechanistic policing. Most police departments have cultures that are not conducive to community policing; officers are more interested in law enforcement than service, order maintenance, or problem solving (Gaines & Kappeler, 2011).

Training can have an impact on these attitudes and foster more effective community policing efforts. For example, Zhao and his colleagues (1995) in a survey of police executives found that they believed that community policing training facilitated the implementing of community policing, but officers and supervisors often resisted it. This resistance often was the result of not understanding community policing. Kratcoski and Noonan (1995) examined departments that did not provide officers with training before implementing community policing and found officers to be highly resistant and uncommitted to it. They suggested that community policing training be integrated into academy or basic police training. These findings point to a need to develop training that departs from traditional modes of policing and incorporates community policing principles.

States require officers to receive basic or academy training, which may consist of 400 to 600 training hours, and veteran officers are required to receive in-service training ranging from 20 to 40 hours annually. Community policing must be integrated into this training, which can be difficult. Essentially, most police training revolves around nuts and bolts—completing reports, stopping suspect vehicles, obtaining warrants, physical fitness, first aid, firearms training, and the like. Coverage of community policing topics such as problem solving, community relations, and community building are secondary and often receive inadequate attention or emphasis. Many police officers, especially probationary officers, are resistant to this training. As Buerger (1998) notes, police officers come to the occupation with preconceived ideas about what policing is, and they often are resistant to job specifications that run counter to those ideas. Training administrators must ensure that officers are as proficient in community policing areas such as community relations and problem solving as they are in firearms, first aid, or report writing. For example, Cheurprakobkit (2002) examined community policing attitudes in a medium-sized department and found that concepts relating to community policing tactics were accepted by officers, but philosophical and organization issues were not understood and officers resisted them. Cheurprakobkit concluded that training must concentrate on all facets of community policing if it is to be accepted and integrated into the department's operation.

Finally, Haarr (2001) found that community policing training positively increased officers' attitudes toward community policing and problem solving, but these positive attitudes dissipated over time after officers were assigned to field training officers. Thus, implementing community policing at the academy level is not sufficient. Community policing tactics and procedures must be a principle component in field officer training. Community policing cannot be implemented without it being integrated comprehensively in all aspects of police training. King and Lab (2000) advise that without proper training, officers are less likely to understand the philosophy of community policing and how to translate that philosophy into effective programming and practice.

Tactical Planning and Operations

The strategic planning process is engaged in developing goals and objectives for operational units and is responsible for monitoring the units to ensure that tactics and operations achieve the established goals and objectives. Essentially, unit commanders then develop and implement programs or tactics to meet the pre-established goals and objectives. In this sense, unit commanders are involved in tactical planning. There are several critical elements of tactical planning including: supervision, geographical focus, and reoriented police operations and problem solving.

Supervision

In terms of supervision, police administrators must ensure that supervisors and middle managers are committed to and understand community policing. DeJong, Mastrofski, and Parks (2001) noted that officers' behavior and attitudes often mimic those of their superiors in an effort to secure positive performance evaluations and promotions. **Supervision** is the key to the successful implementation of community policing, and administrators must ensure that middle managers and supervisors understand and embrace it. This is best achieved though training, policies, and direction.

Engel (2002) investigated police supervision, especially as it relates to community policing. In her studies, Engel identified four distinct types or styles of police supervisors. First, the traditional supervisor expects aggressive policing from subordinates. They are task oriented and are interested in "bean counting" where numbers of arrests, citations, response time, and paperwork are most important. They may give lip service to community policing, but they tend to emphasize traditional measures of policing. Second, there are innovative supervisors who embrace community policing. They understand and value problem solving and community relations and de-emphasize "bean counting" activities. They mentor and counsel subordinates as a way of achieving a commitment to community policing from their subordinates. Third, there are supportive supervisors who are relationship oriented. They attempt to provide a buffer between officers and management policies. They are not necessarily interested in "bean counting" or community policing. They want to remain "friends" with subordinates. This obviously can result in a lack of control. Finally, there are **active supervisors**. They are very active in the field, often making arrests and writing citations, as well as supervising officers. They essentially are street officers who have not come to understand or accept the responsibilities of supervision. She found these four styles of supervision were fairly evenly distributed within police departments.

Theoretically, police departments that are committed to community policing should attempt to select and train supervisors in the innovative style. However, Engel found these supervisors, although embracing the idea of community policing, were no more effective than their counterparts. The innovative supervisors tended to concentrate on the administrative duties associated with community policing rather than community policing itself. This finding suggests that police departments must do more to prepare supervisors and mid-level managers for community policing. It appears that departments have not successfully implemented all facets into their management model. This is best attained though better training, direction, elaboration of goals, and systems of accountability such as COMPSTAT.

Geographical Focus

Police administrators must ensure that line officers and units have a **geographic focus**. This is often accomplished by assigning patrol officers to specific beats and districts or precincts. It is also important that officers are assigned to those beats on a consistent basis. Almost 50 years ago Wilson and McLaren (1963) discussed the concept of territorial imperative. **Territorial imperative** is where officers come to know and associate with the area and people they patrol or police. When officers come to associate with the people and their beats, they tend to take more pride in their work and tend to exert more effort in preventing crime in their beat areas. The idea of territorial imperative holds true today—police officers must come to associate with their beats and the people they police (see Kane, 2000). How else can they develop community partnerships and engage in community building?

To accomplish territorial imperative, police executives must ensure that the beat layout provides officers the opportunity to develop relations with people. This is accomplished by examining officers' workload. A police officer's time can be categorized as committed time and patrol time, when answering a call or self-initiated activity (see Gaines & Kappeler, 2011). Patrol time essentially is uncommitted time where officers patrol and observe for suspicious activities or problems. Officers should have 30 to 40 percent of their patrol time uncommitted to engage the community. Police administrators should constantly monitor the workload of individual beats, and when necessary, restructure the beat configuration.

The patrol time can then be used for community policing activities such as meeting with people, business owners, and juveniles in the neighborhoods and identifying and solving problems. Such activities can foster better relations with the police and confidence in the police. Skogan (2009) advises that when people have more confidence in the police, they are less fearful of crime—an important police objective. Parks and his colleagues (1999), however, found that when officers met or engaged people, they spent a majority of their time with people they knew or people that had no problems. Supervisors should encourage or otherwise direct officers to connect with unfamiliar people and expand the base of people who connect with their beat officers. Supervisors should also consult with officers and identify problems in the beat area and design solutions. Individual police officers are often reluctant or never get around to problem solving without supervisor encouragement. These activities are key tasks in community policing departments. One must also remember, that under community policing, beats are not just constructed from a police perspective or work; they must take into account numerous human interactions that give shape to a location's "natural" geography.

Reoriented Police Operations and Problem Solving

A majority of police activities are still incident driven—officers responding to calls for service and investigating crimes. Typically, officers respond to calls for service and provide one of the following responses: (1) make an arrest, (2) issue a citation, (3) advise the complainant to obtain a warrant or restraining order, (4) provide some type of service, or (5) provide information. These responses often do little to solve the problem, and when problems are not solved, officers must repeatedly respond to the same address to continually deal with the problem. Officers must go beyond this narrow range of services.

However, recognizing that officers have uncommitted or patrol time, administrators and supervisors should develop tactics that center around community building, community members, crime prevention, and problem solving that can be implemented by officers during their patrol time. What this means is that unit commanders and supervisors, in conjunction with officers, should identify problems to be solved by officers. Once problems are identified and prioritized, tactics should be deployed that directly address the problems. Here, officers must use creativity and innovation. Officers must have a toolbox of tactics that can be deployed to address specific problems. The COMPSTAT process is helpful in reorienting police operations. As noted above, COMPSTAT consists of periodic meetings where operational personnel and administrators discuss progress being made in solving problems. Administrators should attempt to foster open dialog among participants discussing innovative strategies that have effectively been used to deal with problems. Participants should also be encouraged to put forth untried solutions to problems. Thus, COMPSTAT meetings can be used as a technology transfer and organizational development tool. It can also be used to focus police operations on problems and to evaluate the effectiveness of tactics once they have been deployed.

Implementing Community Policing

One aspect of community policing that has received insufficient attention is implementation. Little is known about how one might successfully get such a program under way. Examining the origins of current programs makes it appear that they have developed rather haphazardly. There have been multiple causes for programs in that police administrators have a variety of reasons for deciding to implement community policing. There have also been various levels of involvement from different police department organizational strata, and a fairly wide range of police responses at the operational level. Each organizational level has different perceptions about what community policing should look like and how it should be operationalized. Thus, implementation of community policing has very likely taken a variety of paths. Perhaps the best way to understand implementation is to examine the literature on change. When an agency implements community policing, it, in fact, is implementing change.

For the most part, police departments have approached implementation from two directions (Gaines, 1994). Some departments have attempted to implement it department-wide, having all officers involved. A problem with this strategy is that it tends to diffuse efforts—it is likely that some officers

Table 5.2
Successful vs. Unsuccessful Change Efforts

Successful change efforts	Unsuccessful change efforts
Use data to understand problems and needs and to support the options or plans being implemented	A perception that the change was just one among many that received little or no follow-through; the flavor-of-the-month syndrome
Communicate change to all affected	Bad timing
Be honest with each other and build trust	Failure to achieve input from those affected or with expertise to bear
Learn from past efforts and utilize feedback	Failure to achieve buy-in from those affected
Ensure that change is inclusive, eliciting involvement from those affected	Lack of flexibility
Have enough time for the process to work; stakeholders should be patient	Poorly thought out
Consistent with other goals	No or poor communication
Hove a flexible implementation process	Fear-resistance not addressed
Incorporate follow-up plans	Insufficient will/lack of follow-through
Accomplish through a joint labor-management process	The resources needed to support change were not provided or sufficient

Source: The e-newsletter of the COPS Office, Volume 2, Issue 9, September 2009.

and units do not get involved to the extent necessary. The second method is implementation via a specialized unit that concentrates on problem solving and developing and maintaining **community partnerships**. It also results in many officers not being involved in community policing or buying into the concept. Also, Vito, Walsh, and Kunselman (2005) found that when community policing is implemented using specialized units, there is little communication between the community policing specialists and other officers, resulting in ineffectiveness and, in some cases, conflict. Reaves (2010) surveyed departments and found that 47 percent had full-time community policing officers, but only 15 percent of the responding agencies had specialized community policing units. Thus, only one-third of departments are using these separate units.

Regardless of the strategy used, police administrators must plan for implementation of community policing. Table 5.3 identifies eight steps in the change process that should occur or be approximated when implementing or bolstering a department's community policing efforts (Gaines, 1994). These steps provide an excellent framework to analyze community policing and to identify stumbling blocks to its successful implementation.

Table 5.3
Implementing Community Policing

Step 1—Performance Gap
Step 2—Recognizing a Need for Change
Step 3—Creating a Proper Climate for Change
Step 4—Diagnosing the Problem
Step 5—Identifying Alternative Strategies
Step 6—Selecting the Strategy
Step 7—Determining and Operationalizing Implementation Strategy
Step 8—Evaluating and Modifying the Strategy

Step 1—Performance Gap

Performance gap has caused a number of administrators to contemplate community policing projects. Basically, administrators come to realize that what the department is doing does not effectively address problems and needs. For example, police chiefs receive a great deal of pressure from politicians, other governmental agencies, news media, and people as to what the department should be accomplishing. The chief often uses this input to fashion an idea about where the department is in terms of performance. A performance gap, then, refers to a situation where the department's performance does not match the chief's organizational expectations, or where performance and expectations do not match community members' expectations.

It is extremely important that any performance gap be discussed with some level of specificity. It is not enough to state that crime is a problem or even that homicides are a problem. If homicides are a problem it must be learned where they are occurring, when, and who is involved. General or global discussions of problems fail to provide information about what direction should be taken, and they fail to completely legitimize the move toward community policing. When performance gaps are specified they provide more detail about where the department is and what its community policing program should look like.

Step 2—Recognizing a Need for Change

Realizing that the department is not meeting expectations does not necessarily mean that its administrators will support or introduce improvements or make changes. Police managers often realize that their agencies' performance falls short of optimal expectations or even minimum requirements, but they may still fail to act. Police administrators might rely on traditional, reactive responses to problems rather than attempting community policing. Here, the administrators attempt to improve what the department has always done. They tend to focus on service-delivery systems rather than problems or how effectively the service deals with the problem.

One other point needs to be made relative to recognizing the need for change. In many instances where community policing has been implemented, community situations have deteriorated to the point that radical intervention is absolutely necessary, and even then, it is not absolute that conditions can be drastically improved. In other words, a performance gap may exist, but the police administrator may feel that meaningful improvement is beyond the grasp of the department's capabilities. Are police departments likely to change their operational philosophy if it appears that they cannot succeed?

Step 3—Creating a Proper Climate for Change

Creating the proper climate relates to actions whereby administrators prepare and sell the change to departmental constituents and to people affected by the new program. Regarding departmental constituents, perceptions, values, and commitments must be changed throughout the chain of command. As Skogan (2004) notes, community policing often fails because of resistance from line officers, resistance by police managers, resistance by police unions, and resistance by specialized units. Skogan and Hartnett's (1997:74) study of community policing in Chicago found:

New management philosophies will rub salt in the wounds of those who rose to the top when the command-and-control idea was the rule of the day. In many cities, managers near the top of police organizations have mounted an effective rear-guard action against change, making life difficult for those under them who are caught in the cross-fire.

Not only must program participants such as CPOs be acclimated to the change, but all other members of the department must develop an understanding and commitment to community policing. For example, a patrol officer or a detective may not be directly involved in the community policing program, but he or she can contribute a great deal to assist or derail the program.

Herein lie a number of problems. First, as was pointed out previously, the traditional police value system is incongruent with the culture and value system required for community policing. A large part of the police officer's role, as espoused by police officers, most people, and many politicians alike, is law enforcement (Van Maanen, 2006; Sykes, 2006), and law enforcement has been the core police role for decades. It likely is very difficult to move a department's values, especially those of line police officers (Greene et al., 1994), to come in line with those required for community policing. It would be especially difficult in a large department since so many officers and units would be involved.

Second, when values are in fact changed, do the new values match program needs? We have never addressed the concept of preciseness in value transformation and alignment. There must be some degree of accuracy when changing values, and this issue seems to be omitted from previous experiences with community policing. In other words, we may be able to change officers and the department's culture and values, but can they be moved to where community policing and its various programs are fully accepted?

Third, is a change in values enough to equate to a change in actions? Organizations must be definitive when inducing responsive behaviors from organizational incumbents. Changing values is not definitive; there must be an announced change in departmental goals, reward-punishment systems, management, supervision, personnel practices, and leadership. Sparrow (1988) summarizes the extent to which change must be implemented,

> … movement of the most talented and promising personnel into the newly defined jobs; making it clear that the route to promotion lies within such jobs; disbanding those squads that embody and add weight to the traditional values; re-categorizing the crime statistics according to their effect on the community; redesigning the staff evaluation system to take account of contributions to the nature and quality of community

life; providing in-service training in problem-solving skills for veteran officers and managers; altering the nature of the training given to new recruits to include problem-solving skills; establishing new communication channels with other public services; and contracting for annual community surveys for a period of years.

A comprehensive, organization-wide change of this nature is extremely difficult. Some police departments have the freedom to make the changes that Sparrow suggests. Most police departments, however, are "rationally bound" (March & Simon, 1958) by civil service regulations, union contracts, political-governmental requirements and expectations, and people's expectations for traditional responses to crime. For example, a city human resources office dictates the structure and content of most police departments' performance-evaluation systems. It may be quite difficult to incorporate community policing facets within the performance-evaluation system.

Also, there is evidence that officers do not always enthusiastically accept community policing. Greene et al. (1994) examined the implementation of community policing in Philadelphia and found that the union was opposed to it. Lurigio and Skogan (1994) found officers in Chicago to be fairly ambivalent about the new tasks and responsibilities associated with community policing, and Lord (1996) found that officers in Charlotte-Mechlenburg County became stressed as a result of the implementation of community policing. Hoover (1992:23-24) in an assessment of community policing in Houston observed,

> … at least 80 percent of the patrol officers involved remain strong skeptics. Most are outright cynics. Command staff indicates that at best 20 percent of the officers who have been involved in the neighborhood-oriented patrol effort are supporters. Indeed, skeptical managers point out that the 20 percent support may well represent individuals who have decided that the politically correct way to get ahead in the organization is to support the initiatives of central administration. Keep in mind that these are not patrol officers who have merely received a one-hour orientation to community policing. They have had a great deal of training, have been in numerous discussion sessions on neighborhood-oriented patrol, and have been assigned to neighborhood-oriented patrol areas for a number of years.

Collectively, this research indicates that a number of stumbling blocks exist when community policing is implemented, and extraordinary efforts must be made to ensure that the proper climate exists. Creating the proper climate for a police department to move toward community policing may be very difficult, but it is possible. It requires a total commitment from the police chief and his or her staff. It also requires that they develop an implementation strategy that addresses every part of the department. As Skogan and his associates (2000:33) remark,

> Change can occur only if a department's top managers, as well as senior community leaders, supply leadership and a vision of where the organization is headed. Knowing what they are doing now has to be matched with a clear statement of what they want to be doing in the future. They have to clarify the extent to which community-oriented work is a central mission of the department and how all parts of the organization can contribute to the mission. It is important that senior managers try, every day, to do something to push the organization.

Step 4—Diagnosing the Problem

Police departments are complex organizations. It may be fairly easy to implement community policing in a small police department (Thurman & McGarrell, 2005), but the task is much more complicated for large departments (Silverman, 1995). When implementing a new strategy such as community policing, every officer and unit within the police department must be considered. What problems will exist during implementation? Which groups and individuals will have the greatest resistance to community policing? And most importantly, what should community policing look like or how should it operate? These are all questions that the implementer must address. Community policing should be considered a template of activities that will be over-laid and integrated with the existing police structure. Substantial thought must be given to make it fit. In the alternative, the structure must be changed to match the business of community policing.

Along these lines, Brown (1989:5) provides some guidance on how to proceed when implementing community policing. Actions that should prepare a department for community policing include:

- Breaking down barriers to change;

- Educating its leaders and rank-and-file members for community policing;

- Reassuring the rank-and-file members that the community policing concepts being adopted were not imported from outside the department but instead were an outgrowth of programs already in place; and

- Reducing the likelihood that members of the department would reject the concepts of community policing as "foreign" or not appropriate for the department and the community.

Step 5—Identifying Alternative Strategies

Basically there are two strategies for implementing community policing: piecemeal and comprehensive strategies (Gaines, 1994). The **comprehensive model** attempts to introduce community policing concepts and techniques throughout the department, while the piecemeal approach introduces them to a specialized unit charged with community policing throughout the community or a geographical area where they supplant traditional policing. When geographical implementation is used, it is usually assumed that ultimately it will be implemented throughout the community. The piecemeal approach is commonly used in large departments while the comprehensive approach is used in smaller agencies. It is difficult to drastically and quickly change large complex police departments, so an incremental method must sometimes be used.

Piecemeal implementation of community policing poses a particular problem to administrators. The personnel and units involved in the program may become isolated from the main body of personnel and units within the department. Toch and Grant (2004) used the term "innovative ghettos" to describe units that were out of the mainstream. In their worst form, such units become ridiculed, criticized, and undermined by other units and personnel. Administrators must maintain a balance between the CPOs and other personnel if community policing is to succeed.

How to implement community policing is only one part of the identification equation. The implementation of community policing is rooted in the rationale that the department is not reaching its fullest potential. This means that the community policing units and personnel must perform beyond that which was previously accomplished. This may be a tall order, especially for a program that encounters substantial resistance.

Step 6—Selecting the Strategy

Basically, the police executive must determine if implementation initially will be community-wide, or if it will be implemented piecemeal. If community policing is to be implemented piecemeal, will it be implemented in a geographical area, or will it be confined to a specialized unit that will apply its precepts throughout the community. There are a number of implications for each of these strategies, and the executive must carefully consider the ramifications of each before selecting. Once a strategy has been selected, the administrator must change the organizational structure to facilitate the implementation of community policing. It is virtually impossible to effectively implement community policing within a traditional, bureaucratic police structure.

Step 7—Determining and Operationalizing Implementation Strategy

Two points are relevant here regarding community policing. First, since community policing consists of a decentralized structure, it is most amenable to the development of a flexible, realistic implementation strategy. In many cases, line officers who are constantly involved in daily problems develop the best understanding for what needs to be done and how it should be done. Involvement of line police officers is one of the major advantages of community policing as a strategy. They can contribute to problem identification and solutions. They also can be on the forefront of developing community partnerships.

Second, community policing's benefit in this area is also its greatest liability. It is disadvantageous because it is less structured as compared to traditional arrangements. That is, when it is applied as a philosophy, as Goldstein (1990) and others have suggested, line police officers are not provided adequate guidance on how to respond to problems and how their decisions and actions interact with the activities of other departmental operations strategies. If community policing tactics are to be successful, they must be applied within a structured framework—but not necessarily a highly structured organization. In this situation, community policing becomes one of several tactics available to the administrator when confronting problems. This is especially true when the response to a problem goes beyond the capabilities of the individual officer who is attempting to resolve the problem.

When implementing community policing, it must have some level of preciseness so that officers and supervisors are able to understand what is expected of them. For example, Walsh (1995) found that a lack of support and understanding from patrol supervisors and officers; minimal managerial support; no job descriptions for community policing supervisors and CPOs; and no policy or directives regarding a community policing program tend to be major stumbling blocks for officers involved in community policing. Walsh's findings insinuate that implementation was rather haphazard in the department he studied. Administrators must have a thorough, comprehensive implementation plan if they are to successfully implement community policing.

Step 8—Evaluating and Modifying the Strategy

Whenever a program is implemented, there is a need to determine the program's impact on a problem, group of people, or geographical area. In other words, what happened when community policing was implemented? Were the results any different from police operational arrangements and outcomes prior to its implementation? Did community policing accomplish that which was expected? Once implemented, community policing must be evaluated to answer these questions.

There will always be a need to make adjustments or fine-tuning in a new program. One of the major errors that police administrators traditionally have made is to assume that their programs were properly and correctly implemented and that the programs were producing desired or anticipated results. Seldom is any new program implemented consistently with its implementation plans. Planners have specific ideas about the roles and responsibilities of people throughout the organization, but they often get shifted around and sometimes not performed at all. Once the program is in operation, seldom does it function according to expectations. Middle and upper management have the responsibility of monitoring and evaluating community policing once it is in place. They must identify any irregularities or problems and ensure that operational corrections are made.

Once community policing is implemented, administration must take measures to ensure that it becomes institutionalized. They must develop a reward and reinforcement structure that continuously encourages officers to use community policing. This means that promotional and performance evaluation criteria must be adjusted to emphasize community policing (Alpert, Flynn & Piquero, 2001). In-service and basic training curriculum must be altered to reflect the department's style of community policing. Supervisors must reinforce community policing as they provide direct supervision of officers. Elements opposed to it must be brought into the fold to accept it, isolated to prevent disruption, or removed from the agency. Management must do everything in its power to support and improve community policing. If this does not occur, it will very likely fail.

Table 5.4
Levels of Change for Community Policing

Level of intervention	Change issues anticipated	Community policing outcomes
Environmental →	Linkage with → External organizations and groups Political and economic support Define and maintain an organizational set	Reduced crime/fear Cohesive neighborhoods Increased public safety Greater public support Reduced hazard/violence Community problems solved
Organizational →	Technology → Structure Culture Human resources Effectiveness assessment	Change in information flow Decision making (strategic) Decision making (tactical) Improved training Changing symbols and culture Improved communications Revised performance measures Decentralization Role generalization Improved analysis
Group →	Performance norms → Group composition Interpersonal relations Task definition	Team cohesiveness Task consensus Quality decisions Group effectiveness
Individual →	Task identity → Autonomy Feedback Skills	Increased police officer effectiveness Increased performance Increased job satisfaction Broadened role definition Greater job attachment/ investment

Source: Greene, J. (2000). "Community Policing in America: Changing the Nature, Structure, and Function of the Police." In *Criminal Justice 2000, Volume 3, Policies, Processes, and Decisions of the Criminal Justice System,* p. 324. Washington, DC: National Institute of Justice.

Leadership in the Community Policing Department

Leadership is a critical ingredient when implementing, expanding, or sustaining community policing. Community policing is complicated and very different from traditional policing. Moreover, there are many members of a given police department who are resistant to community policing and change in general. Police administrators must demonstrate a high level of leadership if community policing is implemented correctly. **Leadership**, essentially, is the process of directing and influencing people or groups of people to achieve goals (Hitt, Miller & Colella, 2006). It is a process whereby the leaders, generally the chief and his or her staff, identify where the department should be in terms of activities and performance, and motivate subordinates to accomplish goals or the activities. Leadership is active; doing things as they have always been done is not leadership.

As noted above, many police departments still subscribe to the traditional, bureaucratic model of policing. Although they may have implemented some elements of community policing, they largely remain entrenched in the traditional management model. In order to be a community policing department, it must be implemented completely and throughout the department. This means that quite often a department's structure must be altered, managers and supervisors must develop new priorities and strategies, and officers must approach many aspects of the job differently. It entails that police executives have a vision and, through leadership, move the department toward that vision.

The most appropriate style of leadership when implementing and sustaining community policing is transformational leadership. **Transformational leadership** is a process to change direction. Gaines and Worrall (2012) advise that it is a process where "the leader attempts to broaden the interests and horizons of subordinates and move the organization in a new direction" (p. 173). Schermerhorn (2008) has identified the elements of transformational leadership. First, it requires that the leader have a vision. The vision must consist of a sense of direction; this direction must be communicated to the organization. Second, the leader must have charisma, or the ability to motivate and inspire others toward accomplishing objectives. Third, symbolism is important. Whether it is the creation of new units or commendations, the organization must have visible vestiges of the new direction—community policing. Fourth, subordinates must be empowered to become involved in the new strategy, including subordinate self-motivation as well as direction from top administrators. Fifth, there should be intellectual stimulation. Subordinates must begin to think positively about community policing via training and meetings. They must be challenged to become involved. Finally, the leader must have integrity. This means the leader must be open and honest about changes. Transformational leadership can change an organization. It is a broad-based leadership style that touches everyone and every aspect of the department.

Summary

Administrators have a tall order when deciding to implement community policing. For the most part, every element within the police department must be changed. It is not always easy to move a police department given history, size, and resistance to change. However, there is substantial evidence proving that traditional policing is not as effective as community policing. Therefore, there is ample justification for the effort.

The first step in successfully implementing community policing is to evaluate the department's organizational structure and make changes. Authority must be decentralized to the point that unit commanders, supervisors, and officers have the authority to solve the problems they confront. Police officers' responses to problems must not be confined to a limited number of options, but officers must have the discretion to decide on the best approach to a problem. Once officers are given the proper authority to make decisions, they must be held accountable for solving problems at the beat level. At the same time, commanders must be held accountable for resolving problems in district or precinct areas. It appears that total quality management is perhaps the best vehicle to accomplish this task.

Second, the department's values must be changed. Law enforcement and crook catching have always been at the core of the police role. Community policing dictates that the police must substantially expand their role to include problem solver and concerned community member. Police officers must be concerned with any situation or problem that causes people distress.

The police have a broad, overarching responsibility to attempt to improve the quality of life of the community's residents. The department's management structure should be fashioned so as to constantly reinforce these expanded responsibilities. As total quality management dictates, people must be considered as valued clients or customers and treated accordingly.

Third, internal processes in the department must be modified to reinforce community policing. This means that the selection process should emphasize selecting candidates who have a strong commitment to helping others. The training process should not only provide officers with the skills to be CPOs, but it should constantly reinforce its importance. Performance evaluations and promotion processes should focus on community policing attributes. Finally, the department's management and supervision processes should constantly reinforce community policing.

Fourth, the police must recognize that they cannot do it alone. The police must develop partnerships with community members, groups, and other governmental agencies. Alleviation of many community problems requires a cooperative effort among different groups of people. For example, when dealing with a drug or crime problem in public housing, the police must work with community leaders, public housing officials, social service agencies, and most importantly the residents to devise comprehensive solutions to very complex problems. The police working by themselves do not have the resources to effectively deal with the problem.

Police administrators have a key role to play in community policing. It is not an easy or simple matter to implement it. It requires everyone working together to change the department's course and move it toward a philosophy that provides people with a higher quality of service. Police administrators must be dedicated to this principle.

KEY TERMS IN CHAPTER 5

- active supervisors
- authority
- Chief's Advisory Committee
- classical organizational theory
- commander profile report
- community partnership
- comprehensive model
- COMPSTAT
- crime mapping report
- division of labor
- evaluating
- geographic focus

- leadership
- Max Weber
- neighborhood counsels
- organic organizations
- principle of hierarchy
- quality circles
- special committees
- strategic planning
- supervision
- territorial imperative
- transformational leadership
- unit meetings

DISCUSSION QUESTIONS

1. Describe the six principles of classical organizational theory and discuss whether or not they are relevant to policing today.
2. Define "organic organization" and discuss how it is more conducive to community policing than the military model.
3. Discuss the role of strategic planning in the implementation of community policing.
4. The authors identify eight steps in the change process that should occur or be approximated when implementing community policing. Discuss the four steps you consider to be the most important for any agency contemplating community policing.
5. Discuss the mechanisms available to police administrators that can enhance communication with the community.
6. What roles, if any, do organizational culture and police values play in attempts to implement community policing programs?
7. Describe COMPSTAT and identify its value to community policing efforts.
8. Describe the areas of focus necessary for implementing comprehensive change in a police department.
9. Discuss the role leadership plays in moving a department to community policing.

References

Alpert, G., Flynn, D., & Piquero, A. (2001). Effective Community Policing Performance Measures. *Justice Research and Policy, 3,* 79-94.

Braga, A., & Bond, B. (2008). Policing Crime and Disorder Hot Spots: A Randomized Controlled Trial. *Criminology, 46,* 577-607.

Braga, A., & Weisburd, D. (2010). *Policing Problem Places: Crime Hot Spots and Effective Prevention.* New York: Oxford University Press.

Braga, A., Weisburd, D., Waring, E., Green, L., Spellman, W., & Gajewski, F. (1999). Problem-Oriented Policing in Violent Crime Places: A Randomized Controlled Experiment. *Criminology, 37,* 541-580.

Brown, L. P. (1989). *Community Policing: A Practical Guide for Police Officers. Perspectives on Policing* (No. 12). Washington, DC: National Institute of Justice.

Buerger, M. E. (1998). Police Training as Pentecost: Using Tools Singularly Ill-Suited to the Purpose of Reform. *Police Quarterly, 1*(1), 27-64.

Burns, T., & Stalker, G. (1961). *The Management of Innovation.* London, England: Tavistock.

Cheurprakobkit, S. (2002). Community Policing: Training, Definitions, and Policy Implications. *Policing: An International Journal of Police Strategies & Management, 25*(4), 709-725.

Connors, E., & Webster, B. (2001). *Transforming the Law Enforcement Organization to Community Policing.* Alexandria, VA: Institute for Law and Justice.

DeJong, C., Mastrofski, S. D., & Parks, R. B. (2001). Patrol Officers and Problem Solving: An Application of Expectancy Theory. *Justice Quarterly, 18*(1), 1-62.

Eck, J., Gersh, J., & Taylor, C. (2000). Finding Hot Spots through Repeat Address Mapping. In V. Goldsmith, P. McGuire, J. Mollenkopf, & T. Ross (Eds.), *Crime Patterns: Frontiers of Practice.* Thousand Oaks, CA: Sage.

Engel, R. S. (2002). Patrol Officer Supervision in the Community Policing Era. *Journal of Criminal Justice, 30,* 51-64.

Gaines, L. K. (1994). Community-Oriented Policing: Management Issues, Concerns, and Problems. *Journal of Contemporary Criminal Justice, 10,* 17-35.

Gaines, L. K., & Kappeler, V. (2011). *Policing in America* (7th ed.). Waltham, MA: Anderson.

Gaines, L. K., & Worrall, J. (2012). *Police Administration* (3rd ed.). Clifton Park, NJ: Delmar-Cengage.

Goldstein, H. (1990). *Problem-Oriented Policing.* New York, NY: McGraw-Hill.

Greene, J., Bergman, W., & McLaughlin, E. (1994). Implementing Community Policing: Cultural and Structural Change in Police Organizations. In D. Rosenbaum (Ed.), *The Challenge of Community Policing: Testing the Promises* (pp. 92-109). Thousand Oaks, CA: Sage Publications.

Haarr, R. (2001). The Making of a Community Policing Officer: The Implact of Basic Training and Occupational Socialization on Police Recruits. *Police Quarterly, 4,* 402-433.

Henry, V. E. (2002). *The COMPSTAT Paradigm.* Flushing, NY: Looseleaf Law Publications.

Hitt, M., Miller, C., & Colella, A. (2006). *Organizational Behavior: A Strategic Approach.* New York: Wiley.

Hoover, L. (1992). Police Mission: An Era of Debate. In L. Hoover (Ed.), *Police Management: Issues and Perspectives.* Washington, DC: PERF.

Kane, R. (2000). Permanent Beat Assignments in Association with Community Policing: Assessing the Impact on Police Officers' Field Activity. *Justice Quarterly, 17*(2), 259-280.

Kappeler, V. E., & Potter, G. W. (2005). *The Mythology of Crime and Criminal Justice* (4th ed.). Prospect Heights, IL: Waveland Press.

King, W., & Lab, S. (2000). Crime Prevention, Community Policing, and Training: Old Wine in New Bottles. *Police Practice and Research, 1,* 241-252.

Kratcoski, P. C., & Noonan, S. B. (1995). An Assessment of Police Officers' Acceptance of Community Policing. In P. Kratcoski, & D. Dukes (Eds.), *Issues in Community Policing* (pp. 169-185). Cincinnati, OH: Anderson Publishing Co.

Lord, V. (1996). An Impact of Community Policing: Reported Stressors, Social Support, and Strain among Police Officers in a Changing Police Department. *Journal of Criminal Justice, 24*(6), 503-522.

Lurigio, A., & Skogan, W. (1994). Winning the Hearts and Minds of Police Officers: An Assessment of Staff Perceptions of Community Policing in Chicago. *Crime & Delinquency, 40*(3), 315-330.

Magers, J. (2004). COMPSTAT: A New Paradigm for Policing or a Repudiation of Community Policing? *Journal of Contemporary Criminal Justice, 20*, 70-79.

Maguire, E. R. (1997). Structural Change in Large Municipal Police Organizations during the Community Policing Era. *Justice Quarterly, 14*(3), 547-576.

March, S., & Simon, H. (1958). *Organizations*. New York, NY: John Wiley and Sons.

Morabito, M. (2010). Understanding Community Policing as an Innovation: Patterns of Adoption. *Crime & Delinquency, 56*, 564-587.

Parks, R. B., Mastrofski, S. D., DeJong, C., & Gray, M. K. (1999). How Officers Spend Their Time in the Community. *Justice Quarterly, 16*, 483-518.

Reaves, B. (2010). *Local Police Departments, 2007*. Washington, DC: Bureau of Justice Statistics.

Roth, J. (2000). *Evaluation of the COPS Program—Title 1 of the 1994 Crime Act*. Washington, DC: National Institute of Justice.

Schermerhorn, J. (2008). *Management*. New York: Wiley.

Sherman, L., & Rogan, D. (1995). Effects of Gun Seizures on Gun Violence: Hot Spots Patrol in Kansas City. *Justice Quarterly, 12*, 673-694.

Sherman, L., Gartin, P., & Buerger, M. (1989). Hot Spots of Predatory Crime: Routine Activities and the Criminology of Place. *Criminology, 27*, 27-56.

Silverman, E. B. (1995). Community Policing: The Implementation Gap. In P. Kratcoski, & D. Dukes (Eds.), *Issues in Community Policing* (pp. 35-47). Cincinnati, OH: Anderson Publishing Co.

Silverman, I. (1999). *NYPD Battles Crime: Innovative Strategies in Policing*. Boston, MA: Northeastern University Press.

Skogan, W. (2004). Community Policing: Common Impediments to Success. In L. Friddell, & M. Wycoff (Eds.), *Community Policing: Past, Present, and Future* (pp. 159-167). Washington, DC: Police Executive Research Forum.

Skogan, W. (2009). Concern about Crime and Confidence in the Police: Reasurance or Accountability? *Police Quarterly, 12*, 301-318.

Skogan, W. G., & Hartnett, S. M. (1997). *Community Policing, Chicago Style*. New York, NY: Oxford University Press.

Skogan, W. G., Hartnett, S., DuBois, J., Comey, J., Kaiser, M., & Lovig, J. (2000). *Problem Solving in Practice: Implementing Community Policing in Chicago.* Washington, DC: National Institute of Justice.

Skolnick, J. (1966). *Justice without Trial: Law Enforcement in a Democratic Society.* New York, NY: Wiley.

Sparrow, M. K. (1988). *Implementing Community Policing. Perspectives in Policing* (No. 9). Washington, DC: National Institute of Justice.

Steinheider, B., & Wuestawald, T. (2008). From the Bottom-up: Sharing Leadership in a Police Agency. *Police Practice and Research, 9,* 145-163.

Sykes, G. (2006). Street Justice: A Moral Defense of Order Maintenance Policing. In V. E. Kappeler (Ed.), *The Police & Society: Touch Stone Readings* (3rd ed.). Prospect Heights, IL: Waveland Press.

Thurman, Q. C., & McGarrell, E. F. (2005). *Community Policing in a Rural Setting* (2nd ed.). Cincinnati, OH: Anderson Publishing Co.

Toch, H., & Grant, J. D. (2004). *Police as Problem Solvers* (2nd ed.). New York, NY: Plenum Press.

Van Maanen, J. (2006). The Asshole. In V. E. Kappeler (Ed.), *The Police & Society: Touch Stone Readings* (3rd ed.). Prospect Heights, IL: Waveland Press.

Vito, G., Walsh, W., & Kunselman, J. (2005). Community Policing: The Middle Manager's Perspective. *Police Quarterly, 8,* 490-511.

Walsh, W. F. (1995). Analysis of the Police Supervisor's Role in Community Policing. In P. Kratcoski, & D. Dukes (Eds.), *Issues in Community Policing* (pp. 141-151). Cincinnati, OH: Anderson Publishing Co.

Weisburd, D., & Green, L. (1995). Policing Drug Hot Spots: The Jersey City MDA Experiment. *Justice Quarterly, 12,* 711-736.

Weisburd, D., Bushway, S., Lum, C., & Yang, S. (2004). Trajectories of Crime at Places: A Longitudinal Study of Street Segments in the City of Seattle. *Criminology, 42,* 283-322.

Weisburd, D., Maher, L., & Sherman, L. (1992). Contrasting Crime General and Crime Specific Theory: The Case of Hot Spost of Crime. *Advances in Criminological Theory, 4,* 45-69.

Weisburd, D., Mastrofski, S. D., McNally, A. M., Greenspan, R., & Willis, J. J. (2003). Reforming to Preserve: COMPSTAT and Strategic Problem Solving. *Criminology & Public Policy, 2*(3), 421-456.

Wilson, O. W., & McLaren, R. C. (1963). *Police Administration.* New York, NY: McGraw-Hill.

Zhao, J. (1996). *Why Police Organizations Change: A Study of Community-Oriented Policing.* Washington, DC: Police Executive Research Forum.

Zhao, J., Thurman, Q., & Lovrich, N. P. (1995). Community-Oriented Policing Across the US: Facilitators and Impediments to Implementation. *American Journal of Police, 14*(1), 11-28.

Laws, like the spider's web, catch the fly and let the hawk go free.

—Spanish Proverb

CHAPTER 6   Community Policing and Crime

Challenges to Traditional Crime Control

Since the police reform movement of the 1930s, the primary job of the public police has narrowed to that of crime-fighter. While the merit of paring down the police role to this narrow yardstick is debatable, the presence and absence of crime has been an occupational standard against which police programs were measured. Indeed, part of the impetus for finding new ways of policing stemmed from the failure of traditional policing to meet the challenge posed by the explosion of crime in the 1960s. Although criminal victimization has generally declined over the past 25 years (Kappeler & Potter, 2005), rates of serious crime in this country are far higher than for other Western, industrialized nations. Crime has become a media mainstay, and it has emerged as one of the top issues in every presidential campaign of the past three decades. Media-generated fear of crime, public pressure to find new ways to "combat" crime, and the failure of the traditional policing model helped persuade police to experiment with new ideas, including community policing.

Though supporters of community policing can point to data that suggest that the movement has at least contributed to the recent decline in crime rates (Kelling, 1997), it is also beneficial to remember Mark Twain's (1972:925) warning that there are three kinds of lies—"lies, damn lies, and statistics." It should be remembered that the professionalization movement in policing was predicated on the assertion that police could control crime and that crime fighting was their mandate (Manning, 2006). People wanted the police to be accountable for their performance and police officials actively took responsibility for crime control as part of their professional mandate. As Alpert and Moore (1993:110) observed, "Citizens and their elected representatives have long sought a bottom line to measure police performance. The goals have been to reassure the public that hard-earned tax dollars were being spent to achieve important results and to hold police managers accountable for improving organizational performance. As police agencies matured, four generally accepted accounting practices became enshrined as the key measures to evaluate police performance. These include: (1) reported crime rates (2) overall arrests (3) clearance rates (4) response times." It then followed that these should be the measures of police performance and the idea became institutionalized. The **professional model**, however, had little direct impact on crime rates even after millions of federal dollars were poured into crime-fighting programs.

In the 1990s, as the nation's crime rates were falling, unemployment was declining, and the country bounced back from recession and moved into one of the longest and most significant economic expansions ever experienced. At the same time as well, the percentage of the population in its most crime-prone teenage years was falling, as the last of the baby boomers matured and significant changes occurred in the American youth culture. Another obvious factor is that there has been a tremendous increase in private policing activities. The number of privately employed security personnel now far exceeds the number of public police officers. Some have effectively argued that the police institution's move from the language of crime fighting to that of service was, at least in part, a consequence of this private challenge to the crime-fighting mandate (Manning, 2006a). There has also been an explosion in the punitiveness of American society. From 1972 to 2002 this country has increased its incarceration rate by more than 500 percent (Kappeler & Potter, 2005:317).

In 2006, more than 7.2 million Americans were under some form of correctional supervision (BJS, 2007;2007a). The police are currently making more arrests than at any other time in American history (Sourcebook, 2007). In 2006, police arrested more than 10 million people (Sourcebook, 2007). Of course this is not to suggest that arrest and incarceration have an appreciable impact on serious crime rates because the majority of the increase in the prison population came from the incarceration of relatively minor drug offenders, rather than the serious offenders on which the media and the public seem to focus (Kappeler & Potter, 2005). Yet, the United States leads all other industrialized nations in both crime rates and the number of people under control of the criminal justice system.

In a complex society undergoing rapid and constant change, there are simply too many variables to be able to determine, with any certainty, how much of a role any single factor may play in the rise and fall of overall crime rates. Unlike in a controlled lab experiment, studying changes in the world at large depends on how wisely the researchers choose which factors they will examine. After all, during that same period, there were also dramatic increases in the number of coronary bypasses performed, as well as in the number of compact disc players purchased, yet few would argue these changes made any difference in overall crime rates. Another related problem in determining whether a particular social intervention affects crime is that of philosophy and measurement. Social scientists tend to focus on short-term interventions like crime prevention programs and police tactics and measure outcomes in terms of existing measurements and data that are readily available and easy to collect. When a major philosophical change occurs in a social institution that promises long-term intervention, new measurement instruments must be created and new data collected. Dennis P. Rosenbaum (1996:408) has remarked, "Nearly all of the evaluation research on collective anti-crime strategies focuses on **opportunity-reduction** activities (i.e., 'victimization prevention' behaviors and programs). At present we know little about the effectiveness of neighborhood-based strategies that focus on social problems …."At least for a time, we must rely on logic and reason to determine which changes hold the greatest promise of making a significant impact on crime.

Police Measures of Crime—What Do We Know?

The answer to how much crime exists in the United States is simple—no one knows. At best, indicators such as the **Uniform Crime Reports** (UCR) statistics compiled by the FBI show trends, but they do not provide a true picture of the crimes actually committed at any specific time. Even when the police are notified, changes in reporting procedures, complications, and manipulations of the reporting system make the rates suspect. The UCR really tells us more about police practices than about crime. We do know, however, that police accounting practices and politics affect crime rates (Kappeler & Potter, 2005). Victor G. Strecher (1997:72-73) summarizes the findings of the Crime Reporting Audit in St. Louis in the following passage.

> This program was tested in the early 1960s; its purpose was to assure the accuracy of crime reporting. Certain dispatches were thought to be downgraded (for example, burglary to larceny, aggravated to simple assault) by reporting officers under pressure from district commanders to keep crime rates low.... Initially it was found that numerous calls were, in fact, being downgraded—in some cases improperly classified as "unfounded" reports. These inspection findings were given to field operations command for correction after each audit. In time it found that the proportion of calls being downgraded was equaled by those being upgraded (both now small numbers) to the disadvantage of the reporting unit. After this audit, it was thought the limits of accurate reporting had been reached. It was thought, however, that continued audits were necessary to assure the accuracy of crime reporting, given the pressures upon district commanders to keep crime rates low.

The problem of distortions in crime reporting is not merely a problem of the 1960s. Since the creation of the UCR, and even today, many police departments are involved in the distortion of crime rates. Skogan and Hartnett (1997) noted that in the 1980s investigative reporters uncovered that members of the Chicago Police Department "killed crime" by fraudulently rejecting reports to keep detectives' loads low (see Skogan & Gordon, 1982). While one can argue that the more serious the crime, the more reliable the figures, all suffer distortion. We assume that murder rates are the most accurate of all, since people are very likely to report the discovery of a dead body to the police. Yet even in this case, no one knows for sure how many people are murder victims. When figures for even this most serious of crimes cannot be considered complete, the less serious the crime, the more likely that the statistics should be considered highly suspect as an indicator of what is happening in the real world.

An important issue beyond mere numbers concerns which crimes we consider the most serious, as a society and as individuals. The **UCR** data focuses on eight so-called **Part I Index** or "serious" crimes—four violent crimes (murder, rape, robbery, aggravated assault) and four property crimes (burglary, larceny/

theft, motor vehicle theft, arson). While it might seem that everyone would agree that these are the crimes that deserve the greatest attention—and nearly all countries in the world define these crimes as top priorities—they do not reflect the comparative harm caused by criminality.

Using murder as an example, the Federal Bureau of Investigation figures show there are about 17,000 murders committed in the United States each year (FBI, 2007), but there are also about 42,600 traffic-related deaths every year, and more than 41 percent involve alcohol (NTSI, 2007). Though a direct comparison of both problems ignores obvious difficulties, the realization that drunk driving kills as many people each year as are murdered in this country has made us rethink our priorities. Research on the ability of the police institution to curtail drunk driving finds two serious and surprising barriers to effectively reducing this behavior. First, police officers have traditionally viewed drunk driving as a non-serious crime, and officers in many departments have been reluctant to take enforcement actions (Mastrofski & Ritti, 1992). Second, despite training, a growing public concern about drunk driving, and a change in police attitudes toward drunk driving, many police departments do not provide officers a structured work environment from which to take enforcement action (Mastrofski & Ritti, 1996). In essence, even when officers' attitudes are changed and training in drunk driving enforcement is provided, if answering calls for service is a department's first priority and if a department continues to place a greater value on other police activities, very little progress toward solving this problem takes place. These observations reflect the reality that what we define as serious crime changes over time, and that there is a relationship between how officers view police work and how police departments structure police activities and the ability to address crime-related problems. Crime and policing must be considered in a social and organizational context.

While monitoring trends for Part I crimes over time provides a blurry snapshot of what the police are doing and what people are reporting, the picture remains incomplete. Prior to the Sullivan Act, for example, narcotics were legal, whereas today, drug arrests constitute a significant percentage of all arrests made by the police. Manufacturing, selling, and consuming alcohol were illegal acts under Prohibition, but since Repeal, the police role has been narrowed primarily to controlling open drinking, public drunkenness, drunk driving, and problems with underage drinking. Thirty years ago, the crime of child abuse received relatively little attention, but now claims-makers argue that 2.9 million cases of abuse occur each year (Brott, 1995). The real number is closer to 350,000 (Potter & Kappeler, 2006). Yet, since the early 1970s, the number of unsubstantiated claims of child abuse has almost doubled, making questionable claims of abuse greater than founded claims (Kappeler & Potter, 2005).

Likewise, in the 1970s and 1980s, many states decriminalized **status offenses** (acts by juveniles, such as violating curfew or running away, that would not be considered crimes if committed by an adult), but by 1997, well over 75 of the largest 200 American cities had reenacted or created rigid curfew laws designed to address the public's fear of juvenile crime, which means because of sensational media reporting and a failure to understand the realities of juvenile crime, the pendulum began to swing back.

Certain ideas about crime seem to go in and out of fashion, as our knowledge, sensibilities, and media focus change over time. For example, not only is increasing attention now paid to all rapes, but within the past few years, date rape has been more clearly defined as an offense that victims should report to the police for prosecution. Additionally, sensational media reporting and an attempt by political leaders to appease a fearful public have created new crimes like stalking and carjacking (see Kappeler & Potter, 2005). Advances in technology and changes in business practices have also spawned new categories of crime. Prior to the widespread use of computers, unleashing a computer virus could not have been a crime. This country's increasingly complicated financial system has unleashed new variants of white-collar crime, including electronic embezzlement of funds and new wrinkles in stock manipulations. While street crime is estimated to cost Americans between $10 billion and $13.5 billion a year, white-collar crime is estimated to cost between $400 billion and $500 billion annually (Coleman, 1994; Clinard & Yeager, 1980; see Kappeler & Potter, 2005:150). Yet, local police play a very small role in the detection, investigation, and prosecution of white-collar crime. This is no accident; the crime on which we focus is a complex web of knowledge, politics, and power.

Perhaps if we look at an extreme example we can begin to understand the comparative nature of crime as well as its context and consequences. In an elegant analysis comparing the impact of bank robberies versus stolen bikes, Edmonton (Canada) police inspector Chris Braiden questioned whether police are out of touch with the wants and needs of average people. His study showed that in a single year, 1,069 banks in Canada were robbed, with total losses of $2.8 million. Because of the importance of the crime and because such losses are typically recoverable by insurance or tax write-offs, bank robberies are almost always reported to the police.

In contrast, that same year, 182,000 bikes were reported stolen. Since the reporting rate for bicycle thefts is only 29 percent, Braiden conservatively calculated that these crimes cost Canadians $45 million that year. Comparing the two crimes shows that bicycle thefts involve roughly 100 times as many victims as bank thefts, with 15 times the dollar loss (Braiden, 1987). Yet he notes that when a bank robbery occurs, every available officer responds. When a bike is stolen, many departments will not even send an officer to investigate—instead they ask for a report over the phone.

Braiden's point is not that the police pay too much attention to bank robberies, but that they pay far too little to so-called petty crimes. This does not mean that a fleet of squad cars should come screaming to the scene of a bike theft, sirens blaring, but that the police must have a strategy that allows them to monitor and play a role in dealing with such offenses. In fact, such exaggerations have been used to rhetorically support police focus on street crime and support the traditional crime control model (see Klockars, 1999). Far too many police officers think they are wasting time on finding the person who steals a bike; too many police organizations feel that they have no role to play in addressing white-collar crime because they feel that this detracts from the important job of catching bank robbers.

It is easy to understand the justification for relegating widespread but relatively trivial crimes to lesser status. Compared to an armed bank robbery, a bicycle theft does seem petty—except to the victim. In our quest for justice, we have tried to fashion a criminal justice system where the greatest resources are concentrated on what appear to be the more serious threats, but appearances are deceptive. We have put more resource into the war on drugs than all the murders and acts of domestic violence combined, not to mention the "war on terrorism." The danger is that police departments can lose touch with average people and become indifferent to their valid concerns, and petty and white-collar crimes affect far more people than so-called serious street crime.

While the next chapter deals in greater depth with the problem of fear of crime, any discussion of crime must include recognition of how the threat of victimization affects people. We expect the police to do all they can to protect us. We understand, intellectually, that if a serial killer is on the loose, the police department must shift resources from other services to help protect us from that threat, even though relatively few people are actually at greater risk, and most police departments and communities will never have to deal with a serial killer (see Kappeler & Potter, 2005). Yet in the media's presentation of crime and in the minds of many traditional crime-fighters these seem to be the "real" problems communities face.

While the media and the police community bombard the public with national crime statistics, an average person on the street probably has no idea what the ups and downs in the statistics show about the crime rate in their neighborhood. But when the woman across the street returns home for the second time in six months to find the TV stolen or when a stream of late-night visitors frequent an increasingly dilapidated house two doors down, she may have good reason to fear that her personal risk of victimization is increasing. It is not the serial killer or the bank robber that haunts her walk. Those incidents may not individually or collectively make a noticeable difference in the crime statistics, and even the most sophisticated crime analysis may not identify a trend, but someone attuned to life in that neighborhood knows problems are brewing.

To understand more clearly the special niche that community policing fills, it is important first to understand how traditional policing confronts the entire matrix of crime. Only then can we assess the impact community policing makes.

The Traditional Police Effort

Proponents of the traditional model of crime control and supporters of some of the more modern forms of crime prevention argue, based on a **deterrence** philosophy, that there are three times when police action can influence crime:

- Police action can prevent a crime from occurring;

- Police intervention during the commission of a crime can influence the outcome; and

- Police efforts after the crime has occurred can resolve the situation, ideally by solving the crime, arresting the perpetrator, and, in appropriate cases, restoring stolen property.

Traditional police efforts rely primarily on **motor patrol** as the first line of offense and defense. Special units, high-tech gadgets, sophisticated lab analyses, and investigative follow-up are all designed to complement the use of motor patrol as the primary tactics in the traditional police model of fighting crime. Yet even a cursory examination of this approach demonstrates serious shortcomings in how traditional policing approaches crime:

Prevention: The rationale for having motor patrol officers cruise streets on free patrol is that their visible presence in the community should act as a deterrent to crime. It was thought that criminals would refrain from the commission of crimes by the mere presence of a police car or by creating the illusion that there was a significant chance that the criminally minded would be caught by the police should they attempt a crime. Yet, few research studies support the assertion that traditional random motor patrol is effective in these regards.

The controversial **Kansas City Preventive Patrol study** divided the South Patrol Division's 15 districts into three kinds of beats. In five reactive-only beats, routine preventive patrol was eliminated entirely; patrol cars were dispatched only when calls for service were received. In the five control beats, routine preventive patrol remained at the standard one-car-per-beat ratio. In the five proactive beats, the intensity of routine preventive patrol was increased by doubling or tripling the normal ratio.

The results of the Kansas City Preventive Patrol study had profound implications for the efficacy of the traditional crime control model. Among the findings:

- Rates of crimes reported showed no difference among the beats;

- Victimization studies showed the proactive approach made no discernible impact on the number of burglaries, auto thefts, larcenies involving auto accessories, robberies, or vandalism—the kinds of crimes considered to be most susceptible to deterrence through preventive motor patrol;

- People's attitudes toward police showed few consistent differences and no apparent pattern across the three different types of beats;

- Fear of crime did not decline;

- People's satisfaction with police did not improve in the experimental areas; and

- Experimental conditions showed no effect on police response times or satisfaction with response times (Kelling et a., 1974).

The Kansas City study raised serious debate and controversy. Some have even argued that the findings of the study have been misinterpreted to mean that all forms of patrol have no impact on crime. Obviously such an interpretation is open to question. The study does, however, raise concerns about random motor patrol's immediate ability to prevent crime by its mere presence. It also shows people's satisfaction does not appear to depend on how often they see a patrol car—not only did satisfaction not rise in the beats where patrols were doubled, but it did not decline in areas where officers only responded to calls. The assumption was that random motor patrol would provide short-term prevention, while the addition of crime prevention units would address the need for longer-term, educational efforts. In part because of the finding of the study, others have reframed the basic question about motor patrol to focus on the more important issue of how police spend their time and how patrol activities can be restructured to be more effective in crime prevention (Krajick, 1980; Wilson & McLaren, 1977).

SPOTLIGHT ON COMMUNITY POLICING PRACTICE

Community Policing Success Story: Macon, Georgia, Police Department

Law enforcement agencies of all sizes are under a tremendous amount of pressure to reduce their budgets and expenses, thereby being forced to do more with less these days. However, they must still maintain adequate staffing levels to meet the public's demand for policing services within their jurisdiction. As a result, law enforcement agencies must develop new and innovative ways of policing to ensure that police response time is sufficient, and that the efforts of community-oriented policing are continually focused on building community partnerships, engaging in problem solving, and promoting organizational transformation.

The Macon Police Department, located in Macon, Georgia, has heightened its community policing efforts in order to advance public safety in the city's downtown area, which is a very high-traffic and high-pedestrian area. To enhance the police presence in this area, the Macon Police Department decided to relocate its Bike Patrol Office from Martin Luther King, Jr. Boulevard to the heart of downtown, instead of increasing its police force for this purpose.

The Bike Patrol Office is currently located in a former ice cream shop—the site that was agreed upon during an informal "stroll and search" for downtown office space following a brainstorming session on how the law enforcement agency could enhance police presence downtown. The agency developed strong partnerships for its new downtown Bike Patrol Office, some of whom include Dempsey, New Town Macon, Main Street Project, and Macon Arts Alliance.

The Bike Patrol Office is adorned with an array of local eclectic art donated by Macon Arts Alliance. Longtime police Sgt. Greg Jefcoats, of the Macon Police Department, revamped the former ice cream shop and took pride in crafting a pleasant workplace for his fellow officers. His creativity was a key to cost savings, most notably restoring a dilapidated 8-foot storage unit—which had a cotton candy pink top—into a handsome counter using mahogany floorboards. From start to finish of the Bike Patrol Office rehabilitation, the Macon Police Department spent only about $500 on construction costs. Sgt. Jefcoats' efforts, and the involvement of and kind contributions from others, including private donors, have created a well-furnished, attractive, and pleasant place to work and receive visitors as well as a venue for displaying eclectic public art.

The generosity and friendship extended by those at the helm of their partnership organizations have enabled the Macon Police Department to take downtown law enforcement to a new level, by creating a community-friendly and inviting place where community members and visitors can interface with law enforcement practitioners in a non-traditional manner. The relocation of the Bike Patrol Office has been critical to the security of downtown and serves as a reminder that downtown Macon will continue to be a safe place to work, live, eat, shop, and tour. In fact, on the weekend, the Bike Patrol Office is staffed with local ambassadors who are trained by the Macon-Bibb Convention and Visitors Bureau to provide visitors and locals with timely information on what to do and where to eat, shop, and stay. They also field public concerns.

Source: The e-newsletter of the COPS Office, Volume 4, Issue 7, July 2011.

Perhaps Victor Strecher (1997:17-18) said it best in his advice to police executives: "Forget the time-honored but mistaken imagery of an omnipresent 'patrol blanket' over the entire jurisdiction. There is no blanket. There has never been a blanket. From the time of its enunciation by Vollmer, it has been an illusory doctrine which in recent years has revealed vast holes in its fabric."

Crimes in Progress: In theory, this is the area where motor patrol's ability to provide a **rapid response** should make its greatest contribution to reducing and controlling crime, but another study done on Kansas City raised troubling concerns. It showed that response time was unrelated to the probability of making an arrest or locating a witness for serious crime. Success or failure depended less on how fast the officer arrived and more on how quickly the person reported the crime. Other research confirms this conclusion. Most of the criminal or serious calls to the police are "cold," where the perpetrator has long absconded, or the victim waits an inordinately long period of time before calling the police. A national study of response times showed that approximately 75 percent of serious crimes were cold when the person notified the police (Spelman & Brown, 1984). Delays in calling the police are attributable to:

- apathy;

- skepticism about the police's ability to do anything;

- notifying other persons before calling the police;

- shame over victimization;

- trauma following a victimization; and

- fear of the police.

It seems people wait at least five minutes before calling the police in about one-half of the serious crimes that are reported. These studies clearly indicate that rapid response does not contribute to increased apprehensions in the majority of crimes. A second consideration with rapid response is the perception of police effectiveness. Untimely delays for a police response do cause dissatisfaction with the police (Percy, 1980; Pate, Ferrara, Bowers & Lorence, 1976). However, this dissatisfaction can be reduced and controlled through proper police communications procedures. In most cases, discontent is the result of the police response being slower than that which the police dispatcher indicated or led people to expect. "In short, we have focused on using high-technology dispatching equipment and sophisticated deployment schemes to reduce police response time, when we should also have focused on reducing citizen delays"

(Larson & Cahn, 1985) and informing people about police responses. Research confirms that rapid response led to response-related arrests for Part I crimes in only three percent of calls (Kelling, 1981).

Resolving Crimes Already Committed: Traditional police efforts after the crime has occurred include both motor patrol and investigation. Again, the rationale for relying primarily on motor patrol's quick response is based on the assumption that the officers can therefore do a better job of preserving evidence and locating witnesses. After this initial assessment, many departments then assign investigators to follow up further. Criminal investigators, however, don't have a very good track record in solving crime already committed. The RAND study of the criminal investigation process (Greenwood & Petersilia, 1975) cast serious doubt on one of the basic planks in the traditional crime control model. Victor Strecher (1997:73-74) extracted and summarized the major findings of the study in the following list:

- On investigative effectiveness: Differences in investigative training, staffing, workload, and procedures appear to have no appreciable effect on crime, arrest, or clearance rates;

- The method by which police investigators are organized (team policing, specialists vs. generalists, patrolmen investigators) cannot be related to variations in crime, arrest, and clearance rates;

- On the use of investigators' time: Substantially more than one-half of all serious reported crimes receive no more than superficial attention from investigators;

- [A]n investigator's time is largely consumed in reviewing reports, documenting files, and attempting to locate and interview victims on cases that experience shows will not be solved. For cases that are solved … an investigator spends more time in post-clearance processing than … identifying the perpetrator;

- On how cases are solved: The single most important determinant of whether or not a case will be solved is the information the victim supplies to the immediately responding patrol officer. If information that uniquely identifies the perpetrator is not presented at the time the crime is reported, the perpetrator, by and large, will not be subsequently identified;

- On how cases are solved: Of those cases that are ultimately cleared but in which the perpetrator is not identifiable at the time of the initial police incident report, almost all are cleared as a result of routine police procedures (that is, additional information obtained while investigating other cases, or fortuitous results of traffic stops and field interviews, such as Timothy McVeigh being stopped for a traffic violation);

- On collecting physical evidence: Most police departments collect more physical evidence than can be productively processed.... [A]llocating more resources to increasing the processing capabilities of the department can lead to more identifications than some other investigative actions;

- On the use of physical evidence: Latent fingerprints rarely provide the only basis for identifying a suspect;

- On investigative thoroughness: In relatively few departments do investigators consistently and thoroughly document the key evidentiary facts that reasonably assure that the prosecutor can obtain a conviction on the most serious applicable charges;

- On investigative thoroughness: Police failure to document a case investigation thoroughly may have contributed to a higher case dismissal rate and a weakening of the prosecutor's plea bargaining position;

- On relations between victims and police: Crime victims in general strongly desire to be notified officially as to whether or not the police have "solved" their case, and what progress has been made toward convicting the suspect after his arrest; and

- On investigative organization and procedure: Investigative strike forces have a significant potential to increase arrest rates for a few difficult target offenses, provided they remain concentrated on activities for which they are uniquely qualified; in practice, however, they are frequently diverted elsewhere.

Subsequent research supports the RAND study's findings with a somewhat more positive twist. Eck (1983), upon attempting to refine our understanding of the investigative process, concluded that there were three categories of cases facing investigators: weak cases that cannot be solved regardless of investigative effort (unsolvable cases); cases with moderate levels of evidence that can be solved with considerable investigative effort (solvable cases); and cases with strong evidence that can be solved with minimum effort (already solved cases). Eck found that cases within the "already solved" category did not require additional investigative effort or time, and the "unsolvable cases" should not be investigated because it would be wasted effort. Eck concluded that detectives should be assigned the "solvable cases." Such cases had the potential to be solved and they required additional effort. Brandl and Frank (1994) examined a number of burglary and robbery cases relative to Eck's triage of cases and found that cases with moderate levels of evidence could be successfully investigated. Thus, contrary to the RAND study, criminal investigations can have positive results, but investigators must focus on only those cases that tend to solve themselves.

Traditional motor patrol efforts have little discernible impact on preventing crime, very rarely do they thwart crimes in progress, and they accomplish less than people hope for in resolving crimes after the fact. These findings are offered as an effort to understand the structural limitations of a basically reactive response. Alpert and Moore's (1993:112) consideration of the traditional crime control strategy concluded that "enthusiasm for this strategy of professional policing has waned. The professional policing model has been ineffective in reducing crime, reducing citizens' fears, and satisfying victims that justice is being done. Indeed, … a majority of the population believes that the crime problem has become progressively worse during the past decade. Similarly, citizens have lost confidence in the criminal justice system to protect them" (citations omitted).

SPOTLIGHT ON COMMUNITY POLICING PRACTICE

The Role of Traditional Policing in Community Policing

Traditionally, police organizations have responded to crime after it occurs and, therefore, are structured to support routine patrol, rapid response to calls for service, arrests, and follow-up investigation. Community policing calls for a more strategic and thoughtful incorporation of these aspects of police business into an overall broader police mission focused on the proactive prevention of crime and disorder.

Routine Patrol

Community policing advocates for the strategic application of routine patrol that is conducted with an eye toward desired outcomes. Rather than just conducting routine patrol because "that is how we have always done it," routine patrol should be part of comprehensive problem-reduction and community outreach strategies. Routine patrol, for example, may be used specifically to increase police visibility to reduce fear of crime; or preventive patrol may be increased in a particular hot-spot neighborhood as part of a larger comprehensive crime-reduction strategy.

Rapid Response to Calls for Service

Community policing advocates for the strategic application of rapid response. For the vast majority of police calls for service, decreases in response times do not increase the chances of arrest or prevent harm to victims. Community policing encourages the police and the public to determine how rapid a response is necessary based on the nature of the call for service and to align expectations to match these policies. Community policing also encourages the police to increase the means by which citizens are able to report incidents such as through online reporting systems or the use of trained volunteers who take police reports. These efforts should increase the time available to focus on the development of strategic responses to crime problems.

Arrests

It is well-known to police practitioners and police scholars that the police can seldom arrest their way out of crime and social-disorder problems. Although arrests will always be a vital and important function of the police, arrests alone generally are not an effective or efficient way to develop long-term solutions to crime problems, particularly considering that the vast majority of offenses do not result in arrest. Community policing views arrests as one potential response among many available to the police. Part of the proposed solution to any serious public safety problem likely involves arresting offenders (particularly targeting high-volume repeat offenders). For police activity to bring about long-term solutions to crime and disorder problems, however, a wider variety of responses that limit criminal opportunities and access to victims and decrease the crime-generating features of particular geographic places are typically necessary.

Investigations

Conducting investigations (large and small) will always be central to the police mission. Community policing encourages agencies to have strong investigative functions in order to solve crimes, and also asks law enforcement to enhance the value of these investigations by linking them to broader problem-solving activities. Community policing calls both for full-time investigators and for individual officers who take incident reports to gather and share information to inform crime-prevention efforts. Investigations of thefts from construction sites, for example, can be enhanced by including information about building completion, the names of builders, the status of surrounding buildings, or the security level of the site. Investigations of known gang members and gang affiliations can feed efforts to understand gang relationships that can be used to inform comprehensive gang-reduction strategies. Information gathered through sound investigative techniques can serve as a vital resource to feed problem analysis efforts designed to develop lasting solutions to problems.

(Continued)

Law Enforcement Information Sharing

Finally, traditional policing has generally emphasized the role of partnerships and information sharing with other law enforcement entities at the state, local, and federal level. Information about known or suspected offenders is often shared. Community policing advocates for a broader flow of information between law enforcement agencies regarding potentially effective solutions to crime and disorder problems and crime trends and patterns. It also calls for police to broaden the array of potential partnerships beyond other law enforcement entities to include nonprofits, businesses, non-law enforcement government agencies, individual community members, and the media. Moreover, these partnerships should involve more than the sharing of crime or other relevant information with these groups, but rather should be focused on developing proactive long-term solutions to problems that are of concern to citizens.

Conclusion

Traditional policing activities are at the core of most police departments. These activities are not at odds with community policing; rather, community policing calls for a slightly different perspective. Slight modifications and changes in perspective regarding traditional policing activities can make a significant contribution toward advancing the community policing philosophy and thereby increase the capacity of police agencies to deliver fair, effective, and efficient police services.

Matthew Scheider
Assistant Director
The COPS Office

Source: The e-newsletter of the COPS Office, Volume 1, Issue 3, March 2008.

Let us step back from the research for a moment and put a human face on the consequences of a reactive policing model. Perhaps as early as 1964, there were ominous warnings that the traditional police approach, with its focus on reacting to calls for service, would prove unable to control serious crime. That was the year that Kitty Genovese was mugged and murdered in New York. Though she screamed for help for half an hour as her attackers stabbed and beat her, none of those 38 middle-class neighbors who heard her cries called the police. In a series of articles in the *New York Times,* some of those neighbors said they were too afraid to get involved, while others said they simply did not consider the problem any of their business—that it was a problem for the police to handle, not them (Goulden, 1989).

Some commentators tried to write off the incident as peculiar to New York City, but the case raised serious concerns that something had gone severely wrong with the relationship between people and the police and also that something was seriously wrong with the system. The traditional approach relies on that all-important call for service before the police can spring into action. The millions of dollars spent each year recruiting and training top-notch officers and equipping them with the latest technology ultimately relies on persuading just one person to lift up the phone.

What the Genovese case did was demonstrate that the police, often through the media and political commentary, had oversold themselves as society's **crime-fighters**, to the degree that people wanted to believe they could delegate all responsibility to police professionals—that crime was not their responsibility and getting involved was too risky. That famous case also vividly brought home the depth of the estrangement between people and their police. None of those people in Queens apparently saw the police as trusted friends who could protect them, but as nameless and faceless strangers that they dared not count on. Of course, the New York City police have done much historically to foster this public perception (see Kappeler, Sluder & Alpert, 1998). This incident brought into stark reality the terrifying prospect that the alienation between people and their police was so profound that no one was safe. It drove home the point that a society in which people are not part of the policing process cannot expect to control serious crime, and that police had to find better ways to involve people in efforts to police themselves.

The Dynamics of Serious Crime

To understand the special contribution that community policing can make in extending the overall impact of the police, we will examine the most heinous crime, murder, to show how community policing augments motor patrol's attempts to prevent, thwart, or solve this crime. Homicide (including murder, non-negligent manslaughter, and negligent manslaughter)—is often a crime of passion or profit. In more than 50 percent of the cases of known murders, the victim knew or was related to the killer. While TV dramas perpetuate the image of psychopathic killers roaming the country, picking off victims at random; the drive-by shooting of some innocent by a violent gang member; and the would-be terrorist obsessed with bombing some target (Kappeler & Potter, 2005), the vast majority of murders committed in the United States stem from the escalation of domestic quarrels, arguments between friends or acquaintances, or battles that result from intoxication or those that erupt from conflicts about drugs and drug profits.

Murder can be premeditated or impulsive, but, in either case, the police face obvious limits on their ability to make a difference. Murder of and attacks on political figures like Martin L. King, Ronald Reagan, and Robert Kennedy demonstrate the difficulty of preventing serious crimes. As the murder of President Kennedy—and then his alleged killer—affirmed, even being encircled by police is not always enough to prevent premeditated murder. In impulsive murders that occur when a robbery or burglary goes awry, the police cannot hope to provide much protection except by striving to eradicate and control these other crimes. Ironically, the evidence suggests that the police can do the least with the comparatively few senseless, random acts of violence with which we are most often concerned (Kappeler & Potter, 2005).

One of the most intractable problems is finding ways to prevent domestic violence from escalating to murder. When we look at the dynamics of murders involving family or friends, the reactive nature of traditional police efforts makes dealing with such problems extraordinarily challenging. Until or unless a call is made to the police, either by the victim or by neighbors or other witnesses, there is little chance that a patrol car driving by can have any impact on people arguing behind closed doors, so preventive patrol can do little. Once a call is made, motor patrol officers can reduce the likelihood of repeat violence that always holds the threat of ending in murder by arresting the attacker.

The **Minneapolis Domestic Violence Experiment** in 1981-1982 showed arrest was the most effective of the three standard methods police use to reduce domestic violence (the other two are advising or sending the suspect away for at least eight hours). The research showed that when the police arrested the suspect, the incidence of repeat violence over the next six months was only 10 percent, compared to 19 percent for advising, and 24 percent when the suspect was sent away (Sherman & Berk, 1984). This study also shows that factors traditionally considered outside the province of the police seem to play a role in this potentially murderous violence. One striking finding was that roughly six out of 10 suspects and victims alike were unemployed, while the overall unemployment rate in the area was only 5 percent. Also, 45 percent of suspects were the unmarried male lover of the victim; 35 percent were the victim's current husband. Eight of 10 victims said they had been assaulted by the same person within the past six months, and six of 10 had called the police to intervene within that same period. Slightly more than one in four couples were in counseling at the time. In addition, six in 10 suspects had a prior arrest, and four in 10 had been arrested for an alcohol offense (Sherman & Berk, 1984).

Under political pressure from feminists and people concerned with domestic violence, and facing the ever-increasing threat of lawsuits, legislators were quick to enact presumptive or mandatory arrest laws. Relying on the proof of the well-publicized Minneapolis experiment, they legislatively limited officers' discretion in an attempt to reduce domestic violence. Subsequent studies, which replicated the Minneapolis experiment, were conducted in Omaha, Charlotte, and Milwaukee. Using similar research designs, dramatically different results were reached: making an arrest did not result in fewer subsequent incidents of assault. The danger to the victim is not increased or decreased by an officer's choice to use mediation, to separate the parties, or to arrest the offender (Dunford, Huizinga & Elliott, 1986). While there is sufficient philosophical justification for treating domestic violence as seriously as officers would treat other forms of violence, evidence as to the effectiveness of mandatory arrests in reducing violence is at best uncertain. The **Attorney General's Task Force on Family Violence** (1984) noted that the process of mediation assumes equal culpability in a dispute, which seldom is the case in domestic violence cases. Even if arrest is not as effective as hoped, it remains a temporary solution for law enforcement, but community policing perhaps offers a better solution to the problem than merely relying on arrest.

This paints a vivid picture of couples struggling with problems beyond what a 10-minute visit from a motor patrol officer can hope to solve. Over and over, the police arrive to find a troubled couple, stressed by economic problems, where alcohol helped trigger potentially murderous rage. Yet research demonstrates social intervention can make an impact—if someone asks for help—and this is where community policing can begin to expand the police department's impact. One of community policing's stated goals is to boost people's confidence in the police as a valid source of help, so that they will be quicker to report crimes to the police. By focusing on domestic violence as an example, here are other ways a creative community policing effort could be devised to target murders stemming from this problem:

- Enmeshing the police in the community may allow officers to detect the signs of domestic violence long before they are called by a victim. Such awareness may allow for early intervention.

- Police officers trained in community policing are more likely than those officers with less or no training in community policing to provide victims of domestic disputes assistance in controlling aggressors (Mastrofski, Parks & Worden, 1998:2);

- Community policing officers (CPOs) could be charged with the responsibility to make follow-up home visits periodically, as part of their regular beat activity. If social intervention can substantially impact future violence, repeated visits by an officer at least offers some promise of convincing the aggressor that the police are watching him and that they take the matter seriously. But this is only one aspect of the CPO's role;

- In the role as liaison to other public and private agencies, a CPO might also be able to urge more of the three out of four troubled couples into appropriate and affordable counseling. CPOs can offer information about alcohol abuse programs. CPOs can also offer to escort the victim to a shelter for battered women. They can connect women with information and assistance that will allow them to leave abusive relationships. They can teach community members about the signs of partnership abuse; and

- Long-range, proactive community policing efforts, ranging from career counseling to providing lists of available jobs, help address some of the underlying dynamics, such as unemployment. In addition, community policing efforts that provide relief for families under pressure, such as activities for juveniles, can help ease tensions that can trigger violence. Because we now know that children who see physical violence in their homes while they are growing up often learn to mimic that behavior when they become adults, community policing's added impact in reducing violence today also holds the promise of reducing such violence years from now.

The dynamics of so-called crimes of passion defy easy answers. While traditional, reactive efforts can help, the underlying factors that can impel some people to murderous violence require longer-term interventions, which is where community policing offers the promise of playing a broader role. The difficulty in outlining precisely how community policing can dramatically extend the police role relates to the fact that its strategies and tactics are bounded only by the imagination of the officers involved. Perhaps in ethnic neighborhoods where macho male behavior tacitly condones wife beating, the CPO might work with local religious leaders to develop workshops on how to change cultural attitudes. Prevention efforts might also include giving talks on domestic violence in various high-school classes aimed at both sexes, separately and together. The CPO's opportunity to work with young people, one-on-one and in small groups, in informal give-and-take conversations over a long period of time, can also help to counterbalance the negative impact of growing up in a violence-prone environment. This, however, requires that police become educated in the context, not just the control, of crime. Another quality of community policing is that it does not rest on a rigid, textbook approach, but instead each effort can be tailored to the needs of the particular community.

SPOTLIGHT ON COMMUNITY POLICING PRACTICE

Foot Patrols: Crime Analysis and Community Engagement to Further the Commitment to Community Policing

When community stakeholders discuss strategies for enhancing public safety through community policing, the subject of foot patrols inevitably arises. Sometimes deemed old-fashioned by the rank and file, foot patrols may be effective not only as a means of curbing crime in neighborhoods, enhancing community partnerships, and keeping officers in touch with local activity, but also as a means for departments to lessen the impact of high fuel costs.

Historically, foot patrols are the oldest form of police patrol work. The use of foot patrols decreased substantially in the last century before reemerging as a community policing tool. The benefits, particularly in the form of community goodwill and improved relationships between the police and community, may help to explain the recent resurgence in this practice. Coupled with the high gas prices in 2008, foot patrols are once again being used as a community policing tool.

As with many policing strategies, departments adapt their approaches to community and departmental needs. Historically, foot patrols had a small effect on crime, but significant changes have been recorded with increased community stratification. Departments that take the positive elements of foot patrols and combine their efforts with data analysis that focuses on the time, location, and type of crime may use the findings to develop strategies to decrease crime and enhance the quality of life in their communities.

Crime prevention and community satisfaction with police services, while linked to the number of officers on the streets, do not depend entirely on the visibility of patrol officers. Community engagement, targeted initiatives, strategic use of resources, and data-driven decision making contribute to decreasing crime. Foot patrols should be perceived and promoted as an important component of the department's strategic operating plan.

The following are key initiatives that a department can use to pave the way for foot patrols to succeed:

- Determine the date, time, and location of service calls by type, and create representative maps to aid in efficient and effective deployment.
- Complement statistical analysis with a community survey to obtain the opinions of residents and business owners regarding priority issues.
- Invite the community to participate in planning sessions.
- Recruit a range of individuals (both officers and civilians) to use various models of patrol, demonstrating that both police and civilians can address public expectations through a variety of approaches such as volunteer efforts with neighborhood watch programs and crime-prevention programming.

(Continued)

Strategic Planning

Foot patrols should be developed as part of a proactive, integrated problem-solving strategy and not as a reactive response to an incident. The following are useful steps for developing and deploying successful foot patrols:

- Establish a structure for long-term implementation and evaluation. Plan, coordinate, and integrate program development, training, technology, and community outreach consistent with the objectives of the foot patrol and create evaluation criteria prior to implementation.
- Establish criteria for locating foot patrols in the community. Developing criteria such as identified community problems, unique needs, crime data, and special populations allows strategic deployment of resources in a proactive manner, rather than in response to incidents.
- Establish overarching program goals and objectives for implementing each foot patrol/beat location. Use foot patrols to improve community relations, suppress or prevent crime, or a combination of these objectives. Each objective is viable, yet requires a different approach and should be customized to the needs of the area.
- Establish baseline information on the foot patrol area to assist with developing strategies. An audit of the businesses, schools, social service agencies, parks, shopping areas, and other features in the specific foot patrol area allows the department to better understand areas that could benefit from the foot patrol and will assist with planning the community policing strategy.
- Establish focused areas for the implementation of foot patrols. Conduct a community survey to provide information on the community perceptions of safety needs that can be addressed through foot patrols. Most important, it allows community stakeholders to express ways through which they can support community and department priorities.

Once the overall strategy is developed, the department is in a position to shape the specific elements to be included in each foot patrol or beat.

Implementation

A foot patrol strategy needs to consider assignment of foot patrol locations, available staffing, resources, size of the beats, selection of officers to beats, and safety of the officers. To be successful, it is important that the foot patrol strategy is deployed on a permanent basis; therefore, a department must plan carefully to ensure that resources are not overcommitted.

The size of the foot patrol area has a direct impact on the goals and objectives of the foot patrols within a beat location. The area has to be small enough to allow an officer to patrol it several times during a shift. Larger beats in less-congested areas are suited for a combination of foot, bicycle, "park and walk," or other personal transport systems to patrol the area effectively. Using a combination of patrol styles also allows an officer to cover more than one foot patrol location.

Successful foot patrols include more than just walking around. Specific planned programming and community engagement strategies must be incorporated into the process.

Community Engagement and Programming

Community stakeholders need to be active partners in the deployment of foot patrols. Training community members, businesses, and other stakeholders in crime prevention, environmental issues, neighborhood watch strategies, being effective witnesses, and problem solving will assist in reducing crime.

Stakeholders can contribute by taking action in the form of citizen patrols, graffiti eradication, youth programs, and trash removal. Other municipal agencies can assist with enforcing codes, developing youth programs, enhancing lighting, and removing visual barriers.

Officers assigned to foot patrols must have the training, resources, and support to develop and implement programs that address the specific needs of the beat area. Initiatives could include school presentations designed to curb underage drinking, physical security assessments to decrease the likelihood of crime, coordination of other departmental resources such as traffic or narcotics to address an identified problem, or supporting crime watch groups.

The significant obstacles to foot patrols have been the dwindling numbers of officers and an increase in the coverage area for which they are responsible. Foot patrols may be perceived by some departments as inefficient because vehicles cover more ground more quickly; however, the statement made to the community through a police presence on the street speaks of the investment being made in the safety of every resident. Business owners, patrons, and residents welcome an increased police presence in a community troubled by petty crime and vandalism.

The presence of foot patrols contributes to a feeling of safety. This is especially critical to areas undergoing revitalization and in areas with underserved populations. In addition to a safer community, foot patrols provide the officers with the best possible opportunity for understanding what goes on in the community. Technology has improved, and officers are no longer tied to a patrol car for radio access. The flexibility afforded by this form of patrol should be a consideration for every department as it assesses its resources and develops strategies for providing a powerful and coordinated response to crime. Incorporating foot patrols as part of a department's overarching strategy can bring changes in the community that would be unachievable through traditional vehicle patrol alone. Foot patrols have been critical to many communities across the country, strengthening the bonds between community members and officers while providing a coordinated effort to prevent and solve crime.

A foot patrol strategy that incorporates the planning elements discussed here will result in a cooperative effort between the community and the police and increase the quality of life within the community. This cooperative effort will also lead to a higher level of trust between the community and the police, more citizen involvement, and a community that starts to hold its members accountable.

Kym Craven
Director
Public Safety Strategies Group

Source: The e-newsletter of the COPS Office, Volume 2, Issue 2, February 2009.

As the dynamics involved in these most serious violent crimes indicate, the traditional police response offers little opportunity for officers to make meaningful interventions that hold the promise of making people safer. All too often, the best the police can hope to do is deal effectively with the problems after the fact, and even in that regard, community policing's ability to generate more and better information holds the promise of doing a better job than traditional efforts. Moreover, because of community policing's emphasis on treating people as partners in the policing process and on encouraging police to develop their interpersonal skills to maximum proficiency, community policing allows the department to do a better job of working with victims and witnesses.

Community policing's focus on solving problems rather than just answering calls, making arrests, and handling crimes as individual incidents also makes better sense than traditional efforts because of the relative difficulty in making a difference in the dynamics that result in serious crime. CPOs gather information beyond what traditional efforts can achieve, which allows the department to concentrate its efforts where they will do the most good. CPOs provide a sustained presence in the community, so that they can initiate efforts targeted at troubled families and potentially explosive situations in ways that traditional approaches never could. As people learn to trust their CPOs, they turn to them for help, and CPOs skilled in knowing other community resources that can be tapped for assistance have made dramatic strides in helping to defuse the overall climate of violence by concentrating their efforts on those families and addresses where the greatest potential problems cluster.

Community Policing's Strengths

One reason for the lengthy discussion of the dynamics involved in crime is to show the tremendous difficulty the police face in making a positive difference. The police, as currently structured and organized, can do little about obvious root causes of crime, such as poverty and unemployment; likewise, they can do little to influence policy concerning people's access to guns, social support for single parents, or any of the other factors that may play a role in the overall matrix of crime. The police can play only a limited role in controlling crimes of passion, and society's emphasis on the acquisition of material possessions as a yardstick of success is an attitude that the police can do little to alter. Crime encompasses such a broad range of human activity and unpredictability that no single agency in society, no matter how powerful, can be expected to provide all the answers. Of importance as well is the recognition that the police are only one element in the overall criminal justice system. Yet, police can play a powerful role in the development of social policy by becoming the public's educators on issues of crime and its "root" causes. Also police can become politically active in voicing their concerns about poor public policies and forge partnerships with community members to influence change.

Yet what this discussion is also designed to demonstrate is that the traditional police approach holds little promise of doing a better job than it already does. There is good reason to suppose that tinkering with the traditional approach in the hope of dramatically improving police departments' ability to solve the riddle of serious crime is like rearranging the deck chairs on the *Titanic*—too little, too late. What has become glaringly apparent is that the traditional system focuses the vast bulk of its resources on only one of three times that police action can influence the ultimate outcome of a potentially criminal act.

Current efforts target most sworn personnel, the department's first line of defense, toward maintaining the overall ability to respond immediately to those relatively few times where a quick response is vital. One obvious problem with the traditional system, therefore, is that proactive and follow-up efforts often suffer from lack of resources as a result. Yet an even more serious problem is that the rationale for relying primarily on motor patrol rested on the assumption that encouraging these officers to use their free patrol time on preventive patrol would make a substantial contribution in the fight against serious crime. Unfortunately, this appears to have little, if any, practical value in reducing or controlling crime. Though it rattles the foundations of traditional thinking, research tends to confirm that traditional preventive motor patrol efforts are often no more than an expensive waste of time and fuel.

While that may overstate the case, the fact remains that history fails to show that the traditional approach can cope effectively with most crime. Admittedly, the rates of serious crime in recent years have continued to decline, but these may have as much to do with the maturing of the baby boomers out of their most crime-prone years and the unprecedented strength of a sustained economic boom, as to the contribution the police have made in more than quadrupling the number of people behind bars. The fact remains that this society continues to suffer rates of serious crime that would be considered intolerable in other industrialized Western nations. This reality has sparked and continues to fuel a radical re-assessment concerning whether police departments might find better ways to approach the challenge posed by crime.

What community policing proposes is that the riddle of crime requires understanding that crime incidents cannot be solved in isolation—separate from each other and separate from their relationship to the social and economic context. Though it may sound illogical on the surface, the community policing philosophy suggests that only by broadening the police **mandate** beyond a narrow focus on serious crime incidents as they occur can the police provide short- and long-term answers to the dilemma posed by serious crime. Crime must be understood as a "social intersection" where a complex set of material and ideological conditions in a community come together to forge it.

The subtle and sophisticated community policing approach rests on recognizing that coping with serious crime demands approaching it in context. It is possible that anyone in the United States may at some point in life be swept away by the passion of the moment to commit an irrational act totally out of character, an act that ends up as a crime statistic. In such cases, the police can do little more than to make sure that they will arrive on the scene as soon as reasonably possible after receiving the call, and both the traditional police approach and community policing guarantee that. But an important flaw in the traditional approach is that it is not much of an exaggeration to suggest the prevailing system supposes a world in which it is equally likely that President Bush may one day bludgeon Laura in a fight as that a murder will happen at an address where domestic disputes routinely escalate into violence.

The traditional approach only superficially recognizes that many criminal acts follow their own logic, that they have a context within the structure of community and family life. Households with a history of domestic disputes often end up as places where aggravated assaults and even murders are more likely to occur.

The traditional response to this obvious reality is simply to add more patrol cars in problem areas, at problem times. Since the sight of a patrol car whizzing by is rarely much of a deterrent, this simply makes it more likely a car will be available to respond rapidly to the flow of calls for service. This reactive mode means the police do not accomplish much until the call is placed, and most people either cannot or will not call fast enough so that speed of arrival ends up making much difference in the final outcome. More often than not, by the time a person calls the police, a crime has already occurred. Therefore, this can hardly be viewed as prevention or deterrence. As David Carter notes, "random patrol produces random results."

What community policing does is open up the thinking of the department, so that the police learn to see crime in a broader context. The first challenge is to infuse all officers with the community policing philosophy, so that they learn to look beyond isolated crime incidents, at the underlying dynamics where creative interventions might help solve the problem in ways that need not require arrest. In many cases, this requires looking at the context of crime in a new way. CPOs are beginning to adopt this philosophy. Researchers in St. Petersburg, for example, found that

CPOs generally favored views associated with community policing more than did 911 officers. They were much more likely than 911 officers to say that minor disorders were police business. They were far more likely to rank reducing repeat calls for service as an important goal and far less likely to rank handling their call load or making arrests as important goals.... They were less likely to stress the importance of making arrests, issuing citations, and performing drug and gun interdictions and were more likely to view public involvement in neighborhood improvement and reducing fear of crime as important (Mastrofski, Parks, Reiss & Worden, 1999:1).

Yet community policing goes beyond reducing calls for service and handling minor disorders (1) by broadening the police mandate beyond a narrow focus on crime, and (2) by restructuring the department to carry out this expanded mission more effectively. Though it would seem sensible that the best way to reduce and control serious crime is for the police to focus even more attention on just these crimes alone, community policing approaches the problem from a different direction. This means the police must educate people about what they can do to combat crime. Then the department's community **outreach specialists**, its CPOs, must go further by involving people in efforts to deal with the social problems that promote neighborhood conditions—fixing potholes in the street, helping the homeless find shelter, providing meaningful activities for idle teens, and helping people with the persistent, nagging problems such as unrelenting noise that escalate the underlying tensions and finding women adequate employment and shelter to escape abusive relationships.

Critics contend that community policing detracts from a proper focus on crime by dissipating the energies of the department in efforts that have nothing to do with serious crime. They argue that this broadening of the police mandate squanders resources better spent addressing the serious crime problems that this society faces. One problem lies in thinking that serious crime occurs in a vacuum, whereas it is instead part of the fabric of the community and family, which cannot be separated from its cultural context. Another problem is that this argument supposes that the traditional approach focuses more time and energy on serious crime than the community policing approach does, whereas the reverse may well be true.

Because it is basically reactive, the traditional approach usually requires a call for service to trigger action—the dispatcher receives a call that a serious crime is in progress and sends a motor patrol officer in response. A department that adopts community policing does the same. The next level of priority is a call about a serious crime that has already occurred—someone discovers a body, the bank robbers have fled, a rape victim arrives at the emergency ward. Again, regardless of whether the call comes into a traditional department or one that has adopted community policing, a motor patrol officer is dispatched to the scene. The major difference here concerns what happens before and after the officer arrives, since a department infused with the community policing philosophy asks the officers to look beyond the individual incident to see whether there are underlying pressure points that could influence the likelihood of similar problems in the future. It also requires officer to ask whether a response from the community, one beyond a mere police response, might better address the problem.

The question then becomes how the department uses its resources beyond fulfilling these most basic functions. In traditional departments, motor patrol officers spend their time between calls involving serious crime, on answering relatively minor calls, and on preventive patrol. Those calls can include a so-called petty theft, helping people who are locked out of their cars or homes, tagging an abandoned vehicle, issuing a traffic ticket, or responding to a call about a loud party in progress. Most motor patrol officers see those kinds of calls as nuisance calls, trivial matters that occupy their time until the real business of policing—a call about serious crime—comes over the radio. If they have the luxury of time between even these kinds of nuisance calls, a motor patrol officer may cruise areas, knowing full well that the activity heats up again once their taillights disappear around the corner. As this shows, the traditional approach may well squander precious resources in efforts that hold little promise of addressing the challenge posed by crime.

While it is obviously true that violent crime deserves priority, the existing system often fails to recognize the importance of taking personal and social problems equally seriously. People sense something is askew with police priorities when the department insists it cannot afford to send an officer when a person calls to report that his car has been stolen, yet that same driver knows the police always seem to find the time to write a traffic ticket. And even departments that send officers to take a report on a stolen car may send the wrong message when they refuse to do the same for that 12-year-old whose bike was stolen, but seem to have time to tell skateboarders to move along.

The point is not that the police department must be at the immediate beck and call of each person who asks for service, but community policing allows the department to use the officer's free patrol time to follow up on reports about property crime. A dispatcher who grasps how community policing works explains to the caller that the officer will stop by in the next day or so to discuss the problem, since dispatching a motor patrol officer immediately holds no promise of altering the outcome. During that follow-up visit, the CPO has a chance to find out whether there has been a rash of similar incidents in the neighborhood, and whether the person has any ideas concerning who might be involved. Perhaps that stolen bike was one of five that have disappeared, but only this family placed a call to the police. Only by talking with people in the community will this information come to light.

If nothing else, making that home visit provides the officer a hook to attempt to involve that family in the police process. This could mean challenging them to recruit five other neighbors for an organizing meeting where the CPO can explain Neighborhood Watch and offer some crime prevention tips. It could mean the officer succeeds in enlisting various family members for new community-based initiatives, whether that means recruiting a coach for the new softball league or someone in the family to handle calls at the CPO's local office. It might mean finding a business person to employ a teenager. In short, when we focus only on crime all we find is crime; when we focus on solutions we find them.

Maybe that visit allows the family to share concerns about other problems in the community, as well as their insights and suggestions about possible solutions. Perhaps that casual visit elicits information about the teenager down the street who is rumored to commit thefts, the unexplained bruises on the child next door that they can hear screaming in the night, or the group of teenagers they heard shouting racial epithets at passersby. Unlike motor patrol officers, whose focus is on handling this call as quickly as possible so that they can move on to the next, the purpose in freeing CPOs from those constraints is to have the time and opportunity to use informal interchanges to find out valuable information about the community context of crime, including serious crime.

Freeing CPOs to act as the department's community outreach specialists also allows the department to involve itself in efforts to enhance the quality of community life (see Reisig & Parks, 2004). Again, critics of community policing see this as distracting from a proper focus on serious crime, because they fail to see the community context. Unless the department educates all its officers about the contribution that the community policing mandate can make, some may see it as unimportant—or even stupid. On the surface, it seems ridiculous to suggest that a CPO is helping the department and its motor patrol officers by haranguing the city sanitation department to pick up the garbage on time. Traditionalists suggest it is tantamount to insanity to allow officers to waste their time on such trivial problems, especially in a neighborhood notorious for violent crime. Research, however, shows that police officers working under the traditional model of police waste considerable amounts of time. In St. Petersburg researchers found that the "officers they studied spent, on average, between one-fourth and one-third of their time not on specific tasks, but rather on general patrol or personal business. Contrary to widely held beliefs about the reactive nature of police patrol, 911 officers were typically free of dispatcher or supervisor assignments for 5-6 hours of their 8-hour shift" (Mastrofski, Parks, Reiss & Worden, 1999:1). When these researchers compared traditional patrol officers to CPOs, they found that "911 officers initiated approximately 45 percent of their public contacts; CPOs, approximately 66 percent.... Not surprisingly, CPOs spent substantially more time engaged in problem-solving activities than 911 officers (17% and 7-10%, respectively, depending on the shift). Eighty-three percent of CPOs indicated involvement with a problem-solving project in the past year, as did 57 percent of 911 officers" (Mastrofski, Parks, Reiss & Worden, 1999:1).

Not only do CPOs initiate more contact with the community, but they probably stand a better chance of getting timely garbage service for the area than a barrage of calls from people whose address verifies they carry little clout with City Hall. And that achievement can help gain credibility and inspire confidence among the people whose support is vital in organizing efforts targeted at reducing crime. An enterprising CPO may also be able to capitalize on that initial first step by recruiting kids in the neighborhood to begin picking up litter in exchange for which they receive a donated toy. Perhaps the local shop teacher could involve students in fixing broken benches in the park. The next step might be to involve area businesses in donating paint and shrubs to help spruce up the facility. The park might be a good place to host Neighborhood Watch meetings.

The process of revitalizing the community produces other positive spin-offs. People directly involved in improving conditions in their communities are more likely to protect them. When CPOs involve young people in such efforts, they learn about responsibility, hard work, and doing things for others. Properly structured, they also have the opportunity to learn skills that can enhance their ability to land a part-time job. It also provides CPOs informal opportunities to reinforce positive values. These opportunities demonstrate that the police are not uniformed thugs who thrive on giving kids a hard time, but caring human beings who are willing to help make the community a better and safer place to live.

Involving the police in efforts aimed at juveniles also holds the promise of breaking down the barriers between the police and the adults in the community. Jowanne Barnes-Coney, a foot patrol officer in the Flint experiment, said that by working first on programs aimed at the young people in her beat area, she was able to make in-roads with the parents. Kids are basically more open and trusting, so once she had them on her side, they provided her access to their parents.

Admittedly, the link between community policing's proactive focus and any potential impact on serious crime in the future seems tenuous. Fix a few pot-holes and someday the murder rate will decline? Teach a kid to plant flowers today and he won't rob someone five years from now? The first thing to remem-ber is that the traditional system does far less. An officer whizzing by in a patrol car on preventive patrol accomplishes little. Investing scarce resources in a new radar gun and patrol car to catch a few more speeders will do virtually nothing to cut tomorrow's rates of serious crime.

Given the choice, does it make better sense to confine two educated and highly trained police officers into one patrol car, where they spend most of their time talking to each other, or should departments consider freeing some of those officers so that they can talk to people in the com-munity instead?

History reveals that serious crime is a stubborn problem, not given to easy or quick solutions. Community policing suggests that creativity and innovation are required to approach serious crime from new angles, mak-ing incremental improvements that hold the promise of making long-term substantive improvement. It recognizes the importance of treating all social problems, including property crime, as serious police business. It says arrests alone are not the cure, and crime rates are not the sole measure of success. It focuses special attention on those at risk of becoming offenders and victims. It involves people in efforts to make their communities more crime-resistant, including participating in projects to reduce neighborhood problems. It involves CPOs as community outreach specialists, allowing them to function as the community's ombudsmen to other agencies that can help. Community policing pays particular attention to juveniles, not only because young peo-ple commit crime, but because of the hope that positive police interven-tion at an early age holds a greater promise of discouraging problems in the future.

For some, such efforts still sound more like social work than police work. Traditionalists sincerely believe that the proper police response to serious crime is embodied in the "tough cop" (Crank, 2004) rolling up to the scene, sirens blaring, even though that may only account for a fraction of the time spent on the job. Faced with this ambitious list of other duties that community policing demands, traditionalists ask, why the police? Proponents of community policing argue instead, who better? Who else has the power to act on behalf of the pow-erless and those most in need?

KEY TERMS IN CHAPTER 6

- Attorney General's Task Force on Family Violence
- crime-fighters
- crimes in progress
- deterrence
- juveniles
- Kansas City Preventive Patrol study
- mandate
- Minneapolis Domestic Violence Experiment
- motor patrol
- opportunity reduction
- outreach specialists
- Part I Index crimes
- prevention
- professional policing model
- RAND
- rapid response
- resolving crimes already committed
- status offenses
- Uniform Crime Reports

DISCUSSION QUESTIONS

1. Discuss and explain the four traditional key measures used to evaluate police.
2. Discuss the differences in victimization and incarceration rates in the United States. Explain the discrepancy.
3. Do the media influence how the police enforce or report crime? Explain.
4. In his Canadian study, Chris Braiden found that bike thefts resulted in 15 times the dollar loss when compared to bank robberies. What implications does this study have, if any, for the provision of police services?
5. Identify and discuss the three situations when immediate police action can influence a crime.
6. Discuss the results of the Kansas City Preventive Patrol study.
7. Discuss the reasons for citizen delays when calling the police. Does this have any impact on the police's ability to solve the crime? Why or why not?
8. Describe six of the twelve major findings of the RAND study of the criminal investigation process.
9. Discuss whether or not community policing can be an effective tool in fighting crime. What is the role of the CPO in these efforts?

References

Alpert, G.P., & Moore, M.H. (1993). Measuring Police Performance in the New Paradigm of Policing. In *Performance Measures for the Criminal Justice System*. Washington, DC: U.S. Department of Justice.

BJS. (2007). *Correctional Populations in the United States, Annual, Prisoners in 2006*. Washington, DC: U.S. Department of Justice, Office of Justice Programs.

BJS. (2007a). *Probation and Parole in the United States, 2006*. Washington, DC: U.S. Department of Justice, Office of Justice Programs.

Braiden, C. (1987). *Remarks delivered during the National Neighborhood Foot Patrol Training Seminars.* East Lansing, MI: Michigan State University.

Brandl, S., & Frank, J. (1994). The Relationship Between Evidence, Detective Effort, and the Dispositions of Burglary and Robbery Investigations. *American Journal of Police, 13*(3), 149–168.

Brott, A. (1995). Major Reworking of Child Abuse Law. *Chicago Tribune,* (Feb 1), 10.

Clinard, M., & Yeager, P. (1980). *Corporate Crime.* New York, NY: Macmillan.

Coleman, J. (1994). The Criminal Elite: Understanding White-Collar Crime. Worth Publishers.

Crank, J. P. (2004). *Understanding Police Culture* (2nd ed.). Newark, NJ: LexisNexis Matthew Bender/Anderson Publishing.

Dunford, F. W., Huizinga, D., & Elliott, D. S. (1986). The Role of Arrest in Domestic Assault: The Omaha Experiment. *Criminology, 28*(2), 183–206.

Eck, J. (1983). *Solving Crimes: The Investigation of Burglary and Robbery.* Washington, DC: Police Executive Research Forum.

FBI. (2007). *Uniform Crime Report.* Washington, DC.

Goulden, J. C. (1989). *Fit to Print: A.M. Rosenthal and His Times.* New York, NY: Lyle Stuart.

Greenwood, P. W., & Petersilia, J. R. (1975). *The Criminal Investigation Process, Volume I: Summary and Policy Implications.* Santa Monica, CA: RAND Corporation.

Kappeler, V. E., & Potter, G. W. (2005). *The Mythology of Crime and Criminal Justice* (4th ed.). Prospect Heights, IL: Waveland Press.

Kappeler, V. E., Sluder, R., & Alpert, G. P. (1998). *Forces of Deviance: Understanding the Dark Side of the Force* (2nd ed.). Prospect Heights, IL: Waveland Press.

Kelling, G. (1981). *The Newark Foot Patrol Experiment.* Washington, DC: The Police Foundation.

Kelling, G. (1997). The Assault on Effective Policing. *The Wall Street Journal,* (August 26), 11.

Kelling, G., Pate, T., Dieckman, D., & Brown, C. (1974). *The Kansas City Preventive Patrol Experiment: A Summary Report.* Washington, DC: The Police Foundation.

Klockars, C. (1999). The Legacy of Conservative Ideology and Police. In V. E. Kappeler (Ed.), *The Police & Society: Touch Stone Readings.* (2nd ed.). Prospect Heights, IL: Waveland Press.

Krajick, K. (1980). Evidence Favors Aggressive Patrol. *Police Magazine, 3*(5), 30.

Larson, R. C., & Cahn, M. F. (1985). *Synthesizing and Extending the Results of Police Patrol Studies.* Washington, DC: National Institute of Justice.

Manning, P. K. (2006). The Police; Mandate, Strategies, and Appearances. In V. E. Kappeler (Ed.), *The Police & Society: Touch Stone Readings.* (3rd ed.). Prospect Heights, IL: Waveland Press.

Manning, P. K. (2006a). Economic Rhetoric and Policing Reform. In V. E. Kappeler (Ed.), *The Police & Society: Touch Stone Readings.* (3rd ed.). Prospect Heights, IL: Waveland Press.

Mastrofski, S. D., & Ritti, R. R. (1992). You Can Lead a Horse to Water …: A Case Study of a Police Department's Response to Stricter Drunk-Driving Laws. *Justice Quarterly, 9*(3), 465–491.

Mastrofski, S. D., & Ritti, R. R. (1996). Police Training and the Effects of Organization on Drunk Driving Enforcement. *Justice Quarterly, 13*(2), 291–320.

Mastrofski, S. D., Parks, R. B., & Worden, R. E. (1998). *Community Policing in Action: Lessons From an Observational Study.* Washington, DC: National Institute of Justice.

Mastrofski, S. D., Parks, R. B., Reiss, A. J., Jr., & Worden, R. E. (1999). *Policing Neighborhoods: A Report From St. Petersburg.* Washington, DC: National Institute of Justice.

National Traffic Safety Institute (2007). *Crashes, Injuries, and Fatalities.* Washington, DC: NTSI.

Pate, T., Bowers, R., & Parks, R. (1976). *Three Approaches to Criminal Apprehension in Kansas City: An Evaluation Report.* Washington, DC: The Police Foundation.

Percy, S. (1980). Response Time and Citizen Evaluation of Police. *Journal of Police Science and Administration, 8*(1), 75–86.

Potter, G. W., & Kappeler, V. E. (2006). *Constructing Crime* (2nd ed.). Prospect Heights, IL: Waveland Press.

Reisig, M. D., & Parks, R. B. (2004). Can Community Policing Help the Truly Disadvantaged? *Crime & Delinquency, 50*(2), 139–167.

Rosenbaum, D. P. (1988, 1996). Community Crime Prevention: A Review and Synthesis of the Literature. In G. Cordner, L. Gaines, & V. E. Kappeler (Eds.), *Police Operations: Analysis and Evaluation.* Cincinnati, OH: Anderson Publishing Co.

Sherman, L. W., & Berk, R. A. (1984). *The Minneapolis Domestic Violence Experiment.* Washington, DC: The Police Foundation.

Skogan, W. G., & Gordon, A. C. (1982). A Review of Detective Division Reporting Practices. In *Crime in Illinois 1982.* Springfield, IL: Illinois Department of Law Enforcement.

Skogan, W. G., & Hartnett, S. M. (1997). *Community Policing, Chicago Style.* New York, NY: Oxford Press.

Sourcebook. (2007). *Sourcebook of Criminal Justice Statistics, 2006.* Washington, DC: U.S. Department of Justice, Office of Justice Programs.

Spelman, W., & Brown, D. (1984). *Calling the Police: Citizen Reporting of Serious Crime.* Washington, DC: U.S. Government Printing Office.

Strecher, V. G. (1997). *Planning Community Policing: Goal Specific Cases and Exercises.* Prospect Heights, IL: Waveland Press.

Twain, M. (1972). *The International Thesaurus of Quotations.* Compiled by Rhoda Thomas Tripp. New York, NY: Perennial Library, Harper & Row.

Wilson, O. W., & McLaren, B. (1977). *Police Administration* (4th ed.). New York, NY: McGraw-Hill.

Fear itself carries with it its own danger; because when fear is excessive it can make many a man despair.

—St. Thomas Aquinas

CHAPTER 7   Community Policing and Fear of Crime

LEARNING OBJECTIVES

After reading the chapter, you should be able to:

1. Understand the economic and social damage done to society as a result of fear of crime.
2. Discuss the relevance of the Flint Foot Patrol Experiment.
3. Understand the roles of indirect victimization, community concern, and incivilities in citizens' fear of crime.
4. Describe the demographics of those most fearful and their actual rates of victimization.
5. Discuss the relationship between victimization and fear of crime.
6. Understand the roles of the media and law enforcement in the public's heightened fear of crime.
7. Describe the response of community policing to fear of crime.
8. Discuss the relationship between socioeconomic status and fear of crime.
9. Cite the types of crimes citizens are most fearful of.
10. Describe the theoretical models of fear of crime.

Traditional Policing and Fear of Crime

Traditional police strategies focus primarily on crime reduction, responding to calls for service, and maintaining order in a community. Traditional police departments have a myopic view of their responsibilities. They often neglect to consider the consequences of crime and a sense of disorder. They fail to think outside the box. However, consider the following:

- A woman turns down a promotion because it would mean making sales calls at night and memories of her sister's brutal rape make her too fearful to drive alone after dark.

239

- An elderly couple no longer feels safe walking to local stores, even during daylight, so they now wait for their daughter to take them with her when she shops. Not only do they worry about what they will do if she cannot take them, but also they miss the outings they used to take together, stopping at local shops where everyone knew them.

- A sixth-grader begins feigning illness as an excuse to stay home from school because older boys attacked a classmate, and he is afraid he will be next.

- A husband and wife have watched their middle-class neighborhood decline, but they vowed to stay—until there was a rash of burglaries and muggings nearby. To their shock, they find their home is worth less than it was a few years ago, but they sell and move to the suburbs, though it means additional time and expense to commute to their jobs.

In each of these scenarios, no one was the victim of a particular crime, though all were victimized by crime's insidious shadow—fear of crime. The damage that each person suffered was very real and as serious as what many crime victims endure. What we must not forget is that whenever one person is victimized by crime, that individual's family, friends, co-workers, and acquaintances are also victimized. Even reading about crimes in the newspaper or seeing victims on television reinforces the mythic message that no one can be completely safe (Kappeler & Potter, 2005; Potter & Kappeler, 2006). Anyone can become a victim—at least that is what politicians and media tell us.

Crimes can be committed against individuals or seem ever-present in the environment. For example, people experience physical injuries as the result of robberies and assaults. When people are injured they may not be able to work or have medical bills. Their fear may prevent them from going out on the street or to certain parts of the city. In effect, crime results in a negative response or outcome for the individual exposed to it. The ramifications of fear of crime can be far-reaching to the point that some people become prisoners in their own homes. It must be a legitimate concern for the police. Indeed, fear of crime is the best measure for determining the public's perception of safety and security. As discussed later, crime is a less accurate measure of feelings of safety than fear of crime.

The economic and social damage done to us, as individuals and as a society, as a result of fear of crime has become as important an issue as crime itself. We also must remember that the damage done by the corrosive fear of crime extends beyond individuals and families, to businesses and to our communities as well. The downtown business districts in many cities today are places that people avoid or flee as soon as they leave work. The large department stores and other retail businesses that once pervaded central business districts have long left for the suburbs. They basically followed economic patterns and people who have left the cities in growing numbers because of their fear of crime and other social problems. Many businesses that could not afford to make the transition or that waited too long to try have simply disappeared—the family-owned drugstore, the ethnic bakery, the corner grocery, the shoe repair shop—taking local jobs with them. They, too, have been absorbed by the corporatizing of America.

In many of our major cities, the damage seems rather dramatic. There are so many stores and homes that have been neglected and destroyed that entire areas look as if they have been abandoned. In faltering northern industrial cities like Detroit or Chicago, even many comfortable homes now stand empty, a cruel irony in an era when the ranks of the homeless have been expanded drastically, including families with children. In many cases, parts or sections of our cities appear completely disjointed from "mainstream" society. Fear of crime is not the sole source of the exodus from our cities, but it certainly is a primary contributing factor.

Historically, fear of crime was not a prime concern to the police, and it was not until the 1970s that fear of crime was an issue in the American criminal justice arena. The police, into the 1960s, saw law enforcement, or "crook-catching," as their most important role in society (Gaines & Kappeler, 2011). This vision of policing is rooted in the Depression and Prohibition where the police increasingly began to emphasize law enforcement over the provision of services and order maintenance. Indeed, service and order maintenance were seen not only as peripheral, but also, in some cases, as antithetical to the primary mission of law enforcement. This position dictated that the police see themselves in one-on-one conflicts with the criminal adversaries. The community was omitted from the equation.

Simultaneously, police administrators were attempting to implement major reforms in American policing. The Depression and Prohibition not only caused the police to focus on law enforcement, but they also contributed substantially to corrupting the police. Police corruption was a national problem into the 1950s. In an effort to reduce corruption, police administrators moved to a professional model of policing. They implemented training programs and policies that emphasized distancing the police from the people they served. The police began to adopt a detached, professional demeanor when dealing with people. They tended to behave as automatons, as opposed to public servants. This behavior steadily became ingrained in the individual officer's psyche, and it dominated police practices for several decades. Consequently, the police were not overly concerned with the public or their feelings about criminal justice matters.

In the 1960s the nation experienced a burgeoning crime problem. The period witnessed unprecedented civil unrest as a result of discrimination and the Vietnam War. Riots in many major cities resulted in substantial numbers of deaths and injuries. The riots also caused millions of dollars of destruction, all of which was covered in detail by the nightly news. Crime increased exponentially while America for the first time had an open, widespread drug problem. Crime and drugs became central issues in public and political debate. Presidential and congressional elections, as well as state and local elections, were won and lost on candidates' ability to convince the American people of their effectiveness in controlling crime. Fueled by the news media and political agendas, the American public became obsessed with crime. Many of the political polls of the time showed crime to be the most important political issue.

Additionally, the victims' rights movement began in the 1960s (Young & Stein, 2004). Although there was interest in victims prior to the 1960s, the bulk of this interest centered on how victims contributed to their own victimization (Schafer, 1968). For example, Amir (1971) published a study of rape in Philadelphia in which he maintained that 19 percent of the rapes between 1958 and 1960 were victim-precipitated. Studies like Amir's outraged victims. High crime rates, the drug problem, and widespread disorder contributed to legislators and representatives from the criminal justice system becoming concerned with the treatment of victims and their rights. Conservative members of Congress were concerned over the "coddling" of criminals, so they began to fund programs to assist victims (Weed, 1995). Interestingly, however, Christian (2009) found that Congress tends to allocate more funding for "crime fighting" not when there is an increase in crime, but when the public's fear of crime becomes elevated. For the most part, the victims' movement was buttressed by the women's and children's rights movements. These two movements witnessed genuine concern about how women and children victims were treated. It represented a time when society finally recognized that crime has an impact on its victims and that it was being committed against people as well as against the state.

The message to mainstream criminal justice from the victims' movement was that victims were being treated shoddily. **Victimization** was discussed in terms of primary and secondary victimization. **Primary victimization** occurred when a criminal act was committed against the victim. Here, the victim suffered financial and sometimes injurious losses as a result of the criminal act.

Secondary victimization came with the treatment of the victim by the criminal justice system. For the most part, the police and prosecutors were only interested in victims as witnesses to assist in convicting the criminal perpetrators. They really were not concerned with the health or welfare of the victims (Weed, 1995). The treatment of victims by the criminal justice system outraged victims and victims' advocates, and this outrage translated into pressure for the police and prosecutors to intervene in private lives. An ancillary change as a result of the victims' movement was that the police became more concerned with people' attitudes about police services. Thus, fear of crime became an issue worthy of political attention.

Discovering the "Fear of Crime"

During the 1960s and 1970s, crime became the most important issue to many Americans. It cut through the very fiber of American society. Although there was an increasing number of crime victims and society was finally becoming concerned with their treatment, there was only a general concern within society or the criminal justice arena about people' impressions and fear of crime and its consequences. Policing as an occupation was slow to identify fear of crime as a legitimate social concern. It was seen as being outside the sphere of law enforcement or crook catching, or the police believed they were addressing it indirectly (Scheider, Rowell & Bezdikian, 2003) through enforcement. Fear of crime, however, became a legitimate police objective as a result of the Flint, Michigan, Foot Patrol Experiment (Trojanowicz, 1982).

The Flint Foot Patrol Experiment

The Flint Foot Patrol program began in January 1979, as the result of a $2.6 million grant from the Mott Foundation to Michigan State University. The project was the result of two law enforcement-related problems. First, in many parts of Flint, there were no crime prevention programs or programs to help the neighborhood control crime and other problems. Second, police officers were fairly detached from the people. Up until the foot patrol experiments, the department had relied on traditional police motorized patrols to respond to calls for service and deal with community problems. The project covered 14 diverse neighborhoods containing approximately 20 percent of the city's total population. This format allowed researchers to gauge foot patrols' success across the complete socioeconomic spectrum.

The project began with the employment of 22 officers who were assigned to the foot patrol beats. The objectives of the program were to:

- decrease the amount of actual or perceived criminal activity;

- increase the people's perception of personal safety;

- deliver to Flint residents a type of law enforcement consistent with community needs and the ideals of modern police practice;

> *You can learn more about the Flint Foot Patrol study by going to http://www.cj.msu.edu/~people/cp/uniform.html.*

- create a community awareness of crime problems and methods of increasing law enforcement's ability to deal with actual or potential criminal activity effectively;

- develop volunteer action in support of and under direction of the police department aimed at various target crimes;

- eliminate people's apathy about reporting crimes to the police; and

- increase protection for women, children, and the elderly.

At the end of the third year of the program, roughly 70 percent of the people surveyed reported feeling safer as a result of the foot patrols. Many of the respondents qualified their answer by saying that they felt especially safe when their foot patrol officer was well known and highly visible. This perception of safety increased each year during the three years of the experiment, despite the progressive expansion and increased turnover among foot patrol officers, the result of layoffs and excessive rotations. When the people surveyed in the third year of the program were asked if they felt crime was a more serious problem in their neighborhoods, as compared to other neighborhoods, only 14 percent stated that it was true. Nearly one-half (49%) said their area had fewer crime problems, while another 26 percent rated the crime problem in their area as average.

The Flint study was one of the first police experiments to include fear of crime as a factor. Theretofore, the police adhered to the professional model of policing, which not only meant that fear of crime was not important, but that opinions of members of the community were of little use. The Flint study also nudged policing much closer to a general philosophy of community policing. Flint showed that fear of crime was just as debilitating, if not more, as crime itself. Fear of crime affects many more people than actual victimization, and it has been just as powerful in restricting or changing people's behavior and lifestyle.

The Flint Foot Patrol Experiment, to some extent, served as an early foundation for community policing. One of the tenets of community policing is the development of better relations with communities and members of the community (community partnerships and community building). Fear of crime can serve as a substantial impediment to developing better relations. Police activities and programs may not be able to overcome a community's fear of crime. Thus, community policing takes a holistic approach to building relationships with the community—all aspects of a community's well-being must be addressed.

What Is Fear of Crime?

The preceding sections of this chapter detail how fear of crime came to be recognized as a public safety issue. The Flint Foot Patrol Experiment not only helped law enforcement to focus on fear of crime, but with the inclusion of fear of crime as a mainstream police issue, it helped to usher in the community policing era. Community policing goes beyond traditional policing and focuses on a broad array of problems, including fear of crime. Given the importance of fear of crime, it then is important to understand what it is, and its causes. So, what is fear of crime? Hale (1996) essentially defines **fear of crime** as the physical, social, economic, and emotional vulnerability as a result of the stress from crime. Garofalo (1981:840) elaborates further and defines fear of crime as:

> ...an emotional reaction characterized by a sense of danger and anxiety. We restrict our definition to the sense of danger and anxiety produced by the threat of physical harm. Furthermore, to constitute fear of crime, the fear must be elicited by perceived cues in the environment that relate to some aspect of crime for the person.

Garofalo's definition implies that fear of crime has a number of implications that center around environmental cues as well as firsthand knowledge and behavioral and psychological reactions to those cues and experiences. Levels of fear are determined by our information about crime and our subsequent impressions of its extent, the amount of risk we incur in our daily lives, and the options we have to avoid or cope

> *You can learn more about measuring the fear of crime by going to http://www.skogan.org/FearAbst2.html.*

with potential victimization. Heber (2009) notes that there are two types of fear: personal fear and altruistic fear. **Personal fear** is a result of exposure to cues in the environment that result in stressful feelings. **Altruistic fear** relates to concerns regarding safety and well-being for others such as family or friends. Altruistic fear contributes to one's personal fear.

Rader (2004) and Rader, May, and Goodrum (2007) advise that the threat of victimization consists of three components: (1) the **emotive component**, or generalized fear, where the individual becomes wary of real and perceived disorder, and crime events in the community, (2) the **cognitive component**, which is one's perceived risk and consists of one's assessment of danger, and (3) the **behavioral component**, which is constrained activities or lifestyle (avoidance behavior). Threat of victimization produces an array of emotional and behavioral responses, which are interrelated. In other words, although simplistic on its face, fear of crime is an extremely complex social phenomenon.

Most of the research into fear of crime shows that there is some degree of irrationality associated with it. That is, fear of crime is not consistent with victimization or levels of crime; the people most fearful of crime are the least likely to be victimized. Taylor and Hale (1986) discuss three such inconsistencies. First, the ordering of fear of crime by age or gender sometimes results in the exact opposite of victimization rates. For example, young males are most likely to be victimized, but oftentimes are less fearful than older males. Second, larger numbers of people are fearful than are victimized, even when unreported crime is considered. It appears there are social forces at work that spread the effects of crime over the larger population (Franklin & Franklin, 2009; Rader, May & Goodrum, 2007). Many more people are affected indirectly by crime than are affected directly. Finally, fear patterns within the general population do not match victimization patterns. For example, Gau and Pratt (2008) found that people do not distinguish between disorder and crime; disorder, then, has a similar effect on fear as does crime. It seems that actual crime may only play a small role in fear of crime.

It appears that people become fearful of crime in a variety of ways. For example, Thompson and her colleagues (1992) investigated global fear, fear of property crime, and fear of **violent crime**. Global fear refers to one's general sense of fear from crime, while the other two measures focus on specific categories of crime. Their research indicated that global fear was perhaps the best way to measure or understand people's fear of crime. They also found that all three measures were associated with "perceived seriousness of crime in the community." It appears that global measures as opposed to examining particular crimes provide the best estimate of fear of crime.

Fear of crime does not necessarily have any direct consequences. In fact, the majority of Americans experience some measure of fear of crime, but it does not necessarily mean that they will take any direct actions. Fear of crime,

You can learn more about the fear of crime by downloading http://www.popcenter.org/library/reading/pdfs/ReducingFearGuide.pdf.

however, does affect the quality of life of a number of Americans. Hale (1996) has identified six areas that are the indirect costs of fear of crime in society:

- Fear destroys the sense of community that is necessary for a healthy environment. It causes some public areas to be seen as being dangerous. Once an area has achieved this status, people are much less likely to venture into it;

- It results in more prosperous people taking protective actions to safeguard themselves, their homes, and their property, or they may even move out of the neighborhood or city. This enhances the social and crime problems that already plague the poor;

- Fear of crime hardens our attitudes toward criminals, the poor, and generally those who are different. This reduces the likelihood of finding workable solutions;

- Fear of crime potentially can undermine people's faith in the police and courts' ability to deal with crime. This can lead to vigilante justice and other measures outside the criminal justice system;

- Fear of crime has detrimental psychological effects on people. This is especially true when fear is coupled with cues and patterns of disorder and decay; and

- People who are victimized by fear of crime change their lifestyle and habits. They stay home at night; they refuse to walk in their own neighborhoods; and they tend to purchase protective devices such as burglar alarms, locks, and expansive lighting. They also may purchase firearms, which can result in accidents and additional victimization.

It should be noted that even though fear of crime has these social and psychological effects on people, many people take steps to mediate fear's impact. For example, Jackson and Gray (2010) found that fear of crime was akin to problem solving. In other words, fear was not always dysfunctional, but often resulted in people being more vigilant or taking some type of precaution. These precautions reduced the stress associated with fear of crime and improved the quality of life. Thus, there are mechanisms to counterbalance fear. Community policing officers, through a fear reduction program, can train people on these techniques and on how to be safer in the community.

SPOTLIGHT ON COMMUNITY POLICING PRACTICE

Targeting the Fear of Crime

Fear of crime was at or near the top of the list of police priorities in the United States more than two decades ago in the early 1980s. Many police executives had accepted the premise that reducing fear of crime was an important objective, and several promising practices had been identified. This situation helped spur the development of community policing in the 1980s and 1990s, but, paradoxically, the importance of fear of crime within the explicit missions of most police departments seemed to recede even as community policing expanded. More recently, however, the gap between falling crime rates and stable or even increasing levels of fear (what some call the *reassurance gap*) has led to renewed interest among police in strategies for reducing fear of crime. Also, fear of terrorism arose in America post-9/11, making fear reduction even more salient for local, state, and national officials.

Arguably, fear reduction (making people feel safer) should be included among the explicit components of the modern police mission. This position is based on the following interrelated assumptions:

- Fear matters—it has a negative effect on individuals and communities.
- Fear is real—while it is just a feeling, fear affects behavior, politics, economics, and social life.
- Fear is not as important as crime—the harm caused by fear should not be equated with the tangible and often tragic harm caused by violent crime or significant property crime.
- Fear is important—while making people safe is perhaps the most important purpose of government, making them feel safe is nearly as important, because fear has such negative ramifications for politics, economics, and social life.
- Reducing fear is and should be a police responsibility—the important government purpose of making people feel safe falls to the police logically and of necessity.
- Police can reduce fear—promising fear-reduction strategies and practices have been developed and tested during the past 30 years.
- Reducing fear should be an explicit police priority—unless police specifically target fear of crime, their attention tends to get distracted toward other issues and fear reduction efforts are neglected.
- Fear reduction efforts should be targeted—the preponderance of the evidence on police effectiveness in general is that more targeted strategies work best. This general principle applies to the specific challenge of reducing fear of crime.

Why Target Fear?

Because fear of crime is just a feeling, some might wonder why it is important, particularly as a target for police action. Must not crime itself be more important than mere feelings about crime? And even if fear of crime is of some importance, what can police be expected to do about it?

One expert who has studied fear of crime for more than two decades is Wesley Skogan of Northwestern University. He has also studied and evaluated police strategies, including Chicago's experiment with community policing beginning in 1993. He makes the case for paying attention to fear of crime as follows (2006: 255):

> Fear of crime is a social and political fact with concrete consequences for big-city life. The costs of fear are both individual and collective. Fear can confine people to their homes, and it undermines their trust in their neighbors and, especially, in their neighbors' children. Fear is a key "quality of life" issue for many people. Research also indicates that concern about crime has bad consequences for the neighborhoods in which we live. Fear leads to withdrawal from public life, and it undermines informal and organized efforts by the community to control crime and delinquency. It is difficult to organize activities in neighborhoods where people fear their own neighbors. Fear undermines the value of residential property and thus the willingness of owners to maintain it properly. When customers, and even employees, fear entering a commercial area, the viability of businesses located there is threatened.

Most significant, in Chicago as elsewhere, fear of crime has been one of the most important factors driving residents to the suburbs, encouraging race and class segregation and undermining the political importance of American cities.

Interestingly, Skogan found in Chicago that 84 percent of police officers who participated directly in community policing activities agreed with the statement "lowering citizens' fear of crime should be just as high a priority for this department as cutting the crime rate" (p. 237).

National surveys verify the public's concern about crime and fear of crime. In 2006, 37 percent of Americans said there was an area within a mile of their home where they would be afraid to walk alone at night. This measure had peaked at 48 percent in 1982, then gradually fell to 30 percent in 2001 before beginning to go back up. Consistent with this trend in fear of crime, 68 percent of Americans believed there was more crime in the U.S. in 2006 than the year before, and 51 percent believed that crime in their local areas had increased during the past year. Both measures of the perceived level of crime have increased since 2001.

These increases in fear of crime and perceived levels of crime as measured by Gallup Polls between 2001 and 2006 are at odds with the trend in crime since 2001 as measured by either personal victimization or reported crime.

This kind of disconnect between the public's perceptions and actual levels of crime is not new or even surprising, but it has certainly has frustrated law enforcement officials and political leaders during the past decade, when crime drops have not been matched by drops in fear of crime.

Gary Cordner
Professor of Criminal Justice
Kutztown University of Pennsylvania

Source: The e-newsletter of the COPS Office, Volume 1, Issue 12, December 2008 [citations and figures omitted].

Theoretical Models Explaining Fear of Crime

There has been a substantial amount of interest in fear of crime over the past 20 years. Studies of the topic have resulted in four theoretical models that have been used to describe the fear of crime process. The models include: (1) the **victimization model**, (2) the **disorder model**, (3) the **community concern model**, and (4) the **subcultural-diversity model** (Covington & Taylor, 1991; Katz, Webb & Armstrong, 2003). These models are displayed in Figure 7.1. Also, researchers have combined various aspects of the models when analyzing fear of crime to obtain a more comprehensive picture of the problem (Franklin & Franklin, 2009; Rader, May & Goodrum, 2007; Kruger, Hutchison & Monroe 2007; Scarborough, Like-Haislip, Novak, Lucas & Alarid, 2010).

The **victimization model** explains fear of crime through personal victimization, experiences with others who have been victimized, and perceived vulnerability to victimization. Perceived vulnerability here refers to the information about crime one receives, such as media reporting of crime and reports of crime from friends, neighbors, and family members. Thus, the victimization model posits that one's direct and indirect experiences with crime and victimization affect fear of crime. For example, Kruger, Hutchison, and Monroe (2007) found that being a victim of assault increased people's level of fear. The victimization

Figure 7.1
Theoretical Models Explaining Fear of Crime

model recognizes that crime and victimization cues are ever-present in the environment, and some groups of people are exposed to larger numbers of these cues and people react more definitively to the cues.

The **disorder model** postulates that fear is produced by the amount of perceived disorder that people encounter in their neighborhood, or areas where they travel, such as work, shopping, and recreation (Hinkle & Weisburd, 2008). This model follows Wilson and Kelling's (1982) "Broken Windows" thesis. As people encounter signs of disorder—abandoned buildings, groups of people loitering on the streets, vandalism and graffiti, and the consumption of alcohol or drugs in public—they become more concerned about their environment and their own well-being. These indicators imply some level of perceived lawlessness and a feeling of deterioration of community values, which result in a greater level of fear of crime. Ross and Jang (2000) found that as disorder increases, people stay at home and reduce their ties with the neighborhood. People begin moving out of the neighborhood, further increasing the sense of disorder (Markowitz et al., 2001). Thus, neighborhood cohesion is directly affected by the perception of disorder, and as cohesion is reduced, fear increases. McGarrell, Giacomazzi, and Thurman (2000), Kanan and Pruitt (2002), and Franklin and Franklin (2009) found disorder to be one of the strongest causes of fear of crime. A factor to counter disorder is the length of time a person resides in a neighborhood. Roman and Chalfin (2008) discovered that people living in a neighborhood for a longer period of time have reduced levels of fear of crime. It seems that experience results in a better understanding of a neighborhood and actual victimization probabilities.

One of the primary indicators of disorder in major cities is the presence of gangs. In some neighborhoods, fear of gangs outweighs the fear of crime (Katz, Webb & Armstrong, 2003). Katz and his colleagues and Lane and Meeker (2000) found that minority neighborhoods are more fearful of gangs than are White neighborhoods. This, to some degree, is attributable to gangs being more prevalent in minority neighborhoods. Lane and Meeker (2003) attribute this enhanced fear to the diversity of the neighborhood, the amount of disorder in neighborhoods that have gangs, and concern about the community. Along these lines, Katz (2001) found that African American residents, businesspersons, and police officers attributed high levels of crime in their neighborhoods to gang activity. Thus, the presence of gangs confounds the fear of crime problem by adding an additional dimension of fear.

The **community concern model** posits that fear of crime is related to community dynamics. The community concern differs from the disorder model in that it considers one's feelings or attitudes about factors such as social change, dissatisfaction with neighborhood life, and unease about life circumstances.

Whereas the disorder model focuses on observed disorder and crime, the community concern model focuses on social interaction and community processes. For example, Bursik (2000) and Markowitz et al. (2001) found that neighborhood cohesion contributed to fear of crime. Taylor (1999) found that awareness of neighborhood deterioration contributed to fear of crime. Thus, the dynamics of the broader community contribute to one's level of fear.

The community concern model is the opposite of broken windows. Some researchers have approached the community concern model through social capital theory. For example, Kruger, Hutchison, and Monroe (2007) and Ferguson and Mindel (2007) found that neighborhood social capital mediates or reduces fear of crime. Ferguson and Mindel (2007) define **social capital** as consisting of a "set of components found in social associations and interactions among people that, when activated, empower individuals and facilitate cooperation toward a mutual benefit. In essence, social capital refers to the social support networks, local institutions, shared norms of trust and reciprocity, and collective activities among community members that can be used to produce a common good" (p. 323).

It appears that disorder and social capital are not on a continuum, but represent two different community attributes. Perhaps the best way to understand them is to place them in the context of Weed and Seed. Attacking disorder and crime problems, weeding, will help to restore some resemblance of order in a neighborhood. However, to have a long-term positive effect, community policing officers (CPOs) must seed the neighborhood through partnerships and community building; they must attempt to build the

> *You can learn more about the theories associate with social capital and crime by downloading and reading the article at wcr.sonoma.edu/v4n1/Manuscripts/katzarticle.pdf.*

social capital in the neighborhood. This is accomplished by working with neighborhood groups, ministers, businesspeople, and concerned community members. The objective is to get people in a neighborhood connected.

The **subcultural-diversity model** suggests that some measure of fear of crime is produced from persons living near others who have cultural backgrounds that are different from their own (Lane & Meeker, 2003). That is, as neighborhoods become more heterogeneous or diverse, there is an increase in the residents' level of fear. People from different cultures often do not understand the behavior of those from other cultures. This produces uneasiness and tension, which often leads to fear of crime. For example, Bennett and Flavin (1994) found that those who were racially different from their neighbors often were more fearful of crime. Chiricos, Hogan, and Gertz (1997) found that Whites who perceived themselves to be a minority in their neighborhood were more fearful of crime. This, however, was not the case for African Americans. One might perceive that multiracial or diverse neighborhoods would result in less racism and fear of crime. However, Mears and Stewart (2010) found that interracial contact resulted in more fear of crime on the part of White people and higher income African Americans, but fear decreased for lower income African Americans. Thus, diversity and contact with people of different races may not mediate fear of crime problems. It appears that community heterogeneity affects fear of crime in different ways based on income.

These models provide ample evidence that fear of crime is the result of numerous factors interacting with the individual. They also indicate that victimization does not necessarily predict fear of crime, and indeed, direct victimization may only play a minor role in most people's perception of crime and fear of crime. The research also shows that community concern and people's impressions of their neighborhood in terms of disorder and disintegration are key to one's level of fear of crime. These models also infer that CPOs must address fear of crime comprehensively. That is, people and neighborhoods must be examined using the SARA model to identify specific attributes of problems and responses implemented that attack the problems.

Extent of Fear of Crime

Generally, fear of crime is determined by asking people questions about their fear and activities. In other cases, researchers have attempted to observe behavior, such as people's willingness to visit an area, to make a determination about fear. It is difficult to accurately measure fear of crime, because there are a number of questions that one can ask. Therefore, researchers have taken different approaches in measuring the fear of crime. The Bureau of Justice Statistics regularly publishes information about fear of crime. These studies are from a national sample and represent people's fear of crime fairly accurately.

In 2007, the *Sourcebook for Criminal Justice Statistics* provided information on fear of crime, or perceived victimization. Respondents were asked, "How often do you, yourself, worry about the following things—frequently, occasionally, or never?" The percentages in Table 7.1 show respondents' reactions to specific criminal events.

First, as noted in Table 7.1, identity theft was the crime that produced the greatest amount of fear. Seventy percent of the respondents reported being fearful of identity theft. Identity theft was followed by burglary. Violent personal crimes such as assaults, muggings, and being attacked ranked well below property crime victimization. It appears that property crime, which is the most

Table 7.1
Respondents Reporting Concern about Crime Victimization by Sex and Race, United States, 2010

Question: "How often do you, yourself, worry about the following things—frequently, occasionally, rarely or never?" (Percent responding "frequently" or "occasionally")

	Total	Sex		Race		
		Male	Female	White	Nonwhite[a]	Black
Being the victim of identity theft	70%	66%	75%	72%	66%	71%
Your home being burglarized when you are not there	49	47	52	50	50	55
Having your car stolen or broken into	43	43	43	42	45	47
Your home being burglarized when you are there	34	26	41	32	37	41
Having a school-aged child of yours physically harmed while attending school	32	32	32	31	35	44
Getting mugged	32	24	39	29	38	46
Being a victim of terrorism	29	26	31	28	30	34
Being attacked while driving your car	22	19	25	19	28	37
Being sexually assaulted	20	3	34	18	22	33
Getting murdered	18	12	24	15	24	39
Being the victim of a hate crime	18	15	21	13	31	44
Being assaulted or killed by a co-worker or other employee where you work	6	4	7	5	9	10

Note: These data are based on telephone interviews with a randomly selected national sample of 1,025 adults, 18 years of age and older, conducted Oct. 7-10, 2010.
[a]Includes Black respondents.

Source: Sourcebook (2010). *Sourcebook of Criminal Justice Statistics*. Washington, DC: Bureau of Justice Statistics.

common type of crime, generates the most fear among Americans. Invasions of one's privacy and often results in feelings of helplessness or global or **form-less fear**.

The results of the Bureau of Justice Statistics survey show that patterns of fear are relatively stable over time. The survey found that females were more fearful of being victimized as compared to males. In fact, females were more fearful of the crimes contained in the questionnaire. It is interesting that property crimes generated more fear than the possibility of being sexually assaulted. These findings are perhaps best explained by the victimization model, which postulates that fear is derived from cues in the environment such as the media and by the fact that females often feel that they are less capable of defending themselves.

In terms of race, African Americans were the most fearful of every type of crime with the exception of identity theft. African Americans' greater levels of fear most likely are attributable to the disorder model explanation. The following sections examine in detail a number of demographic factors as they relate to fear of crime.

Victimization and Fear of Crime

Heretofore, the research has been inconclusive regarding the relationship between victimization and fear of crime. Hale (1996) notes that victimization may make one more cautious or wary, but it will not necessarily contribute to fear of crime. The research on prior victimization, however, is rather mixed. For example, Miethe and Lee (1987) found that direct experience as a victim had an impact on fear from acts of violence, but it did not affect people's fear as a result of property crime. Warr (1984) argues that women who have been sexually assaulted or raped tend to be fearful of a host of other criminal acts. Agnew (1985) notes that direct victimization may not affect long-term levels of fear of crime because victims tend to neutralize their victimization. They may blame themselves, disregard the extent of their injuries (physical or economic), or attribute their victimization to helping a friend or acquaintance. Although direct victimization increases people's level of fear, direct victimization coupled with other factors usually determines the extent of their fear. When an individual has direct experience with victimization, the effect of other cues, such as crime and disorder in the environment, may be substantially increased, relative to people who have not been victimized.

Not all people are affected the same by fear of crime. That is, some people are more prone to be afraid, while others tend to disregard the potential consequences of crime regardless of its magnitude. There is substantial research indicating that age, gender, and race play a key role in fear of crime. Since community policing attempts to target fear of crime, it is important to understand the behavioral dynamics related to fear of crime. Even though direct victimization contributes to the fear of crime, research tends to show that the perception of disorder has a more profound impact on fear (Kohm, 2009). The question to ask here is what are the signs and clues that lead people to see something as disorderly?

Gender and Fear of Crime

A substantial body of research shows that females are more fearful of being victimized than males (Jackson, 2009). Research conducted by McGarrell, Giacomazzi, and Thurman (2000) and Hale (1996) indicates that **gender** is the strongest and best predictor of fear of crime. That females are more fearful is uniquely interesting given that young males constitute the group that is victimized most frequently. Young males tend to act irrationally more often and expose themselves to greater victimization risks. Women's fear of crime is directly linked to their vulnerability. Rape and sexual assaults constitute a significant category of crime for females. Callanan and Teasdale (2009) advise that women's increased fear of crime is the result of the potential physical harm that results from sexual assaults, but generally does not affect males. Also, it is very likely that sexual harassment, a common problem in the American workplace and public places, plays a key role in women's higher levels of fear. Sexual harassment can result in an increased sense of vulnerability. As females become older, however, their fear of crime is diminished (Franklin & Franklin, 2009). Perhaps experience teaches women that victimization is not as probable as they once thought. Also, Franklin and Franklin (2009) found that as women's incomes increased, their level of fear declined, but increased income for males had the opposite effect.

Many feminists maintain that significant levels of victimization generate women's fear of crime. They maintain that victimization studies as well as the Uniform Crime Reports substantially under-report female victimization. For example, women are more likely to be sexually assaulted by non-strangers, which contributes to their not reporting substantial numbers of crimes (Young, 1992). Women are also exposed to substantial levels of unreported hidden violence in the form of domestic violence. It is unlikely a majority of the domestic violence assaults are ever reported. Thus, feminists argue that female fear of crime may not necessarily be inconsistent with victimization rates (Walklate, 1994; Hale, 1996).

Another consideration when examining women's fear of crime is children. Heber (2009) described fear for the safety of others as altruistic fear. Women, especially mothers, experience a substantial amount of altruistic fear, especially if their children are exposed to risk factors in the neighborhood or in school. Their fear for the safety of their children transcends everyday life and constantly is a concern for most mothers. Indeed, Warr (1994) found altruistic fear to be just as prevalent as personal fear. Women even experience substantial levels of fear for their children when they live in relatively safe neighborhoods.

This research shows that community police programming must address several specific areas if the police are to reduce the levels of fear among women. First and foremost, the police must continue their efforts to more effectively deal with crimes that target women: rape, sexual assaults, and domestic violence. These crimes cast a pall over women's lives to the point that many become somewhat fearful anytime they venture into public spaces. Secondly, the police must ensure that there are ample safe public recreational areas for children; all too often the police take the safety of ball fields and parks for granted. A police presence should reduce altruistic fear on the part of parents. Third, it appears that a substantial portion of women's fear of crime is generated from their vulnerability. Police-citizen academies and other training for women should emphasize self-defense, victimization response, community safety, and support for victims of crime. Such training may increase women's feelings of safety and reduce their fear of crime.

Age and Fear of Crime

Age is only second to gender in predicting one's level of fear of crime (Hale, 1996). Generally, as people grow older, they become more wary of crime. Indeed, it is commonly believed that the elderly, because of their fear of crime, tend to isolate themselves from larger society. The elderly, to some extent, become captives in their own homes. This heightened level of fear is quite problematic since the elderly tend to be victimized less than any other group in society. Their increased fear likely is the result of their feeling that they are less able to physically defend themselves than younger people.

However, an objective examination of the fear of crime and the elderly produces a number of revealing anecdotal facts that help explain their elevated levels of fear. First, the elderly display heightened levels of fear in high-crime areas, but their levels of fear in non-high-crime areas are consistent with other groups (Jaycox, 1978). Similarly, Clemente and Kleiman (1976) found that age as a predictor of fear was strongest in inner cities and weakest in rural areas and small towns. Akers and his colleagues (1987) found that areas where there were higher concentrations of elderly, as opposed to a mix of ages, produced lower levels of fear. Also, older persons may not venture out of their homes because of health and money rather than because of their fear of crime (Clarke & Lewis, 1982). However, older people with health problems tend to be more fearful of crime (Crossman & Rader, 2011). It seems that older Americans' view of crime and their environment may be no different when they are in normal or relatively safe environments, but they may react or have heightened levels of fear relative to younger persons when confronted with indicators that alert them to danger. This is understandable since the elderly are less able to protect themselves.

As noted, much of the research on fear of crime finds that older people are more fearful than younger people. This research is not consistent, however. For example, Jackson (2009) found the opposite. This may be due to younger people being involved in or observing more risky behavior. Disorder and crime in youths' environment may result in an increase in levels of fear. Involvement in crime also affects fear. Melde (2009) found that as youth become involved in crime and delinquency, their fear diminishes.

The police have long recognized a need to work with the elderly regarding fear of crime. For example, the International Association of Chiefs of Police, the National Sheriffs' Association, and the American Association for Retired Persons developed a national outreach program designed to reduce crime and fear of crime among the elderly. Additionally, many local departments have community policing programs that focus on the elderly. Based on the research, it appears that CPOs should focus on the elderly who reside in areas where there are high crime and disorder rates. The police should emphasize to urban planners that elderly-exclusive housing should be made available throughout the community. Finally, the police should attack disorder problems, especially where the elderly reside, since the elderly tend to interpret cues such as disorder as a greater threat.

Race and Fear of Crime

African Americans tend to be more fearful of crime as compared to Whites (Skogan, 1995). No group of people has a higher rate of victimization from violent crime, particularly homicide, than young, male African Americans. In fact, homicide is the leading cause of death for this group of people. Also, African Americans constitute one of the most impoverished categories of people in the United States. Their poverty forces them to live in some of the most crime-ridden neighborhoods. Given where they reside and their victimization rates, there is no question that African Americans should have a higher level of fear of crime.

It is interesting to study the dynamics of race and fear of crime. First, research tends to indicate that younger African Americans do not have a high fear of crime. Young African American males, because of street culture, more often must project an image of toughness or machismo (Miller, 1958). On the streets, the slightest indication of weakness or fear may very well lead to victimization, resulting in some young African American males' inclinations to act fearless.

Older African Americans, on the other hand, exhibit higher levels of fear of crime. Younger males have significantly higher rates of victimization and criminal perpetration resulting in older African Americans being exposed to increasingly higher rates of violence. Some have advocated that elderly African Americans are caught in a double jeopardy (Ortega & Myles, 1987). On the one hand, they are exposed to higher levels of violence, while on the other, they have the least amount of resources to escape the violence. Also, older African Americans, because of a lack of resources, find it more difficult to recover or cope with criminal victimization.

The diversity of neighborhoods also affects fear of crime. Lane and Meeker (2011) found that people living in diverse neighborhoods are more fearful of crime. When there is diversity, some may perceive that the neighborhood has more disorder as compared to a more homogeneous neighborhood. Here, racism and perceptions of disorder, not crime, drive fear of crime.

Historically, the police have under-enforced the law in poorer sections of the cities where African Americans reside in high numbers. The police have had poor relations with the people, did not understand their problems, and generally attempted to avoid them. Gaines and Kappeler (2011) note that this under-enforcement, as opposed to over-enforcement, generates the largest number of complaints from the African American community. Indeed, the police frequently come under fire from some segments of the African American community when they increase their presence and enforcement levels, but they also receive substantial support from a number of residents, especially the elderly, who are in favor of stricter enforcement. Community policing dictates better relations with the community by working with people on common problems. CPOs must assure people in high-crime areas that the police are there to help and support them. CPOs must also maintain a high level of visibility in these neighborhoods to help alleviate the levels of fear. Also, crafting a solution to the problems that generate fear of crime "with" rather than "for" the African American community is the best possible police response.

Fear of Crime and Schools

Schools represent a special case in terms of fear of crime. First, because a number of our schools have deteriorated substantially as a result of low school funding and the laying off of large numbers of teachers and staff, schools now have lower levels of security or guardianship. Also, many schools serve disadvantaged communities, resulting in the enrollment of large numbers of at-risk youths or delinquents. As a result of these populations, many schools now have school resource officers from police and probation departments. These school resource officers are charged with assisting in maintaining order and checking on students who are on probation or who have a history of problem behavior. Nonetheless, a number of these positions are being cut as a result of budget constraints. Second, there is a degree of altruistic fear on the part of parents who worry about the safety of their children. Nationally, there have been numerous shootings, assaults, and other attacks on students that have been highly publicized, increasing this altruistic fear. Even though research shows that schools are the safest place for young people, media coverage of sensational school crimes increases fear of crime.

A recent study by Dinkes and his colleagues (2009) found that students were victimized at a rate of 42.7 per 1,000 students (Table 7.2). Although the majority of offenses centered around property crime and drugs and alcohol, 27.9 students per 1,000 were victimized in violent offenses. This means that 90 students will be the victims of violent crime each year in a school with 3,000 students. The vast majority of these acts of violence, however, are not serious attacks, and less than 0.02 percent of students in any given year will experience a serious act of violence while attending school.

Bullying is another problem that has become a major issue in schools. Nansel et al. (2003) and Bender and Friedrich (2011) advise that bullying behaviors are precursors to fighting, carrying weapons, and violence. In 2007, about 32 percent of students reported being bullied, and of those reporting the offense, 79 percent reported that the bullying took place in school (Nansel et al., 2003). Bullying is a significant problem and, combined with the amount of crime in schools, results in significant fear of crime on the part of students and many parents. Randa and Wilcox (2010) found that disorder, especially the presence of gangs, and prior experience with bullying increased fear on the part of students and resulted in their avoiding school and places that were seen as dangerous.

Table 7.2

Percentage of Public Schools Experiencing and Reporting Incidents of Crime, Number of Incidents, and the Rate of Crimes per 1,000 Students, by Types of Crime for 2007-2008

Type of crime	Percent of schools	Number of incidents	Rate per 1,000 students
Total	85.5	2,040,800	42.7
Violent incidents	75.5	1,332,400	27.9
Physical attack or fight without a weapon	72.7	812,200	17.0
Threat of physical attack without a weapon	47.8	461,900	9.7
Serious violent incidents	17.2	58,300	1.2
Rape or attempted rape	0.8	800	–
Sexual battery other than rape	2.5	3,800	0.1
Physical attack or fight with a weapon	3.0	14,000	0.3
Robbery with a weapon	0.41	700	–
Robbery without a weapon	5.2	18,700	0.4
Theft	47.3	268,900	5.6
Other incidents	67.4	439,500	9.2
Possession of a firearm or explosives	4.7	5,300	0.1
Possession of a knife or sharp object	40.6	77,000	1.6
Distribution, possession, or use of illegal drugs	23.2	107,300	2.2
Distribution, possession, or use of alcohol	14.9	37,800	0.8
Vandalism	49.3	212,100	4.4

Source: Dinkes, R., J. Kemp, K. Baum & T. Snyder (2009). *Indicators of School Crime and Safety, 2009*, Washington, DC: U.S. Department of Education and U.S. Department of Justice Office of Justice Programs, p. 94.

SPOTLIGHT ON COMMUNITY POLICING PRACTICE

South Fulton County Truancy Reduction & Intervention Project (T.R.I.P)

"Ensuring the safety of our youth is of critical importance," according to COPS Office Director Bernard Melekian, and the COPS Office is committed to improving school safety and reducing child victimization through a variety of grant funded programs as well as seeking those agencies in the field who are committed to the issues facing our children every day. One such example is the commitment of the Fulton County (GA) Police Department to develop a community policing model to prevent, identify, and intervene in truancy situations in targeted areas of South Fulton through their **Truancy Reduction & Intervention Project (T.R.I.P)**.

There is a massive responsibility placed on our school system as classrooms no longer depend solely on teachers, but on teams of administrators, health care workers, security staff, and law enforcement professionals to successfully collaborate with the goal of keeping

(Continued)

America's children safe. Truancy is one of the first indicators of a child who is in trouble. Truancy has been correlated with teen pregnancy, juvenile delinquency, substance abuse, and adult criminality. Truancy is also one of the most effective predictors of educational failure according to a 2002 report that showed that 80 percent of dropouts were chronically truant in the previous year. An estimated three out of ten high school students do not graduate from high school on time, and of the 4.2 million Americans who turn 20 each year, 805,000 do not have a high school diploma or GED. Clearly this can have negative long-term outcomes, as a 2006 report indicated that high school dropouts are 3½ times more likely than high school graduates to be arrested and 8 times more likely to be incarcerated.

The negative impact of truancy significantly affects students, but also has negative outcomes for families, schools, and society. Families may lose children to gangs, risky behavior, and other nonproductive behavior. Schools show declining attendance rates and lose federal and state education funding. The community has a less educated workforce, while crime by truants increases during school hours. The pipeline of citizens who can become contributing members of society is significantly reduced due to the impact of truancy.

The reasons for children choosing to "ditch" school are numerous, but sometimes fear of violence can play a very important role. In 2007, 7 percent of students ages 12–18 reported that they had avoided a school activity or one or more places in school in the previous 6 months because of fear of attack or harm. During the 2007–2008 school year, 85 percent of public schools recorded that one or more incidents of crime had taken place at school. During the same year, 75 percent of public schools recorded one or more violent incidents of crime and 17 percent recorded one or more serious violent incidents. Thirty-eight percent of public schools reported at least one violent incident to police and 13 percent reported at least one serious violent incident to police. During the 2007–2008 school year, 25 percent of public schools reported that bullying occurred among students on a daily or weekly basis, and 32 percent of students ages 12–18 reported having been bullied at school during the school year.

There are many national and local agencies working to identify the best strategies to address truancy and the surrounding issues, and those that are most successful include a broad-based collaborative effort where schools and communities work jointly and proactively to effectively tackle the problem of truancy. School officials, parents, politicians, law officials, courts, community organizations, and social services agencies must all be at the planning table to collaboratively develop targeted truancy intervention strategies.

The mission of the Fulton County T.R.I.P. is to reduce the number of truancies in South Fulton by creating a broad-based community and inter-agency team to address truancy. After witnessing the negative impacts of truancy on their students, families, high school graduation rates, workforce development, and entire community, the Fulton County Police Department partnered with Fulton County Schools to target high school students with the highest rate of unexcused absences. The Truancy Prevention Program team includes Fulton County Housing & Human Services; Fulton County Police Department; Fulton County Schools Police Department; Fulton County Office of Communications; Office of the County Attorney; Office of the Fulton

County District Attorney; Fulton County Juvenile Court; Fulton County Office of Grants & Community Partnerships; MARTA Suppression Unit; Truancy Intervention Project; parents; and community organizations.

The goals of this program are to reduce the number of students loitering in the community during school hours; reduce criminal activity of truants in Commission District 7 during school hours; educate and engage the community-at-large about the impact of truancy by working directly with truants and their families to address factors that contribute to truant behavior; and provide needs-based resource referrals to truant students and their families. This initiative uses a "choices and consequences" approach and builds on the strengths and resources within the South Fulton communities, such as:

- Truancy sweeps by law enforcement every day at Fulton County Schools
- A T.R.I.P. Hotline … to report suspected truancy
- Reduction of crime inflicted upon individuals, businesses, and their property during school hours
- Swift parental/guardian notification of truant child
- Improved communication and relationships among multiple systems, agencies, and stakeholders
- Accountability of truants and parents/guardians for truant behaviors
- Needs-based resources to address underlying causes of truancy
- Civic engagement to become a part of the solution to reduce truancy

Since its institution in October 2009, T.R.I.P has successfully processed over 250 youth through the program and has offered support services that have helped both the youth and their families.

Reginald Padgett
Staff Accountant
The COPS Office

Brian Casal
Captain
Fulton County Police Department

Source: The e-newsletter of the COPS Office, Volume 4, Issue 4, April 2011 [footnotes omitted].

The data demonstrate that school crime increases fear of crime not only on the part of students, but also on the part of parents, teachers, and staff. It is a significant problem and should receive priority from the police. Fear of crime is a complicated problem necessitating that CPOs and school resource officers work with school officials. This may involve working with youths who have high levels of fear, and parents of victims as well as perpetrators. It is important to have direct contact with both groups. In some cases, students should be referred to counselors. Most important, however, is that CPOs and school resource officers attempt to address problems. This may involve student disciplinary actions on the part of the schools.

Media and Fear of Crime

Crime, especially sensational or unusual crime, is of significant interest to reporters and the general public. Graber (1980), in a study of newspapers, found that 22 to 28 percent of the news stories were devoted to crime, and 12 to 13 percent of television news was devoted to crime. Harry Marsh (1991) found similar patterns in his examination of newspaper coverage of crime. More importantly, however, is the fact that the media tends to distort such coverage. Sasson (1995) and Barak (1995) found that journalistic accounts of crime were distorted, emphasizing pathological individuals who commit bizarre acts. Such coverage tends to bias the public and promote fear of victimization that is diametrically opposed to police purposes. The public comes to develop a convoluted view of crime. People tend to believe that there are many more rapes, murders, assaults, and violent crimes than actually occur. Skogan and Maxfield (1981) noted that news coverage could create an impression of higher crime rates by reporting on criminal acts in other communities without clearly specifying where the crime took place. What purposes are served when a Kentucky television station reports on a series of homicides or sexual assaults in California or Florida? For example, the 2005 trial of Scott Peterson who was convicted of killing his wife and unborn child was a staple of national news. Indeed, even though news journalists do not admit it, newspaper and television news reporting too often imitates that of supermarket tabloids. Newsroom editors subscribe to the old adage that "if it bleeds, it leads."

Table 7.3

Attitudes Toward Level of Crime in the United States by Demographic Characteristics, United States, 2010[a]

Question: "Is there more crime in the U.S. than there was a year ago, or less?"			
	More	Less	Same[b]	Don't know/refused
National	66%	17%	8%	9%
Sex				
Male	61	22	8	9
Female	70	13	8	9

Table 7.3

Attitudes Toward Level of Crime in the United States by Demographic Characteristics, United States, 2010[a]—cont'd

	More	Less	Same[b]	Don't know/refused
Race				
White	66	16	9	9
Nonwhite	66	19	6	9
Black	68	17	3	11
Age				
18 to 29 years	64	20	6	11
30 to 49 years	67	17	8	8
50 to 64 years	63	17	9	11
50 years and older	67	16	8	9
65 years and older	70	16	7	7
Education				
College post graduate	43	28	15	14
College graduate	57	21	11	12
Some college	73	14	4	8
High school graduate or less	74	14	6	7
Income				
$75,000 and over	59	19	11	11
$50,000 to $74,999	63	20	8	9
$30,000 to $49,999	74	13	8	4
$20,000 to $29,999	73	18	1	8
Under $20,000	72	12	5	11
Region				
East	62	18	11	9
Midwest	62	16	6	16
South	74	14	6	7
West	61	22	10	7
Politics				
Republican	77	13	5	5
Democrat	63	20	8	9
Independent	59	18	10	13
Ideology				
Conservative	74	14	6	6
Moderate	60	21	10	10
Liberal	59	21	8	11

Note: These data are based on telephone interviews with a randomly selected national sample of 1,025 adults, 18 years of age and older, conducted Oct. 7-10, 2010.
[a]Percents may not add to 100 because of rounding.
[b]Response volunteered.

Source: Sourcebook (2010). *Sourcebook of Criminal Justice Statistics.* Washington, DC: Bureau of Justice Statistics.

It has long been postulated that the media plays a key role in the fear of crime. The media, as a result of their slanted coverage of the news, tend to start what some call "**moral panics**" (Kappeler & Potter, 2005; Potter & Kappeler, 2006). As a result of their coverage, the media may cause an overreaction to a crime problem that did not exist. For example, Williams and Dickinson (1993) found that those newspapers that report crime, especially crimes involving personal violence in the most pronounced form, generally have readers who are the most fearful of victimization. Jurin and Fields (1994) examined newspaper articles about crime and found that the sensational nature of the crime, public interest in the victim or perpetrator, or humorous nature of the crime contributed to it being reported. These practices substantially affect the public's fear of crime.

Although the reporting of news, especially violent and sensational crime, serves to heighten fear of crime, the relationship between the two factors is not straightforward. Liska and Baccaglini (1990) identify three factors that serve to predict the influence of news reporting on fear of crime: (1) locale, (2) degree of randomness, and (3) the bizarreness or violence associated with the act. In terms of locale, when crime was reported from other cities or states, it tended not to increase fear of crime. Reporting on crime in one's neighborhood or hometown, however, did increase fear (Chiricos, Padgett & Gertz, 2000). If the crime was a random act of violence, as opposed to where the perpetrator and victim knew each other or had some preexisting relationship, it resulted in greater levels of fear of crime. Finally, the violent or bizarre crimes tended to increase fear.

The **law enforcement community** has also contributed to the public's unrealistic fear of crime. In many cases police officials became active in the media process and in providing misleading information to the public. During the 1980s and 1990s, a new form of television programming emerged following the format of information commercials; television crime programs began to blend entertainment and government-sponsored messages. These shows used government officials, well-known relatives of crime victims, and law enforcement officers to inform the public about crime. These television programs were broadcast from local stations across the nation under various names like Crime Solvers, "Secret Witness," and "Crime Line." These programs encourage viewers to report crime and criminals in exchange for monetary rewards. They were predecessors to the government's national media campaign, "Taking a Bite Out of Crime," which mustered participation in support of crime prevention, self-protection, and neighborhood cooperation (Kappeler & Potter, 2005; Potter & Kappeler, 2006). These programs resulted in increased viewer participation in the program, heightening the potential for increased fear.

Using police officials as spokespersons gave viewers the impression of official credibility. Television shows like "Unsolved Mysteries," "Rescue 911," "48 Hours," "America's Most Wanted," "Cops," and "Top Cops" reenacted crimes accompanied by narratives from law enforcement officials. "Unsolved Mysteries" had a segment in the show called "FBI Alert." The segment was hosted by FBI director William Sessions and spent its time describing American fugitives (Tunnell, 1992). "Bad Girls" and "Gangs, Cops, and Drugs," both broadcast by the National Broadcasting Company (NBC), featured drug czar William Bennett, who "eschewed any social-structural explanation for drug-related crime. ... As mindless as these depictions were, 'Gangs, Cops, and Drugs' aired two nights during prime time, evidently cashing in on a recent crime fad" (Tunnell, 1992:299). These shows and their spin-offs contributed to an unprecedented level of fear of crime in American society (Cavender & Bond-Maupin, 1998) and relied upon the believability of police officials. Viewers who relied on such information ended up with a distorted view of the world as more dangerous than it really was (Kappeler & Potter, 2005; Potter & Kappeler, 2006).

The **media** contribute to feelings of fear of crime through the reporting of violent, bizarre crimes and the use of sensational law-enforcement TV shows (Kappeler & Potter, 2005; Potter & Kappeler, 2006). Much of this reporting is of crimes that occur in other cities or states. Nonetheless, such reporting has a chilling effect on people's sense of security. Community policing dictates that the police appeal to the news media for more balanced reporting and that the police participate more carefully in media productions. Although crime news is extremely popular, the police should attempt to have the media include more human-interest stories about the police and the community. These types of stories may foster a greater sense of security and help reduce the fear of crime.

Wealth and Fear of Crime

Another factor affecting one's fear of crime is personal wealth (Bennett & Flavin, 1994). People with **wealth**, or those living in wealthy neighborhoods, are less fearful of crime. Such neighborhoods are better able to control crime and disorder as compared to other neighborhoods. Wealth enables a neighborhood to better influence government, resulting in better police services and governmental services in general. For example, the police generally are more responsive to calls for service in higher socioeconomic areas, and people in these areas are able to obtain a more rapid, effective response when reporting problems such as street lights, garbage pickups, or building code violations. Police patrols in these neighborhoods often use more critical criteria when determining who to

investigate—they often see their role in these neighborhoods as preventing outsiders from victimizing or bothering residents. Moreover, such neighborhoods
tend to be exclusive with fewer individuals committing "traditional" crime or
acts of disorder—those acts the media have taught the public to fear the most.
Moreover, many of these neighborhoods are gated communities where access is
highly restricted.

Wealthier residents also have a higher capacity to rebound from victimization. That is, when they are victimized, they often have the financial resources
and insurance to minimize the loss and inconvenience associated with the
criminal act. The recovery time is much shorter, relative to belonging to lower
income socioeconomic groups.

Figure 7.2
Factors Influencing the Fear of Crime

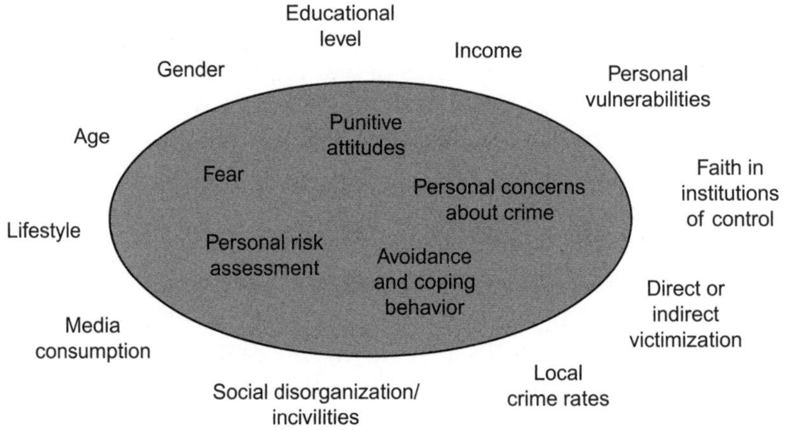

Source: Axel Groenemeyer, Crimprev info n°27bis - Research on insecurity – a lot of answers, but what was
the question? The role of social, political and cultural transformations in constructing contemporary insecurities, *CRIMPREV* [En ligne], CRIMPREV programme, Crimprev Info, URL: http://lodel.irevues.inist.fr/crimprev/
index.php?id=244.

Community Policing and Fear of Crime

The traditional police response to fear of crime has been to disregard it
as a legitimate police objective. The police saw themselves as crime-fighters
whose primary objective was to attack crime. The reduction of crime was seen
as the essence of police work. If fear of crime was reduced, it was a corollary
benefit. Reducing the fear of crime did not fit within the scheme of things for
policing. Since traditional policing relied primarily on routine patrol, which is

basically reactive, there are obvious structural limitations that make it difficult to provide an effective means for confronting the fear of crime separately and directly. Though crime prevention and police-community relations programs have helped broaden the traditional police response in ways that impinge on fear of crime, these peripheral attempts tended to only marginally affect the host of crime and criminal justice concerns facing many people, and they were not intended to have an impact on fear.

It is also important to note that **routine preventive patrol** activities have little impact on people's perception of the police and their feelings of safety. The Kansas City Patrol Study conducted in the early 1970s demonstrated this point (Kelling, Pate, Diekman & Brown, 1974). Essentially, the study demonstrated that variances in levels of patrols did not affect crime or people's perceptions of crime and safety. The Kansas City Patrol Study demonstrated that people pay little attention to the police who ride the streets as a function of routine patrol. It appeared that the public's perception of the police was based on direct contacts and the quality of those contacts. As Skogan (2009) found, reductions in concern about crime flow from increased confidence in the police.

Whereas traditional policing attacks direct sources of fear of crime by attempting to reduce victimization through suppressive tactics, community policing goes beyond this limited perspective by advancing fear of crime as a legitimate police concern or objective. By dealing with issues such as property crime, petty crime, and the signs of disorder in neighborhoods, community policing inspires confidence in people that further contributes to crime and fear reduction. And by expanding the police mission to embrace proactive efforts to address social and physical disorder, community policing directly addresses the indirect fears associated with community problems.

In some ways, community policing provides elements of community action and community development, but as part of a decentralized police approach. Because the job demands learning about the various sources of help available, CPOs can also address fear by linking people with emotional problems to affordable and appropriate counseling and helping the homeless find shelter. If panhandlers plague the area, the CPO can tailor the response to local needs and local resources. It might mean linking people to employment opportunities in the area, with the CPO's office as a clearinghouse. In other cases, it might mean involving juveniles in after-school activities so that they make more constructive use of their time. The virtue of the community policing approach is that the officers understand the nature of the challenge and have the opportunity to work with people on developing new solutions, and the CPO's sustained presence provides an opportunity to monitor the results. If it does not work, the CPO can work with people on trying new ideas. If it is successful, the CPO is there to make sure that it keeps working, altering and refining the initiative to fit changing needs. Here, the police can implement what Skogan (2009) referred to as reassurance policing. **Reassurance policing** simply is police actions that go beyond crime and disorder. The police develop positive relationships with community members to the point that they have confidence in the police and their ability to serve community needs. The police must develop a positive working relationship with people.

Such efforts also demonstrate to people that they can regain control of their communities, and helplessness is an important element of fear. One of the biggest challenges that a CPO faces is the apathy that too much fear can spawn. A healthy dose of fear of crime can inspire positive action, but too much can paralyze people so that they will not take part. Once initial efforts targeted at community conditions begin to make a visible difference, it can galvanize more people to get involved. In this regard, a number of police departments have experimented with a variety of programs to reduce fear of crime.

Police Programming and Fear of Crime

As fear began to become an issue in policing, a number of departments developed programs to deal with it. In some cases, fear of crime was the primary objective, while in others, it was one of several law enforcement objectives. Nonetheless, the police began to view fear of crime as an important objective. Two early endeavors are discussed here, Newark, New Jersey, and Houston, Texas.

In the 1980s, the City of Newark experienced severe budgetary problems that resulted in the department trimming its police force by one-third even though the city had a significant crime problem. Given the crime problem and shortage of officers, Newark represented a city in dire need of a reduction in crime and the fear of crime.

As the result of an extensive planning process, the police department identified three basic sources of fear that should be addressed:

- The lack of local, relevant information about crime and ways to prevent it;

- The presence of social disorder and physical deterioration in a neighborhood; and

- The limited quantity and quality of contacts between police officers and the public (Williams & Pate, 1986:56).

The department implemented a three-prong approach to attack the problem. First, the department began publishing a monthly newsletter, which was mailed to a randomly selected set of households. The newsletter contained information about the neighborhood, police efforts in the area, crime prevention and other safety tips, neighborhood meetings, and other positive news about the neighborhood. The purpose of the newsletter was to provide residents with information about the crime problem and the measures that were taken to address it. Second, efforts were made to reduce the signs of crime. This consisted of two distinct strategies: directed patrols and neighborhood cleanup. The directed patrols conducted high visibility law enforcement to include radar, foot patrols to strictly enforce ordinances to reduce disorder, and road checks to enforce a host of motor vehicle codes. The neighborhood cleanup consisted of coordinating efforts with a number of city departments to clean up trash, repair streets, collect garbage, and improve lighting in the area. The police also worked with the courts to have juveniles provide community service hours to assist in the cleanup. The third prong was community policing, which was coordinated from a storefront police office in the targeted area. Here, officers attempted to implement a number of crime prevention programs including block watches, door-to-door activities, walk-in crime reporting, and referral of people to other agencies to assist with problems. Additionally, police officers were assigned to visit individuals and groups to further enhance the program.

An evaluation of the program found that the community newsletter had no profound effect on crime or fear problems. Although residents voiced an appreciation for receiving the newsletter, few could recall its contents or receiving it. The evaluators attributed this to most people not reading it once they received it. In terms of reducing the signs of crime, the evaluation found that it had very limited effects on crime or fear of crime. Prior victims of crime were even less affected by the program than nonvictims. The community policing program, however, did yield significant effects in several areas. The program resulted in reductions in perceived social disorder problems, reductions in the level of concern about property crime, reductions in actual property crime, and people had improved perceptions of the police.

In Houston, the primary strategy for dealing with problems was routine preventive patrols. This resulted in people having little contact with the police, and in many cases, seldom seeing them involved in law-enforcement activities. The department decided to implement a strategy to deal with the fear-of-crime problem as well as people's feelings of isolation from their police department and city government.

A task force was formed to examine the problem and recommend strategies. The task force eventually decided upon five strategies. First, the department implemented a victim re-contact program where officers re-contacted recent crime victims to express the department's concern over their loss, and to offer additional assistance. Prior to contacting the victim, officers would study the case to determine what possible actions the police could take to help the victim. Unfortunately, the department's paperwork flow resulted in many victims not being contacted until several weeks had passed. Second, as in Newark, the Houston police mailed newsletters to keep people abreast of crime news and police activities. Third, the department implemented contact patrols. Here, officers were instructed to get out of their patrol cars while on patrol and meet with people. Generally, these contacts lasted for several minutes. Fourth, the department opened a storefront office where they held community meetings and implemented after-school programs for juveniles and service programs for adults and the elderly. Finally, a **Community Organizing Response Team** (CORT) was dispatched to create organization in the community by working with community leaders. Organizing was accomplished through block meetings and other means of contact.

Brown and Wycoff's (1986) evaluation of the program found that the victim re-contact program did not produce any desirable results. The evaluators surmised that the officers' contacts were too late. Most of the victims had found services long before the officers contacted them. The contact patrols resulted in less fear of crime, perceived declines in disorder, and better feelings about the police. The researchers report African Americans and renters' perceptions about crime and disorder did not change, while Whites' and Latinos' attitudes changed. The community police station yielded results similar to the contact patrols. Whites' and Latinos' attitudes were affected positively, while African Americans did not register the benefits of the program. Finally, the CORT program resulted in reduced perceptions of disorder and improved evaluations of the police. African Americans registered marginal improvements in their perceptions as a result of the program.

What can be learned from the Newark and Houston experiences? First, because fear of crime is a complex problem, simplistic responses may not produce the desired results. For example, both departments implemented newsletters, but had no effect. Newsletters are a low-cost method of reaching out to the public, but because they result in no one-on-one contact with the public, they have little impact. Second, neighborhoods and ethnic groups respond differently to various police programs. A program may affect one group such as Whites or Latinos, which was the case in Houston, but not other groups. This indicates that programs must be designed to target particular problems. Spellman (2004) and Weisburd and Eck (2004) advise that the police must tailor programs to individual neighborhoods. Neighborhoods are unique and what works in one area may not be effective in another. This is not to say the programs in Newark and Houston were without merit, because they did have an impact on people's perceptions of disorder, amount of crime, and the police. These, too, are important goals, but police departments should note that all three objectives are important, and should develop programs that comprehensively address them. Moreover, the programs in Newark and Houston provide some guidance on how to proceed in the future.

In a more recent study, Scheider, Rowell, and Bezdikian (2003) investigated the effects of community policing on satisfaction with the police, crime prevention behaviors, and fear of crime, in 12 different cities. They found that community policing did not affect people's fear of crime. In fact, they found that crime prevention activities such as distributing crime news or information and engaging in crime prevention activities increased people's fear of crime. However, Zhao and his colleagues (2002a) examined community policing in 50 cities and found that fear of crime was reduced in the majority of them. It seems that providing police presence does not improve people's fear of crime. Indeed, it appears that an increase in "positive contacts" between the police and the people is the best way to reduce fear of crime.

Community policing consists of two primary components: problem solving and community partnerships or community building. Weisburd and Eck (2004) found that programs focusing on community partnerships and community building reduced fear of crime. They found that community partnerships did not have an effect on crime or disorder unless problem solving was part of the police response. Unfortunately, many police departments have neglected the community partnership portion of community policing, and have exclusively focused on problem solving. When departments do not emphasize community partnerships as part of the strategic mix, they are neglecting problems such as fear of crime. Police departments must understand that crime and fear of crime are problems that must be uniquely addressed in all neighborhoods.

Along these lines, Roh and Oliver (2005) examined the impact of community policing on fear of crime and found that when CPOs addressed incivilities and quality of life issues, they were able to reduce people's fear of crime. They found that victimization did not substantially contribute to fear of crime. The work by Weisburd and Eck (2004) and Roh and Oliver (2005) shows that CPOs must engage in community building and community partnerships while engaging in problem solving. When conducting these community policing activities, CPOs should focus on problems that detract from residents' quality of life and incivilities in the community. Reducing fear of crime requires a complex response on the part of the police. Finally, Hinkle and Weisburd (2008) observed that the police must be cautious when attending to problems such as disorder and incivilities. Police interventions without community partnerships or positive contacts may well increase fear of crime, as the interventions may give the appearance of more problems than actually exist. There is no question that a multi-pronged approach is needed to deal with fear of crime and crime itself.

Summary

Fear of crime is a legitimate police concern. Although it does not register in the Uniform Crime Reports or police statistics, it does have a substantial impact on individuals and communities. People should be able to walk the streets and other public places without fear of being victimized. They should be safe in their homes without fear of being burglarized or robbed. Fear directly affects people's quality of life, and government, primarily the police, has an obligation not only to ensure that people are safe, but that they feel safe. Therefore, it can be inferred that fear of crime is a direct responsibility of the police. In many instances, it is just as problematic to a community as crime itself.

Research shows that women, the elderly, and African Americans have the greatest levels of fear. This same research shows that fear does not exist in uniform levels across groups of people. A number of socioeconomic variables mediate and affect how fear affects people. The police should understand how fear is distributed across populations and use this understanding to formulate programs to assure people that they are safe. Reducing fear of crime is just as legitimate as reducing crime itself. In fact, fear may have more detrimental effects on larger numbers of people than crime itself.

There are a number of causes of fear of crime, as exemplified by the four models that have evolved that explain it. Fear emanates from past victimization, disorder, and community interactional processes. This shows that fear of crime is a complex social phenomenon that cannot be adequately addressed with simple programs. Police departments have attempted to reduce fear of crime through a variety of programs. These programs have centered around providing people with information about the police and crime, decentralized operations through storefronts and mini-police stations, and working more closely with people through walking and bicycle patrols, victim re-contact programs, and other programs that emphasize higher quality contacts with people.

Community policing, as a direct result of its emphasis on people, ensures that the police reduce fear. Police managers must continue this trend by developing strategies that focus on specific problems and fear issues within the community and have more positive contacts with people. In other words, fear of crime in a neighborhood is a problem that should receive special attention from the police. It also means that police officers should use the SARA model and deploy strategies that will best reduce fear of crime. This brand of community policing will assist the police in their pursuit of crime reduction and enhancement of quality of life.

KEY TERMS IN CHAPTER 7

- age and fear of crime
- altruistic fear
- behavioral component
- cognitive component
- community concern model
- Community Organizing Response Team (CORT)
- disorder model
- emotive component
- fear of crime
- Flint Foot Patrol Experiment
- gender and fear of crime
- law enforcement community
- media

- moral panics
- Newark and fear reduction
- personal fear
- primary victimization
- reassurance policing
- routine preventive patrol
- secondary victimization
- social capital
- subcultural-diversity model
- victimization
- victimization model
- violent crime
- wealth

DISCUSSION QUESTIONS

1. Discuss the victims' movement and the factors that precipitated the movement.
2. Describe the significance of the Flint Foot Patrol program. Include the factors that led to its implementation, the strategies and objectives of the program, and the results.
3. The research discussed in the text regarding fear of crime indicates some degree of irrationality. Discuss the discrepancies between the results of these studies, including the demographic descriptors of those most fearful and those least victimized by crime.
4. Discuss Garofalo's definition of "fear of crime" and the implications of that definition.
5. Describe and discuss the areas of indirect costs to society because of fear of crime.
6. What does the research suggest about the issue of whether victims of crime are more fearful of crime than nonvictims?
7. Discuss who is most fearful of crime in terms of gender, race, social class, education, and age.
8. Much research indicates that females are more fearful of being victimized than males. Discuss the explanation for that fear.
9. Discuss the ways in which print and television media impact citizen fear of crime. Include a description of the relevant research discussed in the text.
10. In accordance with the philosophy of community policing, identify and discuss five steps police can take to minimize people's fear of crime.
11. Describe efforts taken by the Houston Police Department to reduce fear of crime. What parts of the program were unsuccessful? Which components were successful?
12. Discuss the four models of fear of crime.

References

Agnew, R. S. (1985). Neutralizing the Impact of Crime. *Criminal Justice and Behavior, 12*, 221-239.

Akers, R. L., Sellers, C., & Cochran, J. (1987). Fear of Crime and Victimization among the Elderly in Different Types of Communities. *Criminology, 25*(3), 487-505.

Amir, M. (1971). *Patterns of Forcible Rape.* Chicago, IL: University of Chicago.

Barak, G. (1995). *Media, Process, and the Social Construction of Crime: Studies in Newsmaking Criminology.* New York: Garland Publishing.

Bender, D., & Friedrich, L. (2011). Bullying in School as a Predictor of Delinquency, Violence, and Other Anti-Social Behaviour in Adulthood. *Criminal Behavior & Mental Health, 21*, 99-106.

Bennett, R., & Flavin, J. (1994). Determinants of Fear of Crime: The Effect of Cultural Setting. *Justice Quarterly, 11*, 357-381.

Brown, L. P., & Wycoff, M.A. (1986). Policing Houston: Reducing Fear and Improving Service. *Crime & Delinquency, 33*(1), 71-89.

Bursik, R. (2000). The Systemic Theory of Neighborhood Crime Rates. In S. Simpson (Ed.), *Of Crime and Criminality: The Use of Theory in Everyday Life.* Thousand Oaks, CA: Pine Forge Press.

Callanan, V., & Teasdale, B. (2009). An Exploration of Gender Differences in Measurement of Fear of Crime. *Feminist Criminology, 4*, 359-376.

Cavender, G., & Bond-Maupin, L. (1998). Fear and Loathing on Reality Television: An Analysis of "America's Most Wanted" and "Unsolved Mysteries." In G. W. Potter & V. E. Kappeler (Eds.), *Constructing Crime.* Prospect Heights, IL: Waveland Press.

Chiricos, T., Hogan, M., & Gertz, M. (1997). Racial Composition of Neighborhood and Fear of Crime. *Criminology, 35*, 107-131.

Chiricos, T., Padgett, K., & Gertz, M. (2000). Fear, TV News, and the Reality of Crime. *Criminology, 38*(3), 755-786.

Christian, J. (2009). Fear Mongering and Crime Policy. Paper presented at the Annual Meeting of the American Society of Criminology.

Clarke, A. H., & Lewis, M. (1982). Fear of Crime among the Elderly. *British Journal of Criminology, 22*(1), 49-62.

Clemente, F., & Kleiman, M. B. (1976). Fear of Crime amongst the Aged. *The Gerontologist, 16*, 207-210.

Covington, J., & Taylor, R. B. (1991). Fear of Crime in Urban Neighborhoods: Implications of Between and Within Neighborhood Sources for Current Models. *Sociological Quarterly, 32*(2), 231-249.

Crossman, J., & Rader, N. (2011). Fear of Crime and Personal Vulnerability: Examining Self-Reported Health. *Sociological Spectrum, 31*, 141-162.

Dinkes, R., Kemp, J., Baum, K., & Snyder, T. (2009). *Indicators of School Crime and Safety, 2009.* Washington, DC: U.S. Department of Education and U.S. Department of Justice Office of Justice Programs.

Ferguson, K., & Mindel, C. (2007). Modeling Fear of Crime in 10 Different Dallas Neighborhoods: A Test of Social Capital Theory. *Crime & Delinquency, 53*, 322-349.

Franklin, C., & Franklin, T. (2009). Predicting Fear of Crime. *Feminist Criminology, 4*, 83-106.

Gaines, L. K., & Kappeler, V. E. (2011). *Policing in America* (7th ed.). Waltham, MA: Anderson.

Garofalo, J. (1981). The Fear of Crime: Causes and Consequences. *The Journal of Criminal Law & Criminology, 72*(2), 839-857.

Gau, J., & Pratt, T. (2008). Broken Windows or Window Dressing? Citizens' (In)Ability to Tell the Difference Between Disorder and Crime. *Criminology & Public Policy, 7*, 163-194.

Graber, D. (1980). *Crime News and the Public*. New York, NY: Praeger.

Hale, C. (1996). Fear of Crime: A Review of the Literature. *International Review of Victimology, (4)*, 79-150.

Heber, A. (2009). The Worst Thing That Could Happen: On Altruistic Fear of Crime. *International Review of Victimology, 16*, 257-275.

Hinkle, J., & Weisburd, D. (2008). The Irony of Broken Windows Policing: A Micro-Place Study of the Relationship between Disorder, Focused Crackdowns and Fear of Crime. *Journal of Criminal Justice, 36*, 503-512.

Jackson, J. (2009). A Psychological Perspective on Vulnerability in the Fear of Crime. *Psychology, Crime & Law, 15*, 365-390.

Jackson, J., & Gray, E. (2010). Functional Fear and Public Insecurities about Crime. *British Journal of Criminology, 50*, 1-22.

Jaycox, V. (1978). The Elderly's Fear of Crime: Rational or Irrational. *Victimology, 3*, 329-334.

Jurin, R. A., & Fields, C. (1994). Murder and Mayhem in USA Today: A Quantitative Analysis of the National Reporting of States' News. In G. Barak (Ed.), *Media, Process, and the Social Construction of Crime* (pp. 187-202). New York, NY: Garland Publishing, Inc.

Kanan, J. W., & Pruitt, M. V. (2002). Modeling Fear of Crime and Perceived Victimization Risk: The (In)significance of Neighborhood Interaction. *Sociological Inquiry, 72*(4), 527-549.

Kappeler, V. E., & Potter, G. W. (2005). *The Mythology of Crime and Criminal Justice* (4th ed.). Prospect Heights, IL: Waveland Press.

Katz, C. (2001). The Establishment of a Police Gang Unit: An Examination of Organizational and Environmental Factors. *Criminology, 39*, 301-337.

Katz, C., Webb, V., & Armstrong, T. (2003). Fear of Gangs: A Test of Alternative Theoretical Models. *Justice Quarterly, 20*(1), 95-130.

Kelling, G., Pate, T., Dieckman, D., & Brown, C. (1974). *The Kansas City Preventive Patrol Experiment: A Summary Report*. Washington, DC: The Police Foundation.

Kohm, S. (2009). Spatial Dimensions of Fear in a High-Crime Community: Fear of Crime or Fear of Disorder? *Canadian Journal of Criminology & Criminal Justice, 51*, 1-30.

Kruger, D., Hutchison, P., & Monroe, M. (2007). Assault Injury Rates, Social Capital, and Fear of Neighborhood Crime. *Journal of Community Psychology, 35,* 483-498.

Lane, J., & Meeker, J. (2000). Subcultural Diversity and the Fear of Crime and Gangs. *Crime & Delinquency, 46,* 497-521.

Lane, J., & Meeker, J. (2003). Ethinicity, Information Source, and Fear of Crime, 24 Deviant Behavior 1-26.

Lane, J., & Meeker, J. (2011). Combining Theoretical Models of Perceived Risk and Fear of Gang Crime among Whites and Latinos. *Victims & Offenders, 6,* 64-92.

Liska, A. E., & Baccaglini, W. (1990). Feeling Safe by Comparison: Crime in the Newspapers. *Social Problems, 37*(3), 360-374.

Markowitz, F., Bellair, P., Liska, P., & Liu, J. (2001). Extending Social Disorganization Theory: Modeling the Relationship Between Cohesion, Disorder, and Fear. *Criminology, 39,* 293-318.

Marsh, H. (1991). A Comparative Analysis of Crime Coverage in Newspapers in the United States and Other Countries from 1960-1989. *Journal of Criminal Justice, 19*(4), 67-79.

McGarrell, E., Giacomazzi, A., & Thurman, Q. (2000). Neighborhood Disorder, Integration, and the Fear of Crime. In R. Glensor, M. Correai, & K. Peak (Eds.), *Policing Communities: Understanding Crime and Solving Problems* (pp. 83-96).

Mears, D., & Stewart, E. (2010). Inter-racial Contact and Fear of Crime. *Journal of Criminal Justice, 38,* 34-41.

Melde, C. (2009). Lifestyle, Rational Choice, and Adolescent Fear: A Test of a Risk-Assessment Framework. *Criminology, 47,* 781-812.

Miethe, T., & Lee, G. R. (1987). Fear of Crime Among Older People: A Reassessment of the Predictive Power of Crime Related Factors. *Sociological Quarterly, 25,* 397-415.

Miller, W. (1958). Lower Class Culture as a Generating Milieu of Gang Delinquency. *Journal of Social Issues, 14,* 5-19.

Nansel, T., Overpeck, M., Haynie, D., Ruan, W., & Scheidt, P. (2003). Relationships Between Bullying and Violence Among U.S. Youth. *Archives of Pediatric and Adolescent Medicine, 157,* 348-353.

Ortega, S. T., & Myles, J. L. (1987). Race and Gender Effects on Fear of Crime: An Interactive Model with Age. *Criminology, 25*(1), 133-152.

Potter, G. W., & Kappeler, V. E. (2006). *Constructing Crime* (2nd ed.). Prospect Heights, IL: Waveland Press.

Rader, N. E. (2004). The Threat of Victimization: A Theoretical Reconceptualization of Fear of Crime. *Sociological Spectrum, 24*(6), 689-705.

Rader, N., May, D., & Goodrum, S. (2007). An Empirical Assessment of the "Threat of Victimization": Considering Fear of Crime, Perceived Risk, Avoidance, and Defensive Behaviors. *Sociological Spectrum, 27,* 475-505.

Randa, R., & Wilcox, P. (2010). School Disorder, Victimization, and General V. Place Specific Student Avoidance. *Justice Quarterly, 38,* 854-861.

Roh, S., & Oliver, W. (2005). Effect of Community Policing upon Fear of Crime: Understanding the Causal Linkage. *Policing, 28,* 670-683.

Roman, C., & Chalfin, A. (2008). Fear of Walking Outdoors: A Multilevel Ecological Analysis of Crime and Disorder. *American Journal of Preventive Medicine, 34,* 306-312.

Ross, C., & Jang, S. (2000). Neighborhood Disorder, Fear, and Mistrust: The Buffering Role of Social Ties with Neighbors. *American Journal of Community Psychology, 28,* 401-420.

Sasson, T. (1995). *Crime Talk: How Citizens Construct a Social Problem.* New York, NY: Aldine De Gruyter.

Scarborough, B., Like-Haislip, T., Novak, K., Lucas, W., & Alarid, L. (2010). Assessing the Relationship between Individual Characteristics, Neighborhood Context, and Fear of Crime. *Journal of Criminal Justice, 38,* 819-826.

Schafer, S. (1968). *The Victim and His Criminal: A Study in Functional Responsibility.* New York, NY: Random House.

Scheider, M., Rowell, T., & Bezdikian, V. (2003). The Impact of Citizen Perceptions of Community Policing on Fear of Crime: Findings from Twelve Cities. *Police Quarterly, 6*(4), 363-386.

Skogan, W. (1995). Crime and the Racial Fears of White Americans. *Annals of the American Academy of Political and Social Science, 539,* 571.

Skogan, W.G. (2006). Police and Community in Chicago; a tale of three cities. Oxford University Press.

Skogan, W. (2009). Concern about Crime and Confidence in the Police: Reassurance or Accountability? *Police Quarterly, 12,* 301-318.

Skogan, W. G., & Maxfield, M. G. (1981). *Coping with Crime: Individual and Neighborhood Reactions.* Beverly Hills, CA: Sage Publications.

Spellman, W. (2004). Optimal Targeting of Incivility-Reduction Strategies. *Journal of Quantitative Criminology, 20*(1), 63-89.

Taylor, R. (1999). The Incivilities Thesis: Theory, Measurement, and Policy. In R. Langworthy (Ed.), *Measuring What Matters* (pp. 65-88). Washington, DC: National Institute of Justice.

Taylor, R. B., & Hale, M. (1986). Testing Alternative Models of Fear of Crime. *The Journal of Criminal Law & Criminology, 77*(1), 151-189.

Thompson, C., Bankston, W., & St. Pierre, R. L. (1992). Parity and Disparity Among Three Measures of Fear of Crime: A Research Note. *Deviant Behavior, 13*(4), 373-389.

Trojanowicz, R. (1982). *An Evaluation of the Neighborhood Foot Patrol Program in Flint, Michigan.* East Lansing, MI: National Neighborhood Foot Patrol Center, Michigan State University.

Tunnell, K. (1992). Film at Eleven: Recent Developments in the Commodification of Crime. *Sociological Spectrum, 12,* 293-313.

Walklate, S. (1994). Risk and Criminal Victimization: A Modernist Dilemma? Paper presented at the annual conference of the American Society of Criminology, Miami.

Warr, M. (1984). Fear of Victimization: Why Are Women and the Elderly More Afraid? *Social Science Quarterly, 65*, 681–702.

Warr, M. (1994). Altruistic Fear of Victimization in Households? *Social Science Quarterly, 73*(4), 723–736.

Weed, F. J. (1995). *Certainty of Justice: Reform in the Crime Victim Movement*. New York, NY: Aldine De Gruyter.

Weisburd, D., & Eck, J. (2004). What Can Police Do to Reduce Crime, Disorder, and Fear? *Annals of the American Academy of Political and Social Science, 593*, 42–65.

Williams, H., & Pate, A. M. (1986). Returning to First Principles: Reducing the Fear of Crime in Newark. *Crime & Delinquency, 33*(1), 53–70.

Williams, P., & Dickinson, J. (1993). Fear of Crime: Read All About It. *British Journal of Criminology, 33*(1), 33–56.

Wilson, J. Q., & Kelling, G. (1982). Broken Windows: The Police and Neighborhood Safety. *The Atlantic Monthly*, (March), 29–38.

Young, M., & Stein, J. (2004). *The History of the Crime Victims Movement in the United States*. Washington, DC: Office of Victims of Crimes.

Young, V. D. (1992). Fear of Victimization and Victimization Rates Among Women: A Paradox? *Justice Quarterly, 9*(3), 419–441.

Zhao, J., Gibson, C., Lovrich, N., & Gaffney, M. 2002a. Participation in Community Crime Prevention: Are Volunteers More or Less Fearful of Crime than Other Citizens? *Journal of Crime & Justice, 25*, 41–61.

Zhao, S., Scheider, M., & Thurman, Q. 2002. The Effect of Police Presence on Public Fear Reduction and Satisfaction: A Review of the Literature. *The Justice Professional, 15*, 273–299.

I have often heard that the outstanding man is he who thinks deeply about a problem.

—Livy

CHAPTER 8   Problem Solving and Policing Problem Spaces

LEARNING OBJECTIVES

After reading the chapter, you should be able to:

1. Explain the differences between incidents of crime and seeing crime as a larger social problem.
2. Discuss some of the social conditions that give rise to crime and how these conditions give rise to problem places.
3. Describe the concept of problem solving and how it differs from traditional policing.
4. Give the reason why police need to be involved in problem solving.
5. Explain the differences between dangerous places and crime hot spots and how crime analysis can determine these differences.
6. Describe the stages of problem solving and describe the SARA model.
7. Describe and give examples of how COMSTAT and problem solving can be institutionalized in police agencies.
8. List and describe the methods of problem identification. Know which methods work better than others.
9. Explain the concepts of crime mapping, crime analysis, and crime patterns.
10. List and discuss the reasons many police agencies do not use problem solving.

Historically, policing has been a reactive profession. Although the police patrolled the streets, they, for the most part, depended on people to call them when a crime or problem arose. Once the police received a call, a motorized patrol unit would be dispatched to the scene to handle it. Once on the scene, a police officer would make an arrest, take a report, advise a victim to obtain a warrant or protective order, or provide the person with information about how to handle the problem. Once the officer completed the call, he or she would then continue patrolling, awaiting the next call, often giving little or no thought to the underlying causes of the problem. This was seen as the most effective means of dealing with people and their problems. In this fashion the police could respond to a large number of calls, take action, or push the call off on another social service agency and begin going about the business of law enforcement once again.

The vast majority of contacts the police have with members of the community are initiated by citizens (Reiss, 1971). People either call the police or flag them down when they need assistance. Because most people have access to a telephone, they have instantaneous contact with the police. Police departments across the country have implemented 911 or E911 emergency telephone systems, making it even easier to summon the police. This has not only afforded people with easier access to the police, but it has resulted in a substantial increase in the number of calls the police receive. The 911 telephone number allowed people to call the police no matter how trivial their problem seemed to the police. Many police call takers or 911 operators now are overloaded and cannot adequately respond to the number of calls they receive. Many people calling the police with legitimate emergencies must wait on hold until an operator can take the call. The problem also results in police patrol cars having to respond to calls in queue, and longer response times to the scenes of crimes and calls for service.

The traditional reactive policing model does little to diminish the level of crime, calls for service, or problems community members may be facing. The primary reason is that the traditional police response to people's calls has resulted in the superficial handling of problems. That is, the police responded to the incident and either took action that addressed the problem for the moment or shuffled the person off to another service agency and then left. If the underlying conditions causing the incident were left undisturbed, other incidents were likely to occur, requiring the police to respond repeatedly to the same problem, for example, a bar that serves alcohol to intoxicated patrons resulting in fights; a convenient store where drug dealers hang out resulting in shoplifting complaints; or an apartment where residents are selling drugs resulting in crime in the area. The police, therefore, to be effective, must deal with the underlying causes of problems rather than their symptoms. Solving problems not only represents a better and more effective manner by which to serve the public, but it should also result in a diminished workload for the police. Future calls for service can be eliminated by an effective early response that addresses the causes of problems.

The Nature of Problems and Problem Solving

Today, because of greater reliance on governmental services and a diminishing role of traditional social institutions, the police are the primary social control agency in society. The police are designed to deal with people and activities that are outside the bounds of the existing social and moral order. Although there are numerous public and private agencies that deal with problems such as poverty, unemployment, or public health, the police seem to be the agency of last resort. When these social agencies fail and the problems continue and become even more difficult, they often become matters that must be dealt with by the police. The police deal with not only those problems that society has deemed intolerable but also those that political leaders have failed to adequately address or recognize as problems. Social problems do not just fall from the sky—they are created. The vast major of problems the police deal with are not "caused" by deviant or dangerous people; rather, they are caused by social conditions that are a direct result of poor public policy. So we might say that most "police problems" began their life as "political problems" that were pushed upon the police.

Figure 8.1 provides a diagram showing how problems occur and must be handled by the police. In general, the economic, political, and social structure of our society results in conditions that causes crime. American society is arranged

Figure 8.1
Social Organization of Crime and Disorder

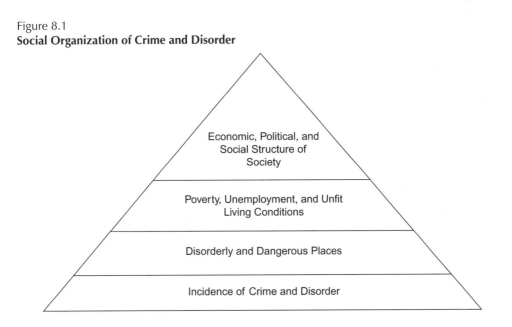

in such as fashion that it produces winners and losers. The winners are able to pursue the "American dream," while the losers do not have the means or life skills to adequately function in society. In many cases, those who are not in a position to be successful legitimately revert to illegal means to do so (Messner & Rosenfeld, 1997). Our social and economic structure results in poverty, unemployment and underemployment, and inferior living conditions for a large segment of our society. There is a wealth of government and private agencies that attempt to mediate these conditions, but as exemplified by poverty and crime, they are unable to wholly deal with the problems. This is simply because we have an economic and political system that allows the few to accumulate vast wealth at the expense of the poor and a political system that responds to that wealth. The poverty, unemployment, and unfit living conditions tend to be spatially segregated into distinct areas. This is to say, the least politically and economically powerful in American society are often forced into living in the less desirable sections of most American cities. Living in these conditions, the political disenfranchisement that comes with poverty, the perception of these locations as dangerous places results in social and economic isolation that can produce inordinate amounts of crime. When viewed by outsiders, these areas certainly seem ripe for abandonment. The police are then called on to address crimes as individual cases, rather than social problems. Obviously, not all crime or even a majority of it is the product of the poor; successful people who are not disadvantaged by social conditions commit corporate crime, white-collar crime, homicides that stem from lust or greed, and many thefts. Yet, our police are directed by political leaders to pay the greatest attention to the crimes of the poor—especially street crime.

The police become involved when social conditions result in incidents of crime. When a problem occurs, it might be observed by a passing police officer, but more often than not, a community member who calls and makes a report usually brings it to their attention. Historically, the police have dealt with incidents failing to see the larger social picture. They seldom ventured into problems at a deep level; instead, they handled calls and moved on. Community policing advocates that the police go beyond incidents and attempt to deal with the causes of incidents and problems. This means that police must begin to deal with crime where it intersects existing social conditions. This is a large mandate because often the police do not control the conditions that lead to crime.

Problem solving represents a tactic that goes beyond traditional policing in that it is an attempt to solve problems that result in fights, public drunkenness, and other incidents that result in a police response. Although we will focus on crime in this chapter, problem solving by the police should not be restricted to crime. Social, health, and quality life problems and issues are all the providence of police problem solving, and as noted above, they contribute to crime problems. Even if a police department successfully and effectively implements community policing and problem solving, it must also respond to calls for services and crime. People expect the police to deal with their problems. Effective problem solving, however, will reduce this workload. Police agencies that use problem solving solely to address crime and enhance their law enforcement agency will quickly lose the support and confidence of the community and find themselves merely enmeshed in addressing symptoms at a more complex level—merely pushing crime around in a community.

In the past, the police would respond to each incident or call. Once on the scene, they would render a service and then return to their cars and wait for the next call. Police responses, in essence, were superficial. They seldom resulted in a problem being solved. Consequently, the police were constantly plagued with repeat calls or calls to the same location for the same reoccurring problem (Goldstein, 1990).

Perhaps a detailed example would demonstrate the importance of problem solving. The example of a rowdy neighborhood bar perhaps best illustrates the point. All cities have bars that are more problematic than others. They generally have a multitude of violations: serving alcohol to minors and intoxicated patrons or allowing gambling, drug dealers, or prostitutes on the premises. These violations and problems lead to other infractions of the law that spill over into the surrounding community. Patrons might leave a bar intoxicated and drive their vehicles, and become involved in a traffic accident. Occasionally, a fight occurs in a bar and later erupts in the street. In some cases, the fight escalates into a shooting or stabbing. Patrons leaving a bar engage in vandalism or commit thefts on their way from the bar. Since the bar has a reputation, it likely draws other criminality to the area. Essentially, a tavern that allows or is conducive to disorder creates a number of calls to the police. If the police were to do something about the bar itself, their overall calls for service and workload might be diminished appreciably.

One must be careful, however, not to equate fights and street crime as the sole indicators of locations where problem solving needs to be implemented. While the police are more likely to be called to a working-class tavern to respond to a call about a fight, upper-class pubs are just as criminogenic. The Wall Street broker who has had a few too many drinks is just as likely to become involved in a vehicle accident, and the high-class pub is just as likely to harbor prostitution and be a source of drug trafficking as is the working-class tavern the police are called to on Saturday nights. The difference here is how political leaders direct police and how the police themselves direct their attention and resources. Attempting to do something about either bar would depart from incident-based policing and focus on places and conditions that often create problems for the surrounding communities, not just problems for the police.

Numerous police departments have been engaging in problem solving since the mid-1980s. Spelman and Eck (1989) have chronicled the differences between traditional reactive policing and problem solving:

- Rather than simply reacting to calls for service, the police actively work to prevent crime and improve neighborhood conditions that are conducive to crime. Prevention efforts must focus on specific problems as opposed to distributing efforts randomly.

- The police must recognize that there are many conditions within society that contribute to crime. The police must analyze these conditions and develop specific responses to each problem or situation rather than depending on rapid response and answering calls for service.

- Crime problems, as depicted in Figure 8.1, are the result of innumerous societal conditions that are outside the control of the police. The police must engage and cooperate with other social agencies to develop a unified strategy for addressing complex problems.

Geographical Policing

If the police depart from focusing on incidents, the next step in the hierarchy of problem solving is identifying "dangerous places" or "crime hot spots." A **dangerous place** is a location that attracts criminals and results in high levels of violent crime. On the other hand, a **hot spot** is a geographical concentration of crime. Whereas a dangerous place is a location, hot spots generally are areas such as a block, apartment building, or an entertainment area. Criminals are attracted to geographical locations by entertainment, potential victims, their work, and their residence. Because of the ways we define crime and because of the type of crime we decide to focus on, crime is not distributed equally across space and time. Most of the crime that the police pay attention to tends to cluster in specific locations and happen during compressed time frames. Locations that have high levels of crime include bars, certain apartment complexes, areas around liquor stores, bus stops, shopping malls, homeless centers, fast-food restaurants, abandoned buildings, and parks. To some extent, dangerous places and crime hot spots can be identified by examining police calls for service. Mapping calls and crime identifies these clusters.

We must, however, remember that the same can be said of political crime, crimes committed by law enforcement officials, and white-collar crime. Political crime is organized in state houses and mansions; police crime happens on the streets and in precinct houses; and white-collar crime follows the path of the dollar. In essence, the crime we choose to focus on determines what places are considered dangerous. Living next to a chemical plant housing environmental criminals can be just as dangerous to one's health as walking down a dark alley in an inner city. It is no accident that some places become seen as dangerous and in need of police attention while other equally dangerous places do not come to attention.

Land use and the configuration or structures of cities play an important role in crime. Those areas adjacent to the central business district in large cities often experience higher levels of traditional crime (Shaw & McKay, 1942). Low-income housing and public housing projects tend to have elevated levels of street crime. These neighborhoods are in transition with fewer permanent residents, which results in less guardianship and increased levels of crime. Additionally, both political leaders and the police have often abandoned these communities (for an example, see Zatz & Portillos, 2004). Houses and businesses on primary roadways leading to high schools tend to experience more vandalism and minor crimes such as larceny as students travel to and from school. Felson (2009) notes that the roadways or transportation corridors used by criminals to go to work, recreation areas such as bars, and their homes are also more susceptible to criminal activity. In fact, more than 60 percent of crimes are committed in relatively few locations (Pierce, Spaar & Briggs, 1988; Spelman & Eck, 1989). Clearly, there are some parts of a city that are more susceptible to street crime and experience more criminal activity relative to other areas of a city.

One of the first studies examining concentrations of street crime was conducted by Sherman (1996). He coined the term "hot spots" to describe the concentrations of crime. He found large areas of cities that were absent of police activities and a small number of areas with a substantial amount of activities or calls that required a police response. He found that these hot spots accounted for an inordinate amount of police activity.

> You can learn more about policing hot spots and crime by going to http://www.nij.gov/topics/law-enforcement/strategies/hot-spot-policing/welcome.htm.

Three percent of the estimated 115,000 addresses and intersections in Minneapolis were the subject of 50 percent of the 321,174 calls to police.... Sixty percent of the addresses and intersections produced no calls to the police at all. Of the 40 percent with any calls, the majority (52%) had only one call, while 84 percent had less than five. The top five percent of the locations with any calls produced 48.8 percent of the calls (p. 217).

Essentially, Sherman found that approximately 5,000 locations in Minneapolis produced almost one-half of all calls to the police. There were 2,606 locations that each produced 20 or more calls. There were 20 locations that produced more than 200 calls each. Sherman found that patrol officers handled an average of four calls per shift. Thus, the top 20 locations consumed 1,000 shifts per year. If the police, through problem solving, could eliminate only a few of the top 20 locations as problems, the police department's workload would be appreciably reduced. Reactive policing cannot accomplish this task. However, problem solving may allow the police to provide a more in-depth response to hot spots to reduce or eliminate them. Thus, problem solving can be an important tool for the police to provide better service and reduce their overall workload.

Since Sherman's groundbreaking study, other researchers have confirmed his findings. Braga, Hureau, and Winship (2008) examined gun violence in Boston and found that hot spots covering only 5 percent of the city's 48.4 square miles accounted for 53 percent of fatal and nonfatal shootings. Weisburd and his colleagues (2004) examined crime in Seattle over a 14-year period and found that 50 percent of the crime consistently occurred in approximately 4.5 percent of the street locations. Not only do crime and police calls occur in dangerous places and hot spots, but they consistently do so. This problem or hot spot consistency was confirmed by Spellman (1995), who found that calls for service at high schools, housing projects, subway stations, and parks in Boston remained fairly consistent over time. The research clearly points to a need for the police to address dangerous places and crime hot spots. Elimination of a crime hot spot may have an impact for several years.

Defining Dangerous Places and Hot Spots

A crime problem or hot spot can be a shapeless and fairly undefined entity. That is, the police may receive a number of calls from a general location, but the crime for that location may be spread over a larger area. There may be instances where several hot spots are located in adjacent areas and their boundaries overlap. If the police are to be successful in solving problems, then they must be adept at recognizing what constitutes a hot spot.

It is important to define dangerous places and hot spots. A definition provides officers with a map or template for action. A clear definition is a benchmark for action. Clarke and Eck (2005) defined them as a reoccurring set of related harmful events in a community that the public expects the police to address. Buerger, Cohn, and Petrosino (2000:139) recognized the importance of defining problems and attempted to generate some rules during their study of hot spots in Minneapolis. Basically, they defined a hot spot as "small clusters of addresses with frequent 'hard' crime call activity, which also had substantial 'soft' crime calls for service.... [They] then limited the boundaries of each spot conceptually as being easily visible from an epicenter ..." Hard crime refers to criminal offenses, usually Part I crimes, and soft crime refers to minor violations. Buerger and his colleagues then constructed rules that are helpful in identifying a hot spot. For example, a hot spot should not exceed a block in size. Hot spots that are located at street intersections should not exceed one-half block in either direction of the hot spot epicenter.

> *You can learn more about dangerous places and crime prevention by going to http://www.popcenter.org/library/crimeprevention/volume_04/.*

Police need to remember, however, that so called hot spots are the product of the data the police collect and with which they are concerned. Hot spots are not necessarily inherent in a location, but rather constructed based on behavior and social interaction. An affluent subdivision maybe a hot spot for domestic violence and a high-rise building may be the prime location for the suit crimes committed by white-collar criminals, but if people do not alert the police of these activities, if police do not investigate these activities, or if police fail to collect data or selectively choose the crimes they consider important, they are shaping the locations of hot spots in their cities. If police view geography as a fixed, bounded location that is predetermined, then they miss the point. A city block is not just a "place," but rather it is a "space" constituted by all the human interactions that take place within that space. Additionally, a block is defined in conjunction with all the other surrounding spaces and interactions that make it distinct. Merely counting and locating crime on a predetermined map does not address the causes of crime; it is just a first step at addressing symptoms. Police must be mindful that what creates "space" is not a bounded and fixed geography but rather human social interactions.

The Mechanics of Problem Solving

Problem solving goes beyond answering calls for service. It represents a complex, multi-stage approach to policing. Problem solving in most police departments today revolves around the SARA model (Spelman & Eck, 1989).

Figure 8.2
SARA: A Problem-Solving Process

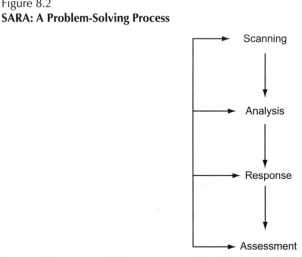

Source: Eck, J.E. & W. Spelman (1987). *Problem-Solving: Problem-Oriented Policing in Newport News,* p. 43. Washington, DC: U.S. Department of Justice, National Institute of Justice.

The model is made up of a sequence of four stages that, when combined, make up the process of problem solving as depicted in Figure 8.2. While there are variations of the SARA model, its basic stages are as follows.

Scanning

Scanning refers to a process whereby individual officers, police units, or the police department collectively examine the community for problems or hot spots. These problems typically are exhibited through high levels of crime or complaints. They also result in large numbers of calls to the police. Scanning can and should be done with the assistance of the community. Community members can often provide valuable insight into problems of which the police might not be aware. Additionally, because traditional policing is often focused on crime control and law enforcement, they might not be aware of the role people can play in solving other types of problems in the community. Using our bar or tavern example, a concern with beer cans being thrown into the yards of residents after the tavern closes might not warrant a call to the police or even be seen as a big deal. This minor problem, however, may appear long before the police are called upon to investigate a shooting or stabbing call in the area.

It is important that the scanning phase explicitly identifies the problem and its boundaries. Many different problems often are co-located in an area, and the individual problems must be disentangled and understood before any analysis. Here, strategies may positively affect one problem, but not others. This likely would lead to a lower than acceptable outcome. Also, Clarke (1998) advises that officers often focus on too simple or too complex problems. For example, a lonely elderly person repeatedly calling the police can be solved without engaging in complex problem solving. On the other hand, a problem of gangs, drugs, and violence may require the identification of multiple problems with different solutions. Fully understanding the problem during the analysis phase is of critical importance.

Analysis

Once a problem, quality-of-life issue, dangerous place, or hot spot is identified, officers attempt to collect information about it. Boba and Crank (2008) advise that the goal of **analysis** "is to determine why a problem is occurring. The underlying, situational causes of the problem are examined in terms of the offenders' motivations, the nature of victims or targets, and the environment of the place(s) where the problem occurs" (p. 390). Basically, they attempt to learn the who, what, when, where, and how of the problem. It is important to note that analysis often goes beyond the location of the calls for service or the place where incidents are happening. For example, disorderly and rowdy behavior at a street intersection may be the result of a bar in the next block selling alcoholic beverages to patrons who then drink on the street. Buerger, Cohn, and Petrosino (2000) note that special care must be taken to ensure that the analysis includes all the area encompassing the problem and at the same time does not include other problems or calls that are not a part of the hot spot or calls.

Officers can use a multitude of sources when analyzing problems. For example, Cordner and Biebel (2005) asked officers in San Diego the sources of information they used when analyzing problems. Figure 8.3 provides a breakdown of their responses. A review of the information sources indicates that officers were doing a superficial job of analyzing the problems or they were addressing simplistic problems since the two most commonly used sources were personal observations and speaking with people. Problems, especially complex problems, require multiple sources of information if they are to be fully understood. Problem analysis can be extremely complex, but a complex analysis will lead to a better understanding of the problem and identification of solutions.

Response

Once a problem or hot spot is clearly identified and analyzed, the police must then structure an effective **response**. This means the police must deal with the cause or causes of the problem rather than its symptoms. The response

Figure 8.3
Sources of Information Used by San Diego Police Officers to Analyze Problems

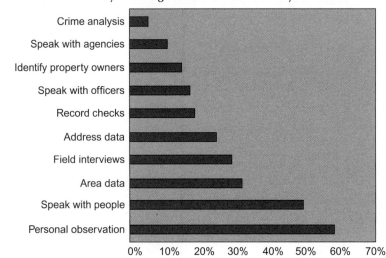

Source: Cordner, G. & E. Biebel (2003). *Research for Practice: Problem-Oriented Policing in Practice*, p. 25. Washington, DC: U.S. Department of Justice.

may involve the police directly or they may serve in a referral role. In some cases, especially complex problems, the response will include other governmental and social agencies. For example, officers might inform the tavern operator of the situation and how they believe his or her actions are affecting the community. If the tavern operator is unresponsive to police requests, perhaps the best way to deal with a bar that is selling alcoholic beverages to inebriates or juveniles is to contact Alcoholic Beverage Control and have the bar's license revoked. Closing the bar may result in an abolition of the problem, but it may also generate additional problems. The police may lose support from the bar's owners, operators, and patrons. Additionally, the closure of the bar can lead to unemployment of some, a loss of pedestrian traffic in the area, and perhaps even an abandoned building that fosters an entirely new set of problems. Engaging people and other agencies, not just enforcement officials, in the problem area allows the police to develop alternatives that are more effective, and it may engender support for police action. Police must begin to view problems, like the tavern example, as nested in communities and affecting a host of social interactions. Merely educating the tavern owner about "cutting off" patrons, or encouraging the opening of a late night diner in the area, or encouraging taxi services to provide free rides home for patrons as a community service might all be more effective means of addressing the problem.

Figure 8.4
Responses Used by San Diego Police Officers in Problem Solving

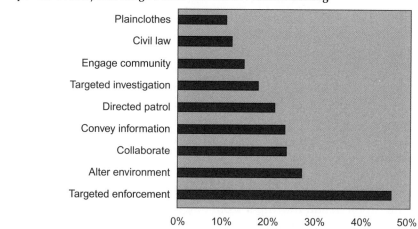

Source: Cordner, G. & E. Biebel (2003). *Research for Practice: Problem-Oriented Policing in Practice*, p. 26. Washington, DC: U.S. Department of Justice.

Police officers should not limit their responses to traditional law enforcement methods or solely depend on departmental resources. Cordner and Biebel (2003) examined responses in San Diego, which are provided in Figure 8.4. Targeted enforcement, a traditional enforcement method, was most commonly used, while altering the environment and collaborating efforts were the second and third most commonly used strategies. Both fit within the community policing and problem-solving paradigm. It appears that San Diego officers had incorporated contemporary problem solving methods into their efforts. Scott (2000), upon examining a number of successful problem-solving efforts, found that on average, departments implemented five different strategies when attempting to solve a problem. Scott's finding demonstrates that successful problem solving requires complex responses—generally multiple strategies.

Assessment

Assessment is one of the most neglected phases of problem solving. Once there is a response by the police or other governmental agency, the police must assess the response to see if it worked and eliminated or reduced the problem. If the strategy did not result in an acceptable outcome, the police must re-analyze the problem and fashion another response. **Assessment** often consists of examining activities that occur in the problem area once the response has been implemented. That is, did the response reduce crime and calls for service?

Cordner and Biebel (2003) found that the assessment tool most commonly used by San Diego police officers was personal observations (51%) followed by an analysis of radio calls (14%) and speaking to residents and businesses (13%).

Too often, officers engaged in problem solving rely on personal observations as their assessment method. Personal observations, however, can be deceiving—personal observations often are cursory and do not always provide a complete picture. Clarke (1998) found that personal observations tend to be the dominant assessment modality, especially for small problem-solving projects. Observation cannot be relied upon for complex problem solving. Cordner and Biebel (2003) found that San Diego police officers used an average of 2.8 assessment tools when assessing their progress. Multiple assessment measures, especially when call and crime data are used, result in a more accurate assessment of strategies. One must, however, be careful that the response is not just dislocating the problem and moving it from one location to another. In the case of police crackdowns on open-air drug markets, law enforcement activities may push drug dealing from the streets into a private residence, making it more difficult and dangerous for the police to address the problem. Rarely will enforcement actions alone eliminate crime from a community. More often than not crackdowns merely displace crime, sometimes making the problem worse.

Skogan and his colleagues (2000) focused on a slightly different problem-solving model that has been used in the Chicago Police Department. The process involved training both the police and community members to implement a five-stage process that included:

- Identifying problems and prioritizing them, incorporating community input.

- Analyzing information about offenders, victims, and crime locations.

- Designing strategies that address the chronic character of priority problems by thinking "outside the box" of traditional police enforcement tactics and using new resources that were developed by the city to support problem-solving efforts.

- Implementing the strategies, a step requiring special skill and effort by the community, police, and other city departments as they attempt to actually put plans in motion.

- Evaluating effectiveness through self-assessments to determine how well the plan has been carried out and what good has been accomplished (p.9).

Skogan and his colleagues essentially attempted to institutionalize problem solving in the Chicago Police Department. Problem solving becomes more commonplace when there are policies and organizational arrangements to facilitate and mandate it. Boba and Crank (2008) developed a similar system for the Port St. Lucie, Florida, Police Department. They attempted to ensure that problem solving was a responsibility for not only officers, but also police managers. Essentially, they integrated COMSTAT with problem solving. Middle managers were held responsible for identifying and responding to problems and were held accountable with COMSTAT data. That is, by examining call and crime data generated by the COMSTAT system, administrators could determine the level of success that officers and managers were achieving when dealing with problems. This accountability prodded managers to become more engaged and provide more supervision and assistance to officers who were conducting problem solving. There is some evidence that institutionalizing community policing and problem solving results in officers' acceptance. Witte, Travis, and Langworthy (1990) found that officers were more likely to be more involved in community policing and problem solving when their supervisors had higher levels of commitment. Institutionalization forces supervisors and middle managers to be more committed.

Methods for Identifying Problems

The first step in problem solving is scanning the environment to identify potential problems that are suitable for police intervention. Problems, as defined here, are a cluster of incidents or calls for service that are of concern to the police and the public (Webster & Connors, 1993). The police must identify those areas that are resulting in large numbers of calls to the police department. When the police engage in problem solving at high volume dangerous places or hot spots, the number of calls to the police should be reduced appreciably. To this end, Webster and Connors (1993) have identified methods the police can use to recognize potential problems: officer observation and experience, complaints, crime analysis, police reports, calls for service analysis, crime mapping, community groups, and surveys.

SPOTLIGHT ON COMMUNITY POLICING PRACTICE

The Role of Crime Analysis in Patrol Work

As a patrol officer, have you asked yourself repeatedly, "What tools and resources can I use that will make my job easier?" The use of crime analysis enables law enforcement agencies to effectively and efficiently engage in problem solving and is an essential component of community policing. Problem solving requires robust analysis capabilities and can be applied

---

(Continued)

to various levels of community problems. Despite the great potential of crime analysis and its importance to proactive problem solving, analysis activities are typically limited to a few individuals within departments. Little information exists about how patrol officers currently use crime analysis information, and little is known about how it is produced for analysis purposes. The COPS office, in partnership with the Police Executive Research Forum (PERF), understands the importance of crime analysis and will study its use through a project called "Integrating Crime Analysis in Patrol Work." Upon completion of this project, the COPS Office and PERF will publish a guidebook describing best practices and highlighting the use of crime analysis and mapping for patrol work.

Problem Solving

Both crime analysis and crime mapping are extremely important tools that can be used to help patrol officers solve problems on their beats. Recall the days when pin maps were displayed on the roll call wall depicting the rash of burglaries that occurred the previous week. With technology advances, crime analysts have the capacity to produce electronic versions of the traditional pin map, as well as more sophisticated mapping products, that will help patrol officers understand crime patterns in their beats. Crime analysis can be used to uncover patterns and trends and identify areas of the neighborhood with hot spot activity. Patrol officers often do not have access to crime analysts or are unaware of the products that the crime analyst can produce that will help them with their jobs. We encourage patrol officers to sit down with the crime analysts at their departments and discuss their needs and what products would be most useful to them in conducting their daily patrols.

Partnerships

The use of crime analysis can encourage partnerships between the local police agency and other law enforcement entities. As a crime analyst at the Albany Police Department, I worked on a grant program aimed at reducing community gun violence. Through statistical analysis and crime mapping, we identified gun violence hot spots. A working group was established that consisted of line level officers who worked the hot spot beats, detectives who were more intimately involved with the cases, probation and parole officers, the District Attorney's office, and federal partners such as ATF and the FBI. The common thread among these key players was the use of analysis and mapping to identify repeat offenders, repeat locations, and offense patterns such as time of day and victim characteristics. Using these analytical tools enabled the Albany Police Department to partner with interested parties to address a specific problem.

Organizational Transformation

The importance of crime analysis and crime mapping must be recognized by the top levels of police administration, from the chief of police or sheriff to the assistant chiefs, and command staff. Executive staff should encourage patrol officers to communicate with their crime analysts about the products they need and what resources would help them do a better job. Crime analysts should be invited to roll call meetings to engage in conversations with patrol officers. They also should also be encouraged to go on routine ride-alongs for a better understanding of the environment they are analyzing and to acquire an insider's view on what officers face every day.

Nicole J. Scalisi
Research Analyst
The COPS Office

Source: The e-newsletter of the COPS Office, Volume 1, Issue 12, December 2008.

Officer Observation and Experience

Patrol officers perhaps possess the most knowledge about what is occurring on their beats. They are usually working there 40 hours each week. Over time, they become intimately familiar with those families that have high levels of domestic violence. Some families experience violence on a regular basis, and officers can identify those families and persuade prosecutors and judges to require social service intervention. They come to know those bars that serve inebriated patrons. Here, officers can contact the operators and ask for help, make additional arrests, or have the Alcoholic Beverage Control Unit inspect the premises more frequently to observe for violations and have the license revoked or pressure owners to follow the laws more closely. Patrol officers often can identify those intersections where drug dealers hang out to sell drugs. Once they identify these locations, they can intensify patrols, initiate additional field interrogations, or have the drug unit initiate counter measures to reduce the level of drug trafficking. Experience also tells them which businesses are more likely to be robbed. Patrol officers can notify crime prevention officers to work with the businesses and can notify the detective unit to request periodic stakeouts. Patrol officers, through their experiences, can identify problem locations and can cooperate with other units in the department to attack them.

> *You can learn more about problem identification and policing by looking at the course materials at http://www.cppsi.com/en/courses/community-police/community-policing-advanced-course/.*

As a result of patrolling and answering calls for service, they also come to identify the people who reside, work, or come to entertainment establishments in their beats. Most likely, in any given area, there is a small number of individuals who are responsible for a significant amount of crime. Over time, patrol officers can come to identify these individuals. Once this occurs, officers can target them for field interrogations on a more frequent basis. Patrol officers can work with detectives in an attempt to make stronger cases against them and get them off the street. They can also contact prosecutors to encourage them to seek longer sentences for criminals engaged in repeat offenses or those who participate in hard crimes. All these possibilities hinge on two principles of community policing; assigning officers to fixed beat assignments and developing partnerships outside the police department.

Community partnerships are one of the key ingredients in community policing. As a part of building community partnerships, patrol officers can develop positive relationships with people in the community or neighborhoods where they patrol. If positive relationships are forged, people should be more forthcoming with information about problems in their neighborhoods. People often know who is dealing drugs, committing burglaries, fencing stolen property, or involved in gang activities. This information can be used by the patrol officers in solving problems, or it can be forwarded to other units in the department to solve cases or to initiate strategies to counter crime. When beat officers take the time to know their beats, they become an invaluable resource for crime control and problem solving in the neighborhood.

One informative method of identifying problems in a community is to poll police officers. Figure 8.5 provides a sample of problems identified by officers from the Albany, Georgia, Police Department. The officers met in groups and developed lists of problems. The lists were then compiled by the department and used for strategic planning and personnel allocation.

The Albany police officers identified a variety of problems. The most common problems identified were drug trafficking and disorder. In the majority of cases, these problems focused on open or public drug trafficking. The drug trafficking generally occurred at locations such as parks, ball fields, and street intersections or adjacent to public housing or apartment complexes. Public drug trafficking generally occurs where large numbers of people congregate. This is because it allows the drug traffickers to blend into the crowd and essentially hide from the police, and the large numbers of people allow for the acquisition of a larger customer base.

Other problems identified by the officers were areas where large amounts of thefts occurred. There were several stores, a movie theater, and a shopping mall that were theft targets. Additionally, there were several apartment complexes with high rates of thefts from automobiles. In many instances the parking lots were isolated or adjacent to wooded areas which facilitated the thieves entering and leaving the parking lots. Several subdivisions were noted to have high rates of burglaries. These were generally middle-class neighborhoods where most if not

Figure 8.5
Albany, Georgia, Police Department Problem Areas

Location	Problem	Solution/Partnership
1300 Blk. W. Highland	Gang activity, intimidation of residents, increase in burglaries.	Neighborhood watch, increase patrols, youth programs and activities.
2601 Dawson Rd. (Albany Mall)	High levels of shoplifting from stores.	Post pictures of shoplifters, monitor items taken to dressing rooms.
Detour 21 Night Club 2700 Dawson	Trashing parking lot, underage drinking.	Cite owner for trash in parking lot, frequent patrols to reduce underage drinking and cite owner for ABC violations, use cleaning the parking lot as community service for violators.
Willie Pitts & Gordon Ave. (Ball Park)	Traffic, overcrowding, drug dealing. Mainly refuse to leave when the park closes. Usually teens and young adults.	Additional patrols, horse patrol. Have Parks Department install metal gates which are closed at a specific time.
1600 McAuther (housing area)	Drug sales, young people loitering, traffic. Citizens previously had filed a petition about the problem.	Additional patrols, perform field interrogations, change street to a cul-de-sac, neighborhood watch, cite people for loitering, road blocks, bike patrols.
K&S Food Store 1104 Newton Rd.	Drug sales, drunks, loitering around store. People buy alcohol across street at a liquor store owned by the person who owns the food store.	Police attempt to clear parking lot but owner protests as long as people have money. He calls the police when they run out. Citizens cannot complain to the police as it is the only grocery store in area. Need a park for kids to congregate.
Disco Palace Talafax & Community	Overcrowding, fighting, public intoxication, underage drinking, drug sales, large number of burglaries and robberies in area.	Have fire inspections, enforce 75 patron limit.
Tremont & Sunrise Sunnyside Subdivision	Daytime burglaries and thefts as a result of excessive foot traffic.	Middle-class neighborhood with everyone working, no guardians, and truancy problems. Wooded area adjacent to parking lot where perpetrators escape.
300 Blk. W. Oakridge & 2000 Blk. ML King	Pedestrian accidents where drunks cross the street from liquor store. Poor lighting, speeding.	Enforce laws relative to crossing street in crosswalks and public intoxication law.

(Continued)

Figure 8.5—Cont'd

Location	Problem	Solution/Partnership
Gillianville Rd. & Slappy Movie Theater	Breaking into autos while patrons are in theater. Females often leave purses in plain view.	Have suggested extra lighting, video cameras, and signs to owner but the owner will not cooperate.
Washington & Roosevelt—Businesses	Public urination, burglaries, trash, old furniture, homeless congregate to look for jobs, panhandling which frightens patrons away.	Find a new area for the "grey line." Establish time limits to seek jobs. Place toilets in area. Work with churches to establish a homeless shelter.
600 Blk. Residence	Gangs, drug activities, loitering, graffiti, vandalism, burglaries using lookouts, low-income substandard housing. Perpetrators usually 13-38 years of age.	Improve lighting, undercover sting operations, more patrols, work with churches in outreach programs.
Jackson & Whitney	Public drinking, loitering, vandalism, prostitution.	Enforce codes, parking, traffic, and open container laws. Have fire marshal inspect premises.
Highland Ave. (Red Fox)	Public drinking, loitering, vandalism, prostitution.	Enforce codes, parking, traffic, and open container laws. Have fire marshal inspect premises.
W. Oglethorpe (Kristol restaurant)	Juveniles loitering, drinking, drugs, fighting. Kids hang out there in the early morning hours.	Increase patrols, use roadblocks.
Clark Ave. & Cordell Rd.	Traffic problem where tractor trailer trucks run traffic light causing crashes.	Intensify enforcement and public education.
Beachview Area	Residential burglaries by juveniles who play in the area and drug abuse and dealing by unemployed adults.	Field interrogate suspicious persons, neighborhood watches, operation ID of property, increase patrol.
600 Blk. Bonnie View	Fights, drug and gang activities, public intoxication. Problem is one large family with extensive drug and alcohol abuse.	Police constantly receive calls and respond by making arrests. Have caused the family to move on at least one occasion.
333 S. Mockrow (Hidden Oaks Apts.)	Thefts from autos, auto theft, truancy.	Increased public presence, neighborhood watch.

(Continued)

Figure 8.5—Cont'd

Location	Problem	Solution/Partnership
1800 Blk. W. Gordon	Domestic violence, fights, disorderly conduct, drug sales, public intoxication, thefts. Suspects are teens and young adults who have been evicted from public housing.	Enhanced patrols. Increase the number of arrests, which has not worked with the area.
Double Gate Subdivision	False alarms.	City has refused to pass a false alarm ordinance.
Ebony Ln., S. Jackson & Emily Ave.	Vacant houses from the flood used for drug trafficking. Children and young teens often hide for days in the houses.	Had street lights replaced, but they were knocked out. Have tried for years to get FEMA to destroy buildings. Try rolling roadblocks and stakeouts.
CME Albany Housing	Many young mothers in public housing draw males who fight, drink, and sell drugs.	Work with public housing to reduce the number of young mothers in the facility. Implement a trespass program, call social workers when problem involves children, work with public housing on evictions.
600 Sands (Wild Pine Apts.)	Thefts from autos, thefts, and drunk and disorderly.	Increase the number of patrols, video cameras, crime prevention.
2701 Gillionville Rd., 8th & Slappy, 2605 N. Slappy, 2923 N. Slappy	Gas station drive offs.	Educate clerks and management to collect money before allowing patrons to pump gas.
1101 Dawson, 712 N. Westover, 1100 Gillionville	False bank alarms.	City had not passed a false alarm ordinance.
1800 Blk. Newton	Speeding in school zone.	Place radar trailer in area, work with schools to educate students, increase number of citations.

all of the adults in the area worked during the day. The work schedules reduced the level of guardianship in the neighborhood, which allowed easy access to many of the homes. Finally, several service stations were named as having a high rate of "drive-offs," where patrons left without paying for their gasoline.

Several bars or clubs were named as being problems. For the most part, they were disorderly where the owners allowed the number of patrons to exceed maximum capacity and large numbers of patrons would become inebriated. This often resulted in fights in and around the bar. It also resulted in a substantial amount of disorder in the adjacent neighborhood. A correlative problem was that when the bars closed, many of the patrons would then travel to nearby restaurants where additional fights and disorder would ensue. Consequently, individual bars would often result in a significant amount of work for the police, especially during weekends.

The officers identified some locations that were traffic problems. There were intersections that had large numbers of traffic crashes. One was a busy intersection where large trucks would speed up to get through a traffic light. This resulted in a large number of accidents, and because the accidents involved trucks, the accidents were often serious. Several neighborhoods were named as having a substantial amount of speeding. This was often dangerous because of children playing in the area or large amounts of pedestrian traffic. Several accident-prone locations were the result of drunks buying alcohol at a liquor store and then crossing the street to drink on a street corner.

The officers pointed out a number of juvenile problems. Notably, juveniles tended to congregate at locations where there were high levels of disorder and drug trafficking. Young adults were the primary instigators of the problems, and they furnished drugs and alcohol to the juveniles who worsened the problems. Several bars were known to serve alcohol to juveniles, which often resulted in other problems for the police. There were a few instances where the officers identified juvenile gangs in a neighborhood. Although there were a number of juvenile problems, most were unorganized and not the result of a gang problem.

Bichler and Gaines (2005) studied police officers' identification of problems. They found that officers generally used the number of calls as the primary criterion for identifying a problem. They focused on locations with numerous calls, regardless of the nature of the calls. Thus, officer input is important, but their information should be supplemented with other information to ensure that problem solving addresses the most serious crime and disorder problems, which may not necessarily occur at high-crime locations. Nonetheless, officer input does provide an excellent starting point for problem solving.

The officers were also queried about possible solutions to the various problems. Most of their solutions focused on more intensive law enforcement. Although a number of solutions included more patrols, they also attempted to tailor solutions for the problems at hand. In some instances, the officers conjured up solutions that involved other governmental agencies such as Alcoholic Beverage Control and Building Inspections, using what Green (1996) termed "third party policing." **Third party policing** involves the police pressuring not the people directly causing the problems but the people who have control over the locations in which a problem is occurring. These people may include tavern and store owners, the owners of rental houses and apartments, as well as the parents and guardians of juveniles. In other words, officers should encourage owners to become more involved in place management.

The information in Figure 8.5 points out that police officers develop a wealth of information about the beats they patrol. In addition to identifying problems, they generally have some good ideas about possible solutions. Information provided by officers should not serve as a single source of problem identification information since officers often do not have a "big picture" view of crime. As evidenced in our discussion, police have a tendency to identify problems associated with crime more often than quality of life problems that affect the community, because quality of life issues have a lesser impact on the police themselves. Police, too, are often quick to craft law enforcement solutions to problems when less formal or more social responses might be better alternatives (Kappeler & Kraska, 1998; 1998a). More effective solutions to substance abuse might be to advocate the development of rehabilitation and drug treatment problems in the community; reductions in petty crime might be better accomplished by linking crime-prone individuals with work training and employment possibilities and the energies of juveniles might be redirected into meaningful experiences like athletic leagues, supervised social activities, after-school programs, or mentoring programs. Police thinking and information should be augmented with the ideas and information from people in the community. Essentially police must be careful to address not only "police" problems, but "community" problems. They must seek out not only police solutions, but community-based solutions.

Complaints and Community Groups

When a person calls the police, it results in a patrol officer being dispatched to the scene. Large- and medium-sized police departments receive thousands of calls each year. As an example, Mazerolle and her colleagues (2005) found that the Baltimore Police Department received about 1 million calls per year. Gaines and Kappeler (2011) found that the police in Boston and Seattle receive approximately 500,000 calls per year. In the past, many police departments dealt with these calls on an individual basis. Today, many more departments are examining the aggregate data rather than looking at each call. Here, police departments are attempting to analyze the content or subject of the calls to determine if problems in specific locations can be identified.

People also have a different perspective than the police when it comes to identifying problems. Although many people are fearful of crime, they generally are more concerned with problems that directly affect them, or problems they experience on a fairly regular basis. When polled, people often cite problems such as speeding cars, loitering on street corners, unruly juveniles, and panhandling as their primary concerns. Such problems are foremost in people's minds because they must confront them constantly. Disorder and minor violations of the law tend to dominate people's perceptions of "neighborhood wellness."

Analyzing complaints from an area or neighborhood may only provide the police with a piecemeal description of their concerns. There may be large numbers of people in a neighborhood that have concerns but never call the police. An effective way of dealing with this problem is to hold neighborhood meetings. Such meetings can be held in churches, schools, business meeting rooms, or government facilities. It is best to select a location that is as close to the neighborhood as possible. This generally results in a larger number of people coming to the meeting. Police officials can then hold an open forum to allow residents to discuss any concerns.

The police should be mindful of their demeanor at such meetings. In the past, some departments would send a large number of officers to these meetings. When this occurs, it may appear to be confrontational to the people. It is also important, especially in the early stages of establishing a relationship with a neighborhood, that high-ranking police officials attend. If only low-ranking officers are sent to these meetings, it communicates that it is not a high priority to the department. Once a relationship has been developed, specific officers can be introduced to the neighborhood and assigned to attend future meetings.

Two of the benefits of community meetings are that they serve as an excellent opportunity to gather information and develop better relations with people. For example, if a person raises an issue, other participants may provide other information about the problem. It also allows the police to query people about the problems. When people raise issues, they often are more willing to discuss them and provide the police information about who is causing the problem. If the police have a positive exchange with people, they may be willing to be more forthcoming with information in the future. This should provide the police with information about crime, criminals, and other problems.

One important point about community meetings is that once they have occurred, the police should initiate some response. That is, they should address issues raised by the people. When people meet with the police and discuss problems and the police fail to do anything about them, people become frustrated, lose their support for the police, and tend to disengage themselves from the police. They see the meetings as little more than manipulation on the part of the police. The object of these meetings is to develop a long-term relationship with the neighborhood residents.

Another important form of community meetings is when police officials meet with service clubs such as the Lions, Rotary, Chamber of Commerce, or Jaycees. These groups represent people from the community who have a common interest. These meetings provide an excellent opportunity to gauge public opinion about issues and problems. They also provide the police an opportunity to cement a good relationship with influential civic leaders in the community. These are, however, the "easy" groups for police to develop relations with because they are often supportive of the police. Police must give equal attention to those less popular groups and those groups that are often less supportive of the police. While these groups many vary from community to community, police officers must begin to work with groups that they have historically viewed as the "opposition." These groups might include labor unions, the ACLU, civil rights activists, environmental coalitions, animal rights activists, students, and others. Many "police" problems, including riots and violent protests, could have been avoided had the police developed better relationships with all community groups—not just those who meet for lunch on the first Tuesday of every month. In fact, engaging groups that have been traditionally viewed as hostile to the police can lead to problem solutions that are more acceptable to a community and reduce the probability of blowback.

Crime Mapping

The past several decades have seen significant strides being made in the use of computers in police departments. Today, many departments are able to map crime and other incidents using computer systems. When the police receive calls for service or reports of crime, the information is entered in the department's **computer-aided dispatch** (CAD) system. The CAD represents the front end of the **records management system** (RMS) where records are stored. The CAD/RMS system contains all the information related to each incident including location, time, nature of police response, police response time, and criminal report numbers. Information from the CAD/RMS system can then be loaded into a mapping program. Crime mapping is not a recent phenomenon. Harries (1999) notes that the New York City Police Department used crime maps as early as 1900. These early maps consisted of street maps with pins denoting the location of specific incidents or crimes. Officers could then view the maps and develop a better understanding of the problems on their beats. The problem with pin maps was that they were "static" and could show the locations of crimes for only a finite time period. With the passage of time, a map would contain so many pins that it was virtually useless to the officers who were attempting to extract information from it. Because the mappers had to begin with clean maps periodically, it was impossible to follow crime trends over time. Pin maps, however, did provide officers with a "limited picture" of the crimes in their beats or patrol areas.

A computerized map of crime and police call data represents a flexible method allowing officers to "see" crime and calls for service. Vasiliev (1996) notes that computerized mapping allows the police to manipulate time and space when viewing activities. The police are able to view activities several ways:

- *Crimes or calls across the community or within a specific area or time*: For example, investigators may want to visually examine all the rapes or robberies in an area to determine if there is a geographical pattern. The crimes could be plotted for any given period thus allowing the investigator to see if a pattern emerges. Likewise less sensational crimes like loud music and vandalism or quality of life issues could be selected for examination.

- *Activities for a particular shift or watch*: Commanders might better deploy patrol personnel or redesign their patrol beats by examining activities during individual shifts. Because crime patterns change over time, the configuration of beats should probably change to remain abreast with the changes in police and crime activities.

- *Activities for a particular beat or police district:* Commanders can visually examine what is occurring in a beat or district which allows them to determine if the area is properly staffed or to identify specific problems in the area which require additional attention by patrol or specialized units.

- *Activities around a "hot spot" or concentration of crime:* Crime and calls for service tend to concentrate in small geographical areas that may cut across beats and police districts. Mapping allows the police to identify hot spots and to examine activities in and around these geographic concentrations.

- *Concentrations of activities in an area over time:* It is sometimes worthwhile to view areas over time, that is, across six months, a year, or several years. This allows the administrator to see if the concentrations are changing over time or to determine if a problem-solving intervention has had an effect.

- *Compare police activities with social and ecological characteristics:* Here, crime and other activities can be mapped in conjunction with attributes in the environment that may contribute to crime. For example, LaVigne and Wartell (1998) discuss how mapping street robberies in relation to street lighting can provide insights into where robberies are more likely to occur in an area that is plagued with high robbery rates. The Redlands, California, Police Department has been mapping crime in relation to measures of community disorder to better identify community interventions by community policing teams. For example, Figure 8.6 provides a map of the city of Redlands, California. The map provides a visual display

Figure 8.6
Redlands Police Department 1999 "Hot Spots" for Residential Burglaries

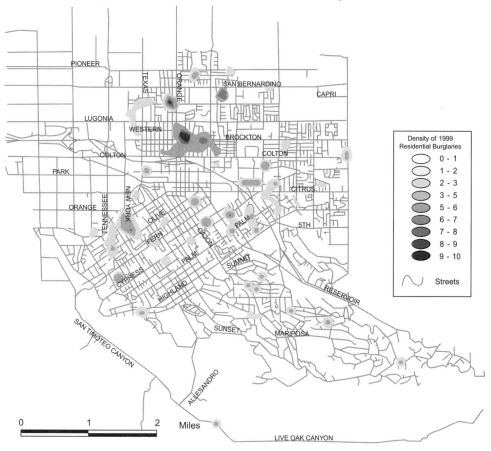

of residential burglaries. Although fairly well dispersed throughout a large area within the city, there are some areas with higher levels of burglaries than others. Given this information, the Redlands Police Department is able to couple enforcement programs with crime prevention and community building programs to alleviate the conditions that result in residential burglaries. Historically, we have depended on patrol to reduce problems such as burglary, but community policing demands that we develop comprehensive solutions. Mapping helps to pinpoint problems and assists in designing solutions.

Police Reports, Calls for Service Analysis, and Crime Analysis

Most police data analysis functions are housed in crime analysis units. These units generally are a part of or work in conjunction with the records unit to store and analyze reports and information. Daily police operations create a vast amount of data and information. Police officers make reports on most every activity in which they are involved. These reports include offense, supplemental, arrest, field contact, intelligence, and special analysis reports. The reports represent a data bank containing a wealth of raw information. Crime analysis is the act of analyzing the available raw data to provide crime patterns and trend information in a form that is easily usable for police officers.

Once the crime analysis unit receives the information, it produces reports which can be used by management, operational units, and individual officers. Examples of reports produced are crime summaries, known offender information, crime pattern information, crime correlation information, and special deployment plans. Figure 8.7 shows how some of this information can be utilized.

As noted in Figure 8.7, crime analysis information is useful to every unit in the department. It provides a wealth of information to aid officers in identifying problems and fashioning solutions.

In the past, police departments depended on pin maps and daily bulletins to provide officers and units with crime information. The pin map consisted of a map of the community with pins positioned where criminal activity occurred. The daily bulletin contained a listing of all criminal activity during a given period of time. Officers were supposed to examine the daily bulletins to keep informed of what was happening in their beats and in the community. There are a number of problems associated with this manual system of information dissemination, especially in larger departments where daily crime activities are quite high. First, in many

Figure 8.7
Crime Analysis Information Flow

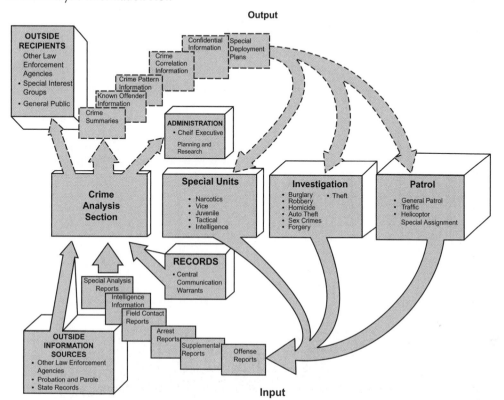

Source: Buck, G.A. (1973). *Police Crime Analysis Unit Handbook (Prescriptive Package: Law Enforcement Assistance Administration and National Institute of Law Enforcement and Criminal Justice*, p. 10). Washington, DC: U.S. Government Printing Office.

departments, the daily bulletin did not order or organize crime information in a useful manner. The bulletin would contain crime information about a particular part of the city or a listing of the various locations for a specific type of crime. It did not cross-reference the various pieces of information: victim type, time of day, geographical location, **modus operandi**, suspect information, and type of property stolen. It is difficult for officers to discern and thoroughly understand crime patterns without collating these crime variables. Finally, the daily bulletins failed to provide officers with information about crime and disorder over extended periods of time. Officers would have to piece together the information from a number of the daily bulletins. Today, computer mapping allows for a more informational display of crime information, and police CAD/RMS systems allow crime analysts to overcome these problems.

Crime analysis in a number of departments now assists officers in identifying and understanding problems. The factors, which are useful in the crime analysis function, include types of crimes, times of occurrence, locations of occurrence, suspect information, victim information, *modus operandi,* and physical evidence. Analysis of this information is directed toward the identification of crime patterns and early identification of crime trends. There are two broad types of crime patterns: (1) geographic concentration patterns and (2) similar offense patterns.

Geographic Concentration Pattern

The geographic concentration pattern is where a number of crimes or activities are concentrated in a specific geographical area. Figure 8.8 displays the Part I crimes for a three-month period in Redlands, California. Vast areas of the city

Figure 8.8
Part I Crimes for Redlands, California

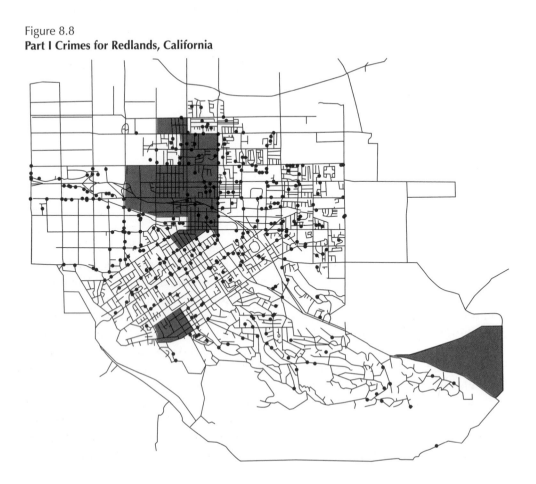

are without crime. Other areas, however, have large amounts of Part I crimes. The map allows the police to concentrate their efforts on those areas that have the highest levels of crime.

Geographic concentrations with large numbers of police activities in a very small area are hot spots, as discussed earlier. When examining a hot spot, not only is it important to look for crimes, but the analyst should also examine the area for all sorts of related activities. It is important to examine geographical concentrations for other types of calls. For example, an area with a concentration of assaults may also have a high concentration of fight or disorder calls. An examination of all the calls most likely will tell the analyst precisely where the problem lies. Once the problem is specified, a police intervention strategy can be developed.

Woodby and Johnson (2000) document an example of this procedure in Austin, Texas. In March 1999, a series of indecent exposures occurred near the University of Texas campus. Within a relatively short period, the police recorded eight different offenses. In each instance, the victims provided the police with similar descriptions of the perpetrator. Crime analysts mapped the crimes. They then examined the area for clues. There was a state hospital and a group home in the area, and the group home was located in the center of the pattern of offenses. Detectives then focused their investigative efforts on the residents in the group home and quickly identified the offender.

Similar Offense Pattern

Similar offense patterns are developed in a similar fashion as the geographic concentration patterns. **Similar offense patterns** can be concentrated in an area, as was the example of the serial indecent exposures discussed above, or they may be spread over a large geographical area as is the case of most serial rapists, serial armed robbers, or burglars. Here, suspect, victim, crime type, and *modus operandi* information are studied for similarities. If similarities exist, then an assumption is made that the same offenders may have committed the crimes.

For example, the analyst may search through all the rapes occurring in the community, searching for unique characteristics. In essence, the analyst is able to combine all the information from the various related reports. The analyst will review a number of factors associated with each case: victim appearance, victim activities at the time of the rape, location, type of location such as a parking lot or building, suspect description, amount and type of force used, and sexual acts engaged in by the perpetrator. Each report where the crime appears to be linked or related, based on the number of matching factors, may contain pieces of information not contained in the other reports and the combined total information provides investigators with more investigative leads. The information from the combined reports simplifies the investigation of all the cases and provides operations personnel with better information to develop crime prevention measures.

Community Surveys

Community surveys are a way of measuring people's attitudes about the police and police performance as well as problems in the community. Numerous police departments across the country are using surveys to measure attitudes on a variety of topics. Police departments are asking people about fear of crime, the amount of crime in their neighborhood, and the types and amount of crime that they observe. They are also surveying people's attitudes about the police. These surveys contain questions about the quality of service, how often they call the police, and general impressions about the police.

Community surveys are a method by which the police can collect information from a variety of segments of the population. For example, the police may identify a neighborhood that has a high crime rate. The police may want to survey the neighborhood to identify specific problems, ideas about solutions, and police priorities. Survey results often show that residents have a different view of what problems are relative to the police impressions of problems (Kappeler & Kraska, 1998; 1998a). A neighborhood survey also serves as a good prelude to neighborhood meetings. Survey results provide the police with information and statistics to discuss with neighborhood residents at such meetings.

In some cases, the police want to survey the population within their city. This provides a general impression of people's perceptions of the police. In some cases, this can be an expensive endeavor, and many residents do not respond. The Lexington, Kentucky, Police Department came up with an innovative way of overcoming these obstacles. They developed short surveys and had them distributed by the County Clerk as people were completing applications for their driver's license. People were asked to complete the short police department survey while they were waiting for the driver's license to be processed. Because people had to renew their driver's license every four years, the department was able to collect a good sample of responses without a great deal of expense.

Webster and Connors (1993) describe how the Tempe, Arizona, Police Department used community surveys to develop beat profiles for their officers. A community policing squad was used to administer questionnaires door-to-door. Residents and businesses in the neighborhood were contacted. The questionnaires contained questions about the respondents' socioeconomic status, observed crime, perceptions of the area's drug problems, city services, and their willingness to participate in police crime prevention programs. The questionnaire served to identify people who would be willing to participate in crime prevention programs and to work with the police to alleviate problems in the neighborhood.

The questionnaire also queried residents about problems such as loitering, buildings where drug dealers and youth hung out, trash problems, gang membership, gang graffiti, disorder problems, and areas such as parks or street corners where disorders occurred. The police were able to take the information and develop a profile of beats. The profiles identified problems and residents who were willing to assist the police in solving problems. Armed with the beat profiles, patrol officers could identify hot spots and take a proactive stance against them.

As noted, surveys can be used to identify and measure a number of problems in a city, neighborhood, or area. Figure 8.9 provides part of a survey used to measure people's perceptions of problem in San Bernardino, California.

The questions used in the survey attempt to measure a number of problems and issues. The survey provides police officers with priorities based on people's view of their neighborhood. In many cases, such surveys result in a different ordering of problems relative to police perceptions of problems. Moreover, the survey measures problems that fall within the domain of other governmental agencies, resulting in the need for the police department to forge partnerships with these agencies.

The preceding provided detailed information about a variety of methods that departments can use to scan the environment to identify problems. These methods can be used in combination or singularly to identify a number of problems. Once a problem is identified, it is important that a thorough analysis be conducted to ensure the problem is totally understood. In terms of analysis, it is important for police problem solvers to think "outside the box." Prior to community policing and problem solving, the police relied too heavily on traditional methods of solving problems which generally involved enforcement (Kappeler & Kraska, 1998; 1998a). The police must search for different and more effective means of solving problems. This search will involve engaging a variety of private and other governmental agencies. They often have the resources to better handle problems that come to the attention of the police.

Finally, once the police fashion and implement a response, they must ensure that it has the intended results: reduction or eradication of the problem. In the past, the police have implemented programs, but failed to ensure that they worked. For example, the police would often increase patrols in an area that was experiencing problems. The additional patrols frequently had no effect on the problem. To ensure that a response works, the police must constantly review calls for service, people's perception of safety, and crime to see if the response indeed worked.

Figure 8.9
Survey Used to Measure Crime and Disorder

Rate the Problems Listed Below in Terms of their Severity in your Neighborhood	
Please **circle** a number from **one to five**, with **1 = no problem** and **5 = severe problem**	
Abandoned cars	1 2 3 4 5
Abandoned buildings/vacant lots	1 2 3 4 5
Public use of drugs & alcohol	1 2 3 4 5
Street drug dealing	1 2 3 4 5
Prostitution	1 2 3 4 5
Gangs	1 2 3 4 5
Speeding & not stopping at stop signs	1 2 3 4 5
Rowdy groups of people in the street	1 2 3 4 5
Trash in the streets	1 2 3 4 5
Truancy – kids not going to school	1 2 3 4 5
Graffiti	1 2 3 4 5
Street lighting	1 2 3 4 5
Stray or loose dogs/cats	1 2 3 4 5
Police stopping people without good reason	1 2 3 4 5
Lack of after school programs for kids	1 2 3 4 5
Lack of recreation sports for kids	1 2 3 4 5

Police Problem Solving

A number of situations present themselves that are amenable to problem solving. The following provides a number of diverse situations where officers have used problem solving to attack persistent community and neighborhood problems.

Spelman and Eck (1989) discuss how the New York City Police Department used problem solving to eliminate a drug problem. Essentially, the department was experiencing a drug trafficking problem at a park located at

49th Street and 5th Avenue. The police had attempted a number of proactive strategies including additional patrols and buy-bust operations. The police were able to make a number of minor possession and loitering charges, but these arrests were of little consequence to the offenders. The drug offenders always returned. The community policing officer discovered that most of the drug dealers were hiding their drugs in the park and would retrieve them when they made a sale. This prevented the police from apprehending them with enough weight to make a substantial charge. Officers met with tenants of nearby apartment buildings to discuss the problem. They found that many of the residents were elderly and were at home during the day. They were asked to watch the park and call the police with the locations of where the drug dealers were hiding their drugs.

As a result of the meetings, a number of calls were made to the police. The police would then go to the park and retrieve the drugs. This resulted in a number of financial losses to the drug traffickers and, because many of them received their drugs from suppliers on credit, they were not able to repay the suppliers. Ultimately, it forced the drug traffickers to carry their drugs with them. The police were then able to make more significant charges against the suspects. Eventually, as a result of the police actions, the drug traffickers left the neighborhood.

A similar problem occurred in Lexington, Kentucky. Drug traffickers were selling drugs at a street corner that was adjacent to a park. Many of the drug traffickers stood around watching or participated in basketball games in the park area. The police intensified patrols and performed a number of field interrogations with no success. Finally, the police department had the basketball nets removed from the area. The local newspaper condemned the police for the action. However, the police pointed out there were still a number of nets in the park that were not adjacent to the street corner, and the action significantly reduced the amount of drug trafficking in the area.

The San Diego Police Department had a major drug problem on University Avenue (Brito & Allan, 1999). It had become an open-air market attracting large numbers of drug pushers and users. The San Diego police used a combination of programs to attack the problem. First, officers interviewed residents, users, and arrestees about why the area attracted so many drugs. They stated that the area had a reputation for being a place where drugs could be scored safety. Officers first identified a high-intensity zone (HIZ) in the area. The HIZ represented the area with the greatest amount of problems and the area where the greatest enforcement would occur. Next, the officers adopted a zero-tolerance policy and began making large numbers of arrests in the HIZ. Officers encouraged users to tell their friends that the area was no longer safe. This was done to eliminate the appearance of safety in the area.

The second phase of the program was to intensify arrests and confuse the drug dealers and users. The police spread the word through the area that there was going to be a major crackdown in the area. Shortly afterward, the police initiated a large crackdown using large numbers of officers and making significant numbers of arrests. After the crackdown had been conducted, the police continually spread the word that another crackdown was eminent. This kept the dealers and users confused and they began to avoid the area. The final phase of the police action was to steer offenders to a rehabilitation program. This was done on a voluntary basis and with the cooperation of the San Diego Drug Court.

The above three examples show how the police can use problem solving to attack drug trafficking. The examples also show that effective problem solving generally uses tactics that are outside the normal police response. They also show how the police can engage people and solicit their help in reducing drug problems.

Problem solving can be used to address a variety of other police problems. Stedman and Weisel (1999) discuss how Dallas, Baltimore, and San Diego attempted to use problem solving to reduce their burglaries. An analysis of the burglaries in the three cities showed that there was a high percentage of repeat burglaries: 11.5 percent for single-family residents and 27.8 percent in multiple-family dwellings in Baltimore, 10.1 percent for single-family residents and 53.8 percent in multiple-family dwellings in Dallas, and 4.1 percent for single-family residents and 10.9 percent in multiple-family dwellings in San Diego.

Officials found that crime prevention and target-hardening efforts had been rather haphazard in the past. Typically, the departments' resources only allowed the departments to take a report. In a number of instances, the reports were taken by a clerk or a reports desk by telephone and no officer visited the scene. The departments attempted to rectify the problem. After reported burglaries, the departments sent crime prevention specialists to visit each victim. In addition to discussing crime prevention techniques with the victim, they also advised the victims of the probability of a repeat burglary. This was done to encourage the victims to take action to prevent a future occurrence. Officers also performed neighborhood checks and advised neighbors of the previous burglary and encouraged them to take preventive measures. This was done because some burglars typically operate in the same area.

Brito and Allen (1999) document how the Nassau County, New York, Police Department used problem solving to attack a problem of fraud being committed on the elderly. Twenty-one percent of the county residents were elderly. The department found that a number of con artists were perpetrating a variety of scams on the residents with an average loss of $2,500. The department held meetings with a number of senior groups and found that the victims were not reporting a majority of the offenses. They too often were embarrassed as a result of their mistakes. Another problem was that historically the police viewed such crimes as civil matters or falling within the jurisdiction of other governmental agencies, while other agencies viewed the problem as a police matter. Consequently, no agency was addressing the problem. The end result was that con artists had found a fairly lucrative crime with minimum risk.

The police contacted a number of organizations to obtain information on the problem: the American Association of Retired Persons, the National Association of Bunko Investigators, the Federal Bureau of Investigation, and the U.S. Postal Inspections Service Operations. The officers also contacted the banks in the area, because bank security personnel generally had intimate knowledge of how such frauds were perpetrated. The police also worked with the area utility companies since a number of the con artists were gaining entry into victims' homes by posing as a utility company employee.

The police developed a multi-constituency training program. Three courses were developed for the police department: one each for command officers, in-service training, and recruit or academy training. These courses were designed to make officers more aware of the problem and ways of dealing with specific crimes. A fourth course was developed for the banking industry. Bank tellers were trained about scams and frauds, how to conduct discreet interviews with seniors, and to watch for instances where seniors make large cash withdrawals. For example, when a senior would request a large cash withdrawal, in some cases, a teller would try to suggest a cashier's check to protect the senior. A fifth course was developed for the utility companies. The utility companies were asked to provide customers with information about the problem and how to identify utility company employees and telephone numbers to check out utility officials who appear unannounced. Finally, a course was developed for the seniors. This course provided information about the kinds of frauds that were being used, how to protect themselves from fraud, and how to contact the police. The Nassau County Police Department partnered with a variety of agencies and developed a strategy that comprehensively addressed the problem.

Finally, the Fontana, California, Police Department used problem solving to address a homeless problem in the city (Brito & Allan, 1999). Fontana serves as a transportation center. It has two major interstate highways running through it, and it has a large number of trucking terminals that serve Ontario International Airport. This ultimately results in a large number of homeless making their way to the city.

The department established a transient enrichment program. Officers were able to obtain an office in a local shopping center to coordinate the program. Volunteers raised money and assisted in rehabilitating the office. Officers then established a provider network to assist the homeless. Initially, the officers believed their priority would be to provide basic services to the homeless. Later, they expanded the program to provide job counseling and employment services. The office served as an intake facility. Once a homeless person was brought to the facility, he or she would be offered food, lodging, and employment services.

In the past, officers felt that little could be done for or with the homeless and had not been aggressive in enforcing nuisance laws against them. The establishment of the office led to patrol officers being more aggressive. When officers encountered a homeless person, they would advise him or her of the program. In many instances, homeless persons were more willing to volunteer, especially with the officers more aggressively enforcing nuisance laws. Officers found panhandlers who were not homeless, and as a result of stricter enforcement, many of them left the community.

During the first 18 months of the program, 510 people entered the program. All but 13 remained in the program. More than 50 percent of the clients had permanent housing. Sixteen percent had permanent jobs. A number of the clients returned to their homes in some other community after the program. The year after the initiation of the program, the city had a 15 percent drop in Part I crimes. Although the drop in crime cannot be attributable to the program, the program certainly had some influence. The number of calls for service involving the homeless has dropped by 50 percent since program implementation. It appears that the transient enrichment program helped a number of people and had an impact on police workload.

The above examples show how problem solving can be used to address many community issues. Crime and drug problems as well as social or service problems can be handled using problem solving. Every unit in a police department can engage in problem solving, whether it's patrol or criminal investigation. Also, effective problem solving often involves developing working relationships with units outside the police department. The following box shows how problem solving can be used within a police department.

SPOTLIGHT ON COMMUNITY POLICING PRACTICE

High Fuel Costs: A Problem-Solving Challenge

As rising fuel costs put the squeeze on law enforcement department budgets, chiefs and sheriffs are searching for ways to sustain their current level of operations while using less gasoline. Some are finding their solutions in differential responses to calls for service, modified patrol methods, and use of vehicles with improved gas mileage or alternative fuels.

With the average price of regular unleaded gasoline approaching $4.00 a gallon and no end to the increase in sight, departments across the country might not yet be feeling the pressure to drive less, but they certainly are taking notice of the impact on their budgets, especially as we head into the traditionally high-demand, price-increasing summer months. For those faced with the puzzle of how to meet the increasing demands on police services while minimizing fuel costs, there are no easy answers. Officers, particularly those who patrol and answer 911 calls, need cars, and cars need gasoline.

Our review of recent news coverage of higher fuel costs as well as conversations with a variety of law enforcement officials suggest that there are a number of ways that agencies can mitigate the impact on their agency budget. This article strives to highlight some short-term as well as potentially long-term solutions we found—an important consideration because gas is unlikely to return to the lower prices enjoyed in the past.

We were pleased to discover that many agencies were looking to community policing and problem solving to help them keep fuel consumption under control without the need to invest in new equipment or reduce police services. Chief Dan Flynn of the Marietta, Georgia Police Department, for example, advocates the "use of a community policing, problem-solving approach" to develop strategies that reach reasonable goals in fuel reduction. He cautioned against reducing police patrols in response to rising fuel costs. He believes that police visibility is vital to the community's feelings of public safety and that there is a correlation between uniformed patrols and the absence of crime.

Some agencies have issued caps (or recommended caps) on per-shift mileage. This may help with budgeting, but as the Eau Claire County (Wisconsin) Sheriff Ron Cramer has noted, in the 1980s deputies in his county were limited to 125 miles per shift, but that also limited effectiveness in a county with 630 square miles to patrol. A different approach to reducing mileage might be offered by technological advances in patrol cars. The Catawba (North Carolina) County Sheriff's Office deputies have access to field-based reporting, allowing them to reduce the number of trips taken to headquarters. Deputies are allowed to sign in from their cars in their assigned communities at the start of their shifts instead of gathering at headquarters for daily squad meetings. Both measures actually increase the law enforcement presence in the community while reducing the number of miles driven for administrative duties.

Other agencies have considered eliminating their take-home car programs or restricting off-duty mileage for take-home cars. As with per-shift mileage caps, this potentially reduces police visibility in the community because marked cruisers are driven less. Still others have instituted reimbursement programs for the use of take-home cars with officers paying one rate for portal-to-portal use and another rate for off-duty personal use of the vehicles. An additional cautionary note is that changes in take-home car programs could have an adverse impact on morale.

In some departments, the program may even be a job benefit that is subject to contract negotiations.

The unintended consequence of some fuel-saving solutions could be a reduction of police services, but what about saving fuel while also improving service and community

(Continued)

interaction? The Hickory (North Carolina) Police Department is encouraging its officers to walk or ride bikes in their assigned communities. They are also encouraged to get out of their car for 10 minutes per hour on duty to do property checks on foot. Similarly, the Claremont (North Carolina) police officers are being encouraged to park their cars for 15 minutes every hour to do community networking and traffic patrolling. These sorts of policies are seen by some chiefs as having a positive side effect that encourages officer/citizen interaction and communication, something they have been striving for as they try to enhance their community policing efforts.

Alternative call-management strategies, many of which are discussed in the COPS Office guidebook, Call Management and Community Policing, can also help agencies save on gas. Residents, for example, can be encouraged to use telephone reporting for minor property crimes, or to meet officers at substations to make reports. This would allow one officer to take many reports without having to drive from house to house.

The approaches to tackling this problem will likely be as varied as the nearly 18,000 state and local law enforcement agencies across the U.S. No solution is going to work for all agencies, so perhaps the best advice we can offer is what we heard in one of our interviews—encourage agencies to use the problem-solving process they use to address crime and disorder problems. Why not turn the SARA process inward? Scan and Assess to identify the biggest fuel drains in your agency and the vehicle priorities. Identify and involve all stakeholders to develop and implement Responses that will reduce fuel use, acknowledging the geographic, technical, and possibly political realities of the agency. Take the time to Analyze how those responses have worked or have not worked in having an impact on the budget and on crime and the community. Then the agency can make policy adjustments that take into consideration not just the current price of fuel, but also the needs of the agency staff and the community they serve.

Rising fuel costs probably will affect policing for the foreseeable future. The need to find innovative ways to save on fuel costs while continuing to provide the level of service communities have come to expect is likely to remain a long-term challenge for police chiefs and sheriffs.

Karl Bickel
Senior Policy Analyst
The COPS Office

Deborah Spence
Senior Social Science Analyst
The COPS Office

Source: The e-newsletter of the COPS Office, Volume 1, Issue 5, May 2008.

Why Police Departments Do Not Engage in Problem Solving

The San Diego Police department is one of the most progressive police departments in the country and is the home of a number of innovations. However, Cordner and Biebel (2005) examined problem solving in the department and found that problem solving as practiced by street officers fell far short of the ideal model. San Diego is not atypical. Police departments across the country have committed to problem solving, but their efforts often are in name only. Departments and their officers often do not have the skills necessary to effectively solve problems and rely too heavily on traditional policing. For example, Scott (2000) advises that many officers have difficulty in distinguishing between problems and incidents.

Problem solving obviously can be productive. There are a variety of problems that can be addressed through the problem-solving process. Many departments, however, do not use problem solving, or do so only haphazardly. Eck (2004: 190-193) has identified nine reasons why problem-solving efforts in many departments are mediocre.

- ***Police officers do not have the analytical skills required to analyze problems:*** In many cases, officers have not received adequate training to solve problems. Also, supervisors and managers fail to mentor officers in the problem-solving process. They often have only a superficial understanding of problem solving.

- ***Police managers and supervisors do not know how to foster problem solving:*** Too often, the department has not developed a framework or structure to facilitate problem solving. It is not one of the tools that are commonly used. Thus, managers and supervisors have difficulty in integrating it in day-to-day police work.

- ***Police agencies resist change:*** Traditionally organized police departments have had great difficulty in understanding or integrating community policing, particularly problem solving, into their operational format. Officers throughout the chain of command resist change. This problem is indicative of a department that has not embraced the true spirit of community policing.

- ***Police workloads prevent anything but superficial analysis:*** Many police departments have remained incident driven. They have failed to take action to better manage their resources. They must examine workloads and make the time for officers to engage in problem solving.

- ***There is too little involvement of communities, and communities do not cooperate:*** Generally, when a department does not have a cooperative relationship with the community, it is the department's fault; it has not put forth the effort to forge such relationships. This is not to say that building relationships with the community is easy, but it can be done with substantial effort.

- *Local governmental agencies provide too little support:*
  Community policing, to be effective, often requires working with
  other governmental agencies. They often are resistant to working
  with the police, especially on projects that are outside their normal
  scope of work. Here, the police executive must use political processes to gain necessary support.

- *Little is known about what works under what circumstances:*
  Police officers often do not know which tactic or strategy is best suited
  for a particular problem. However, the same can be said of conventional
  or traditional responses to crime and disorder problems. Police officers
  must experiment and evaluate the results. Did the action resolve the
  problem, and if not, what other solutions may be tried?

- *The problem-solving process used is linear, but most problem solving is nonlinear:* Here, officers are resistant to using the
  four-step SARA process. Their responses to problems often are hit or
  miss, resulting in failure, or they fail to fully comprehend the nature
  of a problem and tend to focus on a symptom or a small part of the
  problem. All problems can be understood and addressed.

- *We do not know how to solve problems because we do not
  understand the problem:* The analysis step in the SARA model
  requires all information about a problem be collected and analyzed.
  Too often police officers only superficially analyze complex problems. This often leads to failure.

To a great extent the nine reasons identified by Eck are not reasons, but
excuses. As we noted in Chapter 1, community policing is a comprehensive
alteration of traditional policing, and it requires substantial effort to be implemented correctly and effectively. Too many police departments have failed to
put forth the effort. This is not to say that all problems can be solved. There are
complex problems involving larger society that are beyond the police departments' reach. But, police departments can solve a substantial number of problems confronting the community and the department, and have a positive effect
on the community's quality of life.

Summary

This chapter has addressed problem solving in policing. Problem solving and
community partnerships are the two principle components of community policing. Problem solving represents a strategy that goes beyond traditional policing.
It necessitates that the police not only respond to crime, disorder, and calls for

service, but also investigate their root causes. Once the causes are identified, the police can more effectively deal with problems.

Problem solving is a multi-stepped process using the SARA model. It includes: scanning, analysis, response, and assessment. Scanning is the search for problems. The police can use a variety of techniques to identify problems, and it is important that those problems that are the most problematic to the community be addressed. Analysis is the process whereby the police attempt to fully understand the problems and their symptoms. Response is the police reaction to the problem, and typically is in-depth, working with other agencies in the community. Finally, assessment is a process where the police evaluate their response to ensure that it is successful. Police departments too often fail to assess their programs, which results in a continuation of the problem.

If the police successfully attend to problems, especially dangerous places or hot spots that generate large numbers of calls and crime, the police will become more effective and efficient. They will be effective by reducing problems in the community. Problem solving is much more desirable than responding to calls for service, which is historically how the police responded to problems. It is efficient in that it will ultimately reduce the number of calls for service the police department receives; which can free up officers for community policing. Thus, problem solving and community policing can have a significant impact on the police department and its community.

KEY TERMS IN CHAPTER 8

- analysis
- assessment
- community surveys
- computer-aided dispatch (CAD) system
- dangerous place
- drive-offs
- geographic concentration pattern
- hard crime
- hot spot
- *modus operandi*

- police crime
- political crime
- records management system (RMS)
- response
- scanning
- similar offense patterns
- soft crime
- third party policing
- white-collar crime

DISCUSSION QUESTIONS

1. Discuss the relationship between wealth and the conditions that cause crime to be concentrated in specific spaces.
2. Discuss and describe the reasons why one location in a city may become defined as a problem place while another location with crime might not be defined that way.

3. Discuss the reasons why some social problems like crime come to the public's attention while other social problems are given very little attention.
4. Describe and discuss the stages of problem solving. What are the taken-for-granted assumptions implicit in the SARA model?
5. Describe the difference between traditional policing and problem-solving policing. Which is the better model for communities?
6. Discuss the difference between dangerous places and hot spots. Given that all "space" is created by a complex networks of social interaction, is there really any such thing as place? List as many factors as you can think of that define social space.
7. Discuss the limitation of problem solving based solely on crime analysis, crime mapping, and crime patterning.
8. Many police departments do not use problem solving and some of the reasons for this are listed in the text. Discuss other reasons the police have been slow to adopt problem solving.
9. List and discuss the methods that can be used for problem identification in a community. What are the pros and cons of these different methods?
10. What are the dangers of allowing the police to be the major social institution that addresses social problems in the community?

References

Bichler, G., & Gaines, L. (2005). An Examination of Police Officers' Insights into Problem Identification and Problem Solving. *Crime & Delinquency, 51*(1), 53-75.

Biebel, E., & Cordner, G. (2003). "Repeat Calls for People with Mental Illness: An Application of Hot-Spots Analysis." *Police Forum, 13*(3), 1-8.

Boba, R., & Crank, J. (2008). "A Model for Institutionalizing Problem-Solving." *Policing: An International Journal, 9*(5), 379-393.

Braga, A., Hureau, D., & Winship, C. (2008). Losing Faith? Police, Black Churches, and the Resurgence of Youth Violence in Boston. *Ohio State Journal of Criminal Law, 6*, 141-172.

Brito, C. S., & Allan, T. (1999). *Problem-Oriented Policing: Crime-Specific Problems, Critical Issues, and Making POP Work* (Vol. 2). Washington, DC: PERF.

Buerger, M. E., Cohn, E. G., & Petrosino, A. J. (2000). Defining Hot Spots of Crime: Operationalizing Theoretical Concepts for Field Research. In R. Glensor, M. Correia & K. Peak (Eds.), *Policing Communities: Understanding Crime and Solving Problems* (pp. 138-150). Los Angeles, CA: Roxbury Press.

Clarke, R. (1998). Defining Police Strategies: Problem Solving, Problem-Oriented Policing and Community Oriented Policing. In T. O'Connor Shelly & A. Grant (Eds.), *Problem-Oriented Policing: Crime-Specific Problems, Critical Issues, and Making POP Work*. Washington, DC: Police Executive Research Forum.

Clarke, R., & Eck, J. (2005). *Crime Analysis for Problem Solvers: In 60 Small Steps*. Washington, DC: Office of Community Oriented Policing Services.

Cordner, G., & Biebel, E. (2005). Problem-Oriented Policing in Practice. *Criminology and Public Policy, 4*, 155-180.

Eck, J. E. (2004). Why Don't Problems Get Solved? In W. Skogan (Ed.), *Community Policing* (pp. 185–206). Belmont, CA: Wadsworth.

Felson, M. (2009). *Crime and Everyday Life* (4th ed.). Thousand Oaks, CA: Pine Forge Press.

Gaines, L., & Kappeler, V. (2011). *Policing in America* (7th ed.). Waltham, MA: Anderson.

Goldstein, H. (1990). *Problem-Oriented Policing*. New York, NY: McGraw-Hill Book Co.

Green, L. (1996). *Policing Places with Drug Problems*. Thousand Oaks, CA: Sage.

Harries, K. (1999). *Crime Mapping: Principle and Practice*. Washington, DC: NIJ.

Kappeler, V. E., & Kraska, P. B. (1998). A Textual Critique of Community Policing: Police Adaption to High Modernity. *Policing: An International Journal of Police Strategies and Management*, *21*(2), 293–313.

Kappeler, V. E., & Kraska, P. B. (1998a). Policing Modernity: Scientific and Community Based Violence on Symbolic Playing Fields. In S. Henry & D. Milovanovic (Eds.), *Constitutive Criminology at Work*. Albany, NY: SUNY Press.

LaVigne, N., & Wartell, J. (1998). *Crime Mapping Case Studies: Successes in the Field*. Washington, DC: PERF.

Mazerolle, L., Rogan, D., Frank, J., Famega, C., & Eck, J. (2005). Managing Calls to the Police with 911/311 Systems. *NIJ Research in Practice*, *5*, 3–15.

Messner, S. F., & Rosenfeld, R. (1997). *Crime and the American Dream*. Belmont, CA: Wadsworth.

Pierce, G., Spaar, S., & Briggs, L. (1988). The character of police work: strategic and tactical implications. Boston, MA: Center for Applied Social Research, Northeastern University.

Reiss, A. (1971). *The Police and the Public*. New Haven, CT: Yale University Press.

Scott, M. (2000). *Problem-Oriented Policing: Reflections on the First 20 Years*. Washington, DC: Office of Community Oriented Policing Services.

Shaw, C., & McKay, H. (1942). *Juvenile Delinquency and Urban Areas*. Chicago, IL: University of Chicago Press.

Sherman, L. (1996). Repeat Calls for Service: Policing "Hot Spots." In G. Cordner, L. Gaines & V. Kappeler (Eds.), *Police Operations: Analysis and Evaluation* (pp. 277–292). Cincinnati, OH: Anderson Publishing Co.

Skogan, W. G., Hartnett, S., DuBois, J., Comey, J., Kaiser, M., & Lovig, J. (2000). *Problem Solving in Practice: Implementing Community Policing in Chicago*. Washington, DC: National Institute of Justice.

Spellman, W. (1995). Criminal Careers of Public Places. In J. Eck & D. Weisburd (Eds.), *Crime and Place. Crime Prevention Studies 4*. Monsey, NY: Criminal Justice Press.

Spelman, W., & Eck, J. E. (1989). Sitting Ducks, Ravenous Wolves, and Helping Hands: New Approaches to Urban Policing. *Public Affairs Comment*, *35*(2), 1–9.

Stedman, J., & Weisel, D. L. (1999). Finding and Addressing Repeat Burglaries. In C. Brito & T. Allan (Eds.), *Problem Oriented Policing: Crime Specific Problems, Critical Issues, and Making POP Work* (Vol. 2, pp. 3–27). Washington, DC: PERF.

Vasiliev, I. (1996). Design Issues to Be Considered When Mapping Time. In C. Wood & C. Keller (Eds.), *Cartographic Design: Theoretical and Practical Perspectives*. Chichester, UK: John Wiley & Sons.

Webster, B., & Connors, E. F. (1993). Police Methods for Identifying Community Problems. *American Journal of Police, 12*(1), 75-102.

Weisburd, D., Bushway, S., Lum, C., & Yang, S. (2004). Trajectories of Crime at Places: A Longitudinal Study of Street Segments in the City of Seattle. *Criminology, 42*, 283-322.

Witte, J., Travis, L., & Langworthy, R. (1990). Participatory Management in Law Enforcement: Poice Officer, Supervisor, and Administrator Perceptions. *American Journal of Police, 9*, 1-24.

Woodby, K., & Johnson, A. (2000). Identifying a Serial Indecent Exposure Suspect. In N. LaVigne & J. Wartell (Eds.), *Crime Mapping Case Studies: Successes in the Field* (Vol. 2). Washington, DC: PERF.

Zatz, M., & Portillos, E. (2004). Voices from the Barrio: Chicano/a Gangs, Families, and Communities. In F. Esbensen, S. Tibbetts & L. Gaines (Eds.), *American Youth Gangs at the Millennium* (pp. 113-141). Long Grove, IL: Waveland.

A state is not a mere society, having a common place, established for the prevention of mutual crime and for the sake of exchange.... Political society exists for the sake of noble actions, and not of mere companionship.

—Aristotle

CHAPTER 9   Community Crime Prevention

LEARNING OBJECTIVES

After reading the chapter, you should be able to:

1. Understand the social conditions that gave rise to the crime prevention movement.
2. List and explain the theoretical foundations of crime prevention.
3. Understand the various forms of public and private social control.
4. List and distinguish between the five basic strategies for crime prevention.
5. List and explain the concept of situational crime prevention and its elements.
6. List and distinguish between the three basic types of community crime prevention programs.
7. Explain the purpose of the variation of neighborhood watch called "community anti-drug campaign."
8. Explain the roles that community policing and problem solving play in crime prevention.

Police departments began to implement crime prevention programming in the 1980s and 1990s. The intensified interest in crime prevention was fueled primarily by problem solving, fear of crime, Wilson and Kelling's (1982) treatise on "broken windows," and a realization that the police could not control crime without the assistance of the community. Problem solving represented a new mantra for policing. It represented a departure from routine preventive patrol to a philosophy whereby the police attempted to identify problems, especially concentrations of crime and disorder known as hot spots, and implement tactics to ameliorate the causes. It also emphasized thinking outside the box; that is, officers were encouraged to search for solutions that might be nontraditional in nature. This resulted in prevention becoming more important.

Fear of crime, primarily fueled by the media's construction of the crack cocaine epidemic and the war on drugs, resulted in the police seeking new strategies that, if not more effective, would at least involve the public, which would result in better support and cooperation. Crime prevention, in many cases, was a hands-on approach whereby officers interacted with people. This engendered better relationships with members of the community and reduced fear, especially targets of the crime prevention programming, and it was seen as a method of diminishing the crime problem. Positive police interactions as a result of programs were seen as a method of attacking a variety of problems.

Wilson and Kelling's "broken windows" thesis declared that if the police concentrated on disorder and minor crimes, it would have an impact on more serious crime in a neighborhood. It was reasoned that small problems, if left unchecked, ultimately would result in more serious crime problems. The police in numerous communities began to concentrate on reducing disorder. They enforced crimes against panhandling, loitering, drinking in public, and other minor violations that were seen as detracting from the civility in a neighborhood. These activities philosophically resulted in the police becoming more concerned with neighborhood conditions and provided a stimulus for more active crime prevention.

Hughes (1998) notes that part of the impetus for crime prevention was that traditional police response, bureaucratic methods such as rapid response to calls and crime and arrest and incarceration were not effective in stemming the rising crime problem. This resulted in the police seeking assistance from people via crime prevention and community policing tactics. The public had to become involved in the fight against crime; the police could not be successful alone. Thus, crime prevention was seen as a way of involving the community in crime fighting, and it was a method by which to make criminal activities more difficult.

This approach not only attempts to engage people in crime prevention, but it also recognizes that other governmental and private agencies can contribute to the cause. For example, code enforcement is now used as a tool to attack drug trafficking locations (Green, 1996). Drug houses are inspected for code violations and closed when they have ample and unrepaired violations. Public nuisance ordinances can be used to close houses of prostitution. Public mental health services can be used to treat homeless people who are mentally ill. Finally, there are numerous churches and other non-profit organizations that can provide services to at-risk individuals and families, especially in drug- and gang-prone neighborhoods. The police can take the lead and make referrals to these agencies, coordinate activities, and in some cases develop partnerships that provide comprehensive services to a community.

SPOTLIGHT ON COMMUNITY POLICING PRACTICE

Partners vs. Stakeholders

In talking about the importance of partnerships in effective community policing, the words "partner" and "stakeholder" are often used interchangeably. While the two are similar, they are not true synonyms. Partners and stakeholders serve different purposes and make different contributions. Before beginning any new project, it is important to be clear on who your agency's partners are, who the project's stakeholders are, what each can bring to a project, and how the project is going to make the most effective use of both.

Partners

A partner is a person or organization associated with another in some action or endeavor and who shares in both the risks and rewards of the joint effort. It is possible for partners to have different levels of investment in a project and, therefore, a proportional share of the risk. The key is that a partner brings something to the table, knowledge, skills, and/or resources, and stands to benefit in some way from the success of the project. For example, a police department looking to address citizen complaints about chronic speeding in residential neighborhoods can determine if the problem really exists and may quickly reach the conclusion that increased enforcement alone will not solve the problem permanently. Alternative measures, such as the creation of bypasses, enhanced signage, and traffic-calming measures, are not the purview of a law enforcement agency, however. Partnering with the government agencies responsible for sign and road building and maintenance is necessary to achieve those goals. It may take not just their knowledge and skills to find the best solution to the problem, but also their budgets. A united front of agencies interested in working together to address the speeding problem may be more likely to secure the funds necessary than any one agency seeking funding alone.

Stakeholders

A stakeholder is a person or group having an investment or interest in an enterprise. They may share in some risk or reward, particularly if their investment is monetary, but what they stand to gain may not be tied directly to their contribution in the same way as that of the project partners. Stakeholders are often those who are vested in how a project is designed and whether it is successful, but they may not have direct responsibilities and tasks that influence project completion. The primary stakeholders in a police-led project are the citizens who are affected by the problem or issue being addressed and who will benefit from the solution. The voice of those residents is most often provided through organizations and community groups. To return to the example of the problem of speeding in a residential neighborhood, knowing what residents think of the problem is not enough; it is also important to know what

(Continued)

these stakeholders who have a vested interest in the solution think of the possible responses. Convening groups of residents, or organizations representing their interests, would be a valuable tool in planning which traffic-calming devices to implement. Traffic engineers might recommend speed humps or tables, but they also pose a potential burden on the residents. Establishing whether it is a burden residents are willing to accept in exchange for slower moving traffic in their neighborhood is important to the long-term success of the project, and the only way to determine that is to talk with the stakeholders before the work in rectifying the problem begins.

The Importance of Knowing the Difference

At times, participants in police-led public safety efforts can be both partners and stakeholders simultaneously, and sometimes the dividing line may be subtle. The difference between a partner and a stakeholder is more than semantics and must be understood. Stakeholders who are treated as partners may find themselves at regular project meetings wondering why the demand is being placed on their time when they have nothing to offer on the details of implementation. Partners misidentified as stakeholders might be missing from those meetings, leading to significant delays in implementation simply because they are not there with their needed expertise at the time a decision is made. They may not understand why the response is necessary or say why the issue is important and initially lack commitment.

When partners' and stakeholders' roles and responsibilities in a project are clearly defined and understood, you can be sure that each will be integrated into the project's activities and decisions in ways that are appropriate to their levels of investment, risk, and reward.

Deborah Spence
Senior Social Science Analyst
The COPS Office

Source: The e-newsletter of the COPS Office, Volume 1, Issue 8, August 2008.

Today, most large- and medium-sized police departments have a crime prevention unit or component within its community policing operations. Hickman and Reaves (2006) report that 74 percent of all police departments have crime prevention programming. Crime prevention officers work closely with crime analysis personnel to identify crime and disorder problems. Generally, these officers attempt to identify hot spots or areas with large concentrations of crime. They then apply the SARA model of problem solving to intervene in the problem. In addition to enforcement actions, crime prevention specialists work with people to reduce conditions that can lead to a reduction in crime. To a large extent, crime prevention is about community involvement.

Theoretical Foundation for Crime Prevention

Crime prevention has a theoretical foundation. Essentially, there are three theories that can help to explain the workings of crime prevention programming. They are: (1) social disorganization theory, (2) rational choice theory, and (3) routine activities theory. The first helps explain how crime becomes concentrated in certain areas, while the latter focus on criminals' calculus when committing a crime.

Social Disorganization Theory

Shaw and McKay (1942), in a landmark study, examined delinquency in Chicago and developed the basis for **social disorganization theory**. They found that delinquency and crime rates were higher in inner-city areas that were characterized as transitional. That is, in those areas that had the highest levels of population turnover, crime generally was highest. Crime persisted in these areas over time, because the same areas tended to have a high population turnover. Essentially, impoverished groups would move into the area and, over time, they were able to improve their socioeconomic status and move to other more affluent areas, usually middle-class neighborhoods. However, they would be replaced by new, lower socio economically bound individuals.

Neighborhood structure contributed to the high crime rates. The areas had high levels of disorder (broken windows), and because there was a constant turnover of neighborhood occupants, social networking or networks did not evolve. Thus, there was little guardianship or sense of community to combat crime and disorder. Shaw and McKay's findings are true today. In most, if not all, communities, the highest crime rates are in areas that have large proportions of rental property and where residents move in and out on a fairly frequent basis. Social disorganization is a significant factor in crime rates.

Bursik and Grasmick (2002) expanded on Shaw and McKay's social disorganization theory by examining the types of social control that may exist in a community or neighborhood. They identified three levels of social control: (1) private, (2) parochial, and (3) public. **Private social control** mechanisms refer to the family and social networks that develop within neighborhoods. Private social control is the primary and most effective form of social control in a neighborhood. When private social control is weak or absent, which is the case in many crime-ridden neighborhoods, it results in crime, or the need for other forms of social control. **Parochial social control** consists of churches and schools. One-half century ago, there were neighborhood schools and churches that substantially influenced the community. Today, these institutions have virtually vanished in many neighborhoods. They do not have the positive impact on people and neighborhoods that they once did. Finally, **public social control** mechanisms include the police and other governmental agencies. Public social control mechanisms are the last line of defense in a community. Unfortunately, the police cannot control crime, delinquency, and deviant behavior without the assistance of the community. If the police are to be effective, they must work with community members to strengthen or create private social controls in high-crime areas.

Rational Choice Theory

Cornish and Clarke (1986) assert that criminal behavior is not random but is the result of choices that criminals make. **Rational choice theory** claims that there is a calculus, or decision-making process, or people perform when deciding to commit crime. To the outside observer, the decision may not appear to be rational, but it makes perfect sense to the criminal. Criminals make decisions to commit crime to fulfill some need or purpose. For examples, they may commit crime to obtain food or pay rent for their family or to obtain drugs, purchase a car or accessories for their car to enhance their reputation within the community, party, pay bills, or buy jewelry (Miethe, McCorkle & Listwan, 2006). When a criminal has a need, he or she is motivated to commit a crime. The criminal searches for a possible target. A crime is committed when the criminal believes or decides the reward from the crime outweighs the risk when committing the crime.

Routine Activities Theory

We discuss routine activities theory, which builds on rational choice theory because it is an aspect of certain forms of problem solving, and can dovetail with community policing. Basically, **routine activities theory** posits that a crime consists of three elements: (1) a motivated criminal, (2) a target or object of a crime, and (3) the absence of guardianship (Felson, 2009). A motivated criminal is one who is looking to commit a crime in order to obtain money to fulfill some need. If the need is acute, the criminal is willing to take more chances and to commit riskier crimes. There are also opportunistic criminals who observe a relatively safe and easy criminal opportunity that will yield a return. The target is something of value, and it must be something that the criminal can readily convert into cash, or barter for drugs, or whatever he or she desires. Finally, the absence of guardianship means that the criminal perceives that it is safe and easy to commit the crime—no one is protecting the target.

Crime prevention methods can do little to influence the highly motivated criminal, but they can lead to better guardianship. Crime prevention attempts to make crime a more formidable task. Crime prevention attempts to encourage people to better protect themselves, their families, and their property. It also encourages people to watch out for their neighbors and neighborhood. Collective involvement in crime prevention activities can substantially increase individuals' protection from victimization.

Types of Crime Prevention Strategies

Lab (2007) and Linden (2007) as well as others have developed crime prevention models or typologies that describe approaches to crime prevention and approaches by which to achieve reductions in crime. Lindon's model is displayed in Figure 9.1. It includes a comprehensive listing of strategies that focus on crime at all levels. He has identified general types of crime prevention: (1) social development programs, (2) situational prevention, (3) community crime prevention, (4) legislative/administrative programs, and (5) police programs.

Figure 9.1
Crime Prevention Strategies

Strategy	Activities
Social development programs	Programs to improve potential criminals' life skills
Situational prevention	Efforts to increase target hardening and surveillance to deter crime
Community crime prevention programs	Programs to enhance participation in crime prevention
Legislative/administrative programs	Laws enacted to reduce crime and opportunities
Police programs	Traditional police methods aimed at reducing opportunities or arresting criminals

Social Development Programs

Social development programs attempt to reduce the number of motivated offenders in society. They focus on the conditions that contribute to crime. There are areas or neighborhoods that have higher concentrations of crime and have greater numbers of criminals. This clustering of crime and criminals often is the result of neighborhood and social conditions. For example, Zatz and Portillos (2004) studied crime and gang activities in a neighborhood or barrio in Phoenix. They found that gang activities and crime had been substantially higher in the neighborhood for generations. The response had been traditional policing in which the police patrolled the area and made arrests. However, Zatz and Portillos pointed out that nothing would change in the neighborhood as long as nothing was done to improve the social environment. Government had to improve the socio economic conditions, or there would continue to be crime problems for generations to come.

Normally, the police can do little about such disorganized neighborhoods, but the police working with other private and government agencies can perhaps have some impact. Community policing dictates that the police build community partnerships in neighborhoods. Such partnerships not only assist the police with law enforcement, but if people become involved they can build a community. It can build a community's political power where governmental officials would provide more resources to the area. In other words, elected leaders listen more to those people who are organized, bring political pressure on leaders, vote, and express a voice in governmental affairs. Community building would necessitate that police, working with other agencies, meet and organize people. It would result in people identifying problems and priorities in the neighborhood that the police could address.

To be successful, the police must develop alliances and partnerships with other agencies to address a host or wide spectrum of problems that cause crime and disorder. In the past, the police have implemented partnerships with criminal justice agencies to attack crime problems (Parent & Snyder, 1999; Worrall & Gaines, 2006; Jordan, 1998). However, the police can also work with other agencies such as departments of children's services, recreation departments, public health agencies, economic development agencies, code enforcement departments, school districts, city attorney's offices, and private agencies such as churches and civic organizations. The police, when working with these organizations, can provide a variety of services to a community or neighborhood. Code enforcement personnel can assist in cleaning up neighborhoods; public health personnel can focus on sexually transmitted diseases that usually occur at higher rates in poor, high-crime neighborhoods; the recreation department can provide positive sports and recreational opportunities to juveniles; economic development agencies can provide residents with job training and assistance in obtaining housing; the school district can work with the police implementing after-school tutoring programs; the city attorney's office can assist with gang injunctions, the condemnation of public nuisances, and other legal matters that can improve a neighborhood; and church groups and community organizations can often provide a number of programs to enhance the quality of life in neighborhoods. Communities can be improved when there is a concerted effect to reduce numerous inter-tangled problems.

An example of a social development program where the police work with other agencies can be found in San Diego's Truancy Control Project (U.S. Department of Justice, 2000). The police surveyed truant juveniles and found that 73 percent committed crimes and 87 percent were victimized while not at school. Officers worked with school officials and identified chronically truant students. Officers then met with the truant juveniles' families to determine the causes of the problem. Officers counseled families, explained truancy laws and used court intervention, and dealt with criminal violations like family members using drugs or abusing children. The program resulted in a decrease in daytime crimes.

In summary, social development programming is the prevention of crime through social reform. Governments often are reluctant to expend resources in high-crime, poor neighborhoods. The key to social development is organizing and bringing political pressure on officials. It is important to note that when the right partnerships exist and there is a multi-agency approach to improving social conditions and reducing crime, successes can be achieved.

Situational Crime Prevention

Situational crime prevention is defined as opportunity-reducing tactics that, "(1) are directed at highly specific forms of crime, (2) involve management, design or manipulation of the immediate environment in as systematic and permanent way possible, (3) make crime more difficult and risky, or less rewarding and excusable as judged by a wide range of offenders" (Clarke, 1999:4). Linden (2007) notes that situational crime prevention attempts to make potential targets less attractive. It targets opportunities as opposed to the desire to commit a crime. Essentially, there are two primary modes of situational crime prevention: (1) **crime prevention through environmental design** (CPTED) and (2) criminal behavioral change. CPTED is discussed in more detail below. **Criminal behavioral change** refers to making changes that discourage criminal behavior. Such changes fall within social development types of crime prevention as discussed above.

Crime Prevention through Environmental Design (CPTED)

Newman (1972) pioneered defensible space. Newman advocated that the potential for criminal victimization should be a consideration when planning buildings and social space. Architectural design of structures could reduce crime. Essentially, he noted that buildings and public areas could be constructed in such a fashion as to deter criminals. For example, he was critical of large buildings where residents or occupants did not know one and other. Essentially, the design of the building contributed to crime. Jeffery (1971), on the other hand, examined the problem in terms of crime prevention through environmental design. Whereas Newman focused primarily on buildings, Jeffery noted that any private or public area could be designed to reduce opportunities for crime. When social structures and communities are designed based on cost or aesthetics, they too often are conducive to criminal behavior. Environmental engineering should focus on the potential for crime. There are a number of CPTED tactics that can be used to prevent crime. These tactics or measures attempt to harden targets, making them more difficult to victimize.

Access Control

Access control essentially attempts to ensure that only those individuals who have a legitimate interest to enter an area are allowed access. It reduces the opportunities for crime by keeping potential criminals out of an area, and it makes it more difficult for motivated criminals to enter an area. Access control often uses hardware such as gates, locks, bars on windows and doors, fences, and any other devices that make it difficult for a criminal to enter and exit an area or premise. For example, today there are many gated communities that control who is allowed into the community. This increases safety by keeping criminals out of the area, thereby eliminating their opportunity to commit crime in the protected area. Another example is the Transportation Security Administration, which screens passengers at airports. These screenings reduce the possibility of a terrorist attack and the transportation of illegal drugs. The screening process makes access more difficult for criminals.

The police role in access control focuses on advice and advocacy. The police should provide advice to individuals involved in the planning of buildings, homes, subdivisions, and other construction projects. They can provide information on how such projects can be constructed to deter crime (environmental design). Their advocacy role revolves around placing pressure on the legislative branch to incorporate physical control and access control in zoning and construction ordinances and laws. For example, in addition to advocating the mandated use of proper locks and windows, the police should attempt to ensure that new residential streets and neighborhoods are constructed in such a fashion that the possibilities of crime are reduced.

Target Hardening

Target hardening is where measures are taken to make it more difficult to commit a crime. For example, the police commonly have crime prevention programs that advocate the use of deadbolt locks and more secure windows and patio doors. There is evidence that this type of target hardening works. Bennett and Wright (1984) found that burglars considered the quality of locks and windows when they selected a target. For example, smaller windows were easier to break, and stronger locks provided an extra deterrent.

Along these same lines, Buck and Hakim (1993) found that security alarms tended to deter burglaries. Repetto (1974) found that burglars often checked for alarms before attempting a break-in. However, even though some security devices deter criminals, there is some question as to how successful the police can be in getting homeowners to purchase and install these devices. Even if the police are successful in educating the public, the overall effectiveness of the program may falter if people subsequently do not implement protective measures.

Another form of target hardening the police use is a property identification program. Basically, the police work with individuals or groups to encourage them to permanently mark their property for identification in the event that it is stolen. People are encouraged to engrave their social security numbers or names on their valuables. It is reasoned that engraving social security numbers on property will make it more difficult to re-sell and easier to trace if it is stolen. Window decals or other insignia should also serve as a deterrent to would-be thieves. Laycock (1985) found that property identification did have a short-term effect on burglaries when large numbers of people became involved in the program. Rosenbaum (1988) found that property identification leads to higher rates of apprehension of burglars and property recovery.

The police can work with businesses to incorporate target hardening as a method of reducing crime. Convenient stores and gasoline service stations are more frequently targeted for robbery. Managers should be encouraged to have safes and only allow a small amount of money to be in the cash register. This tends to reduce robberies since the potential reward is reduced. These same businesses should employ more than one clerk late at night, which would reduce the likelihood of robbery. Business owners should be encouraged to have clerks check identification when taking credit cards. This reduces the use of stolen credit cards and identity theft. Hannah, Bichler, and Welter (2007) found that damage to hotel rooms and fraud was reduced when hotel clerks checked identification for registrants who previously booked using a credit card. People were using stolen credit cards to book rooms via internet reservations. Identification checks thwarted such activities. The police can encourage businesses to make it more difficult to commit crime.

Surveillance

Surveillance according to Lab (2007) is any action that increases the probability that offenders will be observed. Using Felson's routine activities theory, surveillance is a way to provide enhanced guardianship. There are several methods of enhancing surveillance. One method is "natural" surveillance. Natural surveillance refers to efforts to entice people to be more observant in their physical environments. Natural surveillance can consist of physical changes or it can consist of programs that encourage people to observe their neighborhoods more closely. The police should work with individuals and neighborhood groups and encourage them to take notice of suspicious people and activities in their neighborhoods. This includes forming neighborhood groups whereby people learn about their neighbors and begin to help protect each other's property. Many neighborhoods actually are not neighborhoods in the traditional sense. People do not know each other and therefore do not attempt to watch over their neighbors. Community meetings can develop a sense of neighborhood and encourage collective protective measures.

People should be encouraged to examine the physical environment of their homes and businesses. Overgrown shrubbery provides burglars with ample places to hide before committing burglaries. Backyards that are unfenced allow burglars easy access to unobserved backyards, windows, and doors. The police, as a part of a comprehensive crime prevention program, should perform, or assist people in performing, assessments of their property to reduce crime by modifying the physical environment.

There are a variety of physical measures that can be taken to increase surveillance. Lighting is an important measure. In many areas, streetlights are inadequate or damaged, resulting in unlighted areas that are inviting to potential criminals. People and the police should report broken streetlights and demand that they be repaired. Community members can leave porch and other lights on at night to increase surveillance. Lighting can be a strong deterrent. Painter and Farrington (1997) conducted an experiment where lighting was increased in an area. The additional lighting resulted in a 41 percent decrease in crime incidents in the area. Increased lighting can also result in a decrease in the fear of crime and an enhanced satisfaction with the neighborhood. Thus, improved lighting can garner a number of positive benefits.

Closed circuit television (CCTV) is being used more extensively to control crime and promote security. CCTV on a large-scale basis began in England (see Brown, 1995). The British government has funded several hundred CCTV projects, and now many urban areas are under surveillance via CCTV. Communities within the United States are implementing larger numbers of CCTV, especially in the wake of the 9/11 attacks in New York City. Research indicates that CCTV impedes crime. Brown (1995) and Ditton and Short (1999) found that when CCTV was installed, there was a reduction in crime. More recently, Welsh and Farrington (2002) reviewed evaluations of CCTV. The CCTV systems were deployed in center city, public housing, parking garages, or public transportation centers. They found the results to be mixed with some of the studies showing a decrease in crime, while other areas witnessed no changes.

CCTV can be enhanced with loudspeaker systems. For example, the Redlands, California, Police Department has CCTV for schools and a major park in the city. When they observe intruders or problems, they warn violators to leave or to stop their inappropriate conduct or they will be arrested. This usually results in compliance. CCTV can be used for schools, street fairs, sporting events, and other public gatherings that occur on a fairly regular basis.

The New York Police Department initiated the Lower Manhattan Security Initiative as a result of the 9/11 attacks. The Lower Manhattan Security Initiative is similar to "London's Ring of Steel" whereby the city installed CCTV throughout vulnerable portions of the city. When the project has been completed, there will be approximately 3,000 cameras installed. Additionally, the police supplement their CCTV with privately owned camera systems that currently operate in banks and other businesses.

CCTV not only deters crime but it also assists police in observing criminal behavior, which allows officers to respond more quickly, and it increases the likelihood that a criminal apprehension will be made. When criminal behavior is observed, police officers can immediately be dispatched to the scene with a description of the criminal event and perpetrators. This could lead to more arrests and perhaps a reduction in crime. As an example, the London police were able to quickly identify suspects in the London subway bombings through CCTV information.

Community Crime Prevention Programs

Community crime prevention programs are geared specifically to get people more involved in crime prevention. Most efforts in community crime prevention have centered on: (1) neighborhood watches, (2) community anti-drug programs, and (3) public media campaigns.

Neighborhood Watches

Neighborhood watches, block watches, or private patrols are probably the primary methods used by the police for community crime prevention programming. These programs are initiated by the police and, once they begin, people develop more cohesive relations and actively participate in crime prevention. Garofalo and McLeod (1989) identify two primary expectations for neighborhood watches:

> First, it is meant to reduce crime, both directly, through the "observe and report" function, and indirectly, by being a vehicle for the encouragement of other crime prevention practices. Second, there is a more general hope that NW [neighborhood watches] will kindle a sense of community among residents by giving them a common purpose, and by getting them to talk to each other and watch out for each other (1989:334).

Although surveillance is the primary motive for neighborhood watch programs, they are also involved in numerous other crime prevention activities: operation identification, streetlight improvement, block parenting, household security surveys, and the deployment of other security measures (Lab, 2007). Thus, when a neighborhood group begins a program, it actually has several purposes (Garofalo & McLeod, 1989). In other words, a block watch or citizen patrol can be used as the impetus for a number of other crime prevention measures.

The extent to which neighborhood watches are used in this country is unknown. O'Keefe et al. (1996), in a national survey, found that 31 percent of respondents reported belonging to a neighborhood crime prevention organization. MacGillis (1983), using the data from an ABC News poll, estimated that approximately 20,000 communities and five million people were involved in such programs. Generally, each program has approximately 10 to 15 households involved, and new programs are constantly being developed. However, old programs are waning, which makes it difficult to estimate the actual number of programs at any given time.

Neighborhood watches, like other volunteer organizations, are difficult to develop and maintain. They tend to be organized in middle- and upper-middle-class, well-established neighborhoods. Participants generally have lived in the area for several years. Unfortunately, they are less prevalent in high-crime, lower socioeconomic neighborhoods, because these areas often do not have a traditional sense of community. Watches tend to begin as the result of a sensational criminal event in a neighborhood and unravel or become disorganized over time. Participants tend to lose interest. This is because they tend to be somewhat unorganized from the beginning. Meetings are infrequent, and information dissemination among members is sporadic (Garofalo & McLeod, 1989), and they often lack leadership. For these programs to be effective, the police must meet with participants periodically to motivate them, encourage them, and attempt to keep the groups focused. When these programs fail, it is often due to a lack of community policing.

The effectiveness of neighborhood watch programs and citizen patrols is mixed, at best. In most cases, the programs provide a high profile for a brief period of time. They also provide an outlet for police-community relations, and are effective to the extent that they do develop some level of neighborhood cohesiveness that lasts for periods of time. These programs also provide police with contact points for future community intervention. In terms of long-term effectiveness, most of these programs fail to remain active unless some external threat to the neighborhood is present. Even then, it is difficult to maintain interest among people for long periods of time.

Community Anti-Drug Campaigns

A variation of neighborhood watch is the **community anti-drug campaign**. Here, people band together to fight drugs in their neighborhood and focus exclusively on drug trafficking and the crime associated with the drug trade. Community anti-drug campaigns employ a variety of measures: anti-drug rallies, reporting and surveillance programs, citizen patrols, code enforcement where drugs are sold, group meetings, drug trafficking hotlines, and drug house abatement (Rosenbaum, Lurigio & Davis, 1998). These programs attempt to band people together in an effort to fight neighborhood drug problems. To some extent, these programs can be measured by the degree to which social cohesion is enhanced in the program area.

Lurigio and Davis (1992) evaluated community anti-drug campaigns in Miami, Seattle, Philadelphia, and Baltimore, and found that they significantly increased social cohesion or a sense of community in the neighborhoods. Roehl and his colleagues (1995) evaluated several of these programs and found them to be loosely organized with low community participation. It is difficult to get residents involved, especially in areas with large amounts of drug trafficking and crime. Fear and ambivalence tend to play important roles in these programs. Also, there are a number of residents in these areas who may be profiting from drug trafficking and therefore are not interested in seeing improvements in the neighborhood.

These programs can have a number of benefits, especially when aligned with the police. They can result in enhanced police patrols and enforcement, better relations with the police, and an increase in arrests in the neighborhood. The police can provide members of these programs with information and ideas on how they can assist in resolving the drug problem in their neighborhood. Participants are more willing to provide officers with drug trafficking and crime intelligence. When creating these programs, the police should maintain a liaison to coordinate activities and to help maintain them over time.

A relatively new community crime prevention campaign revolves around terrorist threats. A number of police departments have been asking people to report suspicious persons and activities that may be related to possible terrorist threats. For example, people are being asked to report suspicious purchases of explosives or materials that can be used to make explosives. As an example, on May 9, 2007, the FBI arrested six subjects who had planned to attack and kill soldiers at Fort Dix in New Jersey. One of the subjects had videotaped the suspects training for the attack, and attempted to have the video converted to DVD at a local photo store. The clerk watched the video and called the FBI, which investigated, and ultimately made arrests.

Public Media Campaigns

Police departments began to use public education programs or public relations techniques in the 1960s and 1970s to overcome negative police-community relations. These efforts naturally evolved into crime prevention where the police used the media and other methods of communications to inform the public about the crime problem, how best to assist the police in their fight against crime, and measures that community members could take to neutralize certain crimes and public problems. The police also use the media to control their public image. That is, there is a symbiotic relationship between the police and the media. The media need the police for easy access to crime news, and the police need the media to help manage people's views of the police and the job they are doing

(Kasinsky, 1994).To this end, Bowers and Johnson (2005) note that the media can be used to increase actual and perceived risk to potential offenders, encourage crime prevention or safety practices, and reassure the public.

Media reporting of crime information is the most common type of public education. Crime, especially sensational or unusual crime, is of significant interest to reporters. Surette (1998) notes that about 25 percent of television programming is crime related, and Chermak (1994) found that about half of all crime reporting deals with violence. More importantly, however, is the fact that the media tends to distort such coverage. Surette (1998) found that journalistic accounts of crime were distorted, emphasizing pathological individuals who commit bizarre acts. Such coverage tends to bias the public and promote fear of victimization that is diametrically opposed to police purposes. The public comes to develop a distorted view of crime. People tend to believe that there are many more rapes, murders, assaults, and violent crimes than actually occur (Kappeler & Potter, 2005). Liska and Baccaglini (1990) report that local sensational crime stories tend to increase the level of fear among people. News coverage can create an impression of higher crime rates by reporting on criminal acts in other communities without clearly specifying where the crime took place— creating the appearance of a crime wave.

The best-known crime-prevention media campaign has been "Taking a Bite out of Crime" which was developed by the Advertising Council. In 1991, more than $160 million worth of airtime had been donated to the program with 75 percent of television stations having aired segments (O'Keefe et al., 1996). O'Keefe and his colleagues found that 80 percent of the respondents in their national study had reported viewing "Take a Bite out of Crime" segments. The program had mixed effects in that respondents reported feeling more competent about crime prevention, but on the other hand, became more concerned about crime.

The "Crime Stoppers" program, another media crime prevention technique, consists of a police hotline where people report crime-related information based on wanted persons information supplied by the police. Crime Stoppers provides rewards up to $1,000, depending on the nature of the crime. There are an estimated 1,200 communities using the Crime Stoppers program (CrimeStoppers International, 2006). Basically, the program attempts to increase the flow of criminal intelligence information to the police through rewards and depicting or acting out specific criminal events on television.

Crime Stoppers International reports that programming has resulted in more than one million cases being solved with 625,000 arrests, the recovery of more than $1.6 billion in property, and about $6 billion in narcotics being seized by law enforcement (Crime Stoppers International, 2006). Rosenbaum et al. (1989)

found that most of the tips received by the police came from other criminals attempting to eliminate a competitor or even an old score or "fringe players" who hung around or associated with the criminals whom they reported. A problem with crime stoppers is that it can overburden law enforcement with worthless calls and tips (Kelley, 1997). CrimeStoppers remains a high-profile program that creates a high level of crime prevention awareness in the community.

There are a variety of media programs available to police departments. For example, there have been specialty campaigns focusing on such topics as: fraud against seniors, bullying prevention, identity theft, and internet safety. Selection of a particular program should be based on need and how the program fits other crime prevention efforts. Police executives too frequently attempt to use a shotgun approach where everything available is implemented. Such an approach is unproductive and sometimes can result in destructive or negative effects such as fear of crime and victimization.

The media can be useful in crime prevention. It should be a part of a department's overall crime prevention approach. Media campaigns should be used in conjunction with other programs.

Legislative/Administrative Programs

Legislative and administrative programs are efforts to make changes in administrative policies or statutes that enhance crime prevention. Over the years, there have been numerous efforts to change policies and statutes. For example, most states have changed the presumptive alcohol content for driving while under the influence from .10 percent to .08 percent. The rationale was that this ultimately would reduce the number of impaired drivers on the road and lead to a reduction in traffic crashes. States have enacted statutes requiring arrest for domestic violence. These statutes were intended to reduce domestic-related assaults and homicides. Gang enhancement statutes add additional prison time to gang members convicted of crimes. These statutes were intended to increase the level of protection afforded society from violent gang members. They also were intended to deter gang members from committing crimes and to deter juveniles from joining gangs. Some states, like California, have enacted statutes that allow for the impounding of vehicles being driven by persons without driver's licenses, or with improper vehicle registration. This often forces the vehicles' owners to adhere to vehicle registration and licensing statutes. Gun registration and purchasing waiting periods are seen as a way to reduce crime.

Legislative and administrative changes can provide new tools to law enforcement to fight old problems. Today, many departments use building and nuisance code enforcement and public health regulations to counter prostitution and drug problems. Law enforcement must examine existing statutes and administrative regulations to determine if they can be used to counter different problems. In some cases, law enforcement should lobby for changes in the law that will result in better control over crime and disorder problems.

Police Programs

Throughout this book, we discuss the various programs and strategies for implementing community policing. If police departments are to meet today's challenges, they must be extensively involved in community policing. It should be remembered that even though departments have embraced community policing, these departments remain engaged in numerous traditional police activities, and these activities cannot be neglected. The police must still respond to calls for service, conduct investigations, and arrest perpetrators of crimes. Community policing, in reality, coexists with traditional police tactics and they work hand-in-hand.

Traditional police tactics include rapid response to crimes, routine patrol, criminal investigations, making arrests, and inspecting licensed premises such as bars, adult entertainment, and other areas that are gathering places for people that can erupt in disorder or crime. Indeed, community policing often uses these traditional measures. For example, if there is a hot spot of drug activity, the police department may use saturation patrols and community anti-drug campaigns to counter the problem. There are numerous cases where traditional police measures can be coupled with crime prevention and other community policing strategies to have an effect on a community problem.

SPOTLIGHT ON COMMUNITY POLICING PRACTICE

From Community Policing to Community Governance

Police agencies throughout the country have worked toward adopting the principles and practices associated with community policing. Instead of reacting to crime only after it occurs, community policing calls on the police to implement organizational changes that support the proactive prevention of crime and social disorder through partnerships and systematic problem solving. These principles and practices can be used to address a host of issues confronted by any unit of local government, be it a state, county, city, or tribe. This translation of the community policing philosophy to broader local governance has been termed "community governance."

(Continued)

Although there is no commonly agreed-on definition, in general, community governance is a philosophy focused on improving the quality of life of citizens and their satisfaction with local government services through government-wide organizational changes designed to support proactive collaborative problem solving and interagency and community partnerships. This philosophy, based in large part on community policing, can guide units of local government in their quest to improve the overall quality of life for their citizens. Closely paralleling community policing, the basic concept can be broken down into three interrelated parts: partnerships, problem solving, and organizational transformation.

Partnerships

Like community policing, a central component of community governance is the development of strong partnerships to foster trust and collaborative problem solving. These partnerships may range from informal relationships to true two-way partnerships with regular meetings, shared resources, and clearly defined goals. Community governance encourages strong partnerships and coordination among all government entities and between these entities and the broader public at large to address issues of shared responsibility and mutual concern. Each segment of local government has different resources, expertise, and perspectives that it can bring to respond to jurisdiction-wide issues. It is a matter of strategically coordinating these efforts, making them seamlessly experienced by the public, and developing more effective responses that add greater value to the public service being provided.

Community governance also encourages reaching out in systematic and strategic ways to develop working relationships with the business community and nonprofit and community groups such as victim services, neighborhood associations, faith-based organizations, service clubs, support groups, and advocacy groups. Governments can take a strategic approach to these partnerships by identifying the universe of potential partnerships that may occur and examining the resources and input that these groups can bring to specific public service issues.

Problem Solving

Problem solving has a recent and rich tradition in policing, from which lessons can be translated to broader government applications. The problem-solving model (often operationalized in the form of four distinct phases: Scanning, Analysis, Response, and Assessment, or SARA) offers a framework for approaching crime problems that also can be applied to address a wide range of public service issues that confront many jurisdictions such as traffic flow, neighborhood improvement, school and educational issues, park and facilities use and maintenance, pedestrian safety, uncollected trash, nuisance pay phones, car alarms, or overgrown weeds.

In the past, police departments handled incidents or calls for service as separate and essentially unique occurrences and only infrequently looked beyond individual crimes or criminals to examine the underlying conditions that gave rise to these problems. More recently, in addition to tracking down *individual* burglars or rapists, agencies have begun to address the *overarching* problems of burglary and rape. It is likely that this conception of problems parallels the experiences of other government agencies. A public works department, for example, may treat incidents of graffiti, trash, broken street lights, and abandoned automobiles as individual occurrences. In addition to responding to these individual incidents, community governance encourages the systematic identification and analysis of recurring problems in the hopes of developing coordinated, long-term solutions in cooperation with other stakeholders (both within and outside of the local government bodies). Moreover, the responses can be implemented jointly or in coordination with these stakeholders to bring all appropriate resources to bear on the problem and maximize the likelihood that improvements will be sustained.

Organizational Change

Community governance promotes specific organizational changes to support partnerships and problem-solving efforts. These changes can comprise including principles into strategic planning and broadening outcome measures that are used to evaluate government services. It also involves hiring people who are oriented toward public service, problem solving, and critical thinking, thereby increasing their decision-making authority at lower levels, holding them accountable for their performance, and evaluating them based on these principles. One of the most common manifestations of community governance involves implementing multidisciplinary teams of government employees who are responsible for the community welfare in specific neighborhoods. These groups can be organized around SARA-like problem-solving processes to develop a more complete understanding of what is taking place in that neighborhood that feeds into comprehensive and innovative solutions to their prioritized problems. Community governance also encourages altering the culture so that government employees think of themselves first as a representative of a larger proactive jurisdictional government and second as a member of their specific agency. Finally, integrated technology and information systems, including 311 call systems, facilitate the move toward a more unified and proactive government. Integrated technology can improve the flow of information within a city government and enhance the analytical capacity of governments to improve their understanding of problems.

Conclusion

The police have recognized that including other government entities such as parks and recreation, legislative bodies, sanitation, public works, public safety (fire, EMS), utilities, community services, and community development can greatly enhance their efforts to improve public safety. If governments as a whole are encouraged to adopt similar models, community policing/community governance can provide the basis for more effective and efficient delivery of services to address the host of difficult issues confronted by jurisdictions.

Matthew Scheider, Ph.D.
Assistant Director
The COPS Office

Source: The e-newsletter of the COPS Office, Volume 1, Issue 5, May 2008.

Complex problems cannot be solved using simple responses. Historically, police departments, when faced with a problem, would increase patrols in the problem area or increase investigative efforts. Today, police departments must be more innovative. They must recognize that in many cases, multiple, complementary programs are required to resolve crime and disorder problems. This often entails the coordination of traditional and community policing measures.

Summary

Crime prevention is an important component in a comprehensive community policing approach. There are a number of crime prevention programs that not only reduce crime, but also foster better relationships with the community. Crime prevention is rooted in disorganization theory, rational choice theory, and routine activities theory. These theories help to explain how crime prevention can be successful. According to Linden (2007) there are five levels or strategies of crime prevention programming.

The first is social development programs that attempt to negate the factors that influence juveniles and adults to engage in criminal behavior. In the long term, social development programs have the most potential to reduce crime as compared to any other type of crime prevention. If we can keep youths from entering a life of crime and drug abuse, we will have a more drastic impact on crime. Unfortunately, political leaders have not invested in these types of programs. The second crime prevention strategy is situational crime prevention. Situational crime prevention attempts to make crime more difficult through environmental design and enhanced surveillance. It involves making crime more difficult and increasing the risk to potential criminals. In essence, situational crime prevention attempts to deter criminals. The third strategy is community crime prevention programming. The essence of community crime prevention is community involvement. The police have long understood that efforts to combat crime can be successful only when people are actively involved in assisting the police. Examples of these programs include neighborhood or block watches, citizen patrols, the identification of property, and media campaigns. The fourth category of crime prevention strategy is legislative/administrative strategies. Programs within this strategy include efforts to pass statutes and administrative regulations that prevent crime or enhance law enforcement's ability to tackle a particular crime problem. Over the years, there have been a number of legislative changes relating to domestic violence, gangs, driving while under the influence, and municipal code enforcement that have provided law enforcement with new tools to counter a particular crime or disorder problem. Finally, police programs include traditional police responses to crime. Community policing departments must maintain some level of traditional methods of combating crime. However, when these methods are coupled with community policing and crime prevention activities, the police generally experience more success.

The advent of community policing has resulted in numerous changes in law enforcement. One important change has been an increased awareness of how crime prevention can have an impact on a number of traditional police problems. When implementing crime prevention, it is important for the police to "think outside the box." Police officers should use the SARA model of problem identification and strategy selection and consider as many alternatives as possible. Success comes through innovative thinking. Past practices have not always been the best practices. Crime and disorder should be approached from a number of directions.

KEY TERMS IN CHAPTER 9

- access control
- community anti-drug campaigns
- community crime prevention programs
- CPTED
- criminal behavioral change
- legislative/administrative programs
- neighborhood watches
- parochial social control

- private social control
- public social control
- rational choice theory
- routine activities theory
- situational crime prevention
- social development programs
- social disorganization theory
- surveillance
- target hardening

DISCUSSION QUESTIONS

1. Discuss the relationship between traditional policing and the rise of the crime prevention orientation of the police. How do these two forms of crime control differ?
2. Discuss the three theoretical foundations of crime prevention. How adequate are these theories to understanding how and why people commit crime?
3. Discuss as many forms of social control that you can. Which forms of social control seem most effective at controlling people's behavior?
4. Discuss which of the five basic strategies for crime prevention you think is most effective. Why?

5. Discuss how situational crime prevention can be used in your college, university, or community.
6. Discuss the various forms of community crime prevention programs. Can you think of other programs that might be used to reduce crime in your community?
7. Discuss the roles community policing and problem solving play in crime prevention.
8. Discuss how the concept of governance can be used to prevent crime and empower people in communities.

References

Bennett, T., & Wright, R. (1984). *Burglars on Burglary*. Brookfield, VT: Grower.

Bowers, K., & Johnson, S. (2005). Using Publicity for Preventive Purposes. In N. Tilley (Ed.), *Handbook of Crime Prevention and Community Safety*. Portland: Willan Publishing.

Brown, B. (1995). *CCTV in Town Centres: Three Case Studies*. London: Home Office.

Buck, A., & Hakim, S. (1993). Burglar Alarms and the Choice Behavior of Burglars: A Suburban Phenomenon. *Journal of Criminal Justice, 21*, 497–507.

Bursik, R., & Grasmick, H. (2002). *Neighborhoods and Crime: The Dimensions of Effective Community Control*. New York, NY: Lexington Books.

Chermak, S. (1994). Body Count News: How Crime Is Presented in the News Media. *Justice Quarterly, 11*, 561–582.

Clarke, R. (1999). *Situational Crime Prevention: Successful Case Studies*. Guiderland, NY: Harrow and Heston.

Cornish, D., & Clarke, R. (1986). *The Reasoning Criminal: Rational Choice Perspective on Offending*. New York, NY: Springer-Verlag.

CrimeStoppers International (2006). http://www.c-s-i.org/.

Ditton, J., & Short, E. (1999). Yes, It Works, No, It Doesn't: Comparing the Effects of Open-Street CCTV in Two Adjacent Scottish Town Centres. In K. Painter & N. Tilley (Eds.), *Surveillance of Public Space: CCTV, Street Lighting and Crime Prevention*. Monsey, NY: Criminal Justice Press.

Felson, M. (2009). *Crime and Everyday Life* (4th ed.). Thousand Oaks, CA: Pine Forge Press.

Garofalo, J., & McLeod, M. (1989). The Structure and Operation of Neighborhood Watch Programs in the United States. *Crime & Delinquency, 35*, 326–344.

Green, L. (1996). *Policing Places with Drug Problems*. Thousand Oaks, CA: Sage Publications.

Hannah, M., Bichler, G., & Welter, J. (2007). Fraudulent Online Hotel Booking. *FBI Law Enforcement Bulletin, 76*(5), 1–8.

Hickman, M., & Reaves, B. (2006). *Local Police Departments, 2003*. Washington, DC: Bureau of Justice Statistics.

Hughes, G. (1998). *Understanding Crime Prevention*. Philadelphia, PA: Open University Press.

Jeffery, C. (1971). *Crime Prevention through Environmental Design*. Beverly Hills, CA: Sage.

Jordan, J. (1998). Boston's Operation Night Light. *FBI Law Enforcement Bulletin*, *67*(8), 1-6.

Kappeler, V., & Potter, G. (2005). *The Mythology of Crime and Criminal Justice* (4th ed.). Newark, NJ: LexisNexis Matthew Bender/Anderson Publishing.

Kasinsky, R. (1994). Patrolling the Facts: Media, Cops, and Crime. In G. Barak (Ed.), *Media, Process, and the Social Construction of Crime*. New York, NY: Garland Publishing.

Kelley, J. (1997). Police Lines Often Clogged with False, Unreliable Clues. *USA Today*, (Jan. 31), 1-2.

Lab, S. (2007). *Crime Prevention: Approaches, Practices, and Evaluations*. Newark, NJ: Lexis Nexis Matthew Bender/Anderson Publishing.

Laycock, G. (1985). Property Marking: A Deterrent to Domestic Burglary? In *Crime Prevention Planning Unit: Paper 3*. London: Home Office.

Linden, R. (2007). Situational Crime Prevention: Its Role in Comprehensive Prevention Initiatives. *IPC Review*, *1*, 139-160.

Liska, A., & Baccaglini, W. (1990). Feeling Safe by Comparison: Crime in the Newspapers. *Social Problems*, *37*, 360-374.

Lurigio, A., & Davis, R. (1992). Taking the War on Drugs to the Streets: The Perceptual Impact of Four Neighborhood Drug Programs. *Crime & Delinquency*, *38*, 522-538.

MacGillis, D. (1983). *Crime in America*. Radnor, PA: Chilton Book Co.

Miethe, T., McCorkle, R., & Listwan, S. (2006). *Crime Profiles: The Anatomy of Dangerous Persons, Places, and Situations*. Los Angeles, CA: Roxbury.

Newman, O. (1972). *Defensible Space*. New York, NY: Macmillan.

O'Keefe, G., Rosenbaum, D., Lavrakas, P., Reid, K., & Botta, R. (1996). *Taking a Bite out of Crime: The Impact of the National Citizens' Crime Prevention Media Campaign*. Thousand Oaks, CA: Sage Publications.

Painter, K., & Farrington, D. (1997). The Crime Reducing Effects of Improved Street Lighting: The Dudley Project. In R. V. Clarke (Ed.), *Situational Crime Prevention: Successful Case Studies* (2nd ed.). Gulderland, NY: Harrow and Heston.

Parent, D., & Snyder, B. (1999). *Police Community Partnerships*. Washington, DC: National Institute of Justice.

Repetto, T. (1974). *Residential Crime*. Cambridge, MA: Ballinger.

Roehl, J., Wong, H., Huitt, R., & Capowich, G. (1995). *A National Assessment of Community-Based Anti-Drug Initiatives: Final Report*. Pacific Grove, CA: Institute for Social Analysis.

Rosenbaum, D. (1988). Community Crime Prevention: A Review and Synthesis of the Literature. *Justice Quarterly*, *5*, 323-396.

Rosenbaum, D., Lurigio, A., & Davis, R. (1998). *The Prevention of Crime: Social and Situational Strategies*. Belmont, CA: Wadsworth.

Rosenbaum, D., Lurigio, A., & Lavrakas (1989). Enhancing Citizen Participation and Solving Serious Crime: A National Evaluation of CrimeStoppers Programs. *Crime & Delinquency*, *35*, 401-420.

Shaw, C., & McKay, H. (1942). *A Study of Rates of Delinquency in Relation to Differential Characteristics of Local Communities in American Cities*. Chicago, IL: University of Chicago Press.

Surette, R. (1998). *Media, Crime, and Criminal Justice: Images and Realities*. Belmont, CA: Wadsworth.

U.S. Department of Justice (2000). Truancy Control Project: Removing Attendance Barriers Lessens Daytime Crime. In author (Ed.), *Excellence in Problem-Oriented Policing: The 1999 Herman Goldstein Award Winners* (pp. 37–41). Washington, DC: Author.

Welsh, B., & Farrington, D. (2002). *Crime Prevention Effects of Closed Circuit Television: A Systematic Review*. London: Home Office.

Wilson, J., & Kelling, G. (1982). Police and Neighborhood Safety: Broken Windows. In V. Kappeler (Ed.), *The Police & Society: Touch Stone Readings* (3rd ed.). Prospect Heights, IL: Waveland Press.

Worrall, J., & Gaines, L. (2006). The Effect of Police-Probation Partnerships on Juvenile Arrests. *Journal of Criminal Justice*, *34*, 579–589.

Zatz, M., & Portillos, E. (2004). Voices from the Barrio: Chicano/a Gangs, Families, and Communities. In F. Esbensen, S. Tibbetts, & L. Gaines (Eds.), (pp. 113–141). Long Grove, IL: Waveland Press.

The wrong that men do can be traced to those who mistaught them.

—Sophocles

CHAPTER 10   Community Policing and Drugs

LEARNING OBJECTIVES

After reading the chapter, you should be able to:

1. Understand the nature and extent of the drug problem.
2. List the six goals that should guide police decision making when implementing drug strategies.
3. Describe high-level and retail-level law enforcement strategies and the limitations of each.
4. Understand the importance of directing prevention efforts at juveniles.
5. Understand how community policing can use problem solving to effectively deal with the drug issue.
6. Describe how community policing can be effective at information gathering for the purpose of drug enforcement.
7. Describe how community policing drug enforcement efforts are dependent upon the public and the importance of community involvement.
8. Understand the ways that community policing can direct police responses in the war on drugs.

Since at least the 1960s, America has been coping with a drug problem. Although drugs have always been present in some form or another, it was not until the 1960s that they became the focus of attention of large segments of society. This period also witnessed public display of drug use. Drugs remain a problem that concerns many Americans and constantly remains at the forefront of American politics and governmental policymaking. Many see drugs as a stimulant for crime, especially violent crime, while others are concerned with addiction's devastating effects on people. The drug problem has so occupied attention that several American presidents, beginning with President Nixon, have declared war on drugs. Talk of war has helped to mobilize support and stir people's emotions. It should be noted, however, that we have never had a war against drugs. Although stated as such, drug wars actually have been aimed at people, and to this end, the war has had no limits. In many instances, it has been a no-holds-barred, all-out assault on those who are associated with drugs or perceived to be associated with drugs.

The war on drugs is cloaked in imagery. In the classic sense, it is good versus evil. It is claimed that there are good people within society who are being corrupted or harmed by evil drug dealers. The drug war is shrouded in moralism with disgust, disdain, and fear of drugs, their users, and their sellers (Gaines & Kraska, 2003; Christie, 2000). The drugs problem causes society to paint with a broad moral brush. Our condemnations and attacks focus on broad categories of persons, sometimes irrespective of the nature or extent of their involvement in the drug problem (Kappeler, 1998). Subsequently, our fears, concerns, and reactions to drugs result in substantial levels of covert as well as overt racism (Lusane, 1990; Kappeler & Potter, 2005; Kappeler, 1998). The drug problem is used by politicians to further disenfranchise the poor and minority groups. Law, law enforcement practices, and court sentencing have been tailored to target selected drugs and selected groups in society. Drug enforcement practices drive a wedge between the poor and other classes within society. From this perspective, there has been a substantial measure of immorality inherent to the "moral drug war."

> **You can learn more about the history of the war on drugs by going to http://www.drugalcohol-rehab.com/war-on-drugs.htm.**

This **moral drug war** has placed the police in the middle of a quagmire. On the one hand, addiction can have a destructive influence on society. Addiction can disrupt and destroy people's lives. Addiction is associated with crime although the amount of crime as a result of drugs most likely is far less than most predict (McBride & McCoy, 1993). Consequently, drugs are a problem that requires an effective police response. On the other hand, community policing dictates that the police develop programs to help the disadvantaged within society. It dictates that we must work with the disadvantaged to develop solutions to community problems. We must empower minorities and the disadvantaged so they can develop their own solutions to community problems. In this sense, it is counterproductive to declare war on whole classes of people, especially when the police must at some point attempt to develop working relationships with them. For example, if you consider the most crime and drug-ridden neighborhood in the United States, it must be remembered that the overwhelming majority of people residing there are law abiding and are being victimized by a small number of criminals and only some are drug dealers.

Community policing requires that we abandon the all-out law enforcement assault on drugs and adopt solutions that focus on problem solving. Within this framework, the police should identify practices that effectively counter them. Drug dealers and drug-dealing locations should be targeted for problem solving. At the same time, it is ineffective to use tactics that hassle large numbers of people, typically the poor and minorities, who obviously are not involved in drugs. The police, in conjunction with people, must work with other public and private agencies and groups to reduce crime and alleviate the conditions that result in crime and drug abuse. The police must utilize a public health approach whereby the "health" of a community is of primary concern, rather than producing numbers of arrests and citations or focusing on one dominant problem.

SPOTLIGHT ON COMMUNITY POLICING PRACTICE

American Medicine Chest Challenge: Safe Disposal of Prescription Drugs

A one-day seizure of 10 tons of dangerous drugs would be deemed a successful bust by any law enforcement agency; however, November 13, 2010 marked a national raid of an unlikely source—the bathroom medicine cabinet! The American Medicine Chest Challenge (AMCC) is a national public health initiative centered on a one-day event to collect and safely dispose of unused and expired medicine stored in U.S. homes, which according to recent reports is the number one source of drugs among young teens.

According to the DEA, 15 percent of teens abuse prescription drugs regularly, due in part to the easy accessibility of drugs like Xanax and Oxycontin. An amazing 70 percent of abusers admit using drugs that were meant for family and friends. One such teen, Corey Stevens, started stealing unused Oxycontin pills, prescribed for a grandparent. Finding himself addicted, Stevens escalated to stealing medication when in the homes of neighbors and friends. Stevens, currently in drug rehab, appeared at the annual kick-off of the AMCC to warn others about the dangers of unsecured prescription drugs and to encourage families to adopt smart disposal policies for solid and liquid medications.

According to AMCC's mastermind, Angelo Valente, the initiative not only shines a spotlight on home security but raises public awareness and attention on prescription drug abuse. He said, "The goals of AMCC were clear: to get the word out about prescription drug misuse and encourage the five easy steps to secure medications."

These steps include taking an inventory of medications, properly securing medicine chests, taking medicine only as prescribed by your doctor, disposing of unused and expired medicines, and most importantly, talking to family members about the dangers of prescription drug abuse.

(Continued)

Through a website, and TV and radio ads, the AMCC disseminates valuable facts on how medications affect the water table—clarifying which medications are suitable for flushing—and provides tips on how everyday household items such as coffee grounds and cat litter can be used to prevent the improper use of discarded medications. More information about safe home disposal is available on www.smarxtdisposal.net.

This year's nationwide event was built on the success of a 2009 statewide pilot program in New Jersey. That event, run in conjunction with the Sheriffs' Association of New Jersey and Drug Enforcement Administration–New Jersey Division, netted over 9,000 lbs of prescription drugs with a street market value of over 35 million dollars. "With the overwhelming response to the statewide event, replicating this successful model was a vital step in gaining national momentum," said Valente.

A crucial component of the initiative was national and local partnership: Collaboration with PhRMA and the American College of Emergency Physicians, who highlighted the dangers of this national epidemic, complemented local partnerships with law enforcement, community groups, direct social service agencies, and the media to create a multi-tiered approach to publicize collection and drop-off points, provide education on drug treatment options, and disseminate materials and resources for parents and schools.

Participation among law enforcement agencies became pivotal as over 50 police departments across the country entered into agreements to not only act as collection sites but ensure that local, state, and federal disposal guidelines were adhered to.

One such partnership involved the Mt. Vernon Police Department in Iowa, who in coordination with pharmacies, health services, and community groups collected over 20 lbs of dangerous prescription drugs from neighboring homes. Chief Mark Winder from Mt. Vernon PD commented on the collaboration of all stakeholders as vital in the success of the collection. "The collection of prescription drugs needed to be carefully orchestrated to ensure that these drugs have no opportunity to end up in the wrong hands—this was only possible with coordination with local groups working with us to encourage the community to act." Mt. Vernon PD was also able to garner the assistance of a local pharmacy that donated funds to ensure that a large banner was available to hang in town to get the word out about the event. Chief Winder, buoyed by the community support for the event, is eager to participate in AMCC in 2011.

National public health initiatives such as the American Medicine Chest Challenge mark a new era in law enforcement and community collaboration, by proactively addressing a potential threat lurking in U.S. homes. With AMCC 2011 in the planning stages, long-term success will be measured by millions of parents, grandparents, and caregivers looking at their medicine chest through new eyes and in turn saving more teen lives.

Lydia Nylander
Grant Monitoring Specialist
The COPS Office

Source: The e-newsletter of the COPS Office, Volume 4, Issue 2, February 2011.

Nature and Extent of the Drug Problem

The drug problem must be fully understood before effective strategies can be developed to counter the problem. Although everyone is aware of the drug problem and most people have misgivings about it, few have taken the time to try to understand it. That is, how bad is America's drug problem? What toll does it take on society and quality of life? The media, politicians, and, to some extent, the police would have us believe that it is one of the most important issues facing society today. Certainly, however, there are other problems that are just as pressing. Juvenile crime and violence, poverty and joblessness, treatment of the mentally ill, a lack of quality education in many parts of the country, and discrimination are all problems needing attention. In fact, if many of these problems were alleviated, it is very likely that we would realize a significant reduction in the drug problem. Drug abuse is just one problem within a set of interrelated problems that beg for attention.

In terms of the scope of the drug problem, the Office of National Drug Control Policy (2011) reports that in 2009, 28.1 million Americans ages 12 and older had used an illicit drug in the month previous to the survey. Additionally, it was found that 5.3 million people over the age of 12 used a prescription pain reliever for non-medical purpose. In other words, millions of Americans have abused an illicit drug and have used prescription drugs to get high or for non-medical purposes. Data from emergency rooms in 2009 indicate that drugs were mentioned in slightly more than 211,655 emergency room cases (SAMHSA, 2011). Also, data from inmate populations show that approximately 50.9 percent of federal prison inmates were incarcerated for drug offenses (DrugWarFacts.com, 2011). These data indicate that illicit drug use is a significant problem in society.

However, such global figures are of little value to the police in describing or estimating a local drug problem. Although millions of Americans have used drugs, to what extent is their drug usage a problem? Most of the drug use relates to marijuana, and for the most part, marijuana has not been associated with crime or police problems other than its illegal consumption and distribution. Certainly, most drug users have not been debilitated by their drug usage. Alcohol very likely has had a more negative effect on society than any illicit drug (Kappeler & Potter, 2005) and history tells us how prohibition turned out. If we scan our environment, there are few indications of a drug problem except in a few areas where drugs are used openly and extensively by some people, and these areas

> *You can learn more about the extent of the drug problem by going to http://www.ncjrs.gov/htm/chapter2.htm.*

often suffer from a host of social problems that have for decades remained unattended. Even the emergency room admissions are misleading. Although illegal drugs were mentioned in over 211,000 instances, it should be noted that drug use, in most cases, was not the primary cause for these people being admitted to the hospital, but was only mentioned at the time of admission. This is also true for inmates. A history of drug use or using drugs 30 days before the commission of a crime or incarceration is hardly evidence of a causal linkage between drugs and crime. Indeed, McBride and McCoy (2003) argue that drug use and crime are highly correlated, but they are caused by the same socioeconomic factors. Goode (2005) advises that some drugs are more criminogenic. Alcohol, cocaine, and heroin are linked to more criminality as compared to other drugs.

The nature and extent of a particular community's drug problem is best understood from a problem-solving perspective. That is, how do drugs adversely affect a community in terms of quality of life, crime, and disorder? Although drug education and drug prevention are important police objectives, the police should focus their primary attention on specific problems, neighborhoods or areas, and people that constitute visible or identifiable problems. The police must concentrate their resources on these real problems if they are to have an impact on community life.

SPOTLIGHT ON COMMUNITY POLICING PRACTICE

Shutting the Door on Foreclosure and Drug-Related Problem Properties: Two Communities Respond to Neighborhood Disorder

Problem properties create more than just an eyesore. They act as a drain on police resources, create hazardous environments, and lessen the quality of life for neighbors and community residents. Two communities, one large and one small, have implemented innovative community policing responses to break the cycle of repeated calls for service associated with these properties.

Using Community Prosecution in Milwaukee's Third District

Police in the Third District of Milwaukee (Wisconsin) have implemented a number of problem-solving initiatives through their Community Prosecution Unit to tackle the problem of drug-related properties. For those experienced in community policing, the ideas behind community prosecution may sound familiar. Together with law enforcement and the community, prosecutors build long-term, problem-solving partnerships to address public safety issues proactively. Instead of simply arresting offenders and prosecuting cases after a crime has been committed, community police and prosecutors work closely to prevent crime and solve specific neighborhood problems.

The long-standing Community Prosecution Unit comprises law enforcement officers, city and district attorneys, probation and parole officers, a domestic violence advocate, and a nuisance abatement staff assistant. Their mission is to reduce crime, fear, and disorder by using public-private collaborations to target nuisance activities. "The key to the success of this unit," according to Assistant Chief James Harpole, "has been the empowerment of the assigned police officers to discover, develop, plan, coordinate, and execute innovate ideas of their own design."

One such innovative idea came about as two Community Prosecution Unit officers, Misty Torres and James McNichol, met with a local utility company, WE Energies, to shut off an illegal electrical hookup. Aware that the home in question was a frequent nuisance property, the officers realized that targeting illegal electrical hookups may be one tactic to gaining access to other drug- and gang-related properties. After developing a strong partnership with WE Energies and other municipal agencies, the members of the Community Prosecution Unit have been able to increase greatly the number of nuisance properties they have shut down.

Focusing on illegal electrical hookups has allowed the police to stop criminal activity, even in homes where other traditional methods such as attempting a drug buy, setting up a meeting with an uncooperative landlord, or providing a visible police presence have failed. An illegal hookup creates a serious risk to human habitation through the potential overload of the electrical wiring. Because of this danger, police and other municipal agencies are allowed to enforce an immediate evacuation of the property. Law enforcement, therefore, can eliminate both criminal activity and the potential for fires and other hazards.

Fighting Foreclosure Problems in Manhattan, Illinois

The small community of Manhattan, Illinois prepared itself to face a different type of problem property: the foreclosed home. The village of Manhattan is a residential community of about 6,897 people south of Chicago. It has more that doubled in size since 2000. With larger, nearby towns facing serious foreclosure problems, Manhattan's police department and village administrators decided to take preventive action before their problem grew too large to control.

The village created a database, updated weekly, of all properties in the various stages of foreclosure. Using the database as a guide, the Police Department, Code Compliance, Public Works, and Finance are responsible for a four-point approach to tracking and securing foreclosed structures: monitoring and securing the buildings; enforcing city codes; shutting off water service; and placing liens, if necessary, on delinquent accounts. Law enforcement officers regularly monitor the vacant houses, check for signs of vandalism, and conduct outreach to neighbors in adjacent properties through a Neighborhood Watch program.

(Continued)

Village officials and the Manhattan Police Department have considered these efforts a success. After checking all vacant structures, Manhattan Police found that 27 percent of the area's vacant houses were not locked. They secured the houses and, using their monitoring system, identified additional potential problem properties. Since the initiative was put into place, one concerned neighbor alerted the authorities about a distressed homeowner illegally stripping his house and selling all valuable construction material and appliances on craigslist.

Preserving Quality of Life

These two examples represent how police can effectively monitor problem properties with the goal of preserving quality of life for their citizens. In Milwaukee, the Community Prosecution Unit set a goal of shutting down gang and drug activity that was disturbing area residents and contributing to neighborhood disorder and danger. In Manhattan, a village-wide initiative sought to preserve property values and prevent the foreclosure-related crime that had affected nearby cities. While these goals were different, both communities attacked their problem through frequent collaboration with other stakeholders, engaging in problem-solving policing, and building trust with the community.

Zoe Mentel
Policy Analyst
The COPS Office

Source: The e-newsletter of the COPS Office, Volume 2, Issue 7, July 2009.

Police Drug Strategies

The drug problem is expansive, cutting across many segments of the population. As such, it is impossible for the police to eliminate drugs. Therefore, the police should make **harm reduction** the criterion by which to guide drug enforcement planning and to evaluate enforcement programming. Because the police will never eliminate drugs as a law enforcement or social problem, they must expend their energy and resources in such a way that the harm to the community as a result of drugs is minimized. Priority must be given to solving problems that are the most harmful to people and the community. This means the police should target problems as opposed to apprehending offenders without regard to activities and impact. The police should focus on problem solving as opposed to bean counting.

To this end, Moore and Kleiman (2003) have identified six goals that are useful in guiding police decision making when implementing drug elimination strategies. They are:

- Reduce the gang violence associated with drug trafficking, and prevent the emergence of powerful organized criminal groups;

- Control the street crimes committed by drug users;

- Improve the health and economic and social well-being of drug users;

- Restore the quality of life in urban communities by ending street-level drug dealing;

- Help prevent children from experimenting with drugs; and

- Protect the integrity of criminal justice institutions.

The first two goals identified by Moore and Kleiman relate to law enforcement, and the next three establish objectives for community partnerships and community building, while the final goal causes us to realize that drugs have long had a corrupting influence on the police and others within the criminal justice system (Kappeler, Sluder & Alpert, 1998). If corruption is not controlled, then it is virtually impossible for any kind of enforcement to be effective.

Moore and Kleiman's two law enforcement goals connote a hierarchy of drug dealing. At the top of the hierarchy are the so-called drug kingpins who are responsible for smuggling and distributing drugs to street dealers. At the bottom are the street dealers who receive drugs from low-level wholesalers and then sell small quantities of drugs to individual customers or users. If law enforcement could successfully disrupt the flow of drugs at any level of this hierarchy, then the problem could be substantially reduced. However, law enforcement for the past 30 years or so has not been able to accomplish this objective. Thus, it is useful to examine the drug **trafficking hierarchy** relative to how law enforcement may address the problem.

Figure 10.1
Hierarchy of Drug Enforcement

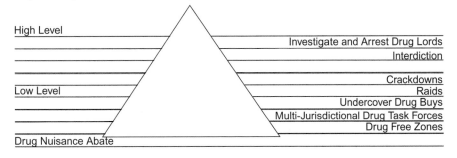

High-Level Enforcement

High-level enforcement is designed to attack the drug problem at the top of the drug trafficking hierarchy. It is designed to arrest those individuals who are involved in smuggling large quantities of drugs into the United States, manufacture large quantities of drugs, or distribute drugs to large, expansive drug networks. The reasoning behind high-level enforcement is that if a drug kingpin is eliminated, the whole network will be rendered useless, and it will cause a large gap in street drug supplies. If enough drug networks can be rendered inoperable, then the supply of drugs to the street will be substantially disrupted.

The responsibility for high-level enforcement has fallen on the shoulders of federal enforcement agencies: the Drug Enforcement Agency; Federal Bureau of Investigation; Bureau of Alcohol, Tobacco, and Firearms; and U.S. Customs and Border Protection Agency. **The Drug Enforcement Agency** is responsible for stopping drugs from coming into the United States. They do this by working with foreign governments in obtaining drug smuggling intelligence and seizing the drugs as they are smuggled into the country. The Federal Bureau of Investigation is responsible for attacking the criminal organizations that are responsible for distributing large quantities of drugs. The FBI targets organized crime and other criminal syndicates that are involved in distributing drugs. The Bureau of Alcohol, Tobacco, and Firearms works closely with state and local police agencies in attempting to target mid-level drug wholesalers and dealers. The **U.S. Customs and Border Protection Agency** has the responsibility of interdicting drugs that are intermingled with exports coming into the United States. The U.S. Customs and Border Protection Agency inspects goods as they are imported into the United States across our borders and through ports of entry.

Federal agents use a variety of tactics to apprehend drug dealers and to seize drugs. Kleiman and Smith (1990:82-83) summarize how federal law officers approach the problem:

> ... long term, high-level undercover operations: developing informants, often by making cases against low-level dealers which can then be bargained away in return for their help against their suppliers ("working up the chain"); searching through police files, financial records, telephone logs, and the like to demonstrate connections; and, most powerful but most expensive, electronic surveillance (wiretaps and less frequently, bugs).

Drug enforcement against high-level smugglers and wholesalers is expensive and time consuming. Indeed, some high-level investigations take years before an arrest is made. Federal agencies with their vast resources are best equipped to handle high-level investigations. Local law enforcement agencies, on the other hand, do not have the resources to devote to long-term investigations. Local law enforcement has the primary responsibility of controlling street drug dealing.

Essentially, high-level drug enforcement has used two primary tactics: interdiction and concentrating enforcement and apprehending leaders of drug cartels or organizations. **Interdiction** is the interception of drugs. The Drug Enforcement Administration is the federal agency responsible for intercepting drugs coming into the United States. The DEA has agents located in a number of countries. They work with local authorities and attempt to destroy or intercept drugs before they leave the originating countries. If they are unsuccessful, they provide intelligence to agencies such as the U.S. Coast Guard or the Customs and Border Protection Agency so that these agencies can intercept the drugs as they come into the United States. On the other hand, apprehending drug cartel leaders entails the identification of cartels and large smuggling rings and attempting to build cases against them so they can be criminally prosecuted in the United States or their home country.

Interdiction is guided by the classic, but very limited and misguided economic theory that has driven drug enforcement policy in America for decades. The theory goes like this: the economics of supply and demand dictate that anything that substantially reduces supply increases price. The price of coffee in the United States jumped dramatically a number of years ago when a drought in Colombia reduced the supply. The same unsound reasoning has been applied to the price of grain and gasoline. If either nature or law enforcement interfered sufficiently with the amount of South American cocaine or Mexican black tar heroin reaching city streets, one would expect to see a similar rise in price. If the price becomes too great, users will not be able to afford to purchase drugs; there will be a decline in drug usage. The United States has continually increased its enforcement efforts since the early 1980s, especially in terms of interdicting drugs coming into the United States from foreign countries. Indeed, there are approximately 3,000 agents assigned to the Drug Enforcement Agency (DEA) whose primary responsibility is to cut off drugs coming into the United States.

Even though the DEA and local and state law enforcement agencies have successfully interdicted large quantities of drugs, the price of cocaine, heroin, and other drugs has steadily dropped and the number of users has not diminished significantly. For example, Mazerolle, Soole, and Rombouts (2007) examined several interdiction studies and found that seizures did not affect the price, purity, or availability of drugs. These disheartening statistics indicate that increasingly larger quantities of drugs have been smuggled into the United States despite enhanced enforcement efforts.

A number of years ago, Reuter, Crawford, and Cace (1988) examined the impact of drug interdiction for the Pentagon. The purpose of the study was to determine how military interdiction might affect drug trafficking at the borders. The Pentagon proposed to use military ships and aircraft to seal the borders from drug trafficking. Members of Congress, as well as many other politicians, have long advocated militarizing the war on drugs. Reuter and his colleagues found that increased interdiction was futile. They concluded that 75 percent of the money spent on cocaine went to street dealers and their immediate suppliers. Only 10 percent of the price of cocaine went to drug production and smuggling. At the time, the Coast Guard found drugs on only one in eight boats it boarded. Even if the Navy were to double the number of boats being inspected, it would have only a minimal impact on smuggling. Reuter suggested that, at best, the volume of cocaine would be reduced from 120 metric tons of cocaine per year to 90 metric tons per year. The supply would not be reduced significantly or to the point that street supplies would be appreciably disrupted.

The arrest of drug cartel leaders has a fairly long history. For example, when cocaine became a major problem in the 1970s, American law enforcement officials worked with Columbian police and prosecutors to arrest the heads of the Columbian drug cartels. Today, the United States is working with Mexico in attempting to deal with cartels. An unfortunate consequence of high-level enforcement is that the high-level dealers that the police catch may well be the sloppiest or weakest, so that law enforcement is inadvertently toughening the remaining drug dealing organizations (Kleiman & Smith, 1990). Also, high-level enforcement assumes that a void will occur when the head of a drug dealing organization is arrested. However, there are often many lieutenants willing to take their boss' place, and there are other organizations that would quickly fill any void in market territory. For example, when American and Columbian officials arrested the leaders of the Medillan cartel, its operations were quickly

> You can read more about the threat of Mexican drug cartels by going to
> http://www.hstoday.us/blogs/the-kimery-report/blog/cartel-threats-attacks-on-us-law-enforcement-and-the-question-of-spill-over-violence/19546dea1864ba1008378ba598069fa4.html.

taken over by the Cali cartel. When American drug lords are arrested, their organizations frequently are taken over by lieutenants or other drug trafficking organizations. Drug trafficking vacuums are quickly filled. The real law of supply and demand is that when there is a demand, someone will provide the supply.

As Kleiman (2003) notes, one of the primary goals of any police strategy is to reduce the violence and health consequences associated with drug trafficking. Violence, especially random violence or violence victimizing innocent bystanders, is much more problematic than drug trafficking. Arresting high-level dealers likely increases the risks of triggering a round of violence, as lieutenants and other drug trafficking organizations battle for the vacated territory. Such violence tends to undermine enforcement efforts and create public hysteria, which is counterproductive to community policing and law enforcement in general. This type of enforcement does little to effectively negate health consequences of drugs to the community since such policies have little impact on the availability of drugs. This is not to say that law enforcement should not concentrate efforts on drug lords, but when designing strategies, they should consider whether there will be collateral damage and how to minimize it.

In the end, high-level enforcement has little impact on the availability and price of drugs on the street. At best, high-level enforcement keeps smugglers from being too blatant, and it serves to discourage more people from becoming involved in smuggling. Large seizures of drugs serve as a public relations tool. The public sees such police actions as victories in the war on drugs even though they effectively are meaningless in terms of supply. The real war on drugs, for any community, remains at the retail level.

Retail-Level Enforcement

If police strategies that aim upward in the drug distribution hierarchy have failed, what about those that focus downward, at the street level? **Retail-level** enforcement strategies attempt to reduce "discreet" and "indiscreet" drug dealing, with the latter more susceptible to control. Indiscreet drug dealing includes open street dealing, as well as crack houses and shooting galleries used exclusively to sell drugs to large numbers of customers. Transactions that take place in people's homes, offices, nightclubs, and other locations where drug dealing is not the facility's sole reason for being are considered relatively discreet and are much more difficult to attack.

Generally, when a city or area within a city has a substantial amount of indiscreet drug trafficking, it indicates that the problem is out of control. For example, Zimmer (1990:48) described such an area in the Lower East Side of Manhattan:

> … the area gained a local reputation as a "drug supermarket" and a national reputation as "the most open heroin market in the nation. Police videotapes… . show long lines of double-parked cars, hundreds of people milling around waiting to purchase heroin and cocaine, sellers shouting out the "brand names" and prices of their drugs, and others openly advertising "works"—hypodermic needles—guaranteed clean for two or three dollars. Enterprising young men and women sometimes searched the crowd looking for novice customers who might be willing to pay to have someone else "score" for them. When long lines formed behind dealers, waiting buyers at the end of the line were sometimes offered "express service," for a fee. On some blocks, vendors set up their carts, selling hot dogs and sodas to the crowd; portable radios competed with the shouting. The unaware might have thought for a moment that they had stumbled upon a block party or street festival.

Indiscreet drug trafficking also means the police have failed to protect people who reside in those neighborhoods where drug dealers work. Indiscreet drug trafficking usually indicates the presence of collateral crime and disorder. Unchecked, the problem will eventually spread into surrounding areas and the quality of life in the affected neighborhoods will continue to deteriorate. Thus, the police should make indiscreet drug trafficking their first priority. Attacking indiscreet drug trafficking will ultimately result in the greatest harm reduction in the community.

Over time, the police have used a number of different tactics to deal with retail-drug operations. Before discussing them, it is important to consider these tactics as tools. Each tool is used to perform a different job. Therefore, the police should consider the nature and scope of a particular drug problem and select the appropriate tool or tactic when attempting to counter it (see Weisburd & Eck, 2004). The nature of the drug problem and the environment determine the tactics that should be implemented and which ones will be most effective.

Discreet drug trafficking, on the other hand, presents a different problem. First, because it is discreet and very likely widespread in many communities, it is virtually impossible for the police to stop. Police undercover operations and buy-busts will result in a few arrests, but such arrests are costly in terms of the amount of time and effort devoted to making each arrest. Second, discreet drug dealing seldom results in collateral crime and disorder problems. People discreetly purchase their drugs and then consume them out of public view.

When the police concentrate their efforts on indiscreet drug trafficking, it generally results in larger numbers of minority arrests and subsequent charges of discrimination on the part of the police (Lusane, 1990).

One tactic used by the police has been **crackdowns**. Davis and Lurigio (1996) defined crackdowns as "abrupt escalations in law enforcement activities that are intended to increase the perceived or actual threat of apprehension for certain offences occurring in certain situations or locations" (p. 86). Essentially, they consist of a substantial increase in the number of officers in a location or an increase in the number of undercover operations in the location. Crackdowns generally are used in high crime and drug trafficking areas. Once a drug trafficking location becomes established, it generally will grow in terms of the number of people visiting the location and the volume of crime and disorder. These locations draw customers, as they are reliable places to find drugs (Boyum, Caulkins & Kleiman, 2011). When drugs are the target, officers generally concentrate on hard drugs such as crack, cocaine, or heroin (Mazerolle, Soole & Rombouts, 2007).

The primary objective of a crackdown is to reduce the supply of drugs in the targeted location. Generally, these crackdowns target the drug trafficking associated with the underclass, outdoor drug markets and indoor inner-city drug trafficking locations like crack houses. Research indicates that crackdowns only have a short-term impact on the drug problem location. Once the crackdown is completed, the problem eventually returns. Sherman (1990) has suggested that this short-term effect can be increased by conducting a series of random crackdowns at the target location, and additional crackdowns over time will have a more significant impact on the location. Regardless, for a crackdown to have a long-term impact, it must be followed by other tactics. Otherwise, the drug market location will once again become a problem.

Another tactic similar to crackdowns is a raid. Mazerolle and her colleagues (2007) note that **raids** are "specifically localized search and seizure type operations. Raids generally target residential and commercial (i.e., clubs, motels, etc.) properties that are sources of numerous drug, crime, and disorder problems (i.e., calls for service, arrests, complaints)" (p. 125). Raids can target retail or mid-level wholesale drug trafficking operations. Raids' primary objective is to remove drugs from the street. Like crackdowns, raids have a short-term impact on the drug trafficking location unless they are followed by other additional raids or other drug reduction tactics. Moreover, Cohen, Gorr, and Singh (2003) found that a number of risk factors in a target area make the target more resistant to interventions such as raids and crackdowns. As an example, the number of bars in a city block contributes to higher levels of violence and crime (Ronsek & Maier, 1991).

Police typically use undercover operations in areas with drug problems. Some of the tactics used are undercover drug buys, buy-busts, use of informants, and reverse stings. **Undercover drug buys** consist of officers working undercover who attempt to buy drugs from street dealers in order to make arrests and cases. Generally, the officers will attempt to get close to the dealers in order to identify other dealers and purchasers. **Buy-busts** are similar to police undercover drug buys, but here officers will immediately or within a short time arrest the seller to avoid identity problems or flight. Informants often play a key role in drug enforcement. **Informants** are people who provide officers with information about drug dealing. One way to use informants is to have a person who is familiar with an area buy drugs and provide the information to the police officer, and then the officer uses the information to obtain a search warrant. In other cases, the officer will use a low-level user or drug dealer in the same fashion in return for reducing criminal charges against the informant. Finally, **reverse stings** are where officers pose as drug dealers and arrest people who attempt to buy drugs from them. Reverse stings are used to diminish drug dealers' customer base. There is no evidence that these operations have a lasting impact on drug dealing.

Another tactic that is commonly used is multi-agency drug task forces. **Multi-jurisdictional drug task forces** consist of large drug enforcement units comprising officers from a number of jurisdictions. Since drug problems often span several jurisdictional boundaries, these task forces are not limited by jurisdictional boundaries. Multi-jurisdictional drug task forces generally encompass large geographical areas and focus on arrests as opposed to abating a specific problem or drug. One benefit derived from these operations is that police departments involved in the task force increase their level of inter-agency communication, thus facilitating enforcement efforts (Smith, Novak, Frank & Travis, 2000). Research indicates that even though these task forces generated a large number of arrests and seizures, they did not necessarily increase drug arrests (see Mazerolle, Soole & Rombouts, 2007).

Numerous cities and counties across the country have implemented drug free zones. A **drug free zone** is an area that is legally identified, usually around a school, playground, or church or a high drug trafficking area where drug trafficking has been concentrated. When people are caught dealing in a drug free zone, there generally is a punishment enhancement—increase in fines or prison time. Drug free zones concentrate on locations as opposed to a particular drug or drug trafficking method. Even though they are popular, there is no evidence that they reduce drug trafficking. For example, Brownsberger and his colleagues (2004) examined drug free school zones in three Massachusetts cities and found they did not push drug dealing away from schools. There were two primary reasons. First, many drug dealers sell drugs close to home, and many schools are located in areas where drug dealers reside. Second, there were so many schools that discerning the boundaries for the drug free zones was difficult. It appears that drug free zones do little to control drugs. It may be that drug free zones are more effective in areas that are not experiencing a significant drug program. There likely is a tipping point where they become ineffective.

Teacher Arrested for Using Drugs in Front of Fourth-Grade Class

Joan M. Donatelli, 59, a substitute teacher, was arrested after two female students, a 10-year-old and a 9-year-old, in her 4th grade class at Lew-Port school in Lewiston, New York witnessed her using cocaine at her desk on February 1, 2007.

According to Lewiston police Sgt. Frank J. Previte, at least two students saw Donatelli use the end of at least two pen caps to "repeatedly" scoop cocaine out of the green-colored bag and inhale the drug into her nose, while she was teaching the class. The students were sitting no less than five feet from the teacher's desk at the time of the incident.

The children who reported the incident are being called "credible."

"First of all their candor, their account of everything in stating what they saw. They were very specific about the color of the bag, the color of the pen caps that were used, which all again, we were able to back up," added Previte.

Previte also stated that Donatelli admitted to using the drug only after police searched the classroom and found trace amounts of cocaine on her desk. Donatelli then got rid of the evidence and drugs by throwing the items out in a trash bin inside a bathroom.

"She stated that she had a problem, that she has an addiction, something she's been struggling with," stated Previte.

The superintendent of Lewiston-Porter Central Schools, Don Rappold, sent a letter home to parents of the students saying:

"On Thursday, February 1, 2007, it was reported that a substitute teacher in your child's classroom may have a substance abuse problem. This letter is to inform you that the Lewiston-Porter School District responded to the report by advising the police. The matter is now under investigation, and the District is fully cooperating with the authorities. Pending the outcome of the investigation, the substitute teacher has been prohibited from being on our campus."

Donatelli is being charged with at least two counts of endangering the welfare of children and seventh-degree criminal possession of an illegal substance. She is expected to appear in the Lewiston Town Court on February 21, 2007. More counts of endangering the welfare of children may be added, but only after police can confirm that other students in the class witnessed the incident.

Source: *Wikinews* (2007). Saturday, February 10, 2007.

Drug nuisance abatement is a strategy that is not used extensively, but it represents an effective tool in dealing with drug problem locations. Drug nuisance abatement consists of civil remedies and third party policing. Mazerolle, Price, and Roehl (2000) describe civil remedies and third party policing:

> Civil remedies are procedures and sanctions, specified by civil statutes and regulations used to prevent or reduce criminal problems and incivilities ... . Civil remedies typically aim to persuade or coerce nonoffending third parties to take responsibility and action to prevent or end criminal or nuisance behavior.... Civil remedy approaches often target nonoffending third parties (e.g., landlords, property owners) and use nuisance and drug abatement statutes to control problems. These types of abatement statutes include repaint requirements, fines, padlocking/closing, and property forfeiture and seek to make owners and landlords maintain drug- and nuisance-free properties (pp. 212-213).

There have been a number of examples of the police using civil remedies and third party policing. Mazerolle and her colleagues (2007) reviewed the research literature and found that civil remedies and third party policing has had a positive impact. They found that the tactic reduces drug trafficking, crime, especially property crime, and disorder. Essentially, the tactics contributed significantly to the quality of life in the areas targeted. Landlords and business owners are more likely to try to control their properties when there is a threat of some civil action. This results in a shared responsibility between the police and community members.

Evaluations of a number of the tactics discussed above showed dismal effects: they often did not achieve positive outcomes. In several cases, it was noted that in order for some of these tactics to be effective, they should be implemented in conjunction with other tactics. For example, crackdowns by themselves were shown to be ineffective; however, if a crackdown were to be implemented with other tactics, the outcome likely would be more favorable. There are numerous cases where multiple tactics have been deployed in unison. For example, in an Arizona study, police officers responded to neighborhood problems by creating a unit that enforced zoning laws, a civil remedy approach, and by creating a police unit that aggressively enforced municipal codes and county laws in the area. The initiative resulted in positive results relative to crime and disorder (Katz, Webb & Schaefer, 2001). In a Jersey City program, the police deployed a three-prong attack on drug market hot spots. Once targets were selected, the police conducted crackdowns in the area that aimed to close the drug markets. The crackdowns were tailored based on the type of location and type of drug problem. If the crackdown was unsuccessful, it was followed by additional crackdowns. Once the drug problem had subsided, detectives used surveillance techniques to ensure that the target areas remained clear. If problems resurfaced, patrols, including foot patrols, were deployed (Weisburd & Green, 1995). The program resulted in a decrease in disorder calls to the police. These examples demonstrate that effective drug countermeasures often require a combination of tactics, and they must be tailored for the specific drug problem.

This section described a number of tactics or tools that can be used to address drug problems. Some of these tools are reactive, while others are proactive. When selecting a tool, officers should not select the one that is easiest to deploy or one that has been used in the past. The tools should fit the job—the drug reduction tactic should be aimed at the specific drug problem. In Chapter 8, the SARA model of problem solving was addressed. The first step in the SARA model consists of scanning the environment to identify problems. The second step is analysis. Here, once identified, drug problems should be thoroughly examined so that they are completely understood. Then, the proper tools should be selected. The tools should theoretically and practically meet the scope and nature of the drug problem.

Efforts Aimed at Juveniles

The police should place a high priority on reducing the drug problem among juveniles. These efforts should focus on prevention as well as enforcement. Statistics point out that larger numbers of younger people use drugs. For example, SAMHSA (2010) reported that in 2009, 10 percent of youth between the ages of 12 and 17 reported having used an illegal drug in the past month prior to the survey. The most commonly used drug was marijuana, followed by the non-medical use of prescription psychotherapeutics. Additionally, juveniles in this age bracket abuse alcohol, and a number of them engage in periodic binge drinking. Hopefully, this drug use is experimental in nature rather than long-term, heavy usage. Nonetheless, the police should make special efforts to reduce juvenile drug usage.

A number of police departments use suppression tactics to attack juvenile drug usage. This means that the police should have an increased presence at places and events that draw juveniles. The police should patrol areas where juveniles congregate. This may mean having officers check skating rinks, drive-in restaurants, and similar businesses on a regular basis. It also means having officers check more closely adults who loiter in these areas. For the most part, the police tend to avoid such places unless they are dispatched there on a call. The lack of attention to such areas may allow a drug problem to develop or escalate.

A special case for police concern is raves. **Raves** are extremely large gatherings of juveniles and young adults, sometimes 1,000 or more, where there is music, drugs, and alcohol. There have been a number of cases where rave participants have overdosed on drugs and alcohol. There also have been instances where they were involved in automobile crashes upon leaving the raves. Raves represent a dangerous location, and the police must respond to them. There are two methods by which to control raves. The first is to encourage government officials to ban them entirely from the community. This eliminates the problem. Second, if they are not banned, the government should pass ordinances requiring a significant police presence, to be paid for by the rave operators. If no such legal requirement exists, the police should aggressively patrol the rave and make arrests to reduce the amount and level of illegal behavior.

The police should also be involved in juvenile drug prevention. Involving police officers in drug education is fairly common, and many departments have adopted the model provided by the **Drug Abuse Resistance Education** (DARE) project that was developed by the Los Angeles Police Department. DARE began in 1983 when the Los Angeles Police Department began sending officers into the schools to teach children about drugs. The questionable rationale behind DARE is that police officers have more credibility and expertise on drug issues than most teachers, so generally they can make a lasting impact on children's future attitudes and behavior. More comprehensive than simply urging kids to "Just Say No," the program is based on the assumption that most kids experiment with drugs because of an inability to withstand peer pressure, problems with low self-esteem, and lack of training in values clarification. DARE was first implemented in a few grades in elementary school; now, however, there is a curriculum for all levels of elementary and secondary education (Carter, 1995).

Unfortunately, research on DARE indicates that it is not successful in reducing drug usage by juveniles (Wysong, Aniskiewicz & Wright, 1994; Rosenbaum et al., 1994). Juveniles exposed to the program have similar usage rates and attitudes toward drugs as those who were not enrolled in the program. Obviously, these results are discouraging, but they point to a need to further examine curriculum and program activities and to question whether police are viewed as legitimate educators on drug issues. It means that we should continue to experiment and attempt to develop a program that will reduce future drug usage among juveniles.

> You can learn more about research on the DARE program by reading the GAO report at http://www.gao.gov/new.items/d03172r.pdf.

Another common program is school police and school probation officers (sometimes referred to as school resource officers). According to Reaves (2010), nationally, about 38 percent of police departments have officers assigned to schools. Here, police or probation officers are assigned to specific schools. Their responsibilities include law enforcement, counseling, and teaching (Burke, 2001). Brown (2006) provides a detailed description of their duties:

> ... patrolling school grounds to maintain a visible law enforcement presence, traffic supervision at the beginning and end of the school day, assisting with the control of disruptive students, attending parent and faculty meetings, intelligence gathering for local criminal justice officials, giving presentations at faculty in-services, parent–teacher gatherings, and community meetings, assisting with delinquency prevention programs such as Drug Abuse Resistance and Education (D.A.R.E.), serving as a liaison between local law enforcement, parents, students, and schools, providing a positive role model for students, and traveling with athletic teams to away games (p. 592).

The duties of school probation officers are essentially the same as police school resource officers. The exception is that school probation officers have a list of students who are on probation. The probation officers can check on these students' attendance, suspensions, and grades and report to the students' probation officers. Since school success is often a term of juveniles' probation, the probation officer has readily accessible information and can apply pressure on juveniles who do not do well in school or who are violating the terms of their probation. Since juveniles tend to get involved in a variety of criminal activities, especially before and after school, these programs may have a preventive effect.

Community Policing and Drug Problems

It may well prove to be a mistake for the police to treat drugs as the exclusive province of a special unit within the department. Perhaps an important lesson to be learned from the drug usage forecast data, which showed that drugs are involved in the arrests of as many as four of every five people arrested in some cities, is that drugs are deeply woven into the total fabric of police work, from child abuse to homicides. Though drugs are not the cause of all the problems the police face, the drug usage forecast data show that they play some role in the lives of the vast majority of people arrested in major cities, but so too do poverty, lack of education, and underemployment.

Furthermore, the police cannot be expected to do the job alone. A three-pronged approach, involving law enforcement, drug education, and drug

treatment, appears to hold the best promise of making a long-term difference, but it also implies a tug-of-war among the three perspectives for scarce
resources. For example, Boyum, Caulkins, and Kleiman (2011) advise that
80 percent of total U.S. drug control spending is for enforcement and incarceration, which leaves very little for prevention and treatment. While it is
vital to educate young people about the threats drugs pose and help them
learn how to resist drugs, and it seems tantamount to scandal that many who
seek drug treatment must wait months before it is available, people question
whether too much money has been devoted to enforcement and not enough
to prevention and treatment (Skolnick, 1990).

Because of the vast number of different kinds of problems that drugs create, a
community problem-solving approach obviously makes better sense than simply
responding to individual incidents. Community policing also allows the department to fashion responses tailored to local problems and needs, without focusing
exclusively on arrest, which often engages the rest of the expensive criminal justice system with little effect. As a department's community outreach specialists,
community policing officers (CPOs) have a particularly vital role to play in controlling crime and improving relations between the department and the community.

Davis and Lurigio (1996) have provided perhaps the best taxonomy by which
to understand how the police interact with the public in the war on drugs. They
analyze the interaction in terms of the people and government involvement;
maximum involvement comes from indigenous community anti-drug activities.
These activities have occurred when people have become frustrated with the
drug and crime problems in their neighborhood and have taken action on their
own. Davis, Smith, Lurigio, and Skogan (1991) found three factors that generally
contributed to community initiatives: (1) they occur in less affluent, high-crime
neighborhoods, (2) activism is strongly related to a neighborhood's capacity
to initiate marches, rallies, and civilian patrols, and (3) the existence of a "community" leader to initiate and sustain activities. Thus, some neighborhoods are
more capable of initiating problem solving than others. If a neighborhood has
not or is not capable of such action, the police should implant programs. Cook
and Roehl (1993) note that the more successful programs are those that consist
of partnerships among large numbers of agencies and constituent groups. Thus,
when the police attempt to transplant a program, they must attempt to secure
a number of commitments.

The following should be considered a partial list of what community policing can do and a blueprint for how it might be used to accomplish more in the
future:

**Community policing directly addresses both discreet and indiscreet
retail-level drug dealing.** If the police are to maintain public confidence, they

must find effective ways to address retail drug dealing, selecting the right tool for the problem. Retail drug dealing, especially when it is indiscreet, occurs in the neighborhoods and in the streets where people live. This type of trafficking directly threatens people's perception of the community; it may result in higher levels of collateral crime; and it can destroy community life when left unchecked. A sense of fairness would seem to dictate that both indiscreet and discreet dealing should receive equal police attention, but open dealing is even more pernicious because it reinforces the public perception that drugs have careened out of control, a singularly dangerous message to send to people, especially young people. Open dealing also makes it far too easy for casual and first-time users as well as addicts to find a ready supply of drugs.

Community policing can provide the department's first line of defense against both indiscreet and discreet dealing. The shift from focusing on responding to calls and making arrests to solving community problems reorders overall department priorities to a proper emphasis on helping people feel safer from the threats drugs pose. The importance of reducing or eliminating the fear of crime is discussed extensively in Chapter 7. Through its CPOs, community policing provides a permanent, citywide, neighborhood-based approach to drug problems. When CPOs are permanently assigned to beats or areas of the city, they can build bridges between the police and the people whose support and participation are crucial in bringing retail-level dealing under control.

Enlisting CPOs directly in addressing retail-level dealing may require a shift in thinking or a change in policy. Traditionally, the police have been call-oriented as opposed to neighborhood-oriented. That is, the police would respond to each call, and once they had responded to a call, they would wait for the next call. Community policing dictates that police not only take care of calls for service, but that they survey their beat or neighborhood, identify crime problems, and respond to them. In many instances, the responses are nontraditional and may require the cooperation of the community or other elements of government.

In North Miami Beach, CPO Charles Reynolds was assigned to a low-income neighborhood notorious as a supermarket for drugs. Once Reynolds gained the trust of the people in the area, he tackled problems personally by warning low-level dealers that he would make it his business to arrest them if they persisted—but that if they wanted help in finding a job, he would provide that as well. Reynolds then proceeded to back up both his threat and his promise. He made cases against those who continued to sell drugs and commit other crimes, and he also provided individualized and broad-based assistance to help people find work.

Each week Reynolds posted in his office a list of jobs available in the community, and he referred people to companies that he knew were hiring people requiring their skills. Reynolds also worked with business and professional leaders to host a job fair in the community-policing office. That event provided classes on a wide range of topics including how to dress for an interview, and how to write a resume, and it involved people in role-playing so that they could assess their performance in mock job interviews. By tailoring the police response to community needs, Reynolds was able to bring open dealing under control without mass arrests that might have resulted in resentment and distrust toward the police on the part of the neighborhood people. Positive action often is more meaningful than negative action.

In Lansing, Michigan, Lt. James Rapp reported success with using foot patrol officers to make repeated visits each day to knock on the doors of known dope houses. Sometimes the officers just stood outside and watched and talked with people who attempted to go to the drug house. Having officers appear in front of drug houses meant a disruption of business, and in some cases the traffickers inside flushed their drugs because they never knew when an officer's arrival might signal a bust. The officers' visible presence also helped drive customers away, which reduced profits even further. The officers also signaled to the neighborhood residents that the police cared about their problems and were doing something about them.

Metropolitan areas plagued by widespread, open dealing require more drastic actions. For example, the department may have to implement an aggressive enforcement program such as a raid or crackdown. Because such tactics often are seen as harassment and create resentment in the community, the department could use its CPOs to prepare the affected people. This could be accomplished by talking with community leaders and individuals, explaining the situation, and requesting their support. Such actions should reduce the negative police-community relations once the tactic is implemented. Once the problem has ebbed somewhat, CPOs could enter the area and implement community-based programs to maintain control. In other cases, it might prove necessary to increase the number of CPOs or other police personnel so that there are ample personnel to attend to the most severe drug problems. Not only would they be able to sustain gains made by coordinating their efforts with the drug sweeps, but also they would be free to pursue new initiatives aimed at a broad range of community concerns.

The problem with relying on sweeps and focused crackdowns that are not part of a community policing approach is that these tactics often alienate the people the police are trying to protect. Community policing coupled with limited enforcement results in people accepting and, to some extent, cooperating with the police. Community policing recognizes that people must accept their responsibility to become involved in efforts to address problems in their own neighborhoods. One of the worst things a police department can do is to roll into a neighborhood, make mass arrests, and then abandon it.

In a notoriously drug-infested area of the District of Columbia, members of the Nation of Islam have achieved notable success by working with residents directly to develop initiatives to eliminate open dealing. Their success demonstrates what a relatively small but dedicated group of people can do to develop grassroots community support and attack community problems. The goal of the police should be to use CPOs as the initiators and supervisors in community-based efforts, because this model offers the opportunity for success (Davis & Lurigio, 1996).

Once the immediate priority of controlling open dealing has been achieved, community policing can then address indiscreet dealing in new ways. A single mother with two sons who was studying at Hunter College moved into a housing project on the Lower East Side of New York City. She soon found that a major crack and marijuana dealer operating from an apartment in the building dominated the complex. Although no fan of the police, the woman felt she had no choice but to ask for their help. She contacted the community patrol officer program (CPOP) team in her area. Together they developed a strategy that included making vertical patrols of the apartment building and offering to escort customers inside, which scared many of them away.

Community policing can gather more and better information about drug dealing with less danger and expense than traditional undercover operations. It bears repeating that two groups of people have information about crime: criminals and the people who are unwillingly exposed to these criminal operations. Traditional police efforts focus on getting the criminals to "roll over," or provide information on their associates in exchange for money or deference on some criminal charge (see Kappeler, Sluder & Alpert, 1998). Community policing instead works on developing the trust between the police and community so that people will provide information about crime and suspicious activities that occur in their neighborhoods. CPOs, as a result of the positive relationships they develop with people, often are in a position to gather intelligence about drug dealing beyond that which can be obtained using traditional methods. Research shows that the visible presence of officers in a neighborhood leads to improvements in opinions about the police (Hawdon & Ryan, 2003; Reisig & Parks, 2003). When people have positive opinions about the police, they are more likely to provide them with information about crime and criminals.

Bruce Benson, a member of the Flint, Michigan, Police Department found that narcotics officers were routinely frustrated because people would call with a tip, but they rarely provided more than an address before hanging up.

The officers would try to follow up, but often found little to go on. The caller often would call again to complain that the police were not doing their job. Once the Flint foot patrol program began, people began to personally provide officers with information. Community policing resulted in people providing in-depth information about drug operations, not just the address, but the names or license plate numbers of the dealers and customers, hours of operation, kinds of drugs sold, and physical descriptions of the drug houses. Even if the people did not know the details, they were often willing to work with the officer to find out what the police needed to know. The foot patrol officers would then transmit the information to the narcotics squad, so that they had enough information to secure a warrant to make a successful investigation and arrest.

Flint was not an isolated case. When a new community policing effort was launched in Morristown, New Jersey, the officers and the administration were amazed at how much information people would pass on about drug dealing during routine visits with people. One woman was able to provide police enough detailed information to break up a broad-based drug-dealing ring shortly after the new program started, the result of an unrelated home visit.

CPOs say that the answer often lies in finding someone in the neighborhood who is interested or concerned about the neighborhood. For example, retired people often keep track of neighborhood activities, including the neighborhood's drug problems. The inherent drawback in the traditional approach is that a motor patrol officer rarely has the time or opportunity to develop the level of trust necessary for people to divulge information, or the officer is there for other reasons and does not have time to devote to cultivating contacts and collecting information.

Another reason that community policing often elicits information that traditional police cannot obtain stems from the fact that home visits and chats on the street are routine. Criminals and drug dealers are not able to identify who in the neighborhood is providing information to the police. A CPO on foot, on a bike, or even on horseback is more approachable than officers in patrol cars. When people see CPOs walking the same streets as them, they know that the officers have good reason to care about what goes on in the neighborhood. For example, Reisig and Parks (2003) found that residents in neighborhoods where police used bike and foot patrols resulted in people being more satisfied with the police. This also can inspire people to venture out of their homes, provide officers with information, and participate in police-sponsored programs.

In Tulsa, Oklahoma, CPOs assigned to a public housing complex patrolled on horseback. The horse acted as an icebreaker, especially with kids. This allowed both adults and children the opportunity of petting the horse as they provided the CPOs information about problems, including drug dealing, in the neighborhood. The horses allowed the people to cooperate with the police without drawing attention to themselves. In one instance, the CPOs were able to rescue a mother who literally was being held captive by cocaine dealers who had taken over her apartment.

Community policing addresses drug dealing in ways that need not always engage or overwhelm the criminal justice system. In the District of Columbia during a two-year period, police sweeps succeeded in arresting roughly 45,000 people without making any dent in the drug-related violence or the amount of open dealing visible on the streets. Meanwhile, the rest of the criminal justice system was overwhelmed; prison costs alone increased 400 percent during an eight-year period (Pooley, 1989).

Similarly, the tally on Detroit's crack problem showed that 144 (more than 10%) of the 1,041 people arrested on felony drug charges during a three-month period never appeared after they had been released on bond or freed because of jail overcrowding. A report prepared by Detroit Recorder's Court seeking more funds to add more judges said that 86.7 percent of all people arrested on drug charges go free on bond because of backlogged dockets and jail overcrowding.

Instead of sending the message that the system has the ability to deal with drug traffickers, the criminal justice response instead seems to ensure that the dealer arrested today will be back in business tomorrow—hustling even harder to pay for legal fees. Community policing approaches the overall problem from a different perspective, by employing arrest as only one of the tools in its arsenal. The traditional police response to a problem often stresses the number of arrests made as a measure of success, but particularly with the problem of open dealing, this yardstick may not always be the best solution. In some cases, actions and outcomes other than arrest may benefit the community.

The account of the CPOP efforts in New York City highlights the importance of solving the problem without focusing on felony drug busts as the primary goal. In that case, using misdemeanor disorderly conduct charges discouraged users from making buys, as did having CPOs and tenants offer to escort them inside. In Wisconsin, an enterprising neighborhood watch group boldly held its meetings across the street from open dealing, thereby driving customers and eventually the dealers away.

The hallmark of the community policing approach is its ability to generate creative, new, community-based, police-supervised approaches. It recognizes that generating arrests beyond what the criminal justice system can handle risks creating bottlenecks that can undermine confidence in the entire system. Community policing shifts the focus from arrest as the primary means of achieving solutions to one that recognizes it as an expensive and time-consuming option.

Community policing can make the best use of police presence to reduce open dealing. One way for the police to address open dealing without always engaging the rest of the criminal justice system involves the judicious and lawful use of presence. A neighborhood group, with a CPO in the lead, making periodic sweeps of streets infested with open drug dealing, can have the same effect as those vertical sweeps floor-by-floor that the CPOP officers used in apartment houses. Perhaps one of the best examples of people harassing drug dealers occurred in Houston. There, approximately 100 residents from the Acres Homes neighborhood banded together and literally chased drug dealers out of the neighborhood (Phillips, 1989).

Creative CPOs and neighborhood residents working together can also employ a host of other tactics to make dealers nervous enough to dispose of their drugs and drive customers away, such as visibly taking down license plate numbers of potential buyers or clicking cameras (without film) at people making dope deals on the street. The purpose is not to assemble lists, but to make buyers and sellers think that they are under surveillance. One CPO even posted signs in his beat area saying that drug dealing would not be tolerated. The goal is to turn up the heat as much as possible, so that the police and people together demonstrate that they will not let up.

Community policing develops and bolsters community participation in antidrug efforts. Areas overwhelmed with drug problems promote apathy and despair because people feel there is nothing they can do that will make a difference. Community policing sometimes requires that only one committed person spark an effort that can achieve a measure of success, and that, in turn, can result in others becoming directly involved in recovering their neighborhoods. Wehrman and De Angelis (2011) note that when CPOs engage people in partnerships, they are more willing to assist the police. The CPO's job is to be a catalyst or motivator to get people involved. Once people are involved, the CPO must constantly expand community efforts.

If a focused crackdown achieves success, but the officers are then removed, only to have the drug dealers return, people can rightfully feel abandoned and betrayed. Many people have expressed concern that traditional efforts ignore them—their needs and concerns and their potential support and participation as well. Community policing pays attention to average people, allowing them a voice in setting priorities and fashioning solutions tailored to their concerns. The community policing alternative to flooding an area with a lot of police for a short time is to substitute a smaller number of CPOs who are stationed in the community permanently, so that they can recruit people in the community to help themselves. Regardless, there is evidence that people living in community policing neighborhoods who have a connection with the police and an understanding of the crime problems are more supportive of the police when the police attack drug and crime problems as compared to people not residing in neighborhoods where there is community policing (Lombardo, Olson & Staton, 2010).

Most often, the first goal in many areas is to reduce open dealing, to stabilize the neighborhood, and then there is a focus on indiscreet dealing to maintain the pressure. As the area begins to improve, the CPO can brainstorm with people in the community about new ways to address the broader spectrum of drug problems. This might mean linking addicts to proper treatment. Or it could include working with area businesses to provide jobs for recovering addicts. Community policing provides a way for the police to link arms with people who understand that they must become part of the answer if drug problems are to be brought under control.

Community policing provides a way to involve the entire department in anti-drug efforts with the least risk of corruption and abuse of authority. Historically, much of the reluctance by many police departments to involve line officers in street-level anti-drug initiatives stems from the unwarranted fear that it would promote corruption and abuse. Many police reforms, beginning in the 1950s, stemmed from efforts to thwart police corruption. Even today, there are periodic police corruption scandals that revolve around drug enforcement. For example, the Mollen Commission in New York City found officers who were openly involved in drug abuse and corruption. Many police managers fear the potential corrupting influence that drugs and drug money have on law enforcement.

The dynamic most likely to promote widespread corruption and abuse appears to be when an elite unit is put on the task, especially a unit cloaked in secrecy (Kappeler, Sluder & Alpert, 1998). A system that also focuses on the number of arrests as the sole or primary measure of success can pressure police to cross the line into abuse, entrapment, and fraud. The structure can promote an "if you can't beat 'em, join 'em" mind-set. The officers involved in the drug corruption scandal in the 77th Precinct in New York, where narcotics officers allegedly robbed dealers and resold the drugs, apparently thought of themselves as modern-day equivalents of Robin Hood even after they were exposed.

Yet police administrators still worry that putting an officer into a beat in a drug-ridden neighborhood invites corruption or abuse of authority. No doubt this stems from concern that when officers band together and begin to see themselves as part of a cohesive brotherhood (Crank, 2004), they can also adopt an unofficial code of silence that demands that they refuse to report a fellow officer's transgressions (Kappeler, Sluder & Alpert, 1998). This bonding is why departments plagued by problems with officers using excessive force often find the situation difficult to reverse.

Ironically, one of community policing's supposed drawbacks may actually be one of its greatest strengths. Because CPOs spend so much time working with people rather than with their fellow officers, they are more likely to identify with the needs of the people they serve. CPOs are less likely to adopt the traditional police mind-set of us (the police) against them (everybody else) (see Skolnick, 1994). Because CPOs are community based, their traditional fellow officers sometimes view them as a breed apart. While that can cause problems of internal dissension, it also makes CPOs less likely than their traditional counterparts to indulge in abuse of authority.

Community policing can help reduce the overall profitability of drug dealing. As explained before, strategies that target high-level drug smugglers and dealers have not had much impact on reducing the drug problem. Every time a high-level dealer is arrested, there is another to take his or her place. By focusing the bulk of its attention on disrupting and reducing retail-level dealing, community policing reduces the overall profits of the drug trade in ways that do not threaten a price increase. **Street-level drug enforcement** attempts to reduce the demand by arresting or otherwise frightening drug buyers. Demand reduction will harm drug dealers and their profitability much more than interdicting the drug supply.

Community policing can best employ problem-solving tactics aimed at drug dealing. Problem solving has become the centerpiece for modern police work. As discussed in Chapter 1, it basically asks officers to look beyond individual incidents and analyze and come to understand underlying crime patterns and dynamics. The purpose is to identify possible pressure points where police intervention can have an impact on a specific problem. CPOs, because of their intense and sustained community involvement, are often the best candidates to identify, launch, and supervise problem-solving initiatives, adjusting them as needed based on their evaluation of the results.

Low-level dealing and user crime can both lend themselves to problem-solving techniques. Perhaps it means having the CPO persuade the city to install high-intensity streetlights in areas where open dealing takes place at night. In North Miami Beach, Florida, the city officials in charge of code enforcement have actually been moved into the department, in part because of the hope that CPOs can work with them to use the regulations as a means to close dope houses. In Lexington, Kentucky, police officers used cutting torches to remove several basketball hoops in a city park. The hoops were located next to the street, and drug dealers were using basketball games to disguise drug dealing. The police made sure that there were ample hoops in the park to handle all of the legitimate sports activities.

Problem-solving tactics can also prove useful in addressing drug-related crime. Research tends to indicate that drug users often commit most of their crimes within a close radius of their homes. CPOs could counter this problem by working with people to implement crime prevention programs in high-crime and drug-usage areas. CPOs could help develop strategies to reduce robberies, burglaries, and other property crimes by improving outdoor lighting and clipping back bushes where muggers can hide. Such efforts to alter the environment potentially can have a substantial impact on crime. It could mean working with the manager of an apartment complex on a system to issue identification cards and visitor passes or a no-trespass system in public housing to discourage outsiders from coming in to make buys—and robbing residents to pay for the drugs. Problem solving means that the police must use imaginative, nontraditional ways to address old problems.

Community policing can focus on youth gangs for special attention. As discussed in the next chapter, the police have the opportunity to play an expanded role in addressing the problem of youth gangs, not only in targeting existing gangs for special attention, but by providing lawful alternatives. The problem with many youth gangs today is that they have discovered the potential profits available in drug dealing. Also, traditional enforcement aimed at youth gangs largely has been ineffective. Community policing can play a unique and important role in working with youth gangs, to reduce open warfare, to gather intelligence, and to help prevent wannabes or potential recruits from becoming hard-core gangbangers.

Kids join gangs for identity, for the recreational activities they provide, and for protection, including protection from the gangs themselves. Community policing focuses on juveniles for special attention, an important part of its overall mandate, and many CPOs have been instrumental in working with individuals and businesspeople to organize alternative activities for young people. Involving CPOs in youth clubs and sports and recreational activities for young people also adds that vital element of protection, and CPOs can also enlist adults willing to provide additional security for youngsters who need a lawful alternative. For example, a number of police departments, as a part of their community policing efforts, have created Police Athletic Leagues for the purpose of organizing sports activities in disadvantaged neighborhoods. A number of departments have also helped to establish after-school tutoring programs to assist disadvantaged kids to assimilate into mainstream activities.

Community policing can focus on juveniles, particularly high-risk youngsters, with efforts to reduce the likelihood that they will become drug abusers or dealers. For example, in Flint, foot patrol officer Jowanne Barnes-Coney took the proactive approach of trying to identify high-risk youngsters so that she could work with them and discourage them from experimenting with or selling drugs. Her rapport with the youngsters in her beat area allowed her to gather a list of young people at risk—those kids whose friends said they worried about them because they were either dabbling in drug use or they had talked about wanting to become a dealer someday. Barnes-Coney first visited the parents of these youngsters potentially at risk, explaining her concerns and offering to work with them on ways to intervene, including involving teachers in the effort.

In the role of community liaison, Barnes-Coney attempted to link families to appropriate community counseling. She developed a program that rewarded young people for arriving home by the curfew set by their parents. She also worked with people in the community to host broad-based efforts, such as a drug-free rally where each child who participated received a T-shirt. Barnes-Coney became persuaded that many of the youngsters she saw turned to drugs because they did not feel good about themselves. As a result, she organized teen self-esteem clubs designed to boost a positive self-image. Barnes-Coney's efforts demonstrate how the police can initiate a number of grassroots programs that attack the drug problem. Because CPOs have close relationships with people and neighborhoods, they are best qualified to identify those programs with the greatest potential and elicit the highest level of support and participation on the part of those who are in need.

The police have an important role to play in drug education, and community policing can go beyond programs like DARE by reaching out beyond schools to the truants and dropouts who may well be at greatest risk. CPOs make presentations in classrooms, and many work within schools. But they also initiate community-based initiatives and activities designed to include youngsters in positive activities as an alternative to drug use. Because they have the opportunity to work with youngsters over time, CPOs can develop informal, one-on-one relationships with youngsters who need special attention. They can also reinforce the anti-drug message in group activities, whether that includes a summer softball league or classes on child care for teen mothers.

The problem with many well-meaning educational approaches is that they find their warmest acceptance among those at least risk, whereas the challenge lies in developing a wide range of approaches in the hope of reaching a broad spectrum of young people with different problems and needs. CPOs have the opportunity to serve as positive role models themselves in a variety of initiatives aimed at young people, so that they can transmit and reinforce the anti-drug message directly and indirectly. Though they remain adult authority figures, their personal relationship with the juveniles in their beat areas holds some promise that CPOs can breach the problem of teenage rebellion. Their sustained presence in the community as a trusted adult also allows them to identify new drug and crime problems and assist in launching countermeasure efforts.

As the example above demonstrates, community policing allows the police to employ proactive strategies designed to support families in their anti-drug efforts. All too often, the only time that many families see the police is when they arrive as adversaries, seeking information or to make an arrest. Community policing allows youngsters and adults to enjoy positive interactions with the police, so that they are not simply authority figures who "will take you away if you are bad."

A hotly debated law in Los Angeles led to the arrest of a mother who was charged with failing to stop her son from becoming involved in gang activity. Parental responsibility is an important component in juvenile drug abuse and drug dealing. The police must not only sanction youths' transgressions and crimes, but also provide families the support they need in controlling their youngsters.

Another problem the police must begin to contend with more directly is abuse within families. Unfortunately officials at all levels in the United States are only beginning to grapple with the high levels of child abuse and neglect that occur in many families, and no one would argue that efforts thus far have been less than adequate. This is an area where CPOs can have a real impact. CPOs can link families to appropriate help, and they can work to initiate community-based efforts to provide support to troubled families. They could encourage an alcoholic parent to obtain counseling or otherwise help protect family members who are being abused by another family member who is substance dependent. But most importantly, CPOs can work with social service organizations to provide direct intervention where necessary. When CPOs identify homes with abuse and neglect, they should demand direct social service intervention. If these kinds of family problems go unattended, it substantially increases the probability that the children will encounter problems later.

Community policing can serve as the link to public and private agencies that can help. There are some public and private agencies that are more capable than the police at intervening in social problems. In the past, police departments worked with or otherwise cooperated with other agencies. They saw their roles simply as referral agents. That is, if the police encountered a problem they believed was in the domain of another agency, they referred the person to the other agency, effectively washing their hands of it. Community policing dictates that the police understand that they have a vested interest in devising effective responses to community problems, and the most effective responses sometimes involve working with a myriad of other public and private agencies.

Police departments must make concerted efforts in developing working relationships, as opposed to mutually exclusive relationships, with a variety of other agencies. When the police team up with other agencies, they can have a profound impact on problems. This can occur only after the department identifies agencies and establishes a liaison with them. Furthermore, officers must be trained to identify problems that can be handled by or in conjunction with those agencies, and they must be taught to call on them for help. Supervisors must constantly reinforce these efforts. As a part of the supervision process, first-line supervisors should attempt to determine if other agencies could be effective in providing assistance.

There are numerous partnerships they can forge. For example, the police should work with parks and recreation departments to ensure that youths living in problem neighborhoods have adequate recreational activities. Juveniles often do not have access to such programs, and consequently associate with other juveniles who are involved in drugs and crime. The police should work closely with schools to reduce truancy. When juveniles are not in school, they are more likely to get involved in criminal behavior. The police can work with city redevelopment agencies to have drug houses torn down, making it more difficult for drug dealers and their customers. There are a number of private agencies such as churches, boys clubs, and boy and girl scouts that can provide developmental opportunities for juveniles in drug-ridden neighborhoods.

The police can work with agencies to develop programs for adults as well. Many cities operate employment agencies, and the police can assist people in getting access to this type of information. The police can work with code enforcement to force landlords to improve living conditions in rental properties that are substandard. Also, the police can link people with social agencies such as mental health, child services, and welfare agencies that can assist people who have severe problems. When the police assist people, they develop better relations with them, and any assistance they receive may result in reduced involvement with drugs or crime.

Community policing provides a logical mechanism for disseminating information on AIDS and other diseases related to IV-drug use. Failure to involve the police in efforts to reduce the potential number of AIDS victims is shortsighted. Not only are the police one of the most logical candidates for the job because they come in contact with many IV-drug users, but also it is in their enlightened self-interest to do all they can to reduce the spread of these diseases. AIDS not only imposes an expensive financial toll on society, but also it results in substantial human misery. The disease creates a street population desperately in need of police and social services.

CPOs should be encouraged to use their local offices as clearinghouses for information on preventing AIDS and other diseases such as hepatitis B caused by sharing infected drug needles. They can also enlist community support in informational efforts, such as how to use bleach to clean and disinfect needles. CPOs can also disseminate information about agencies that offer assistance to those already afflicted. Educating the community about the threat of AIDS can also enlist cooperation and support for efforts aimed at closing down so-called shooting galleries, where addicts often share infected needles. AIDS, perhaps, is the best example of a community problem that demands everyone's attention.

Community policing adds both scope and continuity to the overall police effort, providing sustained, citywide retail-drug enforcement without under-utilizing scarce resources. By using CPOs as the backbone of the department's antidrug efforts, police departments automatically extend their anti-drug efforts beyond what any special unit, such as a narcotics division, can provide. In essence, considering and further exploiting the ability of community policing to fashion short- and long-term solutions to the entire spectrum of problems associated with drugs is a way to make drugs the top police priority overall, as it is with most people.

The mistake in talking about the drug crisis is that the traditional police response to a crisis is to look for ways to make massive, short-term interventions to bring the emergency under control, but without any coordinated follow-up—or prevention. It can be argued that drugs have reached emergency status in some areas of certain cities, in part, because of the failure to provide sustained, proactive police efforts in the past. Street-sweeps and focused crackdowns allow the police to have a temporary impact on the drug problem, but the problem floods back once the massive police intervention is withdrawn. An important prescription that community policing fills best, because it is not a single-purpose approach, is that it consists of effective, creative ways of providing basic police services.

Community policing may help reduce the risk of civil disturbances and rioting that could be triggered by aggressive anti-drug initiatives. Frustration with open dealing has increased the pressure to take drastic action. A number of departments have deployed militarized police units to patrol high-crime and drug areas (Kraska & Kappeler, 1997). Such units do not have problem solving as their primary objective, but for the most part, they are there to send a message to the community and to produce numbers of arrests. Their primary function is to make a statement for the police. Unfortunately, the message is unsound and random arrests seldom accomplish little in terms of improving the quality of life for people or reducing the drug problem. Also, aggressive police actions alienate the public and ultimately lead to direct confrontations with people. Historically, if we examine most of the major riots in the United States, they were touched off by some police incident (National Advisory Commission on Civil Disorders, 1968).

A community policing approach may offer substantially more than a militarized movement in areas with high levels of drugs and crime. Not only can community policing help reduce tensions between the police department and the community, particularly in the area of race relations, but it can also be used to address a number of problems that contribute to crime and drug abuse.

Summary

It seems increasingly urgent to explore what community policing can offer in solving the drug problem. For more than a quarter of a century, police and the criminal justice system have responded to drugs with a tough, aggressive response. Unfortunately, it does not appear that this response has had much of an impact on the problem. Indeed, the drug problem does not appear to have subsided one iota. The drug problem results in mounting frustration within society. This frustration has led to a continuation of the same old draconian solutions. Their failure should suggest that something else must be attempted.

When confronting drug problems, the police have a variety of tools or tactics. It is important for the police to select the proper tools. A tool should be selected in terms of whether it will provide the most positive outcome, and whether it is the least intrusive or problematic in a community. In the past, the police have relied on the same tactics. However, to be effective, the police must think outside the box; they must use the SARA model and select tactics that best fit the problem. This not only leads to a reduction in drug problems, but also results in better police-community relations.

Community policing offers a commonsense approach to the drug and crime problems. Community policing is more than the Weed and Seed programs. Those programs were designed to couple enforcement with community building. Planners believed that enforcement (weeding) was necessary to clear an area before community building programs (seeding) could be implemented. Roehl (1995) evaluated the programs and found that the police concentrated on weeding and gave little consideration to seeding. As history has proven, the police will not be successful in ridding society of drug and crime problems by focusing singularly on enforcement; the police also must be actively involved in community building. Community building as a police strategy must be ever-present, especially when there is active law enforcement.

KEY TERMS IN CHAPTER 10

- Bureau of Alcohol, Tobacco, and Firearms
- buy-busts
- corruption
- crackdowns
- DARE
- discreet drug trafficking
- drug abuse resistance education
- Drug Enforcement Agency
- drug free zone
- drug nuisance abatement
- Drug Usage Forecast
- Federal Bureau of Investigation
- harm reduction
- high-level enforcement
- indiscreet drug trafficking
- informants
- interdiction
- moral drug war
- multi-jurisdictional drug task forces
- raids
- raves
- retail-level
- reverse stings
- street-level drug enforcement
- trafficking hierarchy
- undercover drug buys
- U.S. Customs Service

DISCUSSION QUESTIONS

1. The authors make the statement: "The war on drugs is cloaked in imagery." First describe what is meant by this statement and then discuss how this imagery impacts certain segments of society.
2. At what level of the drug distribution market (e.g., high level, street level) are local police best equipped to attack? At what level are police least equipped to attack?
3. One drug control strategy has been to interdict shipments of illicit drugs and narcotics by focusing on high-level dealers. What effect has this strategy had on drug kingpins and their organizations? On the price and availability of illicit drugs?
4. Should police allocate the majority of their resources toward stopping discreet or indiscreet drug sales? Why?
5. When and where were DARE programs implemented? What have research studies concluded about the effectiveness of DARE programs?
6. If sweeps or crackdowns are to be employed in a neighborhood, what role should the community policing officer play in the process?
7. How can visual harassment be used in community policing to reduce illicit drug activities?
8. List and briefly discuss the reasons cited in the text as to why community policing is a viable approach in addressing the illicit drug problem in communities.
9. Discuss the ways in which community policing efforts could be directed at juveniles to prevent drug use.

References

Boyum, D., Caulkins, J., & Kleiman, M. (2011). Drugs, Crime, and Public Policy. In J. Wilson & J. Petersilia (Eds.), *Crime and Public Policy* (pp. 368–410). New York: Oxford University Press.

Brown, B. (2006). Understanding and Assessing School Police Officers: A Conceptual and Methodological Comment. *Journal of Criminal Justice, 34,* 591-604.

Brownsberger, W., Aromaa, S., Brownsberger, C., & Brownsberger, S. (2004). An Empirical Study of the School Zone Anti-Drug Law in Three Cities in Massachusetts. *Journal of Drug Issues, 34*, 933-949.

Burke, S. (2001). The Advantages of a School Resource Officer. *Law and Order, 49*(9), 73-75.

Carter, D. (1995). Community Policing and DARE: A Practitioner's Perspective. *BJA Bulletin*. Washington, DC: Bureau of Justice Administration.

Christie, N. (2000). *Crime Control as Industry: Toward Gulags, Western Style* (3rd ed.). New York, NY: Routledge.

Cohen, Jacqueline, Wilpen, Gorr & Piyusha, Singh (2003). Estimating Intervention effects in Varying Risk Settings: Do Police Raids Reduce Illegal Drug Dealing at Nuisance Bars? *Criminology, 41*, 257-292.

Cook, R., & Roehl, J. (1993). National Evaluation of the Community Partnership Program: Preliminary Findings. In R. Davis, A. Lurigio, & D. Rosenbaum (Eds.), *Drugs and the Community* (pp. 225-250). Springfield, IL: Charles C Thomas.

Crank, J. P. (2004). *Understanding Police Culture* (2nd ed.). Newark, NJ: LexisNexis Matthew Bender/Anderson Publishing.

Davis, R. C., & Lurigio, A. J. (1996). *Fighting Back: Neighborhood Anti-drug Strategies*. Thousand Oaks, CA: Sage Publications.

Davis, R. C., Smith, B. E., Lurigio, A. J., & Skogan, W. G. (1991). Community Response to Crack: Grassroots Anti-Drug Programs. *Report of the Victim Services Agency, New York, to the National Institute of Justice*.

DrugWarFacts.com. (2011). *Prisons, Jails, & Probation Overview*. http://www.drugwarfacts.org/cms/Prisons_and_Jails#Data Accessed 06.04.11.

Gaines, Larry K., & Peter Kraska, (Editors), (2003). Drugs, Crime and Justice Contemporary Perspectives (second edition). Waveland Press, Inc.

Goode, E. (2005). *Drugs in American Society*. New York: McGraw-Hill.

Hawdon, J., & Ryan, J. (2003). Police-Resident Interactions and Satisfaction with Police: An Empirical Test of Community Policing Assertions. *Criminal Justice Policy Review, 14*, 55-74.

Kappeler, V. E. (1998). Can We Continue to Incarcerate Non-Violent Drug Offenders? In C. B. Fields (Ed.), *Issues in Corrections*. New York, NY: Allyn & Bacon.

Kappeler, V. E., & Potter, G. W. (2005). *The Mythology of Crime and Criminal Justice* (4th ed.). Prospect Heights, IL: Waveland Press.

Kappeler, V. E., Sluder, R., & Alpert, G. P. (1998). *Forces of Deviance: Understanding the Dark Side of Policing* (2nd ed.). Prospect Heights, IL: Waveland Press.

Katz, C., Webb, V., & Schaefer, D. (2001). An Assessment of the Impact of Quality-of-Life Policing on Crime and Disorder. *Justice Quarterly, 18*, 825-876.

Kleiman, M., & Smith, K. (1990). State and Local Drug Enforcement: In Search of a Strategy. In M. Tonry & J. Wilson (Eds.), *Drugs and Crime* (pp. 69-108). Chicago, IL: University of Chicago Press.

Kraska, P. B., & Kappeler, V. E. (1997). Militarizing American Police: The Rise and Normalization of Paramilitary Units. *Social Problems*, *44*(1), 1-18.

Lombardo, R., Olson, D., & Staton, M. (2010). The Chicago Alternative Policing Strategy: A Reassessment of the CAPS Program. *Policing*, *33*, 586-606.

Lusane, C. (1990). *Pipe Dream Blues*. Boston, MA: Beacon Press.

Mazerolle, L., Price, J., & Roehl, J. (2000). Civil Remedies and Drug Control: A Randomized Field Trial in Oakland, California. *Evaluation Review*, *24*, 212-241.

Mazerolle, L., Soole, D., & Rombouts, S. (2007). Drug Law Enforcement: A Review of the Evaluation Literature. *Police Quarterly*, *10*, 115-153.

McBride, D.C., and McCoy, C.B. (1993). The drugs-crime relationship: An analytical framework. *The Prison Journal*, *73*(3-4), 257-278.

McBride, D. C., & McCoy, C. B. (2003). The Drugs-Crime Relationship: An Analytical Framework. In L. Gaines & P. Kraska (Eds.), *Drugs, Crime, and Justice*. Prospect Heights, IL: Waveland.

Moore, M., & Kleiman, M. (2003). The Police and Drugs. In L. Gaines & P. Kraska (Eds.), *Drugs, Crime, and Justice* (pp. 248-267). Prospect Heights, IL: Waveland.

National Commission on Civil Disorders (1968). *Report of the National Advisory Commission on Civil Disorders.* New York, NY: Bantam Books.

Office of National Drug Control Policy (2011). *Fact Sheet: 2009 National Survey on Drug Use and Health.* Washington, DC: Author.

Phillips, C. (1989, September 6). Houston Group Battles, Reclaims Park. *The Wall Street Journal*, Sec. A, 10-11.

Pooley, E. (1989, January 12). Fighting Back against Crack. *New York Magazine*, 39.

Reaves, B. (2010). *Local Police Departments, 2007.* Washington, DC: Bureau of Justice Statistics.

Reisig, M., & Parks, R. (2003). Neighborhood Context, Police Behavior, and Satisfaction with Police. *Justice Research and Policy*, *5*, 37-65.

Reuter, P., Crawford, G., & Cace, J. (1988). *Sealing the Borders: The Effects of Increased Military Participation in Drug Interdiction* (R-3594-USDP). Santa Monica, CA: The RAND Corporation.

Roehl, J. (1995). *National Evaluation of the Weed and Seed Initiative.* Washington, DC: National Institute of Justice.

Ronsek, D., & Maier, P. (1991). Bars, Blocks and Crimes Revisited: Linking the Theory of Routine Activities to the Empiricism of Hot Spots. *Criminology*, *29*, 725-753.

Rosenbaum, D., Flewelling, R. L., Bailey, S. L., Ringwalt, C. L., & Wilkinson, D. L. (1994). Cops in the Classroom: A Longitudinal Evaluation of Drug Abuse Resistance Education (DARE). *Journal of Research in Crime and Delinquency*, *31*(1), 3-31.

SAMHSA (2010). *Results from the 2009 National Survey on Drugs and Health: Volume I, Summary of Findings.* Rockville, MD: Office of Applied Statistics, SAMHSA.

SAMHSA (2011). *Drug Abuse Network*. https://dawninfo.samhsa.gov/data/. Accessed 06.04.11.

Sherman, L. (1990). Police Crackdowns. *NIJ Reports*, March/April. Washington, DC: National Institute of Justice.

Skolnick, J. (1994). *Justice without Trial* (3rd ed.). New York, NY: John Wiley & Sons.

Skolnick, J. H. (1990). A Critical Look at the National Drug Control Strategy. *Yale Law and Policy Review*, *8*(1), 75-116.

Smith, B.W., Novak, K.J., Frank, J. & Travis III, L.F. (2000). Multijurisdictional Drug Task Forces: An Analysis of Impacts. *Journal of Criminal Justice*. 24(6), 543-556.

Wehrman, M., & De Angelis, J. (2011). Citizen Willingness to Participate in Police-Community Partnerships: Exploring the Influence of Race and Neighborhood Context. *Police Quarterly*, *14*, 48-69.

Weisburd, D., & Eck, J. (2004). What Can Police Do to Reduce Crime, Disorder, and Fear? *Annals of the American Academy of Political and Social Sciences*, *593*, 42-65.

Weisburd, D., & Green, L. (1995). Policing Drug Hot Spots: The Jersey City Drug Market Analysis Experiment. *Justice Quarterly*, *12*, 712-735.

Wysong, E., Aniskiewicz, R., & Wright, D. (1994). Truth and DARE: Tracking Drug Education to Graduation and as Symbolic Politics. *Social Problems*, *41*(3), 448-471.

Zimmer, L. (1990). Proactive Policing Against Street-Level Drug Trafficking. *American Journal of Police*, *9*(1), 43-74.

Non-violence is an unchangeable creed. It has to be pursued in the face of violence raging around you. The path of true non-violence requires much more courage than violence.

—Gandhi

CHAPTER 11   Community Policing and Special Populations

By counterbalancing the emphasis on reacting to calls for service with a proactive focus on solving problems, community policing addresses many needs that would otherwise be left unmet as a result of traditional law enforcement tactics. Community policing requires that the police extend personalized services to many groups whose concerns historically have been overlooked. Traditional policing tends to limit the department's response to crimes and those who commit them. Community policing broadens the police mission, sending community policing officers (CPOs) into the community as outreach specialists, so that they can learn about community problems and provide a measure of service to a wide variety of constituent populations.

Even as early as the latter part of the nineteenth century, the police singled out special groups for attention. The police worked with the infirm and sick, the homeless, juveniles, criminals, and women (Douthit, 1975; Whitehouse, 1973). During this period, the police were very service-oriented. Local politicians knew that they could garner more votes and support from people when their police officers helped people as opposed to arresting them or issuing citations. In fact, in many instances, the police totally neglected their law-enforcement duties. This philosophy resulted in the police providing a wide variety of services to the public. Politicians, rather than the needs and desires of the community, however, most often drove the provisions of these services.

This orientation disappeared in the 1950s as professional policing came to dominate police thinking. During the professional era, the police implemented a bureaucratic, monolithic organization and concentrated on law enforcement and crook catching. Providing services to people was seen as being outside the purview of police duties. This remained the case into the 1960s when large-scale urban and campus rioting caused the police to rethink their position. The human relations problems of the 1960s made the police realize that law enforcement alone was not adequate in serving the people. Since the 1960s, many police agencies have adopted a service orientation that continues today with community policing. Community policing provides a new organizational model that encourages the police to address the problems of groups who have not routinely turned to the police for help. Community policing also fosters the idea that the police cannot handle crime problems alone. The police must engage the public in a partnership and cooperatively address complex problems.

Community policing, without question, has caused the police to be more attentive to people's needs and concerns. In the past, the police relied on the political process to help guide policy decisions. That is, people would contact governmental officials such as city council persons who then would discuss problems with the police. Unfortunately, many groups such as the poor, elderly, minorities, and youth were neglected as a result of the process, because they have little or no clout or access to government. Community policing results in direct communication between the police and the public in an effort to ensure that all constituent groups are considered and serviced. Essentially, policing becomes people-oriented, whereby the police favor no singular group and attempt to meet everyone's needs.

Critics of the police working more closely with people note that it may very well contribute to renewed police corruption. Part of the impetus for the professional movement was to separate the police from the public and reduce police corruption (Gaines & Kappeler, 2011). During the 1950s, insulating the police from the public, along with closer supervision and better management practices, was thought to decrease police corruption. It is feared that community policing may indeed result in a renewed cycle of corruption or in civil liability (Kappeler, 2005) as the police are better able to forge closer working relationships, some of which have unwholesome designs, with a variety of people.

The potential benefits from community policing far outweigh its potential problems. Many groups, often those who suffer the highest rates of victimization, are literally disenfranchised from the American political system, and community policing is the most appropriate way for the police to identify these individuals and groups and attempt to bring them back into the system. For example, the homeless do not have a fixed address so they generally are not represented in the political system. Juveniles are too young, and many immigrants have no vote and are too fearful to become involved in the political process. Residents of many of the highest-crime areas are also among the groups least likely to exercise their franchise. Many such groups also fail to organize, they lack the money to lobby for their concerns, and their relative lack of social standing means they are unlikely to gain formal and informal access to those who hold power. Community policing as a political modality allows such individuals to have input into government and receive some measure of service.

Community policing's ability to involve the disenfranchised and to reach out to groups who are reluctant to contact the police offers everyone in the community grass roots input into the police process. The following is a discussion of specific groups that are likely to benefit from community policing.

Juveniles

Juveniles represent a special problem for community policing. On the one hand, juvenile crime, especially violent crime, is portrayed as increasing. It is politicized to the point that many legislative bodies passed stricter laws in terms of penalties and how juveniles are processed in the criminal justice system. On the other hand, juveniles remain one of the most victimized groups in society (Kappeler & Potter, 2005). Advocates claim that child abuse, neglect, and abandonment have substantially increased over the past several years. For example, in 2008, American child protection service agencies investigated over 2 million reports of child maltreatment involving 3.7 million children, and 24 percent of the cases investigated were substantiated (OJJDP, 2010). Children are twice as likely as adults to be victims of serious violent crime and twice as likely to be assaulted (OJJDP, 2000). The National Child Traumatic Stress Network (2011) reports that in any given year, there are 200,000 homeless children. Of those who end up homeless, 80 percent report being the victim of sexual abuse at home (Taylor, 1986).

There is evidence that child abuse and neglect create a **cycle of abuse**. The cycle of abuse is created when a child is abused and that abuse becomes a factor or contributes to the child becoming an abuser in adulthood. Malinosky-Rummell and Hansen (1993), Widom and Maxfield (2001), and Finkelhor and his colleagues (2010) note that children who are physically abused or neglected tend to become offenders later in life. Fisk (1996) found that child abuse often results in mental disorders later in life. The cycle of violence implies that the police can prevent a substantial amount of crime, delinquency, and abuse by effectively dealing with it.

Mounting evidence also suggests a link between childhood sexual victimization and adult sex offenses. Of the 255 sex offenders in the Massachusetts Treatment Center, 90 percent reported they were sexually abused as children (Brand, 1987). While these estimates are most certainly inflated (Kappeler & Potter, 2005), children represent a special population as well as a distinctive victim population. Community policing must address both problems within the juvenile population.

> You can learn more about juvenile victimization and crime by going to http://bjs.ojp.usdoj.gov/index .cfm?ty=pbdetail&iid=1041.

In terms of juvenile victims, Fleisher, (1995) in a study in Seattle, found that on some nights there were more children on the streets at 2:00 A.M. than there were at 4:00 P.M. Many of these children were runaways, castaways, or out on the streets because their parents did not want them or care about them. Introduction to the street life generally meant that they eventually became criminals who were in and out of jails and prison all their lives as the path to survival consists of panhandling and crime. When a juvenile is encountered at 2:00 A.M., the police should make sure that something is done.

An investigation by the police and social agencies should be initiated, and action should be taken to ensure that the juvenile is cared for. Not only is it an indictment on the police, but it is also telling of society when we have children walking the streets in the early hours of the day.

In terms of abused children, the police must take an active role in discovering, investigating, and prosecuting such cases. They must come to see themselves as the first line of defense in protecting the nation's children. The police can deploy three general strategies to accomplish this objective. First, the police must become more active in attempting to identify abused and exploited children. For example, how often do police officers check on children when they answer calls at a residence? Because child abuse is more common in homes where other forms of domestic violence occur, the police should always check on the well-being of any children, even though they may not be a part of the original complaint. The same holds true for those homes where problems of alcoholism and drug abuse are apparent. When there are suspicious circumstances, the police should thoroughly investigate them. Police officers should be trained to recognize signs of abuse, and they should know how to respond to it. When the police otherwise come into contact with children, they should take the opportunity to talk with them and inquire into the possibilities of abuse.

It is also important for the police to cooperate with the social agencies, such as children's protective services and other family service agencies, which are directly involved in investigating child abuse and neglect. In the past, the police and social workers functioned independently, often conducting parallel investigations. These parallel investigations often were incomplete and contained conflicting information. Realistically, both agencies have similar goals, the welfare of children. The Louisville, Kentucky, Police Department has developed a working relationship with the Kentucky Department of Social Services whereby officers and social workers meet to discuss cases, and in some cases perform joint investigations. This not only leads to more effective investigations, but officers are able to fairly quickly provide services to children in need. Close working relationships between the police and social workers can result in less bureaucratic red tape as cases and problems arise. It also results in criminal charges being placed when appropriate and children being removed from dangerous homes or environments more quickly.

Third, in the role of community liaison, a CPO can also link families to public and private agencies who can help, whether that is in the form of affordable counseling for the juvenile or perhaps a substance abuse program for one or both of the parents. CPOs' intense involvement with the community allows them to reach out to families who need assistance; at the same time it increases the likelihood that people will trust them enough to ask for help. CPOs, when appropriate, should act as family counselors and encourage adults to get help for problems that lead to abuse and delinquency. When they fail to seek help on their own, CPOs should bring in social workers to appraise the situation and take action to alleviate dangerous or unacceptable situations.

Juvenile Crime and Violence

Substantial attention to juvenile violent crime began in the 1980s. Juvenile violent crime escalated as a result of America's increasing drug problem. In the 1990s, there were a number of school shootings involving multiple victims. Some predicted that juvenile violent crime would become epidemic (Snyder & Sickmund, 1995). However, this was not the case. In 2009, there were approximately 7,200 homicides in the United States, and juveniles committed only 652. There were 390,328 total violent crimes, with juveniles committing only 51,740. Juveniles

committed approximately one-quarter of all property offenses, with larceny/
theft being the most common crime committed by juveniles (FBI, 2010). Juvenile
crime, like crimes committed by adults, has been decreasing. Nonetheless, it
remains a problem, and community policing has an important role in combating
it. Criminologists have long studied juvenile crime and developed a number of
theories explaining it. Some of these theories explain crime in terms of socialization, social bonding, association, social disorganization, conflict, or strain. However,
the most useful theory is **life-course theory**. Life-course theory states that much
criminal behavior begins at an early age as a result of exposure to multiple interwoven social, economic, and educational problems (Piquero & Mazerolle, 2001).
When there are multiple problems, the juvenile develops a cumulative disadvantage. This cumulative disadvantage starts a juvenile on the path of criminality.
It also postulates that there are intervening factors, such as a job, marriage, and
success in school, that can bring the criminality to a halt. These factors have come
to be known as risk factors. Howell (2004) has identified the risk factors that can
result in criminality.

Figure 11.1 lists a multitude of factors that can contribute to delinquency and
crime. They include community, family, school, peers, and individual factors. As the
number of risk factors increases for a juvenile, it increases the likelihood that he
or she will become involved in delinquency or crime. Life-course and risk factors
are useful in that they provide guidance on the development of juvenile crime
prevention programming. They also demonstrate that delinquency and crime prevention generally cannot occur using a simplistic approach. That is, prevention is
most effective when multiple risk factors for a given juvenile are addressed.

There are additional causes of violence among young people. The National
Coalition of State Juvenile Justice Advisory Groups (1992) report the following
to be causal factors:

- Abuse and neglect;

- Economic, social, and educational conditions;

- Gangs; and

- Accessibility of weapons.

Martin (1994) suggests other causes:

- Hopelessness and exposure to violence;

- Weakening of the family unit;

- Media celebration of violence; and

- Drug culture leading to a gun culture.

Figure 11.1
Risk Factors for Young Gang Membership

Domain	Risk factors	Sources
Community	Social disorganization, including poverty and residential mobility	Curry and Spergel, 1988
	Organized lowerclass communities	Miller, 1958; Moore, 1991
	Underclass communities	Bursik and Grasmick, 1993; Hagedorn, 1988; Moore, 1978, 1985, 1988, 1991; Moore, Vigil, and Garcia, 1983; Sullivan, 1989
	Presence of gangs in the neighborhood	Curry and Spergel, 1992
	Availability of drugs in the neighborhood	Curry and Spergel, 1992; Hagedorn, 1988, 1994a, 1994b; Hill et al., in press; Kosterman et al., 1996; Moore, 1978, 1991; Sanchez-Jankowski, 1991; Taylor, 1989
	Availability of firearms	Lizotte et al., 1994; Miller, 1992; Newton and Zimring, 1969
	Barriers to and lack of social and economic opportunities	Cloward and Ohlin, 1960; Cohen, 1960; Fagan, 1990; Hagedorn, 1988, 1994b; Klein, 1995; Moore, 1990; Short and Strodtbeck, 1965; Vigil, 1988
	Lack of social capital	Short, 1996; Sullivan, 1989; Vigil, 1988
	Cultural norms supporting gang behavior	Miller, 1958; Short and Strodtbeck, 1965
	Feeling unsafe in neighborhood; high crime	Kosterman et al., 1996; Vigil. 1988
	Conflict with social control institutions	Vigil, 1988
Family	Family disorganization, including broken homes and parental drug/alcohol abuse	Bjerregaard and Smith, 1993; Esbensen, Huizinga, and Weiher, 1993; Hill et al., in press; Vigil, 1988
	Troubled families, including incest, family violence, and drug addiction	Moore, 1978, 1991; Vigil, 1988
	Family members in a gang	Curry and Spergel, 1992; Moore, 1991; Moore, Vigil, and Garcia, 1983
	Lack of adult male role models	Miller, 1958; Vigil, 1988
	Lack of parental role models	Wang, 1995
	Low socioeconomic status	Almost all studies
	Extreme economic deprivation, family management problems, parents with violent attitudes, sibling antisocial behavior	Hill et al., in press; Kosterman et al., 1996
School	Academic failure	Bjerregaard and Smith, 1993; Curry and Spergel, 1992; Kosterman et al., 1996
	Low educational aspirations, especially among females	Bjerregaard and Smith, 1993; Hill et al., in press; Kosterman et al., 1996
	Negative labeling by teachers	Esbensen and Huizinga, 1993; Esbensen, Huizinga, and Weiher, 1993
	Trouble at school	Kosterman et al., 1996
	Few teacher role models	Wang, 1995
	Educational frustration	Curry and Spergel, 1992
	Low commitment to school, low school attachment, high levels of antisocial behavior in school, low achievement test scores, and identification as being learning disabled	Hill et al., in press

Source: Howell, J.C. (2004). "Youth Gangs: An Overview." *Juvenile Justice Bulletin*, August:6-7.

(Continued)

Figure 11.1—Cont'd

Domain	Risk factors	Sources
Peer Group	High commitment to delinquent peers	Bjerregaard and Smith, 1993; Esbensen and Huizinga, 1993; Vigil and Yun, 1990
	Low commitment to positive peers	Esbensen, Huizinga, and Weiher, 1993
	Street socialization	Vigil, 1988
	Gang members in class	Curry and Spergel, 1992
	Friends who use drugs or who are gang members	Curry and Spergel, 1992
	Friends who are drug distributors	Curry and Spergel, 1992
	Interaction with delinquent peers	Hill et al., in press; Kosterman et al., 1996
Individual	Prior delinquency	Bjerregaard and Smith, 1993; Curry and Spergel, 1992; Esbensen and Huizinga, 1993; Kosterman et al., 1996
	Deviant attitudes	Esbensen, Huizinga, and Weiher, 1993; Fagan, 1990; Hill et al., in press; Kosterman et al., 1996
	Street smartness; toughness	Miller, 1958
	Defiant and individualistic character	Miller, 1958; Sanchez-Jankowski, 1991
	Fatalistic view of the world	Miller, 1958
	Aggression	Campbell, 1984a, 1984b; Cohen, 1960; Horowitz, 1983; Miller, Geertz, and Cutter, 1962; Sanchez-Jankowski, 1991
	Proclivity for excitement and trouble	Miller, 1958; Pennell et al., 1994
	Locura (acting in a daring, courageous, and especially crazy fashion in the face of adversity)	Moore, 1991; Vigil, 1988
	Higher levels of normlessness in the context of family, peer group, and school	Esbensen, Huizinga, and Weiher, 1993 Short and Strodtbeck, 1965; Vigil, 1988
	Social disabilities	
	Illegal gun ownership	Bjerregaard and Lizotte, 1995; Lizotte et al., 1994; Vigil and Long, 1990
	Early or precocious sexual activity, especially among females	Kosterman et al., 1996; Bjerregaard and Smith, 1993
	Alcohol and drug use	Bjerregaard and Smith, 1993; Curry and Spergel, 1992; Esbensen, Huizinga, and Weiher, 1993; Hill et al., in press; Thornberry et al., 1993; Vigil and Long, 1990
	Drug trafficking	Fagan, 1990; Thornberry et al., 1993
	Desire for group rewards such as status, identity, self-esteem, companionship, and protection	Curry and Spergel. 1992; Fagan, 1990; Horowitz, 1983; Horowitz and Schwartz, 1974; Moore, 1978, 1991; Short and Strodtbeck, 1965
	Problem behaviors, hyperactivity, externalizing behaviors, drinking, lack of refusal skills, and early sexual activity	Hill et al., in press; Kosterman et al., 1996
	Victimization	Fagan, 1990

The causes of violence have direct implications for community policing. First, and perhaps most importantly, it seems that violence begets violence. Many of the teens who are committing violent acts are themselves victims of violence or are subjected to it on a fairly regular basis (Potter & Kappeler, 2006). Effective programming must be multiple-pronged, and it must involve CPOs working closely and partnering with other agencies and service providers. As many risk factors as possible should be addressed by the CPOs and partner agencies.

Juvenile delinquency and crime are not equally distributed across space; there are geographical concentrations. When developing juvenile crime prevention programs, CPOs should first concentrate on those areas where the problem is concentrated. This results in a larger number of juveniles being targeted. The first step when addressing these hot spots is to attack neighborhood disorganization. Vital, functioning neighborhoods have less crime and are more resistant to crime. To this end, CPOs should become involved in community or neighborhood building. CPOs can work with neighborhood leaders to develop cohesiveness in the neighborhood. When this occurs there is more place management whereby citizens are more likely to report problems to the police and take proactive actions themselves. There are a number of activities the police can facilitate, including neighborhood rallies, block watches, citizen patrols, and an increased police presence. People and the police both must understand that the problem cannot be solved without cooperation.

The police must also become involved in providing recreational, civic, and cultural services to the area. The Lexington, Kentucky, Police Department, with the support of the Public Housing Authority and the Parks and Recreation Department, operates a **Police Athletic League** (PAL) to provide a variety of services to disadvantaged youth. The program offers youth a variety of sports including football and basketball. The department attempts to have sporting programs in place most of the year. The PAL centers are equipped with computers that are used to provide classes to both youth and adults. The computers are also equipped with a variety of game and entertainment software to provide meaningful recreation to area youth. The department has a mentoring program whereby local celebrities such as University of Kentucky basketball players make appearances and give talks. The Public Housing Authority sponsors a number of cultural events including ballet, modern dance, and self-esteem and pride training. A great deal of juvenile crime is the result of youth not being occupied with productive activities. Recreational activities occupy them and help to instill positive values and relations with positive role models.

Crime in Schools

In the 2008-2009 school year, there were an estimated 55.6 million students enrolled in schools throughout the United States (Snyder & Dillow, 2010). Schools have a substantial volume of crime as a result of the concentration of children and young adults. In 2009, 31 percent of students in grades 9-12 reported they had been in a physical fight at least once in the previous 12 months, 17 percent of students reported carrying a weapon at least once in the last 30 days, and 8 percent of students reported being threatened with a weapon (Robers et al., 2010). Schools, however, are some of the safest places for children. As Figure 11.2 indicates, children are less likely to be the victims of a homicide in schools as compared to any other place.

These statistics demonstrate that schools have concentrations of minor crimes, with some schools having higher levels of crime than others. Traditionally, the police have left school crime problems to school officials. The police must work with school systems to reduce the levels of crime and violence. This will require more programs where police officers are involved in the intervention of crime and crime prevention in schools. CPOs are ideally prepared for these programs. As a result of their jobs and training they are better able to develop rapport with students, and they can easily work with school officials.

Felson (2009) attributes a great deal of the problem to the fact that school systems for the past several decades have been merging smaller high schools into larger, cost-efficient high schools. Many high schools now have in excess of 1,000 students. These larger schools remove the intimacy, where, in the past, principals, teachers, and staff knew, or at least recognized, all the students. Now students are able to blend into the unknown crowd when they commit assaults

Figure 11.2
Number of School-Associated Homicides and Suicides of Youth Ages 5-18, by Location: 2007–2008

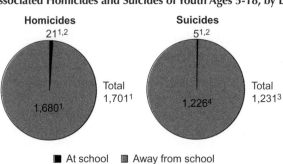

Source: Robers, S., J. Zhang, J. Truman & T. Snyder (2010). *Indicators of School Crime and Safety: 2010.* Washington, DC: U.S. Department of Education and U.S. Department of Justice Office Justice Programs.

You can learn more about crime in schools by going to http://bjs.ojp.usdoj.gov/index.cfm?ty=tp&tid=974.

and other criminal acts. School staff now control crowds rather than individual students. Felson (2009) also notes that routes to these larger schools are where a great deal of crime occurs. Large groups of teenagers are able to congregate unsupervised, which can lead to vandalism and other criminal acts.

SPOTLIGHT ON COMMUNITY POLICING PRACTICE

Bullying and the LGBT Community: Trends and Solutions from the Office of Safe and Drug-Free Schools

Carl Joseph Walker Hoover is a name that the members of New Leadership Charter School will not soon forget. Known as a bright and ambitious 6th grader, on April 6, 2009, his body was discovered by his mother after he hung himself in an upstairs room of their Springfield, Massachusetts home. It was discovered that Carl was the target of a daily barrage of anti-gay language and taunts from bullies at his school. The constant terror every day was enough to make Carl want to end his own life, even when his sexual orientation was not known to be gay. Most disturbingly, these cases of "bully-cide" have become increasingly common. In recent years, episodes of bullying related to anti-gay sentiments have resulted in suicides like that of college freshman Tyler Clementi in 2010, who chose to jump off the George Washington Bridge rather than continue to face harassments stemming from his sexual orientation. These are the tragic stories that anti-bullying advocates such as Assistant Deputy Secretary Kevin Jennings of the Office of Safe and Drug-Free Schools, U.S. Department of Education hope will generate a better understanding of what bullying entails, and what forces within schools and beyond can do to help. In a discussion centered on understanding bullying at the U.S. Department of Justice's RFK building on January 26, 2011, Jennings emphasized the need for recognizing not only why some groups are targets for potential bullying, but also what needs to be done through policy and other support to combat this trend.

Two out of the top three reasons for being bullied were because people perceived the victim as either gay, lesbian, or bisexual, or by how masculine or feminine they seemed. These descriptors target populations of lesbian, gay, bisexual, and transsexual (LGBT) students who are more likely to be at risk for encountering physically or emotionally damaging taunts, language, and threats due to sexual orientation or affiliation with LGBT individuals. Bullying can make them feel enough shame to even hide the trouble from loved ones, resulting in a sense of hopeless isolation that restrains them from seeking help and can result in the taking of desperate measures instead of suffering the victimization any longer.

What can society and schools themselves do to deter bullies who target those perceived to be a member of, identify with, or are affiliated with LGBT groups? Although the Equal Access Act, implemented in 1984, guarantees the rights of students to form clubs such as gay-straight alliances, there is no federal anti-bullying law in place to protect LGBT students from harassment from their peers. Where does one start to find the solutions necessary to build up the policies essential to ensure a student's safety?

Jennings presented many optimal solutions, with the ultimate goals being that, "In a truly safe school, every student feels like they 1) belong, 2) are valued, and 3) are physically and emotionally safe." In order to meet such standards, Jennings suggested that schools must adopt principles that will educate faculty, staff, and parents about how to recognize bullying and how to intervene early, and also that places of education adopt policies that teachers and other school officials can stand behind and uphold when bullying incidences do occur.

At the federal level, the U.S. Department of Education has helped the inception of such solutions by awarding 11 states money from a pilot grant program known as Safe and Supportive Schools. These states have received federal funds to implement and measure progress in improving the conditions for learning in their schools. The goal is to increase feelings of safety (physical, emotional, and the absence of substance abuse) as well as measure what types of support students receive (or don't) in regards to their relationships at school, their participation in school activities, and aspects of their environment that do or do not promote well-being.

Not only does the apparent need for grant funds being expressed at the state level bring encouragement, it is also promising to see agencies at the federal level, including the COPS Office and other Department of Justice entities, collaborating in Bullying Prevention Working Groups. Together these partners have accomplished great things, such as the organization of the National Bullying Summit, held in August 2010. Their action plans have promoted best practices in bullying policies, as well as what research needs to be done regarding "bully-cides" and their prevention.

The Office of Safe and Drug-Free Schools is highly invested in deterring the bullying epidemic. With the U.S. Department of Education and other federal allies at the helm of such policies, the end goal of maintaining students' safety, support, and feelings of belonging are of the utmost importance. Every student has the right to feel safe and secure in their learning environment, and with the proper awareness and implementation of policies being done today, we can intervene and prevent incidences like Carl Hoover's suicide from happening.

Danielle Ouellette
Program Specialist
The COPS Office

Source: The e-newsletter of the COPS Office, Volume 4, Issue 3, March 2011 [citations omitted].

Youth gangs are a particular problem in some schools. Although many gang members abhor school, many attend schools and see schools as a part of their turf. They recruit members from within schools and assault and intimidate students. Robers and her colleagues (2010) report that 20 percent of public schools report having gangs, and 23 percent of students reported there were gangs in their schools. Figure 11.3 shows some of the problems in public schools.

Figure 11.3

Percentage of Public Schools Reporting Selected Discipline Problems That Occurred at School, by School Level: School Year 2007-2008

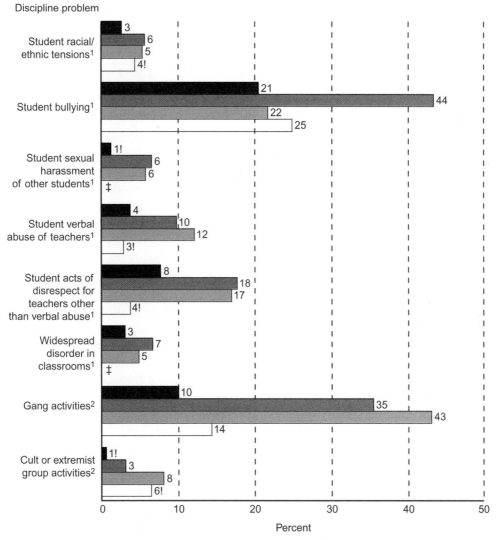

Source: Robers, S., J. Zhang, J. Truman & T. Snyder (2010). *Indicators of School Crime and Safety: 2010.* Washington, DC: U.S. Department of Education and U.S. Department of Justice Office Justice Programs.

School administrators must recognize the existence of such problems and act on them when they occur. The Office of Juvenile Justice and Delinquency Prevention (1994) has identified three components of an effective school-based gang control strategy:

- The development of a school gang code, with guidelines specifying an appropriate response by teachers and staff to different kinds of gang behavior, including a mechanism for dealing with serious gang delinquency;

- The application of these rules and regulations within a context of positive relationships and open communication by school personnel with parents, community agencies, and students; and

- A clear distinction between gang- and non-gang-related activity, so as not to exaggerate the scope of the problem (1994:18).

CPOs should be assigned to work with school officials in developing programs within the schools to reduce drug abuse, crime, and violence. The police should take a more active role in investigating drug and crime problems on school property. In the past, the schools have unfortunately attempted to handle such problems internally and cover them up effectively. When the schools did take action, it usually was in the form of suspensions or expulsions, which, for the most part, are ineffective in dealing with problem students. In fact, denying educational opportunity seems a certain recipe for increasing crime. School officials must understand and accept that in some cases the juvenile justice system is better equipped to deal with problems. A number of states have now passed laws that require schools to report criminal violations to the police.

> You can learn more about school safety by going to http://bjs.ojp.usdoj.gov/index .cfm?ty=pbdetail&iid=2231.

Conversely, the police should cooperate with the schools. A number of departments now have programs where they provide the school system with information on arrests of juveniles who are charged with drug or weapons offenses. Although the schools do not necessarily take any action, it does alert the school staff to the problems, and it may allow teachers and staff to monitor these students' activities more closely. Such information also may assist individual teachers in protecting themselves by carefully monitoring potentially violent students who are in their classes. There are, however, many issues, such as privacy and labeling of juveniles, which make this practice problematic.

Community policing substantially expands the police role regarding juveniles. In the past, the police merely monitored trouble areas and detained juveniles who committed criminal acts. Community policing requires that the police work with a variety of public and private agencies throughout the community in identifying problems and developing solutions to them.

Urban Youth Gangs

Urban youth gangs have become one of law enforcement's most difficult problems. Gangs not only exist in major cities, but they now have spread to medium-sized cities. A national survey estimated that in the United States there were approximately 27,900 youth gangs with approximately 774,000 members (Egley, Howell & Moore, 2010). The gangs are substantially involved in drug trafficking and indiscriminate violence. In one study, Curry and his colleagues (1994) found that gangs were responsible for 1,072 homicides and 46,359 crimes within a 12-month period, and in a similar study Maxson (2004) reported that about half of the homicides in Los Angeles County are gang related. More importantly, their violent nature has resulted in numerous deaths of innocent bystanders, which has caused public rage and massive fear. Youth gangs represent a problem that the police must make every effort to effectively handle. Moreover, they no longer are confined to urban areas; they are found in many suburban and rural communities.

Given the public attention provided to gangs, it would appear that they are a relatively new phenomenon. However, gangs have existed throughout history. A number of the organized crime groups that dominated American crime in the early and middle decades of the twentieth century began as gangs. Movies such as *Blackboard Jungle* and *West Side Story* focused public attention on the problem decades ago, but for the most part, until the 1980s, gangs existed almost exclusively on the east and west coasts and in Chicago (Miller, 1991). The spread of gangs into America's heartland has been attributed to drug trafficking. As the crack markets in the larger cities became saturated, the gangs formed in other cities or markets where there was little or no competition. The gangs also found that the police were inexperienced in dealing with them, which made it much easier for them to become entrenched in the community.

Given the public concern, and in some cases hysteria, associated with gangs, it is important to fully understand what a gang is. Too often the public and officials tend to label any group of young African Americans, Latinos, and in some cases, Asians, as gangs when in fact they do not constitute a gang. Indeed, it is important to note that many social or playgroups often are labeled as gangs. It is also important to note that although many people and officials equate gangs with minority groups, youth gangs exist within all racial groups (Freng & Winfree, 2004).

There is substantial disagreement and confusion as to what constitutes a gang (Esbensen et al., 2004). A large part of the confusion comes from the fact that there are degrees of "gangness." There are different classes or types of gang members. For example, Maxson (1998) discussed gang membership in terms of wannabe, core, fringe, associate, hardcore, and O.G. (original gangster). The wannabe and fringe members are generally on the periphery and are not involved in the more serious criminal activities. The associates are generally involved in drug trafficking and other criminal activities, while the hardcore or **O.G. gangsters** run the gang in terms of managing criminal enterprises and conflicts or wars with other gangs. Membership is often changing. Some research has found that many gang members come and go (e.g., wannabes, fringe, and associate players). Research has shown that on the average a gang member remains in a gang for less than one year (Hill, Lui & Hawkins, 2004).

As noted, it is difficult to accurately define a gang. Miller (1980) offers the following definition:

> A youth gang is a self-forming association of peers, bound together by mutual interests, with identifiable leadership, well-developed lines of authority, and other organizational features, who act in concert to achieve a specific purpose or purposes, which generally include the conduct of illegal activity and control over a particular territory, facility, or type of enterprise (1980:121).

In another definition, Klein (1971) identified three attributes of a gang:

- Generally perceived as a distinct aggregation or group by others in the neighborhood

- Recognize themselves as a denotable group, invariably with a group name, attire, or colors

- Have been involved in a number of delinquent and criminal acts to call for a consistent negative response from neighborhood residents and the police

It is important for the police to accurately identify gang members, especially the hardcore or O.G. gang members. Typically, some departments label any minority youth who gives them problems a gang member. Such a practice tends to exaggerate the problem and prevent the police from developing meaningful solutions. It can also enrage community members when the truth comes to light, or it may incite fear, complicating police-community relations. Sanders (1994) has perhaps developed the best criteria to be used by the police in identifying gang members:

- Admits to being a member of a gang;

- Has tattoos, clothing, or other paraphernalia which is associated with a particular gang;

- Police records or observations confirm association with other known gang members;

- Has been arrested with gang members while committing a gang-related crime; and

- A reliable informant confirms membership in a gang.

It should be noted that all sorts of gangs exist, but here we are more concerned with the youth gangs that have spread across the country. Youth gangs are cultural or entrepreneurial in nature. The **cultural gangs** are those which evolve in a particular neighborhood. They seem to originate as a result of social needs. Their members band together as a result of their familiarity with one another and the need for self-protection. Some have discussed the cultural gang in terms of the extended family where the gang serves to provide some of the belonging and nurturing functions that are often absent in many inner-city homes. They tend to establish a turf area and protect it from intrusion from other youth gangs. The **entrepreneurial gangs** tend to form as a result of the pecuniary benefits associated with drug trafficking. They band together to form a criminal business enterprise. This does not mean that cultural gangs are not involved in drug trafficking. They also deal in drugs as a result of the lucrative profits, but their primary objective is to fulfill a variety of social and cultural needs, especially in the area they see as their turf.

Some gangs have a distinctive organization. Gangs often are organized into sets, like the Bloods and Crips on the west coast. A set represents a particular neighborhood. For example, there are several thousand Bloods in Los Angeles. They are organized into sets, and each set is fairly independent from the other sets. In some cases, sets within the same gang may go to war with each other. Also, each set has an organization:

> The sets are structured along lines of seniority and function. They have caste-like sub-divisions within each set, notably (1) original gang members (O.G.); (2) gangsters, the hard-core members, whose ages range from 16 to 22; (3) **baby gangsters**, who are between nine and 12; and (4) in some cases, **tiny gangsters**, who are even younger. While some age groups go into the late 20s and early 30s, the most violent and active members are those between 14 and 18; many of the them are "**wanna-bees**" who want to prove themselves in order to be accepted by other gang members and who are precisely the ones most useful as soldiers in gang activities (Attorney General, 1989:33).

Gangs can develop throughout a city. For example, Figure 11.4 shows the organization of gangs for a section of Chicago. Chicago has three primary gangs and a host of other, smaller gangs. The map also depicts the patterns of violence. Note the areas are fairly evenly divided between turf-related violence and drug-related violence. There are also a number of areas that are relatively free of violence.

Between 1987 and 1990, there were 288 street gang-motivated homicides in Chicago. Only eight were drug-related. The data seem to indicate that the

Figure 11.4
Street Gang-Motivated Homicide, Other Violence, and Drug Crime

relationship between drugs, gangs, and homicide is rather weak and overstated. Indeed, research shows that gang violence is more often associated with turf and gang disrespect than with drug trafficking (Howell, 2004). Also, 51 percent of the city's gang-related homicides and 35 percent of nonlethal gang violence occurred in ten community areas. There was some level of variation in gang activities in the various community areas. In some cases, gangs were selling heroin, while gangs in other areas were concentrating on crack cocaine. All the gangs were engaged in a variety of criminal activities (Block & Block, 1993).

There seems to be some agreement about why kids are attracted to and join gangs. Howell (2004) has identified several reasons. First, gangs provide juveniles with prestige or status that otherwise is not available through conventional means. Cloward and Ohlin (1960) saw gangs form as a result of sparse access to legitimate means for accomplishing traditional goals or attaining success. Gangs represent an illegitimate means to accomplish goals such as wealth, power, and societal or neighborhood recognition. Second, gangs provide an opportunity for juveniles to be with others who are like themselves, causing girls to be attracted to gangs. Gangs are social networks that provide social and economic opportunities to their members. Third, gangs provide excitement. Juveniles and young adults often seek opportunities to engage in risky behavior for the excitement. Fourth, gangs often provide protection from other gangs. Many juveniles see gang membership as self-survival. Finally, gangs provide mentor members; they help members adjust to social problems. Since many gang members' families are dysfunctional, they have no one else to protect and guide them. There are a number of implications as a result of the research on gangs. First and perhaps foremost is that gangs form as a result of disorganization and disintegration that occur in neighborhoods. This, of course, is not a naturally occurring feature of communities, but rather a result of poor public policy and failed strategies. Failure of political leaders to invest in communities, people, and the social and economic infrastructure necessary to produce well-functioning communities causes disorganization and disintegration. These conditions are a direct result of poor public policy, a lack of investment in communities and people, and an unresponsive political system. Community policing is a comprehensive strategy that can be used to help rehabilitate neighborhoods and bring pressure to bear on local political officials. Essentially, neighborhoods, not gangs, are the problem. Improvements in neighborhoods can lead to a reduction in gang problems. Second, the police must develop a keen understanding of any gang problems and develop strategies tailored for individual problems. The research shows that a variety of gang problems can develop, and no individual strategy will be effective in every case. The police must collect data and information on problems, diagnose them fairly, and then deploy their resources accordingly. Perhaps most importantly, police must refrain from using the gang problem to generate people's fear.

As noted above, there are two general categories of gang members, fringe and hardcore. In terms of hardcore members, the police should maximally apply the law in an effort to remove these individuals from neighborhoods. The wannabes and fringe actors are a different story. They often have not become fully immersed in the gang. Community police officers should attempt to engage these youths and get them involved in pro-social activities. There is a high probability of success here, especially considering that many of these youths will disengage from the gang on their own

Community Policing and Gang Intervention Programs

Youth gangs represent a complex problem for law enforcement. Gang problems intertwine themselves throughout a community, which results in the opening of a number of fronts which require police action. All too often, police strategies have been reactive and fail to address gang problems comprehensively. The police must develop a host of strategies and tactics that address all aspects of the problem. The Office of Juvenile Justice and Delinquency Prevention (1994) identified tactics that have the potential to reduce gang problems:

- Targeting, arresting, and incarcerating gang leaders and repeat violent gang offenders;

- Referring fringe members and their parents to youth services for counseling and guidance;

- Providing preventative services for youths who are clearly at risk;

- Crisis intervention or mediation of gang fights; and

- Patrols of community [gang] hot spots.

An excellent example of how a department developed a comprehensive community policing approach to its gang problems is Reno, Nevada. The department established a Community Action Team (CAT) to deal with the expanding gang problem. The first step the CAT took was to gather intelligence about the gangs and their membership. The team was issued gang kits that consisted of cameras, field interview cards, and tape recorders. Police officers, suspects, and informants were interviewed in an effort to develop information about gang activities and membership. CAT members routinely visited the jail and interviewed prisoners to gather additional information. Once collected, the information was collected in a gang-related database.

CAT members then attempted to identify the most violent gang members and the ones most involved in criminal activities (hardcore or O.G.). A majority of the gang-related crime was found to be committed by 10 to 15 percent of the city's gang members. Five local departments and the Federal Bureau of Investigation created a Violent Crime Task Force to target the gang members who were involved in the greatest amount of criminal activities.

The CAT team then implemented a community awareness program. The team had a brochure printed that provided parents information about gangs and community services in dealing with the gang problem. When officers encountered gang members, the officers would speak with the parents and provide them a copy of the brochure. It was hoped that the parents would seek help from the counseling services provided in the brochure. At the same time, the department initiated a number of neighborhood advisory boards to provide feedback to the department relative to its gang-related programs. By emphasizing assistance and cooperation, the police were able to garner higher levels of public support for the program.

The CAT team also initiated an intervention program. CAT officers operated a bicycle shop that employed gang members to repair bicycles. The repaired bikes were then donated to needy children in the area. CAT officers also established a job-apprenticeship program for gang members. Here, a number of construction companies, body shops, and other businesses provided employment opportunities to gang members as a result of police referral. The intervention program focused on getting the neophyte gang members out of the gang milieu. It also showed other gang members that opportunities other than gang membership existed.

Finally, the department was instrumental in creating the **Gang Alternatives Partnership** (GAP). GAP was created to coordinate the efforts of the many private and public agencies that were involved in the gang problem. Agencies included: police departments, the district attorney's office, juvenile probation, the school district, private agencies, and private businesses. Members of the group recognized that singularly they had little impact, but collectively, they could perhaps make some significant inroads. GAP began to serve as a single source of information to the community as well as to coordinate agencies' efforts. Ultimately, a full-time executive director was hired, which helped to sustain the group's efforts.

Another way to attack gangs is through civil injunctions. Civil injunctions are court orders obtained by the police that prohibit specifically identified gang members from associating with each other, prevents them from being in specific places such as a specific neighborhood or area such as a park, and prohibits them from engaging in certain activities such as possessing drugs. When the conditions of the civil injunction are violated, the police can bring criminal charges and take other civil measures. Civil injunctions have been shown to be effective in controlling specific gangs and gang neighborhoods.

In summary, gangs represent a unique challenge for law enforcement and communities. The very existence of gangs evidences traditional law enforcement's failure. Community policing appears to be the only viable way to confront the gang problem. Even then, departments must develop comprehensive programs that cut across a variety of fronts.

Helping the Homeless

It is virtually impossible to obtain an accurate count of the homeless people in a given community, let alone for the nation. However, anytime one visits a major city in the United States, he or she is likely to encounter homeless people. It is a problem that appears to have been growing in magnitude for several decades. Today, the best estimate of the number of homeless people was done by the National Law Center on Homelessness and Poverty which found that approximately 3.5 million people, 1.35 million of which are children, will experience homelessness in any given year (National Law Center on Homelessness and Poverty, 2009; National Coalition for the Homeless, 2006; 2009). Estimates also indicated that about 1 percent of the U.S. population experience homelessness each year. The "homeless" are a diverse group of people and do not constitute a single group or a single social problem; treating them as such is an oversimplification. About 39 percent of the homeless are children, 17 percent are single women, and 33 percent are families with children. While almost all homeless people are poor, many are employed. Poverty and a lack of adequate shelter seem to be the only binding thread that unites the people we call homeless.

> *You can learn more about the homelessness problem in the United State by going to http://www.nationalhomeless.org/.*

Snyder and Hombs (1986) attributed the growing numbers to several problems:

- A shortage of affordable housing. The past decade has witnessed a substantial decrease in the amount of federal spending for subsidized housing, and the trend continues;

- The careless and wholesale depopulation of the nation's mental hospitals. When nondangerous mental patients were de-institutionalized, many of them ended up on the streets. The American Psychiatric Association estimates that there are one million homeless who are in need of mental health services;

- The cumulative effects of cuts to a variety of federal programs have resulted in many people becoming homeless. When recent changes in the welfare system come to fruition, there will be an additional round of homeless;

- Although unemployment is the lowest it has been for several decades, the unskilled remain jobless or underemployed. Technology and the business enterprise seem to be bypassing a large number of Americans;

- The minimum wage has not kept pace with the cost of living. Unskilled jobs pay at the bottom of the pay scale, and such wages make it impossible for families to afford any kind of housing; and

- The breakdown of the traditional family has contributed to the homeless problem. In past decades, it was unheard of for families to allow other family members to become homeless.

Each of these "causes" of homelessness points, once again, to poor public policy and a lack of caring by political leaders. A shortage of affordable housing is no accident, depopulation of the nation's mental hospitals was a public policy decision, changes in the welfare system were voted on by political leaders, jobs were outsourced, and training programs were not funded. Congress sets the minimum wage, and the viability of extended family has been all but destroyed by creating a high-modern, mobile, and largely disposable labor force. None of these conditions came about by accident and police are now called upon to deal with the consequences of poor public policy.

New York City Homeless Man Allegedly Torched by Teenagers

Police in New York are searching for three teenagers accused of setting a homeless man in New York City on fire yesterday. Felix Najera was bedded down outside the Iglesia Christiana Betania on East 103rd Street in the East Harlem section of Manhattan. Reports indicate that the teenagers threw a gasoline-soaked towel on the man, and set him on fire.

Homeless advocates are calling this incident one of the most senseless and severe acts in recent memory. Mary Brosnahan, the executive director of the Coalition for the Homeless said, "I haven't heard of an incident like this in many years in New York."

Najera is an alcoholic and often asks passers-by for cigarettes, but many residents consider him to be harmless. "It's a shame. He doesn't bother anybody," said Gary Williams. Another resident said, "They don't have no respect for life itself." Pastor Ariel Soto said, "It's an act of evil."

Officials say that Najera suffered second and third degree burns to nearly 75 percent of his body. Najera is 49 years old and is in critical condition at Cornell Medical Center.

Police say no arrests have been made thus far.

Source: *Wikinews* (2007). New York City Homeless Man Allegedly Torched by Teenagers. Saturday, October 6, 2007.

The homeless constitute a two-fold problem for police. People are most fearful of potentially menacing, loitering strangers. Even though no figures exist concerning how many homeless people commit crimes, their desperate straits make people uneasy. Anyone who has walked past the ragged, homeless people who dot the tunnels in New York City's subways or the streets of any large city's central business district knows that they inspire an anguished mix of feelings that include fear, guilt, revulsion, and shame. Their hand-lettered signs detailing real or embellished horror stories about why they have been reduced to begging constitute a grim litany of modern problems—AIDS, veterans who cannot find work, pregnant women with nowhere to go, and children who have been evicted from their homes. These conditions can result in the homeless committing a variety of crimes. However, for the most part, their crimes are minor and generally relate to the acquisition of food, shelter, and drugs or alcohol (Fischer, 1988; Solarz, 1985). In fact, homeless people are more often the victims of crime rather than the perpetrators (National Coalition for the Homeless, 2010).

The second concern is the alarming rates of victimization that the homeless suffer (Table 11.1). There is growing awareness that the children in shelters for the homeless are targets of sexual abuse. Generally, homeless children are with their mother. In some sensational cases, children are bartered for food, alcohol, or drugs by a parent. A study of the elderly homeless in Detroit showed that more than one-half had been beaten, robbed, or raped the preceding year, and many of them report they do not stay in shelters because of the fear of victimization (Chandler, 1988; National Coalition for the Homeless, 2010). These are people whose lack of a permanent address already robs them of their right to vote, which effectively muzzles them from having a direct say in the political process.

The homeless cannot simply pick up a phone to call the police when they are threatened, yet traditional policing depends on a call for service as the primary impetus for taking action. Community policing, in contrast, "goes looking for trouble" before problems erupt into a crisis. Just because the homeless have no votes, no political action committee (PAC) money, and no telephones should not mean they are excluded from police priorities. Their complex dilemma requires more

Table 11.1

Comparison of FBI Defined Hate Crime Homicides v. Fatal Attacks on Homeless[1]

Year	Homicides classified as hate crimes (FBI data)	Fatal attacks on homeless individuals (NCH data)
1999	17 (9 racially, 2 religiously, 3 sexual orientation, 3 ethnically motivated)	49
2000	19 (10 racially, 1 religiously, 2 sexual orientation, 6 ethnically motivated)	43
2001	10 (4 racially, 1 sexual orientation, 5 ethically motivated)	18
2002	13 (4 racially, 3 religious, 4 sexual orientation, 2 ethnically motivated)	14*
2003	14 (5 racially, 6 sexual orientation, 2 ethnically, 1 anti-disability motivated)	8*
2004	5 (3 racially, 1 religiously, 1 sexual orientation motivated)	25
2005	6 (3 racially, 3 ethnically motivated)	13
2006	3 (3 racially motivated)	20
2007	9 (5 sexual orientation, 2 racially, 2 ethnicity motivated)	28**
2008	7 (5 sexual orientation, 1 racially, 1 ethnically motivated)	27
2009	(FBI data unavailable at this time)	43
11-Year Total	103	288

*Note: Upon receipt of further information, these numbers have been decreased by one.
**Note: Upon receipt of further information, these numbers have decreased by three.
[1]Chart compiled by using data from the Center for the Study of Hate & Extremism (California State University, San Bernardino): Analysis of data from the FBI and the National Coalition for the Homeless.

Source: National Coalition for the Homeless (2010). *Hate Crimes Against the Homeless: America's Growing Tide of Violence*. Washington, DC: National Coalition for the Homeless.

than crisis intervention, and this is yet another niche where community policing offers unique opportunities to make a positive difference.

In the role of community liaison, CPOs can help link homeless people to public and private agencies that can help. CPOs are also the logical candidates to enlist and work with community volunteers on improving security in shelters and on the street. The police response must include more than rousting the homeless whenever

You can learn more about homelessness in America by going to http://www.nationalhomeless.org/publications/index.html.

their unnerving presence inflames taxpayers to demand visual relief or arresting those homeless people who take over abandoned, federally owned houses. In New York City, the Transit Authority officers have had to balance the rights of the homeless with the rights of the general public. This means protecting the homeless' right to take shelter in the public subway tunnels, free from harm. At the same time it means people must be allowed unobstructed access to the system, and they must be protected from harassment. It took years to create the current crisis, so even a concerted and well-funded effort will no doubt take years to undo. This is an obvious area where community policing can help.

Balancing the needs of the homeless with society's "right" to not be harassed by the homeless has not been an easy task for the police. The police often are caught in the middle when people desire to have the homeless removed, but the police do not have anyplace to take them. Plotkin and Narr (1993) found ample examples of the problem. In Santa Cruz, California, the police were bombarded with complaints ranging from business groups to the American Civil Liberties Union over the treatment of the homeless by police officers who were enforcing "no camping" and other anti-homeless ordinances. The Miami Police Department was sued after it stepped up enforcement of "no sleeping in public and loitering in parks after hours" ordinances. At one point, the Santa Monica city prosecutor refused to prosecute "offenses related to economic status" because of the criminal justice system's inability to deal with the problem. Perhaps the most dramatic case came from Santa Ana, California, where the police department was required to pay $400,000 after officers chained 64 homeless people to benches and wrote identification numbers on their arms. It becomes extremely frustrating for the police when, on one hand, there are demands to deal with the homeless who are making a nuisance of themselves, while on the other hand, there are inadequate resources to effectively deal with the problem.

When dealing with the homeless, CPOs must realize that there are different types of homeless. For example, the police in Kansas City have devised a typology consisting of four groups:

- **Socioeconomic homeless** are those who are homeless as a result of losing a job, being under-employed, spouse abuse, or a divorce. People in this classification were a part of society, but they became homeless as a result of some economic or social event. They lost their ability to "make it" in the real world;

- **Mentally ill homeless** are those who have mental problems but are not institutionalized or have been abandoned or thrown out by their families. These individuals generally are not ill enough for institutionalization, but they are disruptive, angry, or violent to the point that family members and friends are not able to care for them;

- **Homeless lifestyle** includes those individuals who have chosen the streets as their lifestyle. They feel comfortable with their lives, and they tend to view a change toward conventional styles as threatening; and

- **Immigrants** represent a sizable homeless population in a number of cities and small towns. They do not report being victimized to the police for fear of being deported (Plotkin & Narr, 1993).

Police officers will encounter all types of homeless persons and, as such, no singular program will be adequate in addressing the needs of all four types. Police officers must be adept at recognizing the root cause of homelessness in each case, and act accordingly. This is especially true because many homeless suffer from alcohol and drug abuse problems. Along these same lines, police departments must recognize that a variety of programs will be needed to address the homeless problem. When officers encounter homeless persons who require some type of social service or other assistance, the help should be readily available.

Perhaps the most important component of a police response to the homeless is deciding upon the department's goals and policy regarding the problem. The first step here is to come to grips with the scope of the problem itself. For example, Plotkin and Narr (1993) in their national study of homelessness found that almost 50 percent of the police agencies in their survey reported that the homeless were a minor problem, while about 17 percent reported that they were a major problem. The Santa Monica Police Department found that calls relating to the homeless accounted for 26.9 percent of all police calls. The homeless accounted for 35.4 percent of all bookings in the jail. Santa Monica is probably atypical, but the homeless remain a significant problem for police agencies. It appears that the homeless problem varies from community to community, and perception of the homeless may be more a reflection of available resources. Those departments with adequate resources, a small homeless population, and few complaints about the homeless are more apt to view the homeless as a minor problem. Regardless, the vast majority of large municipalities have a homeless problem.

Many police departments do not have specific written policies to guide police officers when dealing with the homeless. These departments depend on ordinances such as public intoxication, loitering, emergency mental health commitments, and other public disorder ordinances to contend with the homeless problem. Other cities such as Los Angeles and Santa Monica developed special units to deal with the homeless. However, the units' primary objective was to make enforcement and order maintenance more efficient as opposed to providing the homeless assistance. Most traditionally organized departments depend almost exclusively on enforcement as the way to deal with the homeless.

Community policing dictates that the police combine enforcement with the delivery of services as the best approach to the homeless problem.

The Los Angeles Police Department implemented the Safer Cities Initiative (SCI) (Braga, 2010; Berk & MacDonald, 2010). Los Angeles has had a significant homeless population, primarily located in concentrated encampments. These encampments attracted prostitution, drug dealing, property crimes, and some violence. The department under the guise of disorder policing assigned large numbers of officers to these areas who made arrests, issued citations, and forced residents out of the encampments. Once the resident homeless population was removed, the encampments were cleared. Essentially, SCI dispersed the homeless population. The result was a nominal decrease in crime in the affected areas (Berk & MacDonald, 2010), but it did not solve the homeless problem; it dispersed it. Although crime in particular areas of Los Angeles was reduced, the homeless problem was left unresolved.

Another method by which police departments have dealt with the homeless has been the trans-jurisdictional transport of troubled persons, or dumping (King & Dunn, 2004). Here, officers pick up homeless people, mentally ill people, prostitutes, and other problem persons and dump them in another political jurisdiction. King and Dunn identified four American cities where police engaged in dumping: Cleveland, Miami, Washington, DC, and Schenectady, New York. For example, Washington, DC, transported 24 prostitutes to Arlington, Virginia, and Miami was the recipient of dumping by cities in the area. These practices resulted in several lawsuits. This practice obviously does not solve the homeless problem. Police departments must develop programs in concert with social agencies that more effectively deal with the homeless. Moving them about a jurisdiction or dumping them in another jurisdiction does little to solve the problem.

The first step beyond traditional responses to the homeless is where the department adopts policies for dealing with the homeless in emergency situations. For example, the New York City Police Department has an inclement weather and communicable disease policy for the homeless. In terms of the inclement weather policy, when the temperature drops below 32 degrees, police officers search the city for homeless persons. Once located, they are taken to shelters or turned over to the City Human Resource Authority, which provides lodging. Supervisors maintain logs of the numbers of persons removed to shelters, which serves as a motivating force for officers and allows the department to evaluate how well areas are being policed for homeless. This policy is used to reduce the number of cold-weather deaths. The communicable disease policy outlines how officers are to handle homeless individuals with tuberculosis who are refusing treatment. In these cases, the policy is used to guide officers in the removal of those individuals from shelters and how medical treatment is sought (Plotkin & Narr, 1993).

The adoption of community policing would dictate that departments go well beyond these measures and develop cooperative relations with a variety of social organizations to deal with the problem. Although most communities are not provided the resources to adequately handle the homeless, more can be done in most communities. First, the police must make a special effort to provide the homeless with adequate police protection. Patrols should periodically check areas where the homeless congregate. And reports of crime should be taken seriously and investigated thoroughly. The homeless are easily victimized, and special efforts should be made to reduce victimization where possible. Second, the police should serve as referral agents to provide the homeless with access to food, shelter, and medical care. This is accomplished by ensuring that officers are familiar with facilities and policies regarding admission or access. Third, the police should avail themselves to facilitate the homeless access to employment opportunities and job training. Although not all homeless are interested in services, some, especially those who are homeless as the result of socio-economic problems, very well may be.

Policing the Mentally Ill

The homeless and the mentally ill represent two problem populations with significant overlap. Many of the homeless are mentally ill, but there are many who are not. At the same time, there are substantial numbers of mentally ill people who are not homeless. Nevertheless, police officers come into contact with large numbers of mentally ill persons in a variety of settings. As a special population, they cause a number of problems, and unfortunately, in many jurisdictions, there are not adequate social service agencies to assist the police in effectively dealing with them. To some extent, the mentally ill become the responsibility of the police.

One of the primary functions of police is order maintenance (Gaines & Kappeler, 2011). Police officers are often called upon to quell disturbances or calm rowdy people. The root of many of these calls is someone with a mental illness. For example, it is estimated that between 7 and 10 percent of all law enforcement contacts involve people with mental illness (Hails & Borum, 2003; Deane et al., 1999; Janik, 1992). In one study of three police departments, 92 percent of patrol officers advised that they had encountered at least one mentally ill person in crisis in the month previous to the survey (Borum et al., 1998). This is compounded by the fact that many people with mental problems also use alcohol or drugs. For example, studies show that more than half of the male arrestees in urban areas are impaired by drugs or psychiatric disorders such as schizophrenia or dementia (Taylor et al., 2001; Teplin, 2000). Another study showed that 20 percent of people with severe mental disorders who were hospitalized had been picked up by the police at some time in the four months before their hospitalization. Violent behavior and the combination of medication noncompliance and substance use significantly increased the odds of arrest (Borum et al., 1997). There is no question that police officers encounter large numbers of persons with mental problems, sometimes resulting in dangerous situations.

Studies show that police encounters with persons who are mentally ill are more likely to involve police use of force as compared to dealings with individuals who are not impaired (Engel, Sobol & Worden, 2000; Garner, Maxwell & Heraux, 2002; Terrill & Mastrofski, 2002). Ruiz and Miller (2004) have identified five reasons why people with mental disorders are likely to be combative when confronted by police officers. First, people with disorders become fearful because they are often put under the control of people they do not know. Second, people experiencing a mental health crisis tend to not cooperate with police officers or other officials. Third, they become fearful of the police officer's uniform or the officer's overpowering attitude. Fourth, officers often do not understand the mentally ill or have compassion for them. Finally, many officers fear persons with mental illness, which has a tendency to escalate the situation.

In the 1960s and 1970s mental illness was decriminalized. Today, police officers cannot commit someone who has a mental disorder unless the person poses a danger to him- or herself or to others. Consequently, when police officers confront someone who is mentally disturbed but poses no danger, the officer often arrests the person for some minor crime such as vagrancy, disorderly conduct, or trespassing. This is especially true when the individual is creating a problem and no other social services are available to the officer. Essentially, police officers serve as the gatekeepers for our mental health establishment (Patch & Arrigo, 1999). This places police officers in a precarious situation; they often must arrest people when other alternatives would serve the individual and society better or more effectively.

The current arrangements present a number of problems for police officers when dealing with the mentally ill. First, departments should have policies that prescribe how officers should and can deal with the mentally ill. An important part of these policies is the local social service agencies that can assist the police or mentally ill persons. Many departments, however, do not provide officers with adequate guidelines (Patch & Arrigo, 1999). One study found that half of all departments did not have adequate guidelines for the management of persons with mental illness (Ruiz & Miller, 2004). When there are no policies, police officers have little or no guidance on how to deal with problems that arise when dealing with the mentally ill. When this occurs, they often resort to traditional police responses when dealing with the mentally ill.

A second issue is training. Although many police departments and training academies provide officers with instruction on the mentally ill, it often is insufficient (Cordner, 2006). Borum (2000) advises that the training programs "are probably not harmful and may be helpful ... there is good reasons to believe that they are not sufficient to fundamentally change the nature of police encounters with mentally ill people in crisis" (p. 333). Too often, this training is general in nature and provides officers with too little information for dealing with the intricacies that exist in many of the encounters. Police departments should ensure that all officers have adequate training given the number of incidents involving people with mental illness and the dangers they pose. It is also helpful if there is a cadre of CPOs who are provided in-depth training for handling the mentally ill. The CPOs then can assist patrol and other officers when responding to problems involving mentally ill persons.

Some departments have adopted specialized training models. For example, in Memphis, Tennessee, and Louisville, Kentucky, the departments provided a cadre of patrol officers with enhanced training. These officers are dispatched to calls involving persons who are mentally disturbed. In Memphis, the officers handled 95 percent of all mental disturbance calls. The program resulted in a reduction in the time spent waiting for mental health admissions, arrest rates for mentally ill persons were lowered,

> You can learn more about mental illness and crime by going to
> http://www.nij.gov/pubs-sum/184208.htm.

referrals to mental health services increased, and callouts for SWAT teams were decreased (Strauss et al., 2005). Here is a clear case where adequate training and police responses can result in a reduction of violence.

Third, police departments should develop relations with social service agencies that can assist the police when dealing with the mentally ill. Cordner (2006) advises that the police should develop programs with the mental health community and hospital emergency rooms including protocols, procedures, and referral agencies. These facilities are on the front line for dealing with the mentally ill, and mental health professionals can help provide police officers with training on how to diagnose and handle people with mental disorders. Today, many mental health facilities are private, but nonetheless, police agencies must identify agencies, be they public or private, that can assist them and develop working relationships with them.

The arrest and incarceration of mentally ill offenders is quite expensive and largely a waste of resources; incarceration does little to reduce future problem behaviors. It is economically more sensible to provide more appropriate and effective services. In those cases where mentally ill individuals have been arrested, offenders should be diverted to mental health programs that can provide more effective services. Community policing and problem solving dictate that jurisdictions find services that are effective. It reduces future calls for service, it reduces costs, and it decreases violent confrontations.

Minorities and the Police

While minorities do not represent a special population that is served by the police, police-minority relations represent unique issues. In fact, the minority population in the United States is approaching half of the total population. Minorities are the majority in a number of communities in this country. However, the negative relations between the police and minorities warrant special consideration, especially when community policing is concerned. Historically, a substantial amount of resentment existed between the police and minorities. For the most part, the police have seen themselves as the servants of the ruling class and tended to be opposed to cultures outside the mainstream. Also, minorities tended to be poor and had little if any representation in the political system. Only recently have the police made strides in providing better services to all people regardless of their race or culture. This movement began in the 1960s as police departments implemented police-community relations programs to reach out to the underprivileged classes. Today, many police departments have embraced the idea of multiculturalism and have made substantial efforts to provide all people better services. This has become a cornerstone in community policing. However, race remains a volatile police issue because of the:

- alarming rates of victimization many minority groups endure;

- disproportionate number of minorities arrested and incarcerated;

- debate about how best to promote minority hiring and promotion in police departments;

- role of race as a common factor in police brutality;

- concern that racially motivated incidents and attacks are on the rise; and

- worrisome emergence and growth of new militant groups, such as skinheads and other right-wing groups, who openly advocate violence against minorities.

The police will no doubt face even greater pressure to deal with these issues as the racial balance in the United States continues to shift. According to a recent report by the Census Bureau, America will become dramatically less

White this next century. In a study projecting population trends 100 years into the future, the Census Bureau projected that by 2080, White, non-Latinos will be close to losing majority status to today's three major minority groups—African Americans, Asians, and Latinos (Scanlan, 1989). As America moves toward greater diversity, the police must be ready and equipped to protect all people when conflict occurs.

Minorities, African Americans and Hispanics in particular, were long excluded from political power. When the reform era substituted the law for politics as the source of police power, this made a difference for the White mainstream, but not for African Americans or Hispanics. The application of the law for White people often was different from that for minorities. The concern even now is that the politically powerful influence the allocation of police resources so that community policing will be implemented in strong communities where community or business organizations have access to the political leadership, rather than to disintegrating minority neighborhoods with less political influence. This is the avenue that crime prevention took in the late 1970s and early 1980s. It was not until community policing was accepted by law enforcement that the police began to respond to many minority community needs.

Even today, a number of problems remain. In many instances police departments have failed to adequately address minority relations or have given them a low priority. Minorities have continued to voice a number of complaints against the police. Radelet and Carter (2001) summarize the complaints:

- Substandard or poor police protection;
- Substandard or poor service to minorities, especially inner-city residents;
- The expectation that the police will not treat them fairly;
- Numerous incidents of verbal abuse and harassment;
- Stereotyping of minorities as criminals, particularly in "stop and frisk incidents";
- Police use of excessive force; and
- Discrimination in police personnel administration.

A number of studies show that community policing can make positive inroads in minority communities. Community policing activities such as foot or bike patrols and community meetings frequently improve the relationship between the police and minority residents (Reisig & Parks, 2004; Weitzer &

Tuch, 2006), and Skogan (2006) notes that many police departments implemented community policing at the insistence of minority residents. Community policing, however, is not a mantra that will solve all problems. There is research that demonstrates that community policing did not improve minority relations. Basically, when there was failure, it was the result of the police implementing community policing improperly (focusing on traditional police practices as opposed to problem solving and community partnerships) or failing to coordinate their programming with the community. People saw the programs as intrusive, with officers not having a genuine commitment to the people in the neighborhood (Grinc, 1994; Williams, 1996).

If community policing is to be effective in improving minority relations, it must be well planned. For the planning to be effectual, it must include residents so that the police fully understand the problems and residents' expectations. Community policing requires the involvement of civilians. Neighborhood goals should be identified as well as strategies to achieve those goals. More importantly, officers involved in the programs must be committed to community policing and the neighborhood they are policing. Finally, all officers should be given additional training on the divergent cultures in their communities and community policing practices and goals.

Lightning Rods of Racial Tension

There have been a number of highly visible incidents within the past several years demonstrating the volatile relationship between the police and minorities. Many of these incidents have made national headlines and resulted in accusations of police brutality and racism. Several police chiefs lost their jobs or retired as a result of racially charged incidents, most notably the chiefs in Riverside, California, and Louisville, Kentucky. In 2001, riots erupted in Cincinnati, Ohio, after a series of police shootings of minorities.

The following provides a sketch of some of the most publicized incidents of racial tension.

The Rodney King Incident

In 1991, California police officers stopped Rodney King for speeding. King had led a number of officers on a chase that exceeded 100 MPH. Once King was stopped, a total of 21 police officers from several different police agencies arrived on the scene. Once King was removed from his vehicle, he was shocked twice with a 50,000 volt taser. He was also severely beaten by two other officers while between 21 and 27 officers watched. When it was over, King suffered 11 skull fractures, a broken cheekbone, a fractured eye socket, a broken ankle, missing teeth, kidney damage, external burns, and permanent brain damage.

The incident was captured by an amateur video camera enthusiast and was later played on national television. The incident proved to be shocking to many Americans who watched the officers repeatedly beat King. As a result of the public outrage, the city of Los Angeles appointed a commission to study the King incident and the Los Angeles Police Department. The commission found widespread problems in the LAPD. The organizational structure emphasized crime control over prevention. Police officers were encouraged to be "hard-nosed" when dealing with the public, and the department did too little when investigating citizen complaints of police misuse of force (Christopher Commission, 2008).

The Abner Louima Incident

In 1997, one of the most gruesome police brutality cases in the nation came to light. Louima, a Haitian immigrant, was arrested in a Brooklyn nightclub as the result of a fight that had broken out between two other patrons in the bar. Louima was arrested for assault, resisting arrest, disorderly conduct, and obstructing justice. Louima was arrested because one of the officers believed that Louima had assaulted him while he was attempting to break up the fight. Officers beat Louima as they transported him to the police precinct station.

Once at the precinct station, officers stripped Louima from the waist down. Louima was handcuffed, and Officer Volpe, one of the arresting officers, then took a stick and shoved it up Louima's rectum and then into his mouth. While doing so, the officers taunted him with "We're going to teach niggers to respect police officers" and "This is Giuliani's time, not Dinkins' time." Louima suffered broken teeth, and surgery was performed to repair a ruptured bladder and punctured lower intestine.

The Amadou Diallo Incident

In 1999, New York City police officers in an anti-crime unit were searching for a suspect in a Bronx neighborhood. They spotted Diallo, who fit the description of a suspect, and decided to investigate him. Upon being confronted by the officers, Diallo ducked into the vestibule of a building. He reached into his pocket to retrieve his wallet. The officers thought that Diallo was reaching for a gun and opened fire. They fired 41 shots, striking Diallo 19 times.

The Rampart Division Scandal

The Los Angeles Police Department developed a national reputation for police brutality as a result of the Rodney King incident. In 1999, this reputation was solidified with the Rampart Division scandal. A police officer in the Rampart Division was arrested on charges stemming from the theft of cocaine from a police evidence room. As a part of his plea bargain, he agreed to provide investigators information about the illegal activities of other officers in the Rampart Division. The officer described widespread corruption and violations of civil rights in the Division. He advised that it was not uncommon for officers to fabricate charges and to plant evidence on primarily Latino suspects. It seemed that this had become a common practice among Rampart officers.

The Rampart scandal has had monumental consequences on the Los Angeles Police Department and policing nationally. Although the investigation was continuing at the time of this writing, more than 30 police officers had been suspended or fired. More than 80 felony convictions had been overturned, and many more are sure to follow. There have been estimates that the civil suits associated with the scandal will cost the city hundreds of millions of dollars. The U.S. Justice Department is investigating the Los Angeles Police Department, and it appears that the courts ultimately will impose some form of supervision over the department. Ultimately, the Rampart scandal will have a significant impact on the future of policing and the LAPD.

Driving while Black

Another criticism of the police commonly voiced today is the problem of **driving while Black** (DWB). Civil rights leaders across the country are pointing out that minorities are stopped by the police at a higher rate than are White people. They also note that minorities are more likely to receive a traffic citation or to be arrested. For example, the Columbus, Ohio, Police Department was recently sued because it was alleged that officers targeted minorities disproportionately. A number of police departments are examining their arrest and ticketing practices. For example, the San Jose Police Department recently released a report detailing the numbers of stops, citations, and arrests based on race.

There is no question that minorities have more negative encounters with the police than do White people. Although some police officers are most likely racists and some departments have overall racist tendencies, many departments and officers in this country do not allow racism to enter in their decision making process. The war on drugs has contributed to the problem. The courts have substantially reduced restrictions on vehicle searches and seizures, especially as they relate to drugs. The police are now using even the slightest pretense to stop vehicles to conduct drug investigations. This has resulted in the police often being overly aggressive, especially when minorities are concerned.

Each of these problems, as well as others, has received national attention. They have served as lighting rods for criticism of the police. Critics have generalized them to other problems that occur in many local communities. Critics are calling the police racists, brutal, and insensitive to minority needs. It poses a unique problem for police administrators and community policing. It basically means that the police must work even harder to develop better relations with minority communities. It means that the police must endeavor to implement partnerships and cooperatively work with people to solve many of the problems that plague minority communities. It also means that police agencies must do a better job at weeding out racist officers from among their ranks.

Community Policing and Immigrant Communities

Since the terrorist attacks on the World Trade Center and the Pentagon in 2001, American politicians and the public have been preoccupied with issues surrounding immigration. There are two primary areas of focus. First, it is feared that Muslim or Arab terrorists will immigrate, legally or illegally, into the United States to conduct terrorist attacks. This has resulted in the close scrutiny of people from Muslim countries. For example, after the 9/11 attacks, the U.S. Attorney General requested that local police officials assist the FBI in collecting information on 5,000 Muslims in the United States (see Ridgley, 2008). Second, there is public hysteria in some quarters regarding the number of undocumented people crossing into the United States from the southern border. The federal government, states such as Arizona and Alabama, and cities have passed laws and restrictive ordinances to control Hispanics, particularly Mexicans. In some cases, the police have been placed in the middle, shouldering the responsibility for enforcement. They are in the middle because the police need assistance from all community members in solving crimes, providing information about criminal and terrorist enterprises, and enacting crime prevention programs. For example, when Arizona passed its restrictive law requiring police officers to check suspects' legal immigrant status, many law enforcement groups and police departments opposed the measure on the grounds that it would prevent people from cooperating with the police.

Ridgley (2008) notes that cities have taken two different routes when dealing with undocumented immigrants. Some cities have cooperated with the federal government aggressively, assisting with the identification and eventual deportation of immigrants, while other cities, such as San Francisco, have maintained "sanctuary policies," according to which the police were prevented from questioning immigrants about their residency status unless they were charged with a crime. Additionally, a number of cities, while initially going one route, have changed direction. This has resulted in inconsistent policies for police departments across the nation (Decker et al., 2009).

Precise figures regarding undocumented immigrants are obviously difficult to obtain. The best estimate is that there are now approximately 13 million undocumented immigrants, comprising more than 2 percent of the total United States population. It is also estimated that this number increases by more than 275,000 each year (McDonald, 1997). "Mexicans make up over half of undocumented immigrants—57 percent of the total, or about 5.3 million. Another 2.2 million (23%) are from other Latin American countries. About 10 percent are from Asia, 5 percent from Europe and Canada, and 5 percent from the rest of the world" (Urban Institute, 2008) (Table 11.2). Within the ranks of new arrivals are those who have some hope of remaining legally, if they can prove they fled political repression and face retaliation if returned home. Those who left their homes because of economic problems are routinely deported, and Mexican nationals automatically fall into this category, as do Canadians and people of most European and Asian countries. Haitians have also had notable difficulty in establishing political grounds.

Table 11.2
Country of Birth of the Unauthorized Immigrant Population: January 2006 and 2000

	Estimated population in January		Percent of total		Percentage change	Average annual change
	2006	2000	2006	2000	2000 to 2006	2000 to 2006
All countries	11,550,000	8,460,000	100%	100%	37%	515,000
Mexico	6,570,000	4,680,000	57	55	40	315,000
El Salvador	510,000	430,000	4	5	19	13,333
Guatemala	430,000	290,000	4	3	48	23,333
Philippines	280,000	200,000	2	2	40	13,333
Honduras	280,000	160,000	2	2	75	20,000
India	270,000	120,000	2	1	125	25,000
Korea	250,000	180,000	2	2	39	11,667
Brazil	210,000	100,000	2	1	110	18,333
China	190,000	190,000	2	2	-	-
Vietnam	160,000	160,000	1	2	-	-
Other countries	2,410,000	1,950,000	21	23%	24%	76,667

Source: U.S. Department of Homeland Security (2007). Estimator of the Unauthorized Immigrant Population. Washington, DC.

SPOTLIGHT ON COMMUNITY POLICING PRACTICE

The U-visa:An Important Tool for Community Policing

- Eva is married to a man who has assaulted her in the past—and now it has happened again. But this time she is even more frightened. She is about to have the couple's first baby, and her husband has just threatened her once more, only this time he's said that if she reports him to the police, he will have her deported.
- The owner of a small restaurant says he is concerned about one of his employees. The employee is undocumented and was robbed recently after leaving work one night. The owner says,"He's afraid to talk to the police and he has seen these guys before. These guys are going after people they know aren't from this country because they figure they are walking ATMs. They always have cash on them—not credit cards or debit cards—cash."

Both of these are actual cases that illustrate a challenge to officers who do community policing—the challenge of how to get undocumented immigrants to report or admit that they are victims of crime. In recent years, a tool has been developed to help police build a bridge to the neighborhoods they serve and solve crimes in: the U-visa. This visa, designed for immigrant victims of crime who cooperate with law enforcement, was intended to make them more likely to report such offenses. Growing awareness about the U-visa certification process is enabling police departments throughout the United States to take advantage of this tool that can help in the investigation and prosecution of serious crimes and improve public safety. Yet, many officers know little about this visa and how it can be a resource in their work.

Congress created the "U" nonimmigrant classification, or U-visa, in the Violence Against Women Act under the Victims of Trafficking and Violence Prevention Act of 2000. The U-visa strengthens the ability of law enforcement agencies to detect, investigate, prosecute, and solve cases of domestic violence, sexual assault, trafficking, and other types of criminal activity.

Lawmakers recognized that a victim's cooperation, assistance, and safety are essential to the effective detection, investigation, and prosecution of crimes. Victims who fear deportation, however, are often unlikely to come forward to assist in investigative efforts. With the incentive of the U-visa, the purpose of which is to give immigrant victims of certain crimes temporary legal status as well as temporary work eligibility in the United States, not only will the police benefit, but so will the victim. Police agencies do play an important role by certifying that an individual is eligible to apply for a U-visa; however, applications are ultimately approved or denied by the U.S. Citizenship and Immigration Services (USCIS).

In October 2009, the U.S. Department of Justice's Bureau of Justice Assistance awarded a three-year grant to the Vera Institute of Justice and Legal Momentum to develop, field-test, and distribute tools to inform law enforcement agencies about the U-visa certification process. Staff from the two nonprofit organizations work together on a project called the National Immigrant Victims' Access to Justice Partnership, which has already collaborated with 13 law enforcement agencies throughout the country to create a training curriculum for police

(Continued)

personnel. The project has developed a tool kit for law enforcement that includes training modules and other materials related to the U-visa, such as a model policy and a FAQ sheet. Several related resources, such as webcasts, webinars, and podcasts will also be created.

Through this project, trainings focus on issues important to an officer's understanding and use of the U-visa, including:

- the U-visa application procedure;
- enhancing an officer's capacity to work with immigrant victims;
- the U-visa certification process; and
- reasons that law enforcement agents may not be signing U-visa certifications.

Deputy Chief Pete Helein of the Appleton (Wisconsin) Police Department participated in training on the U-visa in 2010. He considered it valuable for future work in the community, particularly with immigrants who are reluctant to report crimes. "Once we get the word out as to what our role is in the U-visa process, it may have some deterrent effect on people who would prey on immigrants," he said. "We want to get the message out that we are going to take action."

Understanding the U-visa process can enhance community policing. For example, an officer can explain the U-visa process and the criminal process to immigrant crime victims—and often to their families or other people who may have witnessed crimes—showing them that the police need their help, and will help them in return. Such interactions can start a dialogue, develop rapport, and build trust, making members of the community more likely to share information with officers they now know. Individuals who have had a favorable experience with police are likely to tell other members of their community about it, and in turn this may make people more willing to report criminal activity in the future.

For officers who are concerned about their role and responsibility in a process that could lead to someone obtaining legal status after just a limited interaction with that individual, it is important to know that police don't determine who receives a U-visa and who does not. The certification process involves documenting that a person has been helpful—or is expected to be helpful in the future—in the detection, investigation, or prosecution of specific criminal activity. This certification is just one step in a longer process, which concludes when USCIS reviews the application and decides whether to issue a U-visa. (By law, a maximum of 10,000 U-visas are issued annually.) Just as passing an eye exam isn't sufficient to obtain a driver's license, certification of eligibility doesn't guarantee that a person will receive a U-visa. But it can be an important and beneficial step for crime victims who have cooperated and assisted with law enforcement.

As familiarity with the U-visa process grows, more officers may come to rely on it. In the big picture, it is a tool that can make community policing more effective and neighborhoods safer.

Sergeant Inspector Tony Flores
San Francisco Police Department

Rodolfo Estrada
Senior Program Associate
Vera Institute of Justice's Center on Immigration and Justice

Source: The e-newsletter of the COPS Office, Volume 4, Issue 1, January 2011.

Like with the homeless, the real undocumented immigrant situation is often contrary to public perception. Women make up a substantial share, more than 40 percent of the adult undocumented immigrants, or about 3.2 million people. About 1.6 million children under 18 in the United States are undocumented immigrants and about 3 million children with undocumented parents are U.S. citizens. Virtually all undocumented men work (Urban Institute, 2008).

Undocumented immigrants pose a difficult challenge for police, because fear of deportation often makes them reluctant to report crimes committed against them—which also makes them easy prey. They can also fall victim to crimes related to their vulnerability—scams include extortion, fees for phony documentation, supposed bribes to judges, and other creative cons. Without legal status, many take jobs in the grey economy, and employers often exploit their status by underpaying them or refusing to pay them at all. Because so many arrive with little or no money and have difficulty making a living, undocumented immigrants often cluster in low-income, high-crime areas.

Although some politicians claim that undocumented immigrants are involved in a substantial amount of crime, they are not overrepresented in the criminal population. For example, a 1994 study estimated that there were 21,395 undocumented immigrants in prisons in seven states, with California holding more than 70 percent of them and New York next with 10 percent (Clark, Passel, Zimmerman & Fix, 1994). Studies in San Diego and El Paso, two cities with large undocumented immigrant populations, showed that undocumented immigrants constituted 12 and 15 percent respectively for serious crime (McDonald, 1997). In 2000, Mexican men had an incarceration rate of less than one percent, which is more than eight times lower than the 5.9 percent rate of U.S.-born males of Mexican descent. And generally, native-born men have an incarceration rate 10 times higher than that of foreign-born men. These statistics indicate that undocumented immigrants are not overly represented in criminality. More recently, Akins, Rumbaut, and Stasfield (2009) examined homicides in Austin, Texas, and found that the increasing Latino population did not contribute to an increase in homicides, and Kubrin and Ousey (2009) examined homicides in large urban areas and found that cities with large undocumented populations had a lower homicide rate as compared to cities that did not have large numbers of undocumented people. Lee and Martinez (2009) examined the research on immigrants and crime and found that undocumented people did not increase the crime rate and in some cases suppressed it. There is substantial misconception relative to immigrants and crime. The fear of rising crime rates has been used to demonize immigrants.

The victimization of undocumented immigrants seems to enjoy less attention from political leaders. The smuggling of immigrants has mushroomed into a major crime problem in the United States. For example, gangs in New York City were charging residents of China between $15,000 and $50,000 to be smuggled into the United States. It was estimated that the Chinese smuggling market alone was worth approximately $3.5 billion. Most of the immigrants would pay a down payment of about $1,500 and the rest upon arrival. In many cases, the immigrants would be required to work much like an indentured slave to pay the remainder of the fee. In 1995, Central America became a free trade zone, which allowed government officials to sell visas and passports to the Chinese. This allowed the Chinese to leave for the United States by plane, which was far safer than illegal arrangements. The transporting of undocumented immigrants very likely is far safer and more lucrative than smuggling drugs, at least for the smugglers.

Police officials in states and localities that strictly enforce immigration laws have been using the tactic of roundups. **Roundups** are where large numbers of police officers are assigned to an area to check the immigration status of anyone who appears to be an undocumented immigrant. Romero (2006) analyzed a five-day raid that occurred in Chandler, Arizona. She found that the police targeted people for their "Mexicanness," the color of their skin, shopping in neighborhoods highly populated by Latinos, and their English speaking ability. She found that residents felt they were treated as "second class citizens," demeaned, and humiliated. The raids and similar police strategies drive a wedge between the police and immigrant communities. They also result in less support and cooperation between people and the police.

A recent roundtable of police executives found that these tactics are foremost in immigrants' minds when they encounter local police. The primary concerns of the immigrant community with the police included:

- Fear of deportation. News of arrests (also known as "raids" or "sweeps"), detentions, and deportations of illegal immigrants by Immigration and Customs Enforcement (ICE) travels fast across immigrant communities and even the country, sometimes spreading panic in immigrant populations. Within any immigrant family, there may be both documented and undocumented individuals. Regardless of their documentation status, immigrants may be afraid to go about their daily business for fear that they or their families will be subject to ICE actions and deportation.

- Concern about local law enforcement's role in immigration enforcement. There is no federal law or regulations on what immigrants can expect from local law enforcement regarding immigration enforce-

ment, and local agencies have vastly different policies. In one jurisdiction, law enforcement may have a policy of not asking about
immigration status; while in another jurisdiction, it may be utilized
but only in criminal investigations; and in yet another jurisdiction,
law enforcement may pursue immigration enforcement actively.
It is often unclear to immigrants how their documentation status
may affect law enforcement's response to crime, including whether
undocumented crime victims will be turned over to immigration
authorities. This uncertainty and concern about local law enforcement's role in immigration enforcement causes many immigrants
to fear that any contact with officers could potentially bring about
their deportation and/or that of undocumented family members.
An avoidance of law enforcement, however, makes immigrants
especially vulnerable to all types of crime and civil violations, for
example, domestic violence, sexual assault, gang activity, human trafficking, nonpayment by employers, and financial scams.

- Negative impact of news reports about ICE actions. The media—both
mainstream and ethnic—sometimes distort and sensationalize the
facts surrounding ICE actions. These distortions further exacerbate
panic in immigrant communities and resentment toward law enforcement in general. News about ICE actions also triggers polar-
izing public debate about immigration issues, which can increase
immigrants' sense of isolation from the larger community (Enhancing Community Policing with Immigrant Populations, 2010: 15-16).

As discussed above, undocumented immigrants place the police in a rather
precarious position. On the one hand, they are violating federal laws, while on
the other, they are often in need of police protection and services. In order to
deal with this problem, the San Diego County Sheriff's Department issued the
following policy:

The primary responsibility for the enforcement of immigration laws
rests with federal authorities. Nonetheless, the Sheriff's Department
has a responsibility to guarantee the safety and well-being of all people living within this county. The scope of this responsibility includes
the enforcement of applicable Federal and State statutes concerned
with illegal immigration into the United States and the County of San
Diego to ensure the safety and well-being of illegal immigrants of this
county.

Although the department recognizes its responsibility for enforcing immigration laws, it seems that the department's priority rests with providing all persons within the county with a reasonable level of service. This philosophy seems to be spreading to non-border states. For example, the State Attorney's office in Montgomery County, Maryland, started a "theft of services" unit, whose primary objective is to obtain justice for undocumented immigrants who are cheated by employers. Undocumented immigrants are a challenge to community policing. However, it seems logical that the plight of people often outweighs the need for strict enforcement.

McDonald (1999) has identified several responses that the police should incorporate when dealing with immigrant populations:

- Increase foreign language capability of the department

- Provide officers with cultural diversity training to make them more sensitive to different cultures in the community

- Increase the diversity of the department's officers

- Provide immigrants and their communities with educational programs about the police and criminal justice process

- Implement police-community coalitions in neighborhoods

- Appoint liaisons between the police and immigrant communities

- Implement specially tailored crime prevention programs in immigrant neighborhoods

Tourists and Transients

Many summer and winter resort communities, as well as cities that are popular entertainment centers, face problems because of the influx of tourists and part-time residents who swell the population at different seasons of the year. An obvious concern is that people who have no long-range stake in the community adopt the conventioneer syndrome where they behave recklessly and irresponsibly. They exhibit drunkenness, vandalism, or skipping out on bills. They tend to victimize the community they visit. The reverse of this problem is where tourists such as those in some of the gambling cities of Atlantic City or Las Vegas are targeted as victims by local robbers, prostitutes, or even local merchants. Without a doubt, tourists and transient populations create problems for the police, and the police must develop strategies for dealing with them. Community policing is the ideal solution to many problems associated with tourists and transients.

A number of resort cities have specialized problems. For example, cities such as Daytona Beach, Ft. Lauderdale, and Panama City, Florida, are inundated with students during spring break. These cities are literally overwhelmed with partying college students. Similarly, Louisville has the Kentucky Derby, New Orleans has Mardi Gras, and Indianapolis has the Indianapolis 500 race. Such activities require the police to apply the precepts of community policing, especially if they are to maintain some semblance of order. The police must control the situation while allowing the visitors to enjoy themselves and engage the local businesses. Such a process requires large numbers of police officers with exceptional personal skills. It requires that the police department develop operational plans that assist in controlling crowds while at the same time allowing the tourists to enjoy themselves.

Victimization of tourists has evolved into a major problem for some communities. Over the past several years there have been several tourists, including foreign nationals, who have been robbed and murdered in south Florida, which has resulted in worldwide publicity. Florida has developed an extensive tourist information program to educate tourists about some of the dangerous areas in south Florida and how to protect themselves. Law enforcement officials have stepped up patrols and enforcement at interstate highway rest stops where some of the crimes have occurred. In some cases, the police have stopped tourists to warn them of the dangers of certain areas. Although the cases of murdered tourists are rare, the problem is not unique to Florida. Several rest areas on interstate highways in

You can learn more about tourism and crime by going to http://www.popcenter.org/problems/crimes_against_tourists/.

Kentucky were closed because of robberies. A number of states have developed state plans to educate tourists and provide them with better protection.

The protection of tourists is a major concern in a number of convention cities, especially in those areas with reputed vice districts. Tourists are seen as a viable, rich market for prostitution, escort services, adult entertainment, and drugs. Too often tourists or convention-goers seek out vice areas and become victimized because of their unfamiliarity with the dangers associated with vice activities. This poses a special problem for the police as they attempt to protect somewhat naive people who wander into dangerous areas. CPOs must actively solicit the assistance of hotels and other business establishments in providing tourists with information about how to safely navigate through the city. In some instances, this includes advising people to avoid certain areas of the city. Officers patrolling in dangerous areas should be watchful of people who appear to be out of their environment.

Summary

This chapter cannot explore all the potential benefits that particular groups may derive from community policing, but it is obvious that community policing has profound changes on the police in terms of their treatment of various groups. As noted in previous chapters, community policing necessitates philosophical changes in the way police departments do business. The foremost change is that the police begin to view people as customers who are to be "satisfied," as opposed to viewing them as hindrances or as the enemies. It also means that the police should emphasize quality of service, as opposed to bean counting where the department measures productivity in terms of numbers of arrests, numbers of citations issued, or response time.

Policing must come to grips with the fact that we live in a culturally diverse society. For example, 10 years ago Kentucky had a fairly homogeneous society. However, this has changed substantially in the past decade. Toyota built a major automobile manufacturing plant in Kentucky, and dozens of other Japanese plants followed. Kentucky farmers now use thousands of migrant workers, many of whom have remained in the state. This factor illustrates that the state is seeing a number of cultural changes. For example, several Kentucky police departments are now recruiting officers who are bilingual, something that would have been considered absurd just 15 years ago. Regardless, there are numerous communities in Kentucky that now have significant minority populations.

Police departments and police officers must recognize the existence of diverging cultures. Police officers must be trained in understanding and dealing with different types of people. This may include training on customs as well as language. This is not to limit police responsibility to ethnic or national cultures; the poor, the homeless, and other disadvantaged groups represent cultures with distinct sets of values and living conditions which must be understood by police officers. Police departments must embody the philosophy of multi-culturalism and service throughout the agency.

KEY TERMS IN CHAPTER 11

- Abner Louima incident
- Amadou Diallo incident
- baby gangsters
- child abuse
- Community Action Team (CAT)
- community liaison
- disorganization
- driving while Black
- excessive force
- gangsters
- GAP
- homeless
- homeless lifestyle
- immigrants
- juveniles
- mentally ill homeless
- O.G. gangsters
- Office of Juvenile Justice and Delinquency Prevention
- Police Athletic League
- professional policing
- Rampart Division scandal
- Rodney King incident
- socioeconomic homeless
- tiny gangsters
- tourists
- undocumented immigrants
- urban youth gangs
- wannabees

DISCUSSION QUESTIONS

1. Discuss the special groups the authors are referring to when they write about "special populations." What unique problems do these groups have with respect to the delivery of police services?
2. Of the special populations discussed in the text, which group, in your estimation, presents the greatest difficulties for the police? Why?
3. Discuss the reasons juveniles represent a special problem for community policing.
4. The National Coalition of State Juvenile Justice Advisory Groups has identified several factors contributing to violent crimes committed by juveniles. List and briefly discuss four of the factors.
5. What is a youth "gang"? What steps can be taken by community policing officers to address gang problems in areas they police?
6. Explain what the authors are referring to when they say that the homeless constitute a two-fold problem for the police.
7. Discuss specific steps that community policing officers can take to address the needs of homeless persons.
8. What factors can be cited to account for the rise in the homeless population?
9. Describe the four groups of homeless people as they are presented in the text. Discuss how each one presents a problem for police.
10. Discuss the reasons race remains a volatile police issue.
11. Discuss why undocumented immigrants present special challenges to police.
12. Describe why tourists and transients present special challenges to police.

References

Akins, S., Rumbaut, R., & Stasfield, R. (2009). Immigration, Economic Disadvantage, and Homicide: A Community-Level Analysis of Austin, Texas. *Homicide Studies, 13*, 307-314.

Attorney General of the United States. (1989). *Drug Trafficking: A Report to the President of the United States*. Washington, DC: U.S. Department of Justice.

Berk, R., & MacDonald, J. (2010). Policing the Homeless: An Evaluation of Efforts to Reduce Homeless-Related Crime. *Criminology & Public Policy, 9*, 813-840.

Block, C. R., & Block, R. (1993). Street Gang Crime in Chicago. *Research in Brief*. Washington, DC: National Institute of Justice.

Borum, R. (2000). Improving High Risk Encounters between People with Mental Illness and Police. *Journal of the American Academy of Psychiatry, 28*, 332-337.

Borum, R., Deane, M., Steadman, H., & Morrissey, J. (1998). Police Perspectives on Responding to People with Mental Illness in Crisis: Perceptions of Program Effectiveness. *Behavioral Sciences and the Law, 16*, 393-405.

Borum, R., Swanson, J., Schwartz, M., & Hiday, V. (1997). Substance Abuse, Violent Behavior, and Police Encounters with Persons with Severe Mental Disorder. *Journal of Contemporary Criminal Justice, 13*, 236-250.

Braga, A. (2010). The Police, Disorder, and the Homeless. *Criminology & Public Policy, 9*, 807-812.

Brand, D. (1987). In Massachusetts: Theater Therapy. *Time*, (November 9).

Chandler, M. (1988). Disturbing Plight of Homeless Elderly Studied. *Detroit Free Press*, (December 22).

Clark, R. L., Passel, J. S., Zimmerman, W. N., & Fix, M. E. (1994). *Fiscal Impacts of Undocumented Aliens: Selected Estimates for Seven States*. Washington, DC: The Urban Institute.

Cloward, R., & Ohlin, L. (1960). *Delinquency and Opportunity: A Theory of Delinquent Gangs*. New York, NY: The Free Press.

Cordner, G. (2006). *People with Mental Illness*. Washington, DC: Office of Community Oriented Policing Services.

Curry, G. D., Ball, R., & Fox, R. (1994). *Gang Crime and Law Enforcement Recordkeeping. Research in Brief*. Washington, DC: National Institute of Justice.

Deane, M., Steadman, H., Deane, M., Borum, R., Veysey, B., & Morrisey, J. (1999). Emerging Partnerships between Mental Health and Law Enforcement. *Psychiatry and the Law, 50*, 99-101.

Decker, S., Lewis, P., Provine, D., & Varsanyi, M. (2009). On the Frontier of Local Law Enforcement: Local Police and Federal Immigration Law. *Sociology of Crime, Law, and Deviance, 13*, 261-276.

Douthit, N. (1975). Enforcement and Non-Enforcement Roles in Policing: A Historical Inquiry. *Journal of Police Science and Administration, 3*(3), 336-345.

Egley, A., Howell, J., & Moore, J. (2010). *Highlights of the 2008 Youth Gang Survey*. Washington, DC: Office of Juvenile Justice and Delinquency Prevention.

Engel, R. S., Sobol, J. J., & Worden, R. E. (2000). Further Exploration of the Demeanor Hypothesis: The Interaction Effects of Suspects' Characteristics and Demeanor on Police Behavior. *Justice Quarterly, 17*, 235-258.

Enhancing Community Policing with Immigrant Populations. (2010). Recommendations from a Roundtable Meeting of Immigrant Advocates and Law Enforcement Leaders. New Orleans, Louisiana, August 27-28, 2008: US Department of Justice.

Esbensen, F., Winfree, L., He, N., & Taylor, T. (2004). Youth Gangs and Definitional Issues: When Is a Gang a Gang and Why Does It Matter? In F. Esbensen, S. Tibbetts, & L. Gaines (Eds.), *American Youth Gangs at the Millennium* (pp. 52-76). Long Grove, IL: Waveland Press.

Federal Bureau of Investigation (FBI). (2010). *Uniform Crime Reports, 2009*. Washington, DC: Author.

Felson, M. (2009). *Crime and Everyday Life: Insights and Implications for Society* (4th ed.). Thousand Oaks, CA: Pine Forge Press.

Finkelhor, D., Turner, H., Ormrod, R., Hamby, S., & Kracke, K. (2010). *Children's Exposure to Violence: A Comprehensive National Survey*. Washington, DC: OJJDP.

Fischer, P.J. (1988). Criminal Activity Among the Homeless: A Study of Arrests in Baltimore. *Hospital and Community Psychiatry, 39*(1), 46-51.

Fisk, W. (1996). Childhood Trauma and Dissociative Identity Disorder. *Child and Adolescent Psychiatric Clinics of North America, 5*, 431-447.

Fleisher, M. (1995). *Beggars & Thieves: Lives of Urban Street Criminals*. Madison, WI: University of Wisconsin Press.

Freng, A., & Winfree, L. (2004). Exploring Race and Ethnic Differences in a Sample of Middle School Gang Members. In F. Esbensen, S. Tibbetts, & L. Gaines (Eds.), *American Youth Gangs at the Millennium* (pp. 142-162). Long Grove, IL: Waveland Press.

Gaines, L. K., & Kappeler, V. (2011). *Policing in America* (7th ed.). Waltham, MA: Anderson.

Garner, J. H., Maxwell, C., & Heraux, C. (2002). Characteristics Associated with the Prevalence and Severity of Force Used by Police. *Justice Quarterly, 19*, 705-746.

Hails, J., & Borum, R. (2003). Police Training and Specialized Approaches to Respond to People with Mental Illnesses. *Crime & Delinquency, 49*, 52-61.

Hill, K., Lui, C., & Hawkins, D. (2004). Early Precursors of Gang Membership: A Study of Seattle Youth. In F. Esbensen, S. Tibbetts, & L. Gaines (Eds.), *American Youth Gangs at the Millennium* (pp. 191-199). Long Grove, IL: Waveland Press.

Howell, J. (2004). Youth Gangs: An Overview. In F. Esbensen, S. Tibbetts, & L. Gaines (Eds.), *American Youth Gangs at the Millennium* (pp. 16-51). Long Grove, IL: Waveland.

Janik, J. (1992). Dealing with Mentally Ill Offenders. *FBI Law Enforcement Bulletin, 61*, 22-26.

Kappeler, V. E. (2005). *Critical Issues in Police Civil Liability* (4th ed.). Prospect Heights, IL: Waveland Press.

Kappeler, V. E., & Potter, G. W. (2005). *The Mythology of Crime and Criminal Justice* (4th ed.). Prospect Heights, IL: Waveland Press.

King, W., & Dunn, T. (2004). Police-Initiated Transjurisdictional Transport of Troublesome People. *Police Quarterly, 7*(3), 339-358.

Klein, M. (1971). *Street Gangs and Street Workers*. Englewood Cliffs, NJ: Prentice-Hall.

Kubrin, C., & Ousey, G. (2009). Immigration and Homicide in Urban America: What's the Connection? *Sociology of Crime, Law, and Deviance, 13*, 17-32.

Lee, M., & Martinez, R. (2009). Immigration Reduces Crime: An Emerging Scholarly Consensus. *Sociology of Crime, Law, and Deviance, 13*, 3-16.

Malinosky-Rummell, R., & Hansen, D. (1993). Long-term Consequences of Childhood Physical Abuse. *Psychological Bulletin, 114*, 68-79.

Martin, D. (1994). Teen Violence: Why It's on the Rise and How to Stem Its Tide. *Law Enforcement Technology*, 36-42.

Maxson, C. (1998). *Gang Members on the Move. OJJDP Juvenile Justice Bulletin*. Washington, DC: U.S. Department of Justice.

Maxson, C. (2004). Gang Homicide: A Review and Extension of the Literature. In F. Esbensen, S. Tibbetts, & L. Gaines (Eds.), *American Youth Gangs at the Millennium* (pp. 275-296). Long Grove, IL: Waveland Press.

McDonald, W. F. (1997). Crime and Illegal Immigration. *National Institute of Justice Journal*, (June), 2-10.

McDonald, W. F. (1999). Policing the New America: Immigration and Its Challenge. In C. Brito & T. Allan (Eds.), *Problem Oriented Policing: Crime-Specific Problems, Critical Issues, and Making POP Work* (Vol. 2, pp. 209-250). Washington, DC: PERF.

Miller, W. (1980). Gangs, Groups, and Serious Youth Crime. In D. Schicor & D. Kelly (Eds.), *Critical Issues in Juvenile Delinquency*. Lexington, MA: Lexington Books.

Miller, W. (1991). Gangs, Groups, and Serious Youth Crime. In D. Shichor & D. Kelly (Eds.), *Critical Issues in Juvenile Delinquency* (pp. 115-138). Lexington, MA: D.C. Heath.

National Child Traumatic Stress Network. (2011). *Facts on Trauma and Homeless Children*. http://www.nctsn.org/nctsn_assets/pdfs/promising_practices/Facts_on_Trauma_and_Homeless_Children.pdf. Accessed 31.05.11.

National Coalition for the Homeless. (2006). *Hate, Violence, and Death on Main Street USA*. Washington, DC: National Coalition for the Homeless.

National Coalition for the Homeless. (2010). *Hate Crimes Against the Homeless: America's Growing Tide of Violence*. Washington, DC: National Coalition for the Homeless.

National Coalition for the Homeless. (2009). *How Many People Experience Homelessness?* Washington, DC: National Coalition for the Homeless.

National Coalition of State Juvenile Justice Advisory Groups. (1992). *Myths and Realities: Meeting the Challenge of Serious, Violent, and Chronic Juvenile Offenders*. Washington, DC: Author.

National Law Center on Homelessness and Poverty. (January 2009). *Homelessness in the United States and the Human Right to Housing*.

Office of Juvenile Justice and Delinquency Prevention. (1994). *Gang Suppression and Intervention: Community Models*. Washington, DC: Author.

Office of Juvenile Justice and Delinquency Prevention. (2000). *Children as Victims*. Washington, DC: Author.

Office of Juvenile Justice and Delinquency Prevention (OJJDP). (2010). *Statistical Briefing Book*. http://ojjdp.ncjrs.gov/ojstatbb/victims/qa02102.asp?qaDate=2008. Accessed 30.05.11.

Patch, P., & Arrigo, B. (1999). Police Officer Attitudes and Use of Discretion in Situations Involving the Mentally Ill. *International Journal of Law and Psychiatry*, *22*, 23-35.

Piquero, A., & Mazerolle, P. (2001). *Life-course Criminology*. Belmont, CA: Wadsworth.

Plotkin, M., & Narr, O. (1993). *The Police Response to the Homeless: A Status Report*. Washington, DC: PERF.

Potter, G. W., & Kappeler, V. E. (2006). *Constructing Crime* (2nd ed.). Prospect Heights, IL: Waveland Press.

Radelet, L., & Carter, D. (2001). *The Police and the Community* (7th ed.). New York, NY: Macmillan.

Randolph M. Grinc (with Susan Sadd). (1994). "Innovative Neighborhood-Oriented Policing Programs: An Evaluation of Community Policing Programs in Eight Cities." pp. 27-52 in Community Policing: Testing the Promises, edited by Dennis P. Rosenbaum. Newbury Park, CA: Sage Publications.

Reisig, M., & Parks, R. (2004). Can Community Policing Help the Truly Disadvantaged? *Crime & Delinquency*, *50*, 139-167.

Ridgley, J. (2008). Cities of Refuse: Immigration Enforcement, Police, and the Insurgent Genealogies of Citizenship. *Urban Geography*, *29*, 53-77.

Robers, S., Zhang, J., Truman, J., & Snyder, T. (2010). *Indicators of School Crime and Safety: 2010*. Washington, DC: U.S. Department of Education and U.S. Department of Justice Office Justice Programs.

Romero, M. (2006). Racial Profiling and Immigration Law Enforcement: Rounding Up of Usual Suspects in the Latino Community. *Critical Sociology*, *32*, 447-473.

Ruiz, J., & Miller, C. (2004). An Exploratory Study of Pennsylvania Police Officers' Perceptions of Dangerousness and Their Ability to Manage Persons with Mental Illness. *Police Quarterly*, 7, 359-371.

Sanders, W. B. (1994). *Gangbangs and Drive-Bys*. New York, NY: Aldine De Gruyter.

Scanlan, C. (1989). An Older, Less White America Predicted. *Detroit Free Press*, (February 1).

Skogan, W. (2006). *Police and Communities in Chicago: A Tale of Three Cities*. New York: Oxford University Press.

Snyder, H., & Sickmund, M. (1995). *Juvenile Offenders and Victims: A Focus on Violence*. Washington, DC: Office of Juvenile Justice and Delinquency Prevention.

Snyder, M., & Hombs, M. (1986). Sheltering the Homeless: An American Imperative. *State Government: The Journal of State Affairs*, (Nov./Dec.).

Snyder, T. D., & Dillow, S. (2010). *Digest of Education Statistics 2009*. (NCES 2010-013). Washington, DC: National Center for Education Statistics, Institute of Education Sciences, U.S. Department of Education.

Solarz, A. (1985). An Examination of Criminal Behavior Among the Homeless. Paper presented at the annual conference of the American Society of Criminology.

Strauss, G., Glenn, M., Reddi, P., Afaq, I., Podolskaya, A., Rybakova, T., et al. (2005). Psychiatric Disposition of Patients Brought in by Crisis Intervention-Team Police Officers. *Community Mental Health Journal, 41*, 223-228.

Taylor, B., Fitzgerald, N., Hunt, D., Readon, J., & Brownstein, H. (2001). *ADAM Preliminary 2000 Findings on Drug Use and Drug Markets—Adult Male Arrestees.* Washington, DC: National Institute of Justice.

Taylor, C. (1986). Black Urban Youth Gangs: Analysis of Contemporary Issues. Paper presented at the annual conference of the American Society of Criminology.

Teplin, L. (2000). Keeping the Peace: Police Discretion and Mentally Ill Persons. *National Institute of Justice Journal*, (July), 1-15.

Terrill, W., & Mastrofski, S. (2002). Situational and Officer Based Determinants of Police Coercion. *Justice Quarterly, 19*(2), 215-248.

The Christopher Commission Report, www.hrw.org 1998 Reports, retrieved Nov. 5, 2008.

Urban Institute (2008). *Undocumented ImmigrantFacts and Figures.* Posted to Web: January 12, 2004.

Weitzer, R., & Tuch, S. (2006). *Race and Policing in America: Conflict and Reform*. New York: Cambridge University Press.

Whitehouse, J. (1973). Historical Perspectives on the Police Community Service Function. *Journal of Police Science and Administration, 1*(1), 87-92.

Widom, C., & Maxfield, M. (2001). *An Update on the Cycle of Violence.* Washington, DC: National Institute of Justice.

Williams, B. (1996). *Citizen Perspectives on Community Policing*. New York: State University of New York Press.

Every society gets the kind of criminal it deserves. What is equally true is that every community gets the kind of law enforcement it insists on.

—Robert F. Kennedy

CHAPTER 12 Toward a New Breed of Police Officer

LEARNING OBJECTIVES

After reading the chapter, you should be able to:

1. Identify the two primary sources of individual images and impressions of police.
2. Describe why the police role is paradoxical.
3. Describe the role of patrol officers in traditional policing and implementing community policing.
4. Identify the characteristics of people who have traditionally entered policing.
5. Describe the nature of police work and the research techniques used to glean that information.
6. Discuss the impact of "danger" on the social isolation of police officers.
7. List and describe the reasons for resistance to community policing.
8. Describe the impact community policing has on the role of the police.
9. Identify the characteristics of the ideal candidate for a position in a community policing department.

Images and Impressions

What image comes to mind when someone says police officer? Some people conjure up Norman Rockwell's vision of the friendly cop offering a lost child an ice cream cone. For others, it is Dirty Harry looking down the barrel of his .44, begging some scumbag to "make my day." Some of us grew up being told that police officers are our friends, someone to turn to whenever we are in trouble. Others were raised with the warning to be good or "the police will take you away." Many of us remember the disturbing TV images of the police decades ago letting loose dogs and firehoses on civil rights protesters, then a few years later clubbing protesters outside the Democratic Convention in Chicago. Younger generations are more likely to recall the graphic images of Los Angeles burning after the senseless police beating of motorist Rodney King or LAPD officers beating protesters at the 2007 May Day immigration rally at MacArthur Park. Still others may see the police as battling drug gangs, tracking down international terrorists, or trying to protect school children under siege from some gun-wielding lunatic. Or, perhaps, we recall a long funeral procession for an officer who had died in the line of duty. Maybe our most vivid memory is the police officer who gave us a speeding ticket or arrested a family member.

Police officers, peace officers, law enforcement officers, cops—no matter what term we attach to the job, most people have a vivid, if not always accurate, image of what police work entails, one that might blend awe, respect, disdain, and fear. Our personalized picture is the end result of cumulative exposure to the police in real life and "reel" life—the officers we have met, the ones we have seen in the theater, and the ones we learn about from the media. All too often these are the images the public has of the police and even the way police see themselves and their work.

In American society, where there is great tension between a desire to allow police the power to protect us and, at the same time, a fear that we must circumscribe their role to protect civil rights, the police have always played an ambiguous role. In *Policing in a Free Society,* Herman Goldstein (1977:3) wrote about the "basic pervasive conflict between crime-fighting and constitutional due process which is inherent in the police function in a free society." Kappeler has remarked, "This means the police may be seen by the public in paradoxical roles. To many segments of society, the police represent what has been termed the 'thin blue line' that separates anarchy from order. Seen in this light, the police represent a governmental body whose ultimate mission is to protect the civil liberties of citizens. This responsibility is paradoxical in the sense that police also represent one of the greatest threats to these liberties" (Kappeler, Sluder & Alpert, 1998:2). This is especially true when police officers abuse the authority of their office.

The police have the power to "put us away." The police are also the only agents of formal social control with the right to use force, including deadly force to accomplish their mandate. By emphasizing their role as crime-fighters, we see them as the thin blue line protecting the forces of light from the powers of evil. Not only does this narrow view ignore the complexity of policing, but it reinforces the perception of society as divided into the Good Guys in the White Hats versus a smaller pool of Bad Guys in Black Hats. Though it provides convenient shorthand for both the police and the community when referring to crime situations to divide the world into the law-abiding people who must remain vigilant against predators, the real world is blessed with only a handful of saints above reproach and an equally small number of unregenerate monsters. In between are the vast majority of people.

The danger in oversimplification is that we can fall victim to the temptation to demonize those who break the law or glorify those who enforce it, thereby robbing both of their humanity. How many of us can say with absolute certainty where we would draw the line if we had a sick, hungry child and no money? We must also remember that many people who would never think of committing crimes as adults wince at things they did when they were younger. Many youngsters who threw a rock through a window at school, shoplifted something from a store, or even went joyriding in a "borrowed" car grew up to become valuable members of the community. The line between law-abiding and law-breaking can shift and change at different times and in different circumstances. While there is great nobility in the notion that the police provide a thin blue line of uniformed officers who can protect good people from evil, real life also requires confronting vast and shifting shades of gray. In fact, many behaviors of police officers fall within this area of gray, somewhere between right and wrong (see Kappeler, Sluder & Alpert, 1998; Crank, 2003).

The goal in this chapter is to examine traditional police culture and the police role, to separate myth from reality, to see what it takes to have "the right stuff" for the real job of policing. We will begin by exploring what the job involves in a traditional department, to see the kind of people who are attracted to this career field, and what they find once they are on the job. Then we will look at what a shift to community policing portends. Does it mean departments must find ways to attract and hire candidates with different qualities, skills, and abilities? Does the job of being a community policing officer (CPO) require attributes that differ from what we have traditionally associated with being a police officer? Do we need a new breed of police officer to handle the challenges of the job in the twenty-first century? Can such a dramatic change in the very culture of policing be achieved?

Traditional Police Culture

Individual patrol officers are the backbone of the traditional police approach. They are the "grunts" in the trenches, the individuals in the department who must deal directly with the community every day (Crank, 2003). In that sense, they are the traditional department's bridge to the saints, sinners, and average people who constitute the real world. These officers come into contact with people in the community when they are at their very best and, unfortunately, when they are at their worst. Like most idealists, police officers bring to the job many great, and sometime misguided, expectations. Therefore, to understand what the real job of policing entails in a traditional department, it is important to explore what incoming candidates expect from the job—and what they find once they arrive.

Many candidates say that they are drawn to police work as a career because of a desire to help others or to serve their community. Others enter the field because of variety of practical considerations like job security (Figure 12.1). While police departments must always be alert to the danger

Figure 12.1
Reasons That Recruits Gave for Pursuing a Career in Law Enforcement
Note: The tick marks indicate the average response, and the lines represent the range for 80 percent of the responses.

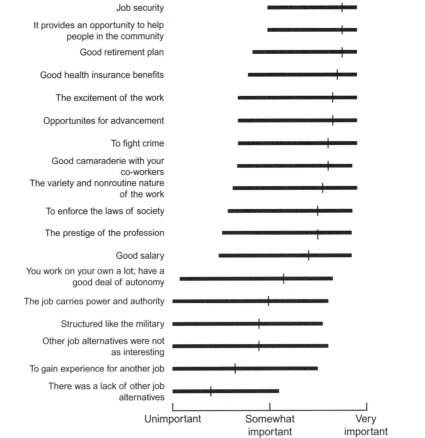

Source: Castaneda, L.W. & G. Ridgeway (2010). *Today's Police and Sheriff Recruits: Insights from the Newest Members of America's Law Enforcement Community.* U.S. Department of Justice Office of Community Oriented Policing Services, p. 14.

that some people will be attracted to the job because of an unhealthy desire to wield power over others, many of the men and women who seek careers in policing are inspired by idealism and altruism. Yet, many of the people who have entered police work also exhibit a tendency toward unhealthy levels of conformity and authoritarianism. Authoritarianism is characterized by conservative, aggressive, cynical, and rigid behaviors. Authoritarians have a limited view of the world and see issues in terms of black and white (Adorno, 1993). For the authoritarian there is little room for the shades of gray that exist in most aspects of life. People are good or bad, likable or unlikable, friends or enemies. These people are said to be extremely conservative, often having "knee-jerk" reactions to people and their problems. Some have labeled these people as "reactionary conservatives" because they are said to instinctively react in a conservative manner regardless of the merit of their position and often without reflecting upon the consequences of their acts (Kappeler, Sluder & Alpert, 1998; see also Loftus, 2010). John J. Broderick (1987:31) has done an excellent job of capturing how the term authoritarian is used in discussions of police:

> Those who ... use it are usually referring to a person who has great respect for power and authority and strongly adheres to the demands of his or her own group. This person is also submissive to higher authority and hostile toward outsiders who do not conform to conventional standards of behavior. The characteristics of willingness to follow orders and respect for authority might seem to be virtues when possessed by police officers, but in the sense used here, the term authoritarian means an extreme, unquestioning willingness to do what one is told and an extremely hostile attitude toward people who are different than oneself.

Carpenter and Raza (1987:16) found that police applicants differ from other occupational groups in several significant ways. First, these researchers found that police applicants, as a group, are psychologically healthy, "less depressed and anxious, and more assertive in making and maintaining social contacts." Second, their findings indicated that police are a more homogeneous group of people and that this "greater homogeneity is probably due to the sharing of personality characteristics which lead one to desire becoming a police officer." Finally, they found that police were more like military personnel in their conformance to authority.

It would seem that the people who have traditionally entered the police occupation share the qualities of idealism and those of authoritarianism. They view the unique power conferred on them as a tool they can use to make a valid contribution in making society a conventional place to live. Loftus (2010) adds that in his observations of the police, "authoritarian ideologies were accompanied by a conservative political persuasion" (p. 9). Power, to officers with this mind-set, is used to force conformity onto a community, not to serve it. Unfortunately, the same people attracted to policing often do not understand the shades of gray we just mentioned. They see the world in terms of good and evil. They also tend to view police work as an exciting, danger-filled occupation.

If these idealistic candidates succeed in becoming patrol officers, many are often surprised to find much of the job involves waiting for something to happen rather than making something happen. "In fact, the average cop on television probably sees more action in a half-hour than most officers witness in an entire career. As a general rule, most police work is quite mundane" (Kappeler & Potter, 2005:212). A variety of research techniques have been employed to study police activities (Greene & Klockars, 1991): radio calls from dispatchers to patrol cars (Bercal, 1970), telephone calls by people to the police (Cumming, Cumming & Edell, 1965), dispatch records (Reiss, 1971), observational data (Kelling et al., 1974), self-reports from police officers (O'Neill & Bloom, 1972), and telephone interviews of people (Mastrofski, 1983). What all these studies show is that relatively little of a police officer's day is taken up responding to serious crime. Jack Greene and Carl Klockars (1991:283) perhaps said it best noting that research "findings in no way lend support to the headline news vision of police work as a violent running battle between police and criminals." Yet, police cleave to these views of the occupation. "A masculine ethos absorbed by the imagery of conflict and danger was one of the most prominent features of the culture … . Although actual episodes of dangerous encounters were rare, officers routinely told each other … stories that glorified violent and confrontational encounters with members of the public" (p. 7). There is far less fighting evil than police recruits might anticipate or even hope for. This situation often comes as a surprise for new police officers.

Police patrol time is also poorly structured. As most research attests, motor patrol officers spend most of their time on patrol, waiting for a call (Payne & Trojanowicz, 1985). While cruising around on patrol, the officers are, in essence, waiting to spot some sign of trouble, whether it's a traffic violation or some suspicious activity on the street. The opportunities to initiate positive action are limited by the need to remain available to handle the next call. The second most time-consuming aspect of the job is handling complaints—and that term can seem particularly apt, since one of the surprises many fledgling officers face is realizing the amount of friction with the community that they encounter on the job. As James Q. Wilson (1970) noted, we often equate crime-fighters with

SPOTLIGHT ON COMMUNITY POLICING PRACTICE

Community Policing Specialists vs. Generalists

Most police agencies are highly specialized, dividing themselves into a number of units, bureaus, or divisions, each with distinct duties. It is not surprising, then, that when some agencies chose to implement community policing, they did so through the creation of specialized community policing units. According to a 2000 survey by the Bureau of Justice Statistics, approximately two-thirds of larger municipal (68%) and county (66%) police departments had full-time community policing units. Other agencies, albeit fewer in number, implemented community policing agency wide by creating community policing generalists and assigning responsibility for community policing activities to all officers. Still other departments have experimented with hybrid models that combine aspects of both approaches. Agencies should consider the advantages and disadvantages of each approach when choosing from among the implementation models.

Community Policing Specialists

Having a group of dedicated officers assigned full-time to community policing offers a number of advantages. This approach ensures that the officers have sufficient time to dedicate to proactive problem-solving and partnership-building efforts. In addition, it is easier for agencies to develop the knowledge and skills necessary to maximize efforts. Finally, specialized units can increase the visibility of community policing activities both within the department and to the community.

Specialized units, however, can breed resentment among other officers who may believe that the units receive special treatment and that their activities do not represent real police work (calling them "Grin and Wave Squads"). In addition, specialized units might encourage the idea that the majority of officers are not responsible for developing collaborative partnerships, engaging in problem-solving activities, or being attuned to the importance of community relations. Specialized units also expose a limited number of officers to community policing training and ideas, making it unlikely that community policing will ever grow beyond the bounds of the special unit. Community policing advocates (like the COPS Office) have generally supported agency wide implementation of community policing, premised on the notion that community policing is a philosophy that should inform all aspects of police business. Generalized models of community policing, however, are not without potential obstacles.

Community Policing Generalists

Adopting agency wide implementation by creating community policing generalists removes any potential tension between a special unit and the rest of the department. It enables agencies to emphasize the importance of proactive problem solving and partnership

(Continued)

development to all officers and builds these activities into their jobs. Agency wide implementation recognizes the belief that community policing principles are applicable to all aspects of police business including routine patrol, investigations, arrests, and traffic stops. Agency wide implementation increases the potential scope and breadth of community policing efforts and facilitates its eventual institutionalization.

On the downside, agency wide implementation can result in a watered-down version of community policing (more reflective of community relations than community policing), with officers actually devoting little time to the core activities of partnership building and problem solving. If officers do not see these activities as integrated into their current duties, they might see them as extra work and resist their implementation. In addition, officers frequently report that they do not have sufficient time to devote to community policing and, therefore, will resist agency wide implementation. In addition, it can be difficult for large agencies to provide adequate training to large numbers of officers in the depth necessary to fully realize the benefits of community policing. Because of these potential concerns, a number of agencies have implemented community policing through a combination of both approaches.

Hybrid Approaches

Some agencies have implemented special units to support the community policing efforts of the entire agency, while encouraging all officers to participate in those efforts. For example, a special unit will set aside sufficient time to engage in in-depth problem-solving efforts for a precinct or an entire city. At the same time, it is made clear to all officers that some problem-solving activities are expected of them, focused on a specific neighborhood or even a single address. In addition, all officers are encouraged to rely on the special unit for assistance in implementing their own community policing efforts, thereby incorporating the special unit into all aspects of police business. Finally, all officers can receive training in community policing that is appropriate and tailored to their position.

Matthew Scheider
Assistant Director
The COPS Office

Source: The e-newsletter of the COPS Office, Volume 1, Issue 4, April 2006.

fire-fighters, as if the jobs were pretty much alike. Yet police officers often feel far more alienated from the community, because they are far more likely to find themselves in adversarial situations where they are perceived as the antagonist.

That feeling of being separate and apart from society at large explains why police officers so often band together for mutual support. The job contains an element of danger, which means officers must rely on each other for their mutual safety. As Skolnick (1966) has observed, danger is one of the most important facets in the development of a police working personality. The relationship between the "real" dangers associated with police work and the police perception of the job as hazardous is complex. While police officers perceive their work as dangerous, they realize that the chances of being injured are not as great as their preoccupation with the idea of danger (Cullen, Link, Travis & Lemming, 1983; Kappeler & Potter, 2005; Loftus, 2010). The disjuncture between the potential for injury and the exagger-ated sense of danger found among police officers is best explained in the remarks of David Bayley (1976:171), who observes:

> *You can learn more about police culture by going to http://sociologyindex.com/police:culture.htm.*

> The possibility of armed confrontation shapes training, patrol preoc-cupations, and operating procedures. It also shapes the relationship between citizen and policeman by generating mutual apprehension. The policeman can never forget that the individual he contacts may be armed and dangerous; the citizen can never forget that the policeman is armed and may consider the citizen dangerous.

Such occupational conceptions foster isolation and antagonism and also encourage police to pull together into a separate subculture of their own. Isolation is an emotional and physical condition that makes it difficult for mem-bers of one social group to have relationships and interact with members of another group. This feeling of separateness from the surrounding community is a frequently noted attribute of police subculture (Skolnick, 1966; Reiss & Bordua, 1967; Manning, 1978; Harris, 1973; Sherman, 1982; Loftus, 2010). The self-imposed social isolation of the police from the surrounding community is well documented (Baldwin, 1992; Clark, 1965; Skolnick, 1966; Cain, 1973; Swanton, 1981). Social isolation reinforces the notion that people outside the police subculture are to be viewed warily as potential threats to the members' physical or emotional well-being, as well as challenges to the officer's author-ity and autonomy. According to Baldwin (1992) and Skolnick (1966), police impose social isolation upon themselves as a means of protection against real and perceived dangers, loss of personal and professional autonomy, and social rejection. Rejection by the community stems, in part, from the resentment that sometimes arises when laws are enforced (Clark, 1965). As no one enjoys receiving a traffic ticket or being arrested, and no one enjoys being disliked, the police tend to look inward to their own members for validation and sup-port (Kappeler, Sluder & Alpert, 1998).

Even the uniform, badge, and gun serve as symbols of being different from the "civilian" on the street. The police, by virtue of their social role, are granted a unique position in the law. Police have a legal monopoly on the sanctioned use of violence (Westley, 1953; Reiss & Bordua, 1967; Reiss, 1971) and coercion (Westley, 1953,1956, 1970; Bittner, 1970) against other members of society. The police are, therefore, set apart from the community because of their unique position in the law and their ability to use violence legally and invoke the force of law. This legal distinction between the people and police sets officers apart from the larger culture and other occupations.

That sense of being separate and apart from the rest of the community is also heightened by the fact that police officers see things that other people do not see. Most people are spared the sight of mangled bodies crushed in cars, battered children, women who have been raped, and decaying corpses, yet this is a small part of what police work entails. The job also requires peeking into people's private lives in ways no other job does, which means the police tend to see people at their worst, not their best. People do not call the police to come share their triumphs and joys, but when they are hurt, angry, frightened, and upset. The exceptional experiences police officers encounter shape their view of the world and the way they respond to their communities.

The need to pull together is also reinforced in traditional departments where those at the bottom of the police pyramid can feel thwarted by the restrictions imposed by working in a paramilitary bureaucracy. Those altruistic candidates who chose police work so that they could make a positive difference can feel frustrated at finding themselves inhibited by a structure where the emphasis on avoiding mistakes seems to overshadow the opportunities to take creative action. Paramilitary bureaucracy stifles innovation and breeds immature personalities, two characteristics that are antithetical to community policing. Police work has been called the most unprofessional profession, because traditional departments often seem to expend more energy in defining the limits of the job than in supporting autonomy, innovation, and problem solving.

The power of traditional police culture can serve as an unhealthy lure for those who want to dominate and abuse others (Kappeler, Sluder & Alpert, 1998). Yet, even the most altruistic candidates can find the job sometimes dangerous and often tedious, one in which they see the horrors that people inflict on each other, horrors they often appear powerless to prevent. Compounding the problem, many find themselves trapped in a system and culture where they receive little support from superiors for taking any initiative. In fact, doing nothing is often seen as the safest choice and a way to stay out of trouble with the department. In some departments, turning to their peers for support requires embracing a macho ethic that puts the highest premium on acting tough and aggressive, regardless of the situation. No matter how well their education and prior experience may have prepared them to understand the full range of human dynamics that impel people to act as they do, that knowledge can be washed out by the combination of the ugliness they see and the callous indifference that their seasoned peers insist is the only way to survive the rigors of the job. Thwarted idealists may struggle against becoming cynics, but cynicism toward the community and toward the police hierarchy may be so potent that few can resist.

SPOTLIGHT ON COMMUNITY POLICING PRACTICE

Discourteous Cops and Unruly Citizens: Mediation Can Help

Achieving a healthy community-police relationship should not be viewed as simply a "warm and fuzzy" or "touchy-feely" aspiration, but rather a necessary objective of any police department. A largely positive relationship between a department and its residents results in safer neighborhoods. Much research suggests that the health of police-community relations (or lack thereof) brings with it very real and quantifiable consequences. When community members hold negative perceptions of police (whether justifiably or not), they are:

- Less likely to alert police when crime is occurring
- Less likely to cooperate with investigations, thereby preventing officers from solving crimes
- Less likely to serve as witnesses, thereby preventing successful prosecution of criminals
- More likely to wait until it is too late to report crime
- More likely to disregard the law, thereby committing more offenses
- More likely to disobey a lawful order by a police officer.

Citizen complaints against the police are inevitable, given the often confrontational nature of police-citizen interaction. Feelings that the police were discourteous, biased in their actions (sexist, racist, etc.), violated one's constitutional rights, or used excessive force frequently lead to mistrust of police officers and a reluctance to cooperate with them or call on them in times of emergency.

Mediation in Denver: As an objective and neutral civilian oversight agency whose mission is to increase public confidence in Denver, Colorado's law enforcement, it is our responsibility to promote policies and initiatives that enhance police-community relations. For the past 3 years, the Office of the Independent Monitor (OIM), in concert with the Denver Police Department, has managed a successful community-police mediation program as a way of resolving police complaints that alleviates misunderstandings, fear, mistrust, trauma, anger, and resentment. In effect, mediation programs should be seen by police departments as

(Continued)

contributing to a larger goal of improving community-police relations, which is essential to enhancing neighborhood safety.

The Internal Affairs Bureau of police departments is charged with investigating citizen- and department-initiated complaints. Traditionally, Internal Affairs would investigate a citizen complaint and command staff would make a finding and, where appropriate, impose discipline. As such, Internal Affairs serves as an internal control mechanism used by departments to assist in managing their employees' behavior. While there have always been questions concerning the difficulty of proving misconduct one way or the other, there were simply no alternatives for dealing with citizen complaints. Unfortunately, this traditional method of complaint-handling, more often than not, has left both complainants and officers dissatisfied with the outcome and process. Ill feelings generally remain unresolved; mistrust of the police department lingers.

Recently, however, there has been some movement toward a more conciliatory and nonadversarial model of complaint handling. That model is mediation. Mediation involves bringing both parties face-to-face in a neutral and confidential setting to discuss the specifics of the complaint. The meeting is facilitated by professional mediators who attempt to get the parties to a point of mutual understanding concerning the actions that led to the complaint.

As the essence of community policing, mediation has the potential to improve the relationship between complainants and officers one case at a time, and often does. Mediation helps prevent an unpleasant experience a citizen might have with one officer from resulting in a negative perception and attitude toward all of law enforcement. In addition, a successful mediation can extend the repaired relationship to the community member's family and friends, some of whom might have been adversely affected by the complainant's personal experience.

The use of mediation in handling citizen complaints against the police is a relatively new phenomenon that is still in its early stages.

Jon Proctor, Ph.D
Management Analyst
Office of the Independent Monitor
Denver, Colorado

A.J. Clemmons
Community Relations Ombudsman
Office of the Independent Monitor
Denver, Colorado

Richard Rosenthal
Independent Monitor
Office of the Independent Monitor
Denver, Colorado

Source: The e-newsletter of the COPS Office, Volume 2, Issue 3, March 2009 [citations omitted].

Left unchallenged and unaddressed, such pressures can make officers feel that their superiors use them as pawns in a cat-and-mouse game in which they must follow rules but their opponents do not. Especially today, an exaggerated sense of the menace posed by drugs and terrorism, can cause patrol officers to see themselves as outmanned, outgunned, underpaid, and bound by rigid rules that the "predators" exploit. The intellectual and emotional leap required to adopt the view that police officers are trapped between an ungrateful community and unthinking superiors can seem small, especially when peers insist that it is emotional suicide to do otherwise.

Resistance to Community Policing

There are reasons that people inside and outside policing will never become fans of community policing. Some resistance comes from a general reluctance to embrace change, no matter how positive. Others have philosophical concerns that have led them to reach an honest difference of opinion. Those who think they fare better under the existing system and culture also have reason to resist change. Resistance to community policing manifests from a tendency of individuals and organizations to fear change. The resistance stems from the fact that police departments are conservative, paramilitary organizations that view change with skepticism. And some resistance comes from traditionalists who disagree with the effort on philosophical grounds, primarily those who feel that the police department's plate is already full enough dealing with "serious crime," and that the police should not broaden their mandate to include problems where they may not have sufficient expertise. Added to them are people inside the department who are the winners under the existing system, those who may see themselves as relative losers under community policing. Fear of change, vested interests, and a singular focus on crime fighting all conspire against community policing.

Regardless of their assignment, anyone who has loudly championed or defended the existing system and culture risks becoming a loser, since the change implies a rejection of the system and culture they probably continue to believe in, one they probably worked hard to make succeed, and one that supports the traditional view of the occupation and their place in it. The change may be viewed not only as a betrayal, but as an insult as well. After all, if the existing system worked well, there would be no need to make any change, especially one as dramatic, fundamental, and far-reaching as community policing.

People who currently hold positions of power within the department can perceive themselves as becoming losers as a result of the change. Yet for the most part, though the police in general may have been reluctant to change, once educated to the benefits of community policing, many police chiefs were at least numbered among the primary proponents responsible for making the shift. But the chief often has the most to lose if the new approach appears to fail or produces embarrassing mistakes. One of the ways in which the traditional system makes the chief a winner is that it promotes predictability and provides great control. By rewarding those who follow rules and procedures closely, the system emphasizes avoiding mistakes. As long as no one challenges whether those rules and procedures do as much to produce the results that people want as community policing, the traditional system often hums along relatively smoothly, causing little unexpected grief for the person at the top, though there have obviously been many examples where this has not been true (see Kappeler, Sluder & Alpert, 1998).

The traditional system also provides at least some "protective cover" when problems erupt. Many times the chief can deflect criticism by pointing out that the mistake occurred because the officers involved violated or ignored rules and procedures. This also allows administrators to cast abuses by police officers as isolated and aberrant behaviors—a few rotten apples—rather than problems that follow directly from the existing system and culture (Kappeler, Sluder & Alpert, 1998). When a police officer abuses a person or when criminal violence erupts, an area suffers a dramatic rise in property crimes, or people complain about new drug problems, the chief in a traditional department can hope to deflect responsibility by pointing to the underlying social problems for which they have no responsibility. Though the traditional approach emphasizes the role of the police as the community's crime-fighters, the chief can usually elicit at least some sympathy by saying that police cannot do anything about poverty and the slum or ghetto conditions it causes, the places that breed crime and drug problems. In a traditional police department, the chief can rail about how officers are doing all they can to help, but the blame for "decaying" neighborhoods lies with city leaders who allow garbage to rot uncollected on the street and who fail to provide idle teens enough summer activities to keep them out of mischief. Police do not create the conditions that breed crime and community problems, but they can bring pressure to bear on those who do.

Community policing puts the chief on the hook for many problems that the traditional system does not. The rotten apple metaphor that is often used to explain away police corruption and deviance is less acceptable when the department has cleaned the barrel by adopting community policing. So, too, are excuses for the use of unnecessary force by police officers since community policing does not rely on the use of force to solve community problems. People are not seen as unruly beasts who only understand and conform by means of violence. Other excuse mechanisms also become problematic and negative behaviors less defensible by the adoption of community policing. It says the department has a valid role to play in making sure that garbage is picked up and children have something worthwhile to do. In granting the responsibility to line officers to tackle a broader range of community problems, it also provides them the authority and power to do more—which means more opportunities for mistakes.

Not only will some creative solutions fail totally, even if they help reduce overall severity or frequency, some people will still take potshots at involving the police in anything that does not focus on arresting the "bad guys" and putting them away, although "putting them away" is as far out of reach for the police as controlling poverty and slum conditions. Doing anything else seems, to them, to ignore getting tough on the people who break the law.

When officers are granted greater autonomy, some will potentially put the chief on the spot by abusing their new freedom. In one case, a person called the department to report that a male CPO and his female counterpart appeared to be sneaking away to an apartment for an afternoon tryst every day. The bad news was that an investigation proved the allegations true, but the good news was that this shows people become so involved in the police process as a result of community policing that they not only act as unofficial supervisors, but trust their department well enough to call and complain. Some police departments have become so alienated from their communities that people will not bother to report even the most serious abuses by the police.

The same problems the chief faces extend to the people in top command, as well as middle managers and especially supervisors. Supervisors, who usually feel caught in the middle regardless of which system is in place, have reason to worry about becoming big losers with a shift to community policing, because the worst part of their job is carrying any bad news to the boss. Middle managers can also feel threatened by a loss of status and control, because community policing requires them to share power with officers beneath them in the hierarchy. In the traditional police department supervisors have a vested interest in both detecting minor problems by officers for sanction as well as ignoring major behavioral problems that would cast their supervision in unfavorable light (Kappeler, Sluder & Alpert, 1998). It is also demonstrably more difficult to supervise community officers, because a true assessment of their performance requires making personal visits to the beat areas to see firsthand how well the CPO is doing. The ability of supervisors to argue effectively that they did not know about a particular problem officer or behavior is less if supervisors are expected to make these personal contacts rather than just check up on officers over the radio.

SPOTLIGHT ON COMMUNITY POLICING PRACTICE

The Role of Performance Appraisal Systems in Community Policing

The primary goals of performance appraisal systems are twofold: to ensure that employees are aware of the expectations the organization has of them, and to assess their activities and performance accordingly. For community policing to be implemented and sustained effectively, it is important that law enforcement agencies adapt their performance appraisal systems to reflect community policing measures, as well as the traditional measures that currently are used. By doing so, agencies will be in a much better position to assess their community policing activities at the individual, unit, and organizational levels.

Adapting existing performance appraisal systems so that they reflect community policing priorities can be complicated. Fully assessing performance in a community policing agency requires a performance appraisal system that includes measures that are easily quantifiable, but also reflects activities and strategies that are employed to achieve the desired results that are more difficult to quantify. In describing the fundamentals of effective police performance management, the United Kingdom Home Office, which has developed a comprehensive set of materials to support its move toward updating police performance reporting and tracking within the U.K., has defined good performance as "doing the right things ("priorities"), doing them well ("quality"), and doing the right amount ("quantity")." Nevertheless, while difficult, developing community policing standards and measures and including them in the performance appraisal system can serve as a linchpin for putting the community policing philosophy in place and institutionalizing the concept.

Performance Appraisals for Officers

Under community policing, line-level officers are encouraged to become intimately familiar with the geographic areas they serve, as well as the people who live and work in that community. Officers are also encouraged to develop ownership for community issues and priorities and to identify and address specific crime problems within that area. Performance appraisal systems that evaluate community policing activities can serve as a valuable tool for these officers by creating the expectations for their work. Moreover, by evaluating officers on their community policing efforts, they are provided with an opportunity to be recognized for the true impact they are making on the community.

The results of performance appraisals may also allow an agency to tailor and focus its training efforts on areas demonstrated of greatest need. Existing reward and promotion systems, which may already reflect community policing and that are used to endorse the desired work of officers, are reinforced when accompanied by a performance appraisal system reflecting consistent values. Moreover, including community policing measures in officer performance appraisals serves as a form of agreement between the agency and officer about not just what is required of him or her while on the job, but also the support, flexibility, and resources the agency needs to invest so that officers can be fully successful.

The Supervisors' Role in Managing the Performance Appraisal System

Supervisors play a fundamental part in helping officers understand their role in community policing. It is their responsibility to translate the philosophy of community policing into expectations for practical activity and then evaluate the officer's performance in meeting these expectations. To accomplish this, supervisors must articulate and demonstrate what is expected, then reinforce the expectations through the performance appraisal process, among other things. Reinforcing successful performance and addressing activities and behavior that are neither desired nor a priority should be addressed not only daily, but also through the formal performance appraisal process.

Whenever possible, supervisors need to remove barriers to the effective implementation of community policing and support the development of skills and knowledge within officers they oversee. Supervisors can identify training needs of their officers by evaluating community policing successes and using performance appraisals to identify areas that need improvement. Ultimately, by encouraging and holding officers responsible for activities such as analyzing crime trends in a service area, mobilizing the community, collecting citizen input on priorities and concerns, and developing problem-oriented policing projects, supervisors become accountable for community policing.

Conclusion

Communities hold their law enforcement agencies to very high standards. A comprehensive performance appraisal system that reflects community policing values can help to determine if the level of service of individual officers, units, and the department as a whole is at the desired level. It can inform strategic planning, performance benchmarking and reporting, and training initiatives and, ultimately, improve the department's level of problem-solving and partnerships with the community.

Performance appraisal systems are perhaps the clearest enunciation of what employees should do and achieve and, in that sense, represent the very essence of an agency. Tracking and evaluating community policing through performance appraisal systems recognizes that the police role is broad and complex, and that working in partnership with the community and engaging in problem-solving are priorities. Performance appraisal systems that do not capture the breadth and depth of activity under community policing may actually discourage community policing activities. Agencies that have maximized the important role that their

(Continued)

performance appraisal system plays in ensuring that officers both understand and are held responsible for meeting community policing responsibilities are likely to see more widespread and effective use of community policing by their employees.

Robert Chapman
Supervisory Social Science Analyst
The COPS Office

Liz Newsom
Research Analyst
The COPS Office

Samuel Mello
Special Contributor
The COPS Office

Source: The e-newsletter of the COPS Office, Volume 1, Issue 10, October 2008.

It would seem that all line officers would benefit under a community policing approach, because of the greater responsibility, authority, and freedom to explore new ways to solve problems. Yet experience shows that much of the resistance to community policing comes from motor patrol officers. This was often more true in the past, when community policing was adopted piecemeal. This often meant that the ranks of the department's motor patrol officers were thinned to field the new CPOs required. Instead of educating and energizing everyone in the department about how to become community problem-solvers, many departments focused first on using community officers as their new, creative thinkers, while motor patrol officers were pretty much told to keep doing the same old thing, with fewer officers.

Eager, open-minded community officers enthusiastic about their new opportunity to work with people directly on a host of challenging new initiatives are obvious winners, yet it is easy to see why their motor patrol peers resented their greater autonomy—especially since CPOs may not work nights or weekends, and they often have additional flexibility in setting their schedules. Motor patrol officers who take great pride in their role as crime-fighters, and who see themselves as potentially risking their lives daily for people in the community they often perceive as ungrateful (see Loftus, 2010), can see themselves as losers if the department begins to emphasize broader goals. The cultural divide between line officers and administrators (Reuss-Ianni, 1983) can widen if a significant number of line officers do not embrace community policing when the administration has full-heartedly endorsed it. Many openly resent the social work approach of community policing, dismissing CPOs as lollicops, the grin-and-wave squad, or "shit magnets" for their propensity to be called to seemingly boring incidents (Loftus, 2010:8).

Victor G. Strecher (1999:77-78) has commented that, "When officers assigned in the CPO mode are asked what they do, they paw the ground, shrug, and give answers such as, 'walk and talk,' 'gin and chin,' 'chat and charm,' 'schmooze,' and often, 'maybe the brass will let us know'" Part of the reasons behind these responses are, of course, not because of a failure of direction or because of a genuine concern with the manner in which the community policing philosophy is operationalized but rather expressions of resistance to a philosophy that directly challenges the traditional police culture as well as the professional identity these officers have developed over years of culturalization into an ethos of crime fighting.

Motor patrol officers pose a thorny problem, since many automatically resent the fact that some community officers may inappropriately keep bankers' hours, with weekends off, and they can also benefit from more flexible schedules. If the motor patrol officers share a commitment to community problem solving as a valid goal and understand how their CPOs can help them, that will help. But many motor patrol officers will at least take time to grasp the benefits. Until or unless this happens, there exists the risk that resentment could become outright hostility.

Many motor patrol officers who believe bravery and toughness are "the right stuff" can rankle when they see people treat their community officers as heroes. The macho myth says that people should not like police officers, but should respect them, as if the two were mutually exclusive. Even though CPOs still use force, when appropriate, many motor patrol officers feel this new kind of officer is just not a real cop.

Community policing requires supervisors to share power with underlings; at the same time they must be willing to work harder to find out if CPOs are doing a good job. The loss of status and control, as well as the new challenge imposed by finding new ways to assess performance, both make the job tougher and challenge the balance of power between line officers and supervisors. Supervisors who see the wisdom of the effort, at first or over time, find the change invigorating, while those who do not like what community policing entails find the new demands draining and perhaps stressful.

Changing Traditional Police Culture

Dramatically altering the educational, cultural, racial, ethnic, and sexual mix of the police officers within police departments implies a tremendous change, even if there has been no change in the organizational structure. It means that modern police departments can no longer be dominated and controlled by White males. Not only does this militate against the danger that the department will adopt an ethnocentric, macho ethic, but an influx of college-educated offi-cers also implies that the officers will demand greater autonomy and flexibility. The job has long attracted idealists who want to make a positive difference, but now that the job increasingly attracts less authoritarian and more innovative college-educated candidates armed with the values and skills of professionals, this increases the pressure on police managers to allow them to function more as professionals within the community. Police agencies must change the way they do business because they are finding it more and more difficult to attract highly qualified people to the occupation.

Yet there are limits inherent in the traditional approach that no doubt have contributed to the concern that the police risk losing these most valued employees to other careers. In a traditional department, the system can only be bent so much before it risks falling apart entirely. The cultural strings that have held policing together—danger, isolation, control, authority—must be severed if community policing is to make a meaningful foothold in the police institu-tion. Yet there are inherent limits on how much freedom officers can be given considering the restrictions of the traditional mandate as crime-fighters and the reliance on violence and traditional police tactics as the best means of achiev-ing that mission.

Many traditional departments have responded to the challenge posed by these dramatic changes in the overall make-up of their line officers by mak-ing at least tentative steps toward broadening the police mandate from crime fighting to community problem solving. Officially and unofficially, police offi-cers have been exploring ways to employ problem-solving techniques. Many departments still restrict their application primarily to crime incidents, insist-ing that other problems are beyond the proper purview of the police. This plays into the hands of traditional police culture because it allows the institu-tion to maintain its unrealistic crime-fighting orientation and further solidifies the negative aspects of traditional police culture. Others have broadened their mandate to include involving officers in efforts to control community prob-lems, but often without allowing officers the time and the sustained presence in one area to develop a feel for the underlying dynamics and the continued presence in the community that may be required to enhance the likelihood of success. This, however, is a limited attempt at community policing because it allows the structuring of police work to limit the full acceptance of the spirit of community policing. Without modifications to organizational struc-ture, which few police departments have made, community policing runs the risk of being little more than lip service. Traditional police culture and organi-zational structure represent formidable barriers to a full conversion to com-munity policing.

Even so, there has been increasing pressure from below on police officials to grant line officers greater professional autonomy, responsibility, and authority. Those idealistic candidates seeking to change their communities for the better through a career in policing have been a major force in promoting experimentation with new ideas. Basically, they are more likely to reject the simplistic notion that communities can become safer and better places to live if line officers embrace an unwritten code that the solution lies in tough cops cracking more heads and making more arrests. Such officers are obviously more likely to think that brains are even more important than brawn and bullets in most situations. The police will always have to exercise the use of force in discharging their duty, but college-educated officers probably tend to generate fewer complaints because they may be more likely to explore other options first, whenever possible (Kappeler, Sapp & Carter, 1992). In general as well, these officers have a greater grasp of the complexity and diversity in the real world, which implies a greater appreciation of those shifting shades of gray.

Part of the problem CPOs face on the job in a traditional department stems from the reality that the traditional model attempts to make sense of the world and make the officer's job easier by casting the police in the role of the tough cops who protect the forces of light from the forces of evil—that thin blue line. Sophisticated and educated police officers often do not find that narrow view comforting, but confining. Instead of being overwhelmed or frustrated by the ambiguities of the real world, they are more likely to find the challenge a stimulating opportunity to see how much they can achieve. This can make the limitations and periods of inactivity that are often part of the traditional approach seem like obstacles that prevent them from accomplishing the goal of making communities safer and better places to live.

What Community Policing Offers

While there may be other theoretical models that might do a better job of capitalizing on some of the attributes, talents, and aspirations of this new breed of police officer who is beginning to permeate the ranks of departments nationwide, community policing comprehensively addresses all of the important issues raised. By broadening the police mandate and making substantive changes that provide organizational support and encouragement for innovation, community policing provides all officers within the department the cultural ethos and structural underpinnings necessary to do more toward that altruistic and idealistic goal of improving the overall quality of life in the community.

By expanding police work to include addressing the full range of community concerns, including crime, fear of crime, and community conditions, community policing gives police officers an expanded agenda that allows fuller expression of their full range of talents, skills, and abilities. And by making that all-important shift from seeing the police officer primarily as a crime-fighter to enlarging their role to that of community builder, this not only opens up the scope of the job, but it changes the basic nature of the police response from an emphasis on dealing with individual crime incidents to attacking the underlying dynamics that detract from the overall quality of life in the community.

If this new breed of college-educated officers is perceived as being more professional, better able to grasp the big picture, and more attuned to community needs, they should therefore be more likely to thrive in a system and culture that grants them more freedom and autonomy to explore proactive solutions to community problems. The police have faced tremendous pressure from college-educated officers to grant them additional responsibility and authority. To attract and retain the best candidates for the job required re-thinking a system and culture that focused more on ensuring control and distributing the use of force (Bittner, 1970) than supporting innovation.

Implications for the Future

Putting all the pieces together, it appears that community policing overall, and the community officer's job in particular, demands a new breed of officer. It means that police departments must recruit a broad mix of individuals so that they can more closely mirror the sexual, racial, and ethnic composition of the communities they serve, and it also means those candidates should be sensitive to, and tolerant of, diversity.

In particular as well, the focus on community problem solving that is an integral part of all officers' jobs in a department that has adopted community policing demands recruiting candidates who can think for themselves. Because the community policing philosophy means a shift from focusing on individual crime incidents and the use of force to address them to exploring creative ways to address the underlying dynamics that create an environment where problems can persist, the best candidates must also be creative and innovative. This is not found among authoritarian conformists who have traditionally entered police service or the veteran officers who insist on transmitting the negative cultural aspects of policing to every new generation of officers. "The values that are often tied to the cop culture stemming from the traditional model of policing include skepticism and cynicism among the police, the development of a code of secrecy to fend off external control and oversight, and often a general disdain for the public at large. Minimizing contact with the public and staying out of trouble, often through work avoidance, have been documented practices of traditional policing" (Greene, 2000:310).

Because community policing grants more freedom and autonomy to line officers, the best candidates will be individuals who can function as true professionals. This means they must be able to act responsibly, without constant supervision, and they must be able to exercise good judgment, consistent with the values and goals of society. This also implies the ability to develop and execute plans aimed at accomplishing realistic and achievable goals. To be professional also implies the capacity to use time wisely and to exercise self-discipline.

The new job of CPO in particular requires all this and more. It appears that the most critical determinant of future success as a CPO is superior communication skills. A good CPO must be able to communicate well with people from all walks of life, one-on-one and in groups. The ability to prepare and deliver speeches and write articles for publication is another obvious plus.

And because the research tends to show that the officers who function in this capacity tend to internalize the orientation and goals of the people they serve, rather than to turn to their fellow officers for guidance and approval, the job perhaps demands an even higher degree of professionalism than almost any other police role. While this is part of the reason for friction between motor patrol officers and CPOs, it is also part of the key in resisting the tendency of the traditional system and its culture to foster an internal climate dominated by the macho ethic of the tough cop.

The day-to-day job of being a community officer also means the best officers will strive to stay abreast of all the various kinds of help that public and private agencies can provide. This implies that the best candidates have experience in seeking out new information, individuals who know how to find what they need on their own. This also means that police departments must restructure themselves and police work to allow officers the time to develop the talents and collect the information necessary to do community policing. No occupation becomes a profession without giving its members the time and opportunity to learn and be well informed. This requires a restructuring of police work to include "intellectual" work, not just "doing the job."

As even this cursory analysis verifies, community policing demands a new breed of police officer, one who possesses specific attributes, qualities, and skills. As this analysis also shows, the college-educated men and women of diverse ethnic and racial backgrounds would have the "right stuff" for the job.

The major problem that police managers will have to contend with is how to hold onto these most highly prized new employees and how to insulate them from the negative effects of police culture. Not only do such candidates tend to chafe under the restrictions and narrowness implicit in the police officer's role in the traditional system, but they usually have other options available to them to enter jobs where their attributes and skills might be allowed fuller expression—and where, in addition, the monetary rewards are greater.

Yet true professionals worry as much or more about their opportunity to make a valid contribution through their work as they do about the size of their paycheck. The idealists attracted to police work because of the altruistic desire to make communities better and safer places in which to live and work find community policing offers more opportunities for job enrichment, job enhancement, job enlargement, and overall job satisfaction (see Pelfrey, 2004).

In particular, the new position as the department's outreach specialist, the CPO, not only provides the best candidates a worthwhile new option, but also provides the autonomy and freedom to allow the most talented individuals a new and unique opportunity to make the most of themselves. The job challenges individuals to see how much they can accomplish, because the boundaries of what can be achieved have yet to be fully defined. Each day, CPOs are discovering and developing new ways to make a positive difference, and the standard of excellence goes up yet another notch as creative and innovative officers find out how they can do even more.

The shift also has implications concerning how criminal justice education must change to meet these new demands. As the Police Executive Research Forum study showed, many police managers suggest that future candidates for police work should be encouraged to take college classes beyond those that directly relate to the "nuts-and-bolts" of police work (Carter, Sapp & Stephens, 1989). A curriculum that emphasizes exposure to the social sciences—psychology, sociology, anthropology—as well as disciplines such as economics and business administration would enhance an individual's overall knowledge about how the real world works; at the same time it would provide future police officers skills in areas that are becoming increasingly important in the job.

The new breed of police officer whose emergence into the field has already changed the composition of police departments will help shape the future of community policing. The basic job description emphasizes the ability to think, act, and communicate. No one knows for sure precisely how community policing will evolve in years to come. What is clear, however, is that the officers who capitalize on the flexibility and autonomy that are the hallmarks of this approach will help define and refine what it can and cannot do in practice. Not only will they be able to help police departments find new ways to meet the challenge of helping communities cope with the problems that they face in the twenty-first century, but this new breed of officer, armed with enhanced skills, will be able to tell us what it will take to do the job well.

KEY TERMS IN CHAPTER 12

- authoritarianism
- autonomy
- change
- communication skills
- cultural divide
- cultural strings
- danger
- force
- idealism
- isolation
- line officers
- middle managers

- paradoxical
- paramilitary bureaucracy
- patrol officers
- professionals
- protective cover
- reactionary conservatives
- reel life
- rejection
- social isolation
- thin blue line
- traditionalists

DISCUSSION QUESTIONS

1. Discuss what factors influence a person's ideological conception of the police.
2. Discuss whether the police truly are the "thin blue line" between anarchy and order.
3. What are the characteristics of authoritarianism? How does authoritarianism affect police officers? Can anything be done to minimize this trait?
4. Discuss what the text says about the characteristics of police applicants. Are these characteristics congruent with, or contrary to, the philosophy of community policing?
5. Briefly discuss what the authors mean by "police patrol time is poorly structured."
6. Why are police officers socially isolated? To whom is social isolationism the greatest problem: individual police officers, the police agency, or the community?
7. Describe and discuss the reasons for resistance to community policing among chiefs.
8. In your estimation what are the two most important explanations that account for officer resistance to community policing?
9. What can be said about the relationship that typically exists between community policing officers and motor patrol officers in agencies embracing community policing?
10. A new breed of highly educated, dedicated, and concerned police officers has been attracted to policing in recent years. These individuals are crucial for the future success of community policing programs. Discuss what negative influences exist in the police culture that present potential impediments for these officers and police agencies using community policing.
11. The authors state, "modern police departments can no longer be dominated by White males." Discuss why is this an important statement and what it means to departments that have not embraced community policing.

References

Adorno, T. W. (1993). *The Authoritarian Personality* (Revised ed.). New York, NY: Harper & Row, Publishers.

Baldwin, J. (1992). *Nobody Knows My Name*. New York, NY: Dell Publishing Company.

Bayley, D. (1976). *Forces of Order: Police Behavior in Japan and the United States*. Berkeley, CA: University of California Press.

Bercal, T. (1970). Calls for Police Assistance. *American Behavioral Scientist, 13*, 681-691.

Bittner, E. (1970). *The Functions of Police in Modern Society*. Chevy Chase, MD: National Clearinghouse for Mental Health.

Broderick, J. J. (1987). *Police in a Time of Change* (2nd ed.). Prospect Heights, IL: Waveland Press.

Cain, M. E. (1973). *Society and the Policeman's Role*. London, England: Routledge and Kegal Paul.

Carpenter, B. N., & Raza, S. M. (1987). Personality Characteristics of Police Applicants: Comparisons across Subgroups and with Other Populations. *Journal of Police Science and Administration, 15*(1), 10-17.

Carter, D. L., Sapp, A. D., & Stephens, D. W. (1989). *The State of Police Education*. Washington, DC: PERF.

Clark, J. P. (1965). Isolation of the Police: A Comparison of the British and American Situations. *Journal of Criminal Law, Criminology and Police Science, 56*, 307-319.

Crank, J. P. (2003). *Understanding Police Culture* (2nd ed.). New York, NY: LexisNexis Matthew Bender/Anderson Publishing.

Cullen, F.T., Link, B. G., Travis, L. F., & Lemming, T. (1983). Paradox in Policing: A Note on Perceptions of Danger. *Journal of Police Science and Administration, 11*(4), 457-462.

Cumming, E., Cumming, I., & Edell, L. (1965). Policeman as Philosopher, Friend and Guide. *Social Problems, 12*, 14-49.

Goldstein, H. (1977). *Policing in a Free Society*. Cambridge, MA: Ballinger.

Greene, J. (2000). Community Policing in America: Changing the Nature, Structure, and Function of the Police. In *Criminal Justice 2000, Volume 3, Policies, Processes, and Decisions of the Criminal Justice System* (pp. 299-370). Washington, DC: National Institute of Justice.

Greene, J., & Klockars, C. (1991). What Police Do. In C. Klockars & S. Mafstrofski (Eds.), *Thinking about Police: Contemporary Readings* (2nd ed.). New York, NY: McGraw-Hill.

Harris, R. (1973). *The Police Academy: An Insider's View*. New York, NY: John Wiley and Sons.

Kappeler, V. E., & Potter, G. W. (2005). *The Mythology of Crime and Criminal Justice* (4th ed.). Prospect Heights, IL: Waveland Press.

Kappeler, V. E., Sapp, A., & Carter, D. (1992). Police Officer Higher Education, Citizen Complaints and Departmental Rule Violations. *American Journal of Police, 11*(2), 37-54.

Kappeler, V. E., Sluder, R., & Alpert, G. P. (1998). *Force of Deviance: Understanding the Dark Side of the Force* (2nd ed.). Prospect Heights, IL: Waveland Press.

Kelling, G., Pate, T., Diekman, D., & Brown, C. E. (1974). *The Kansas City Preventive Patrol Experiment: A Summary Report.* Washington, DC: The Police Foundation.

Loftus, B. (2010). Police Occupational Culture: Classic Themes, Altered Times. *Policing & Society, 20*(1), 1-20.

Manning, P. K. (1978). The Police: Mandate, Strategies and Appearances. In L. K. Gaines & T. A. Ricks (Eds.), *Managing the Police Organization.* St. Paul, MN: West.

Mastrofski, S. (1983). The Police and Non-Crime Services. In G. Whitaker & C. Phillips (Eds.), *Evaluating Performance of Criminal Justice Agencies.* Beverly Hills, CA: Sage Publications.

O'Neill, M., & Bloom, C. (1972). The Field Officer: Is He Really Fighting Crime? *Police Chief, 39,* 30-32.

Payne, D. M., & Trojanowicz, R. C. (1985). *Performance Profiles of Foot Versus Motor Officers. Community Policing Series* (Vol. 6). East Lansing, MI: Michigan State University.

Pelfrey, W. V. (2004). The Inchoate Nature of Community Policing: Differences between Community Policing and Traditional Police Officers. *Justice Quarterly, 21*(3), 579-601.

Reiss, A. J. (1971). *The Police and the Public.* New Haven, CT: Yale University Press.

Reiss, A. J., & Bordua, D. J. (1967). Environment and Organization: A Perspective on the Police. In D. J. Bordua (Ed.), *The Police: Six Sociological Essays.* New York, NY: John Wiley and Sons.

Reuss-Ianni, E. (1983). *Two Cultures of Policing.* New Brunswick, NJ: Transaction Books.

Sherman, L. (1982). Learning Police Ethics. *Criminal Justice Ethics, 1*(1), 10-19.

Skolnick, J. H. (1966). *Justice without Trial: Law Enforcement in a Democratic Society.* New York, NY: John Wiley and Sons.

Strecher, V. (1999). Revising the Histories and Futures of Policing. In V. E. Kappeler (Ed.), *The Police & Society: Touch Stone Readings* (2nd ed., pp. 69-82). Prospect Heights, IL: Waveland Press.

Swanton, B. (1981). Social Isolation of Police: Structural Determinants and Remedies. *Police Studies, 3,* 14-21.

Westley, W. A. (1953). Violence and the Police. *American Journal of Sociology, 59,* 34-41.

Westley, W. A. (1956). Secrecy and the Police. *Social Forces, 34*(3), 254-257.

Westley, W. A. (1970). *Violence and the Police: A Sociological Study of Law, Custom and Morality.* Cambridge, MA: The MIT Press.

Wilson, J. Q. (1970). The Police and Their Problems. In A. Neiderhoffer & A. S. Blumberg (Eds.), *The Ambivalent Force: Perspectives on the Police.* Waltham, MA: Ginn and Company.

Every image should be confronted with another image.

—*Paul Eluard*

CHAPTER 13   Community Policing at the Crossroads

Community Policing: From Theory to Practice

The past few decades have seen exponential growth in the research and literature on community policing. The philosophy has come under close scrutiny by both scholars and police executives. Although community policing has been criticized for lack of continuity with history (Kappeler, 1996; Strecher, 2006), flaws in its parent doctrines (Walker, 2006), and serving as a legitimating tactic (Crank, 1994; Klockars, 1988), police academicians have mostly played the role of community policing advocates. While many scholars and reformers make distinctions between the philosophy of community policing and the many and varied strategies and tactics loosely associated with the philosophy, the phrase has become an umbrella term for almost any innovation in policing. Police chiefs, politicians, and even members of the community now invoke the phrase whenever problems associated with policing or communities surface. For too many people, community policing has become a buzz phrase and a panacea for almost all social problems facing the police and society.

While community policing has come to mean many things to many people, the spirit of community policing was something quite specific, not nearly the catchall phrase it has become today. Whether community policing is described as a philosophy, a paradigm shift, a new model for policing, or a collection of strategies and tactics, community policing was a vehicle for the articulation of values that should guide policing.

In this chapter, with the benefit of hindsight, we will briefly appraise the social context that gave rise to community policing, discuss the ideal form of community policing, and raise issues and questions about the current state of policing and its relationship to the community policing movement. But before we embark on an assessment of the present and possible futures of community policing it is helpful to review the original idea of community policing to demonstrate the depth of that vision, what changes that vision entails, and the difficulties of making it a reality.

A Restatement of the Philosophy of Community Policing

The idea of community policing is a radical departure from traditional notions of policing. Community policing is a **paradigm** shift (Kuhn, 1966) that challenges long-standing conceptualizations of the police and fundamental assumptions about doing police work. As a philosophy, community policing is grounded in a defined set of values that serve as an ethical and moral foundation, values that sought to change both the nature of the tasks police perform and the number of people responsible for determining the desired means and ends associated with policing. The assumptions upon which community policing rest represent a dramatic departure from the past that threatens the values and beliefs embraced by the traditional political system and institutionalized forms of policing.

You can learn more about the concept of a paradigm shift by going to http://des.emory.edu/mfp/Kuhn.html.

Ideally, community policing values people and their concerns relegating the police institution and its law enforcement agenda to a secondary consideration.

By paying attention to human and social problems and by tailoring police service to those problems, communities might be transformed into safer places with an improved quality of life for all people. Solving human problems and making communities safer places in which to live are accomplished by giving average people control over the police agenda. This means a radical redistribution of the power that has traditionally marked the divide between government, police, and people. From this perspective, people are no longer passive actors in the policing process; they are active participants in determining both what constitutes a community problem and how best to address it.

By transforming the values of the police institution, community policing seeks to inject an **ethos of service** into a culture that has historically focused solely on crime rather than social problems. The traditional police institution's obsession with law-enforcement-based tactics is supplanted with an ethos of service and a problem-solving orientation. By retooling policing, the social isolation and inequities inherent in the traditional system are broken down and police form a new partnership with the people they are sworn to serve.

> *You can learn more about hiring police officers in the spirit of community service by going to http://www.cops.usdoj.gov/Default .asp?Item=2011#hiring.*

By allowing line officers and average people, not just police executives and political elites, the power to set immediate priorities and launch new initiatives, police become responsive to community needs.

Community policing, therefore, implies a reduction in the power and control of local political officials and the rich and powerful in a community—the beneficiaries of traditional policing. Conversely, this also means increased empowerment of those groups with less access and clout in the current political system. Community policing allows new groups direct input into the police process, broadening the base of community involvement. Powerful interests in the community are not ignored but harnessed, keeping them from dominating the social agenda. For example, a powerful business person may want the police to do something about the homeless who "scare" customers away from a storefront, but community policing might focus on creating shelters for the homeless and offer new ways to protect the homeless from victimization, which is not what the business owner might have had in mind initially. Rather than relying on enforcement tactics that have a limited impact on social problems, like conducting street sweeps and arresting or displacing the homeless, community policing efforts are directed at some of the underlying causes associated with homelessness—not just the symptoms. Simply responding to the concerns of the business community by pushing out the homeless is not community policing or real problem solving.

Within police departments, community policing redefines power, control, and accountability, allowing those at the base of the organizational pyramid more autonomy and freedom to act independently in achieving the goal of becoming real community servants. This means that police officers become educated in the social and community contexts of crime rather than just the **rule of law** and the tactics of law enforcement. Rather than viewing people as problems, the police begin to see people as partners in problem solving. Community policing recognizes that crime, like poverty, is a problem that has so far defied easy answers, and that despite their efforts, the police will never be able to control it alone. Many of the social problems facing urban centers today are the direct result of poor policy decisions of decades past, not inherent pathologies of cities and their inhabitants. Once understanding is shifted from "bad people" to "bad social policy" and poor community conditions, the equation of policing is dramatically changed. While the police do not dictate the public policies that give rise to the conditions found in American cities, they can make better use of resources so that they can do a better job of reducing and controlling social problems by focusing more attention on their underlying dynamics. Understanding social problems and interacting more closely with the community allows the police to become better advocates of sound public policy. In this way, police do not merely respond to public policy and social problems but they inform policy and mitigate the negative effects of poor public policies. A community policing approach allows the police to expand beyond a narrow focus on crime to address a broader spectrum of community concerns, such as fear of crime, quality of life issues, and neighborhood needs. This allows the police the ability to become advocates for their communities and hopefully affect public policy. Community policing has the potential to hold political leaders accountable for poor decisions and policies that give rise to community problems and conditions, not just the people who must experience the conditions public policy creates.

We can recount the basic values of community policing in the following changes it calls for:

- All people deserve a say in how they are policed, regardless of who they are or what position they hold in society. People have a right to decide both the means and objectives of the police;

- People—and not the police—have the ultimate power to control crime, enhance their own safety, and help improve the overall quality of life in the community. Community policing must empower groups that previously had little or no power and control;

- People are not only vital to policing, they are the reason for policing. People are not problems; they are the solution to problems. To do their job, the police must have access to average people. Average people are no longer the passive recipients of police service, but important partners in the policing process;

- People in the community become important arbiters in determining the relative success or failure of local initiatives, and they have a major role to play in supervising and assessing police performance;

- Police officers must be educated to see themselves as community leaders and builders, not just as crime-fighters. Within realistic limits, they must move beyond responding to calls as isolated incidents, to identifying and altering the underlying dynamics that create social problems—not just their symptoms;

- Police executives must actively demonstrate their commitment to this new philosophy by delegating power and control to line officers and the community; and

- Police executives must shift to emphasizing trust while maintaining accountability, allowing all officers within the department the freedom and autonomy to move beyond responding to calls as isolated incidents, to managing social problems.

The philosophy of community policing is not only a shift in the values that underpin policing but entails restructuring the police organization and rethinking the organization of police work and police agencies. Community policing is a radical shift in the way police departments view and handle police work. It implies both a broader mandate that focuses on community and a structural shift to deliver decentralized and personalized service to the community. Community policing calls for the **decentralization** of police organizations in a manner that allows police officers on the street to have greater organizational power, as well as a working environment that is structured to allow them to engage the community. Line officers must be treated as the professionals they can be.

Community policing means departments are to downsize the number of motor patrol officers on random patrol at any given time. This allows the department to get greater mileage out of its line officers, by retreading many patrol officers into the department's community outreach specialists. The time wasted on random patrol is to be reclaimed under the community policing philosophy and restructured to allow all officers to participate in the new "business" of policing. This does not mean that police officers are merely redeployed in new tactical variations like directed patrol, street sweeps, split force patrol, or SWAT teams; it means that officers are freed from patrol to go out directly to the people in need of service, allowing their input to ensure the department does not lose touch with their needs and values. Police become the community, not just a controlling and occupying force in the community.

Community policing requires a reordering of patrol deployment. Under such a reordering, non-emergency calls do not receive the speediest response, but line officers are freed from patrol duty to serve as community outreach specialists. Until a restructuring of organizational power and a reordering in the work of policing takes place for the entire department, the effort is merely an expensive add-on, one that detracts from a proper focus on the community. Not only must the crime control strategy of the police change, but also the very functions and tasks of the police must be reordered.

Community policing implies changes in the kinds of services the department currently provides (Gaines & Kappeler, 2011). A shift to community policing means that political leaders and community elites no longer have a monopoly on police protection as before. Powerful business interests may suffer a cut in the level of service that they had enjoyed. Non-emergency calls no longer demand the fastest possible response just because they are made by the well-connected or they come from an affluent neighborhood. What makes community policing so threatening is that it is not just a new strategy or technique, but an approach to the business of policing, one that implies a reversal of winners and losers under the current system.

The organizational and structural issues associated with community policing are briefly summarized in the following list of changes:

- Community policing requires changes in the way that **resources** are spent;

- Community policing requires a **reordering** of police work to allow time for problem solving;

- Community policing requires the **decentralization** of organizational power in a manner that allows line officers greater freedom to address human and social problems;

- Community policing requires **flattening** the organizational structure of police departments;

- Community policing requires **educating** the public on the new nature of police work especially as it relates to changes in police responses to calls for service; and

- Community policing requires a new system of **accountability** that allows people direct input into the process of evaluating police efforts.

Before we embark on a discussion of how the ideal form of community policing would be transformed into practice, it is necessary to briefly revisit the social context in which the ideal of community policing arose. Philosophies, theories, and ideals are not created in a vacuum, and historical understanding of the context in which they arose informs us of their meaning and the possibility of transforming practice.

The Social Context of the Community Policing Revolution

To understand fully the issues and challenges involved in shifting to community policing requires taking yet another look at the past to understand the forces that spawned the community policing movement. Much of the resistance to community policing and many of the problems in today's failure to really operationalize the spirit of community policing stems from the fact that the impetus to change came primarily from outside police departments in a time of dramatic social change and institutional crisis. The shift from the professional model of policing to the community policing model was less the product of enlightened reformers than the effect of extreme social pressures on an institution that was facing a crisis in legitimacy. While reformers and advocates of community policing certainly offered the police institution a direction for change, the movement toward community policing was largely the result of social and intellectual pressures outside the police profession itself.

Like any other conservative institution, policing is slow to embrace change. Yet ever since the reform era of the 1930s, the police had little reason to re-examine their basic mission. Reformers helped set the tone for modern policing by repositioning the police from peacekeepers to crime-fighters (Kelling & Moore, 2006). This repositioning also allowed the police to partially divorce themselves from overt political control and reattach themselves to the rule of law and the notion of professionalism. As management and police science began to grow, police departments had good reason to identify themselves with that new mission, especially because it seemed they continued to make progress toward that goal. Some police departments might have to address the occasional "crime wave," but there was general optimism that improved police procedures, new crime-fighting techniques and technologies, and the continued rise in the overall standard of living might someday mean that crime, like polio, would ultimately be conquered. At this stage in the development of the police institution, the conceptual changes to what it meant to be a law enforcement officer and the changes in the language used to characterize that mission might have been more important than any real advances in either science or the actual management of the police. In essence, the idea of policing began to change.

Then that rosy view of an increasingly brighter future was shattered, seemingly overnight. The police soon found themselves under assault on three fronts. On college campuses nationwide, students and other anti-war protesters screamed at the police across the barricades, sometimes spitting on them or hurling rocks. Police more often than not responded with violence. In urban neighborhoods, officers saw themselves as battling for their lives during a frightening series of race riots that seemed to erupt each summer. Again, not only was the police response violent, but the police were often the provocateurs of riots as they attempted to establish their sense of community order.

> You can see some images of the riots that spread across the United States in the 1960s by going to http://www.google.com/search?q=the+watts+riots&hl=en&client=firefox-a&hs=m32&rls=org.mozilla:en-US:official&prmd=ivns&tbm=isch&tbo=u&source=univ&sa=X&ei=zRI8TqewJYyitge8_-iEAw&ved=0CDUQsAQ&biw=1177&bih=703.

Especially in major cities, the rates of serious crime exploded. Because reformers had transformed the police into a crime-fighting institution whose major performance measure was crime rates, the image of the police as efficient and effective crime-fighters was tarnished. For many, this merely affirmed a belief that the police were there not to serve the people, but to control them. Something seemed to have gone terribly wrong, not only with the police institution but also with the "American dream," as more and more social inequities and contradictions began to come to the public's attention. The visible presence of the police on the front lines of the battles taking place on all fronts for social change made them the symbol of society's frustration with the escalating domestic upheaval and a lack of governmental responsiveness to demands for change that seemed unstoppable. In this struggle the police stood squarely on the side of the establishment and against the people calling for social change in the communities they were charged with serving.

In the early 1960s, mainstream America still expressed overwhelming optimism that scientific and technological progress ensured an unbroken march toward utopia. There were still problems to be conquered. Racial integration and equality had not been achieved, but Dr. Martin Luther King Jr.'s nonviolent approach offered hope of peaceful progress toward that goal. The war in Vietnam continued to escalate, but military leaders assured the country of victory

> You can learn more about Dr. Martin Luther King Jr.'s approach to securing civil rights by going to http://www.pbs.org/wgbh/amex/mlk/sfeature/sf_bible.html.

and that they could see light at end of the tunnel—they lied. Technology and science advanced almost as fast as the government's inability to listen to people's concerns about the direction the country had taken. Science and the war metaphor became firmly entrenched in the American view of social problems; we waged wars against poverty, crime, drugs, and foreign adversaries. We lost all these battles. Many people still thought that human and social problems were solvable by waging technological and scientific warfare, and when these tactics did not work we could always call the police. The police were on the streets confronting forces they did not or could not understand.

Community policing arose, in part, as a response to concerns about rising crime and the volatility of police-community relations. Rates of serious crime, particularly violent crime, had risen to levels virtually unthinkable decades before, and people worried that there appeared to be no relief in sight. Almost every large American city experienced race-related disorders and riots, cities burned, and revolution was in the air. There was an overall crisis of confidence that American society could pull itself back from the brink of anarchy portended by the rising tide of violence. There was tremendous pressure on the police to do more, to do something different, and, most of all, to do something that would help rather than fuel more riots. Political leaders, however, did not direct the police toward social problems, but rather they used them in an attempt to blunt social and political change with force.

Important as well is the lesson that the impetus for community policing came from unavoidable pressures from outside the system more than from insiders who were eager to explore new ideas. In fact, the unwillingness of police departments to respond to changing needs and times is what allowed them to be caught off guard. Police departments were also beginning to struggle with the need to address minority concerns and they were bracing for the anticipated rise in crime as those baby boomers started to hit their most crime-prone years. But they were shocked to find themselves figuratively under fire from so many groups at the same time. The police were stunned at the degree of hostility they faced from college students and minorities, but they were perhaps most shocked at criticism leveled at them by those whom they saw as their primary base of political support—the middle-class, White majority. Night after night, it seemed, the public was exposed to images of the police turning dogs loose on protesters or clashing with inner-city youths in violent episodes.

Fears that strained race relations could mean new riots focused police reforms on reaching out to minority communities. Many departments faced increasing pressure to adopt civilian review boards as a way to address abuses of authority. While minorities often correctly viewed a department's willingness to accept such proposals as a bellwether of its sincerity in addressing their concerns, many police chiefs resisted them, arguing that they allowed people who did not understand policing unwarranted intrusion in determining police policy and procedures. Remnants of this type of thinking still haunt police departments today (see Scrivner, 2008:14). Many police departments initially tried to ignore the mounting pressures to change, and dismissed people's concerns. Later, the surprising passage of the **Jarvis Amendment** in California, which cut property taxes in half overnight, sent a brutal message to all government institutions that the people paying bills could revolt in ways that had both political and institutional consequences for the police.

> *You can learn more about the Jarvis Amendment by going to http://www.latimes.com/news/custom/scimedemail/la-oew-prop13cc6jun06,0,7249496.htmlstory.*

The police also began to see the burgeoning growth in the **private security** industry as a growing threat, an ominous indication that people who could afford to pay more to feel safer were turning to the private, not the public, sector. Public policing had steadily lost ground to private policing, though few outside police circles realize that there were far more people employed in private security than there were public police officers. While it would be an exaggeration to say that public policing was on the brink of extinction, the institution faced a direct threat to its occupational mandate—on one side stood the private sector waiting to make a profit and on the other stood the public withdrawing their support.

Even many within policing did not recognize the full ramifications of this trend. One consequence is that those who want more protection and can afford to pay more to feel safer often choose to buy service from private sources. Those who cannot afford to pay more therefore must make do with the level of service that the public police can provide. The added irony, of course, is that those who can afford to buy more private security are often those who are already less likely to be victimized.

Private policing tended to mirror the class distinctions found in American society. On one end of the social spectrum is a family in an exclusive apartment building (or suburban enclave) where a hired security guard monitors the entrance with a video camera, challenging anyone who tries to enter to prove they have a valid reason for being there. On the other end is the inner-city welfare mother who has no phone to dial 911 if she hears someone breaking into her apartment. The harsh reality is that we have a two-tiered system of police protection, one in which the poorest and most crime-riddled areas depend on public policing, while the middle and upper classes must spend more and more of what they make on a mix of public and private services.

Advantages tend to multiply the further up the economic pyramid a person climbs. Affluent areas benefit from a higher tax base, which means more tax dollars for public protection. Those who earn more can also spend for extra security, whether that means buying a burglar alarm or sharing the fee for a doorman or security guard. Even if someone penetrates those superior defenses, money can insulate people of means from many of the consequences of crime. Such people usually have insurance—medical, homeowner's, renter's, or disability—in addition to being better able to bear any out-of-pocket losses in the first place.

As the split between classes in American society became greater and as the public began to lose confidence in the police, the institution was thrown into a state of crisis. The crisis in legitimacy and a growing trend by the public to seek alternative means by which to ensure their safety forced the police institution to once again revisit its mission and rethink its social role. The police had to modify its mission to become socially useful to the vast majority of people. Facing a crisis, how was policing to regain public confidence? How was the emerging philosophy of community policing to become a reality?

Turning the Spirit of Community Policing into Practice

Robert Trojanowicz viewed community policing as the vanguard that would stabilize cities and bring the police institution out of crisis. The idea would forge a new compact between the police and the community, one in which the police would become partners to improve the quality of life in cities and address the conditions that gave rise to the conflicts of the 1960s and the economic divide of the later decades. The philosophy of community policing was to be turned into action by creating **Neighborhood Community Policing Centers** that could grow into **Community Resource Centers**, as new social service agencies sent representatives to reach people where they live. Depending on local needs, not federally directed programs that had been seen as failures, it made sense to move professionals like parole officers into centers, so that they could work together, share information, and share staffing the local office. The next step would be to employ drug counselors, who could work with the community policing officers (CPOs) and the area parole officer to coordinate workable proactive outreach efforts to help people in distress.

Allowing those three new outreach professionals to work together as a community team would allow them to be far more effective together than they hope to be individually. Operating out of such a center, the drug counselor could work with the parole officer to field a roster of former drug offenders who will work with the CPO on making presentations to kids at risk, warning them of the potential consequences they face, and reminding them of the power they have in making positive choices. Unlike the Scared Straight or DARE approaches of dubious value, where the goal is to frighten kids away from bad behavior, such an effort could encourage both ex-cons and reformed drug addicts and kids at risk to work together on helping each other stay drug-free.

The center would also allow CPOs and parole officers to share information. Being in the same facility would give them a chance to work together on helping people on parole readjust and get their lives back together so that they do not fall back on bad habits. This would involve working with area businesses to find jobs, or enlisting the help of adult education teachers to help them sharpen their job skills. The center might provide a home for a volunteer-supported literacy effort. Merely throwing people back into the same social and economic conditions they came from following a prison stint without assistance made little sense.

Trojanowicz envisioned an explosion of possibilities if a public health nurse joined these professionals. The nurse could work with everyone in the center on identifying and helping pregnant women get off drugs, because of the urgent need to prevent the damage that drugs can do. Public health nurses could also work with the CPO to develop community-based initiatives to help single parents struggling to raise infants alone. The public health nurse could play a vital role in helping prevent the spread of AIDS among the IV drug users that the drug counselor sees.

The opportunities would multiply exponentially each time a new outreach specialist joined the team—social workers, adult education teachers, parks, and recreation specialists. Perhaps some might spend a day each week, while others might move into the facility full-time. With the CPO leading the way to ensure their safety, these professionals would enlist others in the cause. Perhaps a physician would visit once a month, to provide immunizations and physicals to youngsters. Maybe a corporation would free a personnel specialist one afternoon a week to help counsel people in how to find and hold jobs. Businesses who recruit employees from the area might be persuaded that their long-term future depends on allowing their successful employees time off to spend working with minority youth in the area, to provide them positive role models.

The Community Resource Center could become the hub of neighborhood activity, the outreach center where local churches and civic organizations hold meetings, coordinate projects, and disseminate information. It would become the place that people turn to for help first, because even if the help was not available there directly, there would always be someone who could tell people where to go or whom to call. Perhaps the concern is finding safe shelter for the homeless or abused women and children. Maybe the challenge is to address minority health concerns, ranging from sickle-cell anemia to high blood pressure, or even the lack of places to shop for healthy food or medication for inner-city residents. It might involve enforcement efforts to prevent illegal toxic dumping or cleaning up the pollution that plagues poor communities. The focus and scope of each effort would be bounded only by the collective imagination of the people involved and the particular needs of the community. And all would benefit from the involvement of the CPO's provision of continuity.

Ironically, of course, this hope for the future harkened back to the past, not of policing, but of social service. Not that long ago, social workers visited clients in their homes; the public health nurse made calls on the elderly, the sick, and young mothers; and truant officers tracked down kids who skipped school. Since then, however, we have pulled back from providing decentralized and personalized service, where professionals worked directly in the community. Pressures to become more "efficient" and more "modern" have favored a centralized system, where the clients came to the professionals. But just as putting police officers into patrol cars inadvertently spawned isolation from the community, centralizing other public services alienated these professionals from the people they serve, and the cost of this new efficiency was often a lack of service.

The first thing that happened when the public system pulled back from direct involvement in the community was that the burden of receiving service fell onto those with the fewest resources. When the social workers of the past visited homes, their transportation expenses were covered as part of the job. Now we also demand that welfare clients pay to take the bus, often with their children in tow, and they often have to wait for hours to be seen. Little thought was given to how these shifts in policy affected the disadvantaged. This change sends a message that the system no longer cares about the client's wants and needs.

Pulling **social agents** out of the community also removed the visible symbols of social control. Though it may be somewhat unfashionable to say so, a visiting social worker was in some sense both a role model and a snoop. The social worker typically brought with him or her middle-class values about what constituted proper behavior, backed with the power to approve or disapprove certain benefits. When the system worked properly, those spot checks could uncover obvious cases of physical, mental, and sexual child abuse and neglect. The downside was the thought of an imperious bureaucrat, arriving unannounced, threatening fearful clients that they would lose their benefits simply because the social worker found the person's lifestyle or customs distasteful. Recall that many initiatives labeled community policing suffered similar undesirable effects when the police and community elites attempted to impose their vision of community revitalization on people.

Another concern was that personalized service led to uneven distribution of aid. A kind hearted social worker might bend the rules to find a way to give enough money to a struggling mother whose kids needed shoes to go to school.

Another might slash benefits to the children of a mother deemed promiscuous. The line between offering help and interfering with individual freedom and dignity has never been easy to draw, which made it easier to retreat from a personalized approach that allowed professionals the opportunity both to use—and abuse—discretion. Community policing is also fraught with the potential for abuse when officers are afforded greater autonomy and power to function in the community.

Adding to uneasiness about personalized service was the tinge of racism. In the past, many social workers were White, while many clients were minorities. The White majority saw this system as a way to use economic coercion as a means of imposing its will and its customs on minorities, in the guise of providing charity and assistance. Yet reform has created a centralized system where people's benefits are determined purely "by the numbers," a system so impersonal that common sense plays no role, and it demonizes those most in need of public assistance. The issues of racism and the loss of personalized service is also a concern with current trends in community and problem-solving policing. As we will discuss later, the criminal justice system's move toward actuarial justice, a "war" on terrorism, a failing economy, and the police institution's unreflective emphasis on problem solving may make service less personal, and practices such as location-oriented policing and sweeping "hot spots" and immigrant roundups could have an adverse impact on minorities, particularly the poor who live in the nation's urban centers.

> *You can read more about social work and the problems of racism by going to http://www.socialworker.com/home/ Feature_Articles/Ethics/Racism%3A_The_ Challenge_for_Social_Workers/.*

Challenges to the Spirit of Community Policing

Many supporters naively believe that community policing ensures a bright future for both communities and the police. Many also believe the movement is too firmly entrenched to be denied. Yet, this ignores the fierce competition in the so-called marketplace of ideas as well as the power of more than half a century of indoctrinating police in their crime-fighting role. These forces as well as the tendency of political leaders to fund innovations only as long as they are spotlighted by the media make holding the course a difficult proposition. The history of modern policing is littered with the remains of promising ideas that faltered and died. **Police-community relations**, **team policing**, and **Weed and Seed** are only a few of the more obvious examples. Each undeniably addressed important problems and was launched with great fanfare and enthusiasm. Yet each failed to change the basic values and operations of the police institution and have all but disappeared, leaving communities and the police little better off than they were before.

There are lessons to be learned from these extinct attempts to transform the police institution. Most of these programs failed because they merely repackaged policing without modifying the core function (Bittner, 1970) and values of the police institution. Likewise, they were often the product of politics rather than real community responsiveness; once the politics of an issue cooled so too did the funding and political leaders' concern. "Community relations issues were more 'eyewash and whitewash' than substantive in many communities, a way for the police perhaps to placate the public. Team policing, by contrast, was an important attempt to change the focus and structure of the police, although by all accounts team policing captured neither the imagination nor the organization of the American police" (Greene, 2000:308). Programs like Weed and Seed helped push poor people out of American cities, yielding lucrative profits for developers; "weeding" became zero-tolerance policing; and of course the "funding seed" for poor communities never came. Once again, a transformation in policing was directed toward serving the people in power, not the people in need.

For more than half a century, police were socialized into a crime-fighting role, political leaders pandered to people's fear of crime, and the media distorted our view of the realities of both crime and the proper response to it (Kappeler & Potter, 2005). Nothing has really changed in this pattern; it repeats itself today in media and political talk about terrorism, immigration, and homeland security.

With such powerful forces shaping our vision of society and the means to improve it, it may be overly optimistic to hope that any philosophy, no matter how revolutionary, can transform social institutions in a few decades. History would seem to instruct otherwise. There have been relatively few social changes in America that have transformed the very fabric of society. History more accurately instructs that change is often a slow, and sometimes violent, process that might be better characterized as a chain rather than a revolution—each social transformation constitutes another link in the chain becoming both dependent on the previous links and making future links dependent upon it.

From this perspective, the spirit of community policing is likely to become absorbed by the traditional orientation of the police institution, packed with new fears and threats, rather than to become a replacement for it. While the introduction of community policing will change the nature of the police institution, it may not fundamentally alter its most basic values and core functions, especially if there is little political will for transformation. We can see the re-emergence of the failed crime-fighting value system in the rise of zero-tolerance policing, the distortion of problem-solving techniques to advance aggressive law enforcement practices, and the tension between police and communities arising over fear of terrorism and hate rhetoric aimed at immigrants (see Table 13.1). The community policing

Table 13.1

Comparisons of Social Interactions and Structural Components of Various Forms of Policing

Social interaction or structural dimension	Traditional policing	Community policing	Problem-oriented policing	Zero-tolerance policing
Focus of policing	Law enforcement	Community building through crime prevention	Law, order, and fear problems	Order problems
Forms of intervention	Reactive, based on criminal law	Proactive, based on criminal, civil, and administrative law	Mixed, based on criminal, civil, and administrative law	Proactive, based on criminal, civil, and administrative law
Range of police activity	Narrow, crime focused	Broad, crime, order, fear, and quality-of-life focused	Narrow to broad, problem focused	Narrow, location and behavior focused
Level of discretion at line level	High and unaccountable	High and accountable to the community and local commanders	High and primarily accountable to the police administration	Low, but primarily accountable to the police administration
Focus of police culture	Inward, rejecting community	Outward, building partnerships	Mixed depending on problem, but analysis focused	Inward, focused on attacking the target problem
Locus of decision making	Police directed, minimizes the involvement of others	Community-police coproduction, joint responsibility and assessment	Varied, police identify problems but with community involvement/action	Police directed, some linkage to other agencies where necessary
Communication flow	Downward from police to community	Horizontal between police and community	Horizontal between police and community	Downward from police to community
Range of community involvement	Low and passive	High and active	Mixed depending on problem set	Low and passive
Linkage with other agencies	Poor and intermittent	Participative and integrative in the overarching process	Participative and integrative depending on the problem set	Moderate and intermittent
Type of organization and command focus	Centralized command and control	Decentralized with community linkage	Decentralized with local command accountability to central administration	Centralized or decentralized but internal focus
Implications for organizational change/development	Few, static organization fending off the environment	Many, dynamic organization focused on the environment and environmental interactions	Varied, focused on problem resolution but with import for organization intelligence and structure	Few, limited interventions focused on target problems, using many traditional methods
Measurement of success	Arrest and crime rates, particularly serious Part I crimes	Varied, crime, calls for service, fear reduction, use of public places, community linkages and contacts, safer neighborhoods	Varied, problems solved, minimized, displaced	Arrests, field stops, activity, location-specific reductions in targeted activity

Source: Greene, J. (2000). Community Policing in America: Changing the Nature, Structure, and Function of the Police. In *Criminal Justice 2000, Volume 3, Policies, Processes, and Decisions of the Criminal Justice System*. Washington, DC: National Institute of Justice, p. 311.

movement faces many challenges and difficulties and it is fraught with obstacles both inherent in the police institution and our political economy.

Contemporary Issues and Questions about Community Policing

While community policing in its purest form represents one of the most profound changes facing the police institution, there are serious issues and questions to be raised about the ability of the police institution to transcend its own past and bring about a "quiet revolution" (Kelling, 1988) rather than merely forging another link in the chain of the troubled relationships between police and society. Some of these difficult questions include:

- Community policing involves a **detachment** of the police institution from the strict rule of law and its professional crime-fighting orientation to develop a true service ethos (Kappeler & Kraska, 1998, 1998a). This means police officers derive their sense of what constitutes acceptable practice from community need, desire, and will rather than from legal and political dictates or professional and cultural desires. In this situation, will police be able to accurately read and discern between their own agenda, what is legally permissible, and what members of the community really want? Will police be able to set aside their desire to achieve the mantle of professionalism by increasing their crime-fighting specializations and technological efficiency to become community servants?

- Community policing entails a **shifting of responsibility** for crime control from the police institution to the people and other social service agencies (Kappeler & Kraska, 1998, 1998a). Could this shift result in an inability of people to make the police accountable for crime control? Will other social service agencies' primary function be adversely affected by an exposure to or transplanting of traditional police ideology and objectives into their agencies? Would every social service agency then have a law-enforcement agenda? Will people still avail themselves of the few remaining social services knowing that these agencies carry out a control function? Will "helping" become the cover language for "detecting" and controlling?

- Community policing involves a dramatic shifting of **police orientation** and public preoccupation with crime to a broader range of human activities and issues. If the police are free to determine what constitutes disorder and problem behavior, will the police institution become more controlling and invasive? Could this mean a dramatic challenge to existing civil rights and liberties? Will the behaviors of the least powerful members of the community continue to be defined as the "disorder" that "causes" crime?

- Modern policing has embraced the high rationality of science along with its tendency toward bureaucratic efficiency. If this movement continues, will the value of **"what works"** supplant the value of "what should be done"? There are many law enforcement tactics that can be used to address crime and make enforcement more efficient, but what is the price tag for these aggressive endeavors? Will the fear of crime be replaced by a greater fear of the police?

- The police adoption of the imagery of service provision and problem solving constitutes a **hierarchical positioning** of police as directors and leaders of the community (Kappeler & Kraska, 1998, 1998a). Will police be allowed to direct "community will" (Sykes, 2006), determine the means by which it is achieved (Klockars, 2006), and interpret the quality of their own performance? Will the police claim credit for declines in crime rates even though they have instructed people and political leaders that this is not the proper measure of police performance, nor is it their sole responsibility?

- Community policing entails the language of **community-based accountability** (Kappeler & Kraska, 1998, 1998a; Kelling, Wasserman & Williams, 1988). Will the police institution surrender its power to define what constitutes a valid complaint about police practice and what actions are appropriate to address police abuses of community trust? Are the police really willing to allow people to determine what constitutes proper police behavior and to make decisions on how to sanction police misconduct?

- Community policing requires a **high level of trust** among all members of the community. Will the fear of terrorism and the political redirection of police toward homeland security, intelligence-led policing, and information collection erode the inroads of trust that community policing has made over the last few decades?

- Finally, community policing requires a **shift in power**. Will the most powerful segments of society, those who have historically directed police action for their own benefit, allow the police institution to be transformed so that it can serve all the people?

These questions are not easily answered or resolved. In many ways they represent the basic paradox of policing in American society. The police represent one of society's greatest assets for the protection of civil rights, liberties, and freedoms, yet they remain one of the greatest threats to those same rights, liberties, and freedoms (Kappeler, Sluder & Alpert, 1998; Gaines & Kappeler, 2011). The language of community policing and the entrenched values of the traditional police culture contain these conflicts.

As the title of this chapter indicates, community policing in America stands at a crossroads—somewhere between a community model and a hyper-rational crime-fighting model (Kappeler & Kraska, 1998). While remarkable strides have been made in our knowledge about crime, policing, and criminality over the last few decades, there are certainly some disturbing practices, dialogues, and trends taking place in society and policing today. Consider a few trends that undermine the spirit of community policing.

Disorder and pathology are dangerous metaphors: The public discussion on community policing has replaced the language of "waging war" on crime with the language of conducting "scientific experiments" into the control of "urban decay" through the deployment of police forces to disorderly "hot spots" and dangerous places (Sherman, Gartin & Buerger, 1989). Unfortunately, these tactics are packaged as "enforcing the community's quality of life and civility" (Bratton, 1995) as expressed in academic theses touted as "fixing broken windows" (Wilson & Kelling, 1982), "acquiring a taste for order" (Kelling, 1999), establishing civil authority (Kelling & Stewart, 1989), and "developing a climate of order" (Bayley, 1994). What these arguments have in common is a lack of tolerance for behaviors that fall outside the desires of the most dominant and politically powerful members of society. Disorder, urban pathology, decaying cities, skateboarders, panhandlers, loud music, and the homeless, rather than poor public and economic policy, are incorrectly seen as the "root causes" of crime. What we must remember is that the imposition of order, whether it is economic, political, social, or legal, creates disorder. Disorder and crime are not "naturally" occurring phenomena—they are made. Disorder and crime are the products of public policy that clusters poverty, unemployment, and lack of opportunity into select communities. We must always ask: 'Whose order' is being imposed and who benefits?"

Policing has taken a tactical rather than a problem-solving turn. This language, while appealing to the public and political leaders in its simplicity, cannot be empirically supported and is often used to restrict civil liberties and promote aggression rather than service practices by the police (see Kraska & Cubellis, 1997; Kraska & Kappeler, 1997; Kappeler & Kraska, 1998, 1998a). The language of disorder and decay has freed the police from some burdensome constitutional constraints that previously limited their proactive authority. More and more cities are enacting statutes that restrict people's behavior—from panhandling to dumpster diving. Now the police enterprise is instructed to scientifically identify and fix "broken windows," "uncivil people," and "decaying urban" places, not through the provision of service but through the use of aggressive law enforcement tactics. "In fact, a new orientation toward zero tolerance—i.e., cracking down on street-level disorder—has risen to effectively challenge community and problem-oriented policing as a means of reducing crime and fear" (Greene, 2000:309).

Police have failed to adequately define and address "quality of life": Within policing and academic circles, the language of policy science is focusing on urban space. Refinements in law enforcement have been advanced with media crime talk, police disorder speech, and an emerging criminology of place. Targets of police control have become scientifically identified "hot spots" (Koper, 1995; Sherman & Weisburd, 1995; Sherman & Rogan, 1995a, 1995b; NIJ, 1996a), and intrusions into public and residential space are rationalized using "street sweeps," "crack house raids," and "weeding and seeding." Coupled with this change is the use of community policing phrases like "quality of life" and "community health." This language has taken on an Orwellian flavor in programs promoted by the Harvard School of Government (HSG) and the New York City Police Department (NYPD). In a novel, albeit distorted, adaptation to the call by police reformers to enhance communities' quality of life, NYPD and HSG sponsored a national training conference (titled COMPSTAT) for police administrators. The program includes a learning module labeled "quality of life enforcement" (Kappeler & Kraska, 1998). True quality of life issues like health care, clean communities, mental health services, controlling the spread of diseases, addressing unemployment, providing community services, providing youth with meaningful activities, and making information available to the most needy in the community have taken a backseat to law enforcement activities wrapped in the language of community policing and quality of life.

We are becoming a society of safety seekers and risk managers: Because of the unrealistic fear of crime, society has developed an obsession with safety and an aversion to risk. People now more than in the past want to make every aspect of life risk-free and predictable. This theme resonates in the desire for uniformity in many aspects of social life, from the fast foods we eat to our daily interactions with others. In our highly modern "society of strangers," prediction becomes both increasingly more desirable and more difficult. These desires have arisen alongside a culturally induced dependence and indifference among many people. The police have become the rhetorical premiere problem-solvers for some of society's most complex difficulties. Politicians and the bulk of the public fall back on juvenile curfews, immigration checks, regulations, order enforcement, and target-hardening as a means to bring order and predictability to a largely unpredictable circumstance—modern living. This trend is destroying the possibility of creating communities where people interact in meaningful ways to solve their own problems without governmental control (Kappeler & Kraska, 1998, 1998a).

We are destroying community as we reorder policing and society: Society is moving in the direction of defensible social ordering. Gated bedroom communities and carefully administered residential areas, isolated by the simulation of nature, punctuate the modern blend of people, places, and purposes. Police use surveillance to scan select parts of American cities, we enter stores designed to move you out as quickly and impersonally as possible so as to deter loitering and perhaps prevent robberies, we have lunch in a fast food restaurant, and all the while behaviors are videotaped and conversations are recorded, just in case! Individual-based suspicion (Skolnick, 1966), the historic cornerstone of police action, is being replaced by surveillance and the control of entire populations and places threatening or defying the new rationality of place and purpose (Kappeler & Kraska, 1998, 1998a). A newly found correlation between public intoxication and robberies can serve as the meager proof of the disorder and broken windows thesis without much thought being given to both relationships and public policy. Residential and formerly private spaces have become redefined and more receptive to intrusion by social control agents through the language of disorder, drug epidemics, family violence, and terrorism. Police activities are moving further into previously undefined, unregulated space, and the daily lives of people (Kappeler & Kraska, 1998, 1998a).

Policing may not be more democratic: Community police reformers repeatedly call for the reading of the community's needs and concerns. Meetings with well-positioned members of the community, discussions with media and political representatives, and especially "citizen" surveys have become popular forums for community involvement. The U.S. Department of Justice has heavily promoted this trend as a type of "democracy in action" (BJA, 1994:4). Yet business owners, corporate executives, community leaders, and the affluent have always been able to make their wishes known through formal and informal contacts. A police executive cannot make time for every person who might call for an appointment, but most will try to make time to meet with the president of a major corporation or the elected leader of a powerful community group.

The traditional system also discourages average people from asking for a formal appointment, especially unless they have a pressing concern. In contrast, the power brokers in the community often interact informally or socialize with police officials at meetings, at luncheons, or as friends. This gives them the chance not only to air specific concerns, but also to share opinions and general impressions. Because the top command in the department often shares much in common with other successful people in the community, in terms of education, values, and lifestyle, they often reinforce each other's perceptions—and biases. The police seem no more accessible today to the poor and disenfranchised than they were decades ago.

Police may not be reading community needs and desires: The citizen-survey approach is packaged as police marketing. It is by far the most popular method by which the police ostensibly allow the people to participate in setting police priorities, and it is used to demonstrate to the community an ethic of public accountability. In addition, these surveys are used as a major indicator of whether or not a police department is "doing community policing," making them an integral part of community policing reform efforts.

Supported by some police academics and by the resources of the federal government, police agencies are using citizen surveys, which have contained within them a traditional law enforcement agenda rather than a service agenda (Kappeler & Kraska, 1998, 1998a). Detailed consideration of the instruments used by the police (see for example, Bradshaw, 1989; Henderson, 1995; NCCP, 1994) demonstrates how the law enforcement agenda is encoded into most community survey measures. These surveys articulate for people the notion that the police are the providers of community solutions to police-identified problems. We can find within these instruments basic tenets of problem solving, but they also instruct people that fear of crime is to be found among distinct populations and activities, that this is the best measure of police productivity, and that solutions to social problems should be enforcement-based. People are to interpret the causes of police-represented problems as stemming from local disorder, the circulation of drugs, violent gangs, unsupervised youths, and community outsiders. Many of the current measures of community concern function as pedagogical tools, framing for people the central tenets of law enforcement rather than a service agenda. Solutions, too, are found in repackaged aggressive policing like zero-tolerance.

Not all police partnerships are created equal: Traditionally, in discussions of policing, one could make a fairly clear distinction between formal and informal social control. One was able to quite effectively argue that police represent one of the most formal institutions of social control and that this institution only had a distant or indirect effect on organizing, managing, and influencing more informal systems and agencies of social control. Today, one of the most dramatic changes in the police institution is the emergence of the police as the organizers and managers of an array of social controls. This phenomenon represents a fundamental change in the alignment of social control. Policing, historically a reactive institution, is emerging as a proactive institution that directs and organizes many social control efforts—from schools to businesses.

Community Policing and Terrorism

Some have argued that community policing died with the terrorist attacks of September 11, 2001. The federal government is beginning to divert funds away from community policing and channel them into gimmicky programs that are said to "attack" terrorism and make the country safer. As federal monies shift and grants are given for different priorities, police departments' priorities also shift. In fact, many police departments have shifted their orientation away from community policing to enhancing security and using aggressive law enforcement tactics to address the possibility of terrorism. Some agencies have expended additional efforts and resources to enhance their abilities as **first responders**—a clear narrowing of the police role. Other agencies have used the fear of terrorism to gain what will be short-lived public support. An LAPD public relations program now fuses the language of terrorism with urban graffiti to provoke people's concern and support. We seem very capable of building and funding fusion centers, but not community service centers.

Given the political and media obsession with the issues of terrorism and immigration, some have argued that the era of community policing is over and that the police institution must return to its traditional crime-fighting orientation, albeit with new intelligence-led policing efforts and programs designed to get inside communities, not for service provision, but for surveillance. This is really a thinly veiled return to tactics that have been shown to be ineffectual at controlling crime and will be shown to be just as ineffectual at preventing terrorism and enhancing public safety. This return to the traditional style of law enforcement overlooks the potential contribution that community policing can make to preventing terrorism and creating safe and secure communities. In fact, community policing offers a better chance at preventing terrorism than does any aggressive enforcement agenda.

You can learn more about the threat that terrorism poses for community policing by going to: http://www.policing.com/articles/terrorism.html.

SPOTLIGHT ON COMMUNITY POLICING PRACTICE

Emergency Management and Community Policing Strategies Work Hand-in-Hand

Fayette County is a suburban county south of Pittsburgh in western Pennsylvania. It borders the states of Maryland and West Virginia, with neighboring counties of Somerset, Greene, Westmoreland, and Washington in Pennsylvania. Fayette County has a population of roughly 150,000 and a service area of 803 square miles. There are 42 municipalities, including two third-class cities, and demographics representing everything from rural to urban. Besides the 20 municipal police departments, the Emergency Management Agency (EMA) provides dispatch services to two state park police agencies, two national parks, and a number of school districts, as well as a hospital-based police department.

Fayette County EMA is responsible for operation of the county 911 Communications Center and the Hazardous Materials Response Team (Team 900), and also assists the facilities that store and use hazardous materials within Fayette County in preparing and exercising their emergency response plans. In the event of a chemical release from any of our facilities, these plans detail facilities and neighborhoods at risk, evacuation routes, and shelter locations.

Presently, all public safety entities in Fayette County are utilizing the Fayette County trunked analog 800 MHz radio (voice only) system. Made operational in January 1996, the EMA presently has over 2,600 subscriber units using the system. Interoperability between all users was a major concern when the system was first deployed. In the 14 years since its inception, numerous situations have occurred that were supported by the EMA systems' efficient interoperable design. With the recent requirements for P25 compliance, the EMA has undertaken a project at a cost in the range of $12 million ($1 million provided through the COPS Technology Program) to update and improve the current system to a digital 800 MHz system that will handle voice and data communications. Achieving P25 compliance and upgrading the system is now more critical than ever because every event that has an impact on the public requires a communication system that will support communications interoperability between agencies.

Once completed, the new system will support data and voice, and will provide a gateway to the neighboring Westmoreland County P25 system for enhanced mutual aid capabilities. It will provide a digital platform that will enable a much more efficient and secure exchange of data for law enforcement, and it will enable state agencies working on different platforms to communicate with local responders in the field.

For an example of the need for interoperable communication, in 1996 just a few weeks after turning our radio system on, Fayette County was hit with a severe ice storm. With our new radio system there was total communications interoperability between our public safety, police, fire, and EMS providers and our public works and local elected officials to effectively manage the huge task of opening our rural roads so that power could be restored.

When the new system is operational, the digital data exchange we will acquire will enhance crisis management even more. Digital mapping can then be used and transmitted as needed to responders to convey road closures, power outages, and emergency shelter locations.

Emergency management is as vital a community policing strategy as any, in that, through efficient emergency management operations—using state-of-the-art technology—emergency management agencies have a greater capacity for assisting the minimization of criminal activities. Criminal acts overlap municipal boundaries constantly and the ability for all of our law enforcement agencies—local and state—to communicate is critical because they assist each other in various situations. In crisis situations—whether they be life threatening or not—reliable interoperable communications are an absolute necessity.

Guy Napolillo
9-1-1 Coordinator/Assistant EMA Director
Fayette County (PA) Emergency Management Agency

Source: The e-newsletter of the COPS Office, Volume 4, Issue 2, February 2011.

Despite the political and media pronouncements about the role of the federal government in protecting communities from terrorism, local police really have the best opportunity for preventing, preparing, and responding to terrorism and natural disasters. Local police departments are the best hope of alleviating unnecessary fear of terrorism. It is unlikely that the Department of Homeland Security or the Federal Bureau of Investigation is going to alleviate people's fear of terrorism, or that they are going to be the ones who first come into contact with potential domestic terrorists. Although rarely mentioned in media accounts of homeland security, government response to natural disasters and providing services to communities following a disaster is an equally important mission of establishing national security (Gaines & Kappeler, 2011). It is equally unlikely that people in a community hit by a natural disaster will see either DHS or FBI personnel in the immediate aftermath. In this sense, homeland security is a local function.

Local police officers, subscribing to a community policing philosophy, provide the best possible response to the threat of a terrorist event, the fear it generates, and occurrence of natural disasters.

SPOTLIGHT ON COMMUNITY POLICING PRACTICE

Community Partnerships: A Key Ingredient in an Effective Homeland Security Approach

The tragic events of September 11, 2001 brought about enhancements to many existing law enforcement approaches in an effort to prevent another attack. As we learn more about the threats we face, and our ability to repel those threats, it is increasingly evident that the

(Continued)

benefits of community policing demand that it become fundamental to any effective homeland security strategy.

Community policing comprises three primary elements, two of which are problem-solving to reduce crime and disorder by addressing their immediate underlying conditions, and implementing associated organizational changes to help ensure that the community policing philosophy can be successfully implemented, sustained, and institutionalized. It is the third element—partnerships—that perhaps best positions law enforcement to protect communities from the threat of terrorism. By engaging important and relevant stakeholders in the community who have tremendous knowledge, resources, and a capacity to collaborate on issues of shared concern, law enforcement can improve responses to problems, reduce citizen fear and concern, and increase the overall satisfaction with police services.

The Value of Partnerships to Homeland Security

Partnerships with the community are integral to any crime-prevention effort and, in many respects, terrorism can be understood and addressed in terms of other crime threats. Just as state and local law enforcement entities serve as partners with their federal counterparts and "are now a critical component of our Nation's security capability as both 'first preventers' and 'first responders,'" so too, do law enforcement partnerships with the community hold tremendous potential for thwarting acts of terrorism. Partnerships help to create trust and improve lines of communication between the police and the community.

Under a community policing approach, the community can become eyes and ears for the police, reporting suspicious behavior and notifying the authorities when something seems amiss. Just as street-level knowledge is important to breaking up narcotics activities in a neighborhood, community partnerships and trusting relationships will inspire the confidence of citizens to pass along information that can help to uncover terrorist individuals or cells. Both here and abroad, those who have first hand experience preventing terrorism incidents enthusiastically promote the importance of community partnerships to defeat terrorism. "It is not the police and the intelligence services who will defeat terrorism," according to Sir Ian Blair, the commissioner of the London Metropolitan Police Service. "It is communities who defeat terrorism." Former CIA Director R. James Woolsey testified to Congress that "only an effective local police establishment that has the confidence of citizens is going to be likely to hear from, say, a local merchant in a part of town containing a number of new immigrants that a group of young men from abroad have recently moved into a nearby apartment and are acting suspiciously. Local police are best equipped to understand how to protect citizens' liberties and obtain such leads legally."

Examples of the value of strong community partnerships have been widely reported. In London, England, a strong, strange odor drifting from a flat and the strange group of visitors to the premises caused a London grandmother to report this activity to authorities, which helped to unravel a terror cell planning a poison gas attack. And in New York City, a resident who worked at an Islamic bookstore located next to one of the city's largest mosques so concerned local residents with his inflammatory anti-American rhetoric that the New York

City Police Department tip line received a number of calls about his behavior. A subsequent investigation revealed plans to attack the Herald Square subway station around the time of the 2004 Republican National Convention.

Partnerships with Immigrant Communities

While most police agencies have established many valuable community partnerships, they may be with specific segments of the community who are accustomed to working with law enforcement. Other communities, however, may not have experience cooperating with police authorities. Some may be reticent to cooperate given their cultural experiences of, and history with, police in their country of origin. Other factors may lead to their hesitation to work with the police, including language barriers, immigration status, and a general mistrust of their local police because of misperception and reputation. Yet these groups may be just the ones who are in the best position to provide information that could lead to the prevention of a terror attack because they often possess information that is unknown outside of what are often insular communities, information that could relate to impending threats before that information would come to the attention of others. To develop and maintain these open lines of communication, diligent, determined, and ongoing efforts are required by all sides. An understanding of, and sensitivity to, different religious and cultural values on the part of the police is also essential.

One final note relates to information gathering by law enforcement and the privacy concerns it raises among some in the community. It is important that law enforcement, especially at the local level, understand these concerns as legitimate even as they work to allay them. Being clear about the safeguards and oversight that exist to protect individual rights and liberties, and acting in a deliberate and transparent way about how and why information is gathered and used, can demonstrate that these are both effective and lawful police activities. Moreover, conveying that these activities actually support other efforts to reduce crime and disorder by helping the police to better understand and prioritize community crime issues and to respond accordingly, can be compelling and convincing to citizens. Better information and stronger partnerships should result in improved citizen satisfaction with police services and reduced levels of fear about crime and disorder—the ultimate win-win situation.

Other Community Partnerships

While numerous potential partners exist, one community in particular that holds much potential are the professionals included under the umbrella of private security. The private security profession is extremely diverse, covering everything from armored guard services, to uniformed security, to corporate security departments, to facility security professionals. They often possess immense technology, skills, and extensive law enforcement and security experience. Additionally, by virtue of their unique responsibilities, they can serve as invaluable partners in the effort to secure communities and public and private assets. By some estimates,

(Continued)

private security provides direct oversight of around 85 percent of the nation's critical infrastructure. Moreover, they outnumber their public sector counterparts by nearly 2 1/2 to 1. Their access to both street-level knowledge and state-of-the-art security technology renders them an important—yet largely untapped—community partner.

Conclusion

A number of specific and tailored federal, state, and local law enforcement strategies have been developed and refined in the years since 9/11. Each brings value in very specific ways to an overall community safety and homeland security strategy. There is value, though, in involving the community as partners in all crime-prevention efforts, including strategies related to homeland security. Community policing strategies, and the development of strong partnerships with the community in particular, offer perhaps the most promise to ensure that the events of 9/11 are not repeated.
Robert Chapman
Supervisory Social Science Analyst
Office of Community Oriented Policing Services

Source: The e-newsletter of the COPS Office, Volume 1, Issue 2, February 2008.

What does community policing offer in terms of "community security"?

- Decentralization of police organizations allows for a faster and more efficient response to any crisis—terrorist or natural disaster. A flat organizational structure allows a faster flow of information and communication within the organization, as well as with the public.

- Community policing's use of a decentralized organization can produce a faster response to incidents because officers are better dispersed across the community and have better knowledge of their communities.

- Empowering line officers with decision-making authority and responsibility can make them better "first responders," who have the ability and authority to really "respond" to the needs of people following a crisis.

- Use of fixed geographic beats allows officers to identify security risks and investigate threats. Who knows the infrastructure in a community better than the officer who works there every day?

- In-depth knowledge of a beat can allow for better collection and development of intelligence data. Perhaps more importantly, community policing officers who have worked with members of the community over the years will be more trusted.

- Community policing officers are more trusted by people and are more likely to be given information about suspicious activities or unusual events in the community long before federal officials become involved. If community policing officers are committed to helping and protecting communities, rather than just collecting information to make arrests, members of the community will trust them.

- Community policing officers are freed from the incessant demands of responding to calls, and are free to pursue leads or investigate suspicious activity.

The potentially destructive abuse of community policing language, fused with the fear-generating language of terrorism, is an attractive lure for some law enforcement officials who do not fully understand the meaning of community policing, and they often use public concern for their own advantage. Some police departments are resorting to the old police tactic of promoting fear among people to gain short-term support for their agendas. The danger in this propaganda approach is two-fold. First, the practice capitalizes on unrealistic fears of both crime and terrorism, by distortion. The simple fact of the matter is that terrorism in the United States is a very rare occurrence (see Figure 13.1).

> *You can learn more about community policing and homeland security by going to* http://www.cops.usdoj.gov/default.asp?Item=143.

Terrorism, like all crime, has been declining for decades (Kappeler & Potter, 2005), and gang-related crime is also on the decline. Just like the unrealistic politicalization and fear of crime used by many police departments in the latter part of the professional era, this practice has a high potential to backfire on the police. Second, the practice trivializes the real destructive nature of terrorism by equating it with urban graffiti; it masks the real causes of terrorism, crime, and community disorder, and offers up simple solutions to complex problems. Notice how the LAPD injects its aggressive police style into the announcement with talk of "zero tolerance," and then packages the entire program as "community policing." This press release is little more than propaganda that is easily detected by the community—reminiscent of the old, failed police public relations programs.

Figure 13.1

International and Domestic Terrorist Incidents by Group Type and Consequences, 1998–2007

International and Domestic Terrorist Incidents by Group Type and Consequences, 1998–2007			
Region	Incidents	Injuries	Fatalities
Africa	439	8,127	2,396
East and Central Asia	128	393	164
Eastern Europe	1,362	4,980	1,943
Latin America and the Caribbean	1,785	2,572	1,653
Middle East/Persian Gulf	12,656	46,634	24,522
North America	120	2,408	2,996
South Asia	4,786	17,672	7,469
Southeast Asia and Oceania	1,462	4,952	1,519
Western Europe	3,071	1,780	401
Total	25,809	89,518	43,063

Source: Data from Memorial Institute for the Prevention of Terror (MIPT) Terrorism Knowledge Base; categories modified.

Hollywood Community and Police Work Together to Wipe Out Urban Graffiti Terrorism

Hollywood: The Hollywood community and police are safeguarding their own freedoms and liberties against urban terrorists by keeping their neighborhoods free from graffiti.

Graffiti is a form of urban terrorism; it creates fear, destroys property and fuels the criminal motives of violent, organized street gangs.

Hollywood's desire to become a zero tolerance gang graffiti zone is closer to reality due to donations from the residential and business communities whose generous contributions have purchased a new Graffiti Paint Truck. During the last months, the Hollywood Police Support Association hired a solicitation firm with the vision of raising enough funds to rid this community of graffiti. The Hollywood Beautification Team will add this new truck to their fleet to paint out graffiti within 24 hours.

By ridding the community of unsightly graffiti, community spirit is energized and the process of restoring peace and order to our neighborhoods begins. With gang crime on the rise, the community/police partnership is crucial and this is one example of community based policing in action. The community/police partnership is strong and we are fighting back. We are fighting back to keep our area free of gang graffiti, while maintaining a safe and clean environment in which to live, work and visit.

Source: This media advisory was prepared by Public Information Officer Jason Lee, Media Relations Section, 213-485-3586. For Release 5:00 pm PDT October 23, 2001.

Summary

Today, policing stands at a crossroads. One path takes policing toward the spirit of community engagement and social responsiveness, whereas the other path takes policing back to the failed crime-fighting traditions of the past. The turbulent forces that led to the rise of community policing still loom on the social horizon. Although we have witnessed the emergence of wonderful technologies and social improvements, many Americans have not enjoyed the prosperity that comes with these changes. These changes also bear the seeds of social forces that can again generate a new crisis for American policing. Communications technology allows people to be better informed than in the past, and the prosperity of some affords people greater opportunity to think and learn about social justice and economics issues. Communities of interest are emerging, and they are better organized and better informed than they were in the past. Abuses of power and a lack of responsiveness by government and social institutions are now projected across communication mediums reaching millions of people almost as quickly as they take place.

One need only look at the events in Seattle and Washington, DC, where protesters demonstrated and fought with police over World Trade Organization and the International Monetary Fund's policies to find well-organized and politically informed challenges to the status quo. Unfortunately, one only needs to look at the police response to these situations to see how quickly reforms can be abandoned.

A similar departure from innovative police practices was experienced in Los Angeles, California, at the site of the 2000 Democratic National Convention (DNC), where police fired rubber bullets and beanbags at young people attending a concert by the band Rage Against the Machine. The young people were protesting the DNC, and just as the conventioneers were beginning to leave the building, police ordered the crowd to disband within 15 minutes. After about 10 minutes, the police opened fire on the crowd and assaulted at least one news reporter.

A less visible stumbling block to community police relations occurred at the 2004 Republican National Convention in New York City. Police officers arrested hundreds of protesters while the Republican National Convention was being held. Because of police perjury and the altering of videotapes, hundreds of charges against protesters had to be dismissed by the courts.

On May Day in 2007, baton-wielding LAPD officers used violence against literally hundreds of peaceful protesters and journalists gathered in MacArthur Park following a march through the city designed to challenge immigration policies.

In response to an increased rate of violence on the south side of Chicago, police deployed SWAT teams into communities, claiming that they were going to stem the violence. Community members, however, "don't see it that way.

They say the SWAT deployment underscores a fundamental rift between police and the communities they serve" (Halasz, 2008:1).

Most recently, in London, fears over terrorism have led to very aggressive police practices like stopping and questioning young people without probable cause. Aggressive police practices coupled with austerity measures imposed by the government and sky-high unemployment rates among youths of color have created a tinderbox of conflict. In 2011, London burned for days and young people rioted following the shooting of an unarmed Black man by police and an alleged attempt by police to cover up the incident. All this came on the heels of a police corruption scandal involving Rupert Murdock's media empire.

Quebec Police Admit They Went Undercover at Montebello Protest

Quebec Provincial Police (QPP) admitted on Thursday that three of their officers disguised themselves as demonstrators during the protest at the North American leaders summit in Montebello, Quebec.

U.S. President George W. Bush, Canadian Prime Minister Stephen Harper and Mexican President Felipe Calderón met in Quebec to discuss a proposed security, resource and trade initiative between the countries called Security and Prosperity Partnership (SPP), but dubbed NAFTA 2.0.

Police said, "At all times, they responded within their mandate to keep order and security." The QPP said, "At no time did the Quebec Provincial Police officers act as agents provocateurs or commit criminal acts. Also, it is not part of the policy of the police force nor is it part of its strategy to act in this manner. At all times, the officers responded to their mandate to maintain law and order."

A video of the incident had been posted on YouTube, which, as of this date, had received greater than 170,000 views. In the video, the three undercover officers could be seen wearing face masks, dark clothes, and boots and milling about with other protesters; one undercover officer could be seen carrying a rock. Some of the gathered demonstrators, notably union leader Dave Coles, could be seen and heard telling the officers to leave, put down the rock, and remove their bandannas: several protesters then tried to remove the officers' bandannas. The undercover officers retreated behind police lines and could be seen being put to the ground and restrained by the riot police.

Those at the protest said the officers were acting like agents provocateurs by provoking violence from within the crowd. Dave Coles, president of the Communications Energy and Paperworkers Union of Canada, confronted the three undercover officers on the protest line. He suggested the officers were there to cause trouble. "We're going to talk to our legal counsel and we'll decide what our next action is going to be," said Coles.

Source: *Wikinews* (2007). Quebec Police Admit They Went Undercover at Montebello Protest. Friday, August 24, 2007.

Exposure of these police practices has damaged many inroads that community policing had made in Seattle, New York City, Los Angeles, Chicago, and London. The social forces that created institutional crises for the police in the 1960s and 1970s still confront them in our time. Whether the police institution will learn from its own history and whether it will be responsive to social change within the framework of community policing and the needs and values of the people remains an issue at the crossroads.

KEY TERMS IN CHAPTER 13

- accountability
- community relations
- Community Resource Centers
- decentralization
- ethos of service
- first responders
- fusion centers
- Jarvis Amendment
- Neighborhood Community Policing Centers

- paradigm
- police orientation
- private security
- resources
- Robert Trojanowicz
- rule of law
- safety seekers
- social agents
- team policing
- Weed and Seed

DISCUSSION QUESTIONS

1. Discuss what the authors mean when they say that community policing is a paradigm shift.
2. Discuss the specific values of policing that serve as its ethical and moral foundation.
3. What are the three most important factors that led to the development of community policing in the late 1960s and early 1970s?
4. Describe and discuss Robert Trojanowicz's vision of Neighborhood Community Policing Centers. Have these centers materialized?
5. Over the past 20 years, have social service agencies centralized or decentralized operations? What are the implications of this for communities?
6. Discuss the authors' concerns about the shift toward community policing. Identify and discuss what you consider to be the four most important questions to be answered about the future of community policing.
7. Has policing become more or less democratic in the past 10 years?
8. Discuss the future of community policing, according to the authors. Do you agree with the authors' conclusions about the status of policing today? Why or why not?
9. What social, economic, and political factors impede the implementation and success of community policing in the future?
10. Briefly describe the six organizational and structural issues associated with community policing.
11. Discuss each of the seven trends that undermine the spirit of community policing.
12. Discuss some current events involving the police and consider their consequences for community policing.

References

Bayley, D. (1994). *Police for the Future*. New York, NY: Oxford University Press.

Bittner, E. (1970). *The Functions of the Police in Modern Society*. Washington, DC: National Institute of Mental Health.

Bradshaw, R.V. (1989). *Reno Police Department's Community Oriented Policing—Plus*. Reno, NV: City of Reno.

Bratton, W. J. (1995). The New York City Police Department's Civil Enforcement of Quality-of-Life Crimes. *Journal of Law and Policy*, *3*(2), 447–464.

Bureau of Justice Assistance (BJA). (1994). *Neighborhood-Oriented Policing in Rural Communities: A Program Planning Guide*. Washington, DC: U.S. Department of Justice.

Crank, J. P. (1994). Watchman and Community: Myth and Institutionalization in Policing. *Law and Society*, *28*(2), 325–351.

Gaines, L. K., & Kappeler, V. E. (2011). *Policing in America* (7th Ed.). Waltham, MA: Anderson.

Gaines, L. K., & Kappeler, V. E. (2012). *Homeland Security*. Boston, MA: Prentice Hall.

Greene, J. (2000). Community Policing in America: Changing the Nature, Structure, and Function of the Police. In *Criminal Justice 2000, Volume 3, Policies, Processes, and Decisions of the Criminal Justice System* (pp. 299–370). Washington, DC: National Institute of Justice.

Halasz, E. (2008). With SWAT on the Streets, Residents Fear Harassment. *Medill Reports*, April 24, 2008.

Henderson, C. (1995). *Community Resource Areas: A Residential Survey*. Hillsborough County, FL: Sheriff's Office.

Kappeler, V. E. (1996). Making Police History in Light of Modernity: A Sign of the Times? *Police Forum*, *6*(3), 1–6.

Kappeler, V. E., & Kraska, P. B. (1998). A Textual Critique of Community Policing: Police Adaption to High Modernity. *Policing: An International Journal of Police Strategies and Management*, *21*(2), 293–313.

Kappeler, V. E., & Kraska, P. B. (1998a). Policing Modernity: Scientific and Community Based Violence on Symbolic Playing Fields. In S. Henry & D. Milovanovic (Eds.), *Constitutive Criminology at Work*. Albany, NY: SUNY Press.

Kappeler, V. E., & Potter, G. W. (2005). *The Mythology of Crime and Criminal Justice* (4th ed.). Prospect Heights, IL: Waveland Press.

Kappeler, V., Sluder, R., & Alpert, G. (1998). *Forces of Deviance: Understanding the Dark Side of Policing* (2nd ed.). Prospect Heights, IL: Waveland Press.

Kelling, G. L., & Stewart, J. K. (1989). *Neighborhood and Police: The Maintenance of Civil Authority*. Washington, DC: U.S. Department of Justice.

Kelling, G. L. (1988). *Police and Communities: The Quiet Revolution*. Washington, DC: U.S. Department of Justice.

Kelling, G. L. (1999). Acquiring a Taste for Order: The Community and the Police. In V. E. Kappeler (Ed.), *The Police & Society: Touch Stone Readings* (2nd ed.). Prospect Heights, IL: Waveland Press.

Kelling, G. L., & Moore, M. H. (2006). The Evolving Strategy of Policing. In V. E. Kappeler (Ed.), *The Police & Society: Touch Stone Readings* (3rd ed.). Prospect Heights, IL: Waveland Press.

Kelling, G. L., Wasserman, R., & Williams, H. (1988). *Police Accountability and Community Policing.* Washington, DC: U.S. Department of Justice.

Klockars, C. B. (1988). The Rhetoric of Community Policing. In J. R. Green & S. D. Mastrofski (Eds.), *Community Policing Rhetoric or Reality* (pp. 239-254). New York, NY: Praeger.

Klockars, C. B. (2006). Street Justice: Some Micro-Moral Reservations-Comment on Sykes. In V. E. Kappeler (Ed.), *The Police & Society: Touch Stone Readings* (3rd ed.). Prospect Heights, IL: Waveland Press.

Koper, C. S. (1995). Just Enough Police Presence: Reducing Crime and Disorderly Behavior by Optimizing Patrol Time in Crime Hot Spots. *Justice Quarterly, 2*(4), 649-672.

Kraska, P. B., & Cubellis, L. (1997). Militarizing Mayberry and Beyond: Making Sense of Paramilitary Policing. *Justice Quarterly, 14*(4), 607-630.

Kraska, P. B., & Kappeler, V. E. (1997). Militarizing American Police: The Rise and Normalization of Paramilitary Units. *Social Problems, 44*(1), 1-28.

National Institute of Justice (NIJ). (1996a). Policing Drug Hot Spots. *Research Preview*, Washington, DC: National Institute of Justice.

Scrivner, E. (2008). Practitioner Perspectives: Community Policing in a Democracy. Washington, DC: U.S. Department of Justice, Office of Community Oriented Policing Services.

Sherman, L. W., & Rogan, D. P. (1995a). Effects of Gun Seizures on Gun Violence: "Hot Spots" Patrol in Kansas City. *Justice Quarterly, 12*(4), 673-710.

Sherman, L. W., & Rogan, D. P. (1995b). Deterrent Effects of Police Raids on Crack Houses: A Randomized, Controlled Experiment. *Justice Quarterly, 12*(4), 755-781.

Sherman, L. W., & Weisburd, D. (1995). General Deterrent Effects of Police Patrol in Crime "Hot Spots": A Randomized Control Trial. *Justice Quarterly, 12*(4), 625-648.

Sherman, L. W., Gartin, P. R., & Buerger, M. E. (1989). Hot Spots of Predatory Crime: Routine Activities and the Criminology of Police. *Criminology, 27*, 27-55.

Skolnick, J. H. (1966). *Justice Without Trial: Law Enforcement in a Democratic Society.* New York, NY: John Wiley and Sons.

Strecher, V. G. (2006). Revising the Histories and Futures of Policing. In V. E. Kappeler (Ed.), *The Police & Society: Touch Stone Readings* (3rd ed.). Prospect Heights, IL: Waveland Press.

Sykes, G. (2006). Street Justice: A Moral Defense of Order Maintenance Policing. In V. E. Kappeler (Ed.), *The Police & Society: Touch Stone Readings* (3rd ed.). Prospect Heights, IL: Waveland Press.

Walker, S. (2006). Broken Windows and Fractured History: The Use and Misuse of History in Recent Police Patrol Analysis. In V. E. Kappeler (Ed.), *The Police & Society: Touch Stone Readings* (3rd ed.). Prospect Heights, IL: Waveland Press.

Wilson, J. Q., & Kelling, G. L. (1982). Broken Windows: Police and Neighborhood Safety. *Atlantic Monthly, 249*(March), 29-38.

GLOSSARY

Abner Louima incident One of the most gruesome police brutality cases in the nation. Louima, a Haitian immigrant, was arrested in a Brooklyn nightclub as the result of a fight that had broken out between two other patrons in the bar. Louima was arrested because one of the officers believed that Louima had assaulted him while he was attempting to break up the fight. Officers beat Louima as they transported him to the precinct station.

abuse of authority Any action taken by a police officer without regard of motive, intent, or malice that tends to injure, insult, tread on human dignity, manifest feelings of inferiority, and/or violate an inherent legal right of a citizen.

access control Essentially, attempts to ensure that only those individuals who have a legitimate interest to enter an area are allowed access. It reduces the opportunities for crime by keeping potential criminals out of an area, and it makes it more difficult for motivated criminals to enter an area.

administration The management of governmental affairs that includes control of the organization and structure of an agency.

administrative discretion The decision-making power granted to administrators that creates a vehicle through which uniform policies and procedures are developed.

administrative reform Initiated by police administration and an important source of change. This type of change was brought about to provide quality law enforcement services to the public and to offset the control and domination exerted by politicians.

agency policy The formal policies and standard operating procedures of an organization that specify the mechanics of performing certain tasks; these regulations set the acceptable limits of an officer's conduct in carrying out sworn duties.

Albert Hunter His book, *Symbolic Communities*, noted the close association among the words "common," "communication," and "community." He argued that both language and shared symbols help identify what he called the "natural community."

allocation of personnel Making decisions about how many officers should be assigned to the various units in the police department.

Amadou Diallo incident New York City police officers in an anti-crime unit were searching for a suspect in a Bronx neighborhood. They spotted Diallo, who fit the description of a suspect, and decided to investigate him. Upon being confronted by the officers, Diallo ducked into the vestibule of a building. He reached into his pocket to retrieve his wallet. The officers thought that Diallo was reaching for a gun and opened fire. They fired 41 shots, striking Diallo 19 times.

analysis Once a problem, quality of life issue, or hot spot is identified, officers attempt to collect information about it. Basically, they attempt to learn the who, what, when, where, and how of the problem.

appointment based on qualifications The principle that holds that only qualified persons should be selected for police service and that the organization has an inherent obligation to train its employees.

arrest Apprehending or detaining a person to answer to an alleged or suspected crime. Generally, an act constitutes an arrest if a reasonable person would assume that they were no longer free to leave and their movement has been restricted in some meaningful way.

assessment Once there is a response by the police, the police assess the response to see if it worked (i.e., eliminated or reduced the problem). If the strategy did not result in an acceptable outcome, the police must re-analyze the problem and fashion another response.

Attorney General's Task Force on Family Violence (1984) Noted that the process of mediation assumes equal culpability in a dispute, which seldom is the case in domestic violence cases.

authoritarian personality Characterized by conservative, aggressive, cynical, and rigid behavior. People having these characteristics are said to have a limited view of the world and see issues in terms of black and white.

authoritarianism A personality type characterized by conservative, aggressive, cynical, and rigid behaviors.

authoritarianism A form of government in which one person or a small number of people control state power, as well as the law, police, military, and other public and semi-public institutions such as school and church.

autonomy A cultural ethos that is evident in the police subculture's use of and concern about discretionary law enforcement.

baby gangsters Gang members ages 9–12.

behavioral component Constrained activities or lifestyle.

Black flight African Americans began moving from the cities to the suburbs in the 1960s.

blockbusting An unethical real estate practice where Whites began selling their houses due to the fear that African American families moving in would inevitably cause property values to plunge.

blue laws A peculiar American phenomenon where religious groups successfully lobbied to make custom part of the criminal law.

bravery A cultural ethos that encourages the display of courage related to the perceived and actual dangers of law enforcement.

broken windows Postulates that, if unchecked, a neighborhood in decline will continue to decline and the number of disorder and crime problems will increase.

brutality When officers willfully and wrongfully use force that exceeds the boundaries of their authority.

Bureau of Alcohol, Tobacco, and Firearms A federal agency that investigates violations of alcohol, tobacco, and firearms crimes and that works closely with state and local police agencies to target mid-level drug wholesalers and dealers.

bureaucracy A form of social organization in which order, rationality, and hierarchy are the most important elements. Bureaucracy is a way of organizing social life to control the behavior of large groups of people and is marked by the formal and uniform application of rules and driven by "rational" goals.

buy-busts Sweeps in which officers attempt to buy drugs from dealers and then arrest them.

CAD/RMS A system that contains all the information related to each crime incident, including location, time, nature of police response, police response time, and criminal report numbers.

Chief's Advisory Committee A support committee that provides broad-based opinions and ideas about community problems and police initiatives.

civilian review boards A group of citizens that attempts to maintain effective discipline of the police, provide satisfactory resolution of citizen complaints against officers, maintain citizen confidence in the police, and influence police administrators by providing feedback and review of police practices.

classical organizational theory Developed by Max Weber, this theory delineates six principles that are used in police departments today.

cognitive component One's perceived risk and consists of one's assessment of danger.

combination laws Prohibited workers from meeting, organizing, and striking against their "masters" to improve working conditions.

Command or Administrative Staff Meetings Police executives who meet periodically with departmental staff and unit commanders to discuss problems, programs, and goal achievement.

Commander Profile Report Serves as a report card on how managers are dealing with their crime problems and their units.

communities of interest Created by either geographical boundaries such as rivers or major highways, by ethnic or racial groups settling together, or by nongeographical groups who share common interests and communications.

community Perhaps one of the most difficult concepts to define and one of the most abused terms in modern sociology. The term can be used in both the concrete and the abstract sense to mean people living together in a social group.

community anti-drug campaigns A variation of neighborhood watch in which people band together to fight drugs in their neighborhood and focus exclusively on drug trafficking and the crime associated with the drug trade.

community concern model Posits that fear of crime is related to community dynamics. The community concern differs from the disorder model in that it considers one's feelings or attitudes about factors such as social change, dissatisfaction with neighborhood life, and unease about life circumstances.

community crime prevention programs Geared specifically to get people more involved in crime prevention. Most efforts in community crime prevention have centered on (1) neighborhood watches, (2) community anti-drug programs, and (3) public media campaigns.

community officer Uses discretion liberally and has a primary objective of helping people.

community policing The first substantive reform in the American police institution since it embraced the professional model nearly a century ago. It is a dramatic change in the philosophy that determines the way police agencies engage the public. It incorporates a philosophy that broadens the police mission from a narrow focus on crime and law enforcement to a mandate encouraging the exploration of creative solutions for a host of community concerns including crime, fear of crime, perceptions of disorder, quality of life, and neighborhood conditions.

Community policing officer (CPO) Has responsibility for a specific beat or geographical area, and works as a generalist who considers making arrests as only one of many viable tools, if only temporarily, to address community problems.

community policing tactics Refer to those where the police use enhanced enforcement coupled with community relations.

community surveys Ways of measuring people's attitudes about the police and their police performance.

community-oriented policing Evolved from work done at Michigan State University that found that the fear of crime was more problematic than crime itself. Researchers advocated that police departments should form partnerships with citizens and citizen groups to address crime and fear issues.

COMPSTAT A program pioneered in New York City by William Bratton and Jack Maples, it is an acronym for computer statistics in some locations, while others refer to it as compare statistics. It has been adopted by a large number of police departments.

constables Among the first law enforcement officers in the American colonies; constables were charged with surveying land, checking weights and measures, serving warrants, and meting out punishment. Constables were often assigned to oversee night watches, many of which later developed into police departments.

corruption The misuse of official authority for personal gain.

CPTED Crime Prevention through Environmental Design.

crime analysis The examination and mapping of crime and calls for service to discover patterns. Once patterns have been discovered, police have better information about criminal activities and how to respond to them.

crime-fighters Zealots who see their role as enforcing the law and view other police activities as being outside "real" police work. They typically are associated with legalistically styled police departments.

crime mapping report Provides commanders with visual accounts of crime and calls for service in their commands.

crime prevention unit A police unit that was manned by staff rather than line officers. The unit's goal was to educate the businesses and community residents about specific measures they could take, such as target hardening, to reduce their likelihood of victimization and thereby help decrease the crime rate overall.

crimes in progress A policing model where motor patrols' ability to provide a rapid response was thought to make a great contribution to reducing and controlling crime.

criminal justice system Composed of three primary and discernible components: police, courts, and corrections.

culture Differences between large social groups; these include varying beliefs, laws, morals, customs, and other characteristics.

dangerous place A location that attracts criminals and results in high levels of crime. Criminals are attracted to geographical locations by entertainment, potential victims, their work, and their residence.

DARE (Drug Abuse Resistance Education) Program that educates fourth, fifth, and sixth graders about the perils of drug use.

deadly force Any level of force that is likely to lead to serious physical injury or death. Deadly force can only be used in instances where the officer believes there is a threat of immediate and "great bodily harm" to the officer or to another.

decentralization The dispersion or distribution of political or police functions and powers; the delegation of power from a central authority to regional and local authorities. In the case of American policing, this means that police forces are controlled at the federal, state, and local levels rather than being centralized at the national level.

deinstitutionalization Occurred in the 1960s and 1970s when thousands of mentally ill patients were released from state hospitals, and laws restricting involuntary commitment of mentally ill people were enacted.

demeanor The attitudes and manners exhibited by citizens when encountering the police. Citizens and offenders who fail to show deference to the police by cooperating are more likely to be treated fairly. When citizens are antagonistic toward officers, their complaints are not taken seriously and the officer is more likely to initiate formal actions.

democracy Concept that includes a belief in such fundamental principles as respect for the rule of law, individualism, civil rights, human dignity, constitutionalism, social justice, and majority rule.

directed patrol Consists of a variety of strategies: saturation patrol, stakeouts, surveillance of suspects, and decoys. Its implementation recognizes that crime and other police hazards are not equally distributed across place and time and that recognizable patterns can often be identified.

discreet drug trafficking Drug trafficking that is discreet and very likely widespread in many communities, and virtually impossible for the police to stop. Police undercover operations and buy-busts will result in a few arrests, but such arrests are costly in terms of the amount of time and effort devoted to making each arrest. Discreet drug dealing seldom results in collateral crime and disorder problems. People discreetly purchase their drugs and then consume them out of public view. When the police concentrate their efforts on indiscreet drug trafficking, it generally results in larger numbers of minority arrests and subsequent charges of discrimination on the part of the police.

discretion The effective limits on a public official's power that leave him or her free to make a choice from among a number of possible courses of action.

discrimination Occurs when officers act on the basis of their prejudices; this overt act results in negative consequences for the person who was the object of the prejudice.

disenfranchised populations The mentally ill, public inebriates, and homeless, although most of the people in these categories are homeless, and society tends to deal with them as homeless.

disorder model Postulates that fear is produced by the amount of perceived disorder that people encounter in their neighborhood, or areas where they travel, such as work, shopping, and recreation.

domestic violence An incident that results in physical harm or threats of harm by one household member against another. This includes partners, spouses, former spouses, parents, children, or others who live or have lived together.

downtime Any time that an officer is not committed to some call or police activity.

drive-offs Where patrons leave without paying for their gasoline.

driving while Black (DWB) The police use of race to determine which drivers to stop for minor traffic violations and the use of race to determine which motorists to search for contraband.

drug abuse Excessive use of a drug (such as alcohol, narcotics, or cocaine) without medical justification to the extent that its use adversely affects the user.

Drug Abuse Resistance Education (DARE) A drug reduction program that began in 1983 when the Los Angeles Police Department began sending officers into the schools to teach children about drugs.

drug cartels Criminal organizations that are extensively involved in the drug business.

Drug Enforcement Agency Federal agency responsible for stopping drugs from coming into the United States. They do this by working with foreign governments in obtaining drug smuggling intelligence and seizing drugs as they are smuggled into the country.

drug marts Locations where large numbers of dealers hawk their drugs; usually located in entertainment districts, high-crime areas, or public spaces.

drug house abatement When police address a specific drug outlet.

economic compulsive violence Crimes of violence, such as robberies or assaults, committed in an effort to obtain drugs, money, or something of value that could be used to obtain drugs.

economic rationale The development and maintenance of an effective criminal justice system is an expensive proposition, and this position argued that frontier towns should not bear the expense, when vigilantism did the job efficiently for free.

economic status discretion Socioeconomic status has been shown to affect the manner in which police respond to requests for service and the probability of being arrested.

emotive component Or generalized fear, where the individual becomes wary of real and perceived disorder and crime events in the community.

Enclosure Acts During the eighteenth and nineteenth centuries, lands that were used by entire communities, called the "commons," were consolidated and privatized with a series of acts of Parliament.

enforcement discretion How officers enforce the law, provide services, and otherwise maintain order.

environmental design Extraordinary steps taken by citizens to make their neighborhood appear difficult to victimize.

excessive force Where an officer applies too much force in a specific situation; unreasonable or unnecessary use of force.

fear of crime An emotional reaction characterized by a sense of danger and anxiety. We restrict our definition to the sense of danger and anxiety produced by the threat of physical harm.

Federal Bureau of Investigation A federal investigative agency responsible for attacking criminal organizations. The FBI targets organized crime and other criminal syndicates and investigates federal crimes.

Ferdinand Tönnies The first sociologist to make an important distinction about communities. In his book *Gemeinschaft und Gesellschaft*, he distinguished between the local community (*gemeinschaft*) versus the larger society (*gesellschaft*).

fixed site Neighborhood sales locations where drug traffickers constantly sell drugs.

fleeing felon doctrine Legal doctrine that allowed police officers to use deadly force against any escaping felon and required that police weigh the dangerousness of shooting a suspect with the probability of immediate or future harm caused by the suspect.

frankpledge system Medieval policing style practiced in England prior to the Industrial Revolution.

Fugitive Slave Laws Laws allowing the detention and return of escaped slaves that were passed by Congress in 1793 and 1850.

gangsters Gang members ages 16–22.

GAP Gang Alternatives Partnership; was created to coordinate the efforts of the many private and public agencies that were involved in the gang problem. Agencies included police departments, the district attorney's office, juvenile probation, the school district, private agencies, and private businesses.

geographic concentration pattern Where a number of crimes or activities are concentrated in a specific geographical area.

geographic focus Police administrators must ensure that line officers and units have a geographic focus.

geography Not a sole matter of place, territory, or location; it is the product of complex human interactions.

government A political institution of the state that uses organization, bureaucracy, and formality to regulate social interactions; is most often recognized among societies that emerge as nation states.

hard crime Refers to criminal offenses, usually Part I crimes in the UCR.

harm reduction The criterion by which to guide drug enforcement planning and to evaluate enforcement programming.

high-level enforcement Designed to attack the drug problem at the top of the drug trafficking hierarchy. It is designed to arrest those individuals who are involved in smuggling large quantities of drugs into the United States, manufacture large quantities of drugs, or distribute drugs to large, expansive drug networks.

homeless A socioeconomic condition whereby people have no fixed permanent residence; a significant part of the population that has been disenfranchised from the rest of society and presents a special challenge for the police.

homeless lifestyle Includes those individuals who have no residence and have chosen the streets as their lifestyle. They feel comfortable with their lives, and they tend to view a change toward conventional styles as threatening.

hot spots Geographic locations that have a disproportionate amount of crime; chronic repeat-call locations.

hundred A unit of law enforcement where every 10 tithings made up a hundred.

indiscreet drug dealing Includes open street dealing, as well as crack houses and shooting galleries used exclusively to sell drugs to large numbers of customers.

interdiction Deterring drug smuggling by seizing drug shipments entering the United States.

investigative commission Panels, boards, or groups, usually appointed by politicians, that investigate police corruption and police practices.

isolation An emotional and physical condition that makes it difficult for members of one social group to have relationships and interact with members of another group.

jurisdiction Political or geographic location in which a police officer may use the authority to enforce the law.

Just Say No A drug reduction program based on the assumption that most kids experiment with drugs because of an inability to withstand peer pressure, problems with low self-esteem, and lack of training in values clarification.

justice of the peace A law enforcement position filled by noblemen appointed by the king. The justice of the peace, with the constable serving as his assistant, eventually refined his role to that of judge; the first official split of the judicial and law enforcement functions.

juveniles Represent a special problem for community policing. Juvenile crime, especially violent crime, is portrayed as increasing. It is politicized to the point that many legislative bodies are passing stricter laws in terms of penalties and how juveniles are processed in the criminal justice system.

Kansas City Patrol study The most frequently cited and perhaps most in-depth study of the effectiveness of routine preventive patrol.

labor riots Around 1835, a series of riots swept through the country. The riots and their devastating effects demonstrated the ineffectiveness of the day and night watch systems in cities. These riots are what caused the watchmen to become a police organization and labor unions to form.

legislative and administrative programs Efforts to make changes in administrative policies or statutes that enhance crime prevention.

London Metropolitan Police First modern English police department; created in London in 1829.

management Processes that occur within the structure of an organization.

Massachusetts State Police Created in 1865, making it one of the oldest statewide law enforcement agencies in the nation.

Max Weber The founder of modern sociology; was the first to outline the principles of organization.

MBO (management by objective) Represents the application of systems theory from the top down within an organization; that is, police executives establish goals for the police department, and then successive units and unit managers within the department establish lower-level goals and objectives.

media image Image presented by the media that policing is all about crime fighting, excitement, and danger.

mental illness Any disease or disorder of the mind that causes behavior or emotional problems that impair a person's ability to function in society.

mentally ill homeless Those who have mental problems but are not institutionalized or have been abandoned or thrown out by their families.

Metropolitan Police Act of 1829 Act abolishing existing efforts and, in their place, establishing a Police Office, administered by justices (commissioners) in charge of planning. It also created the Metropolitan Police District, staffed by paid constables.

militarizing law enforcement Blurring of the lines that separate the military and domestic police forces, a trend made evident with the adoption of military tactics by police agencies.

Minneapolis Domestic Violence Experiment in 1981-1982 Showed that arrest was the most effective of the three standard methods police use to reduce domestic violence (the other two are advising or sending the suspect away for at least eight hours).

multijurisdictional drug task forces A number of police departments banding together and deploying interdiction teams to prevent drugs from coming into their jurisdictions.

neighborhood A small physical area embedded within a larger area in which people inhabit dwellings. Thus, it is a geographic subset of a larger unit where there is a collective life that emerges from the social networks that have arisen among the residents and the sets of institutional arrangements that overlap these networks. That is, the neighborhood is inhabited by people who perceive themselves to have a common interest in that area and to whom a common life is available. Finally, the neighborhood has some tradition of identity and continuity over time.

neighborhood crackdowns Similar to street sweeps, except that the police usually identify an area that they feel deserves concentrated, long-term attention.

neighborhood watches Block watches or citizen patrols are probably the primary methods used by the police for community crime prevention programming. These programs are initiated by the police and, once they begin, people develop more cohesive relations and actively participate in crime prevention.

New Left A loose coalition of groups demanding a variety of social, economic, and political changes, under the umbrella phrase "social justice."

night watch Perhaps the earliest organized law enforcement effort, first established in a Boston town meeting in 1636.

O.G. Original gang members.

omnipresence An appearance that the police are everywhere.

order maintenance role One of four primary roles for which the police are responsible; includes forcing a panhandler or drunk to vacate an area, investigating suspicious persons or vehicles, investigating domestic disturbances, breaking up bar fights, quelling a riot or disorder, and intervening in noisy parties or gatherings.

organization A collective that is brought together to accomplish a mission; distinguished by formal rules, division of labor, authority relationships, and limited or controlled membership.

organizational authority Derived from one's positions within the organization, rather than from personality, standing in the community, or some other source.

organizational documentation The process of ensuring that all or most communications are in writing; serves to inform others about what has previously occurred within the organization and to hold people accountable.

paramilitary unit Officers equipped with an array of militaristic equipment and technology. They often refer to themselves in military jargon as the "heavy weapons unit," implying that what distinguishes them from regular police is power, culture, weapons, and assignments.

parochial social control Consists of churches and schools.

Part I (Index) "Serious" crimes—four violent crimes (murder, rape, robbery, aggravated assault) and four property crimes (burglary, larceny/theft, motor vehicle theft, arson).

participative management Formalized organizational arrangement whereby officers at lower levels of the organization can have input into departmental matters, especially those that directly affect them.

patrol function The primary unit responsible for answering calls, providing police services, and preventing crime.

patrol The practice of covering a district or beat by police officers (e.g., on foot, horse, or bicycle; in automobiles, watercraft, or aircraft), who make observations for the purposes of documentation and the detection or prevention of crime.

Peel, Sir Robert British Prime Minister (1834-1835 and 1841-1846) who established a permanent police force; his name was the source of the word "bobby."

Peelian reform An Act for Improving the Police in and Near the Metropolis, or the Metropolitan Police Act, was introduced by Peel in 1829; the Act provided for a single police authority that would be responsible for an area that covered approximately a 7-mile radius from the heart of the city.

periodic markets Distribution points where drug sales are made at limited times.

police Social control agents or an institution of government that imposes the force of law on the public.

Police Athletic League (PAL) Provides a variety of services to disadvantaged youth. The program offers youth a variety of sports including football and basketball. The department attempts to have sporting programs in place most of the year. The PAL centers are equipped with computers that are used to provide classes to both youth and adults.

police authority Used when police officers take command and control of situations or people by issuing orders or directives.

police force A group of trained officers charged by a government with maintenance of public peace and order, enforcement of laws, and prevention and detection of crime. Police forces are authorized by law to use force to achieve their objectives.

police organization How to structure the department so that goals and objectives are achieved.

police role A basic or standardized social position that carries with it certain expectations.

police-community relations PCR programs represented sincere efforts to reach out and address a host of community concerns by establishing better relations with the community.

policies and procedures Guide the activities of the organization.

political entrenchment A phase of American history in which politicians saw the police as a mechanism for solidifying their power through control of their political adversaries and assisting friends and allies. Not only was the police department responsible for enforcing the city's laws, but, in many respects, it was also the primary social service agency of the time.

prejudice A judgment or opinion developed without the benefit of knowledge or facts.

prevention Refers to ferreting out the problems and conditions that cause crime. In essence, the police must examine the conditions surrounding crime in an effort to develop effective measures of eliminating it.

primary crime prevention Efforts to identify and manage the conditions within the social and physical environment said to cause crime.

primary victimization Occurred when a criminal act was committed against the victim. Here, the victim suffers direct financial and sometimes injurious losses as a result of the criminal act.

principle of hierarchy Each lower officer is under the control and supervision of a higher one.

private security Individuals, organizations, and services other than public law enforcement who work to protect property and assets.

private social control This mechanism refers to the family and social networks that develop within neighborhoods. Private social control is the primary and most effective form of social control in a neighborhood.

privatization Instances in which private security personnel are given full or limited police powers.

problem solvers Police officers who tend to be more sympathetic to people's needs, viewing people as clients, not adversaries. They are community oriented and view the law as one of many instruments that can be used to solve a specific problem.

problem-oriented policing Addresses symptoms of crime rather than crime itself to help reduce the potential for crime to be committed in the first place. There has been little, if any, uniformity in the way it has been implemented.

problem solving Groups organized to focus on a specific problem or a set of problems.

procedural guidelines A system of written rules that include policies (describing the department's position relative to some problem or area of concern), procedures (describing how officers are to perform some function such as documenting the storage of physical evidence), and rules or general orders (explicitly describing what an officer can or cannot do, such as the type of weapons the department will allow an officer to carry while on duty).

professional model of policing Institutionalized in the early 1900s. It dictated that police officers remain aloof and detached from the people they served.

professional officers Officers who consider a complete range of solutions and mediate the "rule of law" and citizen needs when selecting solutions.

professionalism As reform efforts gained momentum and politics played a less obvious and less intrusive role in policing, law enforcement in this country began to be viewed as a profession. The professional phase of law enforcement began in the 1920s and can be analyzed and best understood using three general perspectives: law enforcement role, bureaucratic role, and science and technology.

professionalization Process by which norms and values are internalized as workers begin to learn their new occupation.

professionalized Police narrowed their mandate to "crime-fighting," and motorized patrol replaced foot patrol, with the police rapidly adopting more modern technology.

programmatic dimension Operationalization into specific tactics or programs.

protective cover Where chiefs deflect criticism by pointing out that a mistake occurred because the officers involved violated or ignored rules and procedures. This also allows administrators to cast abuses by police officers as isolated and aberrant behaviors rather than problems that follow directly from the existing system and culture.

public social control Mechanisms include the police and other governmental agencies. Public social control mechanisms are the last line of defense in a community.

quality circles Group of volunteer employees from the same unit or work area who meet on a regular basis to discuss and study problems confronting their area within the department.

racial profiling Occurs when police target someone for investigation, detention, or arrest on the basis of race, color, national origin, or ethnicity.

Rampart Division scandal The Los Angeles Police Department developed a national reputation for police brutality. In 1999, this reputation was solidified with the Rampart Division scandal. A police officer in the Rampart Division was arrested on charges stemming from the theft of cocaine from a police evidence room. As a part of his plea bargain, he agreed to provide investigators information about the illegal activities of other officers in the Rampart Division.

rational choice theory Asserts that criminal behavior is not random but is the result of choices that criminals make. It is claimed that there is a calculus, or decision-making process, that people perform when deciding to commit crime.

reactionary conservatives Said to instinctively react in a conservative manner regardless of the merit of their position and often without reflecting upon the consequences of their acts.

reasonable force The least amount of force necessary for a police officer to effect an arrest or enforce a lawful order.

reform era Long, slow evolutionary process punctuated with numerous gains and losses. For the most part, police reform activities can be discussed in terms of investigative commissions, reform initiated by police administrators, and political reform.

reordering of patrol development Non-emergency calls do not receive the speediest response, but line officers are freed from motor patrol duty to serve as community outreach specialists.

resolving crimes already committed Traditional police efforts after a crime has occurred include both motor patrol and investigation. Again, the rationale for relying primarily on motor patrol's quick response is based on the assumption that the officers can therefore do a better job of preserving evidence and locating witnesses. After this initial assessment, many departments then assign investigators to follow up further. Criminal investigators, however, don't have a very good track record in solving crime already committed.

response Once a problem or hot spot is clearly identified, the police must then structure an effective response. This means the police must deal with the cause of the problem rather than its symptoms.

retail-level enforcement Strategies that attempt to reduce "discreet" and "indiscreet" drug dealing, with the latter more susceptible to control.

reverse stings Where undercover police officers pose as drug dealers and arrest customers who attempt to purchase drugs from them.

right of revolution The United States comes from a tradition of violent revolution, and early framers of the Constitution argued that periodic revolt might be necessary to prevent government tyranny. Part of the American psyche embraces the idea that when something fails to work properly, revolution is as valid as reform.

riots and strikes Around 1835 a series of riots swept through the country. The riots and their devastating effects demonstrated the ineffectiveness of the day and night watch systems in cities. Strikes also played a role in the development of modern-day police organizations. The objectives of police forces were to protect the "scabs," to protect coal company property and factories, and to generally assist in breaking the strikes through arrests and physical violence.

Rodney King incident CHP officers stopped Rodney King for speeding. King had led a number of officers on a chase that exceeded 100 MPH. Once King was stopped, a total of 21 police officers from several different police agencies arrived on the scene. Once King was removed from his vehicle, he was shocked twice with a 50,000 volt taser. He was also severely beaten by two other officers while between 21 and 27 officers watched. When it was over, King suffered 11 skull fractures, a broken cheekbone, a fractured eye socket, a broken ankle, missing teeth, kidney damage, external burns, and permanent brain damage.

routine activities theory Posits that a crime consists of three elements: (1) a motivated criminal, (2) a target or object of a crime, and (3) the absence of guardianship.

routine preventive patrol Provided by officers in marked police vehicles dispersed throughout an agency's jurisdiction. Officers are assigned to patrol specific areas (beats or districts), the geographic boundaries of which are generally based on some form of workload analysis. Agencies attempt to balance the officers' workload by dividing the city into areas that would have equal amounts of activity.

SARA model A four-step process: (1) scanning, (2) analysis, (3) response, and (4) assessment. This is a method of effective problem solving that can be used by police officers.

saturated patrol Attempts to deter crime or problems in a specific area by deploying large numbers of officers; strategies are employed that concentrate officers in a given area to create a total police presence.

scanning Refers to a process whereby individual officers, police units, or the police department collectively examine the community for problems or hot spots.

secondary crime prevention Focuses on persons and the community in an effort to prevent potential crimes and violence.

secrecy The quality or condition of being secret, often the result of a fear of loss of autonomy and authority as external groups try to limit police discretion.

self-preservation This idea justifies vigilantism by arguing that citizens must be willing to kill or be killed when the official system fails to provide adequate protection.

service role One of four primary roles for which the police are responsible; represents the majority of police work, as opposed to the preconceived notion many officers have prior to joining the force that their priority is law enforcement.

shire-reeves Appointed to collect taxes, seize property, and squash political dissent; later known as sheriffs.

shire A group of hundreds was organized into a shire, the rough equivalent of a county.

similar offense patterns Developed in a similar fashion as geographic concentration patterns. They can be concentrated in an area or they may be spread over a large geographical area.

Sir Robert Peel Father of modern policing.

situational crime prevention A form of problem solving; comprises opportunity-reducing measures that (1) are directed at highly specific forms of crime, (2) involve the management, design, or manipulation of the immediate environment in as systematic and permanent a way as possible, and (3) are to increase the effort and risks of crime and reduce the rewards as perceived by a wide range of offenders.

slave patrols Helped to maintain the economic order and assisted wealthy landowners in recovering and punishing their slaves, who essentially were considered their property.

social control Collective practices used by a group to ensure that individuals conform to the norms and values of the group.

social development programs Attempt to reduce the number of motivated offenders in society. They focus on the conditions that contribute to crime. There are areas or neighborhoods that have higher concentrations of crime and have greater numbers of criminals.

social differentiation Developed as villages grew in population and resources, usually beginning with slavery and a surplus of material resources; based on trade, production, warfare, and the exploitation of labor.

Social Disorganization Theory Shaw and McKay (1942), in a landmark study, examined delinquency in Chicago. They found that delinquency and crime rates were higher in inner-city areas that were characterized as transitional.

social norms The types of behaviors that are considered appropriate by society.

society The totality of networks and patterns of social interaction occurring between members of a bounded social group including those interactions within organizations and institutions.

socioeconomic homeless People who are homeless as a result of losing a job, being under-employed, spouse abuse, or a divorce. People in this classification were a part of society, but they became homeless as a result of some economic or social event.

socioeconomic status Refers to an individual's social and economic class.

soft crime Refers to minor violations.

solidarity An effect of the socialization process that breeds a unity of interests or sympathies among the police group.

special committees Special community committees that are appointed to study individual problems occurring in the community or in a neighborhood.

specialization of labor Exists whereby individuals are assigned a limited number of job tasks and responsibilities.

specialization Provides a number of benefits to the department including simplified training, placement of responsibilities, administrative control of operations and activities, and development of expertise for handling complex police problems; in some cases, officers are provided career enrichment.

split force patrol Patrol force split into two separate patrol groups: (1) patrol call answering and (2) criminal interception.

state A political creation that has the recognized authority to use and maintain a monopoly on the use of force within a clearly defined jurisdiction.

strategic dimension Guidelines for the development of specific programs.

strategic planning The identification of goals and objectives and a determination of how they will be achieved.

street sweeps Deploying officers in specific areas to create safer neighborhoods and alleviate the fear of residents living in high crime areas where drug use and sales are high.

street-level drug enforcement Attempts to reduce drug demand by arresting or otherwise frightening drug buyers. Demand reduction will harm drug dealers and their profitability much more than interdicting the drug supply.

subcultural diversity model Suggests that some measure of fear of crime is produced from persons living near others who have cultural backgrounds that are different from their own.

subculture A group that, while sharing many of the values and beliefs of the larger, more dominant culture, also has separate and distinct values.

surveillance Any action that increases the probability that offenders will be observed.

suspect-oriented techniques Agencies direct officers to concentrate on known suspects or classes of individuals.

symbolic assailant Person who, because of his or her characteristics, police believe is likely to be a criminal; tends to take on the characteristics of marginal segments of society that police frequently come into contact with.

target hardening Where measures are taken to make it more difficult to commit a crime.

terrorism The threat or intentional use of violence directed at civilians for the purpose of achieving a political objective.

tertiary crime prevention Directed toward individuals who have committed criminal acts; society and the criminal justice system must try to deal with these individuals in such a way that they will not commit criminal acts in the future.

Texas Rangers Said to be the first state police organization. While the history of the Texas Rangers can be traced to 1823, the name did not appear in legislation until 1874.

The COMPSTAT Report Provides a ranking of the precincts by crime and arrests.

The Flint Foot Patrol Program that began in January 1979, as the result of a $2.6 million grant from the Mott Foundation to Michigan State University. The project was the result of two law enforcement–related problems. First, in many parts of Flint, there were no crime prevention programs or programs to help the neighborhood control crime and other problems. Second, police officers were fairly detached from the people.

The Mollen Commission Investigated corruption in the New York City Police Department; noted that most officers begin their careers by viewing the job honestly and idealistically, but become corrupt over time through progressive stages.

third party policing Involves the police pressuring not the people directly causing the problems but the people who have control over the locations in which a problem is occurring.

tiny gangsters Gang members younger than 9 years of age.

tithings Every 10 citizens constituted a tithing.

U.S. Customs Service Federal agency with the responsibility of interdicting drugs that are intermingled with exports coming into the United States. The U.S. Customs Service inspects goods as they are imported into the United States.

Uniform Crime Reports (UCR) Statistics compiled by the FBI that show trends, but they do not provide a true picture of the crimes actually committed at any specific time.

unnecessary force Any level of unauthorized force that does not contribute to achieving a lawful objective by the police or force used by well-intentioned officers who are unable to handle a situation and resort to violence too quickly or needlessly.

use of force Deadly or non-deadly force used to control the behavior of individuals in order to protect life and property.

vice crimes Criminal activity that is against the public order or public morality; includes activities such as prostitution, gambling, pornography, illegal sale of alcoholic beverages, and trafficking in drugs and narcotics.

victimization model Explains fear of crime through personal victimization, experiences with others who have been victimized, and perceived vulnerability to victimization.

Volstead Act of 1919 Made Prohibition the law of the land.

Walmarting and McDonaldization Corporatizing American businesses resulting in the dislodging of many mom and pop operations and drastically lowering workers' wages.

wannabes Those who want to prove themselves in order to be accepted by other gang members and who are precisely the ones most useful as soldiers in gang activities.

Weed and Seed Police departments across the country were funded to clean up drug-prone neighborhoods, and, once the cleanup was complete, to engage the community and assist in revitalizing it.

White flight Whites moving from cities to the suburbs in the 1950s.

workload analysis Determines the frequency of each activity performed by the unit and the average amount of time spent for each occurrence.

worldview The manner in which a culture sees the world and its own role and relationship to the world.

youth street gangs Highly violent gangs of young persons that have become involved in drug trafficking, crime, and violence.

zero tolerance policing The police have lowered their tolerance and now enforce many minor infractions that historically were ignored.

THE TEN PRINCIPLES OF COMMUNITY POLICING

1. Community policing is both a philosophy and an organizational strategy that allows the police and community residents to work closely together in new ways to solve the problems of crime, reduce fear of crime, and improve neighborhood conditions. The philosophy rests on the belief that people in the community should set the police agenda. It also rests on the belief that solutions to contemporary community problems demand freeing both people and the police to explore creative new ways to address neighborhood concerns beyond a narrow focus on individual crime incidents.

2. Community policing's organizational strategy first demands that everyone in the department, including both civilian and sworn personnel, must investigate ways to translate the philosophy into practice. This demands making the subtle but sophisticated shift so that everyone in the department understands the need to focus on solving community problems in creative new ways that can include challenging and enlisting ordinary people in the process of policing themselves. Community policing also implies a shift within the department that grants greater autonomy to line officers, which implies enhanced respect for their judgment as professionals.

3. To implement true community policing, police departments must also create and develop a new breed of line officer, the community policing officer, who acts as the direct link between the police institution and people in the community. As the department's community outreach specialists, community police officers must be freed from the isolation of the patrol car and the demands of the police radio, so that they can maintain daily, direct, face-to-face contact with the people they serve in a clearly defined beat area.

4. The community police officer's broad role demands continuous, sustained contact with people in the community, so that together they can explore creative new solutions to local concerns involving crime, fear of crime, and community conditions, with private citizens serving as unpaid volunteers. As full-fledged law enforcement officers, community police officers respond to calls for service and make arrests, but they also go beyond this narrow focus to develop and monitor broad-based, long-term initiatives that involve community residents in efforts to improve the overall quality of life in the area over time. As the community's ombudsmen, community police officers also link individuals and groups in the community to the public and private agencies that offer help.

5. Community policing implies a new contract between the police and the people they serve, one that offers the hope of overcoming widespread apathy; at the same time it restrains any impulse to vigilantism. This new relationship, based on mutual trust, also suggests that the police serve as a catalyst, challenging people to accept their share of the responsibility for solving community problems, as well as their share of the responsibility for the overall quality of life in the community. The shift to community policing also means a slower response time for non-emergency calls and that people themselves will be asked to handle more of their minor concerns, but in exchange this will free the department to work with people on developing long-term solutions for pressing community concerns.

6. Community policing adds a vital proactive element to the traditional reactive role of the police, resulting in full-spectrum police service. As the only agency of social control open 24 hours a day, seven days a week, the police must maintain the ability to respond to immediate crises and crime incidents, but community policing broadens the police role so that they can make a greater impact on making changes today that hold the promise of making communities safer and more attractive places to live tomorrow.

7. Community policing stresses exploring new ways to protect and enhance the lives of those who are most vulnerable—juveniles, the elderly, minorities, the poor, the disabled, and the homeless. It both assimilates and broadens the scope of previous outreach efforts, such as Crime Prevention and Police/Community Relations units, by involving the entire department in efforts to prevent and control crime in ways that encourage the police and people to work together with mutual respect and accountability.

8. Community policing promotes the judicious use of technology, but it also rests on the belief that nothing surpasses what dedicated human beings, talking and working together, can achieve. It invests trust in those who are on the front lines together on the street, relying on their combined judgment, wisdom, and expertise to fashion creative new approaches to contemporary community concerns.

9. Community policing must be a fully integrated approach that involves everyone in the department, with community police officers as specialists in bridging the gap between the police and the people they serve. The community policing approach plays a crucial role internally—within the police department—by providing information and assistance about the community and its problems, and by enlisting broad-based community support for the department's overall objectives.

10. Community policing provides decentralized, personalized police service to the community. It recognizes that the police cannot impose order on the community from outside, but that people must be encouraged to think of the police as a resource they can use in helping to solve contemporary community concerns. It is not a tactic to be applied, then abandoned, but an entirely new way of thinking about the police role in society, a philosophy that also offers a coherent and cohesive organizational plan that police departments and communities can modify to suit their specific needs.

AUTHOR INDEX

SUBJECT INDEX

Note: Page numbers followed by *b* indicate boxes, *f* indicate figures, and *t* indicate tables.